Mastering
Turbo Pascal® 6

Fourth Edition

Mastering

Turbo Pascal®

6

Fourth Edition

Tom Swan

HAYDEN BOOKS

A Division of Prentice Hall Computer Publishing
11711 North College, Carmel, Indiana 46032 USA

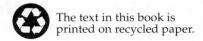
International Standard Book Number: 0-672-48505-2
Library of Congress Catalog Card Number: 91-61702

Publisher
Richard K. Swadley
Publishing Manager
Joseph Wikert
Managing Editor
Neweleen Trebnik
Acquisitions Editor
Gregory Croy
Development Editor
Paula Northam Grady
Senior Editor
Rebecca Whitney
Production Editor
Katherine Stuart Ewing
Editors
Lori Cates, Kezia Endsley, Becky Freeman
Technical Reviewer
Chris Land
Editorial Assistant
San Dee Phillips

Book Design
Scott Cook
Cover Art
Tim Amrhein
Production Coordinator
Mary Beth Wakefield
Production
Claudia Bell
Scott Boucher
Brook Farling
Bob LaRoche
Sarah Leatherman
Laurie Lee
Anne Owen
Cindy L. Phipps
Joe Ramon
Kevin Spear
Dennis Sheehan
Bruce D. Steed
Indexer
Ted Laux

Composed in Garamond and Macmillan Digital by Macmillan Computer Publishing.

Printed in the United States of America.

Trademarks

All terms mentioned in this book that are known to be trademarks or service marks are listed below. In addition, terms suspected of being trademarks or service marks have been appropriately capitalized. SAMS cannot attest to the accuracy of this information. Use of a term in this book should not be regarded as affecting the validity of any trademark or service mark.

Apple and Macintosh are registered trademarks of Apple Computer, Inc.

CP/M is a registered trademark of Digital Research, Inc.

IBM is a registered trademark of International Business Machines, Inc.

MS is a registered trademark of Microsoft Corporation.

Turbo Pascal is a registered trademark of Borland International, Inc.

UCSD-Pascal is a registered trademark of the Regents of the University of California, San Diego.

WordStar is a registered trademark of Micropro International Corporation.

Overview

Contents

3   Action—What a Program Does   37

10 Custom Units and Overlays   *283*

12 More About Numbers

13 Advanced Techniques   425

15 Object-Oriented Programming 581

17 Turbo Vision Tools   *693*

List of Tables

Preface to the Fourth Edition

Every year or so, a computer-industry reporter writes an article that predicts the demise of the software entrepreneur. The article usually begins like this:

> "In the future, all software will be written by teams of programmers employed by giant corporations. The age of the lone-wolf-programmer success story is probably over."

What a tub of hogwash! Over 2 million individuals have purchased Borland International's *Turbo Pascal* compiler, making this easy-to-use product the most popular professional programming language of all time. Some of these *Turbo Pascal* entrepreneurs—hardly a dying breed—have gone on to write their own successful programs. A few have founded software companies that have made their owners wealthy. No, the age of the software entrepreneur isn't over. In fact, despite ups and downs in the computer industry, the opportunities for individual success in the computer software business have never been more promising. If you've been thinking of writing your own software, you couldn't have picked a better time to begin.

You also won't find a better programming language to use than Turbo Pascal, which remains popular among programmers for several reasons. For one, it costs less than comparable C compilers. For another, its high speed is legendary—even on moderately powerful computers, Turbo Pascal runs circles around its competition. Turbo Pascal is also easy to learn, making it the ideal choice for students and self-motivated learners. What's more, Turbo Pascal is a mature product that promises to remain in power for many years to come. Chances are excellent that the time you invest in mastering Turbo Pascal won't be wasted.

For professionals, Turbo Pascal also includes essential features such as overlays, heap management, and separately compiled units. The compiler now has object-oriented extensions, a built-in assembler, and an extensive object-oriented programming library called Turbo Vision—all of which you'll explore in this book.

As in previous editions, the main feature in *Mastering Turbo Pascal 6.0,* 4th Edition, is source code—lots of source code. Over 400 examples show you every nook and cranny of Pascal programming in action. All programs are compatible with Turbo Pascal version 6.0, but many will work with versions 4.0 through 5.5 as well. To learn a new computer language, there's no substitute for typing in *complete* programs and making them run on your own computer. If anything, this book is short on theory and long on practical advice. (See the order form inside the back cover for details on how you can purchase an optional disk of the book's programs or how you can upgrade your disk if you purchased an earlier version. You don't have to purchase the disk. All the programs are printed in full in the text.)

If you're new to Pascal, you'll find a complete tutorial in this book that, I hope you'll agree, doesn't waste time beating around subjects, but gets to the meat in a hurry with real examples that explain key concepts—such as data structures, procedures, functions, units, BGI graphics, and pointers. If you have read a previous edition, I hope you'll enjoy learning about Turbo Pascal's new additions, including object-oriented extensions, a new built-in assembler, and Turbo Vision, to which I've devoted two new chapters.

To the many thousands of readers who have supported previous editions of *Mastering Turbo Pascal,* allow me to add a personal note of thanks. It's been a pleasure to hear from many of you, and to have the opportunity to share Turbo Pascal experiences. Here's to another five great years!

Tom Swan
Compuserve ID: 73627,3241
MCI Mail: TSWAN

Acknowledgments

The following people have contributed greatly to this book. I owe special thanks to Lori Cates, Greg Croy, Kezia Endsley, Kathy Ewing, Paula Northam Grady, Chris Land, Ted Laux, San Dee Phillips, Richard Swadley, Joe Wikert, and all the other employees of SAMS who helped make this book possible.

At Borland, I'm indebted to Eugene Wang, Nan Borreson, Anders Heilsberg, Chuck Jazdzewsky Danny Thorpe, Zack Urlocker, Gary Whizin, and others who provided me with copies of Turbo Pascal and who answered my questions.

Those who helped out on past editions include Jennifer Ackley, Fred Amich, Sara Black, Don Clemons, Jeff Duntemann, Herb Feltner, Wendy Ford, Ronnie Groff, Jim Hill, Marj Hopper, Betty Kish, Kim Kokkonen, Jay Lininger, Paula Lininger, Julie Quackel, John M-Roblin, Glenn Santner, Michael Violano, and Teri Zac.

Special thanks also are due my wife and assistant Anne Swan, who read the entire manuscript and made many useful suggestions.

Introduction

This book describes how to write computer programs in Turbo Pascal. In here you'll find:

- A complete introduction to Pascal programming specifically tailored for Turbo Pascal and assuming no prior programming knowledge.

- Chapters devoted to advanced techniques, pointers, separate compilation with units, and color graphics, as well as using a math coprocessor and mixing assembly language with Pascal.

- Full railroad (syntax) diagrams describing Turbo Pascal syntax, originally introduced in the first edition and now fully updated.

- An encyclopedia describing and listing complete example programs for every Turbo Pascal procedure and function.

- Hundreds of tested examples with line numbers for easy reference from the text.

About the Examples

By typing in and observing the actions of over 400 examples, some only a few lines, some longer, you'll learn how to write your own Turbo Pascal programs. If you don't have the time or patience to type the examples, you can order the programs on disk. You'll find instructions and an order form on the last page inside the back cover.

How to Use This Book

Many tutorials describe how to program with a generic form of Pascal that few professional programmers would actually use to write software. Some textbooks go so far as to use languages that don't even exist on real computers. While these approaches have some merit for generalizing the subject of programming, it's also true that you can't learn how to swim without getting wet! Therefore, I decided to write this book based on a specific language, Turbo Pascal, for a specific computer, the IBM PC and compatible systems.

The best way to use this book is to read the text, type the associated examples, and observe how the programs run. Make changes to the programs to test various theories. Experiment. If something doesn't interest you, or if some of the early material is old hat, jump ahead. Look up procedures and functions in Chapter 18 for more details and consult the index for other references. In general, chapters follow a natural progression from simple to complex subjects, avoiding items not yet introduced. You'll find very few places that discuss material "to be explained later." Even so, this book isn't a novel—you won't ruin the ending by reading the chapters out of order!

The following sections list the materials and equipment you will need, and describe what the chapters do and do not cover.

Required Materials

To begin your study of Turbo Pascal, you need to have the following items:

1. Turbo Pascal version 4.0, 5.0, 5.5, or 6.0.

2. The Turbo Pascal reference manuals.

3. Several blank disks or a hard drive for storing examples.

4. Printer (optional).

5. Any IBM PC or compatible computer.

What This Book Contains

Following are brief descriptions of chapter contents. Each chapter begins with a list of key words and identifiers covered in the chapter and ends with a summary and suggested exercises to test your knowledge. You'll find answers to many exercises at the end of the book.

- Chapter 1, "Programming by Example," introduces Turbo Pascal, explaining the fundamentals of simple programs and variables. You'll learn how to use railroad diagrams as quick references to the language.

- Chapter 2, "Data—What a Program Knows," explains constants and numbers, introduces strings and comments, and shows how to deal with common programming errors.

- Chapter 3, "Action—What a Program Does," adds the concept of a statement to your Pascal knowledge. You'll meet all Turbo Pascal's repetitive and conditional statements here.

- Chapter 4, "Divide and Conquer," begins to show Turbo Pascal in full force, with procedures and functions that divide large programs into manageable chunks. The chapter details the tenets of top-down programming, an organizational method that many professional programmers use.

- Chapter 5, "Adding Structure to Data," expands your knowledge about Pascal's data types, covering subranges and scalar types, arrays, records, and sets.

- Chapter 6, "Files," melts the mysteries of working with disk files as well as accessing devices like printers and modems. You'll learn about text and structured files here.

- Chapter 7, "Pointers, Lists, and Trees," dispels another mysterious subject of Pascal programming—a subject that even some experts avoid. Pointers are not difficult to understand, as this chapter explains.

- Chapter 8, "Strings," completes your study of strings, string procedures, and functions, adding to your knowledge of string handling introduced in Chapter 2.

- Chapter 9, "Introducing the Unit," explains how to use Turbo Pascal's method for compiling programs in separate pieces. The chapter contains descriptions of each of Turbo Pascal's standard units.

- Chapter 10, "Custom Units and Overlays," shows how to write your own units, letting you develop custom programming libraries and overlays.

- Chapter 11, "The Borland Graphics Interface," one of the largest chapters in this book, completely describes every procedure and function in Turbo Pascal's massive graphics unit for writing color graphics programs on CGA, EGA, and VGA systems.

- Chapter 12, "More About Numbers," fully explains Turbo Pascal's integer and real numeric data types, concentrating on specific problems with programming numeric expressions. The chapter also explains how to make good use of Turbo Pascal's math coprocessor data types.

- Chapter 13, "Advanced Techniques," details many of Turbo Pascal's special features for accessing memory, using typecasting and conditional compilation, writing large programs with the Exec function, and declaring structured variable constants. You'll also learn how to design custom exit routines and efficient overlays.

- Chapter 14, "Pascal Meets Assembly Language," takes you down the dark alley of adding machine language to Pascal using Turbo Pascal's new built-in assembler—not really so dangerous once you understand the fundamentals.

- Chapter 15, "Object-Oriented Programming," introduces Turbo Pascal OOP extensions. Object-oriented programming is gaining new acceptance among programmers, and this chapter will help you to enter this brave new world. Many program examples, diagrams, and a glossary explain OOP concepts and terms.

- Chapter 16, "Introducing Turbo Vision," explains how to use Turbo Pascal's extensive object-oriented Turbo Vision library to write programs with pulldown menus, overlapping windows, and dialog boxes—the same features employed in the Turbo Pascal editor. (Note: Some of the text in this chapter and the next was previously published in my *Inside Turbo Pascal* column, *Mastering Turbo Vision,* published by The Cobb Group.)

- Chapter 17, "Turbo Vision Tools," continues the story begun in chapter 16, exploring three important Turbo Vision tools: dialogs, collections, and streams.

- Chapter 18, "Turbo Pascal Encyclopedia," praised in the first edition, is a completely updated reference to all Turbo Pascal's procedures and functions. You'll find this expanded reference valuable long after mastering Turbo Pascal.

What This Book Does Not Contain

Instructions for starting your computer, formatting blank diskettes, making disk copies, and using operating system commands are not covered. Consult your computer manuals or ask teachers and friends if you need help with these subjects.

The first edition of this book explained how to use Turbo Pascal on Z-80-based CP/M computers. Turbo Pascal 4.0 and later versions no longer run under CP/M; therefore, this material has been snipped.

Compiler syntax error numbers, runtime errors, installation instructions, information about how to use the editor, descriptions of the integrated and command-line compiler settings, and other details listed in the Turbo Pascal Reference Manual are not repeated here. Borland's Reference Manual describes Turbo Pascal, the program. This book teaches how to use Turbo Pascal, the language. You need both books to master Turbo Pascal.

For those who are having trouble getting started, though, the next section explains one way to type in example programs. There may be other, even better ways, for typing and running programs, methods you will best learn by reading your reference manual instructions on using the integrated and command-line compilers.

How to Enter Programs

Turbo Pascal comes in two varieties: integrated and command-line. The integrated development system, or IDE, features a multiwindow text editor and can compile and run programs in memory. Because in-memory compilation requires no disk writes, this is the fastest method to compile and run programs. The IDE also can create .EXE code files, which you can run from the DOS command line.

You can use either version of Turbo Pascal to compile the programs in this book. However, you will probably want to use the IDE, which also includes a built-in debugger that lets you examine your program's variables and step slowly through statements while you hunt for bugs.

The following notes describe how to use Turbo Pascal's IDE and command-line compilers to enter, compile, and run this book's example programs.

> **Note:** Turbo Pascal 6.0's IDE was completely rewritten. Although the new IDE has many of the same features in versions 4.0 through 5.5, the new editor is easier to use and more powerful than ever before. You might like to know that Borland's programmers wrote version 6.0's IDE using Turbo Vision, the object-oriented library you'll examine in chapters 16 and 17. If you plan to use Turbo Vision, you'll want to begin using the new IDE now—it is by far the best example of what Turbo Vision can do.

Using the Integrated Development System

1. Prepare your system according to Turbo Pascal's instructions. For best results, when running the automated INSTALL program, specify the base directory name C:\TP rather than the default C:\TURBO. Some of the listings in this book expect Turbo Pascal's home directory to be named C:\TP. If you store the compiler elsewhere, you have to insert the correct path name before the program will run.

2. Make sure C:\TP (or C:\TURBO) is listed in a PATH statement in your AUTOEXEC.BAT file. Then, after booting your computer, use the CD DOS command to switch to a directory where you store files. (For example, create a directory using the command MD C:\MYSTUFF and then enter CD C:\MYSTUFF to make that directory the current one.) It is probably best not to store your own files in Turbo Pascal's directory.

3. Enter TURBO at the DOS prompt to run the IDE. Press Alt-FN to open a blank window. Then enter a sample program's text exactly as printed.

4. Before running a program, it is a good idea to save it to disk. That way, if you made a typing error and are unable to return to the IDE (unlikely, but possible), you can simply reboot and start over. If you forget to save your work, you lose it when you reboot, and you have to retype the program. To save a file, press F2 and enter a file name. From then on, if you make any changes to a file, pressing F2 saves the changes using the same file name. (Note: You can use the *Options:Environment:Preferences* commands to turn on *Auto save:Editor* files. With this option, the IDE automatically saves all modified files before compiling and running programs.)

5. To compile a program, which may be composed of multiple modules called *units,* press F9. This command makes a program, meaning it compiles all its pieces, whether the program has only one module or dozens. (Most programs in this book are self contained in a single module, and do not require making.) To compile *and* run a program, press Ctrl-F9—probably the best way to compile and run most of this book's examples.

6. For most programs, you can leave the Compile menu's Destination setting equal to *Memory,* which compiles a program's text into machine code, stored in memory rather than on disk. This option results in the fastest compilation speeds.

7. If you want to create a stand-alone .EXE code file, which you can run from the DOS command line, change the *Compile* menu's *Destination* setting to *Disk.* When you then press F9 to compile, Turbo Pascal creates a DOS.EXE file containing the current program in binary form, ready to run. You can then quit the IDE (or use the *File* menu's *DOS Shell* command to return temporarily to a DOS prompt) and run the program. After using the *DOS Shell* command, type EXIT to get back to the IDE.

8. Most of the programs in this book are designed to pause at the end so that you can view the program's output before returning to the IDE. After running programs, you might have to press ENTER or ESC to return to Turbo Pascal.

9. After running a program and returning to the IDE, you may view the program's output by pressing Alt-F5. Then, after examining the display, press any key (ENTER or the Spacebar are handiest) to return to the IDE.

10. To quit Turbo Pascal and return to DOS, press Alt-X.

Using the Command-Line Compiler

1. Install Turbo Pascal as suggested in the preceding section. For best results, specify a base directory named C:\TP rather than the default C:\TURBO. Some of the programs in this book expect to find certain files located in C:\TP.

2. Use your favorite ASCII text editor, or the editor in the IDE, to type the program example and save it as NAME.PAS. If you use a word processor to type programs, be sure to save the text as plain ASCII text. Word processors typically add formatting commands and invisible control codes to visible characters, and because Turbo Pascal isn't compatible with every word processor's unique formats, it considers such codes to be typing errors.

3. From the DOS command line, enter the command TPC *name* to compile the file NAME.PAS (you don't have to type the .PAS file name extension) and produce the finished code file NAME.EXE. If you have trouble, be sure the directory containing TPC.EXE is listed in a DOS PATH statement in your AUTOEXEC.BAT file.

4. Unless the compiler has reported an error, run the compiled program by entering its name—just like you run any other program from DOS.

Note: If your computer has an 80286, 80386, or 80486 processor and some extended memory, you can run the alternate protected-mode command-line compiler, TPCX.EXE. Just type TPCX rather than TPC. (You might have to run the TPCXINST.EXE installer before TPCX will operate on your system.) The programs in this book do not require you to use TPCX, which runs more slowly than TPC and the compiler built into the IDE. TPCX is included for developers who want to compile large programs—far larger than any printed in this book. Generally, there is no advantage in using TPCX unless you have run out of memory using the IDE or TPC.

Using the Built-in Debugger

The integrated versions of Turbo Pascal 5.0, 5.5, and 6.0 come with a built-in debugger that can help you find errors in programs and also can help you learn more about programming in Pascal. The debugger can run programs one command at a time, monitor values of variables, and stop a running program at strategic locations.

The following notes explain how to use the built-in debugger's commands. Professional versions of Turbo Pascal come with the more capable stand-alone Turbo Debugger that has many more features and can debug Pascal, C, and assembly language code. (My book, *Mastering Turbo Debugger,* describes how to use the stand-alone Turbo Debugger. Also included with Turbo Pascal Professional is Turbo Assembler, which is described in my book, *Mastering Turbo Assembler.*)

If you are new to Pascal, some of the terms in the following notes might be unfamiliar. But don't let that stop you from using the debugger. As you enter and run the example listings in this book, press F7 to execute statements one at a time. Press Alt-F5 to view the output display and then press any key to return to Turbo Pascal. These commands make it possible for you to examine programs running in slow motion—a useful technique for learning how Pascal works.

Some function keys in the integrated compiler apply only to the debugger; others have more general uses. For reference, the next section lists all function keys, some of which were introduced previously.

Function Keys

F1—On-line help. To get help with specific Turbo Pascal commands, position the cursor on any menu item and press F1. Then follow the on-screen messages to see other help screens. You also can position the cursor on a statement in a program and press F1 for a description of that statement's syntax and requirements. Get used to using Turbo Pascal's *context sensitive* help system—it is a gold mine of facts and tips, and it helps you answer many questions on your own.

F2—Save the current text file. If you never saved the program text before, you are asked to supply a file name.

F3—Load a new file into another window. You can open as many files as memory allows.

F4—Run the program up to the current cursor position. This key is useful for executing just a few statements so that you can see their effects. Place the cursor after the last statement you want to execute. Then press F4.

F5—Zoom the current window to full screen or zoom a full-screen window back to its original size.

F6—Switch to the next window. Active windows have double-line borders. Inactive windows have single-line borders. The editor window must be active before you can enter program text. (Note: Press Shift-F6 to switch to the previously active window.)

F7—Trace the current statement. Use this key to single-step your program, executing one statement at a time. If that statement calls another procedure or function (in other words, a subroutine), the cursor jumps to the first statement in that section of the program. You can then continue pressing F7 to execute the procedure or function one statement at a time.

F8—Step over the current statement. This key works like F7, but if the current statement calls a procedure or function, the cursor does not jump to the first statement in that section of the program. Instead, the subroutine is executed at normal speed, then, after the subroutine returns, the program halts to await your next command.

F9—Compile (make) the program text. Depending on the *Destination* setting in the *Compile* menu, "making" a program stores the executable code in memory or in a disk .EXE file. If the program uses any units (separate modules), pressing F9 compiles all modules that are out of date—that is, those to which you have made changes.

> **Note:** Compiling by pressing F9 is most useful for advanced work. You might want to set the *Compile* menu's *Primary file:* setting to your main program's name. Then, after modifying various modules, set *Destination* to *Disk* and press F9 to recompile only the minimum number of modules needed to bring the entire program to date.

Debugger Menu Commands

The *Debug* menu contains four useful commands you can use to debug a program. The primary purpose of Turbo Pascal's debugger is to let you examine your program in slow motion and view the values of variables so that you can locate the source of problems. Finding bugs is your job; the debugger is only a tool (though a remarkable one) you can use during the hunt.

Get into the habit of using the built-in debugger even when you do not have bugs to track down. When running example listings in this book, if you don't understand how a section operates, run it under the debugger's control. Use the debugger to examine variables. Single-step unfamiliar statements and observe their effects. Learn how to be your own teacher, using the debugger as a guide to how programs work, not only to track down problems.

The following notes describe the commands in Turbo Pascal's *Debug* menu.

Evaluate/modify (Ctrl-F4)

The first command in the *Debug* menu lets you enter expressions and evaluate their results. Select the command to open a dialog window containing three input fields: *Evaluate, Result,* and *New value.* Use the Tab key or a mouse to move from box to box. Press ESC to close the dialog and return to editing.

Enter an expression such as 2 * 3 in the *Evaluate* field. When you then press Enter, the value of the expression appears in the *Result* field. The *New value* field at the bottom of the *Evaluate/modify* dialog lets you give variables new test values. To use this feature, enter a variable's name into the *Evaluate* field and press Enter. You see the variable's current value in the *Result* field. Next, Tab to the *New value* field and enter a new value for the variable. This is a useful debugging technique that lets you experiment with values without having to revise and recompile a program.

You also can call functions and use Turbo Pascal's built-in standard functions such as Abs and Lo in *Evaluate/modify* expressions. For example, enter Abs(V) into the *Evaluate* field to calculate the absolute value (in other words, the positive equivalent) of a variable named V.

> **Hint:** If the *Evaluate/modify* dialog does not seem to work as expected, close the dialog and press F7 to execute at least one program statement. Then reopen the dialog and try your commands again. The program must be "active" for the dialog to be able to find the program's symbols.

Watches

Selecting this command opens a submenu listing four additional commands, each related to a special window called *Watches.* The Watches window lets you *watch* the values of variables while you execute sections of a program. Often, just seeing the values of your variables as they change is enough to lead you to the source of problems. Watching the Watches window is also an excellent way to learn about the effects of statements on variables. The *Watches* menu includes the following four commands:

Add watch (Ctrl-F7)

Use this command to add a new variable name to the Watches window. After selecting the command or pressing Ctrl-F7, you see a dialog box into which you can enter a variable's name. Or, you can press the cursor keys to scroll through a list of variables you entered previously, perhaps to reinsert a deleted variable into Watches.

Instead of entering variable names by hand, you also can position the cursor on any letter of a variable you want to monitor and press Ctrl-F7. Then press Enter to add the variable to the Watches window.

Because variables inside procedures and functions are "visible" to the program only when those procedures and functions are executing, listing such local variables in the Watches window might give "Unknown identifier" error messages. When the program runs those procedures and functions, the variables "come alive," showing their correct values. As a consequence of local variables, Turbo Pascal cannot check whether variable names you enter actually exist. No error is given if you enter MyXQY into Watches when you meant to enter MyXY. This is not a bug in the debugger.

Delete watch

Select this command to delete one variable by name from the Watches window. Rather than use this command, however, it is much easier to activate the Watches window, highlight the variable you want to delete, and press DEL.

Edit watch

This command lets you edit the name of a variable in the Watches window. You also can use *Edit watch* to change the index of an array expression such as MyArray[6] to MyArray[10], for instance, — easier than retyping an entire expression.

Remove all watches

As you might expect, selecting this command deletes all variables listed in the Watches window.

Toggle breakpoint (Ctrl-F8)

The third command in the *Debug* menu adds a breakpoint at the current cursor position. A breakpoint is like a bookmark—it stops a running program just before executing the marked statement, displayed in red or some other attribute that distinguishes the line from other text.

By entering a series of breakpoints in a program, you can run the code to various stopping places. Then, you can use the Watches window and *Evaluate/modify* command to examine the values of variables at strategic locations. For example, move the cursor to any statement in a program, then press Ctrl-F8 to set a breakpoint on that statement's line. (Breakpoints are line oriented—you can set them only for an entire line in a program, which is one good reason to enter statements on separate lines.) To remove a breakpoint, move the cursor to its line and press Ctrl-F8 again.

After setting one or more breakpoints, press Ctrl-F9 to run (and if necessary to compile) the program. When execution reaches the line with the breakpoint, the program halts, showing you the line that is about to be executed. You can then examine variables, press F7 or F8 to step slowly through a program starting from this location, or press Ctrl-F9 to continue running to the next breakpoint or to the program's end.

Breakpoints

The fourth and final *Debug* menu command opens a dialog box that lists every breakpoint currently set in the program. Use this list to review your breakpoints and to examine their conditions and line numbers.

After selecting the *Breakpoints* command, you can choose from a number of options listed as a row of buttons at the bottom of the dialog window. Press Enter or Esc to close the dialog and return to editing. Press D to delete a highlighted breakpoint. Press V to view a breakpoint's line in the program text. Press C to clear all breakpoints.

With the Breakpoints dialog open, you also can press E to open yet another dialog, listing four editing options. Enter an expression into this dialog's *Condition* field to set a condition for a breakpoint to monitor. For example, after setting a breakpoint, if you enter the expression (I > 100) into the breakpoint's *Condition* field, the breakpoint halts the program only if the specified statement is executed *and* if I's value is greater than 100.

Set the Breakpoints dialog's *Pass count* to an integer value representing the number of times you want a breakpoint to be skipped. For instance, if you set the *Pass count* to 10, the breakpoint halts the program only *after* the marked statement is executed 10 times.

You will probably never enter data into the other two fields in the *Edit Breakpoint* dialog. The *File name* field shows the file for which a breakpoint is set. The *Line number* field shows the breakpoint's line number in the specified file's text. Because the IDE can open multiple file windows, it might be useful to examine these fields at times, if only to confirm that a breakpoint is set in the expected file and location.

1

Programming by Example

- Key Words and Identifiers
- The Program Body
- Error Messages
- Introducing Strings
- Reading Railroad Diagrams
- Declaring Variables
- Pascal Input—Reading Strings

1

Key Words and Identifiers

begin, **end**, **program**, Readln, **string**, **var**, Write, Writeln

The best way to master a programming language is to enter programs and make them run on a computer. Books might inspire, but they can never replace your own experience. To help you gain that experience, this book is filled with example Pascal programs of many kinds. Enter them all and do the exercises at the end of each chapter, and you'll be well on your way to mastering Turbo Pascal. With no further delay, then, let's turn to our first example of a complete Pascal program, Program 1-1.

Program 1-1: WELCOME.PAS

```
1:  program Welcome;
2:  begin
3:    Writeln('Welcome to Pascal Programming');
4:    Readln
5:  end.
```

There are five numbered lines in Program 1-1. When you enter the program, exclude the line numbers and colons along the left border. They have been added for reference to most example programs in this book.

The first line of Program 1-1 is the *program declaration,* which has three parts: the key word **program**; a name, or *identifier,* that you make up; and a semicolon. All Pascal programs begin with a similar declaration.

Key Words and Identifiers

Pascal reserves *key words* for special purposes. *Key identifiers,* on the other hand, are built-in commands and symbols in the Pascal language. Other identifiers are words that you create. You can reuse key identifiers, but you risk redefining their original meanings. You can never reuse key words for your own purposes.

For example, Welcome, an identifier from Program 1-1, describes what the program does. You could just as well name the program X29B, but that's no help to others who have to read what you write. **program** is a key word with special meaning to the Pascal compiler. Writeln is a key identifier, a built-in language element.

In this book, key words are in all lowercase, while other identifiers are in upper- and lowercase. In the text, **boldface** words refer to key words. When entering programs, you may type in upper- or lowercase as you prefer. **BEGIN**, **begin**, and **BeGin**, for example, are all the same to Pascal.

When inventing your own identifiers, avoid duplicating key words, or you'll receive an error message from the compiler. Also, try not to use built-in identifiers, or you might redefine their meanings. To help you avoid these problems, chapters begin with a list of the key words and identifiers covered in the chapter. Some identifiers appear in more than one list.

The Program Body

Key words **begin** and **end** mark the body of Program 1-1. Inside the program body are the main actions that occur when you run the program. Notice the period after **end**. A period is the last symbol in all Pascal programs. Turbo Pascal ignores any characters after the **end** and its period.

Writeln (pronounced "write line") is a procedure—a Pascal command—that writes lines of text and other things to the display. (In later chapters, you'll learn how to use Writeln to write to a printer or diskette file, too.) Inside Writeln's parentheses is a *string,* marked with beginning and ending single quotation marks. Together, the Writeln, parentheses, and **string** in line 3 form a *statement*—a description of an action you want Pascal to perform. When you press Ctrl-F9 to compile and run Program 1-1, you see the following message on your display:

```
Welcome to Pascal Programming
```

Readln in line 4 is another procedure, one that causes the program to wait for you to press Enter. When running programs in Turbo Pascal's integrated development environment, or IDE, a fast program's actions may pass by so quickly, you'll never have the chance to see what the program does. For that reason, the Readln statement at line 4 pauses for you to read the program's output. After you do that, press Enter to return to editing. (If you are using another editor and compiling from the DOS command line, you can omit the Readln statement.)

Error Messages

Unfortunately for programmers, computers demand perfection. The tiniest typing error brings the Turbo Pascal compiler to a halt. When that happens, read the error message at the bottom of the display, then press Esc or another key. The error message will help you discover what the compiler did not understand.

Because you probably will make many errors while typing the examples in this book—a perfectly normal, if at times exasperating, experience—it helps to make a few errors on purpose now so you'll know how to deal with them later. Let's see what happens when you introduce a few common mistakes into Program 1-1.

Program 1-2 is the same as Program 1-1, but it has three errors. First, a colon incorrectly replaces the semicolon at the end of line 1. Second, the Writeln statement is misspelled. And third, the period following **end** is missing. When you press Ctrl-F9 to compile and run the program, you receive this error message:

```
Error 85: ";" expected.
```

Program 1-2: WELCOME2.PAS (with errors)

```
1:   program Welcome:
2:   begin
3:     Writelm('Welcome to Pascal Programming');
4:     Readln
5:   end
```

Assuming you are using Turbo Pascal's IDE, you should see the cursor positioned on the faulty colon. Change the colon to a semicolon, and compile the program again. Instead of success, you see another error message at the top of the display:

```
Error 3: Unknown identifier.
```

The cursor is now under the *W* of the misspelled Writelm. Pascal doesn't understand what a Writelm is and, therefore, gives the "Unknown identifier" error. Correct the error by changing Writelm to Writeln, and compile. Once again, you receive an error message:

```
Error 10: Unexpected end of file.
```

That simply means the program text, or *source code,* ended before the compiler found the program's final **end** and period. As you can see, Turbo Pascal insists on a complete program at all times. You can certainly add things to a program, and your work may at times be unfinished, but the program must be officially, or *syntactically,* complete before it will compile. This helpful feature of Pascal lets you compile and test your programs at every stage of development, making sure before going to the next stage that each new addition operates as you expect.

After adding the missing period to the **end** in line 4, compile Program 1-2 again. This time, you should receive no errors.

The process of programming, compiling, correcting errors, and recompiling, over and over, is normal, although in time you'll learn to avoid the more common mistakes. Don't think, however, that because you receive a lot of errors you're doing something wrong. Even top professional programmers make plenty of mistakes and spend a good bit, if not the major portion, of their time getting the bugs out of their programs. Knowing this, perhaps you should change Program 1-2 to display the string, 'Welcome to the club!'

Introducing Strings

Strings are sequences of characters that you want a program to treat as one object. Usually, the characters in a string are visible, constructed from all the letters, digits, punctuation marks, and other symbols available on your keyboard. Less frequently, strings contain invisible *control characters* that perform actions rather than display visible symbols. One example of a control character is Ctrl-I, produced by pressing the Tab key. The tab character is a character just like A or B, but it has no visible symbol. Control characters like Ctrl-I are often abbreviated with a caret, as in ^ I.

To create a string, place single quotation marks, called *delimiters,* at the beginning and end of the characters you want to group. An unbroken string must fit on one line, though you can use plus signs to create strings from fragments on separate lines like this:

```
'One for ' +
'all, and ' +
'all for one.'
```

Although the maximum string length is 255 characters, Turbo Pascal can compile lines containing no more than 127 characters. Even so, the Turbo Pascal editor lets you type practically an unlimited number of characters per line. Other editors may impose smaller maximum line lengths. (Details like these can drive you nuts. Don't worry too much about them.) As you'll learn later, there are ways to avoid these limitations by breaking long strings into pieces.

You already saw one example of a string in Program 1-1. Here's another:

```
'This is a Pascal string.'
```

Try inserting this string in place of the one in the Writeln statement of Program 1-1. Compile and run the program, then remove one or both of the quotation marks, and recompile. Did you receive an error message?

You might wonder, if single quotation marks delimit the beginning and end of a string, how do you display a quotation mark itself? To do that, simply repeat the quotation mark. This tells the compiler to insert a quotation mark into a string, not to mark the string's end. Here, for example, is a string with a contraction:

```
'Don''t give up the ship!'
```

There are no spaces between the single quotation marks in Don"t. Be careful to type *two* single quotation marks and not the double quotation character ("). Insert this new string into the Writeln statement of Program 1-1. When you run the program, you see:

```
Don't give up the ship!
```

Reading Railroad Diagrams

As you learn about the Pascal language, you'll encounter many definitions of various features. For clarity and future reference, there is a precise method for defining these features and explaining Pascal *syntax,* the rules for combining language elements into statements and programs. Language designers use these same methods to create new programming languages and to write compilers like Turbo Pascal.

Pictures, as the saying goes—at least among programmers—are worth a kiloword. And Pascal syntax is often best described in picture-like graphs called *railroad diagrams.*

Figure 1-1 is an example of a railroad diagram, also called a *syntax graph.* To read a railroad diagram, trace the lines with your finger. The diagram is a guide to Pascal symbols, showing their forms and relationships. Each diagram has one entry point (usually at the left) and one exit point (usually at the right). For clarity, some of the diagrams here and in other chapters are modified versions of the full Turbo Pascal syntax diagrams in Appendix A.

program declaration

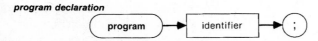

Figure 1-1 Railroad diagram describing the syntax of a **program** declaration, the first line of all Pascal programs.

Compare the diagram in Figure 1-1 with the first line of Program 1-1 while reading the following descriptions of the three essential railroad diagram components.

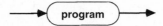

Each encircled part of a railroad diagram contains a symbol, word, or punctuation mark. A single encircled character means you should type that character at this position. Boldface encircled words are language key words. Enter them exactly as spelled. As you learned earlier, the key word **program** is the first word of a Pascal program, a fact the railroad diagram in Figure 1-1 confirms.

A lowercase nonboldface encircled word stands for another symbol or group of symbols with an obvious meaning. For example, the lowercase *digit* tells you that one of the digits 0 through 9 is allowed at this place in a program.

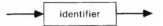

Boxed-in words represent the contents of another diagram. This rule lets simple diagrams serve as building blocks in other more complex graphs while avoiding duplication and clutter. Looking at Figure 1-1, you would expect to find a separate diagram for the boxed *identifier* (see Figure 1-2). You could replace the boxed *identifier* in Figure 1-1 with the entire diagram in Figure 1-2 and still correctly show program declaration syntax.

identifier

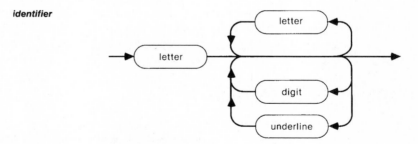

Figure 1-2 An identifier begins with a letter, followed by any number of digits, letters, and underlines.

There are many possible paths through the diagram in Figure 1-2. Notice that some of the arrows point to the left, indicating repetition. The diagram tells you that an identifier begins with a letter, followed by any combination of other letters, digits, and underlines.

By the way, underlines can make long identifiers more readable, as in Speed_of_Light. When using underlines this way, be aware that Turbo Pascal considers Speed_of_Light and SpeedOfLight to be *different* identifiers. (Many other Pascal compilers ignore the underlines.) For this reason, the programs in this book do not use underlines in identifiers.

Compare the identifier railroad diagram in Figure 1-2 with the identifiers in Table 1-1. Listed on the left are correct identifiers; on the right, illegal or badly formed identifiers. Prove to yourself that each word conforms to the rules for well-formed identifiers.

Table 1-1 Identifier rights and wrongs.

Right	Wrong
GoodSym	Bad sym
Fahrenheit_451	32_Degrees
ABCDEFG	876.543
MoneyBags	$Moneybags$
OverWeight	Under-weight

Now that you know the basics of reading railroad diagrams, you should be able to draw a diagram for defining Pascal strings. Try a few designs before looking at the answer in Figure 1-3. How will you diagram the method described earlier for inserting single quotation marks into strings?

string

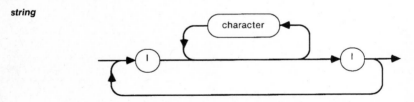

Figure 1-3 Railroad diagram showing how to delimit strings with single quotation marks.

Declaring Variables

In Pascal, as in most other programming languages, *variables* hold data on which a program operates. In the program text, the variable's name represents the value of data stored somewhere in computer memory when the program runs. This value does not have to be numeric, although it often is. You can name variables for numbers, zip codes, and account balances, as well as for strings, names, addresses—even the colors of the rainbow.

Variables are like boxes that hold values, as Figure 1-4 illustrates. Pascal requires you to decide in advance on the type of values that fit in the box. For example, if you declare a variable as an *integer,* meaning a whole number, then that variable cannot hold a string or a floating point value.

```
var
   A, B, C: string[10];
```

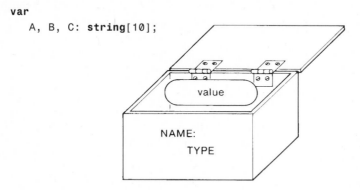

Figure 1-4 A variable is similar to a box with a name and type. The type defines what kind of value goes in the box; the program refers to the value by its name.

Likewise, a string variable may not hold a number. A variable, then, has an associated data *type,* indicating the kind of value it contains. Program 1-3 shows how to declare a string variable, YourName.

Program 1-3: WHO.PAS

```
1:   program WhoAreYou;
2:   var
3:     YourName: string[40];
4:   begin
5:     Write('What is your name? ');
6:     Readln(YourName);
7:     Writeln('Hi there, ', YourName, '!');
8:     Readln
9:   end.
```

Several new elements are in Program 1-3. Lines 2 and 3 make up the *variable declaration,* starting with the key word **var** and declaring a variable YourName. The type of the variable is a string with a maximum character length of 40 in brackets. You can declare string variables with lengths from 1 to 255 characters. When the program runs, the string variable can hold from 0 to its declared maximum number of characters.

If you don't specify a maximum string length in brackets, Turbo Pascal automatically assigns a 255-character limit. For example, the following two strings, StringThing1 and StringThing2, can each hold up to 255 characters:

```
var
  StringThing1: string[255];
  StringThing2: string;
```

All variable declarations start with **var**. After that comes a series of identifiers, each followed by a colon and data type, ending with a semicolon. (See Figure 1-5.) To declare multiple variables of the same type, separate their identifiers with commas. For example, the following variable declaration creates three ten-character strings called A, B, and C:

```
var
  A, B, C: string[10];
```

variable declaration

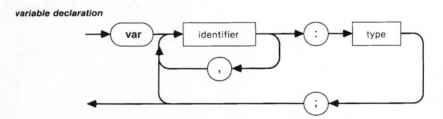

Figure 1-5 The variable declaration part of a program follows the program declaration (see Figure 1-1).

Besides the variable declaration, there's another new feature of Program 1-3 in the four lines between **begin** and **end.** The two previous examples had only single statements in the program bodies. This program has multiple statements separated from each other by semicolons. Together, lines 4-9 form a *compound statement.*

To show its relationship to other parts of the program, each statement is indented on a separate line. You could put all statements on the same line with or without indentations. Turbo Pascal requires only that semicolons separate multiple statements. A statement's physical position and indentation are conveniences for your sake—and for others who have to read your program.

Program 1-3 also shows how to use a Write statement (line 5). Except for one difference, Write is the same as Writeln. Writeln issues a carriage return, moving the cursor to the start of the next line down. Write does not end a line with a carriage return. After Write, the cursor stays on the same line just after the last character written.

Pascal Input—Reading Strings

Line 6 of Program 1-3 contains a Pascal identifier you haven't seen before, Readln. A Readln statement reads information into a variable, in this case, YourName. As used here, Readln takes its input from the keyboard. When the program gets to line 6, it waits for you to enter something. Readln restricts your typing to a maximum of 127 characters, even if the string variable can hold more. Of course, you may use shorter strings, as in the example. In this case, you can still type up to 127 characters, but Pascal ignores characters beyond the declared string length.

Readln lets you edit your typing. You can backspace over mistakes and type corrections before pressing Enter and sending to the program what you type. See Table 1-2 for a list of other editing keys you can use.

Table 1-2 Readln editing keys.

Key	Operation
Backspace	Moves the cursor left, erasing mistakes
←	Works the same as the backspace key
Esc	Prints a backslash (\) and carriage return, cancelling any characters typed so far and letting you reenter the line
Enter	Ends input, placing typed characters in Readln's variable
^C	Ends the program (the caret is shorthand for Ctrl)

When you press Enter, the Readln statement deposits your typing into YourName, which the program then displays in a Writeln statement (line 7). Look closely at this line. Inside parentheses are two literal strings plus the variable YourName separated by commas. Writeln writes these individual elements as though they formed one string. Therefore, when you run the program, "Hi there" is followed by whatever you type into YourName, which is in turn followed by an exclamation point. The ability to combine various elements in a single Write or Writeln statement is powerful, and you'll see this feature again and again in future examples.

Summary

Studying, entering, and running program examples is the best way to master Turbo Pascal. This book has many examples. You should enter, compile, and run them all, and observe how they operate.

Key words are reserved words in Pascal. Key identifiers are built-in language elements. Other identifiers are words that you invent. Statements are descriptions of actions to perform. Railroad diagrams describe the relationships between key words, identifiers, and other symbols and show how to write Pascal statements.

Strings are sequences of symbols, surrounded by single quotation marks. You can store strings, as well as other data types, in declared variables, giving descriptive names to values the program uses. Use two quotation marks to display a single quotation mark.

To display strings, use Write or Writeln. To read strings, letting people enter data into a program, use Readln. To display multiple items in Write and Writeln statements, separate the items with commas.

Exercises

1-1. Write a program to display the following message on your screen.

```
Pack my box with five dozen liquor jugs.
```

1-2. Write a program to display the following two lines. Use multiple Writeln statements. Watch out for the punctuation!

```
"It's eleven o'clock," she said,
"why aren't you in bed?"
```

1-3. Assume that the only parts of English speech are articles, adjectives, nouns, and verbs. Draw a syntax diagram (or diagrams) describing how to compose simple, grammatically correct sentences. Show how to punctuate multiple adjectives with commas, as in "The quick, brown fox jumped over the lazy dog."

1-4. Add a definition for compound sentences to your diagram from exercise 1-3. Identify the key words.

1-5. Using a string variable and a combination of Readln and Writeln statements, write a program that prompts for a string, then duplicates the string three times. For example, if you type "Apple," the program should write "AppleAppleApple." One solution uses five statements. Can you do it using three?

2

Data—What a Program Knows

- The Constant Declaration
- Numeric Constants
- Scientific Notation
- Formatting Numbers
- String and Character Constants
- Boolean Constants
- Variables
- The Assignment Operator
- Comparison Operators
- Declaring Variables
- Common Programming Errors
- Subrange Types
- Range Checking
- Expressions
- Operator Precedence
- Mixing Reals and Integers
- Inserting Comments in Programs
- Compiler Directives
- Variable Constants
- Constant Expressions

2

Key Words and Identifiers

> Boolean, Byte, Char, **const**, Integer, LongInt, Real, ShortInt, **string**, Word

Data are facts that a computer program knows. A program might know your name, your weight, the time of day, the date, the amount of money you have in your savings, and the amount you owe to the telephone company. In Pascal, data that can change are stored in *variables. Constants,* on the other hand, hold data that do not change. This chapter explains how to get data in and out of programs using variables and constants.

The Constant Declaration

Figure 2-1 shows the railroad diagram for a constant declaration, which comes between the program declaration and body but before any variable declaration. Each constant has an identifier and an associated constant value. In a program, you might have constants named Size or Height. After declaring these and other constants, you can use their descriptive names in place of their values.

constant declaration

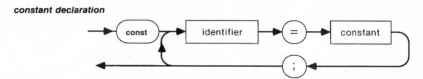

Figure 2-1 Railroad diagram describing the constant declaration part of a Pascal program.

The constant declaration part of Program 2-1 begins with the key word **const**, followed by a list of constants separated by semicolons (lines 2-5). Each constant declaration has an identifier, an equal sign, a value, and a semicolon. The value determines the data type of the constant. For example, line 3 declares a string constant, Name, while lines 4 and 5 declare two integer, or whole number, constants, Weight and Savings.

Program 2-1: CONSTANT.PAS

```
 1:  program Constants;
 2:  const
 3:    Name = 'Anne';
 4:    Weight = 118;
 5:    Savings = 375;
 6:  begin
 7:    Writeln('Name  : ', Name);
 8:    Writeln('Weight: ', Weight, ' pounds');
 9:    Writeln(Name, ' has $', Savings, ' in savings');
10:    Readln
11:  end.
```

As demonstrated in Program 2-1, there are two main advantages to using constants in Pascal. Well-chosen constant identifiers make a program more readable and, therefore, easier to understand. Calling 118 Weight and 375 Savings makes the meanings of the two values harder to confuse.

A second advantage is the concentration of constant values at the top of a program. Although a constant name may appear in many different statements, you can easily change the declared value in the constant declaration. When you recompile the program, all statements automatically recognize the new constant.

As an example, Program 2-1 uses the constant Name in two Writeln statements. If you change Anne to your own name in line 3, the program displays your name in lines 7 and 9. With constants, you avoid hunting through a program for values that need changing. In a typical commercial program with thousands of lines, that advantage is a necessity.

In the special case of string constants, Turbo Pascal stores only one copy of a string in memory, even though you might use the string constant identifier many times throughout the program.

Numeric Constants

Whole number, or Integer, constants range from –32,768 to +32,767. Although commas appear in these numbers to make them more readable in this text, never use commas in a program's numbers. Figure 2-2 shows a few typical integer constants as they might appear in a program's constant declaration.

```
const
  MonthsInYear = 12;
  DaysInWeek   = 7;
  HoursInDay   = 24;
  Altitude     = 15000;
```

Figure 2-2 Examples of Integer, or whole number, constants.

Along with plain integers, Turbo Pascal has four other whole number types. Byte values range from 0 to 255. ShortInt values range from –128 to +127. Word values range from 0 to 65,535. And LongInt values range from a whopping –2,147,483,648 to +2,147,483,647.

Besides their upper and lower limits, the only difference between these four extra numeric types and Integer values is the amount of memory they occupy. Byte and ShortInt values each take one byte of memory. Integer and Word values each take two bytes. LongInt values take four bytes.

When declaring whole number constants, you never have to specify which type to use. As the following example demonstrates, Turbo Pascal automatically selects the most efficient type—the one that takes the least memory—for you:

```
const
  c1 = 200;       { Byte }
  c2 = -2;        { ShortInt }
  c3 = 1024;      { Integer }
  c4 = 55678;     { Word }
  c5 = 2000000;   { LongInt }
```

Real number constants hold larger numbers or values with fractional parts. In mathematics, real numbers include the set of all rational and irrational values. In Pascal, a real number is simply any number with a decimal point. You might declare dollar values or the distance from the earth to the moon as real-number constants. Figure 2-3 lists a few other examples. Notice that values between 0 and 1 must have a leading 0 to the left of the decimal point as in 0.123, and that values with no fractional part must end in a period as in 999. or a period and 0 as in 999.0 to be Real numbers instead of Integer.

```
const
  MinimumWage   = 3.65;
  MilesToMoon   = 238857.0;
  InterestRate  = 0.123;
  MetersPerMile = 1609.344;
```

Figure 2-3 Examples of Real number constants.

Scientific Notation

To see the effect of using real-number constants instead of integers, change the value of Savings in Program 2-1 from 375 to 375.50. When you run the program, it now displays the following line:

```
Anne has $ 3.7550000000E+02 in savings
```

As you can see from that example, real numbers normally display in *scientific notation,* a convenient shorthand for expressing large and small values. Dropping trailing zeros for clarity, the value 3.755E+02 is equivalent to the more common mathematical notation, 3.755×10^2. To read the shorthand value, move the decimal point the number of places indicated by the exponent E. Move the decimal point right for positive exponents. Move it left for negative exponents. Thus, 5.123E+03 is equivalent to 5,123.00. And 6.5E-03 is the same as 0.0065. Moving the decimal place two digits to the right in the previous example, you can see that Anne has 375.50 in savings.

The range of real numbers is much larger than the range of integers. For most purposes, you can assume that real numbers have no limit, although in Turbo Pascal the actual range is approximately plus or minus 2.9E-39 to 1.7E+38. You can extend this range by using a numeric data processor (NDP)—either an 8087, 80287, 80387, or equivalent—or by switching on Turbo Pascal's NDP emulation routines. See Chapter 12, "More About Numbers," for details.

Formatting Numbers

Of course, unless you're fussy about fractions of pennies, two decimal places are sufficient to display dollar amounts. To properly display the real-number Savings constant in Program 2-1, rewrite line 9 to read:

```
Writeln(Name, ' has $', Savings:8:2, ' in savings');
```

The notation :8:2 is a formatting command that tells Writeln to display the value of Savings in eight columns *including* a maximum of two decimal places. Specifying decimal places is optional. Try Savings:8 or Savings:20:4. (The same formatting rules apply to Write and Writeln statements.) Also experiment with different values for Savings in the program's constant declaration. What happens when you use the value 50.459 or 123.456789?

A useful notation is :0:*n*, where *n* is the number of decimal places to display. Even though the 0 appears to specify no columns for the value's whole number part, Turbo Pascal always displays the correct value in cases where numbers require more columns than you specify. Therefore, :0:2 displays any real number with two decimal places but with no leading spaces. To see how this works, change Savings to Savings:0:2 in line 9 of Program 2-1.

Another trick is to use :0:0, which displays the integer part of a Real value rounded to the nearest whole number. Change Savings to Savings:0:0 and experiment with different constant values. For example, 375.49 displays as 375 while 375.50 is rounded up to 376. (Note: Some earlier Turbo Pascal versions rounded 375.50 down to 375 and 375.51 up to 376.)

Using a similar notation, you can also format integer values in Write and Writeln statements. Because integers have no fractional part, specify only the number of columns. To format the integer constant Weight in a ten-character-wide column, replace line 8 in Program 2-1 with this line:

```
Writeln('You weigh ', Weight:10, ' pounds');
```

In addition to letting you create your own constants, Turbo Pascal has two predeclared numeric constants, listed in Table 2-1. You can use MaxInt and MaxLongInt without first defining their values.

Table 2-1 Predefined numeric constants.

Constant	Value	Type
MaxInt	32,767	Integer
MaxLongInt	2,147,483,647	LongInt

String and Character Constants

Figure 2-4 lists a few examples of string and character constants. Single-character constants are type Char. Multiple-character constants are type **string**. You can associate any string of characters with a constant identifier, which you may then use throughout a program in place of the actual, or *literal*, string.

```
const
  LastName      = 'Bush';
  FirstName     = 'George';
  MiddleInitial = 'H';
  Address       = 'The White House';
  CityStateZip  = 'Washington, DC 10000';
  PhoneNumber   = '202-555-1212';
```

Figure 2-4 Examples of string and character constants.

Because single characters are type Char, it apparently is not possible to declare single-character string constants. What type, for example, is MiddleInitial in Figure 2-4? Is it a single character or a single-character string? What's the difference?

To solve this ambiguity, Turbo Pascal's designers rightly chose to allow single characters such as A or X in most places where strings are called for. This allowance may seem vague and unimportant to you now, but it is more understandable when you know that a string is stored in memory along with an invisible value that indicates its length. There is no such value stored with single characters, but there would be with single-character strings. Thus, in your program, the *character* H appears identical to the *string* H, but it is stored differently in memory, a difference that Turbo Pascal conveniently ignores.

Boolean Constants

Type Boolean, named after the nineteenth-century English mathematician George Boole (1815-1864), has two possible values, true and false. The Boolean data type is a critical feature of Pascal, and, because of its use in logical expressions, it's a fair assumption that the self-educated Boole would have approved of this use of his family name. Although Boole's formal education ended after elementary school, he went on to father modern Boolean algebra, without which today's digital computers—and programming languages like Pascal—could not have been designed.

Boolean constants, and Boolean variables, contribute to the readability of Pascal programs while making complex sequences seem logical and appropriate. For example, if you declare a Boolean constant Debugging, your program can test if Debugging is true or false and take appropriate action, perhaps displaying various things that only you, and not your clients, need to see. Used in this way, a Boolean constant is a kind of logical switch, the conceptual equivalent of a test switch that might be found inside a TV or a computer.

Another use for Boolean constants is to keep track of true or false facts. In Program 2-2, the five Boolean constants in lines 3-8 describe facts about a fictitious computer system. The Writeln statements in lines 12-17 display these values in a table. (The lone Writeln in line 18 writes a blank line on the display.) Let's say you're looking for a system that has graphics, is portable, and comes with a printer. Line 19 indicates whether the various settings conform to your specifications. The phrase Graphics **and** Portable **and** Printer is a Boolean expression that evaluates to a single true or false result when the program runs.

Program 2-2: LOOKALIK.PAS

```
 1:   program Lookalike;
 2:   const
 3:      Graphics   = false;
 4:      Compatible = true;
 5:      Dvorak     = false;
 6:      Portable   = true;
 7:      Printer    = true;
 8:      Harddisk   = false;
 9:   begin
10:      Writeln('** Look-alike specifications **'    );
11:      Writeln('------------------------------'     );
12:      Writeln('    Graphics .......... ', Graphics  );
13:      Writeln('    IBM compatible .... ', Compatible);
14:      Writeln('    Dvorak keyboard ... ', Dvorak    );
15:      Writeln('    Portable .......... ', Portable  );
16:      Writeln('    Printer .......... ', Printer    );
17:      Writeln('    Hard disk ........ ', Harddisk   );
18:      Writeln;
19:      Writeln('Good choice = ', Graphics and Portable and Printer);
20:      Readln
21:   end.
```

A Boolean expression may have any combination of Boolean constants or variables plus the key word operators **and**, **or**, **not**, and **xor**. For example, you could replace line 19 with one of the following two Writeln statements:

```
Writeln('Good choice =', Compatible and Printer or HardDisk);
Writeln('Good choice = ', not Portable and Graphics and Printer);
```

Pascal evaluates each Boolean expression into one final true or false value. Each of the Boolean operators has a different effect. **not** changes a Boolean value from true to false or from false to true. **and** combines two Boolean values for a true result only if both operands are true. **or** combines two Boolean values with a true result if one or both operands are true. **xor** (exclusive or) combines two Boolean values with a true result if only one value is true. This relationship is easier to see in a truth table, as shown in Table 2-2, which lists the results of **and**ing, **or**ing, and **xor**ing two operands A and B for all possible true and false combinations.

Table 2-2 Boolean truth tables.

A	*and*	B	=	C
false		false		false
false		true		false
true		false		false
true		true		true

A	*or*	B	=	C
false		false		false
false		true		true
true		false		true
true		true		true

A	*xor*	B	=	C
false		false		false
false		true		true
true		false		true
true		true		false

Variables

Unlike constants, variables may change their values many times while a program runs. In Program 1-3, you learned how to declare a single string variable, YourName. The value of YourName changes to whatever you enter in response to the program's Readln statement. Most programs have many such variables, all of a variety of types: real numbers, integers, strings, and other Pascal data types.

The Assignment Operator

To assign literal values to variables, use Pascal's *assignment operator,* a double character symbol composed of a colon and equal sign. For example, the following statement assigns 125 to the integer variable Height:

```
Height := 125;
```

      The variable on the left takes on the value of the expression or literal value on the right of the assignment symbol. While reading a Pascal program, pronounce := as "becomes equal to" or just "becomes." Don't confuse a simple equal sign with Pascal's assignment symbol. The equal sign states a fact, such as the fact that Height = 125. This is not the same as assigning the value 125 to a variable named Height.

Comparison Operators

      The equal sign is called a *comparison operator* because it compares its two operands—the values on either side of the operator—with each other. Table 2-3 lists other Turbo Pascal comparison operators.

Table 2-3 Comparison operators.

Operator	Meaning	Example
=	Equal	(a = b)
<	Less than	(a < b)
>	Greater than	(a > b)
<=	Less than or equal	(a <= b)
>=	Greater than or equal	(a >= b)
<>	Not equal	(a <> b)

      Having made an assignment to Height, it may then be true that Height = 125. This is intuitive, but many programming languages make no similar distinction between statements of fact and assignments of values to variables. In fact, many languages use the equal sign for both purposes, making programs difficult to understand. In Pascal, you can always differentiate between assignments and statements of fact, an important quality of a professional computer language.

Declaring Variables

      You already know how to declare a single variable. (See the **var** railroad diagram in Figure 1-5.) Declaring more than one variable is equally simple, as Program 2-3 demonstrates.

Program 2-3: VARY.PAS

```
 1:  program Vary;
 2:  var
 3:     Name:    string[20];
 4:     Weight:  Integer;
 5:     Savings: Real;
 6:  begin
 7:     Name := 'Anne';
 8:     Weight := 118;
 9:     Savings := 375.75;
10:     Writeln('Name    : ', Name);
11:     Writeln('Weight  : ', Weight);
12:     Writeln('Savings : ', Savings:4:2);
13:
14:     Writeln;
15:
16:     Name := 'Tom';
17:     Weight := 155;
18:     Savings := 0.25;
19:     Writeln('Name    : ', Name);
20:     Writeln('Weight  : ', Weight);
21:     Writeln('Savings : ', Savings:4:2);
22:     Readln
23:  end.
```

The identifiers in lines 3-5 have the same names as the constants in Program 2-1. This time, though, the program assigns new values to the variables. Unlike constants, variables do not have predefined values. The first thing to do, then, is to initialize a program's variables with assignments.

Lines 7-9 do this by assigning initial values to Name, Weight, and Savings. After that, lines 10-12 display the assigned values. The same process is repeated in lines 16-21, but this time with new values assigned to the same variables. You now have a simple database program recording various facts about people. Try duplicating lines 16-21 yet again, adding another set of facts to the program.

As lines 3-5 in Program 2-3 show, you must declare every variable as a specific data type. This example has **string**, Integer, and Real number variables. You could also declare variables of the other types we've seen, such as Char, Boolean, and Byte. Program 2-4 demonstrates this with six variables of various common data types.

Program 2-4: MANYTYPE.PAS

```
 1:  program ManyTypes;
 2:  var
 3:     Weight:  Integer;
 4:     Age:     Byte;
 5:     Savings: Real;
 6:     Married: Boolean;
 7:     Sex:     Char;
 8:     Name:    string[20];
 9:  begin
10:     Name := 'Marvin';
11:     Age := 42;
12:     Sex := 'M';
13:     Married := True;
14:     Weight := 160;
15:     Savings := 12931.32;
16:
17:     Writeln('Name    : ', Name);
18:     Writeln('Age     : ', Age);
19:     Writeln('Sex     : ', Sex);
20:     Writeln('Married : ', Married);
21:     Writeln('Weight  : ', Weight);
22:     Writeln('Savings : ', Savings:6:2);
23:     Readln
24:  end.
```

When you assign a value to a variable, Pascal checks that the value matches the variable's declared type. This characteristic, known as *strong type checking,* helps prevent one of the most common programming errors—assigning the wrong value to a variable, for example, confusing your age with your golf score. In another language, the variable Married from Program 2-4 might be a simple number, with 0 standing for true and 1 for false. In that case, nothing prevents you from accidentally assigning the value 125 to Married; this is clearly an error, but not something the computer is able to catch. In Pascal, such an assignment would never make it through the compiler. Program 2-4 declares Married as a Boolean data type, which cannot hold a numeric value. Married can be only true or false.

Common Programming Errors

To see what happens when you assign the wrong kind of value to a variable, breaking Pascal's strong type-checking rule, change line 13 in Program 2-4 to read:

```
Married := 500;
```

When you compile the program, you receive:

```
Error 26: Type mismatch.
```

The Boolean data type, remember, has only two values, true or false—numbers are not allowed.

Errors like these are called *syntax errors* because they break one of the syntactical rules of Pascal programming. When you receive a syntax error, check the appropriate railroad diagram in Appendix A. You'll often find your mistake this way.

Syntax errors stop the compiler. A *runtime error,* on the other hand, occurs while the program is running. Syntax and runtime errors are two of the three most common kinds of programming errors. As you learn more about Pascal programming, you'll undoubtedly become old friends—or enemies—with all three.

The third kind of error, a *logical error,* occurs when you assign a value such as 2000 to a variable such as Weight in Program 2-4. Logical errors are the most difficult to correct. The program has no way of knowing that a person can't weigh 2000 pounds—that's your responsibility.

Subrange Types

To help prevent logical errors, you can declare subranges of numeric variables, telling the compiler to limit the low and high values that variables can hold. Specify a subrange as two whole numbers separated with a double period, called an ellipsis. (In typesetting, an ellipsis has three periods. In Pascal, it has two—the economy model.)

Change the 160 in line 14 of Program 2-4 to 2000 and run the program. Although the weight is now incorrect, the compiler doesn't mind. To correct the error, change line 3 to read:

```
Weight: 7 .. 250;
```

You can now compile the program only if the assignment to Weight is in the range of 7 to 250, a reasonable human weight range. The subrange lets the compiler verify assignments to variables. You still could assign the wrong weight value, of course, but at least you get some protection against catastrophes.

Range Checking

One problem with subrange values is that the compiler can check only for literal assignments to variables. If you assign 5000 pounds to poor Marvin, the compiler can stop with an error message. But if you assign a *variable* to a subrange data type, the compiler can't know the variable's value until the program runs. To see the problem, change line 14 to:

```
Write('Weight? ');
Readln(Weight);
```

This prompts for the weight value, letting you type the answer. Run the program and type 2000. Are you surprised by the result? The reason you do not receive an error is that checking subranges takes time—and time is something that Turbo Pascal is rightfully stingy about wasting. When you want to check subranges automatically during program runs, you must turn on an option called *range checking*. To do this, surround the Readln or any other statement with compiler directives:

```
{$R+} Readln(Weight); {$R-}
```

The {$R+} and {$R–} are commands, called *directives,* to the compiler. They tell Pascal to create automatic range checks for statements in between. {$R+} turns on range checking. {$R–} turns it off. Some people place a single {$R+} at the beginning of their programs to turn on range checking for the entire program. This way, after debugging, it's easy to remove the directive and, therefore, remove the time-consuming code that has to perform the limit checks at every assignment to subrange variables.

For another example of a runtime error, add the following two lines between lines 15 and 16 in Program 2-4:

```
Write('How old are you? ');
{$R+} Readln(Age); {$R-}
```

Compile and run the modified program. Type your age when the program asks, "How old are you?" Now rerun the program. This time, lie. Here's what happened when I said I was 500. (If you see "Error 201: Range check error," press Enter then Alt-F5 to see the following.)

```
How old are you? 500
Runtime error 201 at 0000:00C0.
```

The 0000:00C0 is the address in memory where the error occurred. The number you see will probably be different. After you press Enter to go back to the Turbo Pascal editor, the cursor jumps to the Readln statement where the trouble occurred. Error 201 stopped the program at this location because 500 is outside the legal range of a Byte variable, which can hold values only from 0 to 255.

Run the modified program again. This time, if you type A for your age, you receive a different runtime error:

```
Error 106: Invalid numeric format.
```

The letter *A* is not a number. Pascal doesn't let you type letters into the Byte variable, Age.

As you can see from these examples, data types have legal forms and limits, which Pascal can help enforce. Pascal's strong type-checking capabilities encourage you to write correct programs by guarding against common errors that all programmers make.

Expressions

An expression combines constants, variables, and literal values into a single result. If A = 5 and B = 3, the expression (A + B) equals 8. The result of an expression is the same type as its components. Integer expressions have integer results; Boolean expressions, Boolean results. The Boolean expression (A < B), for example, is false, because 5 is not less than 3.

Numeric expressions use the common mathematics programming operators plus (+), minus (–), and multiply (*). Division has two forms. To divide two Byte, ShortInt, Word, Integer, or LongInt values, use the key word **div** this way:

```
IntegerAverage := Sum div Count;
```

To divide two real numbers, use a slash (/). This always produces a real-number result. For example, even if Sum and Count are integer variables, the division result in this statement is a real number:

```
RealAverage := Sum / Count;
```

As an example of using numeric expressions, Program 2-5 converts degrees Fahrenheit to Celsius, named for the Swedish astronomer Anders Celsius (1701-1744), who invented the temperature scale with 0° at the freezing point of water and 100° at the boiling point. There are two real-number variables in the program, Fdegrees and Cdegrees. Lines 1-8 should be familiar. Line 9 shows how to program the conversion formula for Fahrenheit to Celsius as an expression, with the result assigned to Cdegrees. When the program asks for a temperature, type a number such as 100 or 32.5. The program then displays the equivalent temperature in degrees Celsius.

Program 2-5: CELSIUS.PAS

```
 1:  program Celsius;
 2:  var
 3:    Fdegrees, Cdegrees: Real;
 4:  begin
 5:    Writeln('Fahrenheit to Celsius conversion');
 6:    Writeln;
 7:    Write('Degrees Fahrenheit? ');
 8:    Readln(Fdegrees);
 9:    Cdegrees := ((Fdegrees - 32.0) * 5.0) / 9.0;
10:    Writeln('Degrees Celsius = ', Cdegrees:8:2);
11:    Readln
12:  end.
```

Operator Precedence

Notice the use of parentheses in line 9 of Program 2-5. Pascal first evaluates the parts of an expression inside the most deeply nested parentheses before it evaluates the rest of the expression. In the absence of parentheses, the order of operations in an expression follows a predefined *precedence.* (See Appendix E.) Expressions having operators with higher precedence are evaluated before expressions having lower precedence. Some of the operators and data types in Appendix E are introduced in later chapters.

Program 2-6 demonstrates how operator precedence affects expression results. Although the three expressions in lines 6-8 are similar, the results are 610, 610, and 900. Because the multiply operator (*) has a higher precedence than plus (+), lines 6 and 7 evaluate to the same value. The extra parentheses in line 7 do not affect the result. In other words, the following statement is true:

$$(A + B * C) = (A + (B * C))$$

To add variables A and B before multiplying by C requires parentheses to force Pascal to evaluate the expression with the lower precedence first. Therefore, the following statement is also true, at least for the assigned values in Program 2-6. The symbol < > means "not equal."

$$(A + B * C) <> ((A + B) * C)$$

Program 2-6: PRECEDEN.PAS

```
 1:   program Precedence;
 2:   var
 3:     A, B, C: Integer;
 4:   begin
 5:     A := 10; B := 20; C := 30;
 6:     Writeln(A + B * C);
 7:     Writeln(A + (B * C));
 8:     Writeln((A + B) * C);
 9:     Readln
10:   end.
```

Even though extra parentheses are not required, they often clarify complex expressions, as in Program 2-5. Additional parentheses have no effect on the size or speed of a program, and many programmers lavishly use them to avoid any chance of ambiguity. The intention of (A + (B * C)) is perfectly clear, even though the expression (A + B * C) gives the same result.

Mixing Reals and Integers

Although the two data types Real and Integer are different, you may freely mix values of both types in expressions. Although this bends Pascal's strict type-checking rule, it would be awkward if expressions such as (2 * 3.141) were not allowed. The same rule applies for types Byte, ShortInt, Word, and LongInt. In general, you can mix all these types in numeric expressions. However, when you mix real numbers in any expression, the result is always Real, not Integer. Also, when assigning the result of integer expressions, you must be careful to choose variables that can safely hold the expression value.

For an example of mixing Reals and Integers, try changing the real-number variable Fdegrees in Program 2-5 to type Integer. Does the program still run? What happens if you change both Fdegrees and Cdegrees to type Integer? Try to predict the result before compiling and running the program.

Inserting Comments in Programs

Pascal programs tend to be very readable and understandable on their own. Even so, a clarifying comment or two helps explain complicated sections. It's appropriate to introduce comments in this chapter because they are a kind of private data for your eyes only.

Add comments by surrounding text with braces, { and }, or with the alternate double-character symbols (* and *). The compiler ignores the text inside either pair of comment brackets. Comments, therefore, have no effect on the size or speed of the compiled program. Use whichever pair of symbols you prefer.

Program 2-7 converts miles to kilometers while demonstrating how to put comments into a program. The comments in lines 3-5 identify the program's purpose and author, and refer to the source of the conversion factor for kilometers per mile. Other comments attached to lines 8 and 11 further clarify the constant and variable declarations. In lines 17 and 22, the alternate comment brackets (* and *) enclose descriptions about what is happening at various places in the program.

Program 2-7: KILOMETE.PAS

```
 1:  program Kilometers;
 2:
 3:  { Purpose : Convert miles to kilometers }
 4:  { Source  : World Almanac 1984 Units of Measurement pg 763 }
 5:  { Author  : Tom Swan }
 6:
 7:  const
 8:    Kmpermile = 1.609344;   { Number of kilometers in one mile }
 9:
10:  var
11:    Miles: Real;            { Number of miles to convert }
12:
13:  begin
14:    Writeln('Convert miles to kilometers');
15:    Writeln;
16:
17:  (* Prompt operator for number of miles *)
18:
19:    Write('How many miles? ');
20:    Readln(Miles);
21:
22:  (* Print answer *)
23:
24:    Writeln('Kilometers = ', Miles * Kmpermile:8:2);
25:    Readln
26:  end.
```

When using comments, be careful not to fall into the habit of automatically commenting every line. If the purpose of something is already clear, there's no need to add a comment. Commented lines like these are unnecessarily wordy:

```
PersonHeight: Integer;   { Height of person }
B := B + 10;             { Add 10 to B }
```

By the same reasoning, Program 2-7 probably needs no comments—it's perfectly understandable on its own. Because Pascal programs tend to be readable, almost storylike, the programs in this book use comments only where meanings might otherwise be unclear. Most examples have no comments. Try to write programs that are understandable without comments. But, if you think a note or two is needed to clarify program statements, don't hesitate to add as many comments as you need.

Debugging with Comments

Comments can also help you debug a program. Often, an interesting test is to see what happens after removing one or more program statements. Compiling and running a program without some of its vital parts and observing the results often isolate a tricky problem. What happens, for example, to Program 2-7 if you remove the Readln statement in line 20? To perform that test, instead of actually erasing the line, surround it with comment brackets like this:

```
(* Readln(Miles); *)
```

Recompile and run the program, which now has a serious bug—it doesn't request the number of miles to convert. Remove the comment brackets and try again. Now the program works correctly again. When used this way, comment brackets are important programming tools.

Nesting Comments

Turbo Pascal lets you insert a comment inside another comment. Although it may seem strange to want to do that, there's a good reason for being able to nest two comments together. An example explains why. Go back to Program 2-5, Celsius, and add a comment to line 8, changing that line to read as follows:

```
Readln(Fdegrees);   { Get degrees in Fahrenheit }
```

Next, insert the opening comment bracket (* between lines 7 and 8, and the closing comment bracket *) between lines 9 and 10. The lines should now appear like these:

```
(*
Readln(Fdegrees);  { Get degrees in Fahrenheit }
Cdegrees := ((Fdegrees - 32.0) * 5.0) / 9.0;
*)
```

The effect is to "comment out" lines 8 and 9, effectively removing them from the program. Notice that the comment you added to the original line 8 nests inside the larger commented-out portion that now occupies four lines. If Pascal did not allow nested comments, it would be impossible to comment out portions of programs that contain other comments.

A nested comment must always use the other kind of brackets. In other words, you can have the nested comments (*{comment}*) or {(*comment*)}. But the nested comments {(*comment}*) and (*{comment*)} are incorrect—you must use the same kind of bracket at a comment's beginning and end, and you cannot overlap the two different kinds.

I usually reserve the braces, { and }, for permanent comments and save the alternates, (* and *), for temporarily removing sections of programming. That way, I never accidentally nest two pairs of the same comment brackets together.

Compiler Directives

Earlier, you learned how to turn on range checking with the compiler directive {$R+}. A compiler directive is a special kind of comment that gives a command to the compiler, changing the way Turbo Pascal compiles your program.

A compiler directive, also called an option, starts with an opening comment symbol and a dollar sign, for example, {$I-} or (*$R+*). {I-} is a plain comment. The directive's letter, in upper- or lowercase, selects one of several available options. Directive letters might be followed by values, such as {$M 8192,8192,655360}; or a plus or minus switch to turn features on or off, such as {$R+} or {$N-}, respectively; or a string, such as {$L MYCODE.OBJ}.

You can mix compiler directives by separating them with commas. The following compiler directive issues three commands and uses the alternate comment brackets instead of braces:

```
(*$I-,R+,N+*)
```

Appendix C lists Turbo Pascal's compiler options and directives. You'll meet them all in action throughout this book.

Variable Constants

Although the term *variable constant* seems contradictory—an oxymoron like *sweet sorrow*—it's a powerful feature in Turbo Pascal. A variable constant, called a static variable in some other languages, resembles a regular constant but has a colon and data type inserted between its identifier and declared value.

The *Turbo Pascal Programmer's Guide* and other documentation call variable constants *typed constants.* Because all constants have associated data types, the term *variable constant* more correctly describes this Pascal feature and is used throughout this book.

Variable constants are preinitialized variables. Programs can use them wherever regular variables might appear. Constants, as you know, represent predeclared, unchanging values. Variables, on the other hand, have no predeclared values but can change. Variable constants mix these ideas—they have predeclared values like constants but can also change like variables.

Program 2-8 demonstrates one way to use variable constants to save memory. Line 3 is different from previous declarations. The constant identifier (MiscString) has a data type like a variable (**string**[35]) plus a value like a constant ('Welcome...'). Together, these elements create a variable constant.

Program 2-8: PLANETS.PAS

```
 1:   program Planets;
 2:   const
 3:      MiscString: string[35] = 'Welcome to Your Weight and Fortune!';
 4:      Sun     = 27.9;
 5:      Mercury = 0.37;
 6:      Moon    = 0.17;
 7:      Jupiter = 2.64;
 8:   var
 9:      Weight: Real;
10:   begin
11:      Writeln(MiscString);  { Display welcome message }
12:      Write('What is your name? ');
13:      Readln(MiscString);
14:      Write('How much do you weigh in pounds? ');
15:      Readln(Weight);
16:
17:      Writeln;
18:      Writeln(MiscString, '''s weight:');
19:      Writeln(' On the Sun  = ', Sun * Weight:0:0, ' lbs');
```

continued

Program 2-8: continued

```
20:    Writeln(' On Mercury  = ', Mercury * Weight:0:0, ' lbs');
21:    Writeln(' On the Moon = ', Moon * Weight:0:0, ' lbs');
22:    Writeln(' On Jupiter  = ', Jupiter * Weight:0:0, ' lbs');
23:
24:    Writeln;
25:    Writeln(MiscString, '''s fortune:');
26:    Writeln(' You are fortunate not to be living on Jupiter!');
27:    Readln
28: end.
```

The program uses MiscString like any other variable. Line 11 displays the string, welcoming you to the program. Line 13 uses the *same* string as a variable for storing your name, which the program then displays in lines 18 and 25.

Reusing a string variable constant this way saves memory. If the program declared the welcome message as a plain string constant, the message's characters would remain in memory as long as the program runs. But there's no need to keep the message around after displaying it (line 11). By using a variable constant to hold the message, and then reusing that same variable constant for other purposes, the program puts the memory occupied by MiscString to double use.

Even so, don't be tempted to declare all data as variable constants just to avoid initializing variables. There are several reasons why that's a bad idea. For one, all Pascal compilers do not recognize variable constants. Also, variable constants permanently take up memory space. It is possible, as you'll learn later, to declare Pascal variables that are *dynamic,* existing only in the parts of a program where needed. The same is not true of variable constants, which have a voracious appetite for valuable computer memory. Use them sparingly.

Constant Expressions

Beginning with Turbo Pascal 5.0, you can write expressions in **const** declarations. This lets you create constants such as

```
Minimum = 1;
Range = 100;
Maximum = Minimum + (Range - 1);
```

The first two constants are no different from others you've seen earlier. Minimum equals 1. Range equals 100. The third constant uses an expression involving the other two constants to calculate Maximum. With these declarations, changing Minimum or Range automatically affects the value of Maximum. Previous versions of Turbo Pascal required updating all three constants manually, increasing the possibility of errors caused by miscalculations.

All items in a constant expression must be literal values such as 3.14159 or other constant identifiers declared earlier in the program. You may use parentheses along with any of the usual math operators. Variables are never allowed.

Constant expressions are useful for calculating the initial values of variable constants. For example, the declaration

```
StartValue: Integer = (Minimum - 1);
```

assigns to variable-constant StartValue the integer value of Minimum minus 1. However, you can't use similar variable constants in other constant expressions. This declaration will not compile:

```
EndValue = StartValue + Maximum;  { ??? }
```

This expression fails because variable constants can change like variables and are therefore not allowed.

Be sure to understand that constant expressions are calculated when the program is compiled, not later when the program runs. Constant expressions cost you nothing in runtime speed.

Summary

Constants, variables, and variable constants hold and specify data, the facts that a computer program knows. Pascal requires you to declare the data types of variables, and the compiler checks that values assigned to variables match their declared types. Constants automatically assume the types of their values. With its strong type checking, Pascal helps guard against common programming errors, often not prevented in other languages.

The Pascal data types examined in this chapter are Byte, ShortInt, Word, Integer, LongInt, Real, Char, Boolean, and **string**. You can declare variables, constants, and variable constants of any of these types.

Subranges of integers limit the high and low values that variables can hold. The compiler can check for range errors only for literal constant values assigned to subrange variables. To check subranges when programs run, you must turn on range checking with the {$R+} compiler directive.

Expressions combine variables, constants, and other values into a single result. The result of an expression is the same type as its elements. Real-number expressions produce real-number results. Boolean expressions evaluate to true or false. Operator precedence and parentheses determine the evaluation order of an expression's parts. Expressions with a mix of Real and Integer values are always type Real.

Descriptive names for variables and constants make programs more readable, and two kinds of comments let you further clarify a program. One special kind of comment, called a directive, gives the compiler an instruction, selecting among various options.

Variable constants, otherwise known as typed constants, are variables with preassigned values. They can represent fixed values like constants, but they can also change like variables.

Constant expressions let you declare constants that depend on the values of other constants. Only literal values, other constants, and the usual math operators may be used in constant expressions. Variables are prohibited.

Exercises

2-1. Given that water weighs 8.33 pounds per gallon, write a program to prompt for the number of gallons, and compute the weight of that much water. Use a constant to describe the relationship of gallons to weight. The program should accept fractions of gallons (e.g., 5.75 or 10.2) and display the result to two decimal places.

2-2. To convert Celsius to Fahrenheit temperatures, multiply by 9, divide the result by 5, and add 32. Using Program 2-5 as a guide, write this formula into a Pascal program.

2-3. For every 550 feet above sea level, water boils at about 1° less than 212° Fahrenheit. Write a Pascal program to calculate the boiling point of water at any altitude. Document the program with appropriate comments.

2-4. Modify your answer to exercise 2-1 to let someone decide how many decimal places should appear in the result. (Hint: Use an integer variable in the formatting command.) What would be the advantage of using a variable constant instead?

3

Action—What a Program Does

- Compound Statements
- Repetitive Statements
- Conditional Statements

3

case-else, for-to-do, for-downto-do, goto, if-then-else, label, mod, Pred, **repeat-until,** Succ, **while-do**

As the examples in Chapters 1 and 2 demonstrate, a program's many statements normally execute in sequential order, one statement after the other. This chapter introduces two new kinds of statements that change the order in which statements execute. *Repetitive* statements make loops in a program, repeating operations. *Conditional* statements make decisions, selecting one statement over others and changing the program flow.

Compound Statements

A compound statement is a group of individual statements, each separated from the next with a semicolon. As shown in the railroad diagram of Figure 3-1, the key words **begin** and **end** collect the compounded statements into one unit. You can use compound statements at any place in a program where Pascal allows ordinary statements. Railroad diagrams identify those places with the boxed-in word *statement.*

Because you can use single and compound statements interchangeably, from now on *statement* means either a single *or* compound statement.

Looking at Figure 3-1, you can see that the last statement before the key word **end** does not require a semicolon. Semicolons separate statements from each other—they do not terminate statements. In other words, you don't have to end each statement with a semicolon. You do have to separate multiple statements with semicolons.

compound statement

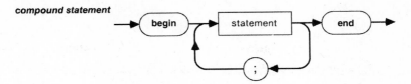

Figure 3-1 Railroad diagram defining a compound statement.

Pascal relaxes its own rule, however, and lets you add an extra semicolon as demonstrated in Program 3-1, line 5. Because there is no actual statement following the semicolon in line 5, you have to imagine the presence of an empty or *null* statement, shown as a comment in Program 3-1. This null statement doesn't do anything except satisfy the syntax of Figure 3-1, which says that a statement, not a semicolon, always precedes **end**. The existence of the null statement is a minor Pascal oddity—don't let it concern you. The extra semicolon before **end** has no effect on the compiled result. Add or delete it as you please.

Program 3-1: SEMICOLO.PAS

```
1:  program Semicolon;
2:  begin
3:    Writeln('Statement #1');
4:    Writeln('Statement #2');
5:    Writeln('Statement #3');   { Null statement }
6:  end.
```

Repetitive Statements

Repetitive statements cause one or more statements to repeat. In Pascal, there are three repetitive statement types: **while**, **repeat**, and **for**.

While Loops

Pascal's **while-do** or, more simply, **while** statement executes another statement while some condition is true. Figure 3-2 shows the railroad diagram for a **while** statement, also called a **while** loop because of the way it causes program actions to cycle in a kind of logical loop.

while statement

Figure 3-2 Railroad diagram defining Pascal's repetitive **while** statement.

The condition can be any Boolean expression that evaluates to true or false. It could also be a simple Boolean variable. While the *expression* is true, the *statement* executes. When the *expression* becomes false, the loop ends, and the program proceeds to whatever follows the *statement.* Because the *expression* may be false to begin with, the statements inside a **while** loop might never execute.

Program 3-2 is a simple example of a **while** loop in action. The program counts to ten and stops. The variable Counter is called a *control variable* because of the way it controls how many times the **while** statement in lines 7-11 executes. First, line 6 initializes the control variable to a starting value, in this case, setting Counter to one. The compound statement in lines 8-11 then executes while the value of Counter is less than or equal to ten.

Program 3-2: WCOUNT.PAS

```
 1:  program WhileCount;
 2:  var
 3:     Counter: Integer;
 4:  begin
 5:     Writeln('While count');
 6:     Counter := 1;
 7:     while Counter <= 10 do
 8:     begin
 9:       Writeln(Counter);
10:       Counter := Counter + 1
11:     end;
12:     Readln
13:  end.
```

Line 9 displays Counter's value. Line 10 adds one to Counter each time through the loop. Eventually, Counter grows larger than ten, which makes the expression Counter < = 10 false, ending the **while** statement and, subsequently, the program.

What is the value of Counter after the loop ends? To find out, add the following statement between lines 11 and 12:

```
Writeln('Value of Counter = ', Counter);
```

Does the final value of Counter make sense? What value would you expect if you change the expression in line 7 to Counter < 10? Sometimes, when trying to answer questions like these, it helps to "play computer," writing down values of variables for statements as you execute the program by hand. What happens, for example, if you use the expression Counter = 10 in line 7? Before running the program, try to predict the results. Will the **while** loop execute? If not, why not?

A control variable can also be a character, as demonstrated in Program 3-3, which prints the alphabet. The program is similar to Program 3-2, but because of Pascal's strict type-checking rule, it can't add one to the character variable Ch as the previous program did to the integer variable Counter. Instead, line 10 uses the standard function, Succ, to return the successor to the value of Ch. (The successor of a character is the next character in sequence. For example, the successor of B is C.) You'll learn more about functions in Chapter 4, but for now, think of a function as a Pascal command that returns a value, in this case, the value that succeeds Ch. A similar function, Pred, returns the predecessor, or preceding, value. For example, Pred('Z') is 'Y'.

Program 3-3: WALPHA.PAS

```
 1:  program WhileAlphabet;
 2:  var
 3:     Ch: Char;
 4:  begin
 5:     Writeln('While alphabet');
 6:     Ch := 'A';
 7:     while Ch <= 'Z' do
 8:     begin
 9:       Write(Ch);
10:       Ch := Succ(Ch)
11:     end;
12:     Writeln;
13:     Readln
14:  end.
```

As in Program 3-2, you can check the value of the character variable Ch when the **while** loop ends. To do this, add a statement between lines 12 and 13 of Program 3-3 to write Ch to the display. What do you think Ch will be? If you don't know, look up the ASCII character set in Appendix D. (ASCII stands for the American Standard Code for Information Interchange.) What character is next in sequence following Z?

Another way to write a **while** loop is to use a Boolean variable for the conditional expression, as Program 3-4 demonstrates.

Program 3-4: WBOOLEAN.PAS

```
 1:  program WhileBoolean;
 2:  var
 3:    Counter: Integer;
 4:    Done: Boolean;
 5:  begin
 6:    Writeln('While Boolean');
 7:    Counter := 1;
 8:    Done := False;
 9:    while not Done do
10:    begin
11:      Writeln(Counter);
12:      Counter := Succ(Counter);
13:      Done := (Counter > 10)
14:    end;
15:    Readln
16:  end.
```

With a well-chosen name, a Boolean variable improves the program's readability, as shown in Program 3-4, which operates similarly to Program 3-2, counting to ten and stopping. This time the program uses a Boolean variable, Done, as the **while** statement control variable. Line 8 initializes Done to false before starting the **while** loop in lines 9-14. You could also write line 9 as follows:

```
while (Done = False) do
```

As shown in Program 3-4, though, the phrase **while not** Done **do** has the same effect and is more readable. Similar uses of Boolean variables often lead to Englishlike programs in Pascal that read more like stories than computer programs. For example, you might have two or more Boolean variables in **while** loops:

```
while Testing and not InError
  do <statement>;
```

Even out of context, you at least get the flavor of what happens at this place in the program. When looking at thousands of statements, you'll appreciate the ability to pick out a lone statement and understand its purpose. Of course, it's up to you to choose names that make sense! The purpose of **while** (A **and** (**not** B **or** C)) **do** is no clearer in Pascal than it is in any other language.

Despite its readability, line 13 of Program 3-4 may appear strange. This assignment is more understandable when you consider that Pascal evaluates the Boolean expression (Counter>10) to a true or false result, which the program assigns to the control variable Done, causing the loop to end when Done becomes true.

What happens if you move line 13 (plus a semicolon at the end of the line) between lines 11 and 12? Predict the result before trying this on your computer. Was your assumption correct?

Repeat Loops

Another kind of repetitive statement is the **repeat-until** or **repeat** loop, diagrammed in Figure 3-3. Notice that a compound statement is automatically allowed in this case, without using **begin** and **end**. The key words **repeat** and **until** already mark the repeating group of statements—surrounding the same group with **begin** and **end** is legal but unnecessary. Multiple statements may appear inside the **repeat** and **until** key words. The *statements* execute repeatedly until the *expression* is true.

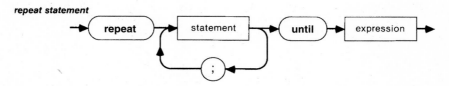

Figure 3-3 Railroad diagram from Pascal's **repeat** statement.

Counting to ten with **repeat-until** is only a little different from doing the same job in a **while** loop. Once again, Program 3-5 uses an integer control variable, Counter, initialized to one in line 6. The program writes successive values of Counter to the screen (line 8), increasing Counter by one in line 9 for every pass through the loop. The loop ends in line 10 when Counter becomes greater than ten.

Program 3-5: RCOUNT.PAS

```
 1:    program RepeatCount;
 2:    var
 3:      Counter: Integer;
 4:    begin
 5:      Writeln('Repeat count');
 6:      Counter := 1;
 7:      repeat
 8:        Writeln(Counter);
 9:        Counter := Counter + 1
10:      until Counter > 10;
11:      Readln
12:    end.
```

A **repeat** loop, unlike a **while** loop, always executes at least one time. If the conditional expression in the **while** loop starts out false (see Figure 3-2 and Program 3-2), its statements never execute. This happens because Pascal evaluates the expression at the top of a **while** loop. But a **repeat** loop evaluates its expression at the bottom (see Figure 3-3 and Program 3-5), which doesn't happen until the statements inside the loop execute at least once.

Program 3-6 is the **repeat** loop equivalent of Program 3-3, which prints the alphabet. Again, the Succ function in line 9 advances the character control variable Ch after initializing Ch to A in line 6. When Ch becomes alphabetically greater than Z, the **repeat** loop, and therefore the program, ends.

Program 3-6: RALPHA.PAS

```
 1:   program RepeatAlphabet;
 2:   var
 3:     Ch: Char;
 4:   begin
 5:     Writeln('Repeat alphabet');
 6:     Ch := 'A';
 7:     repeat
 8:       Write(Ch);
 9:       Ch := Succ(Ch)
10:     until Ch > 'Z';
11:     Writeln;
12:     Readln
13:   end.
```

A **repeat** statement's ending expression might also be a Boolean control variable. In Program 3-7, line 11 sets Boolean variable Done to true or false, depending on the result of the expression (Counter > 10). The **repeat** loop executes until Done is true. When you read this program, the compound statement in lines 8-12, **repeat...until** Done seems natural and understandable.

Program 3-7: RBOOLEAN.PAS

```
 1:   program RepeatBoolean;
 2:   var
 3:     Counter: Integer;
 4:     Done: Boolean;
 5:   begin
 6:     Writeln('Repeat Boolean');
```

```
 7:    Counter := 1;
 8:    repeat
 9:      Writeln(Counter);
10:      Counter := Succ(Counter);
11:      Done := (Counter > 10)
12:    until Done;
13:    Readln
14: end.
```

What does Counter equal after the end of the **repeat** loop in Programs 3-5 and 3-7? What does Ch equal after the loop in Program 3-6? Use Writeln statements to prove your guesses.

For Loops

The third and final repetitive statement in Pascal is the **for** loop, diagrammed in Figure 3-4. Although a **for** loop appears more complex than **while** and **repeat** loops, in practice it often produces more concise programming. To see why, let's look at the same counting program, this time written with a **for** loop.

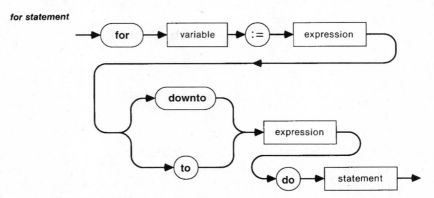

Figure 3-4 Railroad diagram for Pascal's **for** statement.

Program 3-8 counts to ten and stops, but it does it in fewer lines than Programs 3-2 and 3-5, which are similar. Although all three programs do the same thing, using a **for** loop in this case is the easiest and most efficient method.

Program 3-8: FCOUNT.PAS

```
1:  program ForCount;
2:  var
3:    Counter: Integer;
4:  begin
5:    Writeln('For count');
6:    for Counter := 1 to 10 do
7:      Writeln(Counter);
8:    Readln
9:  end.
```

Like other loops, the **for** loop needs a control variable, here the integer variable Counter. In English, line 6 tells you that Counter starts at one, goes up **to** ten, and, for each successive Counter value, the loop should **do** a statement, in this case, the **Writeln** statement in line 7. Line 6 handles the initialization of Counter, the increment by one each time through the loop, and the test for done when Counter is greater than ten—all of the "housekeeping" chores expressly added to the similar **while** and **repeat** loops.

A **for** loop can also count backward, as shown in Program 3-9, which counts from ten down to one. Compare line 6 with its counterpart in Program 3-8. Notice that **downto** replaces the key word **to**. When a **for** loop counts up, use **to**. When it counts down, use **downto**.

Program 3-9: FCOUNTDN.PAS

```
1:  program ForCountdown;
2:  var
3:    Counter: Integer;
4:  begin
5:    Writeln('For count down');
6:    for Counter := 10 downto 1 do
7:      Writeln(Counter);
8:    Readln
9:  end.
```

A **for** loop's control variable can be a character, as it was in the **while** and **repeat** loops. Program 3-10 demonstrates this by printing the alphabet. The program uses a **for** loop to cycle variable Ch through the characters A to Z. Can you rewrite Program 3-10 to print the alphabet in reverse order, in other words, from Z *down to* A?

Program 3-10: FALPHA.PAS

```
 1:   program ForAlphabet;
 2:   var
 3:     Ch: Char;
 4:   begin
 5:     Writeln('For alphabet');
 6:     for Ch := 'A' to 'Z' do
 7:       Write(Ch);
 8:     Writeln;
 9:     Readln
10:   end.
```

From these examples, you might be thinking that **for** loops are more attractive than **while** or **repeat** loops. There are many reasons, though, why you often cannot use **for**. The major restriction is that a **for** loop always counts by one value at a time. It cannot count up or down by two or three—only by one. Second, **for** loops must use simple control variables such as integers and characters. They can't use Boolean expressions, as in Programs 3-4 and 3-7, to control the action of their loops.

And if these restrictions weren't enough, there is another important limitation to **for** loops: *The statements inside the loop must never alter the control variable in any way*. Never write a **for** loop like this:

```
for Counter := 1 to 10 do
begin
    Writeln(Counter);
    Counter := Counter + 1   { ??? }
end;
```

At first glance, you might think this is a clever way to force the computer to count by twos with a **for** loop. Although the compiler accepts such programming, the results can be surprising. To live dangerously, replace lines 6 and 7 in Program 3-8 with this five-line **for** loop, and run the program. In one experiment, the program counted by twos up to 19 and then stopped.[1]

---

[1] Because of changes in Turbo Pascal, the **for** loop now correctly counts by twos, stopping with nine. Even so, I decided to let the example stand from the first edition—it's bad form to change a **for** loop's control variable inside the loop or to assume that the variable will have a specific value when the loop ends. The reason for this restriction is that the Pascal compiler might load the control value into an internal processor register or a memory location rather than use the memory reserved for the variable. This makes the **for** loop run more quickly, but it also makes the variable as stored in memory untrustworthy. Apparently, Turbo Pascal doesn't do this, but more importantly, a future version *might* and still be consistent with the rules of Pascal. This means that you must not change a **for** loop's control variable even when doing so appears to produce no errors! The fact that this example used to fail and now works is fair warning of the consequences of disobeying this important rule.

Similarly, you cannot trust the value of Counter in Program 3-8 or the value of Ch in Program 3-10, after the **for** loop ends. Earlier, in the **while** and **repeat** examples, you inserted Writeln statements to test the ending values of the loop control variables. Although you can do the same thing in Programs 3-8 and 3-10, the results are unpredictable and could be different on other computers. Never write programs that rely on the uninitialized value of the control variable following a **for** loop.

Despite these restrictions, **for** loops are valuable to Pascal programming, as are **while** and **repeat** loops. Of the three types of repetitive statements, a **for** loop, where appropriate, is usually the most efficient and fastest choice. The real problem is knowing how to choose among the three loops.

To help you decide, a few rules of thumb for choosing a **while**, **repeat**, or **for** loop follow. Many times, the best choice is not clear, and you'll have to experiment with the following advice in mind.

When to Use while

Ask yourself, "Is there at least one condition when the statements in the loop should not execute, not even once?" If the answer is yes, a **while** loop probably is the best choice. Because the **while** statement (see Figure 3-2) evaluates its controlling expression at the top of the loop, if that expression is false, the statements in the loop do not execute.

When to Use repeat

If the answer to the question in the preceding paragraph is no, use a **repeat** loop instead. As Figure 3-3 shows, the statements in a **repeat** loop execute before evaluating the controlling expression. Even if the expression is false the first time through the loop, the statements in the loop execute at least one time.

When to Use for

If you know, or the program can calculate in advance, the exact number of loops required, and if a simple control variable is available, a **for** loop is often the best choice. As with a **while** loop, the statements in a **for** loop might never execute. If you replace line 6 in Program 3-8 with the following, it writes nothing to the screen:

```
for Counter := 1 to 0 do
```

Obviously, because zero is less than one and because variable Counter starts with a value of one, the condition to end the **for** loop—namely that Counter is greater than or equal to zero—is true before the loop begins. Therefore, the **for** loop never runs, and the program continues with the next statement. In this example, the program simply ends. On the other hand, the following **for** loop executes exactly one time:

```
for i := 1 to 1 do
```

Repetitive statements add power to all computer languages, and Pascal's menu of three statements—**while**, **repeat**, and **for**—gives you a choice of ways to construct loops. The ability to control the number of times a statement executes is vital to programming in Pascal. Next, you'll learn how a Pascal program selects one statement over another, and makes decisions affecting a program's flow.

Conditional Statements

Deciding which statement to execute based on one condition or another is a common feature among all programming languages. In Pascal, there are three ways to force a program to alter its operational flow. Figure 3-5 diagrams the first of these, the **if-then-else** conditional statement or, more simply, the **if** statement.

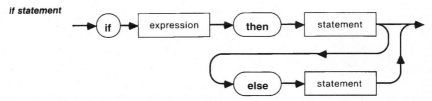

Figure 3-5 Railroad diagram defining Pascal's **if-then-else** conditional statement.

The if Statement

The **if** statement in Pascal is simple to use and operates just the way it sounds. If the *expression* evaluates to true, then the *statement* following the key word **then** executes; otherwise, the *statement* following **else** executes. Notice that the **else** *statement* is optional. As it is in repetitive statements, the *expression* may be any expression that evaluates to true or false, or it may be a Boolean variable. The **then** and **else** statements may be single or compound.

Program 3-11 demonstrates **if** in lines 10 and 11. The example limits a response to a specific range of numbers, in this case, from one to ten. If you enter any other value, the program prints an error message and repeats the prompt. Controlling this action is the Boolean variable Okay, which the program sets equal to true or false in line 9. The **if** statement in line 10 tests this variable and, if it's false, displays an error message.

Program 3-11: CHOICE.PAS

```
 1:  program Choice;
 2:  var
 3:     Number: Integer;
 4:     Okay: Boolean;
 5:  begin
 6:     Writeln('Enter a number between 1 and 10');
 7:     repeat
 8:       Readln(Number);
 9:       Okay := (1 <= Number) and (Number <= 10);
10:      if not Okay
11:        then Writeln('Incorrect.  Try again.')
12:     until Okay;
13:     Writeln('Okay');
14:     Readln
15:  end.
```

Line 9 of this example gives a lot of people trouble on first glance. It's simple to understand, though, if you carefully examine how Pascal evaluates this Boolean expression to a single true or false result:

```
(1 <= Number) and (Number <= 10)
```

Only if Number is inclusively between one and ten is the entire expression true. The program assigns the result of this expression to the Boolean variable, Okay. You could rewrite this with the help of an **if** statement as follows:

```
if (1 <= Number) and (Number <= 10)
  then Okay := True
  else Okay := False;
```

As demonstrated in Program 3-11, there's no reason to go to all this trouble. Instead, you can directly assign the result of any Boolean expression to a Boolean variable—they are, after all, of the same type.

Nested if Statements

if-then-else statements can nest inside one another to make complex conditional decisions. To demonstrate nesting, Program 3-12 has three **if** statements. One statement, starting at line 11 and ending at line 19, tests the value of variable Year. *If* Year is greater than zero, *then* the compound statement in lines 12-19 executes; otherwise, the program goes directly to the **until** in line 20. Notice how indenting lines 13-18 helps make this action clear.

Program 3-12: LEAP.PAS

```
 1:   program Leap;
 2:   var
 3:     LeapYear: Boolean;
 4:     Year: Integer;
 5:   begin
 6:     Writeln('Leap year');
 7:     repeat
 8:       Writeln;
 9:       Write('Year? (0 to quit) ');
10:       Readln(Year);
11:       if Year > 0 then
12:       begin
13:         if Year mod 100 = 0
14:           then LeapYear := (Year mod 400) = 0
15:           else LeapYear := (Year mod   4) = 0;
16:         if LeapYear
17:           then Writeln(Year, ' is a leap year')
18:           else Writeln(Year, ' is not a leap year')
19:       end
20:     until Year = 0
21:   end.
```

Nested inside the compound statement in Program 3-12 are two more **if** statements, the first starting in line 13 and the second in line 16. These statements test for leap years, which are evenly divisible by four, except for new centuries such as 1900 and 2000, which are leap years only if divisible by 400. Therefore, 1900 was not a leap year, but 2000 will be.

The **if** statement in lines 13-15 uses this formula. The **mod** (modulus) operator returns the remainder of an integer division. 15 **mod** 10 equals 5 (10 goes once into 15 with 5 remaining), 8 **mod** 15 equals 8 (15 goes into 8 zero times with 8 remaining), 20 **mod** 20 equals 0, and so on. If the year in question is evenly divisible by 100 (line 13), it's a new century,[2] causing the Boolean LeapYear variable to become true in line 14 if the year is also evenly divisible by 400. Otherwise, LeapYear becomes true in line 15 if the year is divisible by 4. Keep in mind that expressions such as (Year **mod** 4) = 0 evaluate to a single true or false result, assigned here to the Boolean variable LeapYear.

Another **if** statement, starting at line 16, tests the Boolean LeapYear variable and writes a message on the screen to tell you if this is a leap year. Notice also that all these actions occur inside a **repeat** statement (lines 7-20). This lets you enter more than one year without rerunning the program, which stops when you enter zero. The **repeat** statement is the correct choice here to make the statements in lines 8-19 execute at least one time.

Look at the position of the semicolon in line 15 of Program 3-12. Remember, the semicolon in Pascal separates one statement from another. The **if-then-else** in lines 13-15 is a *single* statement and, therefore, the semicolon at its end correctly separates it from the next **if** statement. Try adding a semicolon to the end of line 14 and then recompile the program. Do you understand why you receive an error?

To avoid confusion, it helps to use one of the four popular styles in Figure 3-6 for writing **if** statements. You can have an entire **if-then-else** on a single line, as shown at the top of the figure, or separate the **then** and **else** statements to add clarity to the program. Most programmers prefer to line up an **else** with its corresponding **then.** When nesting multiple **if** statements, it may not be obvious which **else** goes with which **then**, and lining them up improves the program's clarity. The fourth sample shows a newly popular style, placing **then** on the same line as **if**, and aligning **else** with **if** above. Of course, whichever style you choose, the Pascal compiler doesn't care how the program looks. A good-looking style is for your benefit, not the computer's.

Style alone, however, does not guard against the most common **if** statement error, demonstrated in Program 3-13. The example prompts for a value between one and ten, displaying an error message for any other value.

---

[2] Technically, new centuries begin with the first year after those evenly divisible by 100. In other words, 1901 was the start of the twentieth century, and 2001, not 2000, will be the first year of the twenty-first century. There was no year 0000—the first year was 0001; therefore, the one-hundredth year is always the last in its century. I suspect you'll have trouble, though, convincing Times Square revelers that December 31, 1999 is not the end of the twentieth century!

```
if <expression> then <statement> else <statement>;
if <expression>
  then <statement>
  else <statement>;

if <expression>
then
  <statement>
else
  <statement>;

if <expression> then
  <statement>
else
  <statement>
```

Figure 3-6 Four popular **if** statement styles.

Program 3-13: BADIF.PAS (with errors)

```
1:   program BadIf;
2:   var
3:     Counter: Integer;
4:   begin
5:     Write('Value (1..10)? ');
6:     Readln(Counter);
7:     if Counter >= 1
8:     then
9:       if Counter > 10
10:        then Writeln('Error: value > 10')
11:     else
12:       Writeln('Error: value < 1');
13:     Readln
14:   end.
```

Although the **else** in line 11 physically lines up with the **then** in line 8, it logically attaches to the **then** in line 10. The rule is that an **else** statement goes with the closest preceding **then**, regardless of the indentations. When you run the program, entering a legal value between one and ten produces the faulty error message, value < 1.

You can easily correct the bug in Program 3-13 by isolating the inner **if** statement with the key words **begin** and **end**, as shown in Program 3-14. This forms a compound statement in lines 9-12, forcing the **else** clause to go with the **then** in line 8 as originally intended. Running the program now correctly gives the error message for values outside the range one through ten.

Program 3-14: GOODIF.PAS

```
 1:   program GoodIf;
 2:   var
 3:      Counter: Integer;
 4:   begin
 5:      Write('Value (1..10)? ');
 6:      Readln(Counter);
 7:      if Counter >= 1
 8:      then
 9:        begin
10:          if Counter > 10
11:            then Writeln('Error: value > 10')
12:        end
13:      else
14:        Writeln('Error: value < 1');
15:      Readln
16:   end.
```

Short-Circuit Boolean Expressions

Turbo Pascal evaluates Boolean expressions in a special way that helps make conditional statements run more quickly. Consider this:

```
if (<e1> and <e2> and <e3>)
   then <statement>;
```

The symbols <e1>, <e2>, and <e3> represent any Boolean expressions or variables. Only if the three values are true does the entire expression evaluate to true, executing *statement*.

Now, think about what happens if <e1> is false. Because all three values in the expression must be true for the entire expression to be true, if <e1> is false, there is no need to examine <e2> and <e3>—their values are unimportant.

Turbo Pascal knows this and, whenever it can, stops evaluating the parts of an expression *as soon as the result is certain.* The expression *short circuits,* skipping the parts that have no bearing on the final outcome. The three-part Boolean expression could be written:

```
if <e1> then if <e2> then if <e3>
   then <statement>;
```

In fact, this is the only way to achieve short-circuit expression evaluation in versions of Pascal that don't have this capability. There's nothing wrong with this approach, but Turbo Pascal's expression evaluator makes the second two **if** statements unnecessary.

You can turn off Turbo Pascal's capability to perform short-circuit expression evaluation by changing the *Options:Compiler, Complete Boolean eval* setting in the IDE (integrated development environment), or by inserting the compiler directive {$B+} at the start of the program. You can also use the /$B+ command with the command-line compiler. For example, to compile a program named MYPROG.PAS, use the DOS command:

```
tpc /$B+ myprog
```

Usually, the only reason to switch off short-circuit expression evaluation this way is to run programs written for other versions of Pascal (or in previous Turbo Pascal versions) where entire expressions are expected to be evaluated regardless of the outcome. When you learn about functions in Chapter 4, you'll see that it is possible to cause the evaluation of expressions to perform actions, as well as to generate values. In this case, you may have to defeat short-circuit evaluation to ensure that all actions are performed—even if the result of the expression in which those actions participate is known beforehand. This is a shaky rock on which to stand, and you will do yourself a big favor if you never write expressions that require all parts to be evaluated. Use Turbo Pascal's short-circuit Boolean expressions—they make programs run faster and can reduce the complexity of multiple, nested **if** statements.

The case Statement

Multiple **if** statements often lead to a situation demonstrated in Program 3-15, which prints the complementary colors of a standard color wheel you might find in an interior decorating book. (Complementary colors look good together, and the program can pick color pairs for painting a room.) Lines 9 and 10 prompt for a choice of colors and read your single character answer. The program then tests this character, held in variable Choice, in seven subsequent **if** statements. On matching one of the known colors, it writes the color complement. If you enter an unknown character, line 25 displays an error message. Notice that lines 23 and 24 set the Boolean variable UserQuits to true when you type Q to quit the program, ending the **repeat** statement in lines 8-26.

Program 3-15: COLOR1.PAS

```
1:   program Color1;
2:   var
3:     Choice: Char;
4:     UserQuits: Boolean;
5:   begin
6:     Writeln('Complementary Colors #1');
7:     UserQuits := False;
8:     repeat
9:       Write('B.lue, G.reen, O.range, P.urple, R.ed, Y.ellow, Q.uit? ');
10:      Readln(Choice);
11:      if (Choice = 'B') or (Choice = 'b')
12:        then Writeln('Orange') else
13:      if (Choice = 'G') or (Choice = 'g')
14:        then Writeln('Red') else
15:      if (Choice = 'O') or (Choice = 'o')
16:        then Writeln('Blue') else
17:      if (Choice = 'P') or (Choice = 'p')
18:        then Writeln('Yellow') else
19:      if (Choice = 'R') or (Choice = 'r')
20:        then Writeln('Green') else
21:      if (Choice = 'Y') or (Choice = 'y')
22:        then Writeln('Purple') else
23:      if (Choice = 'Q') or (Choice = 'q')
24:        then UserQuits := True
25:        else Writeln('Error: Try again.')
26:    until UserQuits
27:  end.
```

Although there is nothing technically wrong with successive **if** statements as programmed in the example, the excessive clutter is hard to read. Luckily, there is a better way to write the same program.

Pascal's **case** statement (see Figure 3-7) offers an alternative to the multiple **if** statements in Program 3-15. It can replace a series of **if-then-else** statements. An example helps clarify how **case** works. (It's not as difficult to understand as the figure may seem.)

case statement

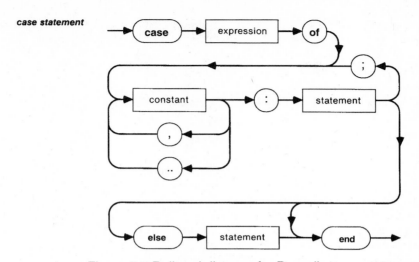

Figure 3-7 Railroad diagram for Pascal's **case** statement.

Program 3-16 does the same job of picking complementary colors but, with the help of a **case** statement, is much easier to read. Except for lines 11-20, Program 3-16 is identical to Program 3-15. The **case** statement evaluates an *expression* (see Figure 3-7) and then applies the resulting value to a list of constants, or *selectors*. Here the selectors are upper- and lowercase characters in lines 12-18.

Program 3-16: COLOR2.PAS

```
1:  program Color2;
2:  var
3:    Choice: Char;
4:    UserQuits: Boolean;
5:  begin
6:    Writeln('Complementary Colors #2');
7:    UserQuits := False;
8:    repeat
9:      Write('B.lue, G.reen, O.range, P.urple, R.ed, Y.ellow, Q.uit? ');
10:     Readln(Choice);
11:     case Choice of
12:       'B', 'b': Writeln('Orange');
13:       'G', 'g': Writeln('Red'   );
14:       'O', 'o': Writeln('Blue'  );
15:       'P', 'p': Writeln('Yellow');
16:       'R', 'r': Writeln('Green' );
```

continued

Program 3-16: continued

```
17:          'Y', 'y': Writeln('Purple');
18:          'Q', 'q': UserQuits := True;
19:          else Writeln('Error: Try again.')
20:      end
21:    until UserQuits
22:  end.
```

If the result of the expression (in this example the character held in variable Choice) matches one of the selectors, the associated statement following the colon executes. If no possibility matches, the optional **else** clause executes instead. If there is no **else** clause, and no matches, the program simply continues after the end of the **case** statement. Remove line 19 to see what happens without the optional **else** clause in place.

When Turbo Pascal compiles a **case** statement, it creates the finished code no differently than it would for a multilevel equivalent **if-then-else** construction. Some Pascal compilers create fast *jump tables* for **case** statements, a method programs can use to skip directly to one **case** selector rather than test each value sequentially. Unfortunately, Turbo Pascal doesn't operate that way, and, in terms of the result, it doesn't matter whether you use **case** or **if-then-else**.

A **case** statement works only with simple constants—you can't use strings or real numbers as selectors. When you must compare a number of strings, you have no choice but to use a series of **if-then-else** statements.

The *expression* in a **case** statement (Figure 3-7) must reduce to a character, an integer, or another scalar type. A type is scalar if it has regular, whole-number steps. Integers are scalar. Real numbers are not. A **case** statement is especially handy, therefore, when writing "menu-driven" programs like Program 3-16 where you make a selection from a menu of choices.

Turbo Pascal allows ranges of selectors in a **case** statement. A range of values looks like this:

```
'A' .. 'D'
```

The double periods form an ellipsis—just as in the integer subranges in Chapter 2—indicating that what you really mean is:

```
'A', 'B', 'C', 'D'
```

This lets you write **case** statements to select actions for a range of selectors. For example, this selects ActionA for uppercase letters, ActionB for lowercase, and ActionC for digits:

```
case Choice of
  'A' .. 'Z' : ActionA;
  'a' .. 'z' : ActionB;
  '0' .. '9' : ActionC
end;
```

To do the same thing in many other Pascal compilers, you have to type each character constant, separated by commas. The Turbo Pascal shorthand is a trick worth remembering.

The statement after each **case** selector may be single, compound, or any other kind. You can use **while**, **repeat**, and **for** loops, insert **if-then-else** decision points, and even use additional **case** statements. Here's an example with no particular purpose but to demonstrate the various kinds of statements you can use inside **case**. Assume **I** is an integer variable:

```
case I of
  1 : Writeln('I=', I);
  2 : begin
        Write('What''s your name? ');
        Readln(YourName)
      end;
  3 : repeat
        Writeln(J);
        J := J + 1
      until J >= 100;
  4 : if (J <> 100) and (J <> 200)
        then J := 0 else J := 100;
  5 : begin
        Ch := 'A';
        while Ch <= 'Z' do
        begin
          Write(Ch);
          Ch := Succ(Ch)
        end
      end
end;
```

The goto Statement

Besides **if** and **case** statements, there is a third way to alter statement flow in a program, a method that has achieved widespread notoriety. The infamous **goto** statement has a nasty reputation because of its capability to jump around at will to nearly any place in a program. This lack of control, according to some, invites programmers to pitch caution away, jumping from here to there, with little regard for the consequences.

Using a lot of **goto** statements can produce what many call *spaghetti code.* If you could draw a line from every **goto** to its destination, a **goto**-infested program would look like that classic refrigerator art work—an explosion in a spaghetti factory.

In practice, with the rich and powerful **while**, **repeat**, **for**, **if**, and **case** statements, few situations require a **goto**. Used indiscriminately, **goto** statements can lead to chaos—but then, so can other Pascal features. In rare situations, though, **goto** statements come in handy and should be used—with care.

The **goto** requires a **label** declaration (Figure 3-8) coming before any program **const** or **var** declarations. Labels can be unsigned (positive) integers or unique identifiers. (In many Pascal systems, they must be integers.) Use commas to separate multiple labels, ending the list of all labels with a semicolon.

label declaration

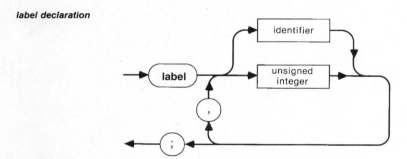

Figure 3-8 Each label to be used in a later **goto** statement must be declared in a **label** declaration.

After defining your labels, you may then use them with a colon in front of any statement to mark that position in a program (Figure 3-9). To transfer control to a labeled statement, use the command **goto** *label*, where *label* is one of your predefined labels. Each label can mark only one position in a program (Figure 3-10).

Program 3-17 demonstrates how to use **goto** statements in Pascal in a situation where another kind of solution would be less elegant. In the example, certain statements repeat for some keypresses, others for other keypresses, and portions of both sequences for still other selections.

labeled statement

Figure 3.9 To mark a statement, precede it with a predefined label and a colon.

goto statement

Figure 3-10 Railroad diagram for a **goto** statement, which transfers control to the statement marked by a label identifier. (See also Figures 3-8 and 3-9.)

Program 3-17: MULTICH.PAS

```
 1:   program MultipleChoice;
 2:   label
 3:      1, 2, 3, 4, 5;
 4:   var
 5:      Choice: Char;
 6:   begin
 7:      Write('Enter A, B, or C: '); Readln(Choice);
 8:      case Choice of
 9:        'A', 'a' : goto 1;   { do statements 1, 3, 4 }
10:        'B', 'b' : goto 2;   { do statements 2, 4 }
11:        'C', 'c' : goto 3    { do statements 3, 4 }
12:              else goto 5    { do no statements }
13:      end;
14:      1: Writeln('statement #1'); goto 3;
15:      2: Writeln('statement #2'); goto 4;
16:      3: Writeln('statement #3');
17:      4: Writeln('statement #4');
18:      5: Writeln('Done');
19:      Readln
20:   end.
```

There appear to be three approaches to solving this kind of problem. One approach repeats each group of statements for each appropriate selection. Another uses Boolean expressions and **if** statements to select which statements to execute. The third uses **goto** statements. Without **goto** statements, Program 3-17 requires either the duplication of one or more statements or multiple, time-wasting, Boolean expressions.

That observation leads to a good rule to follow. If a **goto** avoids repeating the same statement at different places in a program, or if a **goto** saves extra programming steps, use it. Duplication of effort is something to fight courageously in programming, and, on occasion, the **goto** is a useful weapon in the battle. As with all weapons, however, aim your **goto** statements only at things you're sure you want to hit!

One important rule is never to jump into the middle of a **repeat**, **while**, or **for** loop. Ignore this rule at your own peril. Jumping into the middle of a loop may skip an important initialization of the control variable or cause other problems and hard-to-find bugs.

Summary

Compound statements are individual statements, separated by semicolons and surrounded by **begin** and **end**. Pascal allows compound statements anywhere a boxed-in *statement* appears in a railroad diagram.

Repeating a single or compound statement is a common programming operation. Pascal has three repetitive statements to choose from: **while**, **repeat**, and **for**. A **while** loop evaluates its condition at the top and may never execute. A **repeat** loop evaluates its condition at the bottom and always executes at least once. A **for** loop is often shorter and more efficient than the other two loops but requires a simple control variable and always goes up or down by single steps.

Conditional statements, **if-then-else** and **case**, allow programs to make decisions, changing the program's flow. An **if** statement chooses one of two possible statements. A **case** statement chooses one of many possibilities. The notorious **goto** jumps to a specific place in a program, but its power is dangerous if used carelessly.

Exercises

3-1. Modify Program 3-2 or 3-5 to count down from ten to one. Add a prompt for a starting value to begin counting.

3-2. Program 2-5 calculates the Celsius temperature for degrees Fahrenheit, but you have to rerun it for every new temperature. Add a loop to the program, making it repeat until you want to stop.

3-3. The following colors are complementary: yellow-green and red-purple; blue-green and red-orange; blue-purple and yellow-orange. Add these six new colors to Program 3-16. (Hint: Modify the **case** statement to select colors by number; for example, 1=yellow, 2=yellow-green, etc.)

3-4. A factorial, written *n!*, of a nonnegative integer is defined by the equation (using an asterisk for multiplication):

n! = 1 * 2 * ... * n

In other words, *n!* equals all the integer values from 1 up to and including *n* multiplied together. Write a program to calculate *n!* for any positive value of *n*. (Note: The factorial of 0 is 1, not 0. Your program should handle this special condition.)

3-5. Think of a number between 1 and 100. Now, if I try to guess your number, say 50, you tell me if I'm high or low, then I'll make another guess. I bet I can guess your number in seven tries or less. Write a program to play this game with you. What repetitive and conditional statements will you use?

3-6. Modify Program 3-17 to operate without using any **goto** statements.

4

Divide and Conquer

- Top-Down Programming
- Functions
- Passing Parameters
- Nesting Procedures and Functions
- Scope Consequences
- Forward Declarations and Recursion
- Predeclared Procedures and Functions
- Function Side Effects
- Escape Artists: Halt and Exit
- Functions and Evaluation Order
- Procedures That Increment and Decrement

4

Dec, Exit, **function**, **for**, **forward**, **goto**, Halt, Inc, Odd, **procedure**, Upcase, **var**

One approach to designing Pascal programs might be called the "brute-force" method. That is, you state a goal, for example, converting temperatures from Fahrenheit to Celsius, then sit down and write the code. This may be adequate for small programs, but the same approach fails miserably for larger projects, database managers, spreadsheets, and sophisticated games. Such endeavors require too many complex steps to comprehend—much less program—all at once.

Instead of a brute-force, do-it-all approach, most professional programmers follow an organizational method called *top-down programming.* As you'll learn in this chapter, top-down programming and Pascal fit together like a glove on your hand.

Top-Down Programming

Experienced programmers divide large projects into pieces, then conquer each of the more manageable parts one by one. This way, the entire program falls into place while you concentrate on a few simple lines at a time.

This divide-and-conquer method is at the heart of top-down programming. You start at the top, with the main goal, and progress from overall concepts down to finer and finer details. Programmers, of course, are not the only people to use top-down methods in their work. A builder starts with a blueprint and lays the foundation before framing in the walls. A musician begins with a theme or melody before adding the trills. This book started with an idea, then progressed to an outline, and from there grew into chapters, paragraphs, and sentences. The top-down method is a natural, enjoyable way to tackle seemingly overwhelming problems. Pascal encourages top-down design, but you must consciously apply the method for it to work.

One way to divide a large program into smaller parts is to use procedures. A *procedure* is a named group of statements, variables, constants, and other declarations, all with a particular purpose. Anywhere you write the procedure's name, its internal statements run as though you had copied those statements to this place in the program.

For example, you might design a procedure named Calculate. To use that procedure, you write *Calculate* any place in your program. Wherever Calculate appears, the statements in the procedure execute. In this way, procedures extend the Pascal language, letting you invent and name new commands. Procedures also reduce duplication by collecting operations that many other parts of a program require.

You can insert procedures anywhere between the last variable declaration of a program and the **begin** of the main program body. After declaring a procedure, its identifier can be used anywhere in a program to call the procedure into action. Figure 4-1 shows the railroad diagram for a simple procedure declaration. An identifier (naming the procedure) and a semicolon follow the key word **procedure**. After that comes a *block* containing the statements and declarations that apply to this procedure. (Appendix A shows the complete procedure and block diagrams.)

Figure 4-1 Railroad diagram describing a simple procedure.

An example helps clarify procedure declarations while demonstrating top-down programming methods. Program 4-1 is going to be a U.S. Customary to International Metric measurements converter. The program is not finished. Five of the six options listed in lines 20-25 are missing. The only completed option is the first, "Inches to centimeters." This is a typical situation in top-down programming. Parts of the program are finished while others await your attention. After testing the finished parts, you add the rest of the programming, testing each new option before adding the others.

Program 4-1: METRICS.PAS

```pascal
 1:  program Metrics;
 2:  { Metric conversion program }
 3:  var
 4:    Value: Real;
 5:    Selection: Integer;
 6:
 7:  procedure InchesToCentimeters;
 8:  const
 9:    CentPerInch = 2.54;
10:  begin
11:    Writeln(Value:1:2, ' inches = ',
12:      Value * CentPerInch:1:2, ' centimeters')
13:  end;
14:
15:  begin
16:    Writeln('Metrics');
17:    Writeln;
18:    Write('Value to convert? ');
19:    Readln(Value);
20:    Writeln('1 - Inches to centimeters');
21:    Writeln('2 - Centimeters to inches');
22:    Writeln('3 - Feet to meters');
23:    Writeln('4 - Meters to feet');
24:    Writeln('5 - Miles to kilometers');
25:    Writeln('6 - Kilometers to miles');
26:    Writeln;
27:    Write('Selection? '); Readln(Selection);
28:    Writeln;
29:    case Selection of
30:      1: InchesToCentimeters;
31:      else Writeln('Selection error')
32:    end;
33:    Readln
34:  end.
```

You should have no trouble understanding most of Program 4-1. The plan is to enter a value (line 19), select an option (line 27), then do the conversion (lines 29-32). The procedure InchesToCentimeters in lines 7-13 has an obvious purpose—converting inches to equivalent centimeters. Because the procedure name identifies what the procedure does, there's no need to add a comment here.

Notice how the procedure resembles a complete program. It has its own constant declaration and its own **begin** and **end** with a semicolon at the end. In fact, anything that can go in a program can go in a procedure declaration. The only difference is that a procedure's final **end** has a semicolon, not a period.

Line 30 activates the procedure as a selection in the **case** statement, which now has only one selector. The procedure name, InchesToCentimeters, could also go wherever else Pascal allows statements, with one restriction: You cannot use a procedure before declaring it. (Later in this chapter you'll learn how to break even this rule.)

Scope of a Procedure

The procedure in Program 4-1 has a *scope,* a limited range of view, of the procedure's variable, constant, and other declarations. Declarations inside the procedure are *local*—they do not exist outside the procedure's block. To prove this, try adding the following statement between lines 16 and 17, then rerun the program:

```
Writeln(CentPerInch);
```

If you had declared CentPerInch as a constant in the main program, you would not receive an error. But as now written, the procedure declares CentPerInch as a local constant in lines 8-9. Statements belonging to the procedure block can use the constant. Statements outside the procedure's scope can't. When you refer to CentPerInch outside the procedure, you receive:

```
Error 3: Unknown identifier.
```

On the other hand, the two variables Value and Selection in lines 4 and 5 have a *global* scope. Declared in the main program block, which extends from line 2 to line 33, the variables are visible from everywhere in the program—including the procedure statements in lines 11 and 12, where the global Value helps compute inches to centimeters. Global declarations are visible from all places in a program; local declarations are limited to the scope of their declaring procedure.

Continuing with the top-down approach, finish Program 4-1, adding the next option to convert centimeters to inches. First, insert a new **case** selector between lines 30 and 31:

```
2: CentimetersToInches;
```

Next, add the following procedure between lines 14 and 15:

```
procedure CentimetersToInches;
const
   InchPerCent = 0.3937;
begin
   Writeln(Value:1:2, ' centimeters = ',
      Value * InchPerCent:1:2, ' inches')
end;
```

When you're finished, the program has two procedures and two options. Test the program before continuing.

Now add the remaining options until the program is complete. You should be able to write the procedures on your own, using the previous examples as guides. There are 0.3048 meters in 1 foot, 3.28084 feet in 1 meter, 1.609 kilometers in 1 mile, and 0.621 miles in 1 kilometer. In top-down fashion, add and test each formula before going to the next.

Functions

A function is identical to a procedure but for one difference: A function returns a value where its name appears. You may use functions in expressions anywhere you normally could use a constant. Constants, as you already know, have predeclared values. Functions, on the other hand, calculate the values they return. Also, like constants and variables, functions have associated data types. Functions may return Boolean, real, integer, character, or string data types. They may also return other values such as pointers, a subject for Chapter 7, "Pointers, Lists, and Trees."

As the railroad diagram in Figure 4-2 shows, a function declaration starts with the key word **function** and a naming identifier. A colon, data type, semicolon, and block follow. As in a procedure, the block contains the local declarations and program statements belonging to the function, starting with **begin** and ending with **end** and a semicolon.

simple function

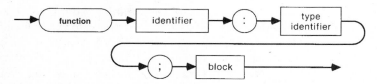

Figure 4-2 Railroad diagram describing a simple function, similar to that in Figure 4-1 but adding a colon and a data type.

Program 4-2 shows a function in action. Before looking at the function, examine the **repeat** loop in lines 18-21. The loop repeats until UserQuits is true, adding one to variable I and displaying I's value for each repetition—just to give the example something to do.

Program 4-2: QUITEX.PAS

```
 1:  program QuitExample;
 2:  var
 3:    I: Integer;
 4:
 5:  { Return true if user wants to end program }
 6:  function UserQuits: Boolean;
 7:  var
 8:    Answer: Char;
 9:  begin
10:    Write('Another value? (y/n) ');
11:    Readln(Answer);
12:    UserQuits := Upcase(Answer) <> 'Y'
13:  end;
14:
15:  begin
16:    Writeln('Quit example');
17:    I := 0;
18:    repeat
19:      I := I + 1;
20:      Writeln('I = ', I)
21:    until UserQuits
22:  end.
```

UserQuits is a Boolean function (lines 6-13) that returns true or false. The function's statements display a prompt (line 10) and request your answer (line 11). Closely examine line 12. If you type Y to the prompt, the program assigns a false result to the function name, UserQuits. If you type any other character, the program assigns a true result. When you run the program, you see a display something like this:

```
I = 1
Another value? (y/n) Y
I = 2
Another value? (y/n) Y
I = 3
Another value? (y/n) N
```

Typing Y and pressing Enter causes UserQuits to report a false value back to the **repeat** loop at line 21. Therefore, the loop repeats. Pressing any other key, which signals that you do not want to see another value, reports a false result, and ends the loop.

There are two important rules to learn from this simple example. First, line 21 uses the function name, UserQuits, in the same way the program might use a Boolean constant. Second, line 12 *inside the function block* assigns a result to the function name, as though it were a Boolean variable. This passes the value back to the place where the function identifier appears in the program.

Line 12 of Program 4-2 uses another function, Upcase, built into Turbo Pascal. The function returns the uppercase equivalent of a character inside parentheses after the function name. For example, this statement displays a capital A:

```
Writeln(Upcase('a'));
```

Usually, you'll pass a variable to Upcase to convert letters to uppercase in statements such as

```
var
  Ch: Char;
repeat
  Readln(Ch)
until Upcase(Ch) = 'Q';
```

The **repeat** loop reads characters from the keyboard until you press the Q key. Because of Upcase, it doesn't matter if you type a lower- or uppercase Q. Without the Upcase function, you would have to write the loop this way:

```
repeat
  Readln(Ch)
until (Ch = 'q') or (Ch = 'Q');
```

Common Errors in Functions

Forgetting to assign a value to a function identifier is a common error. Assuming Value and Factor are global variables the function multiplies, as the following example demonstrates, there is no telling what value a function with such a serious bug returns:

```
function Multiply: Real;
var
  Temp: Real;
begin
  Temp := Value * Factor
end;
```

Although the function calculates the local variable Temp, the programmer forgot to assign that result to the function identifier, Multiply. Being a local variable, Temp has no meaning outside the function's scope. Therefore, when the function ends, the value of Temp is lost. To repair the problem, change the assignment to the following, assigning the result to the function identifier:

```
Multiply := Value * Factor;
```

Or, you can add a new line, assigning the temporary variable Temp to the function identifier:

```
Multiply := Temp;
```

Either way, you ensure that Multiply returns the calculated result. Such errors are all too common in programming and are a leading cause of erratic, hard-to-find bugs. To avoid problems, always assign a value to the function identifier for all possible conditions.

Passing Parameters

Parameters pass values to functions and procedures for processing. With parameters, you can write statements like:

```
Writeln(TenTimes(V):8:2);
```

Earlier, you passed a character parameter to the built-in Upcase function. The parameter—a value the procedure or function needs or processes—appears in parentheses after the procedure or function name. In this example, the parameter value (V) passes to the function (TenTimes), which uses that value in its calculation, returning the result as the function value. Continuing this example, TenTimes declares the parameters it expects to receive, adding them in parentheses to the function declaration:

```
function TenTimes(R: Real): Real;
begin
  TenTimes := R * 10.0
end;
```

Let's say that the program has a real number value V equal to 50.0. These statements then display that value times 10:

```
V := 50.0;
Writeln(TenTimes(V):8:1);
```

The function receives the value of V in its local parameter, R. The value passed to a function must be the same type as the parameter declared in the function, but may have a different name. In this example, V equals 50.0. Therefore, when the program passes V to TenTimes, R—the function parameter—becomes equal to V's value. TenTimes then multiplies R by 10.0 and passes the result back to the Writeln statement, which displays the finished value—500.0 here.

Figures 4-3, 4-4, 4-5, and 4-6 show new procedure and function railroad diagrams complete with parameter lists. Except for the addition of the boxed-in *parameters* in the first two of these figures, the procedure and function definitions are identical to the simple versions presented earlier.

procedure

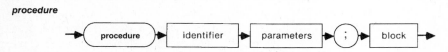

Figure 4-3 The complete railroad diagram for a procedure contains a list of formal parameters.

function

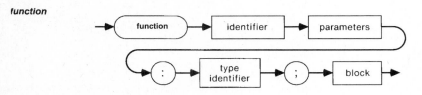

Figure 4-4 The complete railroad diagram for a function contains a list of formal parameters coming before the colon and type identifier.

parameters

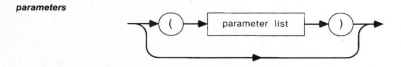

Figure 4-5 Formal parameters may be empty or may contain a parameter list in parentheses.

parameter list

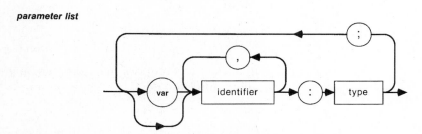

Figure 4-6 A parameter list contains typed identifiers, separated by semicolons, and optionally preceded by **var.**

For both procedures and functions, parameters are listed inside parentheses (Figure 4-5). Parameters are always optional. If your procedures and functions don't need any parameters, just omit them and the parentheses.

Figure 4-6 diagrams a parameter list, which is the same for procedures and functions. Notice the similarity of a parameter list and a **var** declaration. This is no accident. Parameters are named variables inside procedures and functions, just like any other variables. The only difference is that parameters *receive* values from the place in the program that calls the procedure or function. As you can see in Figure 4-6, each parameter has an identifier, followed by a colon and data type. You can separate multiple identifiers of the same type with commas. An optional **var** precedes the first such identifier. For the moment, let's postpone what the **var** does.

As an example of using parameters, suppose you want to calculate the cost of running an appliance for a number of hours at a certain number of watts. On your electric bill, you find the *Cost* per kilowatt hour (kwh) is something like 0.0687. At a certain kwh *Rate,* a certain number of hours, or *Time,* and a certain number of watts, or *Power,* the formula to calculate electric cost in dollars is

$$Cost = Rate * (Power * 0.001 * Time)$$

You can write this same formula as a Pascal function, with the formal parameters Time, Power, and Rate:

```
function Cost(Time, Power, Rate: Real): Real;
begin
   Cost := Rate * (Power * 0.001 * Time)
end;
```

To use the function, insert the function name Cost in your program along with actual values in parentheses. To set real number variable Value to the cost of running a 100-watt appliance for 10 hours, for example, you could use this statement:

```
Value := Cost(10, 100, 0.0687);
```

You must pass as many actual values as there are formal parameters in the function declaration. The following uses of Cost produce compiler errors:

```
Value := Cost(10, 100);   { Too few parameters }
Value := Cost(10, 100, 0.0687, 99);   { Too many parameters }
```

You can also pass variables as actual values. Your program might declare real number variables Watts, Hours, and CostPerKwh. After prompting for those values, display the cost using the statement:

```
Writeln('Cost = ',
   Cost(Hours, Watts, CostPerKwh):8:2);
```

The Cost function returns a real number and, as shown in the previous Writeln statement, you can format it (:8:2) just as you can any other real number. Being able to pass different actual values to the formal parameters of a procedure or function is a powerful Pascal feature. By changing values passed to functions, you can write a program to print a table listing the electric costs for various power ratings over time.

Program 4-3 uses the Cost function (lines 23-27), two procedures, and a Boolean function to print such a table for any number of watts over any length of time. It includes many Pascal features covered in this and earlier chapters. When trying to understand a larger Pascal program like this one, it helps to start not at the beginning, but at the main program body near the end. When you run the program, supply a starting number of hours, an hourly increment, the starting number of watts, an increment for the watts, and the cost per kilowatt hour. When typing the kilowatt-hour value, use a leading zero, as in 0.0625.

Program 4-3: ELECTRIC.PAS

```
 1:  program Electricity;
 2:  const
 3:    MaxRow = 12;          { Number rows in table }
 4:    MaxCol = 8;           { Number columns in table }
 5:  var
 6:    StartHours,
 7:    HourlyIncrement,
 8:    StartWatts,
 9:    WattsIncrement,
10:    CostPerKwh:      Real;
11:
12:  procedure Initialize;
13:  begin
14:    Writeln('Cost of electricity');
15:    Writeln;
16:    Write('Starting number of hours .. ? '); Readln(StartHours);
17:    Write('Hourly increment .......... ? '); Readln(HourlyIncrement);
18:    Write('Starting number of Watts .. ? '); Readln(StartWatts);
19:    Write('Watts increment ........... ? '); Readln(WattsIncrement);
20:    Write('Cost per kilowatt hour (KWH)? '); Readln(CostPerKwh)
21:  end;
22:
23:  { Return cost of running at "Power" watts for "Time" hours }
24:  function Cost(Time, Power, Rate: Real): Real;
25:  begin
26:    Cost := Rate * (Power * 0.001 * Time)
27:  end;
28:
29:  procedure PrintTable;
30:  var
31:    Row, Col: Integer;
32:    Hours, Watts: Real;
```

```
33:  begin
34:     Writeln;
35:     Write('Hrs/Watts');
36:     Watts := StartWatts;
37:     for Col := 1 to MaxCol do
38:     begin
39:       Write(Watts:8:0);
40:       Watts := Watts + WattsIncrement
41:     end;
42:     Writeln;
43:
44:     Hours := StartHours;
45:     for Row := 1 to MaxRow do
46:     begin
47:       Writeln;
48:       Write(Hours:6:1, ' - ');
49:       Watts := StartWatts;
50:       for Col := 1 to MaxCol do
51:       begin
52:         Write(Cost(Hours, Watts, CostPerKwh):8:2);
53:         Watts := Watts + WattsIncrement
54:       end;
55:       Hours := Hours + HourlyIncrement
56:     end;
57:     Writeln;
58:     Writeln;
59:     Writeln('Cost of Electricity @ ', CostPerKwh:0:4, ' per KWH')
60:  end;
61:
62:  function Finished: Boolean;
63:  var
64:     Answer: Char;
65:  begin
66:     Writeln;
67:     Write('Another table (y/n) ? ');
68:     Readln(Answer);
69:     Finished := Upcase(Answer) <> 'Y'
70:  end;
71:
72:  begin
73:     repeat
74:       Initialize;
75:       PrintTable
76:     until Finished
77:  end.
```

Notice that the entire main body of Program 4-3 occupies only six lines, 72-77. Typically, large Pascal programs have tiny main bodies, serving only to call various procedures and functions in some logical order. Figure 4-7 shows an example of the program's output.

```
Cost of electricity
Hrs/Watts     100      110   120   130   140    150    160    170
    4.0  -     0.03    0.03  0.03  0.04  0.04   0.04   0.04   0.05
    6.0  -     0.04    0.05  0.05  0.05  0.06   0.06   0.07   0.07
    8.0  -     0.05    0.06  0.07  0.07  0.08   0.08   0.09   0.09
   10.0  -     0.07    0.08  0.08  0.09  0.10   0.10   0.11   0.12
   12.0  -     0.08    0.09  0.10  0.11  0.12   0.12   0.13   0.14
   14.0  -     0.10    0.11  0.12  0.13  0.13   0.14   0.15   0.16
   16.0  -     0.11    0.12  0.13  0.14  0.15   0.16   0.18   0.19
   18.0  -     0.12    0.14  0.15  0.16  0.17   0.19   0.20   0.21
   20.0  -     0.14    0.15  0.16  0.18  0.19   0.21   0.22   0.23
   22.0  -     0.15    0.17  0.18  0.20  0.21   0.23   0.24   0.26
   24.0  -     0.16    0.18  0.20  0.21  0.23   0.25   0.26   0.28
   26.0  -     0.18    0.20  0.21  0.23  0.25   0.27   0.29   0.30

Cost of Electricity @ 0.0687 per KWH
```

Figure 4-7 Nested **for** loops and the Cost function in Program 4-3 printed this row and column table.

When designing programs with the top-down method, you might start with a short main body and insert *dummy* procedures as placeholders. For example, when I first wrote Program 4-3, I used a dummy PrintTable procedure to hold a place where the actual procedure would eventually go:

```
procedure PrintTable;
begin
end;
```

With its collection of dummy procedures, the program compiles and runs but doesn't do anything. Temporarily, you might also insert Writeln statements in dummy procedures and functions. If you weren't ready to fill in function Cost, you could insert the following dummy function:

```
function Cost(Time, Power, Rate: Real): Real;
var
  Temp: Real;
begin
  Writeln;
```

```
    Write('DUMMY COST. Value? ');
    Readln(Temp);
    Cost := Temp
  end;
```

Eventually, you'll insert the proper formula to complete the function. Meanwhile, the program prompts you for the value that Cost should return. This lets you debug the program, testing what happens when Cost returns various values. After filling in the real programming, you can be confident in the operation of the other tested program statements.

There are a few other highlights you might want to examine more closely in Program 4-3. Procedure PrintTable shows how to use nested **for** loops to print row and column tables, a common computer problem you will encounter repeatedly. Function Finished at lines 62-70 is similar to UserQuits in Program 4-2.

Value and Variable Parameters

Value parameters take their values from the caller of a function or procedure. For example, line 52 of Program 4-3 passes the value of Hours, Watts, and CostPerKwh to function Cost at line 23. When the statements inside Cost execute, the formal parameter Time has the value of Hours; Power has the same value as Watts; and Rate equals CostPerKwh. This is called *passing parameters by value.* Even if Cost were to change the value of Time, the actual variable Hours would not also change. The two variables are distinct even though they have the same value.

The next example will help you to better understand value parameters. Program 4-4 has a single procedure, PrintValues, with three formal integer parameters, X, Y, and Z. The procedure multiplies these three values by 2 and then displays the results in line 9. In line 14, the program assigns initial values 10, 20, and 30 to three global integer variables, A, B, and C. Line 17 passes these parameters by value to PrintValues' formal parameters X, Y, and Z. The program tests the effect of the procedure on the global variables A, B, and C, printing their values (lines 16 and 19) before and after passing them to PrintValues. Running the program produces these results:

```
Before .... A=10, B=20, C=30
During .... X=20, Y=40, Z=60
After  .... A=10, B=20, C=30
```

As you can see, A, B, and C do not change. Although PrintValues multiplies X, Y, and Z by 2 in line 7, the global variables A, B, and C keep their original values before and after the procedure executes, proving that the variables are distinct. PrintValues' formal parameters receive copies of the actual variables passed by value in line 17— the original variables (A, B, and C) are not disturbed.

Program 4-4: VALPARAM.PAS

```
 1:  program ValueParameters;
 2:  var
 3:    A, B, C: Integer;
 4:
 5:  procedure PrintValues(X, Y, Z: Integer);
 6:  begin
 7:    X := X * 2; Y := Y * 2; Z := Z * 2;
 8:    Writeln;
 9:    Writeln('During.... X=', X, ' Y=', Y, ' Z=', Z)
10:  end;
11:
12:  begin
13:    Writeln('Value parameters');
14:    A := 10; B := 20; C := 30;
15:    Writeln;
16:    Writeln('Before.... A=', A, ' B=', B, ' C=', C);
17:    PrintValues(A, B, C);
18:    Writeln;
19:    Writeln('After..... A=', A, ' B=', B, ' C=', C);
20:    Readln
21:  end.
```

Program 4-5 is identical to Program 4-4 except for a new element in the parameter list in line 5. By declaring the formal parameters with the preceding key word **var**, the program has a different effect, producing these results:

```
Before .... A=10, B=20, C=30
During .... X=20, Y=40, Z=60
After  .... A=20, B=40, C=60
```

Now, when procedure PrintValues multiplies X, Y, and Z, the original variables A, B, and C also change to the new values. When declared with the key word **var**, the formal parameters X, Y, and Z are called *variable parameters.* If changed inside the procedure, as in the example, the actual variables passed to the procedure also vary.

Program 4-5: VARPARAM.PAS

```
 1:  program VariableParameters;
 2:  var
 3:    A, B, C: Integer;
 4:
 5:  procedure PrintValues(var X, Y, Z: Integer);
 6:  begin
 7:    X := X * 2; Y := Y * 2; Z := Z * 2;
 8:    Writeln;
 9:    Writeln('During.... X=', X, ' Y=', Y, ' Z=', Z)
10:  end;
11:
12:  begin
13:    Writeln('Variable parameters');
14:    A := 10; B := 20; C := 30;
15:    Writeln;
16:    Writeln('Before.... A=', A, ' B=', B, ' C=', C);
17:    PrintValues(A, B, C);
18:    Writeln;
19:    Writeln('After..... A=', A, ' B=', B, ' C=', C);
20:    Readln
21:  end.
```

Passing values to variable parameters this way is called *passing parameters by reference.* The formal parameters (X, Y, and Z in the example) *refer,* or point, to the actual variables A, B, and C. Changing the value of the formal parameter also changes the value of the actual variable to which it refers.

While you can pass either variable or literal values to value parameters, you can pass only variables to variable parameters. For example, try changing line 17 in Program 4-4 to

```
PrintValues(100, 200, 300);
```

The value parameters in line 5 accept these literal constants. Try changing the same line in Program 4-5, however, and the compiler displays:

```
Error 20: Variable identifier expected.
```

The reason for this error is that variable parameters (line 5) cannot accept literal, constant values. You can pass only variables to variable parameters.

Parameter Names

Parameters in procedures and functions are similar to local variables. Like local variables, parameters are visible only in the routines in which you declare them. You can't refer to parameter names outside the procedure—the parameters exist only when the procedure is running.

Because they are local variables, parameter identifiers never conflict with identifiers declared outside the routine's scope. In other words, you could change line 5 in Program 4-5 to:

```
procedure PrintValues(var A, B, C: Integer);
```

even though the same names A, B, and C are used as global variables at line 3. Inside PrintValues, A, B, and C are distinct variables from the ones with the same names outside the routine.

Usually, though, it's a good idea to choose unique names for identifiers inside procedures and functions. This way, the program is perfectly clear. But if you want to repeat identifier names for global variables, parameters, and local variables inside procedures and functions, you may certainly do so.

Where Are My Parameters?

The *stack* is an area in memory typically used to store return addresses to procedures and functions. When a statement calls a procedure or function, the program "pushes" the address of the called routine onto the stack so that, after the routine finishes, it can *return* to the location following the place that called it.

Value parameters and local variables are also stored on the stack. Unlike global variables, which are fixed in memory while a program runs, stack variables are created only when their declaring routines are called. When those called routines return, the stack variables are discarded from memory, thus making room on the stack for variables created by other routines. For example, in Program 4-5, X, Y, and Z exist only while PrintValues runs.

Local variables and value parameters, then, are *dynamic,* existing only while needed. Turbo Pascal dynamically reserves space for local variables and value parameters on demand, efficiently using memory. In a program with thousands of procedures, only the absolute minimum amount of variable space exists as needed at any one time. Because global variables always exist in memory, even when you don't need them, it's a good idea to use global variables only when you must preserve their values between calls to various routines.

Try to use global variables sparingly, declaring most variables locally inside procedures and functions, and passing parameters for processing. This lets Turbo Pascal dynamically create space for your variables as needed—space that many other routines can share. If you follow this rule, your programs will probably use less memory.

Mixing Variable and Value Parameters

You can freely mix variable and value parameters in a parameter list, but when writing procedures with several formal parameters, you may want to use a style like the one shown at the bottom of Figure 4-8.

```
procedure Test(Param1, Param2: Integer; var Param3:
   Real; Param4: Char);

procedure Test(    Param1,
                   Param2: Integer;
              var Param3: Real;
                   Param4: Char    );
```

Figure 4-8 These two procedure declarations are the same, but the one on top is more difficult to read. The bottom style has each formal parameter declared on a separate line.

As with other stylistic concerns in Pascal, the compiler doesn't care about parameter cosmetics. To the compiler, the two styles for procedure Test in Figure 4-8 are equally beautiful. But a carefully written program is easier to read and understand, especially years later when your original intentions may be unclear. With hundreds or thousands of procedures and functions, many having multiple parameters, the beauty of a good programming style is more than just skin deep— to a programmer, that is.

Turbo Pascal allows two other kinds of parameters. *Untyped parameters* have no data types. *Procedural parameters* are the names of procedures and functions, passed as values to other procedures and functions. Chapter 13 discusses these advanced techniques.

Nesting Procedures and Functions

Procedures and functions can nest inside other procedures and functions. You can have one procedure with other subprocedures and subfunctions, which in turn can have sub-subprocedures, and so on.

A nested procedure or function is local to its surrounding parent. Statements outside the parent cannot call the locally nested procedure, just as they cannot use any locally declared variables or constants.

Program 4-6 demonstrates nested procedures. The program calculates the volume of a sphere from its radius. Designed using the top-down method, the main program in lines 31-36 is simple, writing the program title (line 32) and repeatedly calculating volumes until Done. FindVolume is a procedure (lines 5-29) that prompts for the radius (line 25) and writes the result (line 28). The procedure returns a Boolean variable parameter Quitting (line 6) equal to true if you enter 0, ending the program when the actual variable Done is false in line 35.

Program 4-6: SPHERE.PAS

```pascal
1:   program Sphere;
2:   var
3:     Done: Boolean;
4:
5:   { Compute volume, returning Quitting = true if user is done }
6:   procedure FindVolume(var Quitting: Boolean);
7:   var
8:     Radius: Real;
9:
10:    { Return volume of sphere with radius r }
11:    function VolOfSphere(R: Real): Real;
12:
13:      { Return n*n*n }
14:      function Cube(N: Real): Real;
15:      begin
16:        Cube := N * N * N
17:      end;
18:
19:    begin
20:      VolOfSphere := (4.0 * Pi * Cube(R)) / 3.0
21:    end;
22:
23:  begin
24:    Writeln;
25:    Write('Radius? (0 to quit) '); Readln(Radius);
26:    Quitting := (Radius = 0.0);
27:    if not Quitting
28:      then Writeln('Volume = ', VolOfSphere(Radius):1:3)
29:  end;
30:
31:  begin
32:    Writeln('Volume of a sphere');
33:    repeat
34:      FindVolume(Done)
35:    until Done
36:  end.
```

There are two nested functions in the example. Function VolOfSphere in lines 10-21 calculates the volume according to this formula from solid geometry:

$$V_{sphere} = \frac{4\pi r^3}{3}$$

This formula appears as the expression in line 20. Another nested function returns the cube of a value. Function Cube at lines 13-17 lets line 20 write Cube(R) instead of R * R * R. Notice how the purely stylistic indentation (lines 10, 13, and 19) indicates the level of nesting.

Each nested function in Program 4-6 has a limited scope. For example, function Cube can be seen only from inside its parent function, VolOfSphere. You could not use Cube in the body of the program (lines 31-36) or in procedure FindVolume (lines 23-29). To prove this claim, try adding the following statement between lines 26 and 27 to print the cube of the radius:

```
Writeln('Radius cubed = ', Cube( Radius));
```

The compiler displays:

```
Error 3: Unknown identifier.
```

because the Cube function is local to VolOfSphere and does not exist outside that function's limited scope. To correct the problem, you could move function Cube from its current position at lines 13-17 to between lines 9 and 10. Doing this declares the function local to FindVolume and, therefore, within the scope of everything inside that procedure. Although the modified program now runs, you still cannot access VolOfSphere or Cube from the main body of the program. Those functions are still local to FindVolume.

Limitations of Nesting

Technically, there is no limit to the number of subprocedures that can nest inside procedures on higher levels. You could have procedures inside procedures inside functions inside still other procedures until your program looks like a pyramid toppled onto one side.

In practice, though, nesting is rarely useful to a depth much greater than that shown in Program 4-6. If each nesting level is numbered with the main program at level zero, then procedure FindVolume is at level one, VolOfSphere is at level two, and Cube is at level three. As a general rule, most programs require nesting no deeper than three or four levels.

Another limitation of nested routines concerns the capability to access variables declared locally to other routines. In Program 4-6, variable Radius is local to FindVolume. Both VolOfSphere and Cube can use this variable because these two functions are within FindVolume's scope.

Remember that value parameters and local variables are identical. The only difference is that parameters receive initial values from callers to procedures and functions. Parameter R in line 10 is a local variable inside VolOfSphere. Because of this, FindVolume cannot refer to R. But Cube could use R because Cube is within VolOfSphere's scope. Similarly, parameter N in line 13 is a local variable in Cube. Because Cube is the most deeply nested routine, only its own statements can use N.

If all this seems confusing, just remember that you can refer to items declared only in the same or in outer levels. You can never refer to items declared within inner levels.

It may help to picture this concept as a set of rooms constructed out of one-way glass facing out. Each room, representing a procedure or function, nests inside a larger room. The outermost room is the main program. While standing in any one room, you can see all the way to the outside, but you can't see into any other rooms nested inside the one you're in. You can see the furniture (variables) in outer rooms and in your own, but you can't look into inner rooms to see what they contain. If you fix this image firmly in mind, you'll avoid mixups when working with nested procedures and functions.

Scope Consequences

In Chapter 3, you learned about **goto** and **for** statements. When using these statements in procedures and functions, you need to be aware of two restrictions.

A **goto** inside a procedure or function can jump to labeled statements only within the same block. For example, if you define a global label between lines 1 and 2 of Program 4-4 and label the statement at line 18, you still can't jump to line 18 from inside the PrintValues procedure. This limitation forces you to use **goto** statements only for short hops within the block defining the **goto** label.

Another restriction concerns the scope of procedure and function blocks that contain **for** loops. The control variable for all **for** loops must be a global variable, local variable, or value parameter. You may never use a variable parameter (preceded by **var** in the parameter list) for a **for** loop control. If you try to do this, you receive:

```
Error 97: Invalid FOR control variable.
```

These minor restrictions are rarely problems; you just have to memorize them: Don't be too concerned with the details, though. Turbo Pascal will tell you if you make a mistake—one of the reasons for using a language compiler in the first place.

Forward Declarations and Recursion

Earlier, you learned that you must declare procedures and functions before using them. Sometimes, you'll have to break this rule, using a procedure before declaring it. To handle this problem, Turbo Pascal provides a special key word, **forward**, which Program 4-7 demonstrates.

Program 4-7: ONFIRST.PAS

```
 1:    program WhosOnFirst;
 2:
 3:    procedure B(Ch: Char); forward;
 4:
 5:    procedure A(Ch: Char);
 6:    begin
 7:      if Ch < 'Z' then B(Ch);
 8:      Write(Ch)
 9:    end;
10:
11:    procedure B(Ch: Char);
12:    begin
13:      A(Succ(Ch))
14:    end;
15:
16:    begin
17:      A('A');
18:      Writeln;
19:      Readln
20:    end.
```

The example reads like an Abbott and Costello comedy routine. The program has two procedures A and B. The action begins (line 17) by calling A, which at line 7 calls B if Ch is less than Z. B in turn calls A at line 13 passing the successor of Ch by value back to A, after which A again calls B, which then calls A. Who's calling who?! Although the example may seem silly, it demonstrates a programming situation that often occurs in Pascal.

Program 4-7 is an example of *mutual recursion*. Recursion is what happens when a procedure or function calls itself. Mutual recursion is what happens when procedure (or function) A calls *another* routine B, which again calls A—exactly what happens in Program 4-7. The recursion continues in layer upon layer until the procedures stop calling each other, usually when a variable reaches a certain value or when a condition becomes true or false.

Obviously, even though two mutually recursive procedures call each other, you cannot declare them ahead of each other. Either B must follow A or the other way around. To resolve this conflict, Pascal allows you to declare procedures and functions *forward,* letting both A and B call each other, as shown in Program 4-7, line 3.

The forward-declared B has a normal procedure declaration with an optional parameter list but ends with the key word **forward** in place of the usual block. Now, A may call B, while B may still call A. To understand how the program works, try to execute its statements by hand. The results may surprise you!

When you write the programming for a forward routine (see lines 11-14), you must repeat the procedure or function declaration exactly as it appears earlier with the **forward** key word. If you declare different numbers of parameters in either case, you'll receive:

```
Error 131: Header does not match previous definition.
```

(By "header," Turbo Pascal means the procedure or function declaration.)

Alternatively, you may declare the procedure with its parameters and the **forward** key word and then later delete the parameters altogether. In other words, it's perfectly okay to change line 11 to:

```
procedure B;
```

The reason for this odd rule is that in most other versions of Pascal—and in previous Turbo Pascal versions—you are not allowed to repeat the parameter lists from forward declarations. Therefore, for compatibility, Turbo Pascal lets you declare forward routines with parameters and then write the actual routines without redeclaring those same parameters. If you declare parameters in both places, though, the compiler insists that they match. Use whichever style you prefer.

More About Recursion

Program 4-7 demonstrates mutual recursion. Plain recursion occurs when a procedure or function calls itself. When this happens, several actions occur:

- The procedure or function starts running from its first statement for each time it calls itself.

- New and distinct copies of value parameters and local variables are created on the stack.

- The location that calls the procedure or function is put on hold, in effect pausing while the recursively generated level starts running.

An example helps explain these effects. Program 4-8 contains a recursive procedure, Count, which calls itself from line 5 if the value of N is less than ten. The main program calls Count, passing an initial value of one as a value parameter.

Program 4-8: RECURSIV.PAS

```
 1:    program RecursiveCount;
 2:
 3:    procedure Count(N: Integer);
 4:    begin
 5:      if N < 10 then Count(N + 1);
 6:      Writeln(N)
 7:    end;
 8:
 9:    begin
10:      Count(1);
11:      Readln
12:    end.
```

When Count starts running, N equals one. Because this is less than ten, the **if** statement calls Count a second time, in this case passing N + 1, or two. This causes Count to start over from the top with a distinct value for N. Remember that all value parameters and local variables are distinct for each new level of recursion. Every call to a procedure or function, as you learned earlier, dynamically creates space for local variables and for value parameters. This is true also when routines call themselves recursively, and, therefore, each successive call to Count creates a new and distinct memory space on the stack to hold the value of parameter N.

Eventually, as these actions repeat, N increases to ten, causing the **if** statement to fail. What happens next is the exciting part: The Writeln statement in line 6 executes for the first time.

After the Writeln, Count ends. Because the program calls Count a total of ten times, each successive level of the recursion also ends, unwinding each of the recursive calls until reaching the first. When you run the program, the effect is to count backward from ten!

If you have trouble understanding how this works, imagine that the procedure is like a mirror, with the light striking the glass representing the value passed to the procedure. As you probably have seen, aiming two mirrors at each other causes their light to reflect seemingly forever back and forth between them. Because each mirror "sees" the other as a smaller image, the reflections shrink as they infinitely repeat.

Recursion works like that. And, unless the recursive procedure stops itself at some point down the line, the process continues until the computer runs out of stack space to keep track of the recursive calls and local variables. To prove this, replace Count in Program 4-8 with the following:

```
procedure Count(N: integer);
begin
  Count(N + 1)
end;
```

When you run the modified program, Count calls itself repeatedly, adding one to N for each new call. The recursion never ends—just as the light bouncing between two mirrors presumably never stops alternating back and forth. Actually, though, because computers have limited memory space, when you run the modified program, you quickly receive a "Stack overflow" error. This makes sense because Turbo Pascal stores the successive values of N in memory, stacking each new value along with other items. As you can see, it doesn't take long for memory to fill to capacity, ending the program with an error.

Predeclared Procedures and Functions

Turbo Pascal contains a number of procedures and functions that extend Pascal's standard commands. You learned about one built-in function, Upcase, in Program 4-2. Chapter 18 lists all of Turbo Pascal's built-in routines. You'll meet every one in other chapters as well.

Use built-in procedures and functions the same as those you declare in your own programs. For example, the built-in Odd function returns true if an integer value passed to the function is an odd number. Program 4-9 demonstrates how to use Odd.

Program 4-9: ATODDS.PAS

```
 1:  program AtOdds;
 2:  var
 3:    N: Integer;
 4:  begin
 5:    Write('Type any number: ');
 6:    Readln(N);
 7:    if Odd(N)
 8:      then Writeln(N, ' is very odd')
 9:      else Writeln(N, ' evens the score');
10:    Readln
11:  end.
```

Function Side Effects

Be careful when using functions and procedures not to cause *side effects,* usually as the result of changing a global variable. Program 4-10 demonstrates this danger.

Program 4-10: SIDE.PAS (with errors)

```pascal
 1:  program SideEffect;
 2:  var
 3:    I: Integer;
 4:
 5:  function Even: Boolean;
 6:  begin
 7:    I := I + 1;
 8:    Even := Odd(I)
 9:  end;
10:
11:  begin
12:    I := 1;
13:    while I < 20 do
14:    begin
15:      Write(I:2);
16:      if Even then Write(' : is even');
17:      Writeln;
18:      I := I + 1
19:    end;
20:    Readln
21:  end.
```

Program 4-10 has a bug. The purpose of the program is to write a list of numbers, identifying the even values. Faced with this problem, you might decide to write a function based on the idea that N is even if N + 1 is odd, a reasonable approach, if not the best one. This function is programmed in lines 5-9. Variable I increases by one, making function Even true or false depending on the result of the built-in Boolean function Odd.

The problem is that the main loop of the program also uses I as a control variable inside the **while** loop in lines 13-19. Because the program increases I in line 18 and, unknown to the main program, also in line 7, it lists no even numbers. The side effect of function Even changing the value of the global variable I causes the bug.

Because of the potential for causing side effects, statements inside procedures and functions should rarely, if ever, make assignments to global variables. In a large program, it's easy to forget which procedures affect which global variables. Using those variables elsewhere, as Program 4-10 demonstrates, can lead to difficult problems. To prevent side effects, pass parameters to your procedures. For example, you might rewrite Program 4-10 with the following lines in place of lines 5 and 16:

```pascal
 5:  function Even(I: Integer): Boolean;
```

```pascal
16:  if Even(I) then Write(' : is even');
```

By declaring a formal parameter I in function Even and passing I by value, adding one in line 7 affects only the local parameter, not the global variable of the same name. The side effect is gone, and the program now runs correctly.

Escape Artists: Halt and Exit

Two special built-in procedures let you immediately end a program (Halt) and stop a procedure or function (Exit) at any place you want. Halt is useful when you want to display an error message and end a program:

```
procedure Error;
begin
   Writeln('Error!  Halting program...');
   Halt
end;
```

Exit lets you stop a procedure, rather than let it continue to the end. This is sometimes useful when, deep in the execution of a procedure, you want to escape quickly out of a loop and go on with the rest of the program.

Program 4-11 demonstrates these Pascal escape artists. Procedure A asks you to type X. Procedure B asks you to type Y. If you type a different character, each procedure calls Error at line 3, halting the program. If you type the requested character, procedure A ends rather than calling Error. Procedure B ends a different way: by calling Exit at line 24, thus skipping the call to Error at line 25.

Program 4-11: FASTEXIT.PAS

```
 1:   program FastExit;
 2:
 3:   procedure Error(Ch: Char);
 4:   begin
 5:     Writeln('Error! You did not type ', Ch);
 6:     Readln; Halt
 7:   end;
 8:
 9:   procedure A;
10:   var Ch: Char;
11:   begin
12:     Write('Type X to quit procedure A: ');
13:     Readln(Ch);
```

```
14:    if Upcase(Ch) <> 'X'
15:      then Error('X')
16:  end;
17:
18:  procedure B;
19:  var Ch: Char;
20:  begin
21:    Write('Type Y to quit procedure B: ');
22:    Readln(Ch);
23:    if Upcase(Ch) = 'Y'
24:      then Exit;
25:    Error('Y')
26:  end;
27:
28:  begin
29:    A; B
30:  end.
```

The Exit procedure in a program's outer block ends a program and, in this case, is identical to Halt. Either of the following two replacements for line 29 in Program 4-11 ends the program before calling procedure B:

```
29: A; Exit; B
```

or:

```
29: A; Halt; B
```

Halt has two forms. You can use it with no parameters as in line 6, or you can pass an integer value in parentheses like this:

```
Halt(5);
```

The value passed to Halt goes back to DOS (or to another program that may have run your program). DOS or the other program can use the value for any purpose, but, usually, halt values represent error codes with zero meaning no error. Halt with no parameters is equivalent to Halt(0).

To demonstrate how to use a Halt parameter in DOS, type Program 4-12, save it as TESTHALT.PAS, and compile to disk, creating TESTHALT.EXE. If you're using Turbo Pascal's IDE, toggle the *Compile:Destination* command to *Disk*.

Program 4-12: TESTHALT.PAS

```
1:  program TestHalt;
2:  var N: Integer;
3:  begin
4:    Writeln;
5:    Writeln('Welcome to Test Halt.');
6:    Write('Enter 0 to stop repeating: ');
7:    Readln(N);
8:    Halt(N)
9:  end.
```

Next, type the following five lines and save as RUNHALT.BAT:

```
echo off
:loop
testhalt
if errorlevel 1 goto loop
echo on
```

With RUNHALT.BAT and TESTHALT.EXE on disk, quit Turbo Pascal and type RUNHALT to run this small batch file program. The batch file calls TESTHALT, which asks you to type a number. Type 1, 2, 3, or any other whole number. The value you enter passes back to DOS through the Halt(n) statement in line 8. Back in the batch file, DOS tests this value by checking errorlevel. If the value is greater than or equal to 1, the batch file goes back to :loop, again running TESTHALT. To stop the repetition, type 0.

Functions and Evaluation Order

A subtle side effect can occur when mixing functions in complex expressions. Program 4-13 demonstrates how this situation sometimes clashes with Turbo Pascal's short-circuited Boolean expression evaluator.

Program 4-13: FNEXPRES.PAS (with errors)

```
1:  {$B+}    { Turn off short-circuit evaluation }
2:  program FnExpress;
3:  var
4:    I: Integer;
```

```
 5:
 6:  function Done: Boolean;
 7:  var
 8:    Answer: Char;
 9:  begin
10:    Write('Another value? ');
11:    Readln(Answer);
12:    Done := Upcase(Answer) <> 'Y'
13:  end;
14:
15:  function NextValue(var N: Integer): Integer;
16:  begin
17:    Inc(N);
18:    NextValue := N
19:  end;
20:
21:  function Maximum: Integer;
22:  begin
23:    Maximum := 10
24:  end;
25:
26:  begin
27:    I := 0;
28:    while (NextValue(I) <= Maximum) and (not Done) do
29:      Writeln('Value of i = ', I);
30:    Readln
31:  end.
```

The program declares three functions at lines 6, 15, and 21. A **while** statement at line 28 calls the functions to increment the test variable I, to check whether I is less than or equal to a certain maximum, and to ask, "Another value?" Run the program, answering Y and pressing Enter to each prompt. As this demonstrates, even when I equals the maximum 10, the program still asks for another value. Obviously this is a bug—the program should end when I equals Maximum.

Change line 1 to {$B–}, switching on short-circuit evaluation (the default setting), then run the program again. This time, the **while** loop ends when I equals 10, skipping the call to function Done.

There are two observations to make about these different results. First, with short-circuit evaluation in effect, all functions in a complex expression such as the one in line 28 may or may not be called, possibly skipping a vital operation on which other parts of the program depend. Second, it's dangerous to rely on a specific evaluation order among all expression parts. For example, with short-circuiting switched on ({$B–}),functions NextValue and Maximum are called before Done. With short-circuiting off ({$B+}), Done is called first. If Done changes other values on which the program depends, these actions may affect the results in unexpected ways.

Be aware of these subtle details of expression evaluation. In expressions that call many functions, the results of a complex expression are often difficult to predict. The best solution in these cases is to assign function results in the correct order to temporary variables, then use the variables instead of calling the functions directly in expressions.

Procedures That Increment and Decrement

Program 4-13 demonstrates how to use a versatile procedure, Inc. Use Inc to add 1 to any Byte, ShortInt, Integer, Word, and LongInt variable. For example, if N is a LongInt variable, then these statements are equivalent:

```
N := N + 1;
Inc(N);
```

Because of the way Turbo Pascal evaluates expressions, Inc is faster than adding 1 to a value and assigning the result back to the same variable. Similarly, you can use Dec to decrement (subtract 1 from) a value. These two statements have the same effects:

```
N := N - 1;
Dec(N);
```

You can also use Inc and Dec to increment and decrement values by more than one. For instance, the statement

```
Inc(N, 24);
```

adds 24 to N—in other words, it increments N by 24. Similarly, the statement

```
Dec(N, 5);
```

subtracts 5 from N (it decrements N by 5).

Turbo Pascal generates optimized machine code for Inc and Dec, and these procedures therefore run faster than their equivalent longhand expressions. Use them whenever you can.

Summary

Procedures and functions encourage top-down programming by dividing large programs into small, manageable parts.

Procedures operate as Pascal statements. To activate the statements inside the procedure, simply write the procedure's name.

Functions are the same as procedures except they return values. Use functions anywhere a constant value could go. Unlike constants, functions calculate their values.

Procedures and functions can declare formal parameters. Value parameters (passed by value) copy their initial values from the actual passed parameters. Variable parameters (passed by reference) refer directly to the actual variables passed. A **for** statement may never use variable parameters as control variables.

Procedures and functions have limited scopes. The constants, variables, statements, and other declarations inside procedure and function blocks exist only within the routines. A **goto** statement may jump only to labels defined in the same block.

Recursion is what happens when a procedure or function calls itself. Mutual recursion occurs when one procedure calls another, which again calls the original.

Turbo Pascal has many built-in procedures and functions such as Odd, Exit, and Halt. You can use built-in procedures and functions exactly the same way as those you create yourself.

Beware of side effects, usually caused by procedures and functions making assignments to global variables. To avoid side effects, pass parameters to procedures and functions.

Exercises

4-1. The area of a square, of course, is the product of its length times its width. Other formulas for surface area S are: $S_{pyramid} = (n*b*h)/2$, where n is the number of faces, b is the length of the base, and h is the height; $S_{cube,} = 6a^2$ where a is the length of one side; and $S_{cylinder} = (2*\pi*r)*h$, where r is the radius and h is the height. Using the top-down method, write a program to find the area for those objects. Use procedures and functions to calculate individual formulas and let people select one of several formulas.

4-2. Fuses and circuit breakers are rated by how many amperes it takes to break the connection. Ohm's law says that current measured in amperes equals voltage divided by resistance. Write a program that uses a function Amperes to compute the amount of current for a given voltage and resistance.

4-3. If E equals voltage, I equals current in amperes, and R equals resistance in ohms, then the three variations of Ohm's law are $R = E/I$, $E = I*R$, and $I = E/R$. Expand your program in Exercise 4-2 to calculate all three of these formulas. Use functions, passing the appropriate parameters needed to complete each equation. How can you use the top-down method to make writing this program easier?

4-4. Program 4-3 uses a function Finished as the condition for ending its **repeat** loop. Write a new and more general function. For example, your prompt might simply ask "More? (y/n)."

4-5. What is a formal parameter? What is an actual parameter? Describe the difference between value (passed by value) and variable (passed by reference) parameters.

4-6. Modify Program 4-7 to print the alphabet in normal order.

4-7. Develop a procedure PETC, standing for "Press Enter to Continue." The procedure should display that message and then pause until you press the Enter key. Write a test program for your new procedure.

5

Adding Structure to Data

- The **type** Declaration
- Subranges of Integers
- Scalar Types
- Arrays
- Records
- Sets

5

Key Words and Identifiers

array, **case**, Char, Chr, **in**, Length, MaxInt, **not**, Ord, **packed**, Random, **record**, **set**, **string**, **type**, **with**

Programs in previous chapters declared variables as common Pascal data types, Boolean, Real, Integer, and Char. Many programs, however, require more sophisticated kinds of data. In this chapter, you'll also learn how to define custom data types and then declare variables of those new types. You'll also learn how to add structure to variables, organizing data into arrays, records, and sets.

The ability to create complex data structures is a prime feature of Pascal. With the many different ways to represent data at your fingertips, you can store and manipulate data in ways limited only by your imagination.

The type Declaration

A Pascal **type** declaration tells the compiler about new data types you want it to recognize. After creating a data type, you create variables of the new type for use in expressions or as parameters to procedures and functions.

A type declaration in Pascal (Figure 5-1) begins with the key word **type**, followed by a naming identifier, an equal sign, and a type definition. The type definition can take a variety of forms. One of those forms, the subrange, limits the minimum and maximum range of integer variables. You learned how to create subrange variables in Chapter 2. In the next section, you'll discover that subrange data types are even more useful.

type declaration

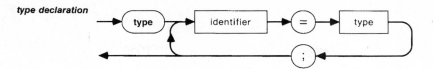

Figure 5-1 Railroad diagram for Pascal's **type** declaration.

Subranges of Integers

Lines 3-4 in Program 5-1 declare a new data type Index as a subrange of the integers 1 through 10. The corresponding railroad diagram is in Figure 5-2. The two periods (called an ellipsis, remember) indicate a range of numbers between two literal constants, 1 and 10 in this example. You must use plain constants to define the minimum and maximum ranges; variable constants are not allowed.

subrange type

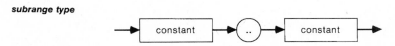

Figure 5-2 Railroad diagram for a subrange scalar data type.

Program 5-1: LIMITS.PAS

```
 1:  {$R+}
 2:  program Limits;
 3:  type
 4:     Index = 1 .. 10;
 5:  var
 6:     I: Index;
 7:  begin
 8:     I := 1;
 9:     while I < 10 do
10:     begin
11:       Write(I:5);
12:        I := I + 1
13:     end;
14:     Writeln;
15:     Readln
16:  end.
```

After defining the new type, the program declares a variable, I (line 6) of type Index, limited to the range of values from 1 to 10. Turbo Pascal then checks that values assigned to I are within this limited range. Assigning a value outside the defined limits causes a runtime "range error."

Instead of declaring a new data type, you could declare I as a subrange type, as explained in Chapter 2. There is no difference between line 6 in Program 5-1 and this:

```
I: 1 .. 10;
```

The new Index data type, though, is available to other parts of the program. You might declare dozens of local variables of type Index. Later, if you need to adjust the range—perhaps from 10 to 20—all you have to do is modify the type declaration and recompile. All the variables of type Index then assume the new subrange limits. If you directly declare variables as subranges, you have to modify each one to change its range. With custom data types, you don't have to work so hard.

Another reason for declaring data type identifiers is to pass parameters of those types to procedures and functions. Parameter types must be simple identifiers, not constructions with multiple pieces like subranges. In other words, you cannot write:

```
procedure Work(I: 1 .. 15); { ??? }
```

Instead, you must declare a data type and then use the type identifier along with the parameter:

```
type Index = 1 .. 15;
procedure Work(I: Index);
```

To tell the compiler you want it to check for range errors, use the option {$R+} as shown in line 1 of Program 5-1. You could also use the alternate style (*$R+*) to do the same thing, or you can turn on range checking by toggling the *Options:Compiler, Range checking* setting in the integrated environment. To see the effect of range checking, change line 9 to:

```
while I <= 10 do
```

When you run the program, you receive a range check error 201, and the program stops. Why did the program fail? When I equals 10, adding 1 to I (line 12) makes 11, which is outside the limited range declared in line 4. With range checking on, Pascal checks that values assigned to variables are within the allowed range.

Turbo Pascal checks for range errors during all assignments to variables, including **for** loops, Readln statements, and other places when values are assigned to variables of subrange data types.

Scalar Types

A *scalar* type is a data type containing a finite number of elements. Two examples of scalar data types are integers and characters. Simple integers such as 1, 2, and 3 are scalar, as are the simple characters A, B, and C. Real numbers are not scalar. Between 1.0 and 2.0 there is a third number, 1.5, and between 1.5 and 2.0 there is 1.75, and so on. Because the steps between real numbers are infinite, real numbers are not scalar.

As you can see in Figure 5-3, you can declare new scalar types as a list of identifiers in parentheses, called an *enumerated* data type. Turbo Pascal allows up to 65,536 scalar elements in an enumerated type, although most such types have only a few elements.

enumerated type

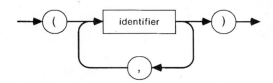

Figure 5-3 An enumerated data type is simply a list of identifiers inside parentheses.

Line 3 of Program 5-2 shows how to declare a new scalar type. In this example, a new enumerated data type, Colors, has the seven scalar values, Red, Orange, Yellow, Green, Blue, Indigo, and Violet. Commas inside parentheses separate the scalar elements.

Program 5-2: RAINBOW.PAS

```
1:   program RainBow;
2:   type
3:     Colors = (Red, Orange, Yellow, Green, Blue, Indigo, Violet);
4:   var
5:     Color: Colors;
6:   begin
7:     Color := Yellow;
8:     Color := Violet;
9:     if Color = Violet
10:      then Writeln('Color is Violet');
11:    Readln
12:  end.
```

Using Enumerated Data Types

When the compiler reads Program 5-2, it translates scalar elements into sequential numbers, starting with 0. Red becomes 0 in the compiled program; Orange becomes 1, and so forth. This is why scalar types like Color are called enumerated data types. The advantage is that instead of having to know that the value 3 represents Green, the compiler lets you ignore this technical detail and use the more descriptive identifier instead. It also ensures that you assign individual colors to color variables. For example, assigning 4 to variable Color in Program 5-2 is not allowed. Instead, you must write:

```
Color := Blue;
```

Using Scalar Variables

You can use scalar variables in loops, expressions, parameter lists, and even as parts of other new data types. Earlier, you learned how to use the built-in functions Succ and Pred to return the successor and predecessor, respectively, of integers and characters. Actually, those functions operate with all scalar data types.

Using the Colors types from Program 5-2, then, Succ(Red) is Orange, Pred (Indigo) is Blue, Succ(Orange) equals Pred(Green), and Pred(Pred(Yellow)) is Red. You can also directly compare scalar elements: (Blue<Indigo) and (Violet>=Orange) are true Boolean expressions.

Boolean variables are also scalar, having the two indivisible scalar elements true and false. If the Boolean data type were not predefined in Pascal, you could create it with the following **type** declaration:

```
type
  Boolean = (false, true);
```

When declaring scalar types with from 1 to 256 scalar elements, a variable of that type occupies one eight-bit memory byte. A scalar variable with 257 or more elements takes two eight-bit bytes. You can associate over 65,000 scalar elements with one enumerated data type, although you'll probably never declare more than a few dozen elements at a time. These details are rarely important, but worth keeping in mind.

Scalar and Ordinal Values

The built-in function Ord returns the underlying ordinal value of a scalar element—in other words, the element's numerical ordering. This is easier to explain with an example. Program 5-3 declares the same scalar type Colors from Program 5-2 and a variable Color of that type.

Program 5-3: SCALAR.PAS

```
 1:  program ScalarValues;
 2:  type
 3:    Colors = (Red, Orange, Yellow, Green, Blue, Indigo, Violet);
 4:  var
 5:    Color: Colors;
 6:  begin
 7:    for Color := Red to Violet do
 8:      Writeln(Ord(Color));
 9:    Readln
10:  end.
```

As shown here, enumerated scalars can be control variables in a **for** loop. The built-in Ord function writes the ordinal number of the successive values for colors Red through Violet. As you can see when you run the program, these values are the integers 0 through 6, the values that the compiler assigns to the seven scalar identifiers.

When using enumerated data types, it's useful to remember that the computer never actually knows anything about real colors. Identifiers such as Red, Blue, Indigo, and Violet are for your benefit, not the computer's. Pascal digests these descriptive names, converting them to numbers, which are, of course, more suited to the tastes of a computer. In the compiled result, therefore, the scalar identifiers no longer exist and do not take up any space. One question I often hear is, "But how does Pascal know what orange is?" The answer is, "It doesn't." The scalar identifier Orange is just a convenience to avoid using numbers in a program that you would otherwise have to remember really mean something else.

Ordinals to Enumerated Types

In the same way that Ord lets you determine the ordinal value of a scalar element, a special Turbo Pascal feature called *typecasting* lets you do the reverse. That is, you can convert or cast an ordinal value, a number, into an enumerated scalar element. Assuming you have a variable Col of the enumerated type Colors, you can assign the ordinal value 3 to Col like this:

```
Col := Colors(3);
```

The number in parentheses after an enumerated type identifier represents the scalar element with that ordinal value. In other words, Colors(3) is equivalent to Green. (Remember, the first element always has the value 0. Green is the fourth scalar element in type Colors and, therefore, has the ordinal value 3.)

If you try to assign a value outside the declared range of scalar identifiers, the compiler squawks with

```
Error 76 : Constant out of range.
```

For example, this statement does not compile:

```
Col := Colors(30);
```

A similar technique converts ASCII values to characters. ASCII values (see Appendix D) range from 0 to 255. To convert a value to a character variable Ch, use the assignment:

```
Ch := Chr(67);
```

This sets Ch equal to the character with the ASCII ordinal value 67—in other words, a C. In Turbo Pascal you can do the same thing using the built-in enumerated type identifier Char:

```
Ch := Char(67);
```

Even though the two methods appear to do the same thing, there is a difference. Chr is a built-in Pascal *function.* Char is an enumerated data type. The value in parentheses recasts the value as a different type, a technique we'll see again in Chapter 13.

Arrays

Arrays are collections of values, all of the same type. When you have many variables to keep track of, rather than store them individually, you can put them into a more manageable array.

Figure 5-4 shows the syntax for declaring arrays. The boxed-in *simple type* can be any subrange or enumerated scalar type enclosed in square brackets, [and]. In place of brackets, you can use the alternate double-character symbols (. and .)—a relic that is included to support keyboards lacking bracket keys. Today, there's little reason not to use square brackets.

In Chapter 1, you learned that a variable is similar to a box that can hold one kind of thing. An array is like a stack of such boxes (Figure 5-5). Each box has a label, or index, so that a program can locate single elements at random. Because it takes no more time to locate element number fifty than it does element number one, an array is known as a *random access data structure.*

index range

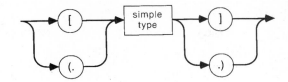

array

Figure 5-4 Railroad diagrams for Pascal arrays.

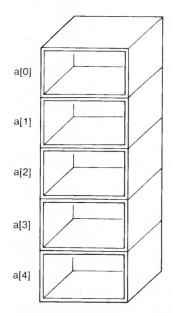

Figure 5-5 An array is like a stack of boxes. To locate one array element, place the element index number inside square brackets.

You can declare arrays as new data types. For example, the following **type** declaration defines an array of ten integers:

```
type
    IntegerArray = array[1 .. 10] of Integer;
```

Or you can directly declare arrays as variables. A program might declare an array of 80 characters like this:

```
var
    CharArray: array[0 .. 79] of Char;
```

Notice that one example uses an index range of [1 .. 10], and the other uses [0 .. 79]. The beginning and ending values are up to you. You could have arrays indexed [100 .. 200] if that makes sense in your program. Pascal is smart enough to not store extra positions [1 .. 99], which are wasted in many other languages that require a starting index of 0 or 1. You can also use negative index values. For example, this is perfectly legal:

```
var
    Score: array[-10 .. +10] of Integer;
```

To locate one element of an array, use the **array** name followed by square brackets around the index of the element you want. To write the fifth element of the integer array declared earlier, you could use the statement:

```
Write(IntegerArray[5]);
```

This is an array of integers, so IntegerArray[N], with N equal to any array index, can go wherever Pascal normally allows integer variables. The identifier IntegerArray stands for the *entire* array. IntegerArray[5], however, stands for a single array element at index five.

Assign values to array variables in the same way you assign values to simple variables. The following statement sets position two in the integer array to the value 1024:

```
IntegerArray[2] := 1024;
```

Be careful when using arrays with indexes beginning with 0. Failing to remember that the zero element is the first item in the array—and therefore, the element at index 5 is the sixth, not the fifth—is a frequent cause of programming bugs. These two arrays illustrate the problem:

```
var
    A1: array[0 .. 9] of Integer;
    A2: array[1 .. 10] of Integer;
```

Both arrays A1 and A2 contain spaces for ten integer values. The fifth value in array A1 is at index 4, referenced in a program by writing A1[4]. The fifth value in array A2 is at position 5, referenced by writing A2[5], because the first index of the array begins at 1.

There is no technical reason to use one method over the other, and you can begin your array indexes at 0 or at 1 (or at any other value). If you want to use the method most programmers prefer, start your arrays at 0—even though you may think it easier to begin with 1. The reason for this is that some languages—C and C++ for example—require arrays to begin with zero indexes. If you define most of your own arrays the same way, your programs will be easier to convert to these languages. Despite this suggestion, though, you should choose array indexes that make the most sense for the job you need to do. If it makes good sense to use array indexes from 12 to 99, then those are the values to use.

Strings and Arrays

A **string** in Turbo Pascal is a specialized array of characters, which you can also index with square brackets. A program might define a string variable and then use indexing to do something with individual characters in the string.

Program 5-4 demonstrates how to index a string as an array of characters. The program contains a handy procedure StringUp that converts from lower- to upper-case all characters in variable parameter S. The **for** loop at line 12 accomplishes this feat by incrementing control variable Index from 1 to the length of the string. (Length, a built-in function, returns the length of a string equal to the number of characters the string contains.) Line 13 converts each character in string S to uppercase through the built-in Turbo Pascal function, Upcase.

Program 5-4: CAPITALS.PAS

```
 1:   program Capitals;
 2:   type
 3:     String80 = string[80];
 4:   var
 5:     S: String80;
 6:
 7:   { Convert characters in string to all uppercase }
 8:   procedure StringUp(var S: String80);
 9:   var
10:     Index : Integer;
11:   begin
12:     for Index := 1 to Length(S) do
13:       S[Index] := Upcase(S[Index])
14:   end;
15:
16:   begin
```

continued

Program 5-4: continued

```
17:    Writeln('Capitals');
18:    repeat
19:      Writeln;
20:      Writeln('Enter any string (<ret> to quit).');
21:      Readln(S);
22:      StringUp(S);
23:      Writeln(S)
24:    until Length(S) = 0
25:  end.
```

Turbo Pascal hides the length of a string at index 0. In other words:

```
Length(S) = Ord(S[0]);
```

In English, this tells you that the ordinal value of the character at index 0—the first byte of the string variable—is equal to the number of characters in the string. Because Turbo Pascal automatically maintains the length of a string, you rarely need to use the length byte directly as shown here. It's nice to know where it is, though, in case you need it. For example, an advanced trick is to change the length of a string artificially by assigning a new value to the length byte. If longString has 25 characters, this statement effectively chops off the last 5 characters:

```
LongString[0] := Chr(20);
```

This works by reducing the string length byte to 20. You must use the built-in Chr function to tell the compiler to assign a character—assigning plain integer 20 is not allowed. (Even though the length byte is not really a character, the compiler thinks it is.)

Use these tricks with care. If you fiddle with the length byte—changing it to 200 or something for a string originally declared to be 80 characters long, you can cause all sorts of strange problems.

Array Range Checking

If you use the compiler directive {$R+}, Turbo Pascal checks that array indexes are within declared boundaries. Normally, range checking is off, just as though you used the directive {$R–}. With this setting, Turbo Pascal does not check array boundaries.

As an example, assume you have an array of ten bytes declared this way:

```
var
  TenBytes: array[1 .. 10] of Byte;
```

The compiler then checks constant indexes against the declared range. Regardless of whether you turn on range checking, the following statement does not compile:

```
TenBytes[11] := 128;
```

Index 11 is outside the declared range. Because 11 is a constant value, the compiler is able to catch the error. The compiler accepts the next statements, though:

```
var I: Integer;
I := 11;
TenBytes[I] := 128;
```

Although those two statements compile correctly with range checking on, you receive:

```
Runtime error 201: Range check error.
```

Pascal checks that the value of I is in the declared array range. But with range checking off, Pascal allows the bad assignment, possibly overwriting another variable in memory, causing a serious, hard-to-find program bug. A good rule is to turn on range checking with {$R+} until you are positive your program operates correctly. Because this generates code to check variable ranges while a program runs, though, most programmers turn off range checking for their finished and tested production versions, gaining every possible bit of speed.

Sorting Arrays

A program that sorts a list of items makes a useful demonstration of arrays. The next example sorts an array of numbers into ascending order, but you can use the same method to sort strings or other values.

Entire books are devoted to sorting algorithms, and there isn't room to compare all methods here. Of them all, though, the method in Program 5-5 offers a reliable compromise between speed and size—as long as the number of things to sort is not too large, no more than about 500 elements. The method is the *binary insertion sort*.

Program 5-5: BINSORT.PAS

```
1:   program BinarySort;
2:   const
3:     MaxElements = 100;  { Maximum array size }
4:   type
5:     Element = Integer;
```

continued

Program 5-5: continued

```
 6:    ElementArray = array[1 .. MaxElements] of Element;
 7:  var
 8:    A: ElementArray;
 9:    I, N: Integer;
10:
11:  procedure Sort(var A: ElementArray; N: Integer);
12:  { N = actual number elements in array a }
13:  { Algorithm = Binary Insertion }
14:  var
15:    I, J, Bottom, Top, Middle: Integer;
16:    Temp: Element;
17:  begin
18:    for I := 2 to N do
19:    begin
20:      Temp := A[I]; Bottom := 1; Top := I - 1;
21:      while Bottom <= Top do
22:      begin
23:        Middle := (Bottom + Top) div 2;
24:        if Temp < A[Middle]
25:          then Top := Middle - 1
26:          else Bottom := Middle + 1
27:      end;
28:      for J := I - 1 downto Bottom do
29:        A[J + 1] := A[J];
30:      A[Bottom] := Temp
31:    end
32:  end;
33:
34:  begin
35:    Writeln('Binary Insertion Sort');
36:    Writeln;
37:    repeat
38:      Write('How many? (2 to ', MaxElements, ')? ');
39:      Readln(N)
40:    until N <= MaxElements;
41:    for I := 1 to N do
42:    begin
43:      A[I] := Random(Maxint);
44:      Write(A[I]:8)
45:    end;
```

```
46:    Writeln; Writeln;
47:    Sort(A, N);
48:    for I := 1 to N do
49:       Write(A[I]:8);
50:    Writeln;
51:    Readln
52:  end.
```

Program 5-5 declares an array in line 6 as a new type ElementArray. The square brackets following the key word **array** surround a scalar subrange indicating the maximum number of things that the array can hold. Line 5 declares single Elements as integers. You could also write line 6 this way:

```
ElementArray = array[1 ... 100] of Integer;
```

Rather than directly using the constant 100 in the array declaration, the constant MaxElements lets other places in the program know what the array limits are. (See lines 38 and 40.) This also makes it easy to change the maximum number of elements in the array—just modify the constant in line 3. For a test, try setting MaxElements to 200. Because such changes are easy to make, it's usually a good idea to let constants rather than literal values define array limits.

Using the Sorting Program

Program 5-5 starts in line 35 by prompting for the number of elements to sort, setting N to this value. A **for** loop at line 41 inserts random values into the array from position 1 to N. In Turbo Pascal, the built-in function Random returns randomly sequenced numbers. (See line 43.) Maxint is a predeclared constant equal to the maximum integer value 32,767. The effect of Random(Maxint) is to select integers at random from the range of 0 to 32,766, one less than the parameter in parentheses. You could use other parameter values, too. For example, Random(100) returns values at random from 0 to 99. (Chapter 12 discusses Random in more detail.)

Notice how in line 43, variable I indexes the array A. Line 44 writes the value of A[I], displaying the raw data before sorting. In a similar way, after sorting, another **for** loop at line 48 writes the now-ordered values in the array.

How the Binary Insertion Sort Works

Exercise 3-5 asks you to invent a number-guessing game. The solution is childishly simple—just keep dividing successive guesses in half, asking if each guess is high or low, until you get the answer. Surprisingly, this simple idea is the basis for the binary insertion sort. It's a *binary* method because of the way it keeps dividing the array of elements in two, bisecting the remaining values, looking for the correct position where each value belongs.

The method operates by starting from the second element (it wouldn't make sense to sort only one number), and proceeding with a **for** loop at line 18, up to the number of elements (N) in the array. The program sets variable Temp equal to each element in turn (line 20) while two other variables, Bottom and Top, specify the range of indexes between I and I - 1, respectively, the portion of the array currently being sorted. This action repeats for successive values of I until the entire array is in order.

The **while** loop (lines 21-27) uses the guessing-game strategy to find where between Top and Bottom the value of Temp belongs. Examine line 23 to see how the program locates the middle of A[Bottom] to A[Top]. After finding where Temp goes, the **for** loop at line 28 shuffles elements greater than Temp upward, dropping Temp into the correct place with an assignment statement in line 30.

If this description seems hard to understand, take eight playing cards ranking from two to nine, shuffle them, and lay them out as though they were the elements of the array. Then play computer, manually following the binary insertion method to put your cards in order. Write down the values of program variables as you go along. A little experimenting—with Program 5-5 as a guide—shows you the inner workings of the binary insertion sort better than any narration of this fascinating algorithm.

Arrays with Multiple Dimensions

An array can have multiple dimensions. Such an array has another array at every indexed position. There are two ways to declare multiple-dimension arrays in Pascal. For example, the following declares two equivalent arrays, A and B:

```
var
   A: array[1 .. 4] of array[1 .. 4] of Char;
   8: array[1 .. 4, 1 .. 4] of Char;
```

Both A and B are arrays of four, four-character arrays. One way to visualize multiple-dimension arrays is to imagine their having rows and columns, as illustrated in Figure 5-6. Every array position has a unique row and column number. Writing B[3,2] locates the element at row 3, column 2. The computer screen you probably have nearby is a multidimensional array of characters that a program could represent like this:

```
var
   Screen: array[1 .. 25, 1 .. 80] of Char;
```

```
                          COLUMNS
                   1       2       3       4
         R   1 | [1,1] | [1,2] | [1,3] | [1,4]
         O   2 | [2,1] | [2,2] | [2,3] | [2,4]
         W   3 | [3,1] | [3,2] | [3,3] | [3,4]
         S   4 | [4,1] | [4,2] | [4,3] | [4,4]
```

Figure 5-6 Two-dimensional arrays form a row and column matrix.

For better compatibility among different computers, though, you'd be wise to declare the maximum screen dimensions as constants and use those constants in the array declaration. That way, you can easily change your program to new display formats:

```
const
   RowMax = 25;   { Number of rows on IBM PC }
   ColMax = 60;   {   monochrome display }
type
   Rows = 1 .. RowMax;
   Cols = 1 .. ColMax;
var
   Screen: array[Rows, Cols] of Char;
```

The new declaration uses constants and subranges of integers, building on those simple elements to finally declare the array variable, Screen. Notice how clear it is that Screen is an array of rows and columns. Because Rows and Cols already define subranges of integers, there is no need to use ellipses in the **array** declaration. Such clarity makes it easy to modify the program, changing the number of columns by revising one constant, ColMax in this example. Redesigning an entire program to operate with a 40-column display also requires a single change—just replace constant 80 with 40. By following a similar approach for all array declarations, you'll make future modifications that much easier—especially in programs with hundreds or thousands of lines.

Beyond the Fourth Dimension

Be careful when declaring multidimensional arrays not to get carried away. While you can have up to 255 multiple dimensions in Turbo Pascal, there are few cases where more than three do much good. The following declares an array of three dimensions, each having ten elements:

```
var
  Cube: array[1 .. 10, 1 .. 10, 1 .. 10] of Char;
```

In the same way that a two-dimensional array has rows and columns, a three-dimensional array resembles a cube, with depth as well as width and height. The cube declared here, though, occupies 1000 (10 x 10 x 10) bytes of computer memory! Adding a fourth dimension of ten elements increases that to 10,000 bytes, and adding a fifth, at 100,000 bytes, makes the array too large for Turbo Pascal to handle as a simple variable. (The maximum size for any variable is about 65,000 bytes.)

Scalar Indexes

Arrays may contain variables of any Pascal type, but array indexes must be scalar data types, such as integers, characters, or your own enumerated data types. For example, you can declare an array of strings, indexed by the scalar Colors type defined earlier:

```
var
  ColorNames: array[Colors] of string[20];
```

This declares an array of four strings, each 20 characters long. Scalar elements such as Blue and Green are the array indexes. The following seven lines assign strings to all array positions:

```
ColorNames[Red   ] := 'Red';
ColorNames[Orange] := 'Orange';
ColorNames[Yellow] := 'Yellow';
ColorNames[Green ] := 'Green';
ColorNames[Blue  ] := 'Blue';
ColorNames[Indigo] := 'Indigo';
ColorNames[Violet] := 'Violet';
```

The statements assign character strings to each array position, associating one string per scalar element. Remember, scalar elements such as Red, Orange, and Yellow are just numbers as far as Turbo Pascal is concerned. The scalar identifiers exist only in the program text; the same identifiers do not exist in the compiled code. If you have a variable Color of type Colors, this means you cannot display the name of the color with the statements:

```
Color := Red;
Writeln(Color); { ??? }
```

If you try this, the compiler complains with

```
Error 64: Cannot Read or Write variables of this type.
```

A variable of type Colors, or of any other enumerated data type, is not something that Writeln can directly display. Instead, you must use the string array of color names. The following corrects the problem:

```
Color := Red;
Writeln(ColorNames[Color]);
```

ColorNames is an array of strings, which, of course, Writeln can display. For an even better example, add the previous seven assignments along with the ColorNames array declaration to Program 5-3. Then change the **for** loop to read:

```
for Color := Red to Violet do
   Writeln(ColorNames[Color]);
```

When you run the program, you see the names of the colors instead of their scalar values, as in the unmodified version. If all of this seems like a lot of trouble just to display seven strings, look back through the examples we've covered and notice how readable they are. The **for** loop is perfectly clear and composed almost entirely of English words.

As these examples illustrate, carefully chosen enumerated types help you to write clear and understandable programs that are easy to modify. Of course, it's up to you to put these features to work!

The Lack of Packing

Many Pascal compilers allow packing of arrays and other variables. Packing squeezes as many variables of a data type into as small a space as possible, usually at the expense of speed. Turbo Pascal, though, has no facilities for packing. If it did, you could declare an array like this:

```
var
   Switches: packed array[0 .. 7] of Boolean; { ??? }
```

In Turbo Pascal, the Switches array occupies eight bytes of memory. With some other Pascal compilers, the same declaration occupies one byte of memory, with each bit of the byte taking one array position. This is possible because Boolean values true and false are represented with only one bit; 0 is equal to false, and 1 is equal to true. Therefore, compilers that allow packing can squeeze eight Boolean variables into one eight-bit byte.

Although Turbo Pascal recognizes the word **packed**, it ignores it. Because of this, you may encounter published programs that do not operate correctly if they rely on packing.

Records

Whereas arrays collect identically typed elements, another kind of collector, the Pascal record, assembles dissimilar elements under one roof. A record can contain any number of any kind of Pascal variables you can devise. To say the least, that's a powerful versatility.

A record declaration (Figure 5-7) begins with the key word **record** and ends with **end**. In between is a *field list* of identifiers and types, which looks similar to a variable declaration. The similarity is no accident. Individual fields in records are just variables that the record contains. Having the fields in one record definition lets a program treat the collection of variables as a unit for some operations, or as individual variables for others.

record

field list

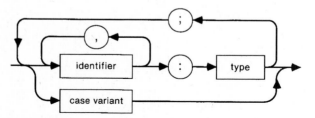

Figure 5-7 Pascal records contain lists of fields; individual fields are variables that the record holds together.

Compare the field list railroad diagram in Figure 5-7 with the diagram for variable declarations (Figure 1-5). Like variables, record fields have identifiers and types separated by semicolons. To save typing, you can declare multiple variables of the same type together, separating their identifiers with commas. For now, ignore the part of the diagram in Figure 5-7 labeled *case variant*. We'll cover that in a moment.

Program 5-6 declares a new type DateRec as a record containing two subrange variables, Month and Day, plus an integer variable, Year. In lines 13-15, the program assigns values to the fields of the Date record variable declared in line 10 as type DateRec.

Program 5-6: DATETEST.PAS

```
 1:  program DateTest;
 2:  type
 3:    DateRec =
 4:      record
 5:        Month : 0 .. 12;    { 0 = no date }
 6:        Day   : 1 .. 31;
 7:        Year  : Integer
 8:      end;
 9:  var
10:    Date: DateRec;
11:  begin
12:    Writeln('Date Test');
13:    Date.Day := 16;
14:    Date.Month := 5;
15:    Date.Year := 72;
16:    Writeln(Date.Month, '/', Date.Day, '/', Date.Year);
17:    Readln
18:  end.
```

To use a field of a record, precede it with a period. The statement Write(Date.Day), for example, writes the Day field of Date. After assigning values to all fields of the Date record, line 16 of Program 5-6 writes the assigned date in common mm/dd/yy format.

A shorthand method avoids typing the record name Date over and over as you did in line 16 of Program 5-6. The key word **with** (Figure 5-8) tells Pascal to associate identifiers with a specific record name, saving keystrokes while making the program more readable. Using **with**, you can use multiple field names without repeating the record name in front. For example, replace lines 13-16 of Program 5-6 with the following compound statement:

```
with Date do
begin
   Day := 16;
   Month := 5;
   Year := 72;
   Writeln(Month, '/', Day, '/', Year)
end;
```

Because of the **with** key word, the compiler knows that Month, Day, and Year are fields in record Date.

with

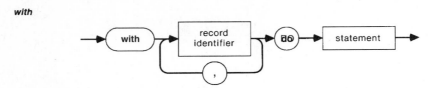

Figure 5-8 The **with** statement railroad diagram.

Keeping Records

One of the most common uses for computers is to store and retrieve information about people and things. Let's say you are elected president of a neighborhood club and you want to computerize data on club members. You might start by inventing a Pascal record for each person's name.

NameRec in Program 5-7 defines a Pascal record containing four fields. The program lets you enter information into each of these fields (lines 15-18). Notice how the **with** statement (line 13) lets you avoid having to type Name.LastName or Name.FirstName. Line 20 displays the fields in correct order.

Program 5-7: NAMETEST.PAS

```
1:   program NameTest;
2:   type
3:     NameRec =
4:       record
5:         LastName  : string[20];
6:         FirstName : string[20];
7:         Initial   : Char;
8:         Preface   : string[8]
9:       end;
10:  var
11:     Name: NameRec;
12:  begin
13:    with Name do
14:    begin
15:      Write('Last name  ? '); Readln(LastName);
16:      Write('First name ? '); Readln(FirstName);
17:      Write('Initial    ? '); Readln(Initial);
18:      Write('Mr, Mrs, Ms? '); Readln(Preface);
19:      Writeln;
20:      Writeln('Name = ',
```

```
21:           Preface, '. ', FirstName, ' ',
22:           Initial, '. ', LastName          )
23:     end;
24:     Readln
25:  end.
```

By storing each part of a person's name in separate fields, you can write names in a variety of ways. For example, a directory listing of all club members would probably look best with names ordered last name first. To do that, replace lines 20-22 of Program 5-7 with this statement:

```
Writeln(LastName, ', ', FirstName, ' ', Initial)
```

At other times, you might want to abbreviate a member's first name for printing on mailing labels: This is easily done by indexing the first character of the field, FirstName. (Remember, strings are just specialized arrays of characters.)

```
if Length(FirstName) > 0
  then Write(FirstName[1], ' ');
Writeln(LastName)
```

Why use the **if** statement? If the length of the string FirstName is zero, indexing the first character of the string causes a runtime range error (if range checking is turned on with the compiler option {$R+}). Although most people have first names, and you may think a blank first name field will never occur, it's a good idea to write programs that work for all cases, especially the unlikely ones.

Records As Building Blocks

Record fields can themselves be records containing still other fields. Such complex structures are easy to construct in Turbo Pascal. Starting with NameRec from Program 5-7, a program could define a new record like this:

```
var
  Couple:
    record
      Husband, Wife: NameRec
    end;
```

Couple is a record variable containing two NameRec records. To write the husband's name, you could use this statement:

```
Writeln(Couple.Husband.LastName);
```

Husband is a field in the Couple record. LastName is a field in the Husband record. The periods and record variable identifiers define a sort of *path* down to the individual field you want, LastName in this example. Similarly, a program could read the wife's first name in a Readln statement:

```
Readln(Couple.Wife.FirstName);
```

From these examples, you can see the value of the **with** statement. Instead of repeating Couple.Wife over and over to write the husband's name, you could use this simple statement:

```
with Couple.Husband do
    Writeln(LastName, ', ', FirstName, ' ', Initial)
```

Nested with Statements

When using multiple **with** statements, you have a choice of two styles. Assume you have the following **record** variable:

```
Student:
  record
    Name: NameRec;
    Age: Integer
  end;
```

To write fields LastName and Age in record Student, you could use the following statement:

```
with Student do with Name do
    Write(LastName, ' is ', Age, ' years old');
```

The double **with** statements tell the compiler first how to find fields Age and Name in Student and then how to find field LastName in Name. You can also use the following statement to do the same thing:

```
with Student, Name do
    Write(LastName, ' is ', Age, ' years old');
```

Separating multiple-level record fields with commas is the same as using multiple **with** statements. In general, the form

```
with r1 do with r2 do with r3 do
```

reduces to the simpler:

```
with r1, r2, r3 do
```

Mixing Data Structures

Pascal allows you to mix complex data structures. A program can have arrays of records, records of arrays, and other combinations. For example, with an array of name records, you have the beginning of a database system for keeping track of club members. Let's say there is a maximum of five members. (Yours is a very exclusive club.) Here's how the first part of the program looks:

```
const
  MaxMembers = 5;
type
  { NameRec declaration from Program 5-7 }
var
  Members: array[1 .. MaxMembers] of NameRec;
  Membership: 0 .. MaxMembers;
```

Members is an array of five NameRec records. Membership holds the number of members currently in the array. To complete the program, you need only a few simple procedures to enter and display individual records in the array. Program 5-8 contains some of these items.

Program 5-8: CLUBDB.PAS

```
 1:  program ClubDataBase;
 2:  const
 3:    MaxMembers = 5;
 4:  type
 5:    Member =
 6:      record
 7:        Name:     string[30];
 8:        Phone:    string[12];
 9:        Charges:  Real;
10:        Payments: Real
11:      end;
12:  var
13:    Members: array[1 .. MaxMembers] of Member;
14:    Membership: 0 .. MaxMembers;
15:    Choice: Char;
16:
17:  procedure AddRecords;
18:  begin
19:    if Membership = MaxMembers
```

continued

Program 5-8: continued

```
20:      then Writeln('Membership is full') else
21:      begin
22:        Writeln('Add new records');
23:        Membership := Membership + 1;
24:        with Members[Membership] do
25:        begin
26:          Write('Name     : '); Readln(Name);
27:          Write('Phone    : '); Readln(Phone);
28:          Write('Charges  : '); Readln(Charges);
29:          Write('Payments : '); Readln(Payments)
30:        end
31:      end
32: end;
33:
34: procedure ListRecords;
35: var
36:   Number: Integer;
37: begin
38:   for Number := 1 to Membership do
39:     with Members[Number] do
40:       Writeln(Number, ' : ', Name,
41:         '  ', Phone, Charges-Payments:8:2)
42: end;
43:
44: begin
45:   Writeln('Club Database');
46:   Membership := 0;
47:   repeat
48:     Writeln;
49:     Writeln('Number of members = ', Membership);
50:     Write('A.dd, E.dit, L.ist, Q.uit ? ');
51:     Readln(Choice); Choice := Upcase(Choice);
52:     case Choice of
53:       'A': AddRecords;
54:       'E': Writeln('Sorry, no editing yet');
55:       'L': ListRecords
56:     end
57:   until Choice = 'Q'
58: end.
```

In Program 5-8, procedures AddRecords and ListRecords enter and display names and phone numbers in the club membership database. The program evolved from a top-down design, starting at the main body in lines 44-58.

Line 46 initializes Membership to zero members. The **repeat** loop in lines 47-57 prompts for choices from a menu displayed by a Write statement (line 50). To simplify the **case** statement selectors, the built-in function Upcase converts character variable Choice to uppercase. The **case** statement in lines 52-56 tests Choice, calling procedure AddRecords if you type A or ListRecords if you type L. Because of pressure from the club business manager to market the program, this early release has an unfinished editing operation. If you type E, the program displays the message, "Sorry, no editing yet."

AddRecords at lines 17-32 adds one new record. First, an **if** statement (line 19) tests if the number of members is already at the maximum. If so, it prints an error message; otherwise, the **else** clause executes in lines 21-31. There, the number of members increases (line 23), and you're prompted for the new name, phone number, charges, and payments. For variety, the Member record definition (lines 5-11) includes two real-number fields, Charges and Payments.

Notice in line 24 how **with** indicates which record to use from the Members array. Without the **with** statement, you'd have to index the array directly in each of the four Readln statements in lines 26-29, something like this:

```
Readln(Members[Membership].Name);
```

Besides cluttering the program and making the poor programmer work harder than necessary, repeating an array index also leads to slower running times. When you index an array, as in this Readln statement, the compiler generates programming to calculate the memory address of an array element. It repeats this time-consuming calculation for every array indexing operation. Using **with**, however, lets the compiler do the address calculation a single time, locating Members[Membership] and then using the same address repeatedly in lines 26-29. Appropriate **with** statements are not purely cosmetic, then. They often contribute to faster-running programs, too.

Procedure ListRecords displays the club database in a **for** loop at lines 38-41. Again, **with** easily—and efficiently—refers to individual member records in the Members array. The Writeln statement (lines 40-41) displays one name and phone number along with the club member's account balance, calculated by subtracting Payments from Charges.

Variant Records

The syntax diagram in Figure 5-9 indicates that a field list may have something called a *case variant* in addition to regular field identifiers and types. A case variant allows records to have different structures dependent on one condition or another.

case variant

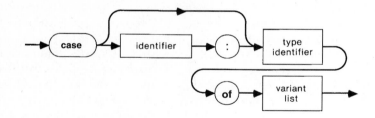

variant list

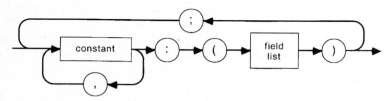

Figure 5-9 Records may contain a case variant part, overlaying different fields at the same physical position in the record.

Looking at the syntax for a case variant (top of Figure 5-9), you see it begins with the key word **case** followed by an optional identifier and colon. After that comes a type identifier, the key word **of** and then a variant list. Together, the identifier, colon, and type make up a *tag field.* For example, a case variant might begin:

```
case Married: Boolean of
```

This prepares two cases: one if the Boolean tag Married is true; another if it's false. Tag fields can also be any scalar type such as Char or Integer. For example:

```
case Number: Integer of
```

The integer Number tag field prepares two, three, a dozen, or more case variants, with an individual record field list for each variation. You might complete the record definition this way:

```
record
  case Number: Integer of
    1: (I: Integer);
    2: (R: Real);
    3: (S: string[10])
  end;
```

You now have three variations: one with an integer field I, another with field R, and a third with field S. Only one variation exists at a time. You can use field I or S, but not both. There is one **end**, not two, at the end of the record and case variant as correctly shown here.

In these examples, tag fields Married and Number are fields in the record definition, just like any other fields. However, the fields that follow them are based on the tag field values. A good example of how to use case variant records is the common database practice of storing certain parameters in the first record, with the real information beginning at record number two. To do this requires a record structure that varies according to what goes in the record. The program starts by defining a scalar type listing the different kinds of records in the database:

```
type
    RecordType = (Active, Deleted, System);
```

A record marked Active contains actual data, Deleted records contain old information, and System records indicate a special use. The record has a tag field of type RecordType, with each scalar element selecting one variation of what goes in the record. Figure 5-10 shows the complete declaration.

```
OneRecord =
    record
        case Kind: RecordType OF
            Active: ( Data: string[30] );
            Deleted: ( Link: Integer );
            System: ( NumRecs: Integer )
    end;
```

Figure 5-10 This record type has three variations selected by the scalar elements Active, Deleted, and system.

Kind is the tag field. If Kind is Active, Pascal selects the Active variation field list in parentheses, allowing a string of Data in the record. If Kind is Deleted, the record contains a Link, an integer variable intended to link together all deleted records. (How that is accomplished is not important here.) The final variation occurs when Kind is System, indicating a record that contains a special value, here the number of active records (NumRecs) currently in the database.

It is important to understand that each variation in a variant record physically overlays the others (Figure 5-11). NumRecs, Link, and Data all occupy the *same* memory space, and therefore, only one variation exists inside the record at a time.

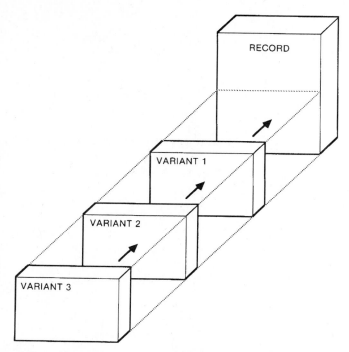

Figure 5-11 Variant parts of a record overlay each other at the same
physical location in the record.

Records with a tag field case variant structure are called *discriminated unions*.
All variations are united in one record definition, discriminated by the values of the
tag field.

To allow for all variations, the total size of the record is equal to the size of the
largest variant. In Figure 5-10, the largest variant is the Data string. Regardless of the
actual tag field value, the record is always large enough to hold a thirty-character
string. Smaller variations, such as the two-byte integer fields Deleted and System,
waste the extra space required by Data fields.

Another example shows how to mix regular fields with a case variant, which
must always come last in the record declaration. Suppose you decide to add a case
variant to the member club records in Figure 5-12. You want to indicate whether a
member is married and, if so, you want to keep the name of that member's spouse
along with a wedding date. For unmarried members, you instead plan to record the
name and phone number of a friend. Combining these exclusive cases—a person
can only be married or not—saves space in the record because the variations
physically overlay each other in memory. Figure 5-12 shows the new record
definition.

```
Member = record
  Name: string[30];
  Phone: string[12];
  Charges: Real;
  Payments: Real;
  case Married: Boolean of
    true: (
      SpouseName: string[30];
      DateMarried: DateRec
    );
    false: (
      FriendName: string[30];
      FriendPhone: string[12]
    )
end;
```

Figure 5-12 The club Member record type redefined with a case variant indicating whether a member is married.

Tag field Married indicates if this member is married. If so, the true variation stores two fields, SpouseName and DateMarried in the record. If Married is false, the false variant takes over, storing a friend's name and phone number. The true and false variations—both contained in parentheses—occupy the same space in the record. A program can test a member record tag field and take appropriate action:

```
with Members[3] do
  if not Married
    then InviteToBachelorParty
```

There is nothing to prevent you, however, from using the wrong variation. This faulty statement causes a bug in the club database program:

```
with Members[3] do
  Writeln('Phone = ', FriendPhone);
```

The variant field FriendPhone exists only if Married is false, a fact the foregoing statement ignores. If Married is true, FriendPhone does not exist, and the program must not use that field. It is up to you to write programs that access only existing fields. The compiler does not check this error for you.

In this example, DateMarried and FriendPhone overlay each other at the same physical location in the record (see Figure 5-11), but it's your responsibility to know which variation is active. From this observation, you can see that case variants let you overlay two fields of different types and use them simultaneously. This ability also lets you easily translate a variable of one type to another. In this case, you don't even need a tag field, leading to one of Pascal's most infamous constructions, the free union.

Free Unions

A *free union* is a case variant record without a tag field. The **case** part of the record declares an unidentified type, a nameless entity that occupies no space. Most typical is the Boolean free union:

```
Trick:
  record
    case Boolean of
      true: (Ch: Char);
      false: (N: Byte )
  end;
```

A Trick record declared as above has two variations, a character variable Ch and a byte N. Because there is no tag field identifier, both variations occupy the same total space taken up by the record. This lets a program trick Pascal into translating characters into bytes. For example, you can write:

```
Trick.Ch := 'A';
```

This assigns 'A' to the character variant of the Trick record. To write this same data as a byte value, use the other variant:

```
Writeln('Value = ', Trick.N);
```

Or you can do the reverse, assigning a value to the byte variant and fooling Pascal into treating that value as a character:

```
Trick.N := 65;
Writeln('Character =', Trick.Ch);
```

Because 65 is the ASCII value for character A and because the freely united fields N and Ch occupy the same space, the foregoing Writeln displays an *A*. As you can see, this effectively subverts Pascal's normal type checking, which ordinarily prevents mixing numbers and characters.

Nesting Case Variants

One case variant may contain another variant, which may contain yet another variant part, and so on. The only restriction is that case variants, however many there are, must be last in the record definition.

With variations on top of variations, you can design complex record structures in Pascal. As an example, imagine you are designing a computer operating system with a disk directory listing the files on a floppy disk. In the file directory, the software needs to differentiate between active and deleted files. It needs also to categorize the active entries further. All this is easily done in a single multivariant record definition, as shown in Figure 5-13.

```
FileEntry = record
  case TypeOfDir: DirKind of
    Deleted: (
      Oldname: FileName;
      DeleteDate: DateRec
    );
    Active: (
      Fname: FileName;
      UpDated: DateRec;
    case TypeOfFile: FileKind of
      TextFile: (
        CharsInFile: Integer;
        Markers: array[1 .. 8] of
          record
            Label: string[8];
            Offset: Integer
          end
      );
      CodeFile: (
        Processor: (P6502, P8080, PZ80, P8088, P8086);
        StartAddress: Integer
      );
      DataFile: (
        BytesPerRec: Integer
      )
  end;
```

Figure 5-13 File name entry record from an imaginary disk operating system
showing that multiple case variants allow complex,
dynamic record structures in Pascal.

The example record makes use of two enumerated data types, DirKind and FileKind, defined as

```
DirKind = (Deleted, Active);
FileKind = (TextFile, CodeFile, DataFile);
```

In a real system, those definitions probably would contain other scalar elements. Each FileEntry record distinguishes its directory type with a case variant tag field, TypeOfDir.

Deleted variants store only OldName and DeleteDate fields; Active variants store a file name and date, plus a second, nested case variant with tag field TypeOfFile. TextFile variants store information possibly needed by a text editor or word processor. CodeFile variants store information about the computer processor. DataFile variants store the file size. With all variations under one tag field stored in the same space, the record compacts its information as much as possible, even if its definition looks long and complicated. Used this way, case variants lead to efficient record sizes.

Although imaginary, Figure 5-13 realistically illustrates how to use case variants. In fact, one operating system, the UCSD p-system, popular in the early 1980s, used a similar record structure for its disk directories.

Sets

Sets define collections of zero or more elements of a certain scalar or subrange base type. The railroad diagram in Figure 5-14 shows that a set starts with the key words **set of** followed by a *simple type,* which might be a scalar type or an integer subrange. For example, you could have a base type of months defined as an enumerated data type:

```
Months = (Jan, Feb, Mar, Apr,
          May, Jun, Jul, Aug,
          Sep, Oct, Nov, Dec);
```

set type

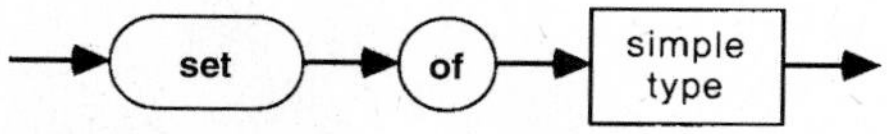

Figure 5-14 Railroad diagram for a **set** data type.

Your program can then define set types and variables of the Month ranges, Jan .. Dec:

```
type
   MonthSetType = set of Months;
var
   MonthSet: MonthSetType;
   Thirties: set of Months;
```

MonthSet and Thirties are set variables of the scalar base type, Months. To such variables, you can assign subsets of base type elements. One way to do this is to enclose a subrange of scalar elements in brackets:

```
MonthSet := [Jan .. Dec];
```

With this assignment, MonthSet defines the set of all 12 months. As it does in an array or integer subrange declaration, the ellipsis indicates a range between two scalar values. The first value must have an ordinal number less than or equal to the second. That's only logical. It would make no sense to write [Dec .. Jan].

Another way to define sets is to bracket individual elements separated by commas. To assign to Thirties the set of months having 30 days, you could write:

```
Thirties := [Sep, Apr, Jun, Nov];
```

Thirties now defines a 4-month subset of its base type—the months with 30 days each. Notice that, unlike a subrange, the order of the individual elements is unimportant.

Sets may also be empty. To assign the empty, or *null,* set to MonthSet, use empty brackets. There aren't any months in this set:

```
MonthSet := [];
```

After assigning a set of elements to a set variable, Pascal's **in** operator tests for the presence of a specific base type element. The following tests if April has 30 days:

```
if (Apr in Thirties)
  then Writeln('Has 30 days!');
```

The Boolean expression (Apr **in** Thirties) evaluates to True or False. Program 5-9 uses a similar expression along with the **in** operator to list which months have 30 days.

Program 5-9: THIRTY.PAS

```
1:   program ThirtyDays;
2:   type
3:     Months = (Jan, Feb, Mar, Apr, May, Jun,
4:               Jul, Aug, Sep, Oct, Nov, Dec);
5:   var
6:     Thirties: set of Months;
7:     MonthNames: array[Months] of string[3];
8:     OneMonth: Months;
9:   begin
10:    Writeln('Thirty Days');
11:    Writeln;
12:
13:    MonthNames[Jan] := 'Jan'; MonthNames[Feb] := 'Feb';
14:    MonthNames[Mar] := 'Mar'; MonthNames[Apr] := 'Apr';
15:    MonthNames[May] := 'May'; MonthNames[Jun] := 'Jun';
16:    MonthNames[Jul] := 'Jul'; MonthNames[Aug] := 'Aug';
```

continued

Program 5-9: continued

```
17:    MonthNames[Sep] := 'Sep'; MonthNames[Oct] := 'Oct';
18:    MonthNames[Nov] := 'Nov'; MonthNames[Dec] := 'Dec';
19:
20:    Thirties := [Sep, Apr, Jun, Nov];
21:    for OneMonth := Jan to Dec do
22:    begin
23:      Write(MonthNames[OneMonth]);
24:      if OneMonth in Thirties
25:        then Writeln(' has 30 days')
26:        else Writeln(' does not have 30 days')
27:    end;
28:    Readln
29:  end.
```

Assignments to the string array MonthNames take up most of Program 5-9. We need the array because compiled programs numerically represent elements of scalar types such as Months, similar to the ColorNames example explained earlier. In other words, when the program runs, Jan = 0, Feb = 1, Mar = 2, and so on. To write the month names, therefore, you have to associate visible strings with each scalar value. This is accomplished in Program 5-9 with the MonthNames array, indexed by the scalar elements of type Months.

Line 20 assigns the 30-day months to set variable Thirties. Then the **in** operator (line 24) tests each month for its presence in the set, displaying an appropriate message.

Relational Set Operators

Relational operators = (equal) and < > (not equal) compare two sets. Both of the following expressions are True:

```
[Jun, Jul, Aug] <> [Apr, May, Jun]
[Jan, Feb, Mar] =  [Mar, Feb, Jan]
```

Inclusion operators < = and > = test if one set is a subset of another. Pronounce < = "is a subset of" and > = "has the subset." If you use this trick to read the following three statements, you immediately see all three are true:

```
[Apr, May, Jun] <= [Jan .. Dec]
[] <= [Jan .. Dec]
[Jan .. Dec] >= [Jan, Dec]
```

Notice that the null set [ ] is a subset of [Jan .. Dec]. By definition, the null set is a subset of *any* set.

Logical Set Operators

Three other set operators combine two or more sets according to the logical rules of *union* (+), *intersection* (*), and *set difference* (–). The example expressions in Figure 5-15 make these operations clear.

Union

```
[Jan, Feb, Mar] + [Feb, Mar, Apr] = [Jan, Feb, Mar, Apr]
```

Intersection

```
[Jan, Feb, Mar] * [Feb, Mar, Apr] = [Feb, Mar]
```

Difference

```
[Jan, Feb, Mar] - [Feb, Mar, Apr] = [Jan]
```

Figure 5-15 Examples of the three set operators: union (+), intersection (*), and difference (–).

The *union* of two sets is the combined set of elements from set A and set B. The *intersection* of two sets is the set of common elements found in set A and set B. The *difference* of two sets is the set of elements found in set A that are not also found in set B.

Program 5-10 demonstrates these concepts. (Lines 29-34 are the same as lines 13-18 in Program 5-9. To save time, you can copy those lines rather than retyping.)

Program 5-10: SETOPS.PAS

```
 1:  program SetOperators;
 2:  type
 3:     Months = (Jan, Feb, Mar, Apr, May, Jun,
 4:                Jul, Aug, Sep, Oct, Nov, Dec);
 5:     MonthSet = set of Months;
 6:  var
 7:     MonthNames: array[Months] of string[3];
 8:     Seta, Setb: MonthSet;
 9:
10:  procedure ShowSet(S: MonthSet);
```

continued

```
11:  var
12:    Separator: string[2];
13:    OneMonth: Months;
14:  begin
15:    Write(' [');
16:    Separator := ' ';
17:    for OneMonth := Jan to Dec do
18:    if OneMonth in S then
19:    begin
20:      Write(Separator, MonthNames[OneMonth]);
21:      Separator := ', '
22:    end;
23:    Writeln(' ]');
24:    Writeln
25:  end;
26:
27:  begin
28:
29:    MonthNames[Jan] := 'Jan'; MonthNames[Feb] := 'Feb';
30:    MonthNames[Mar] := 'Mar'; MonthNames[Apr] := 'Apr';
31:    MonthNames[May] := 'May'; MonthNames[Jun] := 'Jun';
32:    MonthNames[Jul] := 'Jul'; MonthNames[Aug] := 'Aug';
33:    MonthNames[Sep] := 'Sep'; MonthNames[Oct] := 'Oct';
34:    MonthNames[Nov] := 'Nov'; MonthNames[Dec] := 'Dec';
35:
36:    Seta := [Jan, Feb, Mar];
37:    Setb := [Feb, Mar, Apr];
38:
39:    Writeln;
40:    Writeln('Set operators');
41:    Writeln;
42:    Write('SETA = '); ShowSet(Seta);
43:    Write('SETB = '); ShowSet(Setb);
44:    Writeln;
45:
46:    Writeln('Union SETA + SETB');
47:    ShowSet(Seta + Setb);
48:    Writeln('Intersection SETA * SETB');
49:    ShowSet(Seta * Setb);
50:    Writeln('Difference SETA - SETB');
```

```
51:    ShowSet(Seta - Setb);
52:    Readln
53:  end.
```

Lines 47, 49, and 51 apply the three set operators to Seta and Setb. For different results, change the assigned set elements in lines 36 and 37 and rerun the program.

Practical Use of Sets

Besides sets of scalar types, you can also have sets of integers and characters. Turbo Pascal, however, limits sets to a maximum of 256 elements with ordinal values 0 to 255. The following variable declaration, therefore, defines the largest possible integer set:

```
Numberset: set of 0 .. 255;
```

Because Turbo Pascal limits set types to subsets of positive integers, this also limits the size of **set** variables. In memory, each element of a set occupies a single bit, indicating the presence (1) or absence (0) of individual elements; therefore, a set of 256 elements takes 256 bits of memory. At eight bits per memory byte, this maximum-size set takes 32 (256/8) bytes. Sets with fewer defined elements take less room. A set of 0 to 127, for example, takes 16 (128/8) bytes of memory.

Character Sets

One of the more useful kinds of sets is a set of characters. Characters are scalar by nature and, as defined in Turbo Pascal, fall in the ordinal range 0 .. 255. To define a set of characters, use this declaration in your program:

```
type
   CharSet = set of Char;
var
   UpperCase, LowerCase, Digits: Charset;
```

With these declarations, you can assign appropriate character ranges to set variables UpperCase, LowerCase, and Digits:

```
UpperCase := ['A' .. 'Z'];
LowerCase := ['a' .. 'z'];
Digits    := ['0' .. '9'];
```

Because these are character sets, set elements are literal characters surrounded by quotation marks. The set of digit characters ['0' .. '9'] is not the same as the subset of integers [0 .. 9]. The first is a set of characters; the second is a set of positive numbers.

A common programming problem is to prompt for one character from a specific set. The program rejects anything else, perhaps allowing only digits when it asks you to type a number. With character sets, the solution is simple, as demonstrated in Program 5-11.

Program 5-11: CHARSET.PAS

```
 1:  program CharacterSets;
 2:  type
 3:    CharSet = set of Char;
 4:    String40 = string[40];
 5:  var
 6:    UpperCase, LowerCase, Digits: CharSet;
 7:    Ch: Char;
 8:
 9:  { Prompt for a command character }
10:  { Return Command char only if in LegalChars set }
11:  procedure GetCommand(   Prompt:      String40;
12:                             LegalChars:  CharSet;
13:                         var Command:     Char    );
14:  begin
15:    repeat
16:      Write(Prompt);
17:      Readln(Command);
18:      Writeln;
19:      if not (Command in LegalChars)
20:        then Writeln(Chr(7), '*** Entry error!  Try again.')
21:      until Command in LegalChars;
22:    Writeln('Character entered is: ', Command)
23:  end;
24:
25:  begin
26:    Writeln('Character Sets');
27:    Writeln;
28:    UpperCase := ['A' .. 'Z'];
29:    LowerCase := ['a' .. 'z'];
30:    Digits := ['0' .. '9'];
31:    GetCommand('Enter uppercase letter: ', UpperCase, Ch);
32:    GetCommand('Enter lowercase letter: ', LowerCase, Ch);
33:    GetCommand('Enter a digit 0 to 9: ', Digits, Ch)
34:  end.
```

Procedure GetCommand (lines 9-23) takes a character set parameter LegalChars. The routine prompts you to press a key, returning variable Command only if you enter one of the characters from the legal subset. This general procedure works for any subset of characters, digits, punctuation, or letters, and avoids writing complicated logic tests such as

```
if (Ch <> 'A') and (Ch <> 'D') and (Ch <> 'F') and (Ch <> 'Q')
  then Writeln('Error');
```

Character sets allow a more concise statement that accomplishes the same job:

```
if not (Ch in ['A', 'D', 'F', 'Q'])
   then Writeln('Error');
```

Or, with the GetCommand procedure in Program 5-11, use this single statement, limiting variable Ch to a specific set of responses:

```
GetCommand('? ', ['A', 'D', 'F', 'Q'], Ch);
```

A common mistake when using character sets is to attempt a line such as

```
if Ch not in ['A' .. 'Z'] then ...
```

This will not compile because the **not** key word is in the wrong place. The correct form is

```
if not (Ch in ['A' .. 'Z']) then ...
```

The parentheses force evaluation of the Boolean expression (Ch **in** ['A' .. 'Z']). You need to use parentheses because **not** has a higher precedence than **in** (see Appendix E). Without parentheses, **not** incorrectly applies to **Ch**; you cannot negate characters, only numbers or Booleans.

This observation leads to dangerous grounds in Boolean set expressions. If B is a Boolean set, and V a Boolean variable, then:

```
not V in B
```

does not have the expected meaning:

```
not (V in B)
```

Because **not** has a higher precedence than **in**, the expression **not** V **in** B evaluates as though it were (**not** V) **in** B. You must use parentheses as shown previously if that is not your intention.

Another more serious danger occurs with numeric sets. Turbo Pascal permits negating integer values, a permission other Pascal compilers do not often grant. If K is an integer, then **not** K negates all bits in K. In other words, bits take their opposite values: ones turning to zeros, and zeros to ones. The result is called the *one's complement* of K. Be especially wary of set expressions such as these:

```
if not K in [1 .. 50] then ...
if not (K in [1 .. 50]) then ...
```

These two statements may produce different results and, because of the way **not** applies to integers in Turbo Pascal, might cause bugs, especially when you are converting programs from one Pascal compiler to another.

The answer to these problems is to *always* use parentheses to resolve even the slightest potential ambiguity. Especially when programming with sets, this is a rule to follow religiously. Extra parentheses come at no extra cost; the compiler merely uses them to determine the evaluation order of expressions. The parentheses themselves do not end up in the compiled program.

Summary

In this chapter you learned how to declare new data types and add structure to Pascal variables. Subranges limit scalar variables to specific minimum and maximum values. Enumerated types use descriptive names to create new scalar data types.

Arrays collect identically typed elements, whereas records assemble variables of mixed data types. Case variant records allow different fields to coexist in the same record space. Set variables specify subsets of scalar elements.

Pascal lets you mix these and other data structures, making arrays of arrays, arrays of records, and even records of arrays or sets.

Set logical operators let you combine and compare sets in a variety of ways.

Exercises

5-1. How can you prevent illegal date assignments in Program 5-6? Test your solution with illegal dates such as March 42, 1999.

5-2. Write a program to print the ordinal values of the Boolean scalar elements, true and false. What are the ordinal values of the expressions (**not** true), (**not** false), and (**not** (**not** true **and** **not** false))?

5-3. Write a program to prompt for a string and then display individual characters vertically on the screen. Modify your program to write the characters in a diagonal line. Recall that a string is similar to an array of characters.

5-4. Modify Program 5-5 to sort strings instead of numbers. Let the user enter a variety of strings to sort. (Hint: Convert all strings to uppercase before sorting. See Program 5-4.)

5-5. The mileage chart in Table 5-1 is similar to those found in many road maps. Write a program to initialize a multiple-dimension array with these mileages, then let the operator enter the names of two cities, and print the distance between them.

Table 5-1 City mileage chart

	Atlanta	Baltimore	Boston	Chicago	Dallas	Los Angeles	New York
Atlanta	0	654	1108	708	822	2191	854
Baltimore	654	0	427	717	1357	2647	199
Boston	1108	427	0	1004	1753	3017	208
Chicago	708	717	1004	0	921	2048	809
Dallas	822	1357	1753	921	0	1399	1559
Los Angeles	2191	2647	3017	2048	1399	0	2794
New York	854	199	208	809	1559	2794	0

5-6. (Advanced) Finish Program 5-8, adding a procedure to edit the records in the database.

5-7. Add an address field to Program 5-8.

5-8. (Advanced) Add a feature to Program 5-8 to sort the database by last name before listing the records.

5-9. (Advanced) Incorporate the new Member record type (Figure 5-12) into Program 5-8. Modify procedures AddRecords and ListRecords to handle the case variant part of the new record structure.

5-10. Starting with the scalar data type:

```
DaysOfWeek = (Sun, Mon, Tue, Wed, Thu, Fri, Sat);
```

write a program to assign work days to employee records, as might be done in a company scheduling office. Use sets to record data for each employee. A chart listing all employees and the next week's schedule is posted on the company bulletin board. Your program should create this chart.

6

Files

- Text Files
- End of File—Eof
- Closing Files
- Input and Output
- Processing Text Files
- A Utility in Disguise
- Text File Filters
- Adding Line Numbers
- One Char at a Time
- End of Line—Eoln
- Structured Files
- Files of Records
- Sequential Processing
- Chicken and Egg Files
- Testing IoResult
- Random Access Processing
- Seeking and Writing
- Appending Records
- Appending Text Files
- Processing Text Files at Random
- Advanced File Handling
- Special Functions
- Untyped Files
- Passing Files as Parameters

6

Key Words and Identifiers

Append, Assign, BlockRead, BlockWrite, Close, Eof, Eoln, Erase, **file**, **file of**, FilePos, FileSize, Flush, Input, IoResult, Output, Read, Readln, Rename, Reset, Rewrite, Seek, Sizeof, Text, Truncate, Write, Writeln

Computers talk to a variety of devices such as modems, printers, and disk drives. Although most devices have different characteristics, programs need standard ways to communicate with them. Files are the solution.

A file is a kind of magic door (Figure 6-1) through which programs communicate with the outside world. To establish communications, a program *opens* a file to a device. After that, it sends data to the device and, if it makes sense to do so, receives information back. When completed, the program *closes* the file, telling the computer it has finished communicating.

It is important to differentiate Pascal files from disk files. You are probably saving this book's example programs in files on a floppy or hard disk. In this sense, a file is simply a named location, or group of locations, on disk. But in Pascal the meaning of a file is much broader. A Pascal file is a special kind of variable that sets up communication with *any* device. This may include not only named disk files but also printers, modems, and plotters, to name a few examples.

To avoid confusion, from now on *disk file* specifically means a data file stored by name on disk. The word *file* alone, however, refers to any Pascal file, including disk files and also files to communicate with printers, keyboards, and other devices. Figure 6-2 shows the railroad diagram for declaring file types.

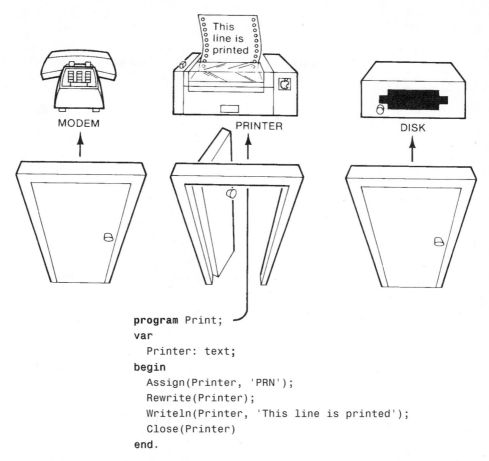

```
program Print;
var
  Printer: text;
begin
  Assign(Printer, 'PRN');
  Rewrite(Printer);
  Writeln(Printer, 'This line is printed');
  Close(Printer)
end.
```

Figure 6-1 A Pascal file is like a magic door through which programs communicate with devices. This figure shows a file named Printer open to the computer's listing device, PRN. The program writes a line of text on paper.

file type

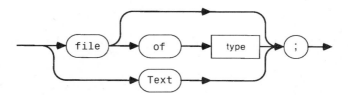

Figure 6-2 Railroad diagram for declaring Pascal **file** variables.

Text Files

Devices that send and receive characters include printers, modems, keyboards, and computer terminals. Pascal programs communicate with these and other character devices through *text files*.

Text is a special file data type in Pascal. To declare a text file in a program, simply create a variable of type Text:

```
var
   Printer: Text;
```

Declared this way, variable Printer is a text file. Here is another way to do almost the same thing:

```
var
   Printer: file of Char;
```

To Pascal programs, Printer is just a file of characters—a place to send text. Both Text and **file of** Char are similar, but not identical, in Turbo Pascal. In general, to read and write text as lines, use Text. To read and write text as individual characters, use either form.

In a similar way, you can declare disk files of integers, strings, real numbers, or other data types. The only data type you can't have in a file is another file. In other words, Pascal does not allow a **file of file**.

Before you use a declared file variable, the first step is to name the device or disk file you want to access. All devices in Turbo Pascal have short three-character names (Table 6-1) that programs assign to file variables with the built-in procedure Assign. For example, to prepare a file for printing, write:

```
Assign(Printer, 'PRN');
```

This links the program text file variable Printer with the physical device or, more accurately, the interface circuit and cable that somewhere, you trust, attach to the printer. Other device names are explained in Table 6-1.

After assigning a name to a text file variable, open the file for output with a Rewrite statement as follows:

```
var
   Printer, Console: Text;
begin
   Assign(Printer, 'PRN');
   Rewrite(Printer);
   Writeln(Printer, 'This is printed');
   Writeln('This is not printed');
end;
```

Table 6-1 Text device file names.

File Name	Description	Input	Output
'AUX'	Auxiliary device (COM1)	Yes	Yes
'CON'	Console and keyboard	Yes	Yes
'PRN'	Printer(LPT1)	No	Yes
'COM1'	Communications port 1	Yes	Yes
'COM2'	Communications port 2	Yes	Yes
'LPT1'	Line printer 1	No	Yes
'LPT2'	Line printer 2	No	Yes
'LPT3'	Line printer 3	No	Yes
'NUL'	Bit bucket	Yes	Yes
''	Standard input and output	Yes	Yes

Assigning a name to Printer and then rewriting the file variable opens the file for later use. Here, a Writeln statement prints a line of text. The second Writeln, which does not have the opened file variable as its first parameter, operates normally, displaying a string on the screen. Including the opened file variable in Writeln (or Write) redirects the text to where you want it to go.

Why *rewrite?* In the olden days of computing, which were not so long ago, a tape drive was the common file device, and Rewrite wound the tape to the beginning and prepared the drive for writing characters to tape—overwriting whatever was there before. Of course it makes no sense to rewind printers and modems. You just have to remember that Rewrite in its modern meaning opens files for output.

When used with a disk file, Rewrite creates a new file on disk ready to receive data. It also erases an old disk file of the same name. Program 6-1 creates a new disk file named MYTEXT.TXT containing four lines of text. Line 5 assigns a name to the text file variable FileVar. Because this name is not a device name from Table 6-1, the file is created on disk. Line 6 creates the new file, and line 11 closes it, locking the new file name in the disk directory and writing any information held in memory buffers to disk.

Program 6-1: MAKETEXT.PAS

```
1:  program MakeText;
2:  var
3:    FileVar: Text;
4:  begin
5:    Assign(FileVar, 'MYTEXT.TXT');
```

continued

Program 6-1: continued

```
 6:     Rewrite(FileVar);
 7:     Writeln(FileVar, 'MYTEXT — A sample text file.');
 8:     Writeln(FileVar, ' This program demonstrates how');
 9:     Writeln(FileVar, ' to create and write to a disk');
10:     Writeln(FileVar, ' text file.');
11:     Close(FileVar)
12:   end.
```

Lines 7-10 do the actual writing, using this form of the familiar Writeln and Write statements:

```
Write([F,] V1, V2, ..., V3);

Writeln([F,] V1, V2, ..., V3);
```

Write or Writeln may include a file variable—which must be of type Text—followed by a comma and the things you want to write. The square brackets indicate that F is optional. If you don't specify a file, output normally goes to the display. Similarly, Read and Readln read text from a file:

```
Read([F,] V1, V2, V3);

Readln([F,] V1, V2, ..., V3);
```

Using Readln with a file variable reads the lines of text from MYTEXT.TXT, which you created with Program 6-1. But with a simple change, the reading program becomes a useful utility, as shown in Program 6-2.

Program 6-2: READTEXT.PAS

```
 1:  program ReadText;
 2:  var
 3:    FileName: string[14];
 4:    FileVar: Text;
 5:    OneLine: string[80];
 6:  begin
 7:    Writeln('Read text');
 8:    Write('File name? ');
 9:    Readln(FileName);
10:    Assign(FileVar, FileName);
11:    Reset(FileVar);
12:    while not Eof(FileVar) do
```

```
13:    begin
14:      Readln(FileVar, OneLine);
15:      Writeln(OneLine)
16:    end;
17:    Close(FileVar);
18:    Readln
19:  end.
```

Instead of using the literal file name 'MYTEXT.TXT,' Program 6-2 lets you enter the name of any file into string variable FileName. Line 10 assigns FileName to the text file variable. Because we don't want to create a new disk file this time, line 11 uses Reset to open the file. Reset opens an existing disk file for reading and writing but does not disturb data already there. (Contrary to Rewrite, which works with all files, Reset works only with disk files and with devices that can send information to the program.)

End of File—Eof

Line 12 of Program 6-2 demonstrates the built-in Boolean function Eof (end of file). Eof is true after the program reads the last line from a text file. In most cases, a Ctrl-Z character (ASCII 26) marks the end of text files. Eof automatically becomes true when Pascal reads that character. For other kinds of files, Eof is true after reading the last unit of data. The **while** loop at lines 12-16 tests Eof, ending the loop after exhausting all text in the file.

Closing Files

To avoid losing information, be sure to close your files as shown in line 11 of Program 6-1. This releases any data temporarily held by DOS in memory, a process called *buffering* because of the way memory, acting as a buffer zone, sits between the program and disk. Accessing disk drives takes time, and buffering data in memory speeds disk operations by reading and writing many bytes at a time.

Closing also tells the operating system to clean up its internal file variables, or *handles,* not normally accessible to your programs. If you forget to close your files, the operating system may eventually run out of handles. If this happens, you can no longer Reset and Rewrite new files.

To force the operating system to write buffered data to disk without closing the file, use Flush:

```
Flush(FileVar);
```

There are two main uses for Flush. When the computer stands idle for a time—for example, while displaying a selection menu—it's a good idea to flush buffered data to disk. Experience teaches that people sometimes turn down the brightness knob on displays. If somebody turns the computer off at that time without checking to see if a program is running, any buffered data would be irretrievably lost. For safety, the menu program could simply Flush all file variables. This method also avoids the time-consuming process of closing and then reopening all program files for each new menu selection.

The second place where Flush comes in handy is in multiuser or networked systems. Local microcomputers in the network—called nodes—may hold buffers of data in memory, making that data unavailable to other users. Multiuser software Flushes a local node's memory, making the buffered information available to all users again. Usually, there are Lock and Unlock commands for making sure that only one node receives a block of information at a time, but these are operating system commands, not part of Pascal.

Input and Output

Without a file variable, Write and Writeln default to the standard file Output, whereas Read and Readln default to Input. In other words, the following statements are equivalent:

```
Readln(S)   =   Readln(Input, S)
Writeln(S)  =   Writeln(Output, S)
```

Input and Output are default text files, automatically supplied for you in the absence of explicit text file variables. They are there if you want to use them, but they usually are not required.

Processing Text Files

A useful program *template,* or shell, to have around is a standard program for reading and writing text files. The program reads lines of text from a file, does something with that text, and then writes the new text somewhere else. With minor modifications, the program converts text to uppercase, counts words, searches for data, and writes output to another file, the console, or maybe the printer.

In its basic form, Program 6-3 simply copies a text file from one place to another. When you run the program, you're asked for input and output file names, which may be device names or the names of disk files. The program contains the dummy procedure ProcessString (lines 21-23), which you can fill in so that it does whatever you want to each line of text from the input file.

Program 6-3: COPYTEXT.PAS

```pascal
 1:  program CopyText;
 2:  const
 3:    Title = 'Copy Text';
 4:  type
 5:    String132 = string[132];
 6:  var
 7:    InFile, OutFile: Text;
 8:
 9:  procedure OpenFiles;
10:  var
11:    FileName: string[14];
12:  begin
13:    Write('Input file? '); Readln(FileName);
14:    Assign(InFile, FileName);
15:    Reset(InFile);
16:    Write('Output file? '); Readln(FileName);
17:    Assign(OutFile, FileName);
18:    Rewrite(OutFile)
19:  end;
20:
21:  procedure ProcessString(var S: String132);
22:  begin
23:  end;
24:
25:  procedure ProcessFiles;
26:  var
27:    S: String132;
28:  begin
29:    while not Eof(InFile) do
30:    begin
31:      Readln(InFile, S);
32:      ProcessString(S);
33:      Writeln(OutFile, S)
34:    end
35:  end;
36:
37:  begin
38:    Writeln(Title);
39:    Writeln;
```

continued

Program 6-3: continued

```
40:    OpenFiles;
41:    ProcessFiles;
42:    Close(Outfile);
43:    Close(Infile);
44:    Readln
45: end.
```

Procedure OpenFiles (lines 9-19) prompts for input and output file names. It then resets the input file and rewrites the output file. Notice that the same string variable FileName holds both input and output names. After assigning FileName to InFile (line 14), FileName is reused in line 16.

Now that the files are open, procedure ProcessFiles reads lines of text from the input file (line 31), calls the dummy procedure ProcessString (line 32), and then writes the string to the output file (line 33). These three steps repeat until reaching the end of the input file, setting Eof to true in line 29.

The **while** loop (lines 29-34) is the correct repetitive statement to use. Why is the following procedure *not* correct?

```
repeat                    { ??? }
   Readln(InFile, S);
   ProcessString(S);
   Writeln(OutFile, S)
until Eof(InFile);
```

The reason this **repeat** loop fails is obvious if you consider what happens when reading empty files. In that case, Eof is true when the program opens the file. The end of an empty file, in other words, is at its beginning. The **repeat** loop, which always executes at least one time, tries to read a line of text from the empty file, causing an error. The **while** loop in Program 6-3, however, never executes if the file is empty. For bug-free results, it's always a good idea to test your programs against unusual cases, such as what happens when processing empty files.

A Utility in Disguise

Program 6-3 has other uses that may not be obvious. In fact, the program is a useful utility in disguise. Of course, it copies disk text files to other disk text files, but it also displays text files on your screen. To do that, enter the name of a disk text file as the input—remember to type in the whole name, for example, MYTEXT.TXT—and then enter CON as the output file. The program reads the disk text file and writes each line to the console.

You can do the reverse, too. Enter CON as the input file and a new disk file name as the output. Don't enter the name of an existing disk file, or the Rewrite statement in line 18 will erase it! Whatever you then type, the program writes to disk, with Program 6-3 functioning as a primitive text editor. To end typing, enter ^Z (Ctrl-Z), the character DOS recognizes as the end-of-file marker.

It may surprise you to learn that Program 6-3 not only copies and creates text but also serves as an electronic typewriter. Enter CON for the input file and PRN for output, and the program prints every line you type, giving you the chance to edit mistakes before pressing Enter to print.

It's certainly impressive that a single program serves in so many capacities—displaying text files, creating new files, making copies of disk files, and running the printer—all by simply changing the input and output files. But let's not stop there. Filling in procedure ProcessString makes the program do even more.

Text File Filters

By modifying Program 6-3 in various ways, you build a collection of text file *filters* to do a number of things. A filter is a program that reads a file, modifies what it reads, and then writes the result to a new file.

As an example of writing text filters, Program 6-3 can be easily changed to convert text files to all uppercase. Insert a new ProcessString procedure (Figure 6-3) in place of lines 21-23. At the same time, change the title in line 3 to read:

```
Title  = 'Uppercase Converter';
```

```
procedure ProcessString(var S: String132);
var
  I: Integer;
begin
  for I := 1 to Length(S) do
    S[I] := Upcase(S[I])
end;
```

Figure 6-3 To convert text files to all uppercase, insert this procedure into Program 6-3, replacing lines 21-23.

You can also make the program display what it's doing—a visual feedback or confirmation of the program's operation—by adding this Writeln statement between lines 32 and 33:

```
Writeln(S);
```

Adding Line Numbers

With an integer variable Line between lines 7 and 8, a statement to initialize Line to 0, and a different ProcessString procedure (Figure 6-4), Program 6-3 adds line numbers to text files. I used a similar program to print the listings in this book.

Add this line between lines 7 and 8

```
Line: Integer;
```

Replace lines 21-23 with this procedure

```
procedure ProcessString(var S: String132);
begin
  Inc(Line);
  Write(OutFile, Line:5, ':  ')
end;
```

Add this line between lines 37 and 38

```
Line := 0;
```

Figure 6-4 Modifications to Program 6-3 to add reference line numbers to text files.

One Char at a Time

Because of the maximum string length of 255 characters, reading text files a line at a time limits you to files with lines that are no longer. Some word-processing programs, however, use carriage returns to separate paragraphs, not lines. In this case, you have no choice but to process text one character at a time.

To demonstrate how to do this, Program 6-4 converts WordStar text files to standard ASCII format. WordStar, a once popular word processing program, stores characters in a special way that makes text unreadable by editors such as Turbo Pascal's.

Program 6-4: WS2ASCII.PAS

```pascal
 1:  program Ws2Ascii;
 2:  { Convert WordStar to ASCII text file }
 3:  const
 4:     TempName = 'TEMP.@@@';
 5:  var
 6:     FileName: string[64];
 7:
 8:  procedure ProcessFile;
 9:  var
10:     I: Integer;
11:     InFile, OutFile: Text;
12:     Ch: Char;
13:  begin
14:     Assign(InFile, FileName);
15:     Reset(InFile);
16:     Assign(OutFile, TempName);
17:     Rewrite(OutFile);
18:     while not Eof(InFile) do
19:     begin
20:       Read(InFile, Ch);
21:       Ch := Chr(Ord(Ch) mod 128);
22:       if Ch = Chr(13)
23:         then Writeln(OutFile) else
24:       if Ch >= ' '
25:         then Write(OutFile, Ch)
26:     end;
27:     Close(InFile);
28:     Close(OutFile);
29:     Erase(InFile);
30:     Rename(OutFile, FileName)
31:  end;
32:
33:  begin
34:     Writeln('WordStar to ASCII Converter');
35:     Writeln;
36:     Write('Convert what file? ');
37:     Readln(FileName);
38:     if Length(FileName) > 0
39:       then ProcessFile
40:  end.
```

To avoid the line-length problem, Program 6-4 reads single characters with a Read statement in line 20. It then forces the character to the ordinal range 0-127 with the expression in line 21, converting eight-bit nonstandard characters to standard ASCII seven-bit format. The **mod** operator returns the remainder of an integer division, here with the ordinal value of the original character.

Lines 22 and 23 convert plain carriage-return characters to carriage returns and line feeds—the output of the Writeln in line 23. Lines 24 and 25 write only characters in the visible ASCII range, skipping control characters whose values are lower than a blank.

Finally in lines 27 and 28, the program closes both input and output files. Notice that all program output initially goes to file TEMP@@@ (see lines 4, 16, and 17). The two lines at 29-30 erase the original input file and then rename TEMP@@@ to whatever file name you enter to the prompt at line 36. This has the effect of preserving the original file until all processing is complete.

End of Line—Eoln

Processing text files a character at a time requires a special function to know when you've reached the ends of lines. Eoln (end of line) returns true when Turbo Pascal detects the end of a line, marked by a carriage return character (ASCII 13), while sequentially reading characters. To process a text file a character at a time with Eoln, use a **while** loop such as this:

```
var
  inFile: Text;
  Ch: Char;
while not Eof(InFile) do
begin
  if Eoln(InFile)
    then Writeln;
  Read(InFile, Ch);
  ProcessChar(Ch)
end;
```

Although this works, I prefer to check explicitly for carriage returns and other control characters such as line feeds as in line 22 of Program 6-4. Most word processors do not adhere to the convention of ending lines with plain carriage returns and, therefore, Eoln is unable to recognize line endings except in standard ASCII text.

Structured Files

Text files are only one of the many varieties of disk files that programs can process. Regardless of how programs interpret file contents, disk files all contain the same thing—binary data bytes. Programs may freely interpret those bytes as they please. One program might interpret them as characters, another as integers, real numbers, Boolean true and false values, name and address records, and other structures. The interpretation of data in disk files is up to you and your program. There is nothing in a file (unless you put it there) to indicate the nature of its contents.

To declare a file of bytes, create a file variable like this:

```
var
   ByteFile: file of Byte;
```

Byte is a predeclared data type with values ranging from 0 to 255, the range of values that fit in one eight-bit byte. With this declaration, a program can open any file as a sequence of bytes, then copy it unchanged to another file. Because the program doesn't change or process the data in the file, it doesn't matter if the data represents other structures, characters, integers, or records.

Program 6-5 is similar to Program 6-3, except it copies any disk file, not only ones containing text. Procedure OpenFiles is unchanged; no matter what kind of files you declare, you open them the same way. Line 3 declares InFile and OutFile as files of Byte. ProcessFiles reads and writes single bytes at a time (lines 25 and 26), and the LongInt variable Size keeps track of the number of bytes processed. (An Integer Size could count no higher than 32,767 bytes, smaller than many common disk files. The LongInt variable lets the program handle files with over 2 *billion* bytes—larger than the total capacity of most personal computer disk drives.)

Program 6-5: COPYBYTE.PAS

```
 1:  program CopyBytes;
 2:  var
 3:     InFile, OutFile: file of Byte;
 4:
 5:  procedure OpenFiles;
 6:  var
 7:     FileName: string[14];
 8:  begin
 9:     Write('Input file? '); Readln(FileName);
10:     Assign(InFile, FileName);
11:     Reset(InFile);
```

continued

Program 6-5: continued

```
12:    Write('Output file? '); Readln(FileName);
13:    Assign(OutFile, FileName);
14:    Rewrite(OutFile)
15: end;
16:
17: procedure ProcessFiles;
18: var
19:    OneByte: Byte;
20:    Size: LongInt;
21: begin
22:    Size := 0;
23:    while not Eof(InFile) do
24:    begin
25:      Read(InFile, OneByte);
26:      Write(OutFile, OneByte);
27:      Inc(Size)
28:    end;
29:    Writeln(Size, ' bytes copied')
30: end;
31:
32: begin
33:    Writeln('Copy any file');
34:    Writeln;
35:    OpenFiles;
36:    ProcessFiles;
37:    Close(OutFile);
38:    Close(InFile);
39:    Readln
40: end.
```

Notice that the program uses Read and Write, not Readln and Writeln, in lines 25 and 26. It can't use Readln because a file of bytes is just a stream of values with no defined structure. You can use Readln only with lines of text that end in carriage returns.

Files of Records

Disk files can hold any Pascal data structure. In Chapter 5, you developed a database for storing information about the members of a fictitious club. A better version saves its data on disk, then reads it back the next time you run the program.

Program 6-6 adds two procedures, WriteMembers and ReadMembers, to the club database in Program 5-8. Procedures AddRecords and ListRecords are copied from Program 5-8.

Program 6-6: CLUBDB2.PAS

```pascal
 1:  program ClubDataBase2;
 2:  const
 3:    MaxMembers = 5;
 4:    FileName = 'CLUB.DAT';
 5:  type
 6:    FileType = (SystemRec, ActiveRec);
 7:    Member =
 8:      record
 9:        case RecKind: FileType of
10:          SystemRec: (NumMembers : Integer);
11:          ActiveRec: (Name      : string[30];
12:                      Phone     : string[12];
13:                      Charges   : Real;
14:                      Payments  : Real    )
15:      end;
16:  var
17:    Members: array[0 .. MaxMembers] of Member;
18:    Membership: 0 .. MaxMembers;
19:    Choice: Char;
20:
21:  procedure WriteMembers;
22:  var
23:    MemberFile: file of Member;
24:    I: Integer;
25:  begin
26:    with Members[0] do
27:    begin
28:      RecKind := SystemRec;
29:      NumMembers := Membership
30:    end;
```

continued

```
31:    Assign(MemberFile, FileName);
32:    Rewrite(MemberFile);
33:    Writeln('Writing ', Membership, ' records.');
34:    for I := 0 to Membership do
35:      Write(MemberFile, Members[I]);
36:    Close(MemberFile)
37:  end;
38:
39:  procedure ReadMembers;
40:  var
41:    MemberFile: file of Member;
42:    I: Integer;
43:  begin
44:    Assign(MemberFile, FileName);
45:  {$I-}
46:    Reset(MemberFile);
47:  {$I+}
48:    if IoResult <> 0 then
49:    begin
50:      Writeln('New file');
51:      Membership := 0
52:    end else
53:    begin
54:      Read(MemberFile, Members[0]);
55:      Membership := Members[0].NumMembers;
56:      Writeln('Reading ', Membership, ' records.');
57:      for I := 1 to Membership do
58:        Read(MemberFile, Members[I]);
59:      Close(MemberFile)
60:    end
61:  end;
62:
63:  procedure AddRecords;
64:  begin
65:    if Membership = MaxMembers
66:      then Writeln('Membership is full') else
67:      begin
68:        Writeln('Add new records');
69:        Membership := Membership + 1;
70:        with Members[ Membership ] do
```

```
71:        begin
72:          Write('Name     : '); Readln(Name);
73:          Write('Phone    : '); Readln(Phone);
74:          Write('Charges  : '); Readln(Charges);
75:          Write('Payments : '); Readln(Payments)
76:        end
77:      end
78:  end;
79:
80:  procedure ListRecords;
81:  var
82:    Number: Integer;
83:  begin
84:    for Number := 1 to Membership do
85:      with Members[ Number ] do
86:        Writeln(Number, ': ', Name,
87:            '   ', Phone, Charges-Payments:8:2)
88:  end;
89:
90:  begin
91:    Writeln;
92:    Writeln('Club Data Base');
93:    ReadMembers;
94:    repeat
95:      Writeln;
96:      Writeln('Number of members = ', Membership);
97:      Write('A.dd, E.dit, L.ist, Q.uit ? ');
98:      Readln(Input, Choice);
99:      Choice := Upcase(Choice);
100:     case Choice of
101:       'A': AddRecords;
102:       'E': Writeln('Sorry, no editing yet');
103:       'L': ListRecords
104:     end
105:    until Choice = 'Q';
106:    WriteMembers
107:  end.
```

One improvement in this new version is a FileName constant in line 4. There's also a new case variant in the Member record type. Its two variations, System and Active, define the record contents. A System record holds the current number of members in the data file, and Active records hold actual data. Other fields in Member are the same.

Another important difference is the array of Members (line 17), which now begins at index 0 instead of 1. The new program stores a special System record at Members[0], keeping track of how many member records are in the array.

This is done in the WriteMembers procedure (lines 21-37). File variable MemberFile, declared in line 23, is a file of type Member. In other words, the disk file contains records with the structure declared earlier in lines 7-15. The **with** statement (lines 26-30) sets tag field RecKind to System and stores the number of members in the NumMembers field. Later, when reading data back from disk, this technique lets the program know how many records are in the disk file.

Sequential Processing

A simple **for** loop (lines 34 and 35 in Program 6-6) writes member records to disk, one after the other, demonstrating one way to process disk files sequentially.

Even so, it is not correct to label the file a "sequential data file." (Later in this chapter is an equally misused term, "random access file.") Disk files are neither sequential nor random. Programs, however, may *process* files in sequential or random order—a subtle though important distinction to remember.

As shown in procedure ReadMembers (lines 39-61), reading a disk file in sequence is simply the reverse process of writing. Again, MemberFile is a file of type Member (line 41). Line 44 is also familiar; it assigns the file name to the MemberFile variable. Line 46 uses Reset to open the existing club disk file. But observant readers might spot a problem with this approach, as described in the next section.

Chicken and Egg Files

Program 6-6 solves a typical problem which might be called the "chicken and egg disk file syndrome." Looking near the end of the program in line 93, you see that the first thing the program does is read the old data file. But the first time the program runs, there is no old file, and resetting the file variable in line 46 causes an error.

To prevent halting the program when this happens, the compiler directives in lines 45 and 47 temporarily switch off input and output (I/O) error checking {$I-}, then switch it back on {$I+} after the Reset command executes.

Normally, Turbo Pascal automatically checks I/O errors during read and write operations on files. If an error occurs, the program stops with an error message. Switching off I/O error checking lets the program test the result, called the IoResult, of file operations and take appropriate actions instead of screeching to a halt.

Testing IoResult

Line 48 in Program 6-6 checks the built-in IoResult integer function for Reset errors from line 46. If IoResult is zero, no error occurred, and the program continues to read the file from disk. But if IoResult is not zero, something went wrong. In this example, the program assumes any error means that the old file doesn't exist, so it sets Membership to zero (line 51) and ends the procedure. A more complete program would test the IoResult code, checking the error type according to the "I/O Errors" list in your *Turbo Pascal Programmer's Guide.* These error codes are identical to those reported by DOS; therefore, you can find descriptions of all codes returned by IoResult—too numerous to list here—in a DOS technical reference.

With I/O error checking off, you must follow every file operation—even simple Readln and Writeln statements—with IoResult checks. This is not optional; you must do it. See Figure 6-5 for a list of file operations that require IoResult checking.

```
Append, BlockRead, BlockWrite, ChDir, Close, Erase, Flush,
GetDir, MkDir, Read, Readln, Rename, Reset, Rewrite, RmDir, Seek,
SeekEof, SeekEoln, Truncate, Write, Writeln
```

Figure 6-5 When you turn off I/O checking with the compiler directive {$I-}, you must check function IoResult following these file operations.

Note: Chapter 13 explains how to use the directory procedures ChDir, GetDir, MkDir, and RmDir, which are listed in Figure 6-5. Chapter 18 lists examples for the special text-file seek functions SeekEof and SeekEoln.

Chapter 4 introduced the subject of side effects caused by procedures and functions that change global variables. IoResult is an example of a function with the *intended* side effect of resetting a global, internally stored error code. You can't reference this code directly—it's private to Pascal. Using IoResult returns the current error setting while resetting the internal value to 0. In other words, the IoResult value is valid only on its *first* use following an I/O operation.

Program 6-7 shows the wrong way to use IoResult. After prompting for a disk file name, the program tries to reset the file, checking IoResult in line 12 to see if any errors occurred. If so, line 14 writes the error code before ending. This doesn't work because checking IoResult in line 12 resets the internal error code to 0. Therefore, even if the program detects an error, it always reports "Error #0." Run the program and type existing and nonexisting file names to see the problem.

Program 6-7: BADCHECK.PAS (with errors)

```
1:   program BadCheck;
2:   var
3:     FileVar: Text;
4:     FileName: string[14];
5:   begin
6:     Write('Reset what file? ');
7:     Readln(FileName);
8:     Assign(FileVar, FileName);
9:   {$I-}
10:    Reset(FileVar);
11:  {$I+}
12:    if Ioresult <> 0
13:    then
14:      Writeln('Error #', IoResult)
15:    else
16:      begin
17:        Writeln('File opened');
18:        Close(FileVar)
19:      end;
20:    Readln
21:  end.
```

Program 6-8 corrects the bug in Program 6-7 by saving IoResult in an integer variable, ErrorCode (line 12). The program then tests ErrorCode (line 14) and, if the value is not 0, correctly displays the error message. Storing IoResult in a variable eliminates the side effect.

Program 6-8: GOODCHEC.PAS

```
1:   program GoodCheck;
2:   var
3:     FileVar: Text;
4:     FileName: string[14];
5:     ErrorCode: Integer;
6:   begin
7:     Write('Reset what file? ');
8:     Readln(FileName);
9:     Assign(FileVar, FileName);
10:  {$I-}
```

```
11:    Reset(FileVar);
12:    ErrorCode := IoResult;
13: {$I+}
14:    if ErrorCode <> 0
15:    then
16:      Writeln('Error #', ErrorCode)
17:    else
18:      begin
19:        Writeln('File opened');
20:        Close(FileVar)
21:      end;
22:    Readln
23: end.
```

Random Access Processing

Processing disk files at random resembles array indexing. The difference is that a file on disk might be much larger than the largest array you could hold in memory. For example, a hard disk drive can store many millions of bytes, but variables in memory are limited to about 65,000 bytes. Future microcomputer devices will store billions of bytes on disk. These *megabyte* and *gigabyte* devices expand the computer's memory but operate more slowly than fast memory circuits. For this reason, programs need special methods for reading and writing large disk files.

To randomly locate one record requires knowing the item's *record number*. A record number is similar to an array index. It uniquely identifies one record in a disk file. To access a particular record by its number, use Turbo Pascal's Seek command:

```
Assign(FileVar, 'CLUB.DAT');
Reset(FileVar);
Seek(FileVar, 2);
Read(FileVar, OneMember);
```

These four statements assign and open a file variable to the club database disk file. The third line seeks, or positions, an internal *file pointer* to the third record stored in the file. (The first record has record number zero. Therefore, seeking the second record number positions the file pointer to the third record, not the second.) Finally, the Read statement transfers a single record from disk to variable OneMember.

Program 6-9 uses this method to prompt for a record number. Then it prints the member's phone number and name. When you enter a record number (lines 27 and 28), the program seeks that record (line 31), reads it (line 32), and prints the phone number (lines 33 and 34). Notice that the program no longer has to read all records into an array. Instead, it reads the record you request, leaving the others on disk.

Program 6-9: CLUBPHON.PAS

```pascal
 1:  program ClubPhone;
 2:  const
 3:    FileName = 'CLUB.DAT';
 4:  type
 5:    FileType = (SystemRec, ActiveRec);
 6:    Member =
 7:      record
 8:        case RecKind: FileType of
 9:          SystemRec: (NumMembers : Integer);
10:          ActiveRec: (Name      : string[30];
11:                      Phone     : string[12];
12:                      Charges   : Real;
13:                      Payments  : Real    )
14:      end;
15:  var
16:    OneMember: Member;
17:    MemberFile: file of Member;
18:    RecordNumber: Integer;
19:
20:  begin
21:    Assign(MemberFile, FileName);
22:    Reset(MemberFile);
23:    Writeln;
24:    Writeln('Club Member Phone Numbers');
25:    repeat
26:      Writeln;
27:      Write('Member number? (0 to quit) ');
28:      Readln(RecordNumber);
29:      if RecordNumber > 0 then
30:      begin
31:        Seek(MemberFile, RecordNumber);
32:        Read(MemberFile, OneMember);
33:        with OneMember do
34:          Writeln(Phone, ' ....... ', Name)
35:      end
36:    until RecordNumber = 0;
37:    Close(Memberfile)
38:  end.
```

Seeking and Writing

With Seek, you can modify individual records without disturbing the others. You might, for example, add the programming in Figure 6-6 to Program 6-9. Now, after reading a record and displaying its phone number, the program lets you correct the number if it's wrong.

Replace line 19 with

```
Ch: Char;
```

Replace lines 33-34 with the following

```
with OneMember do
begin
  Writeln(Phone, ' ....... ', Name);
  Write('Change it? ');
  Readln(Ch);
  if Upcase(Ch) = 'Y' then
  begin
    Write('New number? ');
    Readln(Phone);
    Seek(MemberFile, RecordNumber);
    Write(MemberFile, OneMember)
  end
end
```

Figure 6-6 Modifications to Program 6-9 to change individual member phone numbers.

Notice in Figure 6-6 that another Seek repositions the file pointer before writing the modified record back to disk. Reading the record (Program 6-9, line 32) advances Pascal's internal file pointer to the *next* record. A Write also advances the file pointer one record. To avoid reading or writing the wrong records when processing files at random, always precede each Read or Write statement with a Seek.

Appending Records

A typical large database contains an interrelated collection of many data files. Operators often enter new data into separate disk files, then a simple program appends the new data to a main disk file, ready for sorting and further processing.

Although there are several ways to append records to disk files, the first step is to locate the end of the file. One approach does this by reading records until Eof becomes true:

```
while not Eof(MemberFile) do
   Read(MemberFile, OneMember);
```

Because the file might be empty, **while** is the correct repetitive statement to use. After the loop, a simple Write statement adds a new record at the file's end:

```
Write(MemberFile, OneMember);
```

Another approach takes advantage of the way Program 6-6 stores the number of records in the club database, keeping that value in a system record (record number 0). When you know where to find the last record, seeking the end of the file is easy:

```
Seek(MemberFile, 0);
Read(MemberFile, OneMember);
Seek(MemberFile, OneMember.NumMembers + 1);
```

The first Seek and Read load record 0, containing the case variant with the number of records stored in the file (see Program 6-6, lines 10 and 26-30). Having discovered how many records there are, the third statement seeks past the last record. As with the **while** loop approach, a simple Write can then add a new record.

After appending new records, regardless of the method you choose, the system record (number 0) no longer correctly shows the number of records in the file. To update this record, modify it as follows:

```
Seek(MemberFile, 0);
Read(MemberFile, OneMember);
with OneMember do
   NumMembers := NumMembers + NumAppends;
Seek(MemberFile, 0);
Write(MemberFile);
```

Of course, this assumes you kept track of the number of appended records in the variable NumAppends.

Appending Text Files

To append new text to the end of existing text files, use the Append procedure in place of Reset. Append opens a text file just like Reset, but positions the file to its end, ready to accept more text.

To use Append, first give a text file a name. Then pass Append the file variable. After that, use Write and Writeln statements to write text to the end of the file. Finally, Close the file, preserving your changes. For example, this adds two lines to a file named TEST.TXT:

```
var
  Tf: Text;

begin
  Assign(Tf, 'TEST.TXT');
  Append(Tf);
  Writeln(Tf, 'This is the first appended line');
  Writeln(Tf, 'This is the second appended line');
  Close(Tf);
end;
```

Processing Text Files at Random

Unlike the club database, where all records have identical structures and are therefore the same size, common text files have many lines all of different lengths. There is no easy way to seek a single line of text at random without reading all preceding lines.

Program 6-10 demonstrates one way to access disk text file strings at random. After opening the file in lines 11 and 12, the program prompts for a line number (lines 15 and 16). A **for** loop in lines 20 and 21 advances to that line, which is then displayed in line 22. Try entering the name of an example Pascal program stored in a disk file, then ask for one of the line numbers as printed in this book. As you can see in the **for** loop, Program 6-10 simulates random access by skipping over preceding strings until it finds the one you want.

Program 6-10: SEEKSTR.PAS

```
1:  program SeekStrings;
2:  var
3:    TextFile: Text;
4:    FileName: string[14];
5:    LineNumber, I: Integer;
6:    OneLine: string[80];
7:  begin
8:    Writeln;
9:    Write('Seek strings in what file? ');
10:   Readln(FileName);
11:   Assign(TextFile, FileName);
12:   Reset(TextFile);
13:   repeat
14:     Writeln;
```

continued

Program 6-10: continued

```
17:      if LineNumber > 0 then
18:      begin
19:        Reset(TextFile);
20:        for I := 1 to LineNumber do
21:          Readln(TextFile, OneLine);
22:        Writeln(LineNumber, ': ', OneLine)
23:      end
24:    until LineNumber = 0;
25:    Close(TextFile)
26:  end.
```

The program also demonstrates how to use Reset to reposition the file pointer to the top of the file, similar to rewinding a video tape to its beginning. Every time you enter a new line number (line 16), the program resets the file (line 19). Earlier, you learned that Reset opens existing disk files. When used this way, Reset repositions an already open file to its beginning.

Advanced File Handling

Turbo Pascal has a few special disk file-handling procedures. You can erase a file from disk with the Erase procedure:

```
Assign(MemberFile, 'OLDDATA.DAT');
Erase(MemberFile);
```

When erasing files, do not open them first. Erasing an open file is like closing a door with your foot in the doorway (see Figure 6-1). You could do some serious damage!

Another thing you can do is change the name of a disk file. The following statements rename the club database file to keep a backup copy on disk:

```
Assign(MemberFile, 'CLUB.DAT');
Rename(MemberFile, 'CLUB.BAK');
```

As with Erase, do not open the file before renaming. You could add similar statements to Program 6-6 to create a backup disk file before writing the new records array. Many word-processing programs use a similar method. For example, Turbo Pascal's text editor keeps backup copies of files in case of disk problems, or to allow going back to a previous revision if by mistake you delete something.

To create backup disk files properly, use programming similar to Figure 6-7. First, erase the old backup (if it exists), then rename the current disk file, making it the new backup. Finally, write the new data to disk. This avoids accidentally having the same name appear twice in a directory, a situation DOS does not allow. Rename does not check whether a new file name already exists. That's your responsibility.

Add this new constant between lines 4 and 5

```
BackName = 'CLUB.BAK';
```

Add the following statements between lines 30 md 31

```
{$I-}
  Assign(MemberFile, BackName);
  Erase(MemberFile);
  if Ioresult <> 0
    then { Ignore error };
  Assign(MemberFile, FileName);
  Rename(MemberFile, BackName);
  if Ioresult <> 0
    then { Ignore error };
{$I+}
```

Figure 6-7 Modifications to Program 6-6 to create a backup CLUB.BAK file before writing new records to disk.

Special Functions

FilePos returns the current position of the internal file pointer, equal to the current record number. The function value is type LongInt. Because programs can seek any record number, even outside the range of records stored on disk, FilePos can't detect attempts to seek beyond the end of the file. To catch this error, check IoResult after a disk read operation, not after Seek. If you run the following sample, you'll see that FilePos returns the value last given to Seek, regardless of whether IoResult reports an error:

```
Seek(MemberFile, RecordNumber);
{$I-} Read(MemberFile, OneMember); {$I+}
if IoResult <> 0
  then Writeln('**Error reading file');
Writeln('File position = ', FilePos(MemberFile));
```

Another special function, FileSize, returns the number of records in a file and is also a LongInt value. You can use it to write a handy function that checks for empty files:

```
function FileEmpty(var F: FileType): Boolean;
begin
  FileEmpty := FileSize(F) <= 0
end;
```

Notice the check for a file size less than or equal to 0. Presumably, if the size of the file is negative, something is seriously wrong. But even so, it would be a mistake to return FileEmpty equal to true in that unusual case! Although it might seem adequate to write FileSize(F) = 0, it takes no more time or effort to check FileSize(F) < = 0, which returns a correct value for even the most remote possibility. Covering all possibilities, no matter how unlikely, is a sound programming practice.

Untyped Files

Pascal treats untyped files as sequences of blocks, normally 128 bytes long. To declare an untyped file, use the key word **file** alone. (See Figure 6-2.) The following declares an untyped file, F:

```
var
  F: file;
```

Using BlockRead and BlockWrite

Two special procedures read and write untyped files. BlockRead reads and BlockWrite writes one or more disk blocks at a time. Each has two different formats.

```
{ Format A }
  BlockRead(F, Buffer, N);
  BlockWrite(F, Buffer, N);
{ Format B }
  BlockRead(F, Buffer, N, Result);
  BlockWrite(F, Buffer, N, Result);
```

File F is an untyped file variable; Buffer is any variable, usually an array. N is the number of blocks you want to read or write. In Format B, Result equals the number of blocks actually read or written after calling BlockRead or BlockWrite. If Result does not equal N, something prevented the procedure from completing the request to read or write this many blocks.

These procedures are extremely fast, transferring blocks of disk data to and from memory with no regard for data structure. The procedures might be used in high-speed database systems or in disk backup or copy programs.

Because BlockRead and BlockWrite operate on files in chunks, the file size must be a multiple of the chunk size to avoid an error when reading the last block in a file. In other words, if you are reading 256-byte chunks, the file size must be evenly divisible by 256 or you'll receive an I/O error when trying to read the last partial block.

In truth, all files on disk are stored in multiples of some chunk size—most likely, 512, 1024, or 2048 bytes each. Therefore, you might think that reading files 512 bytes at a time will almost always work. Unfortunately, that's not the case. Even though DOS may physically store data in 512-byte sectors, it keeps track in the disk directory of the actual number of bytes the file uses. This value, representing the usable file size, probably will not be a multiple of 512.

There are two ways around the dilemma, which, by the way, was not a problem in Turbo Pascal 3.0 and earlier versions. First, you can create files with sizes evenly divisible by a certain chunk size with BlockWrite and then read the file with BlockRead. This always works. For example, to create a file with ten, 256-byte blocks, you could write:

```
var
  F: file;
  Buffer: array[0 .. 255] of Byte;
  I: Integer;
begin
  Assign(F, 'TEST.DAT');
  Rewrite(F, 256);
  for I := 1 to 10 do
  begin
    { Insert data into buffer }
    BlockWrite(F, Buffer, 1)
  end;
  Close(F)
end;
```

File F is untyped. The buffer is large enough to hold 256 bytes. After naming the file with Assign, Rewrite creates a new file on disk. The second parameter to Rewrite specifies the block (chunk) size for subsequent BlockWrites, in this case, 256. Then, a **for** loop calls BlockWrite ten times, each time writing one buffer of data to disk. (The example doesn't check for errors, which a real program would, of course, have to do.) How the data gets in the buffer is up to you.

To read this same file a chunk at a time, simply reverse the process, using Reset instead of Rewrite and BlockRead instead of BlockWrite. Here's the code, using the same variables:

```
Assign(F, 'TEST.DAT');
Reset(F, 256);
while not Eof(F) do
begin
  BlockRead(F, Buffer, 1);
  { Process Buffer }
end;
Close(F);
```

After assigning the file name, Reset opens the file, specifying 256 bytes per block for subsequent BlockRead statements. Then, a **while** loop cycles, reading buffers full of data one by one until reaching the end of the file.

These methods of reading and writing files in blocks are extremely useful for rapidly getting data into and out of a program. You might stuff all sorts of things into buffers and transfer them to disk, then reload that same information later in a flash.

Single Byte Chunks

To read and write existing disk files using BlockRead and BlockWrite, open your file variables with a chunk size of one byte. This trick neatly guarantees that file sizes are multiples of the chunk size because every possible file size is, of course, a multiple of one!

Along with the Sizeof function, which returns the number of bytes occupied by a variable or data type, these ideas make it easy to write a fast file copy program. Program 6-11 shows the result.

Program 6-11: COPYFILE.PAS

```
 1:  program CopyFile;
 2:  const
 3:    MaxBuff = 10000;  { Bytes transferred at one time }
 4:  var
 5:    Buffer: array[1 .. MaxBuff] of Byte;
 6:    Original, Copy: file;
 7:    BytesRead, BytesWritten: Integer;
 8:
 9:  procedure OpenFiles;
10:  var
11:    FileName: string;
12:  begin
13:    Write('Original file name? '); Readln(FileName);
```

```
14:     Assign(Original, FileName);
15:     Reset(Original, 1);
16:     Write('Copy to file name? '); Readln(FileName);
17:     Assign(Copy, FileName);
18:     Rewrite(Copy, 1)
19:   end;
20:
21:   begin
22:     OpenFiles;
23:     repeat
24:       BlockRead(Original, Buffer, Sizeof(Buffer), BytesRead);
25:       if BytesRead > 0 then
26:       begin
27:         BlockWrite(Copy, Buffer, BytesRead, BytesWritten);
28:         if BytesRead <> BytesWritten then
29:         begin
30:           Writeln('Disk write error');
31:           {$I-} Close(Copy);
32:           Erase(Copy); {$I+}
33:           Close(Original);
34:           Halt(1)
35:         end
36:       end
37:     until BytesRead = 0;
38:     Close(Copy);
39:     Close(Original)
40:   end.
```

First, the program creates a 10,000-byte buffer (lines 2-5). You can make this byte array any size you want, within Turbo Pascal's usual limits. Original and Copy are untyped file variables. BytesRead and BytesWritten control the copying action.

After typing file names for the original and copy (lines 9-19), a **repeat** loop cycles until the copying is finished or until an error occurs. Carefully examine this loop. It demonstrates the correct way to use BlockRead and BlockWrite to process files of any size.

Line 24 calls BlockRead with four parameters: an untyped file variable, a buffer to hold the incoming data, the size of the buffer in bytes, and a variable, BytesRead. The third parameter tells BlockRead to load 10,000 bytes (or however big you make the buffer), using Sizeof to return the size of Buffer. Of course, the file might not have exactly 10,000 bytes, and in that case, BlockRead reads what it can, setting BytesRead equal to this number.

If BytesRead is not zero (line 25), BlockWrite writes the number of bytes specified by BytesRead from the buffer to the copy file (line 27). If the number of bytes requested to write (the third parameter to BlockWrite) does not equal the number of bytes actually written (BytesWritten), a disk error must have occurred.

Passing Files As Parameters

Files are variables and, as such, you can pass them by reference as parameters to procedures and functions. This lets you write procedures that redirect their input and output.

Program 6-12 demonstrates how to do this; it is a simple program that writes a line of text to three output files. The program passes each file to variable parameter F in procedure WriteText. Because Pascal does not allow passing files by value, you must use the **var** key word as shown here.

Program 6-12: FILEPARA.PAS

```
 1:  program FileParams;
 2:  var
 3:    Printer, Console: Text;
 4:    N: Integer;
 5:
 6:  procedure WriteText(var F: Text);
 7:  begin
 8:    Writeln(F, 'Test string number', N);
 9:    Inc(N)
10:  end;
11:
12:  begin
13:    N := 1;
14:    Assign(Printer, 'PRN');
15:    Assign(Console, 'CON');
16:    Rewrite(Printer);
17:    Rewrite(Console);
18:
19:    WriteText(Output);
20:    WriteText(Printer);
21:    WriteText(Console)
22:  end.
```

Although the example uses the predeclared file Text, you can pass other kinds of files too. However, because of the requirement that parameter types must be simple identifiers, you must first define a new file data type. Let's say you want to design a procedure to operate on integer data files. You might put the following declaration into your program:

```
type
    DataFile: file of Integer;
```

You can then write your procedure header with a formal file parameter DF of type DataFile:

```
procedure Operate(var DF: DataFile);
```

With another special procedure, you can chop the end of a file with Truncate. Let's say you want to limit a file to 100 records. These statements do it:

```
Seek(FileVar, 100);
Truncate(FileVar);
Close(FileVar);
```

Records numbered 0 through 99 remain in the file. Any records above that are now gone.

Summary

Files are like magic doors through which computers communicate with the outside world. Programs can have files for talking to devices such as printers, keyboards, and modems. They can also store and retrieve data in disk files.

Turbo Pascal has a variety of procedures for creating, reading, writing, and appending disk files. Programs can read and write disk files sequentially or at random, plucking out only the records they want. Because all files exist as binary data on disk, programs are free to interpret data as characters, records, single bytes, sectors, or blocks.

BlockRead and BlockWrite read and write data in chunks in sizes from 1 byte to 512 or more bytes. These procedures are useful for rapidly reading and writing to disk files. Another useful procedure is Truncate, which lops off the ends of files from any position.

You can pass file variables as parameters to procedures and functions, but only by reference. Turbo Pascal requires file parameters to be declared with the **var** key word.

Exercises

6-1. Write a program to read a text file and display all its lines backwards.

6-2. Write a program to concatenate (join) two text files into a single, long file.

6-3. Write the reverse program, in other words, a program to split a large text file into two smaller parts. Some text editors have a file size limit, and the program might be used to reduce long files to manageable size.

6-4. How might you increase the speed of Program 6-10? (Hint: Do you always have to reset the file for each new line, or is there another possibility?)

6-5. (Advanced) Write a program to read files as collections of blocks or sectors. Encrypt the file data with a user-entered key. The same key should also recover the original text of a previously encrypted file. Because of the potential for destroying data, test your program thoroughly on copies of files, before trusting it on valuable data.

6-6. (Advanced) Write a program to read lines of text, sort them into ascending order, and then write the sorted lines to a new file. (Use the sorting method described in Chapter 5.)

6-7. Start your own database system. Design a program to read and write disk files of fixed length, eight-character strings. Write procedures to search, edit, delete, sort, and print reports.

7

Pointers, Lists, and Trees

- Creating Pointers
- Using Pointer Variables
- Comparing Pointers
- Pointers to Nowhere
- Notes on Drawings
- Why Use Pointers?
- One-Way Lists
- Memory Management
- Circular Lists
- Trees
- Dynamic Arrays
- Explicit Addressing
- Absolute Variables
- Absolute Pointers
- Overlaying Absolute Variables

7

@, Absolute, Addr, Dispose, FreeMem, GetMem,
Mark,MaxAvail, MemAvail, New, **nil**, Ptr, Release, Sizeof

Memory bytes have addresses, unique values that identify where bytes are located. Ignoring electronic technicalities, when a computer reads a byte's value, it sends the byte's address to memory circuits, which return the value of the addressed byte. To store a new value in memory, the computer again sends the address, followed by the value to store at that location.

In Pascal, a *pointer* variable holds a memory address. That's all a pointer is— a memory address. By specifying an address, a pointer *points* to a unique location in memory. Stored at that location is the actual value the pointer addresses. There is a difference, therefore, between the value of a pointer and the value stored at the location where the pointer points—an important difference to keep in mind.

Pointers can point to simple byte values, integers, real numbers, records, strings—any Pascal data type. The actual value is stored in memory. The pointer locates the first byte of that value.

Creating Pointers

To create a pointer, type a caret, which resembles the point of an arrow, in front of any data type identifier. For example, the following creates a pointer named ValuePointer:

```
var
  ValuePointer: ^Integer;
```

ValuePointer is a pointer to an integer stored somewhere in memory. You can declare pointers to other Pascal types, too. Here are a few more examples:

```
type
  ArrayType = array[1 .. 10] of Byte;
var
  RealPointer: ^Real;
  ArrayPointer: ^ArrayType;
  RecPointer: ^Member;
```

These statements create pointers to a real number (RealPointer), to an array of 10 bytes (ArrayPointer), and to a Member record (RecPointer) borrowed from Chapters 5 and 6. Each pointer is associated with, or *bound to,* a specific type of value. Notice that in the case of the array, you first have to declare an ArrayType identifier and then create a pointer to it. The same is true for records, sets, and other structured types.

Using Pointer Variables

Before a program uses a pointer, it first requests memory space for the type of data the pointer addresses. In other words, a program must initialize its pointers—simply declaring them is not enough. To initialize a pointer, use the New command with any pointer variable:

```
New(ValuePointer);
```

New does two things. First, it reserves space for a value of the type ValuePointer addresses, in this case, an integer, taking two memory bytes. Second, New assigns the address of the reserved memory to ValuePointer. After executing New, ValuePointer points to a two-byte integer stored in memory.

You rarely have to examine or use the actual address of a pointer. In fact, a main reason for using pointers is to eliminate explicit addressing from programs while giving you the advantages only pointers can give. To store a value in memory at the location addressed by ValuePointer, use a caret after the pointer name:

```
ValuePointer^ := 100;
```

This stores 100 at the location addressed by ValuePointer. The caret signifies not the pointer itself, but the intent to access the thing pointed to—an action called *dereferencing the pointer.* When you do want to use the pointer directly, omit the caret. By doing this, you can transfer an address of one pointer variable to another. Let's say you have these two pointers to type integer:

```
var
    PointerA, PointerB: ^Integer;
```

A program can then reserve memory for PointerA and assign the same *address* to PointerB with the two statements:

```
New(PointerA);
PointerB := PointerA;
```

PointerB now addresses the same location in memory as PointerA (see Figure 7-1). The program hasn't assigned a value to this place in memory and, therefore, the value is unknown (shown by a question mark in the drawing):

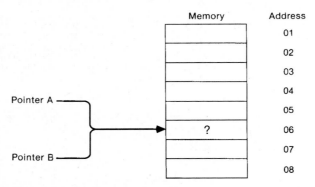

Figure 7-1 After the assignment PointerB := PointerA, the two pointers have the same address and, therefore, point to the same memory Location.

On the other hand, suppose the program reserves two different locations in memory. To transfer the *value* addressed by PointerA to the location addressed by PointerA use carets to signify the things to which the pointers point:

```
New(PointerA);
New(PointerB);
PointerA^ := 100;
PointerB^ := pointerA^ + 1;
```

In these four statements, New assigns to each pointer the address of newly reserved memory space. The third statement then assigns 100 to the location addressed by PointerA (See Figure 7-2). It can do this because the value addressed by the pointer is type integer; therefore, the program can store integers at this place in memory. Finally, as Figure 7-2 illustrates, the fourth and final statement assigns one plus the value at the location addressed by PointerA to the location addressed by PointerB.

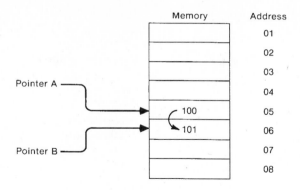

Figure 7-2 The result of the assignment PointerB^ := PointerA^ + 1. After using New to reserve memory for the two pointers, the value stored at the location addressed by one pointer is assigned to the location addressed by the other.

Comparing Pointers

Because pointers ignore the specifics of memory addressing, you can compare them only for equality in expressions. As these **if** statements show, Pascal allows equality and inequality comparisons on pointers:

```
if (PointerA = PointerB)
   then <statement>;
if (PointerA <> PointerB)
   then <statement>;
```

You cannot compare the ordering of pointers with the relative operators <, >, <=, and > =. Because Pascal guarantees nothing about the actual locations of pointer-addressable items in memory, it makes no sense to test if a pointer to one item is less or greater than another. If such comparisons were allowed, they would likely produce different results on computers with different memory organizations.

Despite this limitation, you can compare values addressed by pointers, provided such comparisons would normally be allowed on variables of the same data type. For instance, if PointerA and PointerB point to two integers, then Pascal allows this statement:

```
if PointerA^ <= PointerB^
   then <statement>;
```

With carets attached to the two pointer identifiers, Pascal compares the values addressed by the pointers, not the pointers themselves.

Pointers to Nowhere

Pascal defines a special value, **nil**, meaning no specific address. You can assign **nil** to a pointer of any type:

```
PointerA := nil;
```

Setting PointerA to **nil** signifies that the pointer does not address a valid memory location. If you assign **nil** to all pointers, programs can test the pointers to see if they require initialization:

```
if PointerA = nil
  then  New(PointerA);
```

Notes on Drawings

Throughout this chapter, you will see drawings of data structures, some that have **nil** pointer values. Look ahead, for example, to Figure 7-3. There, an electrical grounding symbol—the three horizontal lines to the right of the figure—represents the value, **nil**.

This drawing and others display pointer-addressable values conceptually and do not necessarily represent actual memory bytes. One of the best ways to understand pointers is to develop a mental model of the relationships between pointers and the data they address. The purpose of the diagrams is to help you develop that image, not to provide an X-ray picture of actual memory circuits.

Why Use Pointers?

If a pointer simply addresses a value—a variable like any other—what's the difference? Why go to the trouble of creating a pointer to a variable? Why not just use a simple Pascal variable instead?

One reason is that pointer-addressable variables occupy memory taken from a pool of bytes called the *heap*. Programs declare pointers and let the system figure out where in the heap to store the actual values. With hundreds or thousands of pointers—a common situation when using pointers to construct lists and trees as explained later in this chapter—it's easier to let the computer calculate where to store new values than to do the address calculations yourself.

The second reason pointers are valuable is their ability to use memory efficiently. As a contrast, consider arrays. Programs have to specify the maximum number of items in an array. If the array is half full, the unused positions are wasted. Pointers eliminate such waste by creating data structures that dynamically expand, taking only as much or as little memory as required. Such programs run on small systems while automatically taking advantage of a larger computer's extra memory. A spreadsheet program that has more "cells" on a larger computer than on a smaller one is a good example of this dynamic approach to memory management.

One-Way Lists

By creating pointers to values in memory and then using other pointers to link the values, programs create lists, which do not have fixed sizes. They might be empty, or they might contain thousands of items. To find individual values, you search through the items in a list as though you were thumbing through the pages of a book.

Lists are easier to understand if you draw them out as in Figure 7-3. Paper and pencil, it turns out, are one of the best tools for learning about lists!

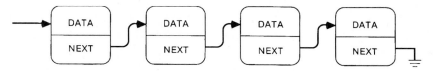

Figure 7.3 Links in values point to other values, creating a list.

If you could see a list in memory, it would appear as shown in Figure 7-3. Each item in the list points to the next item. Items in the list are Pascal records declared as follows:

```
type
  ItemPointer = ^Item;
  Item = record
    Data:  string[20];
    Next: ItemPointer
  end;
```

These type declarations define ItemPointer as a pointer to type Item, a record with two fields. Notice that the pointer type declaration comes *before* Item, the thing to which an ItemPointer points. This is the one time in Pascal where you may use identifiers before defining them. This bending of the rules lets you define a pointer field of the same type inside the record. As shown here, Item's second field, Next, is such a pointer. It points to another Item record of the same structure. This would be impossible if Pascal didn't allow pointer types to be declared in advance of the values they address.

Earlier, you learned about recursive procedures and functions—routines that call themselves into action. In similar fashion, a record type like Item is an example of a *recursive data structure*. It recursively points to a value of its own type.

List Insertion

Inserting a value into a list is a simple matter of requesting memory space for the new value and then adjusting two pointers. If NewItem is a variable of type ItemPointer, and OldItem addresses the value in front of where you want to insert this new record (Figure 7-4), then the following statements insert the new record into the list of Figure 7-3.

```
New(NewItem);
NewItem^.Next := OldItem^.Next;
OldItem^.Next := NewItem;
```

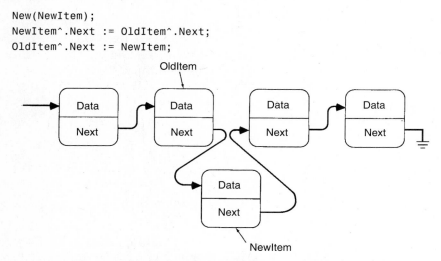

Figure 7-4 Inserting variables into linked lists is a matter
of adjusting two pointers.

Take that process a step at a time, and it's easy to understand. First, New creates space on the heap for one Item record, assigning the address to NewItem. Then, two assignment statements adjust Next pointers to link the new Item record into the list. Notice how the carets access Next fields in the records addressed by the NewItem and OldItem pointers. Remember that these two variables are *pointers,* but with carets attached, NewItem ^ and OldItem ^ refer to Item records, the values to which the pointers point.

List Deletion

Deleting a value from a list is even easier. Again, given pointers NewItem and OldItem as in Figure 7-4, this statement deletes the item addressed by NewItem:

```
OldItem^.Next := NewItem^.Next;
```

After the assignment, the list again resembles Figure 7-3. Assigning the Next pointer field of NewItem ^ to OldItem ^ . Next effectively *unlinks* the item addressed by NewItem. But you don't even need the NewItem pointer. This command does the same thing:

```
OldItem^.Next := OldItem^.Next^.Next;
```

That may look confusing, but it's not hard to follow if you remember Next is just a pointer to another Item, which also has a Next pointer field. A few more examples further explain this idea. Given the list in Figure 7-5, then:

```
A^.Next                 --  addresses B
A^.Next^.Next           --  addresses C
A^.Next^.Next^.Next     --  addresses D
```

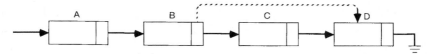

Figure 7-5 Linked lists are joined by pointers inside the variables in the list.

Having pointer A, to delete item C, you can write:

```
A^.Next^.Next := A^.Next^.Next^.Next
```

In English, this statement assigns the Next field of C to the Next field of B, thus skipping C. After the assignment, B's Next field directly addresses D, shown by the dotted line in Figure 7-5.

But, you might wonder, where does the deleted variable go? In Figure 7-5, what happens to deleted C? Ideally, its memory space is automatically reclaimed for use by other pointers and variables later in the program. Unfortunately, Pascal does not realize this ideal and, in practice, leaves deleted variables floating *out there,* scattered wastelands in memory, unreachable by your program. To reuse that space, programs have to manage computer memory carefully, as the next section explains.

Memory Management

As you just learned, procedure New allocates memory space for a pointer-address-able variable. This memory is taken from an available-memory pool called the *heap,* an area of memory independent of the stack, where Pascal stores return addresses, value parameters, and local variables. Manipulating the heap does not affect any other program variables, only those addressed by pointers. In other words, values on the heap are always global—they exist outside of the scope of any procedures and functions.

In Program 7-1, variable NewItem is a pointer to an Item record. The program demonstrates that using New to create variables in memory decreases the amount of total memory available for other values. To test available memory, lines 15 and 23 use a built-in LongInt function MemAvail in Writeln statements similar to this:

```
Writeln('Memory = ', MemAvail);
```

MemAvail returns the number of bytes available on the heap. Usually, this number equals the total amount of memory in your computer minus the memory occupied by DOS, your program, and a few other miscellaneous items.

Program 7-1 calls New 10 times in a **for** loop (lines 17-21). On each pass through the loop, MemAvail displays the amount of free memory left (line 20).

Program 7-1: HEAPDEMO.PAS

```
 1:   program HeapDemo;
 2:   type
 3:     ItemPointer = ^Item;
 4:     Item = record
 5:       Data: string[20];
 6:       Next: ItemPointer
 7:     end;
 8:   var
 9:     NewItem: ItemPointer;
10:     I: Integer;
11:   begin
12:     Writeln;
13:     Writeln('Heap Demonstration');
14:     Writeln;
15:     Writeln('Starting memory = ', MemAvail);
16:     Writeln;
17:     for I := 1 to 10 do
18:     begin
19:       New(NewItem);
20:       Writeln(I:3, ': After new, memory = ', MemAvail:5)
21:     end;
22:     Writeln;
23:     Writeln('Ending memory = ', MemAvail);
24:     Readln
25:   end.
```

As you can see when you run the program, using New reduces the amount of memory available on the heap by adjusting an internal heap pointer that Pascal keeps hidden from view. Figure 7-6 illustrates the heap before and after running Program 7-1. Allocating space for new variables increases the heap pointer by raising the top of the heap and reducing the amount of free memory available for other values. (Higher memory addresses are at the top of Figure 7-6.)

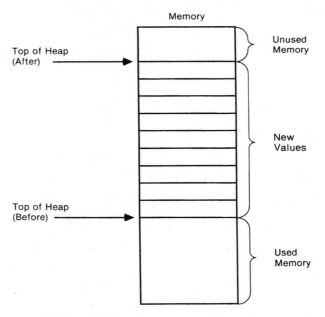

Figure 7-6 New allocates space for variables in a memory area called the heap.

Recording the value of the heap pointer before using New and then restoring that value later reclaims the memory space occupied by pointer-addressable variables. The reclaimed memory is then available for new variables. Two built-in procedures, Mark and Release, manage the usually invisible heap pointer to make this possible.

Except for lines 11, 13, and 25, Program 7-2 is similar to Program 7-1. Line 11 declares Heap of type Pointer, a generic type that is compatible with any other Pascal pointer. In this example, we are interested in the pointer values themselves—not in the variables that pointers address. Generic Pointer variables don't address specific values—they just hold address values.

Mark in line 13 sets Heap equal to the current value of the internal heap pointer. After the **for** loop executes (lines 19-23), Release restores the internal heap pointer to its original value (line 25). When you run the program, the amount of available memory before and after the **for** loop is the same, proving that the used space has been reclaimed.

Program 7-2: HEAPDEM2.PAS

```
 1:  program HeapDemo2;
 2:  type
 3:    ItemPointer = ^Item;
 4:    Item = record
 5:      Data: string[20];
 6:      Next: ItemPointer
 7:    end;
 8:  var
 9:    NewItem: ItemPointer;
10:    I: Integer;
11:    Heap: Pointer;
12:  begin
13:    Mark(Heap);
14:    Writeln;
15:    Writeln('Heap Demonstration');
16:    Writeln;
17:    Writeln('Starting memory = ', MemAvail);
18:    Writeln;
19:    for I := 1 to 10 do
20:    begin
21:      New(NewItem);
22:      Writeln(I:3, ': After new, memory = ', MemAvail:5)
23:    end;
24:    Writeln;
25:    Release(Heap);
26:    Writeln('Ending memory = ', MemAvail);
27:    Readln
28:  end.
```

Using Mark and Release to record and reset the internal heap pointer can be dangerous. After resetting the heap pointer to its original value, variables previously created remain in the unused portion of memory, as shown by "Old Data" in Figure 7-7. Old pointers still may address portions of this memory. There's nothing to prevent you from using them and doing so is likely to cause serious problems if you subsequently create new variables *in the same space,* overwriting any values stored at the old pointer locations.

The rule to remember is: After releasing the heap, never use pointers allocated by New since you last marked the top of the heap. As another example, these statements create two variables on the heap:

```
New(Item1);
Mark(Heap);
```

```
New(Item2);
Release(Heap);
```

Item1 is in protected memory. Item2 is in the unused portion of the heap after Release. Heap is a plain Pointer. Figure 7-8 shows the heap after those four statements execute. When you release the heap pointer, Item2 is in unprotected memory.

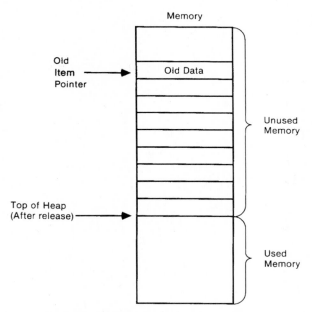

Figure 7-7 One way to reclaim heap space is to Mark the top of the heap and then execute Release to reset the heap pointer to the marked location.

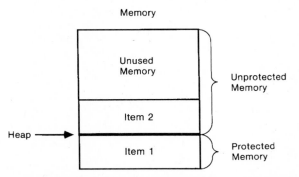

Figure 7-8 A danger of releasing the heap is that old pointers may address unprotected memory.

Disposing Variables

In addition to Mark and Release, Turbo Pascal offers a more sophisticated way to manage heap memory. In this new approach, programs *dispose* individual variables to return their space to the available memory pool. Pascal automatically keeps track of all such disposed items.

As Program 7-3 demonstrates, Dispose reclaims the memory occupied by variables (line 21) allocated by New. After disposal, the same memory space is available for new variables.

Program 7-3: HEAPDEM3.PAS

```
 1:  program HeapDemo3;
 2:  type
 3:     ItemPointer = ^Item;
 4:     Item = record
 5:       Data: string[20];
 6:       Next: ItemPointer
 7:     end;
 8:  var
 9:     NewItem: ItemPointer;
10:     I: Integer;
11:  begin
12:     Writeln;
13:     Writeln('Heap Demonstration');
14:     Writeln;
15:     Writeln('Starting memory = ', MemAvail);
16:     Writeln;
17:     for I := 1 to 10 do
18:     begin
19:       New(NewItem);
20:       Writeln(I:3, ': After new, memory = ', MemAvail:5);
21:       Dispose(NewItem)
22:     end;
23:     Writeln;
24:     Writeln('Ending memory = ', MemAvail);
25:     Readln
26:  end.
```

Because of the way Turbo Pascal manages heap memory, disposing numerous variables can cause *fragmentation,* a condition that shatters the heap into islands of occupied and unoccupied territory. If it weren't for this disadvantage, disposing pointer-addressable variables would attain the earlier-mentioned ideal of automatically reclaiming used memory space. An example illustrates the problem. If a program has four pointers and then executes the following statements, the heap appears as shown in Figure 7-9.

```
New(Item1);
New(Item2);
New(Item3);
New(Item4);
Dispose(Item2);
```

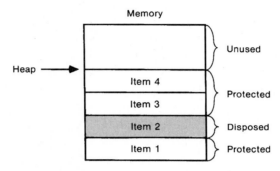

Figure 7.9 Disposing an individual item in the heap reclaims the item's space but can also fragment the heap.

As the shaded portion of Figure 7-9 shows, Item2's disposed space is available for new items. Even so, that space is only large enough for items no bigger than Item2. In seriously fragmented memory, with hundreds or more unconnected, disposed variables, there might be plenty of total memory available but no single space large enough to hold new variables. Although Turbo Pascal can join adjacent items—for example, combining Item3 and Item4 in Figure 7-9 if these records were disposed—memory spaces are not shuffled to maximize the amount of free space available, a process called *garbage collection,* found in some other languages, most famously in Lisp.

Usually, you can minimize fragmentation by applying a few simple rules. First, avoid designing programs that create many small values of different sizes. Larger variables tend to produce less fragmentation; smaller variables, more. You might also add dummy fields to records to make them the same size as others. This way, new records fit neatly into disposed spaces. In fact, if *all* records are identical sizes, the danger of fragmentation is *completely eliminated.* Of course, this drastic solution may not be practical in all cases. Creating variables of sizes in bytes that are multiples of other record sizes (16, 32, 64, and so on) can also help reduce fragmentation.

Turbo Pascal keeps track of disposed variables by linking them together. When a program disposes a variable, Turbo Pascal's heap manager stores a record in the space formerly occupied by the variable's value. This record has the form

```
type
  PFreeRec = ^TFreeRec;
  TFreeRec = record
    Next: PFreeRec;    { Points to next free block }
    Size: Pointer      { Fake pointer = size of block }
  end;
```

A System variable called FreeList addresses the first disposed, or *free,* variable on the heap, in which Turbo Pascal stores an initialized record of type TFreeRec. (The T in TFreeRec reminds you this is a "Type" declaration.) The Next field, of type PFreeRec, addresses the next disposed block, if any. The Size field is declared as a Pointer, but is treated as a 32-bit value divided into two parts. The high 16-bit part represents the number of 16-byte "paragraphs" in the disposed block, and the low 16-bit part represents the number of additional bytes not accounted for by the first part. Together, the two values specify the size of a disposed block in a way that is advantageous to the heap manager's inner workings. (You'll rarely if ever need to refer to these values, so don't be concerned about memorizing these details.)

Since the combined sizes of the Next and Size fields in the TFreeRec record total 8 bytes, variables created by New on the heap must always be at least 8 bytes long. If you attempt to create a 3-byte variable on the heap, Turbo Pascal will reserve 8 bytes, wasting 5. Larger variables have their sizes rounded up to the next multiple of 8 bytes. If you attempt to create a 21-byte variable, the heap manager will reserve 24 bytes, the next highest multiple of 8. Although this scheme may seem wasteful, in practice, it can reduce heap fragmentation, especially in programs that allocate heap variables of arbitrary sizes.

Measuring Disposed Memory

Function MaxAvail returns a value equal to the largest available disposed memory space. This allows you to test whether there is enough space for new variables. MemAvail returns the total space available, which may be greater than MaxAvail after disposing other values on the heap. To use MaxAvail properly, you also need the help of function Sizeof, which returns the number of bytes occupied by a variable or data type. Assuming P is a pointer to type RecType, this **if** statement tests whether there is adequate memory for a RecType variable:

```
if MaxAvail >= Sizeof(RecType)
then
  New(P)
else
  Writeln('Out of memory');
```

Remember that MaxAvail returns the value of the largest unbroken space. MemAvail returns the *total* amount of available memory, including all disposed spaces. In seriously fragmented memory, MemAvail might indicate plenty of room even though no single area of memory is large enough for new variables.

The Avail Stack

A third memory-management technique, one that works under all versions of Turbo Pascal as well as with other Pascal compilers, links disposed variables into a list of available memory space. Although there is no active data in these values, the method uses existing pointer fields to link deleted items.

The list is handled as a stack, a data structure that resembles a stack of dishes in a spring-loaded bin. The first dish placed on the stack is the last taken off. The data structure, a list, operates in the same fashion. The first item inserted, or *pushed,* into the list is the last one to be taken, or *popped,* off.

To use the avail stack method, first declare a pointer Avail as an ItemPointer, addressing a list of disposed variables (Figure 7-10). Initialize Avail to **nil**. To remove an item from the Avail list, use the following **if** statement:

```
if Avail = nil
then
  New(NewItem)
else
begin
  NewItem := Avail;
  Avail := Avail^.Next
end;
```

Figure 7-10 Another method for managing memory is to link disposed items into an Avail stack.

The effect of the **if** statement (Figure 7-11) is to pop one disposed item from the Avail list. If the list is empty (Avail = **nil**), New creates a new variable on the heap. Therefore, additional heap space is taken up only if there are no disposed spaces available.

To push an item onto the Avail stack, do this:

```
NewItem^.Next := Avail;
Avail := NewItem;
```

Those two statements link the disposed item (addressed by pointer NewItem) into the list and set Avail to the item's address, changing Figure 7-11 back into Figure 7-10.

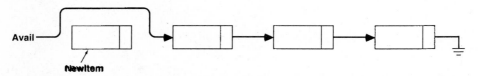

Figure 7-11 Popping the Avail stack removes the first item from the linked list.

To demonstrate these concepts, Program 7-4 declares two lists, Avail and ItemList, both pointers to Item records. Lines 63-64 initialize these pointers to **nil**, emptying both lists at the start.

When you press key A, AddItem (lines 49-54) adds a new item to ItemList. When you press D, DeleteItem (lines 56-60) deletes an item from the list, inserting the item into the Avail list. If you delete more items than you add, the program pushes empty uninitialized items onto the Avail stack. After each addition and deletion, the program displays both lists along with the total amount of free memory (lines 28-47).

The critical procedures in this program are Push (lines 13-17) and Pop (lines 19-26). Push inserts an item into a list. Pop removes one item. Notice that Pop creates a new variable if the list is empty. When writing programs to manipulate lists, it's especially important to handle empty lists correctly. Forgetting to deal with this situation is a common cause of bugs.

When you run the program, you'll see memory decreasing for each newly added item. After making a few deletions and inserting deleted items into the Avail list, you'll see that new items use disposed memory space before taking up new memory from the heap.

Adding a new variable (lines 49-54) is a matter of popping space from the Avail stack and assigning values to the item. To demonstrate this, the example assigns a random integer (line 52) before pushing the item into the ItemList. Of course, in your own programs, you'd assign whatever data you want to insert in the list.

Reversing the process deletes variables. As lines 56-60 show, the program does this by popping the ItemList and then pushing the popped item onto the Avail stack.

Program 7-4: AVAIL.PAS

```
1:    program AvailStack;
2:    uses Crt;
3:    type
4:      ItemPointer = ^Item;
5:      Item = record
```

```
 6:      Data: Integer;
 7:      Next: ItemPointer
 8:    end;
 9:  var
10:    Avail, NewItem, ItemList: ItemPointer;
11:    Ch: Char;
12:
13:  procedure Push(var NewItem, List: ItemPointer);
14:  begin
15:    NewItem^.Next := List;
16:    List := NewItem
17:  end;
18:
19:  procedure Pop(var NewItem, List: ItemPointer);
20:  begin
21:    if List = nil then New(NewItem) else
22:    begin
23:      NewItem := List;
24:      List := List^.Next
25:    end
26:  end;
27:
28:  procedure ShowList(P: ItemPointer);
29:  begin
30:    while P <> nil do
31:    begin
32:      Writeln(P^.Data:8);
33:      P := P^.Next
34:    end;
35:    Writeln
36:  end;
37:
38:  procedure Display;
39:  begin
40:    ClrScr;
41:    Writeln('Memory = ', MemAvail);
42:    Writeln;
43:    Writeln(' Avail list');
44:    ShowList(Avail);
45:    Writeln(' Item list');
46:    ShowList(ItemList)
47:  end;
48:
```

continued

Program 7-4: continued

```
49:   procedure AddItem;
50:   begin
51:     Pop(NewItem, Avail);
52:     NewItem^.Data := Random(Maxint);
53:     Push(NewItem, ItemList)
54:   end;
55:
56:   procedure DeleteItem;
57:   begin
58:     Pop(NewItem, ItemList);
59:     Push(NewItem, Avail)
60:   end;
61:
62:   begin
63:     Avail := nil;
64:     ItemList := nil;
65:     repeat
66:       Display;
67:       Writeln; Writeln('-----------');
68:       Write('A.dd, D.elete, Q.uit ? ');
69:       Ch := Readkey;
70:       case Upcase(Ch) of
71:         'A': AddItem;
72:         'D': DeleteItem
73:       end
74:     until Upcase(Ch) = 'Q'
75:   end.
```

Circular Lists

Stacks are only one of the many kinds of dynamic structures that are easy to create with Pascal pointers. So far, we've created lists organized in only one direction. For example, all the pointers in the one-way list illustrated in Figure 7-10 point the same way.

Adding a second pointer creates a bidirectionally linked list—a structure that's easier to visualize by imagining linear lists of items with pointers to the right and left (Figure 7-12). There are several advantages to using such *doubly linked* lists.

One advantage is the ability to search for items either backward or forward. You must search one-way lists (Figure 7-10) in a forward direction. When a program points to the third item in a one-way list, it has no way to go back to the previous item. But from any place in a two-way list (Figure 7-12), a search can go to the right or left—all items are readily available from any starting place.

Besides being doubly linked, the list in Figure 7-12 is circular. Follow either the right (thin-line) or left (heavy-line) pointers, and you'll discover no beginning or end to this list. (Doubly linked lists do not have to be circular, although they often are. The leftmost L and rightmost R pointers in Figure 7-12 could be **nil**, still linking the list in two ways, but giving it a beginning and end.)

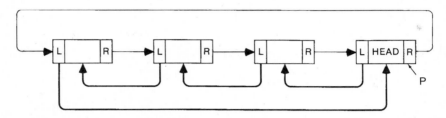

Figure 7-12 Items in doubly linked circular lists have both left and right pointers.

Because a circle has no beginning or end, and therefore no explicit beginning of a circular list for a program to address, managing circular lists is easier with a dummy item, called the *list head*, as one of the variables in the list. As explained earlier, empty lists require careful handling. Unfortunately, with circular lists, the programming tends to be complicated unless the dummy circular list head is never deleted from the list. That way, a circular list is never empty—avoiding, if not solving, the problem. The dummy list head also makes insertions and deletions simple to program.

To create a circular list, first declare a pointer to a record type with Left and Right pointer fields as follows:

```
ItemPointer = ^Item;
Item = record
  Data: string[20];
  Left, Right: ItemPointer
end;
```

Initialize the list by allocating a new variable in memory, setting the item's Left and Right fields to point to their own record:

```
New(P);
P^.Left := P;
P^.Right := P;
```

Pointer P is a variable of type ItemPointer. The statements create the list illustrated in Figure 7-13. If you compare Figures 7-12 and 7-13, you can see that the list is empty when either the Left or Right field of the list head points to its own record. Knowing this leads to a simple Boolean function test for an empty list:

```
function Empty: Boolean;
begin
  Empty := (P^.Left = P)
end;
```

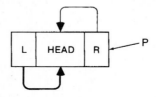

Figure 7-13 A list head, which is never deleted, makes doubly linked circular lists easier to handle. The list head shown here is initialized to point to itself.

However, when $P^\wedge$.Left = $P^\wedge$.Right, the list is not necessarily empty, even though it may appear so from Figure 7-13. Look at Figure 7-14 for an example—the list head left and right pointers are equal (because they address the same item), but the list is not empty.

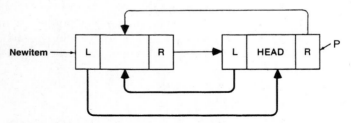

Figure 7-14 Adding a new item to the list head in Figure 7-13 produces this new, two-variable list.

The next four statements insert new items into a circular list. Pointer P addresses the list head. Another pointer NewItem addresses the new item to insert. First execute New(NewItem) and then:

```
NewItem^.Left := P;
NewItem^.Right := P^.Right;
P^.Right^.Left := NewItem;
P^.Right := NewItem
```

These statements applied to Figure 7-13 create the two-element list shown in Figure 7-14. For a better understanding of how this works, execute the four statements by hand.

You can also insert new items anywhere in the list, not only at the list head. To do this, replace P with a pointer to any list variable and execute the same four statements. One of the primary advantages to using doubly linked circular lists is the ability to insert new items given only a single pointer to any list element.

Similarly, it's easy to delete doubly linked items. For example, these statements delete NewItem ^ in Figure 7-14:

```
NewItem^.Left^.Right := NewItem^.Right;
NewItem^.Right^.Left := NewItem^.Left;
```

This reassigns the Left and Right fields of the items surrounding the one to delete. Again, try the statements on paper, applying them to Figure 7-14. You should end up with the list in Figure 7-13. Also, try deleting items from the longer list in Figure 7-12. What happens if, by accident, you delete the dummy list head?

After unlinking NewItem ^ this way, you would normally Dispose it or link it into an Avail stack using one of the methods described earlier.

Trees

A tree is a special kind of linked list. Trees are difficult to describe—there are many variations and many disagreements among computer scientists about how to define them. For our purposes, though, a computer tree is more like a family tree than a tree in nature.

Family trees come in two varieties: pedigree trees listing an individual's ancestors and lineal trees showing the descendants of parents. Computer trees more closely resemble the lineal type. The *nodes* in a family tree are people. When drawn out, these nodes, linked with branching lines, have a treelike structure.

You probably have seen lineal trees like the one in Figure 7-15, which represents the genealogy of the rulers of Tenochtitlan, the nation centered in the land that is now Mexico City. In Pascal trees, pointer variables replace the lines. Records replace the people. By the way, I chose this particular example to illustrate trees because the Aztec names in the figure remind me of the unreadable identifiers Pascal programmers sometimes create.

The analogy between family trees and trees in computer memory is imperfect. Genealogies like the one in Figure 7-15 have several complications normally disallowed in computer trees. For example, the same name often appears more than once, or there might be unusual links as in the case of the prolific Huitziliahuitl (top right of Figure 7-15).

Roots

One similarity between family trees and the computer kind is that both have roots. Your great-great-grandparents might be at the root of your family tree. Opochtzin and Atotoztli are the root parents of the genealogy in Figure 7-15.

In Pascal, the root is simply a pointer to the starting place in the tree. In fact, some authorities recursively define a tree as any structure with a root that is empty or points to the root of another tree. In other words, a tree is a structure composed of subtrees, linked to a common root. Cut off the root, and what's left is a forest of subtrees. Join two subtrees, and you have a single tree with a common root.

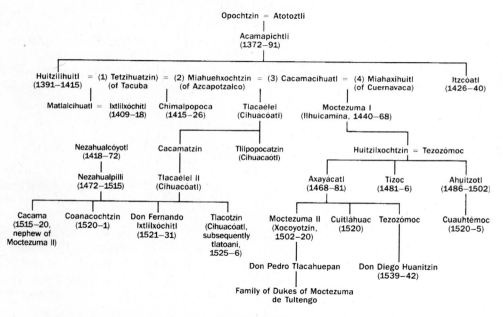

TENTATIVE GENEALOGY OF THE ROYAL DYNASTY OF TENOCHTITLAN

Figure 7-15. Computer trees resemble family trees, similar to this genealogy of the leaders of Tenochtitlan. (Davies, N. The Aztecs. London: Macmillan, 1973. Reprinted with permission of the publisher.)

BinaryTrees

A special kind of tree is the binary tree. Binary trees have roots and nodes each with a maximum of two branches, one to the left and one to the right. Every node in a binary tree, including the root, either points nowhere or points to a subtree. When both branches point nowhere, the node is called a *leaf.*

Figure 7-16 shows a binary tree of fruit names. The root of this fruit tree is MANGO, which has two subtrees, (BANANA, APPLE, CHERRY) and (PEACH, PEAR). Removing the root MANGO makes a forest of two subtrees with roots BANANA and PEACH.

The leaves of the fruit tree are APPLE, CHERRY and PEAR. There are no branches growing from these nodes. PEACH is the root of a lopsided subtree with no branches to the left.

Programs can represent binary tree nodes as Pascal records, defined like this:

```
ItemPointer = ^Item;
Item = record
  Data: string[20];
  Left, Right: ItemPointer
end;
```

Surprisingly, this definition is identical to the Item records used earlier in doubly linked, circular lists. This is an important observation. A structure's organization makes it a tree—not the composition of nodes or the data in them.

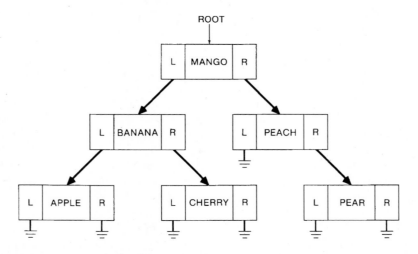

Figure 7-16 A "fruit tree" as it might appear in a computer's memory.

Tree Traversal

Programs traverse binary trees in three ways. Traversing means going from node to node and doing something with the data in each node. The three methods are *pre-order*, *in-order*, and *post-order*.

Clearly, at any single node, a program has three choices. It can move to the node on the left, move to the right, or process the data in the node. The exact nature of what it means to "process the data in the node" is unimportant for now. You might print out a string variable, increment a counter, or assign a value to a node variable. Important here is the concept of *when* a process activates, not *what* the process does.

Table 7-1 lists the three ways of traversing binary trees. It's easy to remember the three methods by observing when node processing occurs. Pre-order traversal processes nodes *before* going left and right. In-order processes nodes *in between* going left and right, and post-order processes nodes *after* going left and right.

Table 7-1 Binary tree traversal methods.

Pre-order	In-order	Post-order
Process node	Go left	Go left
Go left	Process node	Go right
Go right	Go right	Process node

Each of the three traversal methods is recursive. The instruction "Go left" means to follow the left pointer to the next node and then start that traversal method over *from the top*. If a pointer has the value **nil**, then simply go on to the next step.

If "process node" means to write out data stored in that node, then pre-order traversal of the fruit tree in Figure 7-16 produces (MANGO, BANANA, APPLE, CHERRY, PEACH, PEAR). In-order traversal produces (APPLE, BANANA, CHERRY, MANGO, PEACH, PEAR). Post-order makes (APPLE, CHERRY, BANANA, PEAR, PEACH, MANGO). Each traversal order produces a differently ordered list of data from the same tree.

Notice that in-order traversal of the tree in Figure 7-16 alphabetizes the fruit names. This happens because, in this particular tree, nodes branching left are alphabetically less than, and nodes branching right are alphabetically greater than, their parent nodes. In-order traversal respects this ordering, and the list comes out in alphabetic order.

Trees and Recursion

The definition of a tree is recursive because it states that a tree is any root node that points to another tree. Because trees are naturally recursive, it is equally natural to write recursive procedures to manipulate them. This leads to simple procedures for traversing binary trees according to the three traversal methods described in Table 7-1.

Program 7-5 implements the three traversal methods in three recursive procedures: PreOrder, InOrder, and PostOrder. InOrder (lines 18-26) first tests if the passed node is **nil** (line 20). If not, lines 22-24 execute the in-order method, that is, following all left branches, processing the node, then following the right branches. The **if** test satisfies the requirement that the recursion end, as it must if the tree has a finite number of leaves with **nil** branches. The other two procedures (lines 28-36 and 38-46) operate similarly but process the node at different times.

Notice how the procedures in Program 7-5 mirror the descriptions of the three traversal methods in Table 7-1. The algorithm becomes the program—supporting evidence for Pascal's reputation as an *algorithmic* language.

Without recursion, these same procedures are much more difficult to write. There isn't room here to examine the alternative, but it can be done. Recursion is never a requirement, only a convenience. All recursive programs have equivalent, nonrecursive solutions.

Program 7-5 creates a tree by adding new data that you type in—fruit names for example—with calls to procedure Search in lines 48-66. Search also calls itself recursively (lines 62-63).

The procedure does two things. First, in lines 52-59, if Root is **nil**, the program creates a new root node (line 54). It also adds new data to this node and sets both left and right pointers to **nil** (line 57). The actual Root value might represent any root of any subtree, not necessarily the main root.

The second job for procedure Search is to find the correct place in the tree to add new data. This happens in lines 62-64, which execute only if the current Root is not **nil**. In two **if** statements, Search recursively calls itself, tracing the left branches if NewData<Data or right branches if NewData>Data. If the new data is neither greater nor less, then it is already stored in a node, and the program prints the error message in line 64. Right and Left are pointers, remember, and Search takes a variable parameter in line 48. Passing these pointers as the roots of subtrees eventually finds the **nil** pointer to which the new data should attach.

It is remarkable that the entire search and insert procedure is so concisely written while taking only a single pointer as its input. Once again, for a better understanding of the process, execute Search by hand, inserting new nodes into a paper tree.

Program 7-5: TREE.PAS

```
1:   program Tree;
2:   type
3:     String20 = string[20];
4:     ItemPointer = ^Item;
5:     Item = record
6:       Data: string 20;
```

continued

Program 7-5: continued

```
 7:      Left, Right: ItemPointer
 8:    end;
 9: var
10:    NewData: string 20;
11:    Root: ItemPointer;
12:
13: procedure Process(Node: ItemPointer);
14: begin
15:    Write(Node^.Data, '   ')
16: end;
17:
18: procedure InOrder(Node: ItemPointer);
19: begin
20:    if Node <> nil then
21:    begin
22:      InOrder(Node^.Left);
23:      Process(Node);
24:      InOrder(Node^.Right)
25:    end
26: end;
27:
28: procedure PreOrder(Node: ItemPointer);
29: begin
30:    if Node <> nil then
31:    begin
32:      Process(Node);
33:      PreOrder(Node^.Left);
34:      PreOrder(Node^.Right)
35:    end
36: end;
37:
38: procedure PostOrder(Node: ItemPointer);
39: begin
40:    if Node <> nil then
41:    begin
42:      PostOrder(Node^.Left);
43:      PostOrder(Node^.Right);
44:      Process(Node)
45:    end
46: end;
```

```
47:
48:  procedure Search(var Root: ItemPointer);
49:  { Search for global NewData string in tree. }
50:  { If not found, insert it, else give error. }
51:  begin
52:    if Root = nil then
53:    begin
54:      New(Root);
55:      with Root^ do
56:      begin
57:        Data := NewData; Left := nil; Right := nil
58:      end
59:    end else
60:    with Root^ do
61:    begin
62:      if NewData < Data then Search(Left) else
63:      if NewData > Data then Search(Right)
64:        else Writeln('Error: Duplicate data!')
65:    end
66:  end;
67:
68:  begin
69:    Writeln('Tree test');
70:    Root := nil;
71:    repeat
72:      Write('Data (Enter to quit)? ');
73:      Readln(NewData);
74:      if Length(NewData) > 0
75:        then Search(Root)
76:    until Length(NewData) = 0;
77:    Writeln;
78:    Writeln('PREORDER:');
79:    PreOrder(Root);
80:    Writeln; Writeln;
81:    Writeln('INORDER:');
82:    InOrder(Root);
83:    Writeln; Writeln;
84:    Writeln('POSTORDER:');
85:    PostOrder(Root);
86:    Writeln;
87:    Readln
88:  end.
```

Balanced Trees

When you run Program 7-5, enter the fruit names in this order: MANGO, BANANA, APPLE, CHERRY, PEACH, PEAR. What happens if you enter the names in a different order?

If you enter data in alphabetic order, the tree becomes unbalanced (Figure 7-17). An unbalanced tree has all or most of its branches going in one direction. You could balance the tree in Figure 7-17 by making BANANA the root and setting its LEFT pointer to address APPLE, the current root node. A good explanation of balanced trees in Pascal is in Niklaus Wirth's *Algorithms + Data Structures = Programs* (see Bibliography).

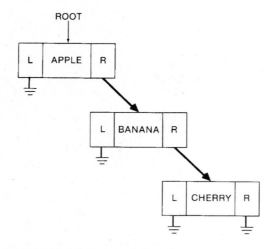

Figure 7-17 This binary tree is unbalanced. All its branches go in one direction.

Dynamic Arrays

One common complaint about Pascal is the inability of a program to change the size of an array at run time. In some languages, you can declare array boundaries as variables, changing the size of arrays as needed when programs run. In Pascal, array index ranges must be constants, and, therefore, array sizes are fixed when you compile the program. If you have this array declaration:

```
var
   BigArray: array[1 .. 100] of string[80];
```

then, to change the size of the array, you have to manually change the 100 to something else and recompile. Some programmers get around the problem by declaring arrays like this:

```
var
   BigArray: array[1 .. 1] of string[80];
```

Because Turbo Pascal normally has range checking off, as though you included the compiler directive {$R–} at the top of all programs, it allows statements such as the following even though BigArray has only one, and not 20, declared elements:

```
BigArray[20] := 'String Twenty';
Writeln(BigArray[20]);
```

Unfortunately, the element at BigArray[20] might be at the same position as other variables or program code in memory! Assignments like the one above can easily destroy data or even wreck your program's code in memory.

Allocating Heap Space

One way to have dynamic arrays and protect memory at the same time is to use two special procedures, GetMem and FreeMem, to allocate and dispose heap space in a way that is different from other pointer methods.

Use GetMem to allocate a specific number of bytes on the heap and assign the address of the first byte to a pointer variable. To dynamically create an array of 20 strings, use the statement:

```
GetMem(P, NumElements * Sizeof(OneElement));
```

Function Sizeof returns the number of bytes occupied by a data type or variable, here OneElement. GetMem reserves enough bytes on the heap for NumElements elements and assigns the address of the first element to P. Assuming P points to an array data type, the following statement assigns a string to element number twenty, and displays it:

```
P^[20] := 'String Twenty';
Writeln(P^[20]);
```

To deallocate space on the heap, use FreeMem with the same arguments to GetMem:

```
FreeMem(P, NumElements * Sizeof(OneElement));
```

FreeMem is equivalent to Dispose except that it gives you full control over the number of bytes to free. After freeing heap space, do not use pointer P. The memory that P addresses is no longer reserved for the program's use!

Program 7-6 demonstrates how to use this idea to create dynamically expanding arrays. Line 12 calls GetMem to allocate space for NumElements array items, which two **for** loops then fill and display (lines 13-16).

The declaration in line 4 may seem odd. (In fact, I frequently receive letters from readers claiming array declarations like this are typographical errors.) Declaring the array boundaries as [0 .. 0] is not a mistake. Although this appears to specify an array with only one index entry [0], with range checking off as it normally is, Turbo Pascal allows programs to ignore the declared boundaries and use indexes like [100] or [50]. Of course, it's up to you to make sure there is a variable at those locations, as done here in line 12.

The program declares Item as type Integer in line 3, using Item in the array declaration (line 4) and again later when allocating memory for the array (line 12). This makes it easy to change the array element type. For example, you can change Integer to LongInt in line 3, and the program still runs correctly.

Program 7-6: DYNAMIC.PAS

```
 1:  program DynamicArray;
 2:  type
 3:     Item = Integer;
 4:     StringArray = array[0 .. 0] of Item;
 5:  var
 6:     Dynarray: ^StringArray;
 7:     NumElements, I: Integer;
 8:  begin
 9:     Write('How many array elements? ');
10:     Readln(NumElements);
11:     Writeln('Memory before = ', Memavail);
12:     GetMem(Dynarray, NumElements * Sizeof(Item));
13:     for I := 0 to NumElements - 1 do
14:        Dynarray^[I] := I;
15:     for I := 0 to NumElements - 1 do
16:        Write(Dynarray^[I]: 8);
17:     Writeln; Writeln;
18:     Writeln('Memory after = ', Memavail);
19:     Readln
20:  end.
```

Explicit Addressing

Usually, you don't have to worry about where in memory Turbo Pascal stores variables. In fact, that's one reason for using a high-level language like Pascal in the first place—to avoid using explicit addresses as you must do in assembly language programming.

Sometimes, though, you will need to know where a certain variable is. Or, you might need to assign specific addresses to pointers. Turbo Pascal contains several features for handling these situations.

To find the address of any variable, procedure, or function, precede the identifier with an @ (at) sign. For example, suppose you have these declarations:

```
var
  Q: Real;
  P: ^Real;
```

Variable Q, a Real number, exists somewhere in memory. Variable P is a pointer to type Real. To make P point to Q, you can type:

```
P := @Q;
```

This assigns the *address* of Q to pointer P. Because P now points to Q, the following statements both assign Pi to the *same* variable in memory:

```
Q := Pi;    { Assign Pi to Q }
P^ := Pi;   { same as above! )
```

There's no practical reason for making such assignments to simple variables—you may as well just use the variable identifier. But there is an advantage to using a similar idea to assign values to array elements, as the next two programs demonstrate.

Programs 7-7 and 7-8 assign Pi to item number 52 of an array of Real numbers. The two **for** loops in both programs repeat this step five million times. (Change the 500 to 50 or lower for PC or XT computers. The program takes about 10 seconds to finish on an 80386, 25-MHz system. It will take longer on slower systems.)

Program 7-7 uses typical array indexing, assigning Pi to A[K] in line 11, with K equal to 52. On my system, five million such assignments takes about 9 seconds.

Program 7-7: ARRAYA.PAS

```
1:  program ArrayIndexA;
2:  var
3:    A: array[1 .. 100] of Real;
4:    I, J, K: Integer;
```

continued

Program 7-7: continued

```
 5:   begin
 6:     K := 52;
 7:     Write('Press Enter to start...');
 8:     Readln;
 9:     for J := 1 to 500 do      { 50 on PC, XT and clones }
10:     for I := 1 to 10000 do
11:       A[K] := Pi;
12:     Write(Chr(7))   { Beep! }
13:   end.
```

Program 7-8 uses the pointer method to assign Pi to the same array element as in Program 7-7. Line 7 of the new program sets pointer P to the address of A[52]. Then, inside the two **for** loops, line 12 assigns Pi to the address to which P points. Because the program no longer has to calculate the same address, as it does in Program 7-7, the results are better—about 6 seconds.

Program 7-8: ARRAYB.PAS

```
 1:   program ArrayIndexB;
 2:   var
 3:     A: array[1 .. 100] of Real;
 4:     I, J: Integer;
 5:     P: ^Real;
 6:   begin
 7:     P := @A[52];
 8:     Write('Press Enter to start...');
 9:     Readln;
10:     for J := 1 to 500 do      { 50 on PC, XT and clones }
11:     for I := 1 to 10000 do
12:       P^ := Pi;
13:     Write(Chr(7))   { Beep! }
14:   end.
```

Even this small improvement could be important in a critical program. Remember that you can always take the address of any variable (@V), assign the address to a pointer to the same data type (P:=@V), and then use the pointer with a caret (P^) in place of the variable identifier (V).

Turbo Pascal has a function, Addr, that you can use in place of @. Both of the following statements assign the address of Q to P:

```
P := @Q;          { Assign address of Q to P }

P := Addr(Q);     { Same as above }
```

The only reason to use Addr instead of @ is if you plan to transfer your programs to other Pascal compilers, which might not recognize the @ symbol. In this case, you could write your own Addr function to return the address of variables and save time modifying your program.

Absolute Variables

Absolute variables exist at specific memory addresses. They can be any data type and exist anywhere in memory. You can declare variables at known locations or declare absolute variables on top of other Pascal variables and let the compiler figure out the addresses. An absolute variable is a sort of antipointer. Instead of using pointers to avoid explicit addressing, you can use absolute variables to force Pascal to use specific memory locations.

The form of an absolute variable is the same as any other variable declaration but includes the key identifier Absolute plus a memory address with both segment and offset values. For example, this declares a variable at the location of the print-screen status byte:

```
var
   Status: Byte Absolute 0000:$0500;
```

Variable status is *not* a pointer to 0000:$0500. It's a variable at a specific location that you specify in the Absolute declaration. Use status like any other variable. For example, this sets the print-screen status byte to 1:

```
Status := 1;
```

Doing this disables the print-screen key by fooling the computer into thinking a print-screen operation is in progress. Change the 1 to 0 to enable the key again.

Absolute Pointers

Another way to fix variables at specific locations is to assign a known address to a pointer variable. With a single pointer, all computer memory is available to your program. Such control is powerful but dangerous. You can easily overwrite portions of your program in memory, the operating system, or both.

Be sure you understand the difference between using an absolute variable and a pointer to a fixed address. To create a pointer variable to the address of the status byte and disable the print-screen key, you would have to write:

```
var
  StatPtr: ^Byte;
begin
  StatPtr := Ptr(0000, $0500);
  StatPtr^ := 1
end
```

The Ptr function takes a segment and offset value, which together specify one location in memory. Ptr returns a memory pointer, assigned here to StatPtr, a pointer to type Byte. Storing 1 at this location disables the print-screen key. Storing 0 enables the key again. Although this has the same effect as using the absolute variable, one extra step is required to assign the address to the pointer variable. Also, four bytes of memory are required to hold the StatPtr pointer. Absolute variables occupy no memory—they merely tell the compiler at which address to store and retrieve values.

Overlaying Absolute Variables

Specifying the identifier of a declared variable in place of a literal address overlays the variable at the same address. When you assign a value to one variable, the value of the other changes, too.

Program 7-9 shows how this works. Line 3 declares a byte variable, ASCII. Line 4 declares a character variable, Ch. The program prints the alphabet by using ASCII in a **for** loop but writing Ch. Although the program assigns nothing to Ch, it cycles through letters A to Z! It does this because at line 4, the program declares Ch to coexist in memory at the absolute address of ASCII.

Program 7-9: DOUBLEUP.PAS

```
 1:  program DoubleUp;
 2:  var
 3:    ASCII: Byte;
 4:    Ch: Char Absolute ASCII;
 5:  begin
 6:    for ASCII := 65 to 90 do
 7:      Write(Ch:2);
 8:    Writeln;
 9:    Readln
10:  end.
```

Summary

An understanding of pointers is vital to mastering Turbo Pascal. In this chapter, you learned that pointers are memory addresses that point to variables in memory. Programs manage the heap, where Pascal stores pointer-addressable variables, and use the Mark and Release, Dispose, or Avail stack methods to reclaim space occupied by old data.

Linked lists and trees are two important data structures, easily managed with the help of Pascal pointers. Using pointers, programs create lists, insert and delete objects, and manage stacks and doubly linked, circular list structures. Trees, recursive by nature, are easily managed with recursive procedures to create, search, and traverse nodes containing data.

By using GetMem, you can allocate memory on the heap, a method that lets you create dynamic arrays. FreeMem disposes the allocated memory.

Explicit addressing techniques let you assign addresses of variables, procedures, and functions to pointers. You can also declare absolute variables at specific locations in memory. Such abilities are powerful but dangerous if used improperly.

Exercises

7-1. Write a program to read a disk file of strings and insert the strings into a one-way list. Include a procedure to display the strings after reading.

7-2. Revise your answer in 7-1 to use a circular, two-way list. Add a procedure to search the list for specific values, printing the previous and next string.

7-3. (Advanced) Develop a procedure to exchange two objects in a circular list. It should take as parameters pointers to the two objects to exchange. Use your procedure in a program to sort a list *without* moving data, only adjusting pointers. Why is this better than the array-sorting method in Chapter 5?

7-4. Revise Program 7-5 to take its input from a disk text file.

7-5. Describe the three methods of memory management and explain the advantages and disadvantages of each.

7-6. Rewrite Program 7-4 *without* using any pointers.

7-7. (Advanced) Write a family-tree program. It should print out nodes in a treelike graph similar to Figure 7-15. Develop a set of general procedures for saving tree nodes on disk. What special problems does this present?

8

Strings

- String Length
- Directly Setting String Length
- String Operators
- String Procedures
- String Functions
- Strings As Parameters
- Writing Your Own String Functions
- Special Characters
- Numbers to Characters
- Character Constants in Strings

8

Key Words and Identifiers

Chr, Concat, Copy, Delete, Insert, Length, **packed**, Pos, **string**

In early versions of Pascal, strings were simple arrays of characters, and the only string operation was assignment. Today, most Pascal compilers, including Turbo Pascal, come equipped with built-in string procedures and a string data type. Previously, you would declare a 20-character string variable like this:

```
var
   Name: packed array[1 .. 20] of Char;
```

The key word **packed** tells some Pascal compilers, but not Turbo Pascal, to place each character in as little space as possible—usually a single byte. Assignments to Name would require exactly 20 characters, including extra blanks:

```
Name := 'Susan               ';
```

Turbo Pascal's string data type simplifies character strings by allowing *dynamic* string variables that expand or contract according to the number of significant characters in the string. You can still declare strings as arrays of characters, but there is seldom a good reason for doing so. (Turbo Pascal ignores the **packed** key word, automatically putting characters into single bytes in character arrays.) To declare a 20-character string variable, type a length value in brackets after the key word, **string**:

```
var
   Name: string[20];
```

Declared this way, the length of Name depends on its contents. The size of the variable in memory—the total amount of space it occupies—doesn't change but can hold anywhere from zero to 20 characters. You now can assign both short and long strings to Name without worrying about trailing blanks.

```
Name := 'Susan';                    { 5 characters }
Name := 'abcdefghijklmnopqrst';  { 20 characters }
```

Figure 8-1 shows the railroad diagram for Turbo Pascal's string data type. Inside the brackets, or the alternate symbols (. and .), you can specify lengths from one to 255 characters. The declared length represents the maximum number of characters that the string may hold. The actual length of the string varies according to how many significant characters the string contains. If you don't specify a string length in brackets, Turbo Pascal creates a 255-character, maximum-length string. In other words, these two declarations create variables of the same lengths:

```
var
  MyString: string[255];
  YourString: string;
```

Program 8-1 demonstrates function Length, which returns the number of characters in a string. Although you can also use Length with character arrays, the value the function returns always equals the number of bytes in the array, rather than the number of significant characters. Therefore, you should normally use Length only with string variables.

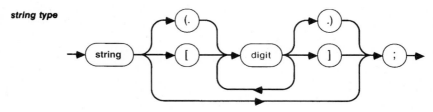

Figure 8-1 Railroad diagram for declaring **string** data types.

Program 8-1: STRLEN.PAS

```
1:  program StringLength;
2:  var
3:    S: string[80];
4:  begin
```

continued

Program 8-1: continued

```
 5:    repeat
 6:      Writeln;
 7:      Write('Enter a string: ');
 8:      Readln(S);
 9:      Writeln('Length = ', Length(S))
10:    until Length(S) = 0
11:  end.
```

String Length

To record a string's actual length, Pascal stores a normally invisible single byte in front of all string variables. For example, the eight-character string in Figure 8-2 has five significant characters (HELLO) and three wasted positions. Because of the added length byte, string variables occupy one byte more than their declared lengths.

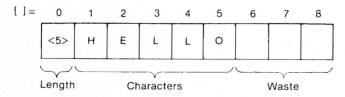

Figure 8-2 In memory, a string variable begins with a length byte followed by an array of characters.

As you can see from Figure 8-2, a string is simply an array of characters with the addition of a length byte. As with other arrays, you can index strings a character at a time. But, you cannot do the same with string constants—you can index only variables or variable constants. To demonstrate in-memory string representation, Program 8-2 is similar to Program 8-1 but shows the indexed characters of whatever string you enter. Enter HELLO, and you'll see a display that resembles Figure 8-2.

Program 8-2: STRINDEX.PAS

```
1:  program StringIndexing;
2:  const
3:    Blank = ' ';    { Single blank }
```

```
 4:  var
 5:    S: string[14];
 6:    I: Integer;
 7:  begin
 8:    repeat
 9:      Writeln;
10:      Write('Enter a string: ');
11:      Readln(S);
12:      for I := 0 to Length(S) do
13:        Write('[', I:2, ']', Blank);
14:      Writeln;
15:      Write(Ord(S[0]):3, Blank:2);
16:      for I := 1 to Length(S) do
17:        Write(S[I]:3, Blank:2);
18:      Writeln
19:    until Length(S) = 0
20:  end.
```

Line 15 of Program 8-2 shows a different way to find the length of a string. We know that the first byte of any string holds the length; therefore, the following statement is true:

```
Length(S) = Ord(S[0]);
```

In other words, the ordinal (integer) value of the byte at string index zero equals the length of the string. Because the Length function returns this value, there are few good reasons for directly accessing the length byte as shown here. At times, however, it's helpful to be able to preset the length of a string to some value before actually assigning any characters:

```
S[0] := Chr(5);
```

This sets the length of string S to five. The first five characters, left over from previous operations, are again made significant. Because all positions in the string are characters, to avoid a "Type mismatch" error, you must use the Chr function to assign the length value.

The result of this assignment is simply to store a five in the length byte of the string. The method works even if you turn range checking on with the compiler option {$R+}. Unlike other arrays, Turbo Pascal always allows you to index S[0], although many other compilers consider zero to be outside the normal string range of S[1] . . . S[N], where N is the declared string length.

Directly Setting String Length

As a practical example of setting the string length byte, procedure DeTrail (Program 8-3, lines 9-20) removes trailing blanks from string parameter S. The procedure searches for the first nonblank character starting from the end of the string and proceeding in a **while** loop to the front. It correctly handles empty strings as well as those with all blanks.

Program 8-3: TRAILERS.PAS

```pascal
 1: program Trailers;
 2: const
 3:   maxLen = 80;
 4: type
 5:   String80 = string[80];
 6: var
 7:   S: String80;
 8:
 9: procedure DeTrail(var S: String80);
10: var
11:   I: Integer;
12:   Looking: Boolean;
13: begin
14:   I := Length(S); Looking := true;
15:   while (I > 0) and Looking do
16:   if S[I] = ' '
17:     then Dec(I)
18:     else Looking := false;
19:   S[0] := Chr(I);
20: end;
21:
22: begin
23:   Writeln('Remove trailing blanks');
24:   repeat
25:     Writeln;
26:     Write('Enter a string: ');
27:     Readln(S);
28:     Writeln('Length before ..... ', Length(S));
29:     DeTrail(S);
30:     Writeln('Length after ...... ', Length(S))
31:   until Length(S) = 0
32: end.
```

DeTrail indexes the string with variable I, while looking for blank characters (line 16). If the procedure finds a blank, it decrements I and continues searching. Otherwise, it sets Boolean variable Looking to false, ending the **while** loop at lines 15-18. The **while** loop also ends if I becomes equal to zero.

String Operators

As with numbers, you can check if two strings are equal or if one is less than the other. The usual mathematics operators (=, < >, <, >, <=, and >=) apply to strings as well as to numeric values. The results, however, depend on the alphabetic order of characters in the string.

In addition to comparing two strings, you can combine them with Concat, short for "concatenate." Concat combines two or more strings into a single string variable. Program 8-4 demonstrates how Concat works. In line 8, the program adds to Result each new string you enter. You could replace line 8 with the following statement, which does the same thing:

```
Result := Result + Entry;
```

When concatenating strings, be careful to keep the result within the maximum declared string length. No harm is done if you exceed the maximum, but Turbo Pascal ignores any extra characters.

Program 8-4: CONCATS.PAS

```
 1:  program Concatenation;
 2:  var
 3:    Entry, Result: string[80];
 4:  begin
 5:    Result := '';
 6:    repeat
 7:      Write('Entry? '); Readln(Entry);
 8:      Result := Concat(Result, Entry);
 9:      Writeln('Result = ', Result)
10:    until Length(Entry) = 0
11:  end.
```

You can combine several strings with one operation. Let's say you have three string variables, Last = 'Smith', First = 'John', and Middle = 'Q'. A mailing label program might concatenate the three strings this way:

```
Name := First + ' ' + Middle + '.' + ' ' + Last;
```

This sets Name to the string, 'John Q. Smith', inserting the proper spacing and punctuation.

Because the plus sign has a higher precedence than the relational operators (see Appendix E), you can safely compare concatenated strings in expressions like these:

```
if S = 'IBM' + 'XT'
   then <statement1> else
if S = 'IBM' + 'AT'
   then <statement2>
```

Turbo Pascal concatenates the literal strings 'IBM' and 'XT' or 'AT' before comparing with S.

String Procedures

There are several procedures and functions available to manipulate strings. Procedure Delete removes a specified number of characters from anywhere inside a string. Insert does the opposite, inserting characters into a string at any position.

Insert requires three parameters: the string or character to insert, the string into which the insertion goes, and the indexed position where the insertion begins. Program 8-5 demonstrates how this works, inserting successive characters from A to K into string S at index 6, in other words, at S[6]. When you run the program, you see characters already in the string move to the right to make room for new insertions.

Program 8-5 also demonstrates Delete, which takes three parameters: a string, the starting position of the deletion, and the number of characters to remove. Line 16 deletes one character from S at indexed position 6 (S[6]). Doing this eleven times removes the previous insertions.

Program 8-5: INSDEL.PAS

```
1:  program InsDelDemo;
2:  var
3:    S: string[80];
4:    Ch: Char;
5:    I: Integer;
6:  begin
7:    S := 'abcdefghijk';
8:    Writeln(S);
```

```
 9:     for Ch := 'A' to 'K' do
10:     begin
11:       Insert(Ch, S, 6);
12:       Writeln(S)
13:     end;
14:     for I := 1 to 11 do
15:     begin
16:       Delete(S, 6, 1);
17:       Writeln(S)
18:     end;
19:     Readln
20:   end.
```

String Functions

Two functions copy strings and search for substrings inside string variables. Function Copy takes the same parameters as Delete, but instead of removing characters, Copy simply transfers them to another variable. If string Name equals 'WASHINGTON', then the following sets Name to 'SHING':

```
Name := Copy(Name, 3, 5);
```

The first Copy parameter is a string variable, the second is the starting indexed position in the string, and the third is the count of characters to copy. This writes the first character of any string:

```
Write(Copy(S, 1, 1));
```

If you ask for more characters than available, Copy returns only as many characters as it can, up to the end of the string. If you use an index beyond the actual string length, Copy returns the null string ('')—a string with zero length.

Function Pos returns the indexed position of one string in another. Pos returns zero if it fails to find the substring. Using Pos, you can easily write a program to search for embedded strings in a text file.

Program 8-6, which demonstrates Pos, prompts for the name of a text file in which to search for strings. (Enter the full file name, for example, PROG1.PAS or TEST.TXT.) The program prints all lines containing your search string. As a programmer's utility, the program finds statements that use a certain variable name. For example, try searching for all uses of Ch and **for** in Program 8-5 (assuming, of course, you saved the program on disk.) What happens when you search for single-character variables such as I or N?

The program holds your search string in variable SubString (line 29). Procedure UpperCase converts all characters in the string to uppercase. Failing to do this would require the exact upper- and lowercase spelling of search strings. (Remove lines 32 and 39 to see the effect of not converting to uppercase.)

Variables OneLine and Temporary hold lines of text. After converting Temporary to uppercase (line 39), function Pos searches for SubString (line 40). Pos takes two parameters: the string to search for and the string in which to search. It returns the indexed position where it finds the first character of SubString, or zero if the string is absent. If SubString = 'SHING' and Temporary = 'WASHINGTON', then:

```
Pos(SubString, Temporary);
```

returns three, indicating the index where SHING starts in WASHINGTON.

Program 8-6: SEARCH.PAS

```
1:  program Search;
2:  type
3:     BigString = string[132];
4:  var
5:     FileName: string[14];
6:     FileVar: Text;
7:     LineNumber: Integer;
8:     OneLine,
9:     Temporary,
10:    SubString: BigString;
11:
12: { Convert all chars in s to upper case }
13: procedure UpperCase(var S: BigString);
14: var
15:    I: Integer;
16: begin
17:    for I := 1 to Length(S) do
18:       S[I] := Upcase(S[I])
19: end;
20:
21: begin
22:    Write('Search what text file? ');
23:    Readln(FileName);
24:    Assign(FileVar, FileName);
25:    repeat
26:       Writeln;
27:       Reset(FileVar);
```

```
28:        Write('Search for? (Enter to quit) ');
29:        Readln(SubString);
30:        if Length(SubString) > 0 then
31:        begin
32:          UpperCase(Substring);
33:          LineNumber := 0;
34:          while not Eof(FileVar) do
35:          begin
36:            Readln(FileVar, OneLine);
37:            Inc(LineNumber);
38:            Temporary := OneLine;
39:            UpperCase(Temporary);
40:            if Pos(SubString, Temporary) > 0
41:              then Writeln(LineNumber:3, ': ', OneLine)
42:          end
43:        end
44:     until Length(SubString) = 0
45:  end.
```

Strings As Parameters

When designing your own procedures and functions with string parameters, Turbo Pascal normally insists that the declared lengths of actual parameters match the lengths of formal parameters. In other words, if you design a procedure with a variable parameter ParamString of type **string**[40], you can pass only string variables of that same size to the procedure.

While this automatic check prevents a dangerous error, it also imposes an often annoying restriction. The danger looms when you pass a string by reference to a procedure or function, and that string is smaller than the type of the formal parameter. In this situation, a concatenation or other operation in the procedure might cause the formal parameter to grow larger than the maximum length of the actual variable, thus overwriting other items in memory. On the negative side, restricting formal parameters to the same size as their actual variables, while preventing this error, also makes it hard to design procedures to operate on all strings, regardless of length.

Luckily, it's easy to turn string length checking off, as Program 8-7 demonstrates with a procedure DownCase that converts strings from upper- to lowercase. Line 11 adds 32 to the ordinal (ASCII) value of each string character found in line 10 to be in the set ['A' .. 'Z'].

The procedure's formal parameter S is of type **string**, with a maximum length of 255 characters. Because the **for** loop restricts index I to the actual string length, you cannot accidentally index past the end of a shorter string. The main program at line 17 passes LittleString, with a maximum of 40 characters, to procedure DownCase. The compiler directives {$V–} and {$V+} temporarily turn off string length checking, allowing the procedure to accept the short parameter.

To see the difference string length checking makes, remove the directives in line 17 and recompile. You receive:

```
Error 26: Type mismatch.
```

because the actual string parameter type is shorter than the declared length of S. You can turn off string parameter length checks by inserting a {$V–} compiler directive at the beginning of a program or by turning off the IDE's *Options:Compiler, Strict var strings* setting. Usually, though, it's best to turn off string length checks temporarily as in Program 8-7. This way, you aren't likely to run programs with the wrong setting in effect.

Program 8-7: MIXLEN.PAS

```
 1:  program MixedLengths;
 2:  var
 3:    LittleString: string[40];
 4:
 5:  procedure DownCase(var S: string);
 6:  var
 7:    I: Integer;
 8:  begin
 9:    for I := 1 to Length(S) do
10:      if S[I] in ['A' .. 'Z']
11:        then S[I] := Chr(Ord(S[I]) + 32)
12:  end;
13:
14:  begin
15:    repeat
16:      Write('? '); Readln(LittleString);
17:      {$V-} DownCase(LittleString); {$V+}
18:      Writeln(LittleString)
19:    until Length(LittleString) = 0
20:  end.
```

Writing Your Own String Functions

Many Pascal compilers restrict function results to scalar and real-number data types. But in the special case of a **string** type, Turbo Pascal breaks the common mold, letting you write functions that return strings. For example, here's a simple function that removes blank characters from a string:

```
function NoBlanks(S: string): string;
var J: Integer;
begin
  J := 1;
  while J <= Length(S) do
    if S[J] = ' '
      then Delete(S, J, 1)
      else Inc(J);
  NoBlanks := S
end;
```

NoBlanks operates on a single value parameter S. After using Delete to remove blanks from S, the final statement in NoBlanks assigns S to the function name, thus passing the edited string back to the caller. To use the function, create a string variable, say MyName. Then, to remove blanks from MyName, write an expression such as:

```
NyName := NoBlanks(MyName);
```

Technically, NoBlanks returns an address, even though it appears to return a **string** data type. The address points to the actual string variable stored somewhere in memory. At most times, you can ignore this detail and use string functions as though they were actual strings. This doesn't always hold true. For instance, you can't index a string function:

```
Writeln(NoBlanks(S)[4]);  { ??? }
```

Although that appears to index the fourth character in the string result of NoBlanks, Turbo Pascal rejects the statement. If you remember the earlier-stated rule that string and other function results may be used where *constants* can normally appear, you'll avoid backing yourself into such corners. (You can't index string constants, either.)

You may be wondering how it is possible for Turbo Pascal to return strings as function results, which are usually restricted to real numbers, integers, and other scalar values. Because string functions actually return addresses that point to string variables in memory, and because functions can, of course, return pointers, string functions obey Pascal's rules by returning a kind of secret string pointer that doesn't require you to use the pointer techniques described in chapter 7.

Related to this is the fact that all arrays, of which strings are merely special subsets, are passed by address to procedure and function parameters. Even if you don't use the **var** key word to declare string and array parameters, the variables are passed by address. Most times, you can ignore this technical detail, which helps keep compiled code running fast. String and array parameters operate like parameters of other types, but you should be aware that Turbo Pascal always passes these items around by address.

When designing your own string functions, you may first have to declare a new string data type. This is necessary because you cannot write function declarations like this:

```
function Name: string[40];    { ??? }
```

Instead, you first have to declare a new string data type. Then you can write the function declaration to return the new type:

```
type
   String40 = string[40];
...

function Name: String40;
```

To demonstrate how to design string functions, Program 8-8 writes the color names for enumerated type Colors (line 4). Function ColorName takes a parameter Col of that type and, with the help of a **case** statement, returns an appropriate string as the function value. The Writeln statement in line 19 activates the function to write the names of the three colors, Red, White, and Blue.

Program 8-8: STRINGEN.PAS

```
 1:  program StringFunctions;
 2:  type
 3:     String8 = string[8];
 4:     Colors = (Red, White, Blue);
 5:  var
 6:     C: Colors;
 7:
 8:  function ColorName(Col: Colors): String8;
 9:  begin
10:    case Col of
11:      Red  : ColorName := 'Red';
12:      White: ColorName := 'White';
13:      Blue : ColorName := 'Blue'
14:    end
15:  end;
```

```
16:
17:  begin
18:    for C := Red to Blue do
19:      Writeln(ColorName(C));
20:    Readln
21:  end.
```

Special Characters

There are two special ways to assign values to character and string variables, methods not usually found in Pascal compilers.

In the ASCII character set, characters with ordinal values 0 to 31 are called *control characters* because, when written to the display or printer, they typically cause actions to occur rather than visible symbols to appear. For example, this statement:

```
Write(Chr(7));
```

rings the bell or beeps the beeper on terminals and computers that recognize ASCII code 7 as the bell control character. Another control character, ASCII 12, advances most printers to the top of a new page. As originally designed, Pascal has a procedure Page that does the same thing. Although Turbo Pascal lacks a built-in Page, it's easy to write your own procedure:

```
procedure Page(var F: Text);
begin
  Write(F, Chr(12))
end;
```

To use the new procedure, Rewrite a text file F to 'PRN' and execute Page(F) to advance the printer to the top of a new page. Some terminals, but not all, clear the screen if you use Page(Output). This doesn't always work because not all terminals recognize ASCII 12 as a screen control character. On the IBM PC, for example, paging the standard Output file displays the astronomy symbol for Venus ♀ (or, depending on your specialty, the biology symbol for a female organism). This may come as a surprise, but it's a good example of why you should not expect all ASCII terminals to understand the same control characters.

In Turbo Pascal, you can also write control characters with a preceding caret. The following statement rings the bell.

```
Write(^G);
```

Pascal translates the symbol ^G (control G) into the equivalent of Chr(7). All other control characters have associated letters starting with ^A = Chr(1), ^B = Chr(2), and so on. The letters correspond to the values generated by pressing the Ctrl key and that same letter on the keyboard. (Although letters are capitalized, you don't have to press the shift key.) For instance, to check if an operator enters Ctrl-E, a program could use these statements:

```
Read(Ch);
if Ch = ^E
   then Dosomething;
```

Numbers to Characters

You can also assign ASCII values to character variables. Precede a value with a number sign (#), and the compiler considers that value to be an ASCII character, not an integer. This is most useful in constant declarations:

```
const
  BellChar = #7;
  CtrlE = #5;
```

To do the same thing with most other Pascal compilers, you'd have to declare a BellChar variable and then assign to it the ASCII value you want. Using such special features may be convenient, but it can also make transporting programs to other compilers more difficult.

Character Constants in Strings

Because values like #7 and ^H are character constants, you can use them in strings as long as you insert the characters with no intervening symbols *outside* the string's quote delimiters. For example, to beep the terminal and display a string at the same time, use the Writeln statement:

```
Writeln(#7'Beep!');
```

One useful application of this idea is in error messages. Because errors might occur at any time during a program run, it's usually wise to first execute a carriage return and then display the message. This way, all messages line up along the left screen border where they are easy to see. Program 8-9 demonstrates the idea and shows how to mix character constants and control characters in literal strings (line 5). Notice that although line 6 executes a Write statement, the error message starts on a new display line because of the carriage return (#13) and line feed (#10) character constants assigned to S in line 5.

Program 8-9: CHARCONS.PAS

```
1:   program CharConstants;
2:   var
3:     S: string[80];
4:   begin
5:     S := #13#10'***'^G'Error!';
6:     Write('I detect an...');
7:     Writeln(S);
8:     Readln
9:   end.
```

Summary

Along with Turbo Pascal's built-in **string** data type, there are a number of procedures and functions for combining, checking length, copying, searching substring positions, and doing other string operations. Early versions of Pascal used character arrays for strings. While you can do the same in Turbo Pascal, dynamic strings are more versatile.

String variables may hold from 0 to 255 characters. Physically, string variables are arrays of characters with a length byte at index 0 (S[0]). The declared string length limits the maximum characters the string can hold. The actual length of the string changes depending on how many characters are in the string. You can index string variables similar to the way you index other arrays. You cannot index string constants.

Length returns the actual length of a string. Concat joins two or more strings. You can use a plus sign (+) in place of Concat. Other string routines, Copy, Insert, and Delete, let you manipulate strings. Pos finds a substring, if it exists, in another string.

Turbo Pascal checks that string parameters to procedures and functions have the same declared lengths. You can turn off this feature with the {$V–} compiler directive at the risk of introducing a bug in your program if you increase a string's actual length beyond the declared maximum.

Even though Turbo Pascal normally limits function results to scalars and real numbers, it breaks the rules for strings, letting you write string functions. Actually, string functions return pointers to string variables, thus obeying Pascal's rules for function data types. Related to this is the fact that Turbo Pascal passes all string and array procedure and function parameters by address, regardless of whether the parameters are declared with **var**.

Exercises

8-1. Design a mailing list program (or several programs) to store names and addresses in a disk file. Let the operator select one of three printout formats: labels, directory, and envelopes. The directory should come out last name first, while labels and envelopes should show names in normal order. Use string procedures and functions in your program.

8-2. Write a utility program to hunt for all key words in a Pascal text and convert them to uppercase.

8-3. Write a search and replace program to hunt for any string in a text file and change it to something else.

8-4. Design a procedure for editing strings. Use control characters to delete characters, move forward and back, and insert blanks. After testing, add your procedure to your program in exercise 8-1.

9

Introducing the Unit

- The **uses** Declaration
- Unit Disk Files
- Using Units in Programs
- The System Unit
- The Crt Unit
- The Dos Unit
- The Printer Unit
- The Turbo3 Unit
- The Graph3 Unit

9

Key Words and Identifiers

AssignCrt, ClrEol, ClrScr, Delay, DelLine, DiskFree, DiskSize, DosVersion, EnvCount, EnvStr, FExpand, FindFirst, FindNext, FSearch, FSplit, GetCBreak, GetDate, GetEnv, GetFAttr, GetFTime, GetTime, GetVerify, GotoXY, HighVideo, InsLine, Intr, Keypressed, LowVideo, MsDos, NormVideo, NoSound, PackTime, ReadKey, SetCBreak, SetDate, SetFAttr, SetFTime, SetTime, SetVerify, Sound, TextBackground, TextColor, TextMode, UnpackTime, **uses**, WhereX, WhereY, Window

A unit is a precompiled collection of Pascal goodies, ready for other programs to share. A kind of programmer's warehouse, a unit stocks raw materials—constants, types, variables, procedures, and functions—in a form that Turbo Pascal can quickly attach to programs.

Although a unit can store anything that you might find in a normal Pascal program, a unit is not itself a complete program. You can't run a unit on its own. Instead, you have to write a *host program* that uses the unit's features, just as though you declared those same features directly in the program.

This chapter explains how to use Turbo Pascal's standard units as well as other precompiled units that you might purchase from software companies. Chapter 10 explains how to write your own units and how to convert units to *overlays,* which can share memory to reduce a large program's RAM consumption.

The uses Declaration

To attach a unit to a program, insert the unit's name in a **uses** declaration, which appears immediately after the **program** line but before any **label**, **const**, **type**, **var**, **procedure**, or **function** declarations. For example, to use unit Crt, you could start your program like this:

```
program UsesOneUnit;
uses Crt;
```

A semicolon must come at the end of the **uses** declaration. To use more than one unit, separate the unit names with commas:

```
program UsesManyUnits;
uses Crt, Dos, Graph;
```

This program uses three units: Crt, Dos, and Graph. For each unit a program uses, Turbo Pascal reads from the unit disk file a special section called the unit interface. Inside the interface are the declarations describing the unit's contents. The compiler needs this information to know what's in a unit.

Of course, you also need to know what's in a unit before you can put the unit's features to work. To find this information, you can't use the IDE to read a unit disk file, which is stored in compiled form for the compiler's use only. Instead, you have to read the unit interface in its original text form. For example, Turbo Pascal's standard units come with .INT text files that describe the unit's contents. Usually stored in your C:\TP\DOC (or C:\TURBO\DOC) directory, these files are purely for reference—you can't modify and compile them to change how units operate. If you purchase units from other companies, you'll probably receive similar files or printed interface documentation.

Table 9-1 lists Turbo Pascal's standard units. The TURBO.TPL (Turbo Pascal Library) file stores multiple units in a single file. The .TPU (Turbo Pascal Unit) files store individual compiled units. Each unit has an associated .INT file. You'll learn about the Crt, Dos, Graph3, Printer, System, and Turbo3 units in this chapter. Chapter 10 describes how to use the Overlay unit. Chapter 11 is devoted to the Graph unit.

Table 9-1 Turbo Pascal standard units.

Name	Disk file	Description
Crt	TURBO.TPL	Fast direct-video display routines
Dos	TURBO.TPL	DOS functions
Graph	GRAPH.TPU	Graphics kernel
Graph3	GRAPH3.TPU	Version 3.0 graphics
Overlay	TURBO.TPL	Overlay manager
Printer	TURBO.TPL	Printer output
System	TURBO.TPL	Standard run-time library
Turbo3	TURBO3.TPU	Version 3.0 miscellaneous

Note: Turbo Pascal comes with several other units such as OBJECTS.TPU, DRIVERS.TPU, and VIEWS.TPU, located in the TVISION subdirectory. These units are part of the object-oriented Turbo Vision library, explained in chapters 16 and 17. The units listed in Table 9-1 are of general purpose, are not object-oriented, and can be used in all Turbo Pascal programs.

Unit Disk Files

Individual units are compiled to files ending in .TPU, which you may transfer to TURBO.TPL for faster loading when using the IDE (integrated development environment). Turbo Pascal reads all of TURBO.TPL into memory, making the library's precompiled units instantly available to host programs. Use the TPUMOVER program (described in Chapter 10) to transfer compiled units in and out of TURBO.TPL. To gain extra memory during compilation, you can remove the Turbo3 and Graph3 units, needed only to compile version 3.0 programs.

If a unit listed in a **uses** declaration is not in TURBO.TPL, the compiler searches for a file *unitname*.TPU in the current directory. If it still can't find the compiled unit, it searches all the paths specified in the IDE's *Options:Directories, Unit directories* setting. This lets you store compiled units in various subdirectories, but still allows the compiler to find them. For example, to make the compiler search for compiled units in the BGI, TURBO3, and MYUNITS subdirectories of C:\TP you could change your *Unit directories* entry to:

```
C:\TP\BGI;C:\TP\TURB03;C:\TP\MYUNITS
```

Using Units in Programs

A simple example demonstrates how to compile programs that use units. Program 9-1 uses the Crt unit (line 2). The program displays a message (line 4) and executes a **repeat** loop (lines 5-7) until function ReadKey returns ASCII character 13, the value generated by pressing the Enter key. When you press Enter, line 8 clears the display by calling ClrScr.

Program 9-1: CLEAR.PAS

```
1:   program Clear;
2:   uses Crt;
3:   begin
4:     Write('Press Enter to clear the screen');
5:     repeat
6:       { Wait }
7:     until ReadKey = Chr(13);
8:     ClrScr
9:   end.
```

Function ReadKey and procedure ClrScr are not part of the Pascal language. They are precompiled routines stored inside the Crt unit. (For more information on these routines, look them up in Chapter 18, which lists all Turbo Pascal procedures and functions in alphabetic order.) Because of the **uses** Crt declaration, the routines are available—just as though they were Pascal natives. To prove this, remove line 2 and recompile. Instead of success, when the compiler reaches ReadKey, it displays the error message:

```
Error 3: Unknown identifier.
```

Because ReadKey is defined in Crt, you must use the unit for the compiler to know what ReadKey means. You would receive the same error at line 8 if the compiler ever reached that point. ClrScr is a routine in Crt. You have to specify **uses** Crt for the compiler to know what ClrScr is. As you can see, using units adds new commands to Pascal, customizing the language to understand how to accomplish new tasks.

The System Unit

The System unit is a phantom, always around even if you don't insert it in your program's **uses** declaration. Inside System are most of Turbo Pascal's standard procedures and functions, such as the string routines described in Chapter 8. You never have to tell the compiler to **use** System—it always will.

Think of the System unit as a kind of shell enveloping every program you write. Chapter 18 lists all of System's many routines, too numerous to discuss individually here.

SYSTEM.INT details the System unit's interface, which does not list standard procedures and functions such as Writeln and Read, even though these and other native routines are actually stored in System, sometimes also called the *runtime library*. System includes several variable (typed) constants that define Turbo Pascal's internal values, for example, the location of the heap and the size of the stack. You'll meet many of these values again in Chapter 13. Also in the System unit are the standard Input and Output text file variables plus a series of pointers in which Turbo Pascal saves interrupt vectors when programs start running. Interrupt vectors are pointers to routines stored in your computer's ROM and in DOS. Because Turbo Pascal hooks into some of these routines, it saves the original pointers for restoring when the program ends.

It's probably best to be aware that the System unit exists—and then forget about it. Because you never have to tell the compiler to use System, you may as well consider this unit's features to be native Turbo Pascal residents.

The Crt Unit

The Crt unit contains constants, variables, and routines to control the display and keyboard. (Crt stands for *Cathode Ray Tube* but, in computer jargon, generally refers to the display and keyboard together.)

Adding the Crt unit to programs does more than simply give you a few neat procedures and functions to use. Using Crt also replaces the Write and Writeln standard text output routines with super-fast, direct-video code. Using Crt, then, has three important side effects:

1. Writing text to the display goes as fast as possible by transferring characters directly to video display memory buffers rather than calling slower BIOS (Basic Input Output System) ROM routines.

2. Program output from Write and Writeln statements can no longer be redirected or piped with the DOS <, > and | command characters. As you'll learn in a moment, there is a way to provide this ability by using a text file along with Crt.

3. Programs might not run correctly under control of some multitasking software, which shares computer time among several programs stored together in memory.

The Crt Unit Variables

This section describes Crt's several variables, which you can examine and change. The unit also declares a number of constants described in the sections that follow:

CheckBreak: Boolean;

Normally true, CheckBreak controls whether programs halt on the *next* Write or Writeln statement to execute after you press Ctrl-Break. Set CheckBreak to false to disable Ctrl-Break checking:

```
CheckBreak := false;  { Disable Ctrl-Break checking }
```

CheckEof: Boolean;

Use CheckEof to control the effect of pressing Ctrl-Z during Read and Readln statements. Normally, CheckEof is false, ignoring Ctrl-Z. When true, pressing Ctrl-Z during input sets Eof to true. A few examples clarify the importance of this action:

```
var
  S: string;
  I, J, K: Integer;
begin
  CheckEof := true;    { Enable Ctrl-Z checking }
  Readln(S);
  Reset(Input);
  Read(I, J, K)
end.
```

With CheckEof true, the Readln statement ends as soon as you press Ctrl-Z, setting Eof true for the standard Input file. If CheckEof were false, then pressing Ctrl-Z in Readln would have no effect—you'd have to press Enter to continue as you normally do in Readln statements.

The Reset statement is necessary after Readln because Eof, once set to true, remains true until resetting the file. If you did not reset the standard Input file and if you typed Ctrl-Z to Readln, the next Read statement would not execute.

The Read statement lets you type three numbers separated with spaces. When CheckEof is true, pressing Ctrl-Z immediately ends input—even before you supply values for all variables. Pressing 5 and then Ctrl-Z sets I to 5, and J, K to 0. When CheckEof is false, pressing Ctrl-Z has no effect; you must supply values for all variables before the Read statement ends.

DirectVideo: Boolean;

Set DirectVideo to false (it's normally true) to disable writing characters directly to video display memory. Because this slows text output by calling inefficient BIOS ROM routines, do this only if you have problems with text I/O when using Crt. If you have this problem, set the variable to false:

```
DirectVideo := false;  { Disable direct video output }
```

Setting DirectVideo to false does not reenable the ability to redirect program output with the <, >, and | DOS command-line characters. To use Crt and be able to redirect program output, Rewrite a text file with a null file name. Program 9-2 demonstrates how this works, attaching a text file to standard output, bypassing Crt's direct video effects on Write and Writeln. Compile the program to disk and type:

```
crtredir >test.txt
```

This redirects the line "This text is redirectable" to file TEST.TXT. You could also type >PRN to redirect output to the printer. The Writeln statement in line 8, though, is not redirectable—the text always appears on screen because of Crt's direct video routines. Setting DirectVideo to false would still not allow line 8 to be redirected.

Program 9-2: CRTREDIR.PAS

```
 1:  program CrtRedirection;
 2:  uses Crt;
 3:  var F: Text;
 4:  begin
 5:    Assign(F, '');
 6:    Rewrite(F);
 7:    Writeln(F , 'This text is redirectable');
 8:    Writeln('This text is not redirectable');
 9:    Close(F)
10:  end.
```

CheckSnow: Boolean;

If you see "snow storms" on some older CGA video systems, especially during scrolling and when clearing the display, set CheckSnow to true. Monochrome and newer EGA and VGA displays do not have this problem.

You might want to include a command in your program's setup procedure to ask people if they see snow on their screens. If so, set CheckSnow to true to cure the problem. Unfortunately, this also slows output so don't take this step unless absolutely necessary. (The variable is set automatically by the Crt unit for most displays.)

LastMode: Word;

When calling TextMode to switch video text modes, Crt stores the mode number in LastMode. (This variable probably would be better named *CurrentMode.*) To switch to a different mode, use programming such as:

```
var
  Mode: Word;
begin
  Mode := LastMode;      { Save current text mode value }
  TextMode(CO40);        { Switch to color 40-column mode }
  ...                    { Commands in color 40-column mode }
  TextMode(Mode);        { Restore previous text mode }
end.
```

TextAttr: Byte;

Normally, use procedures TextColor and TextBackground to change foreground and background colors or attributes such as underlining and bold characters on monochrome systems. When speed is important, though, you can accomplish the same job by storing values directly in the TextAttr byte.

Figure 9-1 shows this byte's format. Bit 7 controls whether characters are solid or blinking. Bits 4-6 specify the background color, 0 to 7. Bits 0-3 set the foreground color from 0 to 15. Use Crt's 16 color constants to set the blink attribute, foreground, and background colors in one assignment statement. Here are a few examples:

```
{ White on blue, no blink }e
TextAttr := White + Blue * 16;

{ Blinking "red alert" warning }
TextAttr := Red + LightGray * 16 + Blink;
```

```
{ Normal white on black, no blink }
TextAttr := White + Black * 16;
```

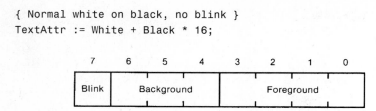

Figure 9-1 The TextAttr byte in unit Crt packs Background and Foreground color
values plus a single Blink bit into one eight-bit variable.

WindMin: Word;
WindMax: Word;

These two variables hold the minimum and maximum display coordinates. The low
byte of each word equals the horizontal (X) coordinate. The high byte equals the
vertical (Y) coordinate. To set four variables to the top-left (X1,Y1) and bottom-right
(X2,Y2) window corners, write:

```
X1 := Lo(WindMin) + 1;
Y1 := Hi(WindMin) + 1;
X2 := Lo(WindMax) + 1;
Y2 := Hi(WindMax) + 1;
```

Notice that you must add 1 to each value for the correct coordinate values.
While WindMin and WindMax range from 0 to the maximum coordinate less 1, Crt's
GotoXY cursor positioning procedure requires coordinate values from 1 to the
maximum.

Controlling the Cursor

One procedure (GotoXY) and two functions (WhereX and WhereY) change and
examine the cursor position. Use GotoXY (some people call it "go-toxy", others say
"go-to-x-y") to position the cursor anywhere on screen. GotoXY(1,1) sends the
cursor to the upper-left corner of the current window. Use functions WhereX and
WhereY to locate the current cursor position. For example:

```
var
  X, Y: Integer;
  YourName: string;
begin
  GotoXY(10, 21);                { Send cursor to X = 10, Y = 21 }
```

```
Write('Enter your name: ');  { Display prompt }
Readln(YourName);            { Get answer from user }
X := WhereX;                 { Assign cursor location }
Y := WhereY                  { to X and Y }
end.
```

Controlling the Display

Crt has a number of routines to help you design good-looking displays. You can clear portions of the screen, turn on special video modes, and select foreground and background colors.

To switch video modes, use TextMode along with one of the constant values from Table 9-2. Each time you do this, Crt saves the mode value in variable LastMode as explained earlier. Remember that this variable always specifies the text mode *now* in effect—not the mode last in effect as its name implies.

Table 9-2 Crt unit TextMode constants.

Constant	Value	Columns	Lines	Display mode
BW40	0	40	25	Black and white
CO40	1	40	25	Color
C40	1	40	25	Color
BW80	2	80	25	Black and white
CO80	3	80	25	Color
C80	3	80	25	Color
Mono	7	80	25	Monochrome
Font8x8	256	80	43	EGA compressed text
Font8x8	256	80	50	VGA compressed text

Notes. BW40, CO40, C40, BW80, CO80, and C80 require a color video system such as CGA, EGA, or VGA. Mono requires a monochrome adapter (MDA), Hercules, or equivalent. Font8x8 must be added to CO80 to select either 43- or 50-line compressed text displays.

Compressed 43- and 50-Line Text

Add the Font8x8 constant to CO80 to select EGA 43-line or VGA 50-line displays:

```
TextMode(CO80 + Font8x8);
```

Use LastMode to leave the video mode unchanged but select between normal and compressed EGA 43-line or VGA 50-line displays. Assuming the display is compressed, this switches to normal 25-line text:

```
TextMode(Lo(LastMode));
```

To switch back to 43- or 50-line text, add back the Font8x8 constant like this, leaving the video mode unchanged while returning to compressed text:

```
TextMode(Lo(LastMode) + Font8x8);
```

Clearing, Inserting, and Deleting Text

Call ClrScr to clear the entire screen or window. ClrEol clears from the cursor to the end of the line. To clear the entire line and leave the cursor position unchanged, insert this procedure into your program:

```
procedure ClrLine;
var
  X, Y: Integer;
begin
  X := WhereX;
  Y := WhereY;
  GotoXY(1, Y);
  ClrEol;
  GotoXY(X, Y)
end;
```

ClrLine simulates the clear-line operation found on many video terminals. To clear from the cursor position to the end of the screen requires a bit more work:

```
procedure ClrEosc;
var
  XX, YY, Y: Integer;
begin
  ClrEol;
  YY := WhereY;
  XX := WhereX;
  for Y := YY to Hi(WindMax) + 1 do
```

```
  begin
    GotoXY(1, Y);
    ClrEol
  end;
  GotoXY(XX, YY)
end;
```

By carefully using ClrEol, WhereY, WhereX, GotoXY, and WindMax, ClrEosc works correctly for all video modes, inside restricted windows (described in the next section) and in 43- and 50-line compressed displays.

To insert a blank line at the current cursor position, call InsLine. All lines from the cursor below move down one line within the current window. The last line in the window is permanently lost. To delete a line at the current cursor position, call DelLine. The deleted line is permanently lost, all lines below the cursor move up one line, and a blank line replaces the last line in the window.

Text Windows

Windows have become such a popular subject in modern software design that any language or product that doesn't have them may have serious trouble competing in the market. Turbo Pascal offers a limited form of text-screen windows demonstrated in Program 9-3. (See chapters 16 and 17 for information about creating more sophisticated text windows.) The Window procedure changes the relative display borders. It has the form:

```
procedure Window(X1, Y1, X2, Y2: Byte);
```

Technically, this is the correct definition as found in Crt's interface. But you might find it easier to work with Window if you pretend it to be declared like this:

```
procedure Window(Left, Top, Right, Bottom: Byte);
```

The four byte parameters represent the screen coordinates of the new corners. Normally, Left and Right range from 1 to 80, and Top and Bottom from 1 to 25.

After setting a new window's parameters, the top-left corner has the coordinate (1,1). In other words, executing GotoXY(1,1) always sends the cursor to the top-left window corner, regardless of where that is on the entire screen. Other procedures such as ClrScr and ClrEol also respect the new window borders.

Program 9-3 demonstrates these ideas. A record type, WindRec, keeps track of the borders of two display windows, Wind1 and Wind2. Procedure OpenWind (lines 16-24) uses the Window procedure to set the new borders and put the cursor in the lower-left corner (lines 20-21). Procedure TextBox (line 64) draws a simple box around the window, using an extended character, ASCII 176.

After initializing two windows (lines 97-98), the program lets you enter a file name (see function OpenFile, line 27). The function returns true only if it can open the file you request.

With the file open, procedure DisplayFile at line 50 reads and displays the file's contents in the larger window. Because line 54 switches to Wind2, the contents of the smaller entry window are not disturbed while lines of text scroll off the screen.

By separating the input and output windows, you can view text but still see the command you gave to open the file. In a way, the program runs as though there were separate computer screens, each with a different purpose. The windows help you form a mental image of what the program is supposed to do, even if they don't actually do much to help the computer complete its task.

Program 9-3: WINDOWS.PAS

```pascal
1:  program Windows;
2:  uses Crt;
3:
4:  type
5:    WindRec = record
6:      WindTop,
7:      WindBottom,
8:      WindLeft,
9:      WindRight: Integer
10:   end;
11: var
12:   Done: Boolean;
13:   Wind1, Wind2: WindRec;
14:   TextFile: Text;
15:
16: procedure OpenWind(Wind: WindRec);
17: begin
18:   with Wind do
19:   begin
20:     Window(WindLeft, WindTop, WindRight, WindBottom);
21:     Gotoxy(1, 1 + WindBottom - WindTop);
22:     Writeln
23:   end
24: end;
25:
26: { True if file open; False if user quits }
27: function OpenFile: Boolean;
28:   var
```

```
29:    ErrCode: Integer;
30:    FileName: string;
31:  begin
32:    OpenWind(Wind1);
33:    repeat
34:      Writeln('Enter a file name');
35:      Write(']');
36:      Readln(FileName);
37:      if Length(FileName) = 0 then
38:      begin
39:        OpenFile := False; Exit
40:      end;
41:      Assign(TextFile, FileName);
42:      {$I-} Reset(TextFile); {$I+}
43:      ErrCode := Ioresult;
44:      if ErrCode <> 0
45:        then Writeln('Error #', ErrCode, #7#13#10)
46:    until ErrCode = 0;
47:    OpenFile := True
48:  end;
49:
50:  procedure DisplayFile;
51:  var
52:    S: string[132];
53:  begin;
54:    OpenWind(Wind2);
55:    Writeln;
56:    while not Eof(TextFile) do
57:    begin
58:      Readln(TextFile, S);
59:      Writeln(S)
60:    end;
61:    Close(TextFile)
62:  end;
63:
64:  procedure TextBox(Top, Bottom, Left, Right: Integer);
65:  var
66:    X, Y: Integer;
67:
68:    procedure TwoChar(X1, Y1, X2, Y2: Integer);
69:    begin
```

continued

Program 9-3: continued

```
70:       Gotoxy(X1, Y1); Write(Chr(176));
71:       Gotoxy(x2, Y2); Write(Chr(176))
72:     end;
73:
74:   begin
75:     for X := Left to Right do
76:       TwoChar(X, Top, X, Bottom);
77:     for Y := Top to Bottom do
78:       TwoChar(Left, Y, Right, Y)
79:   end;
80:
81:   procedure InitWind(var Wind: WindRec;
82:     Top, Bottom, Left, Right: Integer);
83:   begin
84:     TextBox(Top, Bottom, Left, Right);
85:     with Wind do
86:     begin
87:       WindTop    := Top + 1;
88:       WindBottom := Bottom - 1;
89:       WindLeft   := Left + 1;
90:       WindRight  := Right - 1
91:     end
92:   end;
93:
94:   procedure Initialize;
95:   begin
96:     ClrScr;
97:     InitWind(Wind1, 1, 12, 1, 21);
98:     InitWind(Wind2, 5, 22, 26, 80)
99:   end;
100:
101:  begin
102:    Initialize;
103:    repeat
104:      Done := not OpenFile;
105:      if not Done
106:        then DisplayFile
107:    until Done;
108:    Window(1, 1, 80, 25);
109:    ClrScr
110:  end.
```

Controlling the Keyboard

The Keypressed Boolean function returns true if it senses a key was pressed sometime earlier. This lets you write **repeat** loops such as:

```
repeat { Wait } until Keypressed;
```

The loop waits until you press a key. The bracketed comment Wait is not necessary—it merely makes the purpose of the statement clear. Actually, there is a null statement (which isn't really there, of course) between the **repeat** and **until**. You may be amused by this bit of sorcery, but null statements are no joke. If Pascal did not allow them, you could never write a "do-nothing" loop like this one—you'd have to use a real statement. And then, the do-nothing loop would no longer do nothing!

Reading Characters in Silence

For some odd reason, reading a single character from the keyboard without displaying the character is one of those tricky subjects that most computer languages never seem to get right. Even older Turbo Pascal versions made the job unnecessarily difficult. Luckily, the Crt ReadKey character function threatens an end to this controversy once and for all: To read a single character, use the following statement:

```
Ch := ReadKey;
```

(Variable Ch is of type Char.)

The statement pauses for you to press a key, depositing the ASCII result in variable Ch. ReadKey has absolutely no effect on any text now on display, and there is no way to make it have any such effect. If you want to display the character—so people can see what they type—do this:

```
Ch := ReadKey;
Write(Ch);
```

There are other neat tricks you can teach your program with ReadKey. For example, this waits for you to press the Escape key:

```
repeat
  { Wait }
until ReadKey = Chr(27);
```

There's that null statement again inside the **repeat** loop, which waits until ReadKey returns ASCII 27, the code for the Esc control character. Notice that loops like this do not require a program variable.

ReadKey always pauses for input. Often, that's not convenient. Suppose your program is printing a long text file and you want to check periodically if someone has pressed Esc to stop printing. You could write:

```
if Keypressed then
  if ReadKey = Chr(27)
      then Halt;
```

By checking Keypressed *before* ReadKey, the program reads the keyboard only *after* you type something. If you don't type anything, the program continues normally.

Reading Function Keys

All PC keyboards have 10 or 12 function keys plus several other special keys, arrows, Insert, Home, and so on. Unlike regular alphanumeric, punctuation, and control keys, these special function keys generate two ASCII codes, not just one. For this reason, it takes extra care to recognize them properly. Again, ReadKey makes the job easier than in earlier Turbo Pascal versions.

If the first character returned by ReadKey equals ASCII 0, then the next key specifies a key from Table 9-3. Special keys like Home and the up arrow always generate one character following ASCII 0. Function keys F1-F10 produce one of four possible characters depending on whether you press the key alone or hold down the Alt, Ctrl, or Shift keys. For example, to check for Alt-F4, you could write:

```
if Keypressed then
  if ReadKey = Chr(0) then
    if ReadKey = 'k' then
      DoAltF4;
```

Program 9-4 tests these and other key combinations. Run the program and press any key, try out various function keys, and experiment with control and Alt keys. The program displays the visible character that a key produces (except for a few that do not display visible symbols) and lists the ASCII code in parentheses. Press Esc to end the program.

Program 9-4: KEYTEST.PAS

```
1:  program KeyTest;
2:  uses Crt;
3:  var
4:    Ch: Char;
5:    Done: Boolean;
6:
7:  function ASCII(Ch: Char): Char;
8:  begin
9:    Write(Ch, ' (', Ord(Ch), ') ');
```

```
10:    ASCII := Chr(0)
11: end;
12:
13: begin
14:   Writeln('Key test.  Press Esc to quit.');
15:   Done := False;
16:   repeat
17:     if Keypressed then
18:     begin
19:       Ch := ReadKey;
20:       if Ch = Chr(0)
21:         then Writeln(ASCII(Chr(0)), ASCII(ReadKey))
22:         else Writeln(ASCII(Ch));
23:       Done := (Ch = Chr(27))
24:     end
25:   until Done
26: end.
```

Table 9-3 Special function keys.

Key Label	Normal	Alt	Ctrl	Shift
F1	; (59)	h (104)	^ (94)	T (84)
F2	< (60)	i (105)	_ (95)	U (85)
F3	= (61)	j (106)	` (96)	V (86)
F4	> (62)	k (107)	a (97)	W (87)
F5	? (63)	l (108)	b (98)	X (88)
F6	@ (64)	m (109)	c (99)	Y (89)
F7	A (65)	n (110)	d (100)	Z (90)
F8	B (66)	o (111)	e (101)	[(91)
F9	C (67)	p (112)	f (102)	\ (92)
F10	D (68)	q (113)	g (103)	] (93)
Home	G (71)			
Up arrow	H (72)			
PgUp	I (73)			
Left arrow	K (75)			
Right arrow	M (77)			
End	O (79)			
Down arrow	P (80)			
PgDn	Q (81)			
Ins	R (82)			
Del	S (83)			

Note: Some keyboards label keys Page Up, Page Down, Insert, and Delete instead of PgUp, PgDn, Ins, and Del.

Text Attributes

Table 9-4 lists the Crt unit text color constants, which you can use with TextColor and TextBackground to select foreground and background colors. Use the first eight constants for both foregrounds and backgrounds. Use the second eight constants only for foregrounds. This prepares to display yellow text on a blue background:

```
TextColor(Yellow);
TextBackground(Blue);
```

Table 9-4 Crt unit color constants.

Constant	Value	Fg	Bg
Black	0	x	x
Blue	1	x	x
Green	2	x	x
Cyan	3	x	x
Red	4	x	x
Magenta	5	x	x
Brown	6	x	x
LightGray	7	x	x
DarkGray	8	x	
LightBlue	9	x	
LightGreen	10	x	
LightCyan	11	x	
LightRed	12	x	
LightMagenta	13	x	
Yellow	14	x	
White	15	x	

To make characters blink on and off, add another Crt constant, Blink, equal to 128, to any foreground color. (You can't blink the background.) You might use this to display warnings:

```
TextColor(Red + Blink);
TextBackground(LightGray);
Write('You are about to erase your disk!');
```

On monochrome monitors, various color combinations select underlined, dim, bold, and blinking text. Blue and LightBlue constants select underlined text. Other colors from Green to Brown select dim text. LightGreen to White select bold text. Blinking works as it does on color displays—just add the Blink constant to any foreground color. Here are a few examples:

```
TextColor(Blue);
Writeln('This is underlined');
TextColor(LightGray);
Writeln('This is not underlined');
Writeln;
TextColor(LightBlue);
Writeln('This is underlined');
TextColor(White);
Writeln('This is not underlined');
```

Another way to change text attributes is to use the LowVideo, HighVideo, and NormVideo procedures. LowVideo turns off the high intensity bit in the character attribute byte, bit number 3 in Figure 9-1. HighVideo turns the bit on. As you can see from Figure 9-1, LowVideo and HighVideo do not add additional colors or attributes over what you can achieve with color constants. They simply convert between the first and second eight foreground color constant values in Table 9-4. In other words, if the foreground color is Green, executing HighVideo has the identical effect as setting TextColor to LightGreen.

Use HighVideo and LowVideo to intensify and dim letters after selecting the colors you want, as in this example, which intensifies the word *not* in mid sentence:

```
LowVideo;
TextColor(Green);
TextBackground(Red);
Write('Press N if you do ');
HighVideo;
Write('not ');
LowVideo;
Writeln('want to continue');
```

Unfortunately, HighVideo selects several light colors (color numbers 9-13) while LowVideo selects more brilliant hues (1-5)—exactly opposite of what the procedure names suggest. If the color is now green and you execute HighVideo, the color changes to light green. But if the color is light gray, HighVideo changes to bright white—a confusing contradiction we just have to endure.

A final way to change text attributes is to call NormVideo, which resets the TextAttr byte to the value it had when the program started. To restore text to original colors, call this procedure just before your program ends:

```
NormVideo;    { Restore original text attributes }
```

Waiting Around

Usually, programmers spend much of their time making programs faster. Occasionally, though, it's helpful to be able to slow things down—perhaps to let people read text as though it were coming from a ticker tape. To do this, call Delay with a value representing the number of milliseconds you want to pause at this point:

```
Delay(1000);   { Wait a sec. }
```

Don't put too much faith in the amount of delay—it's accurate only to plus or minus about 1/4 second. Turbo Pascal uses a timing loop to set the amount of delay when programs begin, so this feature works whether or not the computer has a built-in clock. One use for Delay is to pause between important text displays—for example, sign-on copyright notices and error messages. Because different computer models run at different speeds, unless you insert Delays, your program's messages may zip by too fast to read on super fast computers.

Sounding Off

Crt's Sound procedure starts a tone at approximately the frequency specified in parentheses:

```
Sound(440);    { 'A' }
```

Sound continues until you call NoSound—even after the program ends! Therefore, in any program that uses Sound, it's a good idea to end with a call to NoSound:

```
NoSound;   { Turn off tone generator }
```

Crt Reassignments

Sometimes, it's nice to give people the choice of printing text or displaying it on screen. A database program, for example, might have a command to preview a report on screen before printing a copy on paper. One way to accomplish this is to design a procedure with a text file parameter, something like this:

```
procedure Report(var F: Text);
var
  I: Integer;
begin
  Writeln(F, 'Report header');
  for I := 1 to NumLines do
    Writeln(F, Lines[I])
end;
```

This is just a simple example and a real report generator would be much more complex, but the idea is to pass text file F to Writeln, optionally redirecting the report to one device or another. For example, this displays the report on screen by specifying the standard Output text file:

```
Report(Output);
```

And this opens a file to the printer, printing a paper copy of the report by writing to a file named PRN:

```
var
  Printer: Text;
begin
  Assign(Printer, 'PRN');
  Rewrite(Printer);
  Report(Printer);
  Close(Printer)
end.
```

These methods work but introduce a nasty problem that may not be obvious. One of the reasons for using the Crt unit is to display text as fast as possible, storing characters directly in video display memory. Redirecting text to the standard Output file as just described defeats this feature, displaying text through the slower BIOS ROM routines.

To have your direct-video text and print it too, use the AssignCrt procedure to attach a text file to the Crt unit. Doing this tells Crt that you plan to use the text file in Write and Writeln statements but that you still want the unit to use its direct-video routines for displaying text on screen. Continuing the earlier report example, instead of specifying the standard Output file, you could write:

```
var
  Console: Text;
begin
  AssignCrt(Console);
  Rewrite(Console);
  Report(Console);
  Close(Console)
end.
```

Except for the AssignCrt statement, this is identical to the earlier method for printing text. By assigning the unnamed text file to Crt, subsequent Write and Writeln statements that use the file go through Crt's direct-video routines. You can now pass to procedures a 'PRN' file to print text but pass the console file to display text as fast as possible.

The Dos Unit

The Dos unit contains constants, type declarations, one variable, and several routines to call DOS functions. The following covers most of the Dos unit routines except for a few advanced subjects postponed until Chapter 13.

Note: To avoid confusion, *Dos* refers to the Dos unit. *DOS* in all capital letters refers to the Disk Operating System software.

Dos Variables

The Dos unit has a single variable, DosError, of type Integer. Table 9-5 lists DosError's possible values. After calling Dos routines, check this variable to see if an error occurred.

Calling BIOS Interrupts

In all PCs, there are many low-level routines available for controlling various computer features. These routines are called "low level" because they directly access computer hardware to control the display, communications ports, timers, disk drives, and other devices. Together, the routines form the ROM BIOS, or *Basic Input Output System*.

Table 9-5 DosError codes.

DosError Value	Meaning
0	No error
2	File not found
3	Path not found
5	Access denied
6	Invalid handle
8	Not enough memory
10	Invalid environment
11	Invalid format
18	No more files

Each BIOS routine has a unique *interrupt number.* An interrupt is a process that stops the computer at whatever it is doing and makes it do something else. When that something else finishes, the original operation resumes where it left off. Except for the time this takes, the interrupted process is normally unaware of the interruption.

There are two kinds of interrupts: hardware and software. *Hardware interrupts* come directly from devices like the keyboard. Every time you press a key, circuits inside the keyboard generate an interrupt signal, which causes a BIOS routine to read your keystroke and store its value in memory where programs can find it. Contrasting that action, *software interrupts* are more like Pascal procedures. You call them by issuing a *software interrupt number.*

To generate software interrupts in Turbo Pascal, use the Dos unit Intr procedure as demonstrated in Program 9-5, line 33. Intr takes two parameters: an interrupt number and a simulated register record, which contains fields that represent the processor registers AX, BX, CX, and others. Figure 9-2 lists the Registers data type.

```
Registers =
  record
    case Integer of
      0: (AX,BX,CX,DX,BP,SI,DI,DS,ES,Flags: Word);
      1: (AL,AH,BL,BH,CL,CH,DL,DH: Byte);
  end;
```

Figure 9-2 The Dos unit Registers record contains fields
to simulate processor registers.

Program 9-5 changes the cursor shape by calling interrupt $10 with register AH equal to 1 (line 32). This selects interrupt $10's cursor style routine, changing the cursor size by specifying its start line in register CH and its end line in CL. Although the cursor looks like a solid block, it's composed of horizontal lines numbered from the top 0 to 7 for color and 0 to 13 for monochrome displays. The two variable constant arrays in lines 9-10 specify start and end line numbers for each of three settings, normal, half, and full, which, when passed to interrupt $10, change the cursor.

After running the program, the cursor may or may not keep its new shape, depending on other software installed in your computer.

Program 9-5: CURSOR.PAS

```pascal
 1:  program Cursor;
 2:  uses Crt, Dos;
 3:
 4:  type
 5:     Settings = array[0 .. 5] of Byte;
 6:
 7:  const                    {  0        1       2    }
 8:                           { ch   cl   ch   cl   ch   cl }
 9:     Monochrome: Settings = (11, 12, 07, 12, 00, 12);
10:     Color      : Settings = (06, 07, 04, 07, 00, 07);
11:
12:  var
13:     Choice: Integer;
14:
15:  { n = 0, 1, or 2 to select Monochrome or Color settings }
16:  procedure SetCursor(N: Integer);
17:  var
18:     Reg: Registers;
19:  begin
20:     N := N * 2;
21:     with Reg do
22:     begin
23:       if LastMode = Mono then
24:       begin
25:         Ch := Monochrome[N];
26:         Cl := Monochrome[N+1];
27:       end else
28:       begin
29:         Ch := Color[N];
```

```
30:          Cl := Color[N+1]
31:        end;
32:        Ah := 1;
33:        Intr($10, Reg)
34:      end
35:  end;
36:
37:  begin
38:    Writeln('Change cursor style:');
39:    Write('-1=No change; 0=Normal; 1=Half block; 2=Full block ? ');
40:    Readln(Choice);
41:    if (0 <= Choice) and (Choice <= 2)
42:      then SetCursor(Choice);
43:    Writeln('Press Enter to end program.');
44:    Write('New cursor style: ');
45:    Readln
46:  end.
```

Calling DOS Functions

Of course, one of the main purposes for the Dos unit is to call routines in the MS-DOS or PC-DOS operating system. These operating system calls are readily available to assembly language programmers and, with the help of the Dos unit, to Turbo Pascal programmers, too. In assembly language, the conventional way to call a DOS routine is to place a function number in register AH, initialize other registers the function needs, and then execute interrupt $21. For example, this fragment displays the character A by calling the DOS character output routine, number 2:

```
DISPLAY:  mov  AH,2
          mov  DL,'A'
          int  21H
```

That, obviously, is not Pascal. The mov AH,2 instruction is assembly language for "move the value 2 into register AH." But in Turbo Pascal, you cannot move values into computer registers, which are physically located on the processor chip inside your system. Instead, you have to use the simulated Registers record of Figure 9-2 and then call the Dos unit MsDos routine, which loads the real registers and calls DOS for you.

There are two ways to call DOS routines: You can call MsDos with simulated register values as just described, or you can call several predeclared Dos unit procedures and functions that simplify common DOS operations. The MsDos method takes a single variable parameter of type Registers:

```
procedure MsDos(var Reg: Registers);
```

For each DOS call you make, be sure to assign appropriate values to the simulated register fields in record Reg. The slightest mistake can cause serious problems and can even erase disk files unexpectedly. Use MsDos carefully. It bites.

In all cases, assign to register AH the number of the DOS routine you want to call. Also assign values to other registers that this routine requires. You don't have to initialize unused register fields. Finally, pass Reg to MsDos. Afterwards, if the DOS routine returns any register values, you'll find them in the same Reg record.

A simple example shows how to use MsDos. Program 9-6 displays the DOS version number—similar to typing VER at the command line prompt. Line 6 assigns the DOS version routine number, $30, to register field AH. Then, line 7 calls MsDos, which passes the version number back in registers AL and AH. Line 8 displays this number.

Consult a DOS technical reference for other interrupt and DOS function numbers and their requirements.

Program 9-6: VERSION.PAS

```
 1:  program Version;
 2:  uses Dos;
 3:  var
 4:    Reg: Registers;
 5:  begin
 6:    Reg.AH := $30;
 7:    MsDos(Reg);
 8:    Writeln('DOS Version = ', Reg.AL, '.', Reg.AH);
 9:    Readln
10:  end.
```

Starting with Turbo Pascal 5.0, you can call the Dos unit's DosVersion function to perform the same action that Program 9-6 demonstrates. DosVersion returns a Word value representing the DOS version. Use the Lo function to extract the major version number from this value. Use Hi to extract the minor revision number. To try DosVersion, replace lines 3-9 in Program 9-6 with:

```
var
  V: Word;
begin
  V := DosVersion;
  Writeln('DOS Version = ', Lo(V) '.', Hi(V))
end.
```

The first statement assigns DosVersion's result to V. This saves time by not calling DosVersion twice in the Writeln statement—a good programming technique to remember. Limiting the number of times a program calls functions and procedures keeps the code running fast.

The System Date

Two routines inspect and change the computer's system date. GetDate reads the current date. SetDate changes the date to anything you want. The procedures are defined as:

```
procedure GetDate(var Year, Month, Day, DayOfWeek: Word);
procedure SetDate(Year, Month, Day: Word);
```

GetDate returns the year, month, day, and day of week. Years are full values like 1988 and 2001. Months range from 1 for January to 12 for December. Days are the day of month. And the day of week equals 0 for Sunday, 1 for Monday, 2 for Tuesday, and so forth.

SetDate takes one less parameter than GetDate. There's no need to specify the day of week when setting the date. Program 9-7 demonstrates these procedures by calculating the day number for dates after January 1, 1980. (DOS stores years relative to 1980, so the program doesn't work with earlier dates.) Line 13 preserves the current date for restoring later in line 20. Lines 17-18 change the date by calling SetDate and then immediately calling GetDate, which returns the day of week.

Program 9-7: DAYS.PAS

```
1:   program Days;
2:   uses Dos;
3:
4:   const
5:     DayName: array[0 .. 6] of string[3] =
6:       ('Sun', 'Mon', 'Tue', 'Wed', 'Thu', 'Fri', 'Sat');
7:
8:   var
9:     OldYear, OldMonth, OldDay,
10:    Year, Month, Day, DayOfWeek: Word;
11:
12:  begin
13:    GetDate(OldYear, OldMonth, OldDay, DayOfWeek);
14:    Write('Year? '); Readln(Year);
```

continued

Program 9-7: continued

```
15:    Write('Month? '); Readln(Month);
16:    Write('Day? '); Readln(Day);
17:    SetDate(Year, Month, Day);
18:    GetDate(Year, Month, Day, DayOfWeek);
19:    Writeln('Day = ', DayName[DayOfWeek]);
20:    SetDate(OldYear, OldMonth, OldDay);
21:    Readln
22:  end.
```

Two similar routines, GetTime and SetTime, inspect and change the system time:

```
procedure GetTime(var Hour, Minute, Second, Sec100: Word);
procedure SetTime(Hour, Minute, Second, Sec100: Word);
```

GetTime reads the current hour, minute, second, and hundredths of seconds. SetTime changes the system time to any values you want. The hundredths parameter Sec100 is not very accurate. In general, you should not expect accuracy of most PC system times to be any greater than about 1/4 second.

If your computer has a hardware clock, the Dos unit date and time routines do not change the clock's internal settings. They change only the date and time that DOS maintains—whether or not the computer has a hardware clock. Therefore, after changing the date and time, you don't have to change it back if you have a hardware clock. You can simply reboot or use the DOS DATE and TIME commands.

File and Disk Routines

A number of Dos unit routines perform special operations on disks and disk files— operations that Turbo Pascal file-handling routines cannot do on their own. Two of the simplest in this set are:

```
function DiskFree(Drive: Byte): LongInt;
function DiskSize(Drive: Byte): LongInt;
```

DiskFree returns the number of bytes available on any drive. DiskSize returns the total of all bytes used and unused on any drive. Specify the Drive as a number with 0 for the current drive, 1 for drive A:, 2 for B:, and so on. These LongInt functions make it easy to display a report of disk usage with only three Writeln statements:

```
Writeln('Disk size  = ', DiskSize(0));
Writeln('Bytes free = ', DiskFree(0));
Writeln('Bytes used = ', DiskSize(0) - DiskFree(0));
```

Procedures GetFAttr (Get File Attribute) and SetFAttr (Set File Attribute) examine and change the single-bit attributes stored with every entry in disk directories. See Figure 9-3 for a description of each attribute bit. Table 9-6 lists corresponding Dos unit constants that you can use to examine and change these bits.

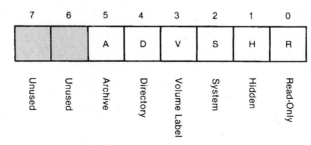

Figure 9-3 The directory attribute byte.

Table 9-6 Dos file attribute constants.

Constant	Hex value	Bit number
ReadOnly	$01	0
Hidden	$02	1
SysFile	$04	2
VolumeID	$08	3
Directory	$10	4
Archive	$20	5
AnyFile	$3F	0-5

To examine a file's attribute, assign the file name to a file variable, which can be any type, and call GetFAttr, passing the unopened file and a Word variable:

```
var
  F: file;
  Attr: Word;
begin
  Assign(F, 'TEST.DAT');
  GetFAttr(F, Attr);
  if DosError <> 0
    then Writeln('Error locating file')
    else Writeln('Attribute = ', Attr);
end.
```

Checking DosError detects errors. If DosError is not 0, the cause is probably a bad or nonexistent file name. To check for specific attributes, use the sum of the first six constants from Table 9-6 logically **and**ed with the attribute byte. For example, this tells you if the archive bit is set, indicating a recent change to the file:

```
GetFAttr(F, attr);
if (Attr and Archive) = 0
  then Writeln('file is backed up')
  else Writeln('file has been changed');
```

You can also change a file's attribute. Again, assign a name to any file and pass the unopened file variable plus the sum of the attributes you want to set. SetFAttr does not preserve the current attribute settings. To do that, precede SetFAttr with GetFAttr as in this example, which sets the file's hidden and read-only bits:

```
Assign(F, 'TEST.TXT');
GetFAttr(F, Attr);
Attr := Attr or (ReadOnly + Hidden);
SetFAttr(F, Attr);
```

Setting the hidden bit this way hides the program name in directories. To undo this change, turn off all attribute bits with:

```
Assign(F, 'TEST.TXT');
SetFAttr(F, 0);
```

File Dates and Times

As you no doubt know, DOS stores the date and time when a file was most recently changed. The Dos unit lets you examine and change this information—but not as easily as it lets you work with the system clock. To save disk space, DOS encodes the date and time in two 16-bit values, which the Dos unit further packs together into one 32-bit LongInt value. Table 9-7 lists the components of this value while Figure 9-4 shows the Dos unit DateTime record, which makes it easy to work with encoded dates and times.

Table 9-7 Date and time packing format.

Field	Range	Bits
Sec	0-59	0-5
Min	0-59	6-11
Hour	0-23	12-16
Day	1-31	17-21
Month	1-12	22-25
* Year	0-99	26-31

* Note: For the correct year, add 1980.

```
DateTime =
  record
    Year, Month, Day, Hour, Min, Sec: Word;
  end;
```

Figure 9-4 The Dos unit DateTime record.

Call PackTime to convert a DateTime record into a packed, 32-bit LongInt variable. Call UnPackTime to do the reverse, unpacking a LongInt value into a DateTime record. These procedures are defined as:

```
procedure PackTime(var T: DateTime; var P: LongInt);
procedure UnpackTime(P: LongInt; var T: DateTime);
```

To read the date and time of any file, assign its name to a file variable and pass the unopened file along with a LongInt variable to GetFTime:

```
var
  Unpacked: DateTime;
  Packed: LongInt;
  F: file;
begin
  Assign(F, 'TEST.DAT');
  GetFTime(F, Packed);
  UnpackTime(Packed, Unpacked)
end.
```

Unpacking the encoded value into a DateTime record makes the date values more accessible. To change a file's date and time, pass the unopened file variable plus a packed LongInt value to SetFTime:

```
with Unpacked do
begin
  { Fill in year, date, month, ..., fields }
end;
PackTime(Unpacked, Packed);
Assign(F, 'TEST.DAT');
SetFTime(F, Packed);
```

Directory Routines

FindFirst and FindNext make listing directories far simpler than in previous Turbo Pascal versions. Both of these handy routines use the record type listed in Figure 9-5. DOS uses field Fill for its own purposes. For each file entry located in a directory, Attr equals its attribute (see Figure 9-3), Time equals the packed date and time (see Table 9-7 and Figure 9-4), Size equals the file size in bytes, and string Name is the file's name.

```
SearchRec =
  record
    Fill: array[1 .. 21] of Byte;
    Attr: Byte;
    Time: LongInt;
    Size: LongInt;
    Name: string[12];
  end;
```

Figure 9-5 The Dos unit SearchRec record.

To read file name entries from a directory, first call FindFirst with three parameters:

```
procedure FindFirst(Path: PathStr; Attr: Word; var F: SearchRec);
```

The Path can be any string you would normally type to the DOS DIR command, for example, *.* or C:\PROG*.EXE. The Attr word equals the attributes you want to find. Use the constant AnyFile (see Table 9-6) to locate all files including those normally hidden from view, subdirectories, plus regular files. The last FindFirst parameter is a SearchRec variable. After FindFirst, any file entries matching the parameters are in this record.

The next step is to call FindNext, this time with the same SearchRec variable filled in by FindFirst. FindNext is defined as:

```
procedure FindNext(var F: SearchRec);
```

Never call this procedure without first calling FindFirst and never modify the Fill field in the SearchRec record. DOS needs the information in this field to continue searching for file name entries after finding the first one.

Program 9-8 shows how to put these ideas together to list a disk directory, displaying file names and sizes in parentheses, and adding the total space occupied by all listed files. Line 13 tests DosError after FindFirst, looping until either this procedure or FindNext in line 17 fail to execute, indicating there are no more matching files to be found. Compile this program to a disk file DR.EXE (or any other name). Then type DR *.*, or DR C:\UTIL*.PAS for a directory.

Program 9-8: DR.PAS

```
 1:  program Directory;
 2:  uses Dos;
 3:  var
 4:    Arg: string;
 5:    Total: LongInt;
 6:    FileStuff: SearchRec;
 7:  begin
 8:    if ParamCount = 0
 9:      then Arg := '*.*'
10:      else Arg := ParamStr(1);
11:    Total := 0;
12:    FindFirst(Arg, AnyFile, FileStuff);
13:    while DosError = 0 do with FileStuff do
14:    begin
15:      Writeln(Name, ' (', Size, ')');
16:      Total := Total + Size;
17:      FindNext(FileStuff)
18:    end;
19:    Writeln;
20:    Writeln('Total size = ', Total, ' bytes');
21:    Readln
22:  end.
```

Taking a Break

As explained earlier, you can disable Ctrl-Break checking for Write and Writeln statements by setting the Crt unit CheckBreak switch to false. DOS maintains a similar variable, called the *Break switch*. When this switch is off, DOS checks for Ctrl-C key presses during console input and output, printer operations, and serial communications. When the switch is on, DOS checks for Ctrl-C at every system call.

To read the current setting of DOS's Break switch, call the Dos unit procedure GetCBreak procedure as in Program 9-9, line 6, passing the name of a Boolean variable. The procedure sets the variable equal to the current Break-switch value. To change the Break-switch setting, pass true or false (or a Boolean variable) to SetCBreak as in lines 8 and 15.

Program 9-9 counts from 1 to 10, pausing for about 1 second between displaying each number. Run the program and press Ctrl-C to stop execution before reaching 10. This works even though CheckBreak is set to false because line 8 turns on the DOS Break switch, causing DOS to check for Ctrl-C during all system calls. In this example, the program halts during the call to DosVersion at line 13. Now, change true to false in line 8 and run the program again. This time, because no DOS I/O is performed, you can no longer break out of the code by pressing Ctrl-C.

> **Note**: The Crt unit CheckBreak switch is not the same as the DOS Break switch, which affects only calls to DOS routines. The Crt unit's fast direct-video routines ignore the setting of the DOS switch. When running BreakOut from Turbo Pascal's IDE, you may be able to halt the program by pressing Ctrl-Break regardless of SetCBreak's setting. For a more accurate test, compile the program to disk (use the Compile menu to set Destination to Disk) and run BreakOut from the DOS command line.

Program 9-9; BREAKOUT.PAS

```
1:  program BreakOut;
2:  uses Crt, Dos;
3:  var I, J: Integer;
4:    OldBreak: Boolean;
5:  begin
6:    GetCBreak(OldBreak);
7:    CheckBreak := false;
8:    SetCBreak(true);
9:    for I := 1 to 10 do
```

```
10:     begin
11:       Write(I, ' ');
12:       Delay(1000);
13:       J := DosVersion
14:     end;
15:     SetCBreak(OldBreak)
16:   end.
```

Trust but Verify

Programmers are trusting souls. They (or, I should say, we) are prone to believing that writing data to disk safely stores the data away, ready for reading later. But that's not always what happens. Despite built-in safeguards in disk controller circuits, it's possible to write data to disk only to discover that same data was somehow changed in the process, usually due to a flaw on the disk surface.

One way to increase the security of saved data is to read the same disk sectors immediately after writing them. If this operation fails, the program can take corrective action. Or, at the very least, it can display an error message. Better to know now than months later that a Save-File command didn't work!

DOS has the ability to read back every disk sector following a disk write operation. To switch on this ability, give the DOS command VERIFY ON. To switch it off, type VERIFY OFF. To see the current setting, just type VERIFY. Most of the time, you'll want to leave the switch off—disk writes go at half speed when verification is in effect.

In Turbo Pascal programs, call GetVerify to read the state of the DOS *read-after-write-verify* switch. Call SetVerify to change the state of this switch. Program 9-10 demonstrates how to use these procedures (see lines 50 ,51, 54, and 55). The program writes four hundred, 512-byte blocks to a test file named TEST.$$$. (Be sure to have at least 204,800 bytes of free disk space before running the test.) Doing this with verification on and then off demonstrates the effect of different switch settings. The program also serves as a useful benchmark of disk performance—you might want to run it to compare drive speeds on different systems.

Program 9-10: DISKBENC.PAS

```
1:  program DiskBenchmark;
2:  uses Crt, Dos;
3:  const
4:    FileName = 'TEST.$$$';  { Test file name }
```

continued

Program 9-10: continued

```
 5:     Blocks = 400;   { Warning: requires 204800 bytes disk space }
 6:   type
 7:     ArrayType = array[0 .. 511] of Byte;
 8:   var
 9:     F: file of ArrayType;
10:     Verify: Boolean;
11:     Hour1, Minute1, Second1, Hundredths1: Word;
12:     Hour2, Minute2, Second2, Hundredths2: Word;
13:     V: ArrayType;
14:
15:   function Seconds(Hour, Minute, Second, Hundredths: Word): Real;
16:   begin
17:     Seconds := (Hour * 3600) + (Minute * 60) + Second
18:       + (Hundredths / 100)
19:   end;
20:
21:   procedure ShowTime;
22:   var
23:     Time1, Time2: Real;
24:   begin
25:     Time1 := Seconds(Hour1, Minute1, Second1, Hundredths1);
26:     Time2 := Seconds(Hour2, Minute2, Second2, Hundredths2);
27:     Writeln('Time1 ........ ', Time1:8:2, ' second(s)');
28:     Writeln('Time2 ........ ', Time2:8:2, ' second(s)');
29:     Writeln('Elapsed time = ', Time2 - Time1:8:2, ' second(s)')
30:   end;
31:
32:   procedure Test;
33:   var
34:     I: Integer;
35:   begin
36:     Writeln('Start: Writing ', Blocks, ' blocks');
37:     GetTime(Hour1, Minute1, Second1, Hundredths1);
38:     Assign(F, FileName);
39:     Rewrite(F);
40:     for I := 1 to Blocks do
41:       Write(F, V);
42:     Close(F);
```

```
43:     GetTime(Hour2, Minute2, Second2, Hundredths2);
44:     Erase(F);
45:     Writeln('End of test');
46:     ShowTime
47:  end;
48:
49:  begin
50:     SetVerify(true);
51:     GetVerify(Verify);
52:     Writeln('-- Testing with Verify = ', Verify);
53:     Test;
54:     SetVerify(false);
55:     GetVerify(Verify);
56:     Writeln('-- Testing with Verify = ', Verify);
57:     Test;
58:     Readln
59:  end.
```

Environmental Concerns

The DOS environment is a block of memory composed of ASCII character variables in the form *name=value.* Standard environment variables such as COMSPEC, which specifies the directory path to COMMAND.COM, and PROMPT, which sets the DOS prompt characters, are stored along with others that you can create with the SET command. For example, to create an environment variable named TMP and assign to it the name of a RAM disk drive E:\, you'd give the command SET TMP=E:\ either directly from the DOS command line or in a batch file.

In Turbo Pascal programs, the Dos unit EnvCount function tells you how many environment variables exist. A simple statement displays this number:

```
Writeln(EnvCount, ' variables');
```

The EnvStr function returns a string equal to a specific variable. To display the value of the first variable, you can write:

```
Writeln('Variable #1:', EnvStr(1));
```

Program 9-11 demonstrates how to use these two functions to display all environment variables. The program operates similarly to typing SET and pressing Enter at the DOS prompt.

Program 9-11: ENVIRON.PAS

```pascal
 1:   program Environment;
 2:   uses Crt, Dos;
 3:   var
 4:     I: Integer;
 5:   begin
 6:     Writeln;
 7:     Writeln('There are ', EnvCount, ' environment strings');
 8:     Writeln;
 9:     for I := 1 to EnvCount do
10:       Writeln(I:2, ' : ', EnvStr(I));
11:     Readln
12:   end.
```

Another function, GetEnv, reads environment variables just as EnvStr does but lets you specify variables by name. For example, this sets a string S to the value of the PATH variable:

```pascal
S := GetEnv('PATH');
Writeln('Path is ', S);
```

If the PATH environment variable doesn't exist, the first statement sets the length of string S to 0.

Using environment variables is a great way to pass information around in DOS. Programs can look for specific variables, using their values in place of various defaults. For example, you might design your program to place temporary files in the current directory, but give people the option to direct those files elsewhere, perhaps to a RAM disk for extra speed. The program uses an environment variable TMP for the directory name:

```pascal
DirName := GetEnv('TMP');
if Length(DirName) > 0
  then Writeln('Writing files to ', DirName);
```

Program 9-12 demonstrates GetEnv and also serves as a useful utility that enhances the DOS CD (CHDIR) command. To use the program, first set up an environment variable CDPATH with a command such as:

```
SET CDPATH=C:\;C:\APPL;C:\PROJ;C:\USR
```

This assumes that your main drive is C: and that you have several subdirectories named APPL, PROJ, and USR. Substitute your actual subdirectory names for these and add others separated by semicolons. You'll probably want to insert this line into your AUTOEXEC.BAT file to create CDPATH automatically when you boot.

Next, compile Program 9-12 and save (or rename) the result to XD.EXE. Copy this file to any file listed in your DOS PATH setting (another environment variable that tells DOS where to look for executable programs and batch files).

After completing these steps, type XD *name,* where *name* is the name of a subdirectory located in any of the directories listed in CDPATH. You may have to try this a few times to understand the value of this utility, but I think you'll be pleased with the results. Suppose, for example, you have two subdirectories named C:\APPL\WS4 and C:\APPL\WORK. To change to WORK, you'd normally type:

```
CD C:\APPL\WORK
```

But, with the XD program, as long as C:\APPL is one of the CDPATH directories, you can instead type the shorter:

```
XD WORK
```

This performs the same task as the CD command with a lot less typing. And it works no matter which directory happens to be current.

Program 9-12: XD.PAS

```
 1:  {$I-}              { Switch off I/O error checking }
 2:  program XDir;
 3:  uses Crt, Dos;
 4:  var
 5:    TryPath, Paths: string[80];
 6:    P: Integer;
 7:  begin
 8:    ChDir(ParamStr(1));
 9:    if IoResult <> 0 then
10:    begin
11:      Paths := GetEnv('CDPATH') + ';';
12:      while Length(Paths) > 0 do
13:      begin
14:        P := Pos(';', Paths);
15:        TryPath := Copy(Paths, 1, P - 1);
16:        Delete(Paths, 1, P);
17:        if Length(TryPath) > 0 then
18:        begin
19:          if TryPath[ Length(TryPath) ] <> '\'
20:            then TryPath := TryPath + '\';
21:          ChDir(TryPath + ParamStr(1));
```

continued

```
22:              if IoResult = 0
23:                then Halt(0)
24:          end
25:        end;
26:      Writeln('Can''t change to ', ParamStr(1))
27:    end
28: end.
```

File and Path Names

Programs that read and write disk files usually store file names in string variables. As long as the files are in the current directory, keeping track of file names is simple. But the best programs are not so restrictive, letting people enter complex path names such as A:\MYWORK\ACCOUNTS.DAT to read and write files on floppy disks and in subdirectories. The Dos unit has three useful routines that help make working with paths easy.

The FExpand function expands a simple file name such as INIT.TXT to its full path, prefacing the name with a drive letter and subdirectories, thereby pinpointing the file's exact location on disk. FExpand returns a PathStr defined along with these other special strings in the Dos unit:

```
Pathstr = string[79];
DirStr  = string[67];
NameStr = string[8];
ExtStr  = string[4];
```

To use FExpand, declare a PathStr variable, perhaps named Path, and then prompt for new file names this way:

```
Write('File name? ');
Readln(Path);
Path := FExpand(Path);
```

The call to FExpand adds drive and subdirectory information to Path, letting the program change the current directory with ChDir but still be able to open the file by specifying the complete path.

FSplit reverses what FExpand does, taking a full path name and splitting it into pieces. FSplit's parameters are four string variables (see Program 9-13, lines 6-9 and 21). Also demonstrated here is function FSearch, which tries to locate a file in a series of subdirectories. For example, assuming Path is a PathStr string variable, to search for INIT.DAT in the three directories, C:\, C:\DOS, and C:\WORK, you can use the statement:

```
Path := FSearch('INIT.DAT', 'C:\;C:\DOS;C:\WORK');
```

If INIT.DAT is found in any of the listed paths, FSearch returns the full path name. If INIT.DAT is not found, FSearch returns a zero-length string.

Usually, you'll call FSearch with the value of the PATH environment variable (or another), using a statement such as:

```
Path := FSearch('PROG.EXE', GetEnv('PATH'));
```

To demonstrate these routines, run Program 9-13 and enter the name of a file to locate among the directories listed in SearchPath (line 4). Try entering GRAPH.DOC and TURBO.EXE. Lines 13, 19, and 21 show the FSearch, FExpand, and FSplit routines in action.

Program 9-13: FINDFILE.PAS

```
 1:   program FindFile;
 2:   uses Crt, Dos;
 3:   const
 4:     SearchPath = 'C:\;C:\TP;C:\TP\UNIT;C:\TP\BGI;C:\TP\DOC';
 5:   var
 6:     Fname, Path: PathStr;
 7:     Name: NameStr;
 8:     Dir: DirStr;
 9:     Ext: ExtStr;
10:   begin
11:     Write('Find what file? ');
12:     Readln(Fname);
13:     Path := FSearch(Fname, SearchPath);
14:     if Length(Path) = 0
15:     then
16:       Writeln('Can''t find ', Fname)
17:     else
18:       begin
19:         Path := FExpand(Path);
20:         Writeln('Path     = ', Path);
21:         FSplit(Path, Dir, Name, Ext);
```

continued

Program 9-13: continued

```
22:        Writeln('Dir       = ', Dir);
23:        Writeln('Name      = ', Name);
24:        Writeln('Extension = ', Ext)
25:      end;
26:    Readln
27:  end.
```

The Printer Unit

The Printer unit is the shortest in Turbo Pascal's standard library. It contains only one text variable, Lst, which makes it easy to send text to the printer.

Use Lst in Write and Writeln statements. You don't have to initialize Lst or close it when your program ends. The Printer unit takes care of these details, attaching Lst to LPT1:, the logical device normally connected to printers. Program 9-14 uses Lst to read and print any text file. Line 12 writes a form feed control character (ASCII 12) to Lst, which advances the paper to the top of a new page. Line 24 shows how to print one line of text.

Program 9-14: LISTER.PAS

```
 1:  program Lister;
 2:  uses Crt, Printer;
 3:  var
 4:    InFile: Text;
 5:    FileName: string;
 6:    OneLine:  string;
 7:    Lines: LongInt;
 8:
 9:  procedure Page;
10:  { Start a new page }
11:  begin
12:    Write(Lst, Chr(12))  { Send form feed command to printer }
13:  end;
14:
15:  begin
16:    Write('List what file? ');
17:    Readln(FileName);
```

```
18:    Assign(InFile, FileName);
19:    Reset(InFile);
20:    Lines := 0;
21:    while not Eof(InFile) do
22:    begin
23:      Readln(InFile, OneLine);
24:      Writeln(Lst, OneLine);
25:      Inc(Lines);
26:      if Lines mod 58 = 0
27:        then Page
28:    end;
29:    if Lines mod 58 <> 0
30:      then Page;
31:    Close(InFile)
32:  end.
```

The Turbo3 Unit

The Turbo3 unit contains two variables and several routines that make it possible to compile most Turbo Pascal version 3.0 and earlier programs.

If you receive the source code to a 3.0 program, which you have trouble compiling, add a **uses** declaration after the program name:

```
uses Turbo3;
```

Often, this is all you need to do to compile an older program. If this doesn't work, though, refer to your Turbo Pascal references for hints on converting older Turbo Pascal programs to work with version 6.0. (The Turbo3 unit contains nothing of value for writing new programs. Unless you have to convert older programs, don't waste your time studying Turbo3.)

The Graph3 Unit

The Graph3 unit contains the programming from Turbo Pascal 3.0's GRAPH.BIN file. Use this unit to compile Turbo Pascal version 3.0 and earlier graphics programs. Like Turbo3, Graph3 is intended only to support older programs—the unit contains nothing of value for writing new code. See chapter 11 for a better approach to writing graphics programs using the new Graph unit.

Graph3 works only on CGA (Color Graphics Adapter) systems. To convert 3.0 graphics programs, remove all references to GRAPH.BIN and GRAPH.P and add this **uses** declaration after the program name:

```
uses Graph3;
```

Summary

Units add new features to the basic Turbo Pascal language by attaching to programs precompiled libraries of procedures, functions, constants, types, and variables. Units are like warehouses, stocked with raw materials that all programs can share.

The **uses** declaration adds everything inside a unit to a program. You can specify one or more units in a **uses** declaration, which must come immediately after the **program** header.

Units are stored in one of two kinds of disk files. TPU (Turbo Pascal Unit) files store individual units. TPL (Turbo Pascal Library) files store one or more units together. The Turbo Pascal compiler automatically loads a special library file, TURBO.TPL, making the units in this file instantly available to programs.

Turbo Pascal comes with several ready-to-use units: Crt, Dos, Graph, Graph3, Overlay, Printer, System, and Turbo3. You do not have to specify the System unit in a **uses** declaration. When compiling programs, Turbo Pascal always includes System, which contains standard runtime procedures and functions. To use the features in other units, you must list the unit names in **uses**.

The Crt unit contains items for controlling the display and keyboard. Crt also improves the performance of Write and Writeln statements with fast direct-video code. The Dos unit makes it easy to call MS-DOS routines. The Printer unit helps you print text. Turbo3 and Graph3 contain declarations that help you to compile Turbo Pascal programs written for version 3.0 or earlier. The Graph unit, described in Chapter 11, contains a powerful set of graphics commands. The Overlay unit, described in Chapter 10, lets you convert other units to overlay modules.

Exercises

9-1. Write a program to display a menu and let people read and view any text file. Use the Crt unit, ClrScr, ClrEol, and other features to create a good-looking display.

9-2. Add a procedure to your answer for exercise 9-1 to let people choose various colors and screen attributes for menus, text, and program messages.

9-3. Write a custom directory lister using the Dos unit to display file names in columns instead of one file name on a line as in Program 9-8.

9-4. (Advanced) Write a procedure to use in any program to select file names by moving a highlighted bar around in a directory. Your program should use the Dos and Crt units.

9-5. Pick any DOS function from a technical reference and use the Dos unit's MsDos procedure to call the function.

9-6. Write a utility to determine the space free and used for all disk drives installed on the computer.

9-7. Write a program to print and view a text file simultaneously. Use the Printer unit.

10

Custom Units and Overlays

- The Parts of a Unit
- Writing Your Own Units
- Declaring Procedures and Functions in Units
- Compiling Units
- Using Your Own Units
- The Unit Directory
- Using the XtraStuf Unit
- Units That Use Other Units
- Circular Unit References
- Multiple Units in Memory
- Unit Identifier Conflicts
- Units in Memory
- Near and Far
- Installing Units in Library Files
- Using TPUMover
- Large-Program Development with Units
- Overlays

10

Key Words and Identifiers

begin, **end**, **implementation**, **interface**, OvrGetBuf, OvrInit,
OvrInitEMS, OvrResult, OvrSetBuf, **unit**, **uses**

By storing your favorite routines in units, you build programming libraries for other
programs to share. You can also divide large programs into pieces, storing different
parts in separate units, which you compile individually. Called *separate compilation,* this process reduces compilation time and helps you to better organize the
many thousands of statements in a large program.

This chapter explains how to write and use your own units. You'll learn about
the design of a unit, how to compile units to memory and to disk, and how to install
compiled units in library files. You'll also learn how to convert units into *overlay
modules,* a technique for constructing programs that are too large to fit entirely in
memory.

The Parts of a Unit

All units have four parts, whether or not you write them yourself. The four parts are:

1. Unit declaration.

2. Unit interface.

3. Unit implementation.

4. Unit initialization.

The *unit declaration* is like a program declaration. It gives the unit a name and tells Turbo Pascal this is a unit and not a program. On disk, precompiled units store the unit's name along with the unit's contents. Programs that use the unit must specify this name in a **uses** declaration in order to use a unit's contents.

The *unit interface,* sometimes called the unit's *public* section, describes all the features inside a unit that host programs, and other units, can share. In text form, the interface contains labels, constants, types, and variables, plus **procedure** and **function** declarations. In compiled form, Turbo Pascal stores an encoded form of the unit interface section along with the unit's other items. When you later compile a program that uses the unit, the interface tells the compiler the syntax of the unit's features.

The *unit implementation* contains items that are *private* to the statements inside the unit. Contained in the implementation are the actual statements that *implement* the procedures and functions described in the interface. The implementation can also contain additional labels, constants, types, and variables—as well as private procedures and functions—that are strictly for the unit's own use.

The last part of a unit is the *initialization,* an optional block of statements that resembles the main body of a normal Pascal program. The statements in the initialization run before the statements in a program that uses the unit, giving the unit the ability to initialize its own variables and automatically perform other jobs immediately before the host program begins. Some units have no initialization section and, therefore, perform no startup actions.

Writing Your Own Units

Writing your own units is as easy as writing programs. Anything a program can do, a unit can do—if not better, at least as well.

To illustrate the basic design of all units, Program 10-1 lists a shell, a starting place for your own unit designs. Line 1 is the unit declaration, which gives the unit a name and tells the compiler this is a unit and not a program. In your own units, replace Shell with your unit's name.

Line 3 begins the unit interface, the public parts you want other programs (and other units) to know about. The comments in lines 5, 7, and 9 show where to insert various declarations such as **uses**, **const**, **type**, **var**, **procedure**, and **function**.

Line 12 begins the implementation containing the unit's private parts. In this section, you can insert a second **uses** declaration in place of the comment at line 14—an advanced technique that allows multiple units to refer to each other in circular fashion. Line 16 shows where you can insert **label**, **const**, **type**, and **var** declarations, all of which are for the unit's internal use—none of these declarations is visible to host programs that use the unit. Line 18 shows where to place procedure and function bodies. Every procedure and function declared in the interface (see line 9) must have a corresponding statement block in the implementation. You may also insert private procedures and functions here.

The final part of the unit shell in Program 10-1 is the initialization, lines 21-25. Insert the statements between **begin** and **end** that you want to execute before a host program begins running. When a host program uses more than one unit, all initialization parts run in the order the units appear in the host's **uses** declaration. If you have no initialization statements to perform, you can write **begin end** with nothing between, or take out **begin** and end the unit with a lone **end**.

Program 10-1: SHELL.PAS

```
 1:  unit Shell;
 2:
 3:  interface
 4:
 5:  { Place a uses declaration here }
 6:
 7:  { Place const, type, and var declarations here }
 8:
 9:  { Place procedure and function declarations here }
10:
11:
12:  implementation
13:
14:  { Place a second uses declaration here }
15:
16:  { Place private label, const, type, and var declarations here }
17:
18:  { Place procedure and function bodies here }
19:
20:
21:  begin   { optional }
22:
23:  { Insert initialization statements here }
24:
25:  end.
```

Declaring Procedures and Functions in Units

An example of a real unit will help you to understand the outline in the unit Shell. Program 10-2 is a collection of seven general-purpose procedures and functions plus one data type that I've been using for years. Precompiling these routines in a unit makes them readily available. To add my favorite library to any program, I simply type **uses** XtraStuf after the **program** declaration.

Program 10-2: XTRASTUF.PAS

```
 1:  unit XtraStuf;
 2:
 3:  interface
 4:
 5:  uses Crt;
 6:
 7:  type CharSet = set of Char;
 8:
 9:  function Dncase(Ch: Char): Char;
10:  procedure GetCommand(var Command: Char; Commandset: Charset);
11:  procedure BumpStrup(var S: string);
12:  function InRange(N, Min, Max: Integer): Boolean;
13:  function Verified(Message: string): Boolean;
14:  procedure PromptAt(X, Y: Integer; Message: string);
15:  procedure Center(Y: Integer; Message: string);
16:
17:
18:  implementation
19:
20:  { Convert ch from upper- to lowercase }
21:  function Dncase(Ch: Char): Char;
22:  begin
23:    if ('A' <= Ch) and (Ch <= 'Z')
24:      then Dncase := Chr(Ord(Ch) + 32)
25:      else Dncase := Ch
26:  end;
27:
28:  { Return command from keyboard from chars in commandset }
29:  procedure GetCommand(var Command: Char; Commandset: Charset);
30:  begin
31:    repeat
32:      Command := Upcase(Readkey)
33:    until Command in commandset
34:  end;
35:
36:  { Convert (bump) string S to uppercase }
37:  procedure BumpStrup(var S: string);
```

continued

Program 10-2: continued

```
38:  var I: Integer;
39:  begin
40:    for I := 1 to Length(S) do
41:      S[I] := Upcase(S[I])
42:  end;
43:
44:  { True if min <= n <= max }
45:  function InRange(N, Min, Max: Integer): Boolean;
46:  begin
47:    InRange := (Min <= N) and (N <= Max)
48:  end;
49:
50:  { True if you type Y or y to message }
51:  function Verified(Message: string): Boolean;
52:  var Ch: Char;
53:  begin
54:    Write(Message, ' ? (y/n) ');
55:    ClrEol;
56:    GetCommand(Ch, ['Y', 'N']);
57:    Writeln(Ch);
58:    Verified := (Ch = 'Y')
59:  end;
60:
61:  { Display message at (x,y), clearing to end of line }
62:  procedure PromptAt(X, Y: Integer; Message: string);
63:  begin
64:    GotoXY(X, Y);
65:    Write(Message);
66:    ClrEol
67:  end;
68:
69:  procedure Center(Y: Integer; Message: string);
70:  { Center message at row y, clearing line }
71:  begin
72:    GotoXY(1, Y);
73:    ClrEol;
74:    Write(Message: 40 + (Length(Message) div 2))
75:  end;
76:
77:  end.
```

Look carefully at Program 10-2's interface (lines 3-15). The seven procedure and function declarations appear without their usual **begin** and **end** key words and do not have any statements. Remember that the interface merely describes what's in the unit—the actual programming comes later. The **type** declaration (line 7) declares CharSet as a set of type Char. Because this declaration is in the interface section, any program using XtraStuf can declare variables of type CharSet as though this were a native Pascal data type.

The implementation section (lines 18-77) contains the programming for the routines declared in the interface. As you can see, the procedures and functions now have bodies and statements that make the routines do their stuff.

When writing your own units, be careful to duplicate all function and procedure declarations in both the interface and implementation parts. This dual format—declaring procedures and functions in the interface and then fleshing them out later in the implementation—resembles the **forward** declarations you learned about in Chapter 4. To demonstrate what happens if you make a mistake, change the parameter type in line 21 from Char to Integer:

```
function Dncase(Ch: Integer): Char;  { ??? }
```

Because Dncase's implementation no longer matches the interface declaration in line 9, compiling the modified unit produces:

```
Error 131: Header does not match previous definition.
```

Turbo Pascal insists that procedures and functions be exactly the same in both the interface and implementation.

If you receive this error frequently, you can optionally remove the parameter lists in the implementation. Turbo Pascal relaxes its own rule and lets you specify procedure and functions with no parameters in the implementation. For an example of how this works, change line 20 to:

```
function Dncase;
```

Even though this new declaration does not match the interface, Turbo Pascal compiles the unit with no errors. If you include parameters, though, the compiler checks that they match their counterparts in the interface. The choice is yours. Some programmers repeat the parameters in both places; others leave them out. In a long unit, it's nice to have the parameters in both places for reference, although you then have to remember to modify both the interface and the implementation if you add or subtract new parameters. Try both approaches until you find the one that works best for you.

> **Note:** If you are following along, undo your changes to the Dncase function now.

Occasionally, you'll see units with their implementation parameter lists surrounded with comment brackets like this:

```
function Dncase(* (Ch: Char): Char *);
```

Of course, this is effectively the same as not declaring the parameter and function type at all. I point this out only because you will see listings that use this style, required by some compilers such as UCSD Pascal and Macintosh Turbo Pascal that do not allow parameter lists to repeat in the implementation. In these systems, the comments are merely references to avoid having to look up parameters in the interface.

Before moving on to the next example, notice that line 77 ends the unit without a **begin**. There are no initializations to perform in this unit and, therefore, no need for an initialization section. This is the only time when an **end** in a statement block does not have to be preceded by **begin**.

Compiling Units

As you can with programs, you can compile units either to disk or to memory. Most of the time, though, you'll compile units to disk files, which end in TPU (for Turbo Pascal Unit). Compiling units to memory is faster than compiling to disk, but it has a serious disadvantage: Host programs can use the units only as long as you remain in Turbo Pascal's IDE. If you compile your units to disk, then you don't have to recompile them for each new programming session.

To compile a unit to disk, first change the *Compile:Destination* command from *Memory* to *Disk.* (Pressing D when the Compile menu is visible toggles this setting, a handy shortcut to remember.) Then press Alt-F9 to compile the unit.

Try this now with Program 10-2. Save the listing text as XTRASTUF.PAS and compile to disk, creating the unit code file XTRASTUF.TPU. You must use the same name for the .PAS file and the unit identifier in line 1. Use the first eight characters for the file name if the unit name is longer. (Previous Turbo Pascal versions recognized the {$U *unitname*} option to refer to units named differently than their disk files. Versions starting with 5.0 no longer permit this option.)

Using Your Own Units

Now that you've written your own unit and compiled it to memory or to disk, you're ready to write a host program that uses the unit's features. You should already have typed Program 10-2, saved the text in file as XTRASTUF.PAS, and compiled to XTRASTUF.TPU on disk.

Next, type Program 10-3 and press Ctrl-F9 to run. This test program demonstrates several of Xtrastuf's features in a design that a larger program might use in a main menu. Press Esc to clear the screen; press A, B, or C to test the GetCommand procedure; press Q to quit.

Program 10-3: TESTXTRA.PAS

```
 1:  program TestXtraStuf;
 2:  uses Crt, XtraStuf;
 3:  const
 4:    TheEndOfTime = false;  { As far as I know }
 5:  var
 6:    Command: Char;
 7:  begin
 8:    ClrScr;
 9:    Center(8, 'A Great New Program');
10:    Center(10, 'from Ugly Duckling Software');
11:    Center(14, '(C) 2001.  No rights reserved.');
12:    repeat
13:      PromptAt(1, 1, 'Menu: A, B, C, Q-uit ');
14:      GetCommand(Command, ['A', 'B', 'C', 'Q', #27]);
15:      ClrScr;
16:      case Command of
17:        'A', 'B', 'C'
18:          : begin
19:              PromptAt(1, 18, 'You typed ');
20:              Write(Command)
21:            end;
22:        'Q'
23:          : begin
24:              GotoXY(1, 24);
25:              if Verified('Do you want to quit')
26:                then Halt
27:            end
28:      end
29:    until TheEndOfTime
30:  end.
```

A few quick experiments with Program 10-3 help explain several other features about writing your own units and host programs. Suppose you make a change to the host (or write a new host). You do not have to recompile the unit—you already did that. For example, add the following line to Program 10-3 between lines 11 and 12:

```
Center(23, '(this is the bottom line)');
```

You can compile and run the new host without recompiling the XtraStuf unit. The only time you have to recompile a unit is if you make changes to the items in the unit.

To handle situations involving many units, some which require recompilation and others that don't, two Turbo Pascal commands automate compiling out-of-date units. Again, a simple experiment helps explain how to use the commands. Reload XTRASTUF.PAS (Program 10-2) and modify line 77, adding an initialization section:

```
77:  begin
78:    ClrScr
79:  end.
```

Because the new initialization section clears the screen, any host program that uses XtraStuf can now assume that the display is clear when the program begins running. If you permanently make this change, remove line 8 from Program 10-3. XtraStuf's initialization statements automatically run before the host program's first statement; therefore, the display is already clear when the program starts.

Having made this and other changes to XtraStuf, there are three ways to recompile both the unit and the host program. These methods assume you either have the host program in the Turbo Pascal editor or you've set the *Compile:Primary file* setting to the name of the host text file. To bring both the unit and host program up to date, follow one of these three steps:

1. Use the *Compile:Make* command. This automatically checks the .PAS text files of all units the host program uses. Any unit text files with dates and times later than the unit's TPU file are recompiled, bringing all units up to date before compiling the main program.

2. Use the *Compile:Build* command, which is identical to *Compile:Make* except that Turbo Pascal compiles all unit .PAS files without checking if any are out of date.

3. Manually recompile each unit the program uses and then compile the program.

The first method—*Compile:Make*—is the best in most cases. You can change various units, modify your program, and use this single command to recompile only the necessary modules to bring the entire project up to date.

The second method—*Compile:Build*—is less helpful, but handy when you have the text files to a multiunit program but not the TPU code files. For example, you might download a multiunit program in text form from a bulletin board or time-sharing system. Use this command to recompile the entire program including all units.

Of course, you can always use the third method, recompiling each unit individually and then compiling (or running) the host program. But, why work so hard when you have easier methods at your disposal?

The Unit Directory

One alternative to storing compiled unit TPU files in the current directory is to change Turbo Pascal's unit directory setting. To do this, use the *Options:Directories* command and type the name of one or more directories in the space labeled *Unit directories.* Separate multiple directory names with semicolons as in C:\TP;C:\MYUNITS. After compiling a unit text file, copy your TPU disk files into one of the specified directories.

Some programmers prefer to store all their TPU files in one place, building a programming library of common routines for many host programs to share. If Turbo Pascal can't find a unit TPU file in the current directory, it looks in the library subdirectory. If it still doesn't find the file needed, the compiler will display the message:

```
Error 15: File not found.
```

Using the XtraStuf Unit

The XtraStuf unit (Program 10-2) contains many useful routines, described in this section. For reference, the procedure and function declarations are repeated here.

function Dncase(Ch: Char): Char;

Pass any character to Dncase to change uppercase letters to lowercase. Only characters A though Z are affected. Other characters are unchanged. Dncase is the reverse of Turbo Pascal's built-in function, Upcase.

procedure GetCommand(var Command: Char; Commandset: Charset);

Use GetCommand to read a single uppercase character from the keyboard, perhaps in a menu as in Program 10-3, line 14. Pass a character variable and a set of characters. GetCommand rejects any characters not in the set. For example, to prompt for a digit from 1 to 4, you could write:

```
var
   Digit: Char;
begin
   Write('Type a digit from 1 to 4: ');
   GetCommand(Digit, ['1' .. '4']);
end;
```

procedure BumpStrup(var S: string);

Pass any string to BumpStrup to convert characters in the string to all uppercase. Characters not in the set 'A'..'Z' are unaffected. To pass short strings to BumpStrup, use the {$V–} compiler directive as in this example which prompts for a file name, converting your answer to uppercase:

```
var
  FileName: string[64];
begin
  Write('File name? ');
  Readln(FileName);
  {$V-} BumpStrup(FileName); {$V+}
end;
```

function InRange(N, Min, Max: Integer): Boolean;

InRange returns true only if N is within the range Min..Max. Use the function in place of **if** statements as in this example, which prompts for a number from 1 to 100:

```
var
  N: Integer;
begin
  repeat
    Write('Enter a number from 1 to 100: ');
    Readln(N)
  until InRange(N, 1, 100);
end;
```

function Verified(Message: string): Boolean;

Verified returns true if you type Y or y to the Message, to which the function adds a question mark and the reminder, (y/n). This function is particularly handy in constructions like this one:

```
if Verified('Do you want to print the report')
  then PrintTheReport;
```

On screen, the message appears as follows, waiting for you to respond yes or no:

```
Do you want to print the report? (y/n)
```

procedure PromptAt(X, Y: Integer; Message: string);

Use this procedure to display strings at any (X,Y) location on screen. I find the routine particularly handy for constructing data entry screens where people type information into *fields*. For example, you could write:

```
PromptAt(1, 10, 'Name              : ');
Readln(Name);
PromptAt(1, 11, 'Address           : ');
Readln(Address);
PromptAt(1, 12, 'City,  State,  Zip : ');
Readln(CityStZip);
```

procedure Center(Y: Integer; Message: string);

Call Center to display Message centered on row Y. For a few examples, see lines 9-11 in Program 10-3.

Units That Use Other Units

Any unit can use any other unit by inserting a **uses** declaration after the **interface** key word. For example, if you write a new unit that needs some of the declarations in XtraStuf, start the new unit with:

```
unit MoreStuf;
interface
uses XtraStuf;
{ Okay to refer to XtraStuf items }
```

Or, hide **uses** inside the new unit's **implementation**, in which case only the unit's implementation details, not items in the interface, can use XtraStuf's stuff:

```
unit MoreStuf;
interface
{ Interface declarations }
{ Can't refer to XtraStuf items yet }
implementation
uses XtraStuf;
{ Okay to refer to XtraStuf items }
```

Having told the compiler that the new unit uses XtraStuf, you can then declare variables of XtraStuf's CharSet data type, and you can call any of the procedures and functions declared in XtraStuf's interface. A host program can also use either or both units. In the previous examples, because MoreStuf uses XtraStuf, both units will be loaded into memory when the program runs. Even so, for the host program to be able to use the features in both units, it must also declare both unit names in a **uses** declaration:

```
program Sample;
uses XtraStuf, MoreStuf;
```

The order of the unit names doesn't matter; you could put MoreStuf first. (Some other compilers such as UCSD Pascal require units to be declared in "nesting" order. In other words, units used by others must be named first.)

Circular Unit References

If UnitA uses UnitB, which uses UnitA—and if these units are listed between **interface** and **implementation**—Turbo Pascal refuses to compile the units, instead displaying the error message:

```
Error 68: Circular unit reference.
```

You might also see this error in cases where UnitA uses UnitB, which uses UnitC, which in turn uses UnitA. The situation is more common than you may suppose. For example, if you write a unit named Math that uses XtraStuf, you may decide later to revise XtraStuf to use one of the procedures declared in Math. But that won't work because it introduces a circular-unit reference, and you'll receive error 68 when you try to compile the units.

Turbo Pascal solves this tricky problem by permitting circular-unit references in a private **uses** declaration inside the unit's implementation (see Program 10-1, line 14). As long as you insert your **uses** declarations into the implementation, multiple units may refer to each other in roundabout order, and the final result will come out correctly. The restriction against circular-unit references applies only to units listed in interface sections.

Unfortunately, this also means that if UnitA uses UnitB, which uses UnitA, then UnitB may not declare new constants, types, and variables in UnitB's interface using declarations from UnitA's interface. In other words, two interface sections may never use each other. You can usually get around this restriction by copying all such circular declarations to another unit, perhaps named GLOBALS.PAS, compile that unit separately, and then insert **uses** Globals in as many other units as you need.

Multiple Units in Memory

Multiple units do not nest inside each other in memory. If UnitA uses UnitC, and UnitB also uses UnitC, then only one copy of UnitC is loaded into memory. UnitC is not *inside* UnitA or UnitB. A unit is a distinct entity even though other units (and the main program) use it. In cases where many units use others—a common situation in a large program—only one copy of each unit exists in memory, no matter how many other units refer to that copy. If 15 units use Crt, Turbo Pascal knows the program doesn't need 15 copies of the same code in memory!

Unit Identifier Conflicts

One common multiunit problem arises when the same identifiers exist in two or more units. For example, suppose you purchase a precompiled unit, let's say it's called Video, that has a ClrScr procedure—the same name as the procedure in unit Crt. You may think that, because of the conflict, you can't use both units. Actually, you can. Here's an example. (Don't try to run this. There is no Video unit in Turbo Pascal.)

```
program Test;
uses Video, Crt;
begin
  ClrScr
end.
```

If both Video and Crt contain a ClrScr procedure, which procedure does this program call? The answer is: the procedure in the unit *last* declared in **uses**. The following program would call the ClrScr procedure in Video:

```
program Test;
uses Crt, Video;
begin
  ClrScr
end.
```

Switching the unit names in **uses** now calls ClrScr in Video, which follows Crt. With many conflicting identifiers, though, this method won't always work. Instead, you can use a technique called *dot notation* to distinguish between duplicate identifiers.

Unit-identifier dot notation is similar to the dot notation in record and field identifiers. Turbo Pascal lets you precede any identifier by a period (the dot) and the name of the unit or host program that declares the identifier. For example, to call the Video ClrScr procedure, but declare the Video unit first in **uses**, you can write the program this way:

```
program Test;
uses Video, Crt;
begin
  Video.ClrScr
end.
```

The dot notation Video.ClrScr tells the compiler to call the ClrScr procedure in Video instead of Crt. If the host program declares a conflicting identifier, you can also use the program name to resolve the problem.

Program 10-4 demonstrates these ideas with an example of dot notation carried to the extreme. The program uses the Crt unit but also declares its own ClrScr procedure, causing an identifier conflict with the Crt procedure of the same name. To call Crt's ClrScr, the program uses this statement at line 27:

```
Crt.ClrScr;
```

The dot notation resolves the conflict, even though the program redefines ClrScr. To call the host program's procedure, use the program name and dot notation:

```
Lotsadots.ClrScr;
```

Other uses of dot notation in Lotsadots show how to refer to global variables when there are identical local variables as I and J in procedure FillScreen (lines 13-22). By writing:

```
for Lotsadots.I := 1 to 25 do
```

the program refers to the global variable. The local integers I and J at line 14 are not used.

Line 26 uses dot notation to call a System unit routine, Readln. Even though the program does not include System in the **uses** declaration (line 2), recall from Chapter 8 that Turbo Pascal always uses the System unit even if you do not specify System in **uses**. Of course, you would have to do this only if the program or another unit redefined Readln and you want to use the System routine instead.

Program 10-4: LOTSADOT.PAS

```
 1:   program Lotsadots;
 2:   uses Crt;
 3:   var I, J: Integer;
 4:
 5:   procedure ClrScr;
 6:   var I: Integer;
 7:   begin
 8:     Crt.GotoXY(1, 25);
 9:     for I := 1 to 25 do
10:       System.Writeln
11:   end;
12:
13:   procedure FillScreen;
14:   var I, J: Integer;    { Not used! }
```

```
15:  begin
16:    for Lotsadots.I := 1 to 25 do
17:    begin
18:      Writeln;
19:      for Lotsadots.J := 1 to 79 do
20:        System.Write('*')
21:    end
22:  end;
23:
24:  begin
25:    Lotsadots.FillScreen;
26:    System.Readln;
27:    Crt.ClrScr;
28:    System.Readln;
29:    Lotsadots.FillScreen;
30:    System.Readln;
31:    Lotsadots.ClrScr;
32:    Readln
33:  end.
```

Units in Memory

Simple programs that do not use any units have four main sections in memory. These sections are:

1. Code segment.

2. Data segment.

3. Stack segment.

4. Heap.

The *code segment* contains all of the program's procedures and functions plus the main program body. The *data segment* contains global variables and variable constants plus a few items for Turbo Pascal's private use. The *stack segment* contains return addresses for calls to procedures and functions plus most local variables declared inside those routines. The *heap* contains nothing until you reserve memory with New and store data in that memory via pointers as described in Chapter 7.

Figure 10-1 shows the relationship of these four sections. (Appendix B contains a detailed memory map, more complete than the simplified version here.) The code, data, and stack segments can each be up to 64K long while the heap takes up whatever remaining memory is available. As you can see from this diagram, discounting the variable-sized heap, the maximum simple program size is about 192K (64 x 3).

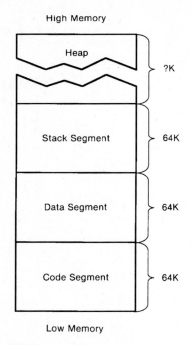

High Memory

Heap

?K

Stack Segment

64K

Data Segment

64K

Code Segment

64K

Low Memory

Figure 10-1 Simplified memory map of compiled Turbo Pascal programs.

Carefully dividing large programs into units can increase the program code-size limit. This works because the procedures and functions in a unit are stored in separate memory segments. Each unit segment, which can be as large as 64K, occupies only as much memory as needed. The unit code segments fit between the main code and data segments, as Figure 10-2 shows. The first units in a **uses** declaration are higher in memory. Figure 10-2 corresponds with this program declaration:

```
program UnitsInMem;
uses UnitA, UnitB, UnitC;
```

Near and Far

All unit public procedures and functions—those declared in the interface section—are *far* routines. Calls to a far routine push onto the stack both the segment and offset addresses after the calling instruction. Because the complete return address is on the stack, far routines can be called from any place in memory, even from other code segments.

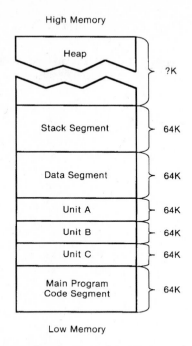

High Memory

Low Memory

Figure 10-2 In addition to the three main segments in Figure 10-1, each unit occupies its own memory segment, which can be as large as 64K. Segmenting programs into units, then, allows programs to grow as large as available memory.

All private procedures and functions—those declared exclusively in the implementation section plus those in the host program—are *near* routines. Calls to near routines push only the offset address. Because the segment address is not saved on the stack, near routines can be called only from inside their own code segment.

Because of the additional address on the stack, far calls are slightly less efficient than near calls. Usually, the difference is minor and nothing to worry about. Be aware, though, that there is a small time penalty for calling far routines declared in unit interface sections.

Despite the fact that each unit's code segment is distinct, all global variables declared in the unit interface and implementation sections are lumped together in a single data segment. This means that the space occupied by all the program's own global variables plus all public and private global variables in all units the program uses cannot total more than 64K. To store more data than that, you must use pointers and reserve memory on the heap as Chapter 7 explains.

Installing Units in Library Files

The TPUMover program on your Turbo Pascal disks collects individual unit TPU files into single library files, ending in .TPL (Turbo Pascal Library). You can also use the program to extract or delete individual units from library files.

Turbo Pascal automatically loads the special library file TURBO.TPL into memory when it starts, making all units in this library file available to programs without additional disk reads. Because this is faster than loading individual unit files from disk, you can store your most-used units in TURBO.TPL to reduce compilation time.

Using TPUMover

Turbo Pascal's TPUMover utility program adds and subtracts compiled units to and from TURBO.TPL. To run TPUMover, exit to DOS (or use the *File:Dos shell* command to return temporarily to a DOS prompt). Then type TPUMover commands in the form

```
TPUMover filename command
```

Usually, the filename should be TURBO.TPL because that's the only unit-library file that Turbo Pascal currently recognizes. You can also enter TURBO without the .TPL extension. Perhaps a future compiler version will work with other .TPL library files, but until then, use the name TURBO.TPL for TPUMover's filename parameter. The command may be

```
+unitname
-unitname
*unitname
```

Enter a plus sign and a unit's name to add a compiled unit to the library. Enter a minus sign and a unit's name to delete a unit from TURBO.TPL. (Be careful with this command. Once you delete a unit from the library, it's gone for good.) Enter an asterisk and a unit's name to extract a unit from the library and store that same unit in a separate TPU file.

For safety, use the asterisk command rather than the minus sign to delete units. For example, if you are not going to compile Turbo Pascal version 3.0 programs, you may as well extract the Turbo3 and Graph3 units from TURBO.TPL. Doing that will gain a little extra memory for the compiler, since it will no longer preload those units into memory. To extract Turbo3 and Graph3 from TURBO.TPL, enter the commands

```
tpumover turbo *turbo3
tpumover turbo *graph3
```

If you receive an error message when entering these commands, the Turbo3 or Graph3 units may not be in the library. Check whether that's the case by entering TPUMOVER TURBO to display a list of the units now in TURBO.TPL along with the sizes of each unit's code and data segments, plus the names of all the units each other unit uses.

For a reminder about TPUMover's commands, you can also enter TPUMOVER with no file name or command. The program will then display brief instructions.

You might want to install the XtraStuf unit (Program 10-2) into TURBO.TPL, especially if many of your programs use the unit. After installing the unit in the library, XtraStuf will be preloaded into memory and ready for instant use. To install XtraStuf in TURBO.TPL, make sure the XTRASTUF.TPU is in the current directly along with TURBO.TPL and TPUMover. Then enter the command:

```
tpumover turbo +xtrastuf
```

You can also use this same command to replace the current XtraStuf unit with a new version. Later, if you decide to remove XtraStuf from the library, enter the command:

```
tpumover turbo *xtrastuf
```

That command will extract XtraStuf from TURBO.TPL and store the unit in a file named XTRASTUF.TPU. If you already have this file, or if you no longer want to keep it, enter the following command to delete XtraStuf permanently from the library:

```
tpumover turbo -xtrastuf
```

Large-Program Development with Units

Besides collecting program libraries of common routines, variables, and other items, units are also useful for writing large programs. Dividing a program into separate units can drastically reduce compilation times.

Programs 10-5 through 10-8 show a typical multiunit, large-program setup. Of course this example is small and you could just as easily write the entire program in one text file. But the design is similar to what you could use in a program with thousands of statements.

To compile and run the complete example, type Program 10-5 and save as UCHOICEA.PAS. Type Program 10-6 and save as UCHOICEB.PAS. Finally, type Program 10-7 and save as UCHOICEC.PAS. You do not have to compile the units at this time.

Next, type Program 10-8 and save as MAIN.PAS. Load Main into memory, then compile the entire program with the *Compile:Make* command. (You could also use *Compile:Build.*) Press Ctrl-F9 to run, and then type A, B, or C to select the ChoiceA, ChoiceB, and ChoiceC procedures in the three units. Press Enter to return to the program's menu. Type Q to quit.

Program 10-5: UCHOICEA.PAS

```pascal
 1:  unit UChoiceA;
 2:
 3:  interface
 4:
 5:  procedure ChoiceA;
 6:
 7:  implementation
 8:
 9:  procedure ChoiceA;
10:  begin
11:    Write('Choice A....');
12:    Readln
13:  end;
14:
15:  end.
```

Program 10-6: UCHOICEB.PAS

```pascal
 1:  unit UChoiceB;
 2:
 3:  interface
 4:
 5:  procedure ChoiceB;
 6:
 7:  implementation
 8:
 9:  procedure ChoiceB;
10:  begin
11:    Write('Choice B...');
12:    Readln
13:  end;
14:
15:  end.
```

Program 10-7: UCHOICEC.PAS

```
 1: unit UChoiceC;
 2:
 3:   interface
 4:
 5:   procedure ChoiceC;
 6:
 7:   implementation
 8:
 9:   procedure ChoiceC;
10:   begin
11:     Write('Choice C...');
12:     Readln
13:   end;
14:
15:   end.
```

Program 10-8: MAIN.PAS

```
 1:   program Main;
 2:   uses Crt, UChoiceA, UChoiceB, UChoiceC;
 3:   var
 4:     Ch: Char;
 5:   begin
 6:     ClrScr;
 7:     repeat
 8:       GotoXY(1, 1);
 9:       Write('Choice-A, Choice-B, Choice-C, Q-uit ? ');
10:       Ch := UpCase(ReadKey);
11:       ClrScr;
12:       case Ch of
13:         'A': ChoiceA;
14:         'B': ChoiceB;
15:         'C': ChoiceC
16:       end
17:     until Ch = 'Q'
18:   end.
```

The importance of this multiunit design is the way each main program operation is in its own unit. This makes it easy to change individual operations without having to recompile the entire program. To see how this works, add a few lines to Program 10-5 (UCHOICEA.PAS). Before loading that file, though, use the *Compile:Primary file* command to make MAIN.PAS the current work file. Then, load UCHOICEA.PAS and replace procedure ChoiceA (lines 9-13) with these statements:

```
uses Crt;
procedure ChoiceA;
var Ch: Char;
begin
   Write('Ch? ');
   Ch := Readkey;
   Writeln('ASCII value = ', Ord(Ch));
   Write('Press <Enter>...');
   Readln
end;
```

Insert the **uses** Crt declaration in place of line 4. Press F2 to save these changes and then press Alt-R to recompile and run the whole shebang. Because you made MAIN.PAS the primary file, you don't have to reload the host program before compiling.

When designing your own large programs, start by dividing the project into sections, each in its own unit. For test purposes, you might also write separate programs and then, after debugging, convert each program into a unit, ready for attaching to the main host. Either way, units help you organize even the most monstrous of projects.

Clearing the Primary File

In the previous section, you used the *Compile:Primary file* command to make MAIN.PAS the current work file. To clear the work file, select the same command, and press Alt-C. You must do this before typing and compiling other programs.

Overlays

Most Turbo Pascal programs fit easily into memory. Even large programs composed of many separate units rarely require more than about 256K of RAM, and most PCs today have at least that much.

But what do you do if your programs grow larger than available RAM? With Turbo Pascal 4.0, the answer wasn't encouraging. If your program didn't fit entirely in memory, you had little choice but to divide your code into separate .EXE files and run the pieces separately from a batch-file menu or under control of another program.

Turbo Pascal 5.0 solved this problem with an *overlay manager* unit, appropriately named Overlay. Version 5.5 added additional enhancements for fine-tuning overlay efficiency. Version 6.0 has the same overlay capabilities as version 5.5. (Chapter 13 discusses these enhancements in detail.)

What are overlays? They are units that remain on disk until needed and, when loaded into RAM, share the same memory addresses with other overlay units. Because there's no practical limit to the number of units that can overlay each other in the same memory, there's no longer any restriction on program size. If your program grows too large to fit entirely in RAM, just divide the code into overlays and let the Overlay unit manage the dirty details of loading the pieces into memory as needed.

Using Overlays

In most cases, writing overlay units is only a little more difficult than writing regular units. The primary rule to remember is: Only entire units may be converted to overlays. Turbo Pascal 3.0 allowed you to write overlay procedures and functions. Versions 5.0 and up restrict overlays to whole units.

Using overlays correctly takes careful planning. A common mistake is to misuse overlays, writing inefficient programs that spend too much time reloading portions of themselves from disk into RAM. One way to avoid this problem is to design your programs in top-down fashion. When following this idea, the main program typically calls various submodules as demonstrated in Program 10-8. Because of this natural organization, each submodule—ChoiceA, ChoiceB, and ChoiceC in this example—is an excellent candidate for converting to an overlay.

To demonstrate how to accomplish that goal, in this section, you'll convert Programs 10-5 through 10-8 into a main program and three overlays. Each overlay must be stored in a unit, and each unit must include the directive {$O+}, which tells the compiler that this unit *might* be called as an overlay. That's a capital O in {$O+}, not the digit zero.

Convert the UCHOICEA.PAS, UCHOICEB.PAS, and UCHOICEC.PAS units to overlays by first copying those files to three new files named OVERA.PAS, OVERB.PAS, and OVERC.PAS. Load the copied files into Turbo Pascal's editor, change each unit's name to match its file, and add the {$O+} directive. For example, change OVERA.PAS's first two lines to:

```
{$O+}
unit OverA;
```

Modify the other two files similarly, but use the unit names OverB and OverC.

Next, enter Program 10-9, a modified version of Program 10-8. Save the new program as OVERMAIN.PAS. Instructions for compiling and running the program follow the listing.

Program 10-9: OVERMAIN.PAS

```
 1:  {$O+,F+}
 2:  program OverMain;
 3:
 4:  uses Overlay, Crt, OverA, OverB, OverC;
 5:
 6:  {$O OverA}
 7:  {$O OverB}
 8:  {$O OverC}
 9:
10:  var
11:     Ch: Char;
12:
13:  begin
14:     OvrInit('OVERMAIN.OVR');
15:     if OvrResult <> OvrOk then
16:     begin
17:       Writeln('Overlay error');
18:       Halt(1)
19:     end;
20:     ClrScr;
21:     repeat
22:       GotoXY(1, 1);
23:       Write('Choice-A, Choice-B, Choice-C, Q-uit ? ');
24:       Ch := UpCase(ReadKey);
25:       ClrScr;
26:       case Ch of
27:          'A': ChoiceA;
28:          'B': ChoiceB;
29:          'C': ChoiceC
30:       end
31:     until Ch = 'Q'
32:  end.
```

Compiling Overlays

Compiling overlay units and programs is different in only one aspect from compiling nonoverlay programs. You must compile all the program's parts to disk. The Turbo Pascal integrated environment can compile, but it can't run overlay programs.

If you are using the integrated environment, set *Compile:Destination* to *disk* and specify OVERMAIN.PAS as the *Compile:Primary file.* Then use the *Compile:Build* or *Compile:Make* commands to compile the entire program. Remember to recompile any units to which you added the {$O+} directive.

If you are using the command-line compiler, just compile as you normally do, using option switches to compile all (/B) or only modified (/M) units.

In either case, the result is two files, in this example, OVERMAIN.EXE and OVERMAIN.OVR. The .EXE file contains the code that stays permanently in memory. The .OVR file contains the overlay code that the Overlay manager loads from disk as needed.

> **Note**: When running this example, you may not see the disk light come on when calling procedures in the overlay modules. This example is so small that overlays aren't needed, and the entire program may therefore be loaded into RAM.

Understanding Overlays

Line 1 of Program 10-9 declares two options. The overlay switch O+ tells the compiler that this program uses overlays. The Far code switch F+ forces all procedures and functions to use far call and return instructions. A far call pushes both the 16-bit segment and offset address values onto the stack. This way, the called code can return to the original location, even if that code is in a different memory segment. Normally, Turbo Pascal assumes that all procedures and functions are near and, therefore, require only the 8-bit offset address of the return location in the same code segment.

When writing overlay programs, if there is any chance no matter how remote that a procedure or function will result in an overlay being loaded from disk, then that procedure or function must have been compiled with the {$F+} directive in effect. Ignore this rule at your own peril. If a near {$F-} procedure or function calls another procedure or function in an overlay unit, the stack may become corrupted because of the way the Overlay manager unit intercepts the call. Every active procedure and function at the time the overlay is loaded *must* have been compiled with {$F+} in effect.

You must obey this rule even in cases where a near procedure calls a far procedure, which activates the overlay. Because the earlier near procedure hasn't yet ended, disaster may strike. For this reason, it's usually wise to add the {$F+} directive to every part of the program unless you are 100% positive that an overlay cannot be activated.

Lines 4-8, repeated here from Program 10-9, list the units that this host program uses:

```
uses Overlay, Crt, OverA, OverB, OverC;

{$O OVERA}
{$O OVERB}
{$O OVERC}
```

List the Overlay unit in the host program's **uses** declaration along with other overlay and nonoverlay units. After that, list each overlay unit in separate {$O unitname} directives. (Again, that's a capital O, not the digit zero.) Together, the **uses** declaration and the directives tell the compiler which units to place in the .OVR file.

In addition to these setup chores, the main program must call an initialization procedure in the Overlay unit. As line 14 shows, pass the name of the overlay disk file to OvrInit:

```
OvrInit('OVERMAIN.OVR');
if OvrResult <> OvrOk then
begin
    Writeln('Overlay error');
    Halt (1)
end;
```

Normally, you'll want to check OvrResult this way, an Integer variable (typed) constant in the Overlay manager. If OvrResult is not equal to OvrOk, then an error occurred and the program must not be allowed to continue. Table 10-1 lists all possible OvrResult values.

Table 10-1 Overlay manager OvrResult values.

Constant	Value	Meaning
OvrOk	0	No error
OvrError	−1	General error code
OvrNotFound	−2	Overlay file not found
OvrNoMemory	−3	Not enough memory for overlays
OvrIOError	−4	Disk I/O error loading overlay
OvrNoEMSDriver	−5	Expanded-memory driver missing
OvrNoEMSMemory	−6	Not enough EMS memory available

When you call an overlay unit (see lines 27-29 in Program 10-9), the Overlay manager automatically intercepts the call and loads the appropriate overlay code from disk. That code is stuffed into an internal buffer that occupies a portion of the heap. When another overlay is needed, the buffer is emptied, and the new code is brought into memory. Actually, the Overlay manager is smart enough to keep multiple overlays in the buffer simultaneously, but that's a subject to which we'll return in Chapter 13.

Most of the time, the preceding steps are all you need to write your own overlays. Here are a few hints and tips that will help you get started:

- Remember to add {$O+} to every overlay unit.

- Add {$O+,F+} to the beginning of the main host program and to any unit that uses another overlay unit.

- With no exceptions, any procedure or function that eventually results in an overlay being loaded into memory must have been compiled with the {$F+} switch in effect.

- Specify the Overlay unit in your host program's **uses** declaration along with your own overlay units.

- List the overlay units in {$O unitname} directives after the host program's **uses** declaration.

- Call OverInit with the name of the overlay file, usually the same as the program name but ending in .OVR. Check OvrResult for any errors, halting the program if the overlay file isn't found.

Finding the .OVR File

When you execute OvrInit('OVERMAIN.OVR');, the Overlay manager tries to open the file OVERMAIN.OVR in the current directory. If this doesn't work and you're running DOS 3.0 or a later version, OvrInit searches for the file in the same directory that contains the main program code file, in this example, OVERMAIN.EXE. If it still can't find the overlay file, OvrInit searches all the directories listed in a PATH command. Only if this fails does the procedure give up, returning error OvrNotFound (see Table 10-1).

Loading Overlays into Expanded Memory

The Overlay unit can load overlay code into *expanded memory* (EMS), the kind of extra RAM that works on all PCs, XTs, and ATs. *Extended memory* works only on ATs and 80386 or 80486 systems. If you have extended memory, your system probably came with a software driver to convert some or all of the extra RAM into simulated EMS. Installing the driver should allow overlays to use extended memory.

To enable the use of EMS RAM, call OvrInitEMS after successfully calling OvrInit. To do this with Program 10-9, change lines 14-19 to:

```
OvrInit('OVERMAIN.OVR');
if OvrResult <> OvrOk then
begin
  Writeln('Overlay error');
  Halt(1)
end;
OvrInitEMS;
```

You can also check OvrResult for errors after OvrInitEMS. If equal to OvrNoEMSDriver or OvrNoEMSMemory, then the Overlay manager either did not find any or enough EMS RAM. But, if there isn't enough EMS RAM to hold the overlays, the program simply uses main memory as it normally does.

If it finds enough EMS RAM, the Overlay manager loads *all* overlays from the .OVR file into memory. Then, instead of loading individual overlay units from disk, Overlay transfers the overlays as needed from EMS to main RAM. Because of this action, EMS RAM doesn't reduce a program's memory requirements—it just makes overlay programs run more quickly.

Changing the Overlay Buffer Size

The overlay buffer size is normally set to the size of the largest overlay unit. If enough memory is available, you can increase the buffer size to a value large enough to hold two or more overlays simultaneously. That way, if two overlay units are used frequently, the program runs faster because the overlays tend to stay in memory longer. The Overlay manager automatically detects this condition, loading overlays from disk only if they are not already in RAM.

> **Note:** Chapter 13 explains how to use advanced features in Turbo Pascal 6.0's Overlay unit to help keep multiple overlays in memory for even longer times. The overlay buffer actions described in this section apply to Turbo Pascal 5.0 through 6.0.

Call OvrGetBuf for the size of the current overlay buffer. For example, to display the buffer size, add this statement between lines 22 and 23 in Program 10-9:

```
Writeln('Overlay buffer size = ', OvrGetBuf, ' bytes');
```

To change the buffer size to 6000 bytes (or any other size), call OvrSetBuf:

```
OvrSetBuf(6000);
```

Do this *after* calling OvrInit but *before* calling New or GetMem to allocate variables on the heap. The overlay buffer occupies the bottom portion of the heap;

therefore, OvrSetBuf ignores a request to increase the buffer size if you've allocated any pointer-addressable variables. (See Appendix B for a memory map showing the overlay buffer location.)

> **Note**: You may not want to increase the overlay buffer size if OvrInitEMS returns OvrOk. In that case, all overlays are stored in EMS RAM and a larger overlay buffer in main RAM offers little or no advantage.

If you're using Turbo Pascal 5.5 or higher, you can combine your .EXE and .OVR files into one .EXE file. For this to work, you must compile all programs and units *without* debugging information for the stand-alone or built-in Turbo Debuggers. If you want to run your overlays under control of Turbo Debugger, you must store your programs in separate .EXE and .OVR files.

To join the OVERMAIN.EXE and OVERMAIN.OVR files from program 10-9, edit line 14 to:

```
OvrInit('OVERMAIN.EXE');
```

Or, because ParamStr(0) under DOS 3.0 or later returns the name of the program code file, you can use the statement:

```
OvrInit(ParamStr(0));
```

After editing OvrInit to open the .EXE file, and after compiling your program, join the result with the DOS command:

```
COPY /B OVERMAIN.EXE + OVERMAIN.OVR
```

The /B option with DOS COPY stands for "binary copy." This attaches OVERMAIN.OVR to the end of OVERMAIN.EXE. You can then delete OVERMAIN.OVR with:

```
DEL OVERMAIN.OVR
```

Summary

Units collect procedures, functions, types, variables, constants, and other items in separate modules, which you compile apart from other program sections. Units are good for collecting libraries of common features for many host programs to share. They are also helpful for dividing large programs into manageable pieces. And, because a unit's code goes in its own memory segment, you can use units to write Pascal programs limited only by the amount of memory in your computer.

Units have four parts: the declaration, interface, implementation, and initialization. The initialization section resembles a program's main body and runs before the statements in a host program.

Use dot notation to resolve conflicts between duplicate identifiers in multiple units and in the main program text. Unit dot notation is similar to the notation used in record and field expressions.

To add a unit's features to a program (or to another unit), type the unit name in a **uses** declaration, which comes after the **program** header or, in another unit, after the key word **interface**. No matter how many units a program and other units use, only one copy of the unit's code is loaded into memory.

Use the TPUMOVER program to install and remove compiled units in library TPL disk files. Installing units in the special TURBO.TPL file lets Turbo Pascal preload the units into memory, speeding compilation but also reducing memory space.

Units may use other units. But, when two or more units refer to each other in circular fashion, the **uses** declaration must appear in the unit's implementation section. Units listed in **uses** in the unit's interface may not refer to each other circularly.

To construct Turbo Pascal programs larger than available memory, you can selectively convert units to overlays. Overlay units can share the same memory. The Overlay manager unit loads overlay units as needed into RAM. Programs can also load overlays into EMS memory.

Exercises

10-1. Create your own unit of favorite routines, culled from programs in your personal library. Or, extract several procedures and functions from other examples in this book and insert them in a unit.

10-2. Write a test program to put your custom unit in exercise 10-1 through the paces.

10-3. Install your custom unit from exercise 10-1 in TURBO.TPL. What effect does this have on memory and compilation speed?

10-4. Where does the unit's code exist in memory? Where are the global variables? Where are the variables declared in procedures and functions inside the unit?

10-5. Describe the difference between a *far* and a *near* procedure or function.

10-6. If UnitA uses UnitB, which uses UnitC, which uses UnitA, Turbo Pascal may not compile the program. Why not? How would you instruct a programmer to fix this problem?

The Borland Graphics Interface

- Choosing a Graphics Mode
- The Borland Graphics Interface
- Setting Up for Graphics
- Viewports and Coordinates
- Plotting Points
- Drawing Lines
- Relative Lines
- Stylish Lines
- Color Palettes
- Changing Display Colors
- In the Background
- Setting the Write Mode
- Shape Routines
- Arcs and Circles
- Drawing Ellipses
- A Slice of Pie
- Bit-Map Images
- Displaying Text on Graphics Screens
- Animation
- Loading Multiple Fonts and Drivers
- Creating a Graphics Application
- Advanced BGI Graphics

11

Key Words and Identifiers

Arc, Bar, Bar3D, Circle, ClearDevice, ClearViewPort,
CloseGraph, DetectGraph, DrawPoly, Ellipse, FillEllipse,
FillPoly, FloodFill, GetArcCoords, GetAspectRatio, GetBkColor,
GetColor, GetDefaultPalette, GetDriverName, GetFillPattern,
GetFillSettings, GetGraphMode, GetImage, GetLineSettings,
GetMaxColor, GetMaxMode, GetMaxX, GetMaxY,
GetModeName, GetModeRange, GetPalette, GetPaletteSize,
GetPixel, GetTextSettings, GetViewSettings, GetX, GetY,
GraphDefaults, GraphErrorMsg, GraphResult, ImageSize,
InitGraph, InstallUserDriver, InstallUserFont, Line, LineRel,
LineTo, MoveRel, MoveTo, OutText, OutTextXY, PieSlice,
PutImage, PutPixel, Rectangle, RegisterBGIdriver,
RegisterBGIfont, RestoreCrtMode, Sector, SetActivePage,
SetAllPalette, SetAspectRatio, SetBkColor, SetColor,
SetFillPattern, SetFillStyle, SetGraphBufSize, SetGraphMode,
SetLineStyle, SetPalette, SetRGBPalette, SetTextJustify,
SetTextStyle, SetUserCharSize, SetViewPort, SetVisualPage,
SetWriteMode, TextHeight, TextWidth

There are few areas in computer programming more satisfying than graphics. Programmers who spend their time designing graphics software live in a heaven of colors, shapes, animations, and three-dimensional objects limited only by their imaginations and their computer's video display circuits.

With Turbo Pascal's extensive graphics commands, anyone can become a computer graphics artist, whether you write business software, games, or simulations, or just like to have fun. Even simple programs can produce remarkable patterns, giving your programs an extra touch that text-only software can never match.

Choosing a Graphics Mode

All PCs can display text—individual characters with fixed bit patterns stored in ROM or, sometimes, in RAM. Although several special characters have fixed line and angle segments giving a limited ability to construct lines and boxes on text displays, the real excitement in computer graphics comes from the ability to control each tiny display dot, called a *picture element,* or *pixel.*

Depending on the type of display and video card or circuits in your PC, you can have from 320 x 200 pixels to 1024 x 768 pixels in as few as two to as many as 256 colors on-screen at one time. That's anywhere from 64,000 to 786,432 pixels at your control. Also called an All Points Addressable (APA) display, a PC graphics screen is the Etch-a-Sketch of many a programmer's dreams.

Perhaps the most difficult aspect of PC graphics is writing programs to choose among the number of display formats, some of which do not exist on various computer models. Turbo Pascal simplifies the process by automatically detecting and initializing the best possible graphics mode available. And, by following a few simple rules, you can write graphics software that runs correctly on all the graphics modes listed in Table 11-1.

Table 11-1 Turbo Pascal graphics modes.

Mode	Description	Interface file
CGA	Color Graphics Adapter	CGA.BGI
MCGA	Multicolor Graphics Array	CGA.BGI
EGA	Enhanced Graphics Adapter	EGAVGA.BGI
VGA	Video Graphics Array	EGAVGA.BGI
Hercules	Hercules Monochrome Graphics	HERC.BGI
AT&T	AT&T 400 Line Graphics	ATTBGI
PC3270	IBM PC 3270 Graphics	PC3270.BGI
IBM8514	IBM PC 8514 Graphics	IBM8514.BGI

Most of the programs in this chapter look best with EGA or VGA color graphics and an RGB (Red, Green, Blue) monitor. You can use CGA graphics or a less expensive color monitor, but the results may not be as colorful or as clear. Hercules and other monochrome graphics systems will also work, although you'll see only shades of green or amber instead of different hues.

The Borland Graphics Interface

The right column in Table 11-1 lists the BGI (Borland Graphics Interface) disk files containing the machine language software for the graphics modes on the left. A BGI file is called a *driver* because it drives the video display. The graphics driver is also known as a *kernel,* an operating system term that refers to a core of low-level routines with some particular purpose.

To run graphics programs, you need at least one BGI driver file on disk. To compile programs, you need only the GRAPH.TPU file, which contains the Graph unit's interface and implementation (see Chapter 9). The information inside GRAPH.TPU tells the compiler how to make calls to the routines inside a BGI driver. When the program runs, Turbo Pascal automatically loads the correct driver, connecting your program with the necessary machine language programming for your graphics system. You do not need GRAPH.TPU on disk to run graphics programs.

If you have a floppy disk system, you can remove the BGI driver files from your compiler disk to save room. You might also remove all but the BGI driver needed by your graphics hardware. If you want to write programs that automatically run on any display, though, it's best to keep all the BGI drivers on disk. (It's also possible to link drivers directly into your compiled code, a subject for later in this chapter.)

Another important disk file type ends in CHR and contains information for drawing text characters. A CHR file is also called (somewhat incorrectly) a *font* file. In typesetting, a font is one type size and style. In Turbo Pascal graphics, a font is a text style, which you can scale up or down to many different sizes. I'll follow the modern trend here and use font to describe a text style in *all* its sizes.

Setting Up for Graphics

The easiest way to prepare your disks for compiling and running graphics programs is to store GRAPH.TPU and all your BGI and CHR files in the same directory as your program files. Assuming this is your setup, Program 11-1 shows the correct way to initialize a graphics mode and draw a circle in the center of the screen.

Program 11-1: ITROUND.PAS

```pascal
 1:  program InTheRound;
 2:  uses Graph;
 3:  var GrDriver, GrMode, GrError: Integer;
 4:    XCenter, YCenter: Integer; Radius: Word;
 5:  begin
 6:    GrDriver := Detect;
 7:    InitGraph(GrDriver, GrMode, '');
 8:    GrError := GraphResult;
 9:    if GrError <> GrOk
10:    then
11:      Writeln('Graphics error: ', GraphErrorMsg(GrError))
12:    else
13:      begin
14:        XCenter := GetMaxX div 2;
15:        YCenter := GetMaxY div 2;
16:        Radius := GetMaxY div 4;
17:        SetColor(Green);
18:        Circle(XCenter, YCenter, Radius);
19:        Readln;
20:        CloseGraph
21:      end
22:  end.
```

If you have EGA or VGA graphics, Program 11-1 should display a green circle in the center of the display. If you have a different graphics system and your circle is not green, don't worry—we'll get to colors and how to change them later. If you don't see a circle, or if you receive an error message, be sure you typed the program correctly and that you have the BGI, CHR, and GRAPH.TPU files on your compiler disk.

Note: If you don't see a circle and you're sure your system supports graphics, try changing Green to White, or remove line 17.

Program 11-1 contains many elements that you will use in all your graphics programs. Lines 6-8 automatically detect and initialize a graphics display mode. The first step is to set integer variable GrDriver to Detect, a constant defined in the Graph unit. Passing Detect to InitGraph (line 7) automatically detects the best graphics mode for your computer. Therefore, the most common initialization sequence is:

```
GrDriver := Detect;
InitGraph(GrDriver, GrMode, '');
```

You can change the third InitGraph parameter to the path where you store the BGI driver and CHR character files. This lets you run graphics programs from other directories and disks. A null string indicates the current drive and directory. If you save your BGI and CHR files in a subdirectory named C:\TPAS\GRAPH, use these statements:

```
GrDriver := Detect;
InitGraph(GrDriver, GrMode, 'C:\TPAS\GRAPH');
```

InitGraph loads the proper graphics BGI driver file from disk, initializes various internal variables and default conditions, and erases the display. The procedure also returns a second integer variable GrMode equal to the mode now in effect for the driver specified by GrDriver.

Table 11-2 explains GrMode and GrDriver values. As you can see, most drivers can handle many different modes with various resolutions and pages. A single page equals the amount of memory needed to hold all the pixels from one display. Multipage modes let you draw off-screen while viewing graphics on other screens—an especially useful technique for animation and slide show programs.

Table 11-2 Graphics modes, resolutions, and pages.

Driver	Mode	Resolution	Pages
CGA	CGAC0	320 X 200	1
	CGAC1	320 X 200	1
	CGAC2	320 X 200	1
	CGAC3	320 X 200	1
	CGAHi	640 X 200	1
MCGA	MCGAC0	320 X 200	1
	MCGAC1	320 X 200	1
	MCGAC2	320 X 200	1
	MCGAC3	320 X 200	1
	MCGAMed	640 X 200	1
	MCGAHi	640 X 480	1
EGA	EGALo	640 X 200	4
	EGAHi	640 X 350	2

Driver	Mode	Resolution	Pages
EGA64	EGA64Lo	640 X 200	1
	EGA64Hi	640 X 350	1
EGAMono	EGAMonoHi	640 X 350	1-2*
VGA	VGALo	640 X 200	4
	VGAMed	640 X 350	2
	VGAHi	640 X 480	1
HercMono	HercMonoHi	720 X 348	2
ATT400	ATT400C0	320 X 200	1
	ATT400C1	320 X 200	1
	ATT400C2	320 X 200	1
	ATT400C3	320 X 200	1
	ATT400Med	640 X 200	1
	ATT400Hi	640 X 400	1
PC3270	PC3270Hi	720 X 350	1
I8M8514	IBM8514Lo	640 X 480, 256 colors	n/a
	IBM8514Hi	1,024 X 768, 256 colors	n/a

*64K on card = one page; 256K = two pages.

Initializing Graphics the Hard Way

If you don't care for Turbo Pascal's automatic mode selection, you can choose a different mode by assigning a driver from Table 11-2 to GrDriver and a mode to GrMode before calling InitGraph. For example, to initialize EGA low resolution, 640 x 200, 16-color graphics, you can write:

```
GrDriver := EGA;
GrMode := EGALo;
InitGraph(GrDriver, GrMode, '');
```

When manually selecting graphics modes this way, it's up to you to determine what graphics hardware the computer has. Usually, it's best to let Turbo Pascal automatically select a graphics mode for you, but you might want to include an option in your programs to let people select specific modes, overriding auto-detection. Be careful when experimenting. Initializing display modes not available on your computer can cause the computer to hang, forcing you to reboot or, in some cases, to shut off power.

One way to avoid these problems is to call DetectGraph instead of passing the default Detect constant to InitGraph. DetectGraph checks the hardware and sets integer variables GrDriver and GrMode to the values Turbo Pascal considers ideal for this system. But, unlike InitGraph, DetectGraph does not initialize the display. The initialization sequence now becomes:

```
DetectGraph(GrDriver, GrMode);
InitGraph(GrDriver, GrMode, '');
```

This is identical to passing Detect to InitGraph as in the previous examples. But, because most graphics drivers can support more than one mode, DetectGraph gives you the option of initializing the display to a different mode. You might use this idea to detect CGA graphics, but initialize the display to 640 x 200 resolution instead of the default 320 x 200 mode. This does the job:

```
DetectGraph(GrDriver, GrMode);
if GrDriver = CGA then
begin
  GrMode := CGAHi;
  InitGraph(GrDriver, GrMode, '');
  ...
  { Graphics statements }
  ...
end;
```

Another possibility is to call function GetMaxMode after InitGraph to find the range of modes supported by the automatically selected driver. To select another display mode, you can then pass a value in the range 0 to GetMaxMode to SetGraphMode, which clears the display and selects a specified graphics mode. For example, to initialize graphics for the highest possible mode number, execute these statements:

```
DetectGraph(GrDriver, GrMode);
InitGraph(GrDriver, GrMode, '');
if GraphResult = GrOk then
begin
  SetGraphMode(GetMaxMode);
  ...
  {  Graphics statements }
  ...
end;
```

Prior to Turbo Pascal 5.0, the only way to detect the maximum mode number was to call GetModeRange, which returns two values representing the low and high modes for a graphics driver. Unlike GetMaxMode, you may call GetModeRange before InitGraph, as in this fragment, which selects the lowest possible mode number for the default graphics driver:

```
DetectGraph(GrDriver, GrMode);
GetModeRange(GrDriver, LoMode, HiMode);
InitGraph(GrDriver, LoMode, '');
```

LoMode and HiMode are Integer variables. One drawback with this method is that it works only with standard BGI drivers. As you'll discover later in this chapter, starting with Turbo Pascal 5.0, it's possible to link in custom graphics drivers. GetMaxMode returns the maximum mode number for custom and BGI standard drivers. GetModeRange works only with the standards.

You can also pass the Graph unit constant CurrentDriver to GetModeRange instead of calling DetectGraph. This may be useful for obtaining the mode range values after calling InitGraph. The previous code then becomes:

```
GrDriver := Detect;
InitGraph(GrDriver, GrMode, '');
if GraphResult = GrOk then
begin
    GetModeRange(CurrentDriver, LoMode, HiMode);
    SetGraphMode(LoMode);
    ...
    { Graphics statements }
    ...
end;
```

Note: If your computer has VGA graphics, depending on how much memory your hardware has, you may have some trouble running programs that use multiple display pages. If you see "garbage" on-screen or a band of interference patterns, you may have to force Turbo Pascal to initialize graphics in EGA mode in order to run the program. Most programs in this chapter initialize the default mode by setting GrDriver to Detect. For most VGA displays, this selects 640 x 480, 16-color graphics. To initialize a VGA card for EGA 640 x 350, 16-color graphics, change Detect to EGA. That should clear up any problems.

Detecting Graphics Errors

The final step in preparing a graphics mode is to check whether the initialization worked. InitGraph, as well as several other routines, stores an internal error code that describes the success or failure of an operation. You can examine this code through the integer function GraphResult. Be careful, though. GraphResult returns the current error code but also resets the code to zero. Therefore, you can check GraphResult only once after any operation. Checking it again always returns zero, the value meaning no error.

Lines 8-11 in Program 11-1 show the correct way to check GraphResult for errors. First, assign the function result to a temporary integer variable, here GrError. All graphics errors are either zero or negative—you must use integer variables to store their values. Line 11 displays an appropriate message if an error occurs (GrError is not equal to GrOk). Table 11-3 lists graphics error values and messages. You could decode the values and display your own messages, but it's easier just to call string function GraphErrorMsg as in line 11, displaying the messages shown in the table. GraphErrorMsg fills empty parentheses (error values –3 and –8, for example) with the offending file names for these errors.

Displaying Driver and Mode Names

After initializing graphics with InitGraph, you can ask the Graph unit for the names of the current driver and mode. To do this, call the string functions GetDriverName with no parameters and GetModeName with a single parameter equal to any valid mode number in the range 0 to GetMaxMode.

To see how these functions work, replace lines 6-21 of Program 11-1 with the following:

```
GrDriver := Detect;
InitGraph(GrDriver, GrMode, '');
if GraphResult = GrOk then
begin
   Writeln('Graphics driver: ', GetDriverName);
   Writeln('Graphics mode:   ', GetModeName(GrMode));
   Readln;
   CloseGraph
end;
```

For the Writeln statements to work in graphics modes, the program may *not* use the Crt unit. This doesn't work with Hercules displays.

Table 11-3 Graphics error numbers and messages.

GraphResult	GraphErrorMsg
0	No error
−1	(BGI) graphics not installed
−2	Graphics hardware not detected
−3	Device driver file not found ( )
−4	Invalid device driver file ( )
−5	Not enough memory to load driver
−6	Out of memory in scan fill
−7	Out of memory in flood fill
−8	Font file not found ( )
−9	Not enough memory to load font
−10	Invalid graphics mode for selected driver
−11	Graphics error
−12	Graphics I/O error
−13	Invalid font file ( )
−14	Invalid font number
−18	Invalid version

Detecting Screen Resolution

Lines 13-21 in Program 11-1 execute if no errors occur when initializing a graphics mode. At this point, the screen is clear and ready for drawing. The first three statements, repeated here for reference, show how to prepare drawings for any of the many possible resolutions:

```
XCenter := GetMaxX div 2;
YCenter := GetMaxY div 2;
Radius := GetMaxY div 4;
```

The integer functions, GetMaxX and GetMaxY, return the maximum horizontal (X) and vertical (Y) coordinate values. By designing your programs around these values, instead of assuming you have so many pixels high or wide to work with, you write programs that work correctly in different modes. Here, XCenter and YCenter are set to the midpoint of the display X and Y axes, while radius is set to one-quarter the height. Because the height is never greater than the width in PC graphics display modes, these three values ensure that the circle drawn in line 18 is centered and is *relatively* the same size, no matter what graphics mode you are using.

Lines 17 and 18 draw the circle, using the command SetColor to choose a drawing color and Circle to draw the figure in that color. The three parameters to Circle specify the X and Y center position and the radius.

Switching Between Text and Graphics

The final two statements in Program 11-1 wait for you to press a key (line 19) and perform an optional deinitialization step (line 20) before the program ends. To return to the display mode in effect before calling InitGraph, end your programs with CloseGraph. If you don't do this, you may confuse people by leaving the computer in an unfamiliar graphics display mode. This is harmless, and you can always reboot or use the DOS MODE command to return to the normal text display. (See your DOS or computer manual for information on using MODE.)

CloseGraph also removes the BGI driver previously loaded by InitGraph. You might use CloseGraph in programs that display graphics and then switch to a text display. To perform this same action but keep the BGI driver in memory, use the method in Program 11-2 to go back and forth between graphics and text.

Program 11-2: MIXEDMOD.PAS

```
 1:  program MixedModes;
 2:
 3:  uses Crt, Graph;
 4:
 5:  const
 6:    Esc = #27;
 7:
 8:  var
 9:    GraphDriver, GraphMode: Integer;
10:    XCenter, YCenter: Integer;
11:
12:  begin
13:    GraphDriver := Detect;
14:    InitGraph(GraphDriver, GraphMode, '');
15:    XCenter := GetMaxX div 2; YCenter := GetMaxY div 2;
16:
```

```
17:    SetColor(Cyan);
18:    Rectangle(XCenter - 50, YCenter - 50, XCenter + 50, YCenter + 50);
19:    OutText('This is the graphics page.  Press <Enter>...');
20:    Readln;
21:
22:    RestoreCrtMode;
23:    Write('This is the text page.  Press <Enter>...');
24:    Readln;
25:
26:    SetGraphMode(GraphMode);
27:    Circle(XCenter, YCenter, YCenter div 2);
28:    OutText('Back on the graphics page.  Press <Enter>...');
29:    Readln;
30:
31:    CloseGraph
32:  end.
```

To save space, Program 11-2 and other programs in this chapter do not check for errors after InitGraph as in Program 11-1. Add these checks to all examples if you want. Lines 17-20 change the drawing color to cyan (blue-green) and display a box with procedure Rectangle, which takes the form:

```
Rectangle(X1, Y1, X2, Y2);
```

Coordinate (X1,Y1) specifies the upper-left corner and (X2,Y2) the lower-right corner of the box. Line 19 displays a line of text in the current font. (You'll meet the OutText command in more detail later in this chapter.)

After you press Enter, line 22 calls RestoreCrtMode to return to the text display temporarily. After you press Enter once more, line 26 calls SetGraphMode, passing the same GraphMode value you originally fed to InitGraph back at line 14. This restores the display to graphics for the Circle command in line 27. Press Enter a final time to end the program.

If you called CloseGraph instead of RestoreCrtMode in line 22, you'd have to call InitGraph again to reload a graphics driver before displaying more graphics. For this reason, RestoreCrtMode is faster, although the graphics driver takes up memory space that only CloseGraph can recover.

Unless you are using a monochrome or CGA graphics mode, you'll notice that the cyan color selected in line 17 changes when switching back to graphics in line 26. Also, the rectangle is gone. SetGraphMode erases the display and resets all graphics parameters to their default settings. There's no easy way to preserve screens when switching modes—except maybe storing a display on disk or in a memory buffer, and then reloading it when going back to graphics.

Graphics Defaults

After changing colors and selecting other graphics features, to return to the default conditions, call procedure GraphDefaults. Doing this does not erase the display.

If you need to know what graphics mode is now in effect, use integer function GetGraphMode. If you don't want to keep a global GraphMode variable as in Program 11-2, you can write:

```
GraphMode := GetGraphMode;
RestoreCrtMode;
...
{ Text display commands }
...
SetGraphMode(GraphMode);
```

This records the current graphics mode in a variable before restoring the text display with RestoreCrtMode. Passing this value to SetGraphMode returns to the graphics screen, erases the display, and resets all default conditions.

Viewports and Coordinates

Every graphics display pixel has unique X and Y coordinate values. The X axis is horizontal; the Y is vertical. The pixel in the upper-left corner of the display has the coordinate (0,0). Positive X coordinates move to the right. Negative Y coordinates move down. In the vertical direction, this is the reverse of common mathematics notation where positive values move up along the Y axis.

All coordinate values in Turbo Pascal graphics are integers, which can be negative or positive. As the inner rectangle in Figure 11-1 shows, the visible portion of the graphics display is merely a restricted view of the entire *logical* surface, or plane, on which programs can draw. This area is called the *viewport*. Drawing outside the viewport is invisible. Only points within the viewport's boundaries are displayed.

At all times, Turbo Pascal stores an internal coordinate, called the *current point* (CP). The CP is the point at which many graphics operations begin. The CP might be the beginning of a line, or it might be the position where text appears. To find out where CP is, use the integer functions GetX end GetY. After initializing a graphics mode, CP equals (0,0). To find out the maximum X and Y coordinates available within the viewport, use the integer functions GetMaxX and GetMaxY. Together, the four functions test whether points are inside the viewport regardless of the graphics mode in effect:

```
if (0 <= GetX) and (GetX <= GetMaxX) and
  (0 <= GetY) and (GetY <= GetMaxY)
 then { CP is inside viewport }
 else { CP is out of view }
```

The total number of horizontal coordinate values equals GetMaxX + 1. The total number of vertical coordinate values equals GetMaxY + 1. By using these functions instead of fixed limits, you can write programs that work correctly in any resolution.

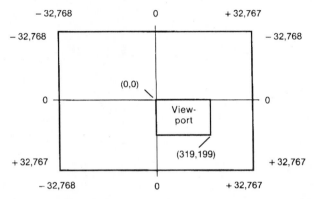

Figure 11-1 A viewport defines the visible area of the logical coordinate surface, or plane.

Clearing the Viewport

To erase the viewport, call ClearViewPort, which paints the screen with the current background color. To erase the viewport and reset CP to (0,0), call ClearDevice. To clear the viewport, reset CP, and restore all default conditions, call ClearViewPort followed by GraphDefaults. Calling ClearDevice in this case would be redundant.

Changing the Viewport

There are two reasons to change the viewport illustrated in Figure 11-1. You can restrict drawing to a portion of the display, protecting graphics in other locations. Or, you can shift the *origin*—the viewport's top-left corner—to make some kinds of graphics operations easier to write.

Program 11-3 calls SetViewPort in line 12 to restrict drawing to the coordinates (0,0) to (100,75). The procedure is declared as

```
procedure SetViewPort(X1, Y1, X2, Y2: Integer; Clip : Boolean);
```

Coordinate (X1,Y1) is the new upper-left corner while (X2,Y2) is the new lower-right corner of the viewport. The four values must be greater or equal to zero, X1 must be less than X2, and Y1 must be less than Y2. Set Clip true to restrict drawing to within these new boundaries. Set Clip false to allow drawing outside the viewport. Instead of true and false, you can use the more descriptive Graph constants ClipOn and ClipOff.

Program 11-3: RESTRICT.PAS

```
 1:  program RestrictedViews;
 2:
 3:  uses
 4:     Crt, Graph;
 5:
 6:  var
 7:     GraphDriver, GraphMode: Integer;
 8:
 9:  begin
10:     GraphDriver := Detect;
11:     InitGraph(GraphDriver, GraphMode, '');
12:     SetViewPort(0, 0, 100, 75, ClipOn);
13:     while not Keypressed do
14:     begin
15:       SetColor(1 + Random(GetMaxColor));
16:       Line(Random(GetMaxX), Random(GetMaxY),
17:              Random(GetMaxX), Random(GetMaxY))
18:     end;
19:     CloseGraph
20:  end.
```

Experiment with different coordinate values in line 12 of Program 11-3. Change ClipOn to ClipOff and observe the difference clipping makes. Add a check to GraphResult to test for bad viewport settings. For example, you could change line 12 to:

```
SetViewPort(0, 0, 100, 75, ClipOn);
if GraphResult <> GrOk then
begin
   CloseGraph;
```

```
   Writeln('Error in viewport settings')
end;
```

After changing the viewport, the upper-left corner again has the coordinate (0,0). This seems confusing at first. Consider the statement:

```
SetViewPort(100, 50, 200, 150, ClipOn);
```

Although this sets the viewport to the coordinates (100,50) and (200,150), plotting a point at the relative viewport location (0,0) appears at the absolute screen coordinate (100,50). You'll avoid confusion if you think of a viewport as having its own coordinate system with (0,0) always in the upper-left corner no matter where the viewport appears on display. Coordinates inside the viewport are relative to the viewport boundaries.

To reset the viewport to the entire display, call GraphDefaults followed by ClearViewPort if you also want to erase the screen. Or, you can write:

```
SetViewPort(0, 0, GetMaxX, GetMaxY, ClipOn);
```

If you need to know the current viewport settings, call GetViewSettings passing a variable of type ViewPortType:

```
ViewPortType = record
  X1, Y1, X2, Y2: Integer;
  Clip: Boolean
end;
```

Another viewport setting you can check is the *aspect ratio,* defined as:

$$\frac{\text{Display width}}{\text{Display height}}$$

NTSC (National Television Standard Code) standard aspect ratio is 4:3, suggesting an ideal display with a multiple of four pixels wide by a multiple of three pixels tall, a ratio equal to 1.333. On Macintosh computers and some VGA modes, the aspect ratio is very nearly 1.000—pixels are just about square. In 640 by 350 EGA display mode on PCs, the aspect ratio is 0.7750—nowhere near the ideal.

Turbo Pascal uses the aspect ratio when drawing circles and arcs to make them round. If it didn't compensate for the display's aspect ratio, a round circle would look oval.

Note that the aspect ratio is *not* equal to the horizontal divided by the vertical *resolutions.* The display resolution has no relation to the aspect ratio. To find the correct aspect ratio for any display mode, call GetAspectRatio with two Word parameters:

```
GetAspectRatio(Xaspect, Yaspect);
```

Run Program 11-4 to display the aspect ratio for the automatically selected graphics mode on your computer.

Program 11-4: ASPECT.PAS

```
 1:   program AspectRatio;
 2:   uses Crt, Graph;
 3:   var GrDriver, GrMode: Integer;
 4:      Xaspect, Yaspect: Word;
 5:   begin
 6:      GrDriver := Detect;
 7:      InitGraph(GrDriver, GrMode, '');
 8:      RestoreCrtMode;
 9:      GetAspectRatio(Xaspect, Yaspect);
10:      Writeln('Graph driver = ', GrDriver);
11:      Writeln('Graph mode   = ', GrMode);
12:      Writeln('Xaspect      = ', Xaspect);
13:      Writeln('Yaspect      = ', Yaspect);
14:      Writeln('Aspect ratio = ',
15:         (Xaspect * 1.0) / (Yaspect * 1.0) :0:3);
16:      Readln
17:   end.
```

In EGA 640 x 350 mode, Program 11-4 displays the following information:

```
Graph driver  = 3
Graph mode    = 1
Xaspect       = 7750
Yaspect       = 10000
Aspect ratio  = 0.775
```

These values indicate that, for graphics driver 3 in mode 1, a one-unit-tall pixel is 0.775 units wide. Assuming the aspect ratio is less than zero, multiplying the height of a line by the aspect ratio compensates for the disparity, letting you draw lines of equal display sizes even though the lines cover different numbers of pixels. Program 11-5 demonstrates how to do this.

Program 11-5: EQUALS.PAS

```
1:  program EqualLines;
2:  uses Crt, Graph;
3:  var GrDriver, GrMode: Integer;
4:    Xaspect, Yaspect: Word;
5:    Ratio: Real;
6:
7:  procedure DrawLines(X, Y, Len: Integer);
8:  begin
9:    Line(X, Y, X + Len, Y);  { Horizontal line }
10:    Line(X, Y, X, Y + Round(Len * Ratio));  { Vertical line }
11:  end;
12:
13:  begin
14:    GrDriver := Detect;
15:    InitGraph(GrDriver, GrMode, '');
16:
17:    Ratio := 1.0;   { No adjustment }
18:    DrawLines(25, 25, 75);
19:
20:    GetAspectRatio(Xaspect, Yaspect);
21:    Ratio := (Xaspect * 1.0) / (Yaspect * 1.0);
22:    DrawLines(110, 110, 75);
23:
24:    repeat until Keypressed;
25:    CloseGraph
26:  end.
```

Program 11-5 draws two right angles. The first in the upper-left corner is not adjusted for the display's aspect ratio. As you can see, the vertical line is longer than the horizontal. Pixels are taller than they are wide; therefore, lines of the same pixel length are similarly taller.

The second right angle to the lower-right adjusts the vertical line length by the aspect ratio, calculated in program line 21. This adjustment makes the horizontal and vertical lines equal lengths on display. If you measure these lines accurately, though, don't be too surprised if the results are imperfect. Minor differences in display monitors can also affect the aspect ratio.

If the default aspect ratio is not correct—in other words, if circles aren't perfectly round—call SetAspectRatio with two parameters representing the X (display width) and Y (display height) axes. The actual values aren't too important. It's the *ratio* of X to Y that matters. For instance, to change the display ratio to the NTSC standard 4:3, a ratio of 1.333, you can execute:

```
SetAspectRatio(4, 3);
```

Shifting the Origin

By turning off clipping and moving the viewport so that (0,0) is at dead center, you can write graphics that use both negative and positive coordinate values. Doing this divides the viewport into quadrants, simplifying some kinds of operations. Figure 11-2 shows the relationship of this new viewport to the entire coordinate plane.

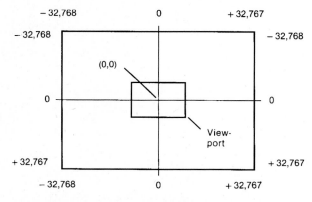

Figure 11-2 Changing the viewport so that (0,0) is at center screen makes some kinds of graphics programs easier to write.

To accomplish this requires a small trick: Set the viewport so that the absolute center of the screen becomes the new (0,0) coordinate and then turn off clipping:

```
XCenter := GetMaxX div 2;
YCenter := GetMaxY div 2;
SetViewPort(XCenter, YCenter, GetMaxX, GetMaxY, ClipOff);
```

Using ClipOn instead would restrict drawing to the lower-right quadrant of the display. With clipping off, the other three quadrants are visible. Even though the viewport is technically in the lower right of the display, positive and negative coordinate values now locate points on the entire screen, with (0,0) in the center. Figure 11-3 shows this new arrangement. Four combinations locate points in the four quadrants according to the scheme:

(–X, –Y) Upper-left quadrant.

(–X, +Y) Lower-left quadrant.

(+X, –Y) Upper-right quadrant.

(+X, +Y) Lower-right quadrant.

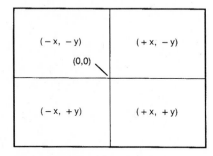

Figure 11-3 With (0,0) at the center, the display is divided into four quadrants.

Plotting Points

Two fundamental routines display and read individual pixels:

```
procedure PutPixel(X, Y: Integer; Pixel: Word);
function GetPixel(X, Y: Integer): Word;
```

A pixel is the Word value equal to the displayed dot's color number. (Later in this chapter, you'll learn how to associate different display colors with color numbers. GetPixel always returns the color number—in other words, the logical color—not necessarily the color you see on-screen.)

PutPixel displays one dot at location (X,Y) in the color number specified by parameter pixel. Program 11-6 demonstrates how to use PutPixel and GetPixel. The program displays dots at random locations (line 17) unless GetPixel discovers a dot already there. In this case, line 16 turns the pixel off by painting it black. The effect is to create a display full of pixels, evenly distributed like sand on the beach. Let the program run for several minutes. This is also a good test of the random number generator as well as a check on your monitor's ability to resolve individual pixels. Line 14 of the program shows how to use function GetMaxColor to determine the maximum color number available for any graphics mode.

Program 11-6: TWINKLER.PAS

```
 1:  program Twinkler;
 2:  uses Crt, Graph;
 3:  var GrDriver, GrMode, GrError: Integer;
 4:     X, Y, XMax, YMax, Color: Integer;
 5:  begin
 6:     GrDriver := Detect;
 7:     InitGraph(GrDriver, GrMode, '');
 8:     XMax := GetMaxX; YMax := GetMaxY;
 9:     Randomize;
10:     while not Keypressed do
11:     begin
12:       X := Random(XMax);
13:       Y := Random(YMax);
14:       Color := Random(GetMaxColor);
15:       if GetPixel(X, Y) <> Black
16:         then PutPixel(X, Y, Black)
17:         else PutPixel(X, Y, Color)
18:     end;
19:     CloseGraph
20:  end.
```

Drawing Lines

Of course you could draw lines by plotting individual pixels along a path between two coordinates. Instead of doing this yourself, it's easier—and much faster—to call one of Turbo Pascal's three line generators: Line, LineTo, and LineRel.

Procedure Line connects two points, (X1,Y1) and (X2,Y2). The procedure is declared as

```
procedure Line(X1, Y1, X2, Y2: Integer);
```

The two points can be anywhere, even off-screen, although you'll see lines only in the visible portion of the current viewport. Program 11-7 demonstrates how to use Line to draw a border around the graphics display. Notice how GetMaxX and GetMaxY (line 8) let this program work correctly for all display resolutions.

Program 11-7: GRBORDER.PAS

```pascal
 1:  program GraphBorder;
 2:  uses Crt, Graph;
 3:  var GraphDriver, GraphMode: Integer;
 4:     XMax, YMax: Integer;
 5:  begin
 6:     GraphDriver := Detect;
 7:     InitGraph(GraphDriver, GraphMode, '');
 8:     XMax := GetMaxX; YMax := GetMaxY;
 9:
10:     Line(0, 0, XMax, 0);
11:     Line(XMax, 0, XMax, YMax);
12:     Line(XMax, YMax, 0, YMax);
13:     Line(0, YMax, 0, 0);
14:
15:     repeat until Keypressed;
16:     CloseGraph
17:  end.
```

Instead of specifying the first (X, Y) coordinate, you can use LineTo to join the current CP to a new (X, Y) location:

```pascal
LineTo(X, Y);
```

Drawing lines with Line, LineTo, or LineRel changes CP to the line's new end point. Calling LineTo then continues drawing with the previous end point as the start for the next line. Because LineTo has two fewer parameters than Line, it runs a tiny bit faster—enough to make a noticeable difference in speed when you have many lines to draw.

Another way to change CP before drawing lines is to use MoveTo. The statements:

```pascal
MoveTo(X1, Y1);
LineTo(X2, Y2);
```

have the identical effect as:

```pascal
Line(X1, Y1, X2, Y2);
```

Program 11-8 duplicates Program 11-7, but uses MoveTo and LineTo to outline the display. The previous program (11-7) is obviously wasteful in lines 10-13 because the end point of each line is the starting point of the next. Therefore, LineTo is faster. The MoveTo statement at line 10 is not necessary in this example because InitGraph positions CP to (0,0). The statement would be necessary, though, if you had previously changed CP.

Program 11-8: BETTERBO.PAS

```
 1:  program BetterBorder;
 2:  uses Crt, Graph;
 3:  var GraphDriver, GraphMode: Integer;
 4:    XMax, YMax: Integer;
 5:  begin
 6:    GraphDriver := Detect;
 7:    InitGraph(GraphDriver, GraphMode, '');
 8:    XMax := GetMaxX; YMax := GetMaxY;
 9:
10:    MoveTo(0, 0);
11:    LineTo(XMax, 0);
12:    LineTo(XMax, YMax);
13:    LineTo(0, YMax);
14:    LineTo(0, 0);
15:
16:    repeat until Keypressed;
17:    CloseGraph
18:  end.
```

Relative Lines

Two procedures, MoveRel and LineRel, move CP to a new coordinate relative to the present CP or draw a line with its starting point relative to CP. With these procedures, it's easy to design figures that display correctly at any screen position. The procedures are defined as:

```
procedure MoveRel(Dx, Dy: Integer);
procedure LineRel(Dx, Dy: Integer);
```

Parameters Dx (delta X) and Dy (delta Y) are integer values representing the change in X and Y. Positive values move down and to the right; negative values move up and to the left.

Program 11-9 shows how to use these routines in a procedure, DrawFigure at lines 6-17, that draws a design centered relative to a point (X,Y). Because of the MoveRel and LineRel statements, the same figure is easy to draw at any screen location.

Program 11-9: RELATIVE.PAS

```pascal
 1:  program Relativity;
 2:  uses Crt, Graph;
 3:  var GraphDriver, GraphMode: Integer;
 4:    XMax, YMax: Integer;
 5:
 6:  procedure DrawFigure(X, Y, Size: Integer);
 7:  begin
 8:    MoveTo(X, Y);
 9:    MoveRel(X - Size, Y - Size);
10:    LineRel(Size, 0);
11:    LineRel(0, Size);
12:    LineRel(-Size, 0);
13:    LineRel(0, -Size);
14:    LineRel(Size, Size);
15:    MoveRel(0, -Size);
16:    LineRel(-Size, Size)
17:  end;
18:
19:  begin
20:    GraphDriver := Detect;
21:    InitGraph(GraphDriver, GraphMode, '');
22:    XMax := GetMaxX; YMax := GetMaxY;
23:    Randomize;
24:    while not Keypressed do
25:    begin
26:      Delay(100);
27:      DrawFigure(Random(XMax), Random(YMax), 10 + Random(40))
28:    end;
29:    CloseGraph
30:  end.
```

Stylish Lines

Two procedures, GetLineSettings and SetLineStyle, examine and change three line characteristics:

- Style
- Pattern
- Thickness

The line style can be one of the following constants:

```
SolidLn   = 0;
DottedLn  = 1;
CenterLn  = 2;
DashedLn  = 3;
```

The first four of these constants specify solid lines (SolidLn), dotted lines (DottedLn), alternating dash-dot lines (CenterLn), and dashes (DashedLn). Two other constants change line width to normal or thick:

```
NormWidth  = 1;
ThickWidth = 3;
```

These are the only automatic thicknesses available. In other words, to draw two-pixel wide lines, you have to draw two lines of normal width.

Call SetLineStyle to change line styles and thickness. For example, to draw a fat center line, dividing the top and bottom of the display, you can write:

```
SetLineStyle(CenterLn, 0, ThickWidth);
Line(0, GetMaxY div 2, GetMaxX, GetMaxY div 2);
```

The second parameter to SetLineStyle is significant only when the first parameter equals another constant, UserBitLn. In this case, the second parameter is the Word bit pattern you want the line generator to use to draw lines. For example, to display a faint line of sparse dots in the center of the screen, write:

```
var
  Pattern: Word;
begin
  Pattern := $1010;
  SetLineStyle(UserBitLn, Pattern, NormWidth);
  Line(0, GetMaxY div 2, GetMaxX, GetMaxY div 2)
end;
```

The custom Pattern equals hex $1010, or in binary, 0001 0000 0001 0000. Each 1 in the pattern becomes a dot on-screen; each 0, an invisible point that is not plotted. Using the UserBitLn constant lets you draw lines with any repeating pattern of 16 ones and zeros.

To read the current line style settings, call GetLineSettings with a record variable defined as

```
LineSettingsType = record
  LineStyle: Word;
  Pattern: Word;
  Thickness: Word
end;
```

The three fields in this record correspond with the three parameters passed to SetLineStyle. Use GetLineSettings to preserve the current line style when you want to change styles temporarily to draw other lines. Here's an example:

```
var
  Style: LineSettingsType;
begin
  GetLineSettings(Style);
  ...
  { Change line style and draw lines }
  ...
  with Style do
     SetLineStyle(LineStyle, Pattern, Thickness)
  end;
```

This technique preserves the current line style in variable Style and then, after changing styles and drawing other lines, restores the previous settings with a call to SetLineStyle, passing the three record fields, LineStyle, Pattern, and Thickness.

Color Palettes

Different graphics modes can display different numbers of colors on-screen at once. CGA graphics shows up to four colors, including the background. EGA and VGA graphics display up to 16 colors. And, by using the special driver VGA256.BGI, available from Borland, VGA graphics can display a full 256 colors. IBM 8514 graphics modes can also display 256 colors.

Because most people have CGA and EGA adapters, it's a good idea to limit your graphics programs to 16 colors—especially, of course, if you plan on distributing your program to others. The following discussion, therefore, assumes that you'll be using a maximum of 16 colors.

In each of these modes, and in other less popular graphics displays, a *palette* controls what actual colors (or shades of gray on monochrome systems) you see on-screen. Changing palettes instantly changes the colors of points already on display. You can't draw a few objects in one set of colors and then change palettes to get more colors on-screen. Changing palettes merely tells the computer what colors to use for all points, whether already displayed or to be displayed in the future.

In memory, a palette is an array of color values. The indexes to each arrayed value represent the *color numbers*—the values programs use to specify the colors of lines and points. When you draw in a certain color, say Red, a Graph unit constant equal to 4, the actual color you see on-screen depends on the color value of palette[4]. If you change that color value to Blue, all the previous red points as well as future red points will be Blue. Turbo Pascal defines a palette this way:

```
const
  MaxColors = 15;
type
  PaletteType = record
    Size: Byte;
    Colors: array[0 .. MaxColors] of ShortInt
  end;
```

A PaletteType record starts with a Byte field Size, which tells how many significant bytes follow. The actual number of bytes changes for different modes but is never greater than MaxColors + 1. To find out how many colors are available, use the function GetMaxColor. Assuming you have a PaletteType record Pt, this always sets the Size field correctly:

```
with Pt do
  Size := GetMaxColor + 1;
```

Remember that a PaletteType variable only represents the actual palette stored somewhere in memory. To load a PaletteType variable with the contents of the in-memory palette, use GetPalette like this:

```
var
  Pt: PaletteType;
begin
  GetPalette(Pt);
  ...
end;
```

GetPalette initializes the Size field in Pt and inserts color values into the colors array. You can then inspect or change the values to create different palettes and pass the result to SetAllPalette:

```
Pt.Colors[1] := Brown;
SetAllPalette(Pt);
```

A value of −1 in the Colors array causes no change to a color. This lets you change some colors while leaving others alone. For example:

```
with Pt do
begin
  Size := GetMaxcolor + 1;
  for I := 1 to Size do
    Colors[I] := -1;
  Colors[1] := Brown
end;
SetAllPalette(Pt);
```

An easier way to change a single color entry is to use SetPalette. This changes the first color to brown:

```
SetPalette(1, Brown);
```

The first SetPalette parameter is a Word equal to the color number—the index into the color palette array. The second parameter is the color value, a ShortInt value, which can be any number from –128 to +127. After this statement, passing 1 to SetColor will draw in Brown—or in whatever actual color or gray shade this value produces in one or another graphics modes.

In most programs, PaletteType records are useful for preparing several different palettes and switching among them with SetAllPalette. To change individual palette entries, use the simpler SetPalette.

Another way to determine the maximum palette number is to call GetPaletteSize, introduced in Turbo Pascal 5.0. The Integer function returns the same value as the size field in a PaletteType record returned by GetPalette. Use GetPaletteSize to check that palette color numbers are within range. Because the maximum value equals GetPaletteSize --1, the correct way to verify that a Word variable color is within limits is:

```
if Color >= GetPaletteSize
   then { Error--color out of range }
   else SetPalette(Color, Red);
```

The Default Palette

The Graph unit maintains a copy of the original palette initialized by InitGraph. To read this palette, call GetDefaultPalette with a variable of type PaletteType. Unlike GetPalette, which returns the current palette, including any modifications you made to palette entries, GetDefaultPalette returns an unblemished copy of the original palette. Assuming Pt is a PaletteType variable, to restore the original palette at any time takes only two statements:

```
GetDefaultPalette(Pt);
SetAllPalette(Pt);
```

Changing Display Colors

Because of the variety of different display modes, it's a good idea to call GetMaxColor early in your program. This tells you the maximum color number (palette index) that you can pass to SetColor, changing the color for subsequent drawing.

Color number 0 is the background color. Values from 1 to GetMaxColor equal the full range of color numbers that you can use. Program 11-10 demonstrates these ideas along with GetMaxX and GetMaxY to fill the screen with randomly positioned lines, in randomly selected colors, for any display mode.

Program 11-10: RANDLINE.PAS

```
 1:  program RandomLines;
 2:  uses Crt, Graph;
 3:  var GraphDriver, GraphMode: Integer;
 4:     XMax, YMax: Integer;
 5:  begin
 6:     GraphDriver := Detect;
 7:     InitGraph(GraphDriver, GraphMode, '');
 8:     XMax := GetMaxX; YMax := GetMaxY;
 9:     Randomize;
10:     while not Keypressed do
11:     begin
12:       Delay(100);
13:       SetColor(1 + Random(GetMaxColor));   { 1 .. GetMaxColor }
14:       LineTo(Random(GetMaxX + 1),          { 0 .. GetMaxX }
15:              Random(GetMaxY + 1));         { 0 .. GetMaxY }
16:     end;
17:     CloseGraph
18:  end.
```

Remove line 12 to increase the speed of this example, slowed for effect. Line 13 calls SetColor with the expression:

```
SetColor(1 + Random(GetMaxColor));
```

to select a drawing color at random between 1 and GetMaxColor + 1. This skips the background color (which would draw invisible lines) and is usually the correct way to generate colors at random in the entire spectrum available for all graphics modes.

If you need to find out the current drawing color, use GetColor, assigning this function's result to any Word variable:

```
var
   TheColor: Word;
begin
   TheColor := GetColor;
   ...
end;
```

In the Background

Two other color procedures examine and change the background color, which always has the color palette number 0 no matter what actual color you see. To change the background to cyan, write:

```
SetBkColor(Cyan);  { Change background color }
```

This is identical to changing the palette entry for color number 0:

```
SetPalette(0, Cyan);   { Change background color }
```

Like other palette changes, the visual effect is immediate. You don't have to clear the screen or perform any other steps to see the new background color. Lines and other shapes are preserved and appear on top of the new background—as long as they aren't of the same color, of course! To find out the current background color, call Word function GetBkColor:

```
var
  TheBkColor: Word;
begin
  TheBkColor := GetBkColor;
  ...
end;
```

Setting the Write Mode

Changing the Graph unit's write mode affects the method used to poke new pixels into the display. Normally, routines such as DrawPoly, Line, LineRec, LineTo, and Rectangle—some of which you haven't yet seen in action—simply turn on the appropriate pixels to draw lines and other shapes. To set the write mode to XOR (exclusive-OR), call SetWriteMode with the predefined constant XORPut:

```
SetWriteMode(XORPut);
```

To change the Write Mode back to normal, pass CopyPut to SetWriteMode:

```
SetWriteMode(CopyPut);
```

When setting the write mode to XORPut, redrawing a line in the same color erases the line. This is useful in graphics programs that display shapes on top of other shapes. After setting write mode to XORPut, you can remove a shape on top of another simply by redrawing the foreground image—without disturbing the shape below.

For a demonstration of how the XORPut write mode works, make a copy of Program 11-10 and replace line 4 with this procedure:

```
{ Recursive XORPut demonstration }
procedure DoLines(N: Integer);
var
  Color, X1, Y1, X2, Y2: Integer;
begin
  Delay(50);
  X1 := GetX;
  Y1 := GetY;
  X2 := Random(GetMaxX + 1);
  Y2 := Random(GetMaxY + 1);
  Color := 1 + Random(GetMaxColor);
  SetColor(Color);
  LineTo(X2, Y2);
  if N < 30 then DoLines(N + 1);
  Delay(50);
  SetColor(Color);        { Must reset color! }
  Line(X1, Y1, X2, Y2)    { Can't use CP! }
end;
```

Next, replace lines 8-16 with:

```
SetWriteMode(XORPut);
Randomize;
DoLines(0);
```

When you run the modified program, you'll see random lines as in the original. This time, because SetWriteMode changes the write mode to XORPut, redrawing lines in the same colors erases the lines one by one, leaving the display clear. Change XORPut to the default CopyPut (or remove the SetWriteMode statement) to see the difference that exclusive-OR drawing makes.

Shape Routines

Turbo Pascal offers three basic shapes, all composed of lines: rectangles, bars, and polygons. You can also fill a shape's insides with various patterns and colors. And, in the case of bars, you can display a pseudo-three-dimensional box, popular for business graphs.

Rectangles

Rectangles are the easiest shapes to draw. Pass the coordinates of the upper-left and lower-right corners of the area to enclose. Then call Rectangle, declared as

```
procedure Rectangle(X1, Y1, X2, Y2: Integer);
```

Line 9 of Program 11-11 calls Rectangle to outline the screen in the default drawing color, usually white. This is far simpler than our attempts to do the same job in Programs 11-7 and 11-8. Program 11-11 calls Rectangle again at lines 15-18, drawing boxes at random locations and colors until you press a key to stop the program. Notice how the Random statements carefully restrict the boxes to within the outline borders.

Program 11-11: RECTS.PAS

```
 1:  program Rects;
 2:  uses Crt, Graph;
 3:  var GraphDriver, GraphMode: Integer;
 4:     XMax, YMax: Integer;
 5:  begin
 6:     GraphDriver := Detect;
 7:     InitGraph(GraphDriver, GraphMode, '');
 8:     XMax := GetMaxX; YMax := GetMaxY;
 9:     Rectangle(0, 0, XMax, YMax);  { Outline screen }
10:     Randomize;
11:     while not Keypressed do
12:     begin
13:       Delay(100);
14:       SetColor(1 + Random(GetMaxColor));  { 1 .. GetMaxColor }
15:       Rectangle(1 + Random(GetMaxX - 1),
16:                 1 + Random(GetMaxY - 1),
17:                 1 + Random(GetMaxX - 1),
18:                 1 + Random(GetMaxY - 1))
19:     end;
20:     CloseGraph
21:  end.
```

Bars

A simple bar, helpful for drawing bar graphs, is just a rectangle painted with a color and a bit pattern. When drawing these and other filled shapes, it's helpful to think of the color as the *paint* and the bit pattern as the *brush*. Executing this command:

```
Bar(X1, Y1, X2, Y2);
```

is the same as calling Rectangle with these same coordinates and then filling the inside of the box with the current paint (white unless you change it) and brush pattern (normally solid). To see an example, replace Rectangle in line 15 of Program 11-11 with Bar and rerun the demo.

If you're following along on your computer, you now see a problem—the color passed to SetColor does not affect the paint color for filled shapes. To fix the problem, replace line 14 in Program 11-11 with:

```
SetFillStyle(SolidFill, 1 + Random(GetMaxColor));
```

SetFillStyle takes two parameters, both Word types. The first parameter is the pattern, which can be any one of the identifiers listed in Table 11-4. The second pattern is the color of paint you want to use. To fill boxes with both random patterns and colors, replace line 14 with:

```
SetFillStyle(Random(12), 1 + Random(GetMaxColor));
```

If none of Turbo Pascal's standard brush patterns will do, you can create your own patterns with SetFillPattern. This procedure takes an array of type FillPatternType, defined as:

```
type
    FillPatternType = array[1 .. 8] of Byte;
```

A custom pattern is an 8 x 8 block, with each bit corresponding to a pixel on display. To fill shapes with tiny boxes, assign values to a FillPatternType array with the appropriate bits.

A simple experiment demonstrates how to design custom patterns. Starting with a copy of Program 11-11, change Rectangle in line 15 to Bar and add a variable between lines 4 and 5:

```
Pattern: FillPatternType;
```

Next, add these assignments between lines 10 and 11 (after Randomize):

```
Pattern[1]:=$00;        {00000000}
Pattern[2]:=$3C;        {00111100}
Pattern[3]:=$24;        {00100100}
Pattern[4]:=$24;        {00100100}
Pattern[5]:=$24;        {00100100}
Pattern[6]:=$24;        {00100100}
Pattern[7]:=$3C;        {00111100}
Pattern[8]:=$00;        {00000000}
```

Table 11-4 Pattern constants for SetFillstyle.

Constant	Value	Fill effect
EmptyFill	0	Background color
SolidFill	1	Solid color
LineFill	2	Lines
LtSlashFill	3	Thin slashes
SlashFill	4	Thick slashes
BkSlashFill	5	Thick backslashes
LtBkSlashFill	6	Thin backslashes
HatchFill	7	Light hatch marks
XHatchFill	8	Heavy hatch marks
InterleaveFill	9	Interleaved lines
WideDotFill	10	Sparse dots
CloseDotFill	11	Dense dots
UserFill	12	Previous SetFillPattern

This creates the custom pattern array, assigning hex values to each of the eight array bytes. For reference, the equivalent binary values are shown in comments to the right of the assignments. Notice that the 1s form a box inside the 8 x 8 grid.

The final step is to pass this custom bit pattern to the graphics kernel. Replace line 14 with:

```
SetFillPattern(Pattern, 1 + Random(GetMaxColor));
```

When you pass a custom pattern to SetFillPattern this way, Turbo Pascal makes a copy of the pattern in memory. Rather than call SetFillPattern a second time, to use the most recent custom pattern, write:

```
SetFillStyle(UserFill, 0);
```

In this case, the color is the value you passed to SetFillPattern. The 0 in this example is ignored.

To preserve the current fill pattern, call GetFillPattern with a FillPatternType variable. You can then restore this pattern by calling SetFillPattern:

```
var
  Pattern: FillPatternType;
begin
  GetFillPattern(Pattern);
  ...
  { Design and draw with custom patterns }
  ...
  SetFillPattern(Pattern, Color);  { Restore pattern }
end;
```

To preserve both the current fill pattern and color, call GetFillSettings. This procedure takes a record defined as:

```
type
  FillSettingsType = record
    Pattern: Word;
    Color: Word;
  end;
```

After calling GetFillSettings, you can restore both the original pattern and color by passing the fields of this record to SetFillStyle. Here's an example:

```
var
  Settings: FillSettingsType;
begin
  GetFillSettings(Settings);
  ...
  { Design and draw with other patterns }
  ...
  with Settings do
    SetFillStyle(Pattern, Color);
end;
```

Three-Dimensional Bars

A special bar procedure, Bar3D, draws a pseudo-three-dimensional box, with three visible sides. The box has no depth and is technically called an *orthographic projection*. Even so, this object is useful for breathing some realism into an otherwise boring two-dimensional bar chart.

Program 11-12 displays a series of three-dimensional bars. When you run the program, you'll see that the face of the bar is filled with a solid color (probably white), while the top and right sides are only outlines. To change the number of bars, adjust constant NumBars in line 5. To change the depth of the pseudo-three-dimensional effect, change Depth in line 4.

Change the face of the bars the same way you changed the brushes and paint colors in earlier examples. Use either SetFillStyle or SetFillPattern. For example, to fill the bars with red slashes, insert this statement between lines 14 and 15:

```
SetFillStyle(SlashFill, Red);
```

When you run this modified program, the bars fill with red slashes instead of solid white—a definite improvement. Notice that the bar outlines remain white, unaffected by SetFillStyle. To change outline color, call SetColor. Try this statement after the SetFillStyle you just inserted:

```
SetColor(Yellow);
```

You now should see red-faced, slash-filled bars, outlined in yellow. On older CGA graphics systems, you might see the reverse—yellow faces outlined in red. This just goes to show that you can't trust the names of color constants to hold true for all graphics modes!

Program 11-12: FANCYBAR.PAS

```
 1:   program FancyBarChart;
 2:   uses Crt, Graph;
 3:   const
 4:     Depth = 14;
 5:     NumBars = 9;
 6:   var
 7:     GraphDriver, GraphMode: Integer;
 8:     Width, Height: Integer;
 9:     I, X1, Y1, X2, Y2, XMax, YMax: Integer;
10:   begin
11:     GraphDriver := Detect;
12:     InitGraph(GraphDriver, GraphMode, '');
13:     XMax := GetMaxX; YMax := GetMaxY;
14:     Randomize;
15:     Width := XMax div NumBars;
16:     Height := YMax - (YMax div 4);
17:     for I := 1 to NumBars do
18:     begin
19:       X1 := Width * (I - 1);
20:       Y1 := Depth + Random(Height);
21:       X2 := X1 + (Width div 2);
```

continued

Program 11-12: continued

```
22:        Y2 := YMax - (YMax div 6);
23:        Bar3D(X1, Y1, X2, Y2, Depth, TopOn)
24:     end;
25:
26:     repeat until Keypressed;
27:     CloseGraph
28: end.
```

Polygons

A polygon is any enclosed shape with sides made of straight lines. Triangles and boxes are polygons. Because there are easy ways to draw such simple shapes, though, a polygon is usually a more complex object with many sides.

One good analogy to the way Turbo Pascal draws polygons is a child's connect-the-dots game. Each dot is a coordinate on the screen. The graphics kernel is the child, connecting the dots to draw a picture.

In memory, a polygon is an array of X and Y coordinates—two integers per coordinate point. The array can be any size within practical limits; the more points you have, the longer it takes to draw the figure. Unlike some other graphics data types, there is no predefined polygon structure. Probably, the best design is to use an array of PointType records:

```
var
   Polygon: array[1 .. NumPoints] of PointType;
```

Each PointType record has two fields, X and Y. To fix the starting point of the polygon to (0,0), you can write:

```
with Polygon[1] do
begin
  X := 0;
  Y := 0;
end;
```

You can also use a two-dimensional array indexed by X and Y values, but this method uses the more efficient **with** statement and a single index operation to get to the X and Y components of each polygon point.

Another good possibility is to use a variable constant prefilled with coordinate values. Program 11-13 uses this idea to define a five-point star, the polygon constant at lines 4-10. Passing this array to DrawPoly at line 18 draws the star by connecting the points in the array.

The first parameter to DrawPoly tells how many coordinates follow—in this case, six. The second parameter is the array itself. Notice that this five-point object requires six array entries to close the shape. Replace line 18 with the following to see what happens if you forget this important rule:

```
DrawPoly(5, Polygon);
```

Program 11-13: STARSTRU.PAS

```
 1:  program StarStruck;
 2:  uses Crt, Graph;
 3:  const
 4:    Polygon: array[1 .. 6] of PointType =
 5:      ((X:  50; Y:   0),
 6:       (X:  90; Y:  75),
 7:       (X:   0; Y:  25),
 8:       (X: 100; Y:  25),
 9:       (X:  10; Y:  75),
10:       (X:  50; Y:   0));
11:  var
12:    GraphDriver, GraphMode: Integer;
13:  begin
14:    GraphDriver := Detect;
15:    InitGraph(GraphDriver, GraphMode, '');
16:
17:    SetColor(Cyan);
18:    DrawPoly(6, Polygon);
19:
20:    repeat until Keypressed;
21:    CloseGraph
22:  end.
```

Filling Polygons

You can fill polygons with patterns and colors the same way you fill two- and three-dimensional bars. Use SetFillStyle and SetFillPattern to select a brush and paint. Then call FillPoly instead of DrawPoly. For a test, replace line 18 in Program 11-13 with these two statements:

```
SetFillStyle(InterleaveFill, LightBlue);
FillPoly(5, Polygon);
```

The 5 is not a mistake. FillPoly operates a bit differently than the sister procedure, DrawPoly. Because painting a polygon with an unconnected side would leak paint all over the screen, Turbo Pascal automatically closes the shape for you. Therefore, FillPoly always requires one less point than DrawPoly. (You can specify the last point with no harm, though, passing 6 instead of 5 to FillPoly with no bad effects.)

When you run this new program, you'll see the star tips filled with light blue, using an interleaved line pattern. Use SetColor to change the color of the lines outlining the polygon.

Flood Filling

So far, you've learned how to draw and fill regular shapes like boxes, bars, and polygons connected with straight sides. To fill other shapes, use FloodFill, declared as:

```
procedure FloodFill(X, Y: Integer; Border: Word);
```

Coordinate (X,Y) specifies a *seed,* which can be anywhere inside the shape. Parameter border is the color of the lines that make up the shape, which must be completely enclosed. If the shape has gaps in its outline, the paint will leak into the surrounding areas, possibly filling the screen and ruining your drawing. Change the paint color and brush with SetFillStyle and SetFillPattern as you did in previous examples. To complete the program, replace line 18 with the next statements. (The earlier modifications are repeated here for reference.)

```
SetColor(White);
SetFillStyle(InterleaveFill, LightBlue);
FillPoly(6, Polygon);
FloodFill(50, 50, White);
```

Arcs and Circles

Three useful procedures round out Turbo Pascal's set of basic graphics commands: Arc, Circle, and Ellipse. A variant of these routines, PieSlice, makes it easy to design pie charts or to draw wedges for other purposes.

To draw an arc, specify a starting (X,Y) coordinate, equal to the center of the circle containing the arc. Also specify the starting and ending angles, as though spokes from the center reached to the arc end points. Finally, specify the circle radius. The complete definition for procedure Arc is:

```
procedure Arc(X, Y: Integer; StAngle, EndAngle, Radius: Word);
```

Figure 11-4 shows how these parameters cooperate to draw arcs. On-screen, only the heavy line is visible. The center point is at (X,Y). The starting angle is at A in the figure. The ending angle is at B. The radius is the dotted line r. Angles and the radius must be positive integers or zero. An angle of zero is at 3 o'clock, with greater angles rotating counterclockwise.

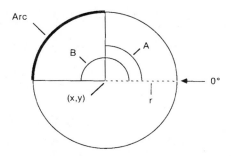

Figure 11-4 Of the many parameters that specify arcs, only the arc itself (the heavy line here) is visible.

Program 11-14 draws a rainbow—not true to nature's colors—by cycling through all colors available on your system, and calling Arc at line 18. To draw full circles instead of arcs, replace that line with:

```
Arc(X, Y, 0, 360, Radius);
```

You must specify a starting angle of 0 and an ending angle of 360 to enclose a circle completely.

Program 11-14: RAINBOW.PAS

```
1:  program Rainbow;
2:  uses Crt, Graph;
3:  var
4:    GraphDriver, GraphMode: Integer;
5:    Color, X, Y: Integer;
6:    Radius: Word;
7:  begin
8:    GraphDriver := Detect;
9:    InitGraph(GraphDriver, GraphMode, '');
10:
11:    X := GetMaxX div 2;
12:    Y := GetMaxY div 2;
13:    Radius := Y;
14:
```

continued

Program 11-14: continued

```
15:     for Color := 1 to GetMaxColor do
16:     begin
17:       SetColor(Color);
18:       Arc(X, Y, 0, 180, Radius);
19:       Y := Y + 10
20:     end;
21:
22:     repeat until Keypressed;
23:     CloseGraph
24:   end.
```

As Figure 11-4 shows, arcs have three important coordinates: the center point (X,Y), the starting point of the first pixel in the arc (X1,Y1), and the ending point of the last pixel (X2,Y2). Call GetArcCoords after drawing an arc to get these points from the graphics kernel.

Program 11-15 demonstrates how to do this with a program that draws a figure similar to the illustration in Figure 11-4. A variable arcCoords in line 7 is declared of type ArcCoordsType, which has the definition:

```
type
  ArcCoordsType = record
    X, Y: Integer;
    XStart, YStart: Integer;
    XEnd, YEnd: Integer;
  end;
```

Six integer fields locate the center, starting, and ending points associated with the arc most recently drawn. Program 11-15 uses this information to draw a blue wedge inside a brown circle with a white arc. (In CGA displays, you'll probably see different colors.)

Program 11-15: GETARC.PAS

```
1:  program GetArc;
2:  uses Crt, Graph;
3:  var
4:    GraphDriver, GraphMode: Integer;
5:    XCenter, YCenter: Integer;
6:    StAngle, EndAngle, Radius: Word;
7:    ArcCoords: ArcCoordsType;
8:  begin
```

```
 9:    GraphDriver := Detect;
10:    InitGraph(GraphDriver, GraphMode, '');
11:
12:    XCenter := GetMaxX div 2;
13:    YCenter := GetMaxY div 2;
14:    Radius := GetMaxY div 3;
15:    StAngle := 0;
16:    EndAngle := 59;
17:
18:    SetColor(Brown);
19:    Circle(XCenter, YCenter, Radius);
20:
21:    SetColor(White);
22:    Arc(XCenter, YCenter, StAngle, EndAngle, Radius);
23:
24:    GetArcCoords(ArcCoords);
25:    with ArcCoords do
26:    begin
27:      SetColor(Blue);
28:      Line(X, Y, XStart, YStart);
29:      Line(X, Y, XEnd, YEnd)
30:    end;
31:
32:    repeat until Keypressed;
33:    CloseGraph
34: end.
```

Program 11-15 also demonstrates the Circle procedure, which has three parameters:

```
procedure Circle(X, Y: Integer; Radius: Word);
```

Circle draws a circle (what else) centered at (X,Y) with a certain Radius. Program 11-16 demonstrates one problem with the Radius parameter, which Turbo Pascal adjusts according to your display's aspect ratio in order to draw round circles.

Program 11-16: RADIUS.PAS

```
1:  program RadiusDemo;
2:  uses Crt, Graph;
3:  var
4:    GraphDriver, GraphMode: Integer;
5:    Color, X, Y: Integer;
```

continued

Program 11-16: continued

```
 6:    Radius: Word;
 7:  begin
 8:    GraphDriver := Detect;
 9:    InitGraph(GraphDriver, GraphMode, '');
10:
11:    X := GetMaxX div 2;
12:    Y := GetMaxY div 2;
13:    Radius := Y div 2;
14:
15:    SetColor(Yellow);
16:    Circle(X, Y, Radius);
17:    SetColor(White);
18:    Line(X, Y, X + Radius, Y);
19:    Line(X, Y, X - Radius, Y);
20:    Line(X, Y, X, Y + Radius);
21:    Line(X, Y, X, Y - Radius);
22:
23:    repeat until Keypressed;
24:    CloseGraph
25:  end.
```

When you run this program, you'll see a circle in the center of the display with a cross in the center. The horizontal lines exactly fit inside the circle. But on most displays, the vertical lines extend beyond the circumference. This happens even though program lines 18-21 use the same radius value. This shows that you cannot assume the radius of displayed circles to have a certain number of pixels along their diameters.

Drawing Ellipses

An ellipse in Turbo Pascal graphics is any oval shape, including perfectly round circles. You can also draw a portion of an oval, similar to what the Arc routine produces, but with finer control over the results. One procedure, Ellipse, draws all these shapes. Ellipse is declared as

```
procedure Ellipse(X, Y: Integer; StAngle, EndAngle: Word;
  XRadius, YRadius: Word);
```

The (X,Y) coordinate is at the center of the ellipse (or ellipse-like arc). Angles StAngle and EndAngle correspond to A and B in Figure 11-4 and have the same purpose as the angle parameters to Arc. The last two parameters control the shape of the ellipse, altering its width (XRadius) and height (YRadius).

Unlike Circle, the ellipse is not adjusted for the display's aspect ratio. This usually means that, if XRadius equals YRadius, the ellipse will not be circular. In other words, to draw a circle with the Ellipse procedure, you must allow for the display's aspect ratio. The graphics kernel does not do this for you.

Program 11-17 demonstrates Ellipse while drawing an interesting shape. A **while** loop (lines 16-22) varies the X and Y radii to draw successive ovals from fat to skinny and short to tall.

Program 11-17: OVALTINE.PAS

```pascal
 1:  program Ovaltine;
 2:  uses Crt, Graph;
 3:  var
 4:    GraphDriver, GraphMode: Integer;
 5:    XMax, YMax, XRadius, YRadius: Integer;
 6:    XCenter, YCenter, MaxColor: Integer;
 7:  begin
 8:    GraphDriver := Detect;
 9:    InitGraph(GraphDriver, GraphMode, '');
10:    XMax := GetMaxX; YMax := GetMaxY;
11:    XCenter := XMax div 2; YCenter := YMax div 2;
12:    MaxColor := GetMaxColor + 1;
13:
14:    YRadius := YCenter div 4;
15:    XRadius := XCenter div 2;
16:    while XRadius > 40 do
17:    begin
18:      SetColor(1 + (XRadius mod MaxColor));
19:      Ellipse(XCenter, YCenter, 0, 360, XRadius, YRadius);
20:      XRadius := XRadius - 1;
21:      YRadius := YRadius + 1;
22:    end;
23:
24:    repeat until Keypressed;
25:    CloseGraph
26:  end.
```

Filling Ellipses

Starting with Turbo Pascal 5.0, a new Graph unit procedure, FillEllipse, operates much like other fill procedures such as FloodFill and FillPoly. The new procedure takes four parameters:

```
procedure FillEllipse(X, Y: Integer; XRadius, YRadius: Word);
```

Except for the missing StAngle and EndAngle fields, the four parameters are identical to those in Ellipse. FillEllipse can't fill in partial ellipses; therefore, the two additional angle values that Ellipse requires aren't needed.

Use SetFillStyle as explained earlier to modify the ellipse fill pattern and color. To see how FillEllipse works, replace lines 14-22 in Program 11-17 with the following statements, which draw a tennis racket (or maybe it's a fly swatter).

```
YRadius := YCenter div 2;
XRadius := XCenter div 4;
SetColor(White);
SetFillStyle(HatchFill, LightRed);
FillEllipse(XCenter, YRadius, XRadius, YRadius);
SetFillStyle(SolidFill, White);
Bar(XCenter - 8, YRadius * 2, XCenter + 8, GetMaxY);
```

Filling Partial Ellipses

Another new routine, with the somewhat unusual name Sector, has the identical parameters as Ellipse:

```
procedure Sector(X, Y: Integer; StAngle, EndAngle,
   XRadius, YRadius: Word);
```

Sector draws a full or partial ellipse filled with the current pattern and color initialized by SetFillStyle. Except for filling what it draws, Sector operates identically to Ellipse. Adjust the two angle parameters, StAngle and EndAngle, as explained earlier to draw partial ellipses or filled ellipses.

To see what Sector does differently from FillEllipse, replace lines 14-22 in Program 11-17 with the following statements, which draw an umbrella (or maybe it's a mushroom).

```
YRadius := YCenter div 2;
XRadius := XCenter div 3;
SetColor(White);
SetFillStyle(HatchFill, LightGreen);
Sector(XCenter, YRadius * 2, 0, 180, XRadius, YRadius);
SetFillStyle(SolidFill, White);
Bar(XCenter - 8, YRadius * 2, XCenter + 8, GetMaxY);
```

A Slice of Pie

A special Graph unit routine, PieSlice, makes it easy to draw pie charts—one of the more common shapes needed in business graphics programming. PieSlice is defined as:

```
procedure PieSlice(X, Y: Integer; StAngle, EndAngle, Radius: Word);
```

Except for its name, PieSlice is identical to Arc. In fact, that's what a pie slice is—a filled arc, or wedge, with its end points joined at the center point (X,Y) (see Figure 11-4). You could use other commands to draw arcs, join their ends, and fill their centers, but using PieSlice is easier.

Each slice of pie has an outline color, changed by SetColor, and a fill pattern and interior color, changed by SetFillStyle or SetFillPattern as described earlier for other filled shapes. If you don't want outlined pie wedges, use the same colors for the interior and outline.

Program 11-18 draws a pie chart from a data set, which you must enter into a separate file. You can specify from one to 50 wedges. For example, type the following lines into a file named PIE.DAT:

```
8
12.0
5.0
7.0
29.0
13.0
22.0
8.0
4.0
```

The first number tells how many values follow, in this case eight. Each value can be any number with or without a fractional part. Usually, the values following the first number should total 100.0 as they do here, but they don't have to.

After saving the data, type Program 11-18, compile, and run. When the program asks for a file name, type PIE.DAT and press Enter. For reference, the program first displays the data in tabular form. Press Enter a second time to see the pie chart.

Program 11-18: SWEETYPI.PAS

```
1:    program SweetyPie;
2:    uses Crt, Graph;
3:
4:    const
5:      MaxData = 50;   { Maximum number of wedges }
```

continued

```
 6:
 7:  type
 8:    WedgeRec =        { Holds precalculated wedge parameters }
 9:      record
10:        StAngle, EndAngle: Integer
11:      end;
12:
13:  var
14:    GraphDriver, GraphMode: Integer;
15:    XMax, YMax, Radius: Integer;
16:    XCenter, YCenter, MaxColor: Integer;
17:    Total: Real;
18:    NumWedges: 1 .. MaxData;
19:    Percentage, Data: array[1 .. MaxData] of Real;
20:    Wedge: array[1 .. MaxData] of WedgeRec;
21:
22:  { Text file format: count, d1, d2, ..., dcount }
23:  procedure ReadData;
24:  var Tf: Text; FileName: string; I: Integer;
25:  begin
26:    Write('Read data from what file? ');
27:    Readln(FileName);
28:    Assign(Tf, FileName);
29:    Reset(Tf);
30:    Readln(Tf, NumWedges);
31:    for I := 1 to NumWedges do
32:    begin
33:      Readln(Tf, Data[I]);
34:      Writeln(I:2, ': ', Data[I]:12:3)
35:    end;
36:    Close(Tf)
37:  end;
38:
39:  { Calculate wedge parameters from data }
40:  procedure Calculate;
41:  var
42:    I, StartAngle, ArcAngle: Integer;
43:  begin
44:    Total := 0.0;
45:    for I := 1 to NumWedges do
46:      Total := Total + Data[I];
```

```
47:    Writeln('=================');
48:    Writeln('Total =', Total:10:3);
49:    StartAngle := 0;
50:    for I := 1 to NumWedges do with Wedge[I] do
51:    begin
52:      Percentage[I] := Data[I] / Total;
53:      if I = NumWedges then ArcAngle := 360 else
54:        ArcAngle := StartAngle + Round(Percentage[I] * 360.0);
55:      StAngle := StartAngle;
56:      EndAngle := ArcAngle;
57:      StartAngle := EndAngle
58:    end
59:  end;
60:
61:  { Display the pie chart }
62:  procedure DisplayChart;
63:  var I: Integer;
64:  begin
65:    for I := 1 to NumWedges do with Wedge[I] do
66:    begin
67:      SetFillStyle(SolidFill, I mod MaxColor);
68:      PieSlice(XCenter, YCenter, StAngle, EndAngle, Radius)
69:    end
70:  end;
71:
72:  begin
73:    ReadData;
74:    Calculate;
75:    Write('Press <Enter> for pie chart...');
76:    Readln;
77:    GraphDriver := Detect;
78:    InitGraph(GraphDriver, GraphMode, '');
79:    XMax := GetMaxX; YMax := GetMaxY;
80:    XCenter := XMax div 2; YCenter := YMax div 2;
81:    MaxColor := GetMaxColor + 1;
82:    Radius := YMax div 3;
83:    DisplayChart;
84:    repeat until Keypressed;
85:    CloseGraph
86:  end.
```

Program 11-18 displays a pie chart by calculating the percentage of 360° for each data value (Lines 50-58) along with the PieSlice angles, stored in an array of

WedgeRec records (lines 8-11 and 20). After this step, procedure DisplayChart (lines 61-70) calls SetFillStyle and PieSlice to display each wedge.

On monochrome monitors, the wedge divisions might be difficult to see. To fix this problem, use different fill patterns. For example, you might change line 67 to:

```
SetFillStyle(1 + (I mod 11), I mod maxColor);
```

When you make this change, each wedge fills with both a different color and pattern, making the pie chart visible on all types of graphics displays.

Bit-Map Images

Three routines, ImageSize, GetImage, and PutImage, copy display pixels into variables and then display those pixels anywhere on-screen. The Graph unit defines these routines as:

```
ImageSize(X1, Y1, X2, Y2: Integer): Word;
GetImage(X1, Y1, X2, Y2: Integer; var BitMap);
PutImage(X, Y: Integer; var BitMap; BitBlt: Word);
```

ImageSize calculates the number of bytes required to store a copy of pixel image within a rectangle with its upper-left corner at (X1,Y1) and its lower-right corner at (X2,Y2). GetImage copies pixels from the display inside a similar rectangle, depositing the image plus width and height information in the untyped variable, BitMap. It's your responsibility to ensure that a BitMap is large enough to store the image. If not, GetImage can overwrite other information or programs in memory, causing serious bugs.

PutImage copies a BitMap image to the screen with the upper-left corner at (X,Y). The BitBlt parameter specifies one of the constants:

```
CopyPut = 0;    { Or NormalPut = 0 }
XORPut  = 1;
OrPut   = 2;
AndPut  = 3;
NotPut  = 4;
```

These values select the logical method used to combine the copied image with pixels already on display. CopyPut overwrites existing pixels. (CopyPut used to be called NormalPut, which still exists for compatibility and has the same effect.) The other four values perform the listed bit-by-bit logical operations—**xor** (exclusive-OR), **or**, **and**, and **not**.

Note: The final PutImage parameter, BitBlt, is a strange but common term in graphics programming. According to many references, BitBlt stands for "bit blitter," a high-speed graphics device found on some computers, but not PCs. Some claim the term BitBlt means "bit blaster," a tongue-in-cheek interpretation that implies blazing speed. Others refer to BitBlt as meaning "bit block transfer," which is probably the correct translation.

Normally, you will use the three routines—ImageSize, GetImage, and PutImage—to copy and display images, following these steps:

1. Draw the image using various Graph unit commands.

2. Use ImageSize to create a variable large enough to hold a copy of the image.

3. Call GetImage to copy pixels from the screen into the variable created in step 2.

4. Call PutImage to display the image, possibly at a different location.

Program 11-19 demonstrates these steps, drawing a green house with DrawPoly (line 30), using the variable constant values initialized at lines 5-14. Line 32 shows how to create a variable to hold the bit image. Two data types are needed:

```
ByteArray = array[0 .. 0] of Byte;
ByteArrayPtr = ^ByteArray;
```

A ByteArray is an array of bytes. Because the actual size of the variable will change, the array dimensions are unimportant. The range [0..0] is typical, although any other legal range values would work equally well. The ByteArrayPtr type is a pointer to a ByteArray, which the program creates on the heap. Line 32 reserves memory for this purpose, calling GetMem with the statement:

```
GetMem(Image, ImageSize(0, 0, 50, 50));
```

Variable image is a ByteArrayPtr. Using the ImageSize function as the GetMem size parameter allocates the correct number of bytes needed to hold the pixels within the rectangle at (0,0) to (50,50). If enough memory is not available, GetMem halts the program with a runtime error. To avoid this problem, see Chapter 16's discussion of HeapFunc, which causes GetMem to return a **nil** pointer if memory is tight. In that case, you'd follow the GetMem call by testing if image is **nil**, in which case the program must not use the image pointer.

This step of reserving memory with ImageSize is vital to writing graphics programs that work correctly in all display resolutions. You could, of course, create a fixed-size variable to hold display pixels but then your program would be fixed to one display mode. Avoid this limitation whenever you can.

After reserving memory, line 35 uses this statement to copy the displayed green house to the location addressed by image:

```
GetImage(0, 0, 50, 50, Image^);
```

The coordinate values must be the same as those used to create the image variable on the heap. GetImage copies the pixels from the display—actually, from the video memory buffer—transferring the data to the location addressed by pointer image. At the same time, the procedure copies the width and height of the image for later use by PutPixel.

Lines 36-37 replicate the copied image at randomly selected locations, calling PutImage to create a rapidly expanding development of little green houses. Try other display mode constants in place of NormalPut, the last parameter to PutImage.

Program 11-19: DEVELOP.PAS

```
 1:  program Developments;
 2:  uses Crt, Graph;
 3:
 4:  const
 5:    House: array[ 1 .. 9 ] of PointType =
 6:        ((X:    0; Y: 50),
 7:         (X:    0; Y: 25),
 8:         (X:   25; Y:  0),
 9:         (X:   50; Y: 25),
10:         (X:    1; Y: 25),
11:         (X:   50; Y: 50),
12:         (X:   50; Y: 26),
13:         (X:    1; Y: 50),
14:         (X:   50; Y: 50));
15:
16:  type
17:    ByteArray = array[0 .. 0] of Byte;
18:    ByteArrayPtr = ^ByteArray;
19:
20:  var
21:    GraphDriver, GraphMode: Integer;
22:    XMax, YMax: Integer;
23:    Image: ByteArrayPtr;
24:
25:  begin
26:    GraphDriver := Detect;
27:    InitGraph(GraphDriver, GraphMode, '');
```

```
28:     XMax := GetMaxX; YMax := GetMaxY;
29:     SetColor(Green);
30:     DrawPoly(9, House);
31:
32:     GetMem(Image, ImageSize(0, 0, 50, 50));  { Reserve memory }
33:     if Image <> nil then
34:     begin
35:       GetImage(0, 0, 50, 50, Image^);  { Copy image from screen }
36:       while not Keypressed do
37:         PutImage(Random(XMax), Random(YMax), Image^, NormalPut)
38:     end;
39:
40:     CloseGraph
41: end.
```

Displaying Text on Graphics Screens

As long as you do not use the Crt unit or a Hercules-compatible graphics adapter, Write and Writeln work the same on graphics and text displays. Using Crt switches to direct-video routines for Write and Writeln, which display characters more quickly on text screens, but which can't show characters on graphics displays.

Another and probably better way to display text with graphics is to use Turbo Pascal's built-in font routines. Fonts are stored in disk files ending in CHR and containing the information needed to display characters on graphics screens. Your Turbo Pascal disks come with several of these files, and you'll probably find others on bulletin boards and advertised in magazines.

There are two kinds of graphics fonts: bit-mapped and vectored, or *stroked*. The default font is bit-mapped—its character shapes are stored as fixed bit patterns, similar to the PC's usual character images in ROM. All other fonts are stroked, formed out of line segments much like the polygon shapes you drew earlier in this chapter.

The advantage of using a stroked font becomes obvious when you enlarge characters. Because the patterns are formed of line segments, characters retain their relative shapes as they grow larger. A B's humps stay round no matter how large they grow. Also, the lines in a character have the same thicknesses in all font sizes. A straight line in an uppercase I, for example, may grow taller, but it won't get fatter.

Bit-mapped fonts are different. As a bit-mapped character grows, jagged edges along diagonals become more pronounced. Each bit—normally a single pixel in the font's default size—grows in all directions, making lines grow fatter as well as taller. You've probably seen this effect on paper banners created by dot matrix printers.

Bit-mapped fonts do have one important advantage over stroked fonts, though—they are faster to display. Because a stroked character is composed of individually drawn lines, it takes longer to display than a bit-mapped image, which the graphics kernel can plop directly into video memory with fast memory move commands. Turbo Pascal handles both kinds of graphics text, letting you choose quality or speed, whichever is more important to you.

An example explains how to load character fonts from disk and display text. Because Program 11-20 does not use the Crt unit, it can display text with Write and Writeln (as in line 11) as well as with Turbo Pascal's two analogous routines, OutText and OutTextXY. When you run the program, you'll see two lines of text, the first displayed by a Writeln statement and the second by OutText.

Program 11-20: GRAPHTEX.PAS

```
 1:  program GraphText;
 2:  uses Graph;
 3:  var GraphDriver, GraphMode: Integer;
 4:  begin
 5:     GraphDriver := Detect;
 6:     InitGraph(GraphDriver, GraphMode, '');
 7:
 8:     SetColor(Blue);
 9:     SetTextStyle(DefaultFont, HorizDir, 2);
10:
11:     Writeln('This text is displayed by Writeln');
12:     MoveTo(0, 25);
13:     OutText('This text is displayed by OutText');
14:
15:     Readln;
16:     CloseGraph
17:  end.
```

Line 9 loads a character font and specifies two characteristics: direction and size. SetTextStyle takes three Word parameters:

```
procedure SetTextStyle(Font, Direction, CharSize: Word);
```

Set Font to one of the numbers in Table 11-5. The default bit-mapped font is number 0 and is always available to programs. Other fonts require a corresponding CHR file in the directory path previously passed to InitGraph (see line 6). For best results, store your BGI graphics drivers and CHR files in the same directory.

Table 11-5 Graphics text fonts.

Constant	Value	Type	Disk file
DefaultFont	0	Bit map	none
TriplexFont	1	Stroked	TRIP.CHR
SmallFont	2	Stroked	LITT.CHR
SansSerif Font	3	Stroked	SANS.CHR
GothicFont	4	Stroked	GOTH.CHR

The Direction parameter displays text horizontally or vertically. Use one of these two constant values:

```
HorizDir  = 0;
VertDir   = 1;
```

The final parameter, size, controls the size of text on-screen. You need only one font in memory for all sizes—Turbo Pascal scales the font patterns up and down as needed. Different fonts do not have the same relative sizes for the same size values. Unfortunately, text sizes have no direct relation to typesetting points, which measure character size in 1/72-inch increments.

Experiment with Program 11-20, inserting different values in the SetTextStyle statement in line 9. If you don't see different font styles, check that your CHR files are on disk. You might also follow SetTextStyle with an error check after loading the font pattern from disk. To do this, add an integer variable GrError and replace blank line 10 with:

```
GrError := GraphResult;
if GrError <> GrOk then
begin
  RestoreCrtMode;
  Writeln('Graphics error : ', GraphErrorMsg(GrError));
  Halt
end;
```

Of course, you might want to take a more friendly action than halting the program. Unlike more serious errors, such as a failure to initialize the graphics display with InitGraph, an error loading a font simply causes text to appear in a different style.

Notice the MoveTo statement in line 12 of Program 11-20. MoveTo changes CP, where OutText displays the upper-left corner of the first character. To prove this, replace blank line 14 with:

```
PutPixel(0, 25, White);
```

When you run the modified program, you'll see a small white dot at the upper-left corner of the cross in the T. (You might have trouble seeing this dot on CGA systems or on poor-quality monitors.)

Instead of using MoveTo to change CP for OutText, you can use the simpler OutTextXY to do both jobs at once. For example, replace lines 12 and 13 with:

```
OutTextXY(0, 25, 'This text...');
```

One important difference between OutText and OutTextXY is the effect on CP. After OutText, CP changes to the next position after the last character drawn. After OutTextXY, CP equals the (X,Y) coordinate passed to the procedure. A little experiment helps make this clear. Replace line 13 in Program 11-20 with:

```
OutText('This is a test');
SetColor(White);
LineTo(GetMaxX, GetMaxY);
```

You should see a line from just after the end of the text to the bottom-right display corner.

Now, change the OutText to OutTextXY with this statement:

```
OutTextXY(0, 50, 'This is a test');
```

This time, the line extends from the first character to the bottom-right corner, proving that OutTextXY changes CP to (0,50).

Text Justification

SetTextJustify changes where OutText displays text in relation to CP or to the coordinate passed to OutTextXY. The procedure takes two Word parameters:

```
procedure SetTextJustify(Horiz, Vert: Word);
```

The Horiz parameter determines whether text starts at CP and moves right, starts at the center, or starts at the right and moves left. The Vert parameter determines whether text is above, below, or centered at CP. For the Horiz parameter, use one of these constants:

```
LeftText    = 0;
CenterText  = 1;
RightText   = 2;
```

For the Vert parameter, use one of the constants:

```
BottomText  = 0;
CenterText  = 1;
TopText     = 2;
```

Combinations of these values change where text displays in relation to CP. Program 11-21 shows all possible combinations of these values and also explains how to display numeric values with OutText and OutTextXY, which can display only character strings. When you run the program, press Enter to redisplay a line of text at different locations relative to CP, represented as a small cross.

Program 11-21: JUSTIFY.PAS

```
 1:  program Justification;
 2:  uses Crt,Graph;
 3:  var
 4:    GraphDriver, GraphMode: Integer;
 5:    XCenter, YCenter: Word;
 6:    Horiz, Vert: Integer;
 7:    Hs, Vs: string[5];
 8:  begin
 9:    GraphDriver := Detect;
10:    InitGraph(GraphDriver, GraphMode, '');
11:    XCenter := GetMaxX div 2; YCenter := GetMaxY div 2;
12:    for Vert := 0 to 2 do
13:      for Horiz := 0 to 2 do
14:      begin
15:        ClearViewPort;
16:        SetTextJustify(LeftText, TopText);
17:        SetColor(White);
18:        Str(Horiz, Hs); Str(Vert, Vs);
19:        MoveTo(0,  0); OutText('Horiz = '); OutText(Hs);
20:        MoveTo(0, 25); OutText('Vert  = '); OutText(Vs);
21:        SetTextJustify(Horiz, Vert);
22:        SetColor(LightRed);
23:        OutTextXY(XCenter, YCenter, 'Justification Test');
24:        SetColor(White);
25:        Line(XCenter, YCenter - 2, XCenter, YCenter + 2);
26:        Line(XCenter - 2, YCenter, XCenter + 2, YCenter);
27:        if Readkey = Chr(27) then Halt
28:      end;
29:    CloseGraph
30:  end.
```

Lines 18-20 display the current Horiz and Vert justification values, calling Str to convert integers to strings. It's necessary to use MoveTo and OutText here because OutTextXY would not leave CP in the correct position to display the string values, Hs and Vs.

Line 21 changes the justification for the OutTextXY statement in line 23. Lines 25-26 draw the cross.

Text Width and Height

To determine how many pixels a character occupies on-screen in the current font and size, call the functions:

```
function TextHeight(TextString: string): Word;
function TextWidth(TextString: string): Word;
```

The two functions help you write programs with graphics that change relatively to the font size. Program 11-22, for example, displays underlined text by using TextHeight and TextWidth to draw a line under a string.

Program 11-22: GRUNDER.PAS

```
1:   program GraphUnderline;
2:   uses Graph;
3:   const S = 'This text is underlined.';
4:   var GraphDriver, GraphMode: Integer;
5:   begin
6:     GraphDriver := Detect;
7:     InitGraph(GraphDriver, GraphMode, '');
8:
9:     SetColor(White);
10:    SetTextJustify(LeftText, BottomText);
11:    SetTextStyle(GothicFont, HorizDir, 4);
12:    OutTextXY(0, TextHeight(S), S);
13:    Line(0, TextHeight(S), TextWidth(S), TextHeight(S));
14:
15:    Readln;
16:    CloseGraph
17:  end.
```

Try changing the font and size in line 11. In every case, the underline automatically grows and shrinks as necessary. In your own programs, try to design text and graphics that work the same for other sizes and styles. This makes modifying your programs much easier.

Controlling Font Size

For finer control over character width and height, use SetUserCharSize with four Byte parameters:

```
procedure SetUserCharSize(MultX, DivX, MultY, DivY: Byte);
```

The four parameters specify two ratios, which the graphics kernel uses to change the width and height of text in the current style and size set by SetTextStyle. The horizontal ratio equals MultX / DivX. The vertical ratio equals MultY / DivY. A ratio of 1 causes no change. A ratio less than 1 reduces the horizontal or vertical size. A ratio greater than 1 increases the size. For example, to display text half as wide as normal, you can write:

```
SetUserCharSize(1, 1, 1, 1);
SetTextStyle(TriplexFont, HorizDir, UserCharSize);
OutTextXY(0, 0, 'Normal width');
SetUserCharSize(1, 2, 1, 1);
SetTextStyle(TriplexFont, HorizDir, UserCharSize);
OutTextXY(0, 40, 'Half width');
```

The first call to SetUserCharSize prepares to display text in its normal size—not necessarily the same as a size parameter of 1, but in the size of a font with no adjustment to the width and height. After SetUserCharSize, you must call SetTextStyle to choose a font and direction. Instead of the usual size parameter, specify UserCharSize, a Graph unit constant equal to 0. This tells the graphics kernel to use your ratios in place of the standards.

The second call to SetUserCharSize in this example prepares for displaying text half as wide as previously displayed. In this case, MultX equals 1 and DivX equals 2, a ratio of 1:2 or 0.5. Notice that you must again call SetTextStyle after changing ratios. (Take this statement out to see the difference.) To display text twice as wide, use the statement:

```
SetUserCharSize(2, 1, 1, 1);
```

This specifies the ratio 2:1 or 2.0—twice as wide as 1:1. Here's another example:

```
SetUserCharSize(2, 1, 4, 1);
```

This displays text twice as wide (2:1) and four times as tall (4:1) as normal.

Reading Text Parameters

When you need to know the current text settings, call GetTextSettings with a record variable of this type:

```
type
  TextSettingsType = record
    Font: Word;
    Direction: Word;
    Charsize: Word;
    Horiz: Word;
    Vert: Word
  end;
```

Turbo Pascal fills in the fields of this record with the current text parameters. You might use GetTextSettings to save the current settings, change to a new font and size, display some text, and then restore the original settings before proceeding. Here's how:

```
var
  Settings: TextSettingsType;
begin
  GetTextSettings(Settings);
  ...
  { Change settings and display text }
  ...
  with Settings do
  begin
    SetTextStyle(Font, Direction, CharSize);
    SetTextJustify(Horiz, Vert)
  end;
end;
```

First, save the current text settings by calling GetTextSettings with a variable of type TextSettingsType. Then, change to other fonts and display text in various sizes. To restore the original settings, pass the five fields in the settings record to SetTextStyle and SetTextJustify as shown here.

Animation

EGA, VGA, and Hercules video modes have enough memory to store more than one display page. With these systems, the graphics kernel lets you choose on which page to draw and which page to view. You can draw on off-screen pages and then switch rapidly to the finished drawing. Because of this action, people don't see your graphics in the process of forming—they see only the final result. Using this technique, you can also store more than one chart, picture, or graph and then switch among them like slides in a projector.

Another use for multipage graphics is in animation. Drawing off-screen while viewing a second page, and then rapidly alternating between the two screens, smoothly animates pictures by hiding the drawing details from your eyes. This process, called *ping ponging* or *page swapping,* is similar to the way cartoons appear to move by showing successive still frames fast enough to produce an illusion of motion.

To change the page you see, call SetVisualPage. To change the page on which drawing commands operate, call SetActivePage. Each of these procedures takes a single Word parameter, Page.

It's up to you to make sure the pages you request exist in your system. The first page is number 0, the second number 1, and so on. Table 11-2 lists the number of pages for various modes. Never attempt to select nonexistent pages—you can cause serious bugs and, in some video systems, even cause the computer to hang.

To animate a sequence, follow these steps:

1. Initialize two word variables. Set Active to 0 and Visual to 1.

2. Execute these statements to draw on the active page and view the other:

```
SetActivePage(Active);

SetVisualPage(Visual);
```

3. Erase any drawing on the unseen page and draw your new figures.

4. Swap the Active and Visual variables and go back to step 2.

An example demonstrates how these steps smooth animations by hiding the drawing details. Program 11-23 draws a "Pac Person" figure, opening and shutting its hungry mouth by changing the starting and ending angles in a PieSlice statement (line 34).

Procedure Initialize first checks that you have an EGA, Hercules, or VGA video system (lines 11-16). If not, the program halts with an error. Otherwise, lines 17-21 prepare for the upcoming graphics. Line 21 initializes the page swapping variables described earlier.

Lines 41-42 set the active and visual page. Then, procedure DoGraphics draws a figure on the off-screen page while you view the other. After lines 44-46 swap Active and Visual, the **while** loop repeats until you press a key to end the program.

A simple experiment proves that page swapping makes the animation work smoothly. Assign 0 to Visual instead of 1 in line 21 and run the program again. This ruins the animation by displaying the details of drawing the Pac Person pie slice.

Program 11-23: PACPER.PAS

```
1:  program PacPerson;
2:  uses Crt, Graph;
3:  var GraphDriver, GraphMode: Integer;
4:    Active, Visual, Temp: Word;
```

continued

```
 5:     XCenter, YCenter, Radius, StAngle, EndAngle: Integer;
 6:
 7:   procedure Initialize;
 8:   begin
 9:     GraphDriver := Detect;
10:     InitGraph(GraphDriver, GraphMode, '');
11:     if not (GraphDriver in [EGA, HercMono, VGA]) then
12:     begin
13:       RestoreCrtMode;
14:       Writeln('Error: Requires multi-page video graphics');
15:       Halt
16:     end;
17:     SetColor(Red);
18:     SetFillStyle(SolidFill, Blue);
19:     XCenter := GetMaxX div 2; YCenter := GetMaxY div 2;
20:     StAngle := 0; Radius := GetMaxY div 8;
21:     Active := 0; Visual := 1
22:   end;
23:
24:   procedure DoGraphics;
25:   begin
26:     ClearViewPort;
27:     if StAngle = 1 then
28:     begin
29:       StAngle := 30; EndAngle := 330
30:     end else
31:     begin
32:       StAngle := 1; EndAngle := 360
33:     end;
34:     PieSlice(XCenter, YCenter, StAngle, EndAngle, Radius)
35:   end;
36:
37:   begin
38:     Initialize;
39:     while not Keypressed do
40:     begin
41:       SetActivePage(Active);
42:       SetVisualPage(Visual);
43:       DoGraphics;
44:       Temp := Active;
45:       Active := Visual;
46:       Visual := Temp
```

```
47:     end;
48:     CloseGraph
49:  end.
```

Loading Multiple Fonts and Drivers

By preloading fonts and drivers into memory, you speed up programs that need to switch modes and character styles. The only disadvantage to this method is the extra memory it takes. The main advantage is speed—sometimes, a lot of speed.

The idea is simple. Load each driver and font you need into a memory buffer exactly as big as required. Then, register the drivers and fonts with the graphics kernel. That's *register,* as in registering to vote. By registering your drivers and fonts, you tell the graphics kernel that they are already in memory. Knowing this, the kernel won't reload the files from disk every time you switch modes and text styles.

An example demonstrates how this idea dramatically improves performance. Program 11-24 displays five lines of text in as many fonts (lines 57-61) and then writes the alphabet, alternating fonts for each character (63-68). Procedures LoadOneFont and LoadFonts load Turbo Pascal's four standard disk-based fonts into memory. Pass the same path name to LoadFonts used later in InitGraph (see lines 50 and 52).

Notice how lines 24-25 calculate the font file size, which is different for different fonts, and then reserve that much memory with GetMem. You could use a different method or even store fonts in global variables, but storing fonts on the heap is easy and, in most cases, best. The BlockRead statement in line 26 loads the font into memory, storing bytes at the location addressed by pointer Fp.

Never load fonts into local variables declared in procedures and functions. When the routines end, the variable space disappears, a fact the graphics kernel won't know.

The final step is to register the font by calling RegisterBGIfont, an integer function, passing the address of the first byte of the font image now in memory (line 28). If the function returns a value less than zero, then an error occurred—probably because the font file is not recognized. (Perhaps you tried to load a file that is not actually a graphics font.) In this case, check GraphResult for the error number (lines 31-32).

That's all you need to do to load multiple fonts into memory. When you later call SetTextStyle to switch fonts, the graphics kernel knows the font is already in memory and won't reload the .CHR file from disk.

Preloading multiple fonts takes extra care and programming, but the results are worth every bit of trouble. For proof, remove line 50 from Program 11-24 and run the program again. Now, because each new font number passed to SetTextStyle loads that font from disk into memory, the program runs sluggishly, especially when displaying the multifont alphabet.

You could use a similar method to load multiple graphics drivers into memory, too. In this case, just replace RegisterBGIfont with RegisterBGIdriver. Everything else is the same except, of course, you will load driver files like CGA.BGI instead of fonts.

Usually, however, loading multiple drivers this way is not as advantageous as loading multiple fonts. It's the rare program that needs to switch rapidly between different graphics modes. The next section explains a superior approach to attaching multiple drivers to programs.

Program 11-24: MULTIFON.PAS

```pascal
 1:  program MultiFonts;
 2:  uses Graph;
 3:  const
 4:    Message = 'Turbo Pascal 6.0';
 5:  var
 6:    GraphDriver, GraphMode, Y: Integer;
 7:    Ch: Char;
 8:
 9:  procedure ShowText(Font: Word);
10:  begin
11:    SetTextStyle(Font, HorizDir, 4);
12:    OutTextXY(0, Y, Message);
13:    Y := Y + TextHeight(Message) + 4
14:  end;
15:
16:  procedure LoadOneFont(FileName: string);
17:  var
18:    F: file;         { Untyped file for reading disk file }
19:    Fp: Pointer;     { Pointer to font in memory }
20:    Bytes: LongInt; { Bytes required to hold font in memory }
21:  begin
22:    Assign(F, FileName);
23:    Reset(F, 1);                { Open with block size = 1 byte }
24:    Bytes := FileSize(F);      { Get size of file }
25:    GetMem(Fp, Bytes);         { Reserve memory for font }
26:    BlockRead(F, Fp^, Bytes); { Read font into memory }
27:    Close(F);
28:    if RegisterBGIfont(Fp) < 0 then  { Register font number }
29:    begin
30:      Writeln('Error loading ', FileName);
31:      Writeln('Graphics Error: ',
```

```
32:          GraphErrorMsg(GraphResult));
33:      Halt
34:    end
35:  end;
36:
37:  procedure LoadFonts(Path: string);
38:  begin
39:    if Length(Path) > 0 then
40:      if Path[Length(Path)] <> '\'
41:        then Path := Path + '\';
42:
43:    LoadOneFont(Path + 'TRIP.CHR');
44:    LoadOneFont(Path + 'LITT.CHR');
45:    LoadOneFont(Path + 'SANS.CHR');
46:    LoadOneFont(Path + 'GOTH.CHR');
47:  end;
48:
49:  begin
50:    LoadFonts('');
51:    GraphDriver := Detect;
52:    InitGraph(GraphDriver, GraphMode, '');
53:    Y := TextHeight(Message);
54:
55:    SetColor(Cyan);
56:
57:    ShowText(DefaultFont);
58:    ShowText(TriplexFont);
59:    ShowText(SmallFont);
60:    ShowText(SansSerifFont);
61:    ShowText(GothicFont);
62:
63:    MoveTo(0, Y + 16);
64:    for Ch := 'A' to 'Z' do
65:    begin
66:      SetTextStyle((Ord(Ch) - Ord('A')) mod 5, HorizDir, 2);
67:      OutText(Ch)
68:    end;
69:
70:    Readln;
71:    CloseGraph
72:  end.
```

Creating a Graphics Application

For programs that you plan to sell or, perhaps, to distribute to the public domain on bulletin boards, it's inconvenient to require people to have Borland's BGI driver and CHR font files on disk. Besides, you certainly don't want to limit your market to only those people who own Turbo Pascal.

One way to proceed is to combine driver and font files directly into your disk EXE code file. Although this makes the disk file grow up to 50,000 or more bytes larger, it makes a convenient package of one file containing all the elements needed to run your graphics program.

The first step is to convert BGI and CHR files into a new form, called *object files,* that Turbo Pascal can link into a program. To do this, locate the program BINOBJ.EXE on your Turbo Pascal disks. Make sure you have in the same directory BINOBJ.EXE along with the four CHR files listed in Table 11-5 plus the first five BGI files listed in Table 11-1. Then from the DOS command line, type the following lines exactly as shown here:

```
binobj goth.chr goth GothicFontProc
binobj litt.chr litt SmallFontProc
binobj sans.chr sans SansSerifFontProc
binobj trip.chr trip TriplexFontProc
binobj cga.bgi cga CGADriverProc
binobj egavga.bgi egavga EGAVGADriverProc
binobj herc.bgi herc HercDriverProc
binobj pc3270.bgi pc3270 PC3270DriverProc
binobj att.bgi att ATTDriverProc
```

Alternatively, you could type these lines into a batch file named MAKEOBJ.BAT, and then just type MAKEOBJ to convert all files at once.

After executing these unseemly instructions, you should have the following object files on disk:

```
ATT.OBJ
CGA.OBJ
EGAVGA.OBJ
GOTH.OBJ
HERC.OBJ
LITT.OBJ
PC3270.OBJ
SANS.OBJ
TRIP.OBJ
```

The *binobj* instructions you just typed to create these files converted the driver and font files from their binary form into object files that, to Turbo Pascal, look like code modules—in other words, procedures and functions, even though that's not what they really are. The next step is to create two units containing these phony procedures. Type Program 11-25, save as GRDRIVER.PAS, and compile to disk as GRDRIVER.TPU. Type Program 11-26, save as GRFONT.PAS, and compile to disk as GRFONT.TPU.

After these steps, you no longer need the .OBJ files on disk, to compile and run graphics programs. In fact, you don't even need the BGI or CHR files any longer. (Don't delete your only copies of these files, though!)

Program 11-25: GRDRIVER.PAS

```pascal
 1:  unit GrDriver;
 2:
 3:  { Graphics drivers }
 4:
 5:
 6:  interface
 7:
 8:  uses Graph;
 9:
10:
11:  implementation
12:
13:  procedure ATTDriverProc; External;     {$L ATT.OBJ }
14:  procedure CGADriverProc; External;     {$L CGA.OBJ }
15:  procedure EGAVGADriverProc; External; {$L EGAVGA.OBJ }
16:  procedure HercDriverProc; External;    {$L HERC.OBJ }
17:  procedure PC3270DriverProc; External; {$L PC3270.OBJ }
18:
19:  procedure ReportError(S: string);
20:  begin
21:    Writeln;
22:    Writeln(S, ': ', GraphErrorMsg(GraphResult));
23:    Halt(1)
24:  end;
25:
26:  begin
27:    if RegisterBGIdriver(@ATTDriverProc   ) < 0
28:      then ReportError('AT&T');
29:    if RegisterBGIdriver(@CGADriverProc   ) < 0
```

continued

Programs 11-25: continued

```
30:       then ReportError('CGA');
31:     if RegisterBGIdriver(@EGAVGADriverProc) < 0
32:       then ReportError('EGA-VGA');
33:     if RegisterBGIdriver(@HercDriverProc  ) < 0
34:       then ReportError('Hercules');
35:     if RegisterBGIdriver(@PC3270DriverProc) < 0
36:       then ReportError('PC-3270');
37: end.
```

Program 11-26: GRFONT.PAS

```
 1:  unit GrFont;
 2:
 3:  { Graphics fonts }
 4:
 5:
 6:  interface
 7:
 8:  uses Graph;
 9:
10:
11:  implementation
12:
13:  procedure GothicFontProc; External;    {$L GOTH.OBJ }
14:  procedure SansSerifFontProc; External; {$L SANS.OBJ }
15:  procedure SmallFontProc; External;     {$L LITT.OBJ }
16:  procedure TriplexFontProc; External;   {$L TRIP.OBJ }
17:
18:  procedure ReportError(S: string);
19:  begin
20:    Writeln;
21:    Writeln(S, ' font: ', GraphErrorMsg(GraphResult));
22:    Halt(1)
23:  end;
24:
25:  begin
26:    if RegisterBGIfont(@GothicFontProc   ) < 0
27:      then ReportError('Gothic');
28:    if RegisterBGIfont(@SansSerifFontProc) < 0
```

```
29:        then ReportError('SansSerif');
30:     if RegisterBGIfont(@SmallFontProc    ) < 0
31:        then ReportError('Small');
32:     if RegisterBGIfont(@TriplexFontProc  ) < 0
33:        then ReportError('Triplex');
34:  end.
```

The two units in Programs 11-25 and 11-26 are similar. Except for the **uses** declaration at line 8, neither has any public items for programs to use. In Program 11-25, five private procedures are declared External, which tells the compiler that the code for these procedures is stored on disk in the files specified by the {$L} directives at the end of each line. Remember that these are only phony procedures—place holders for font patterns and graphics drivers. You never directly call the phony procedures.

Compiling each unit combines the external object files to produce a single unit TPU disk file. When the program runs, the unit initialization parts execute (lines 26-37 in Program 11-25 and lines 25-34 in Program 11-26). The series of **if** statements in these sections register the fonts and drivers with the graphics kernel, telling the system to use the in-memory copies of these items instead of loading them from disk.

To finish your graphics application, simply add Program 11-25 or 11-26 or both to your program's **uses** declaration along with unit Graph. When you compile your program to disk, the resulting EXE file is completely self-contained, runs correctly under any graphics mode, and does not require driver or font files on disk. To convert any of the previous examples to a stand-alone program, follow these steps. We'll use Program 11-18 here, although the same steps work for any graphics program.

1. Load or type Program 11-18 (SWEETYPI.PAS) and save as SWEETY2.PAS.

2. Change the **uses** declaration in line 2 to read:

   uses Crt, Graph, GrDriver;

3. Compile to disk, creating SWEETY2.EXE. Exit to DOS and type SWEETY2 to run the program. Enter the name of a pre-chart data file, such as PIE.DAT.

Simple, no? For an example of how to use both the GrDrivers and GrFonts units, follow these steps for converting Program 11-24.

1. Load or type Program 11-24 and save as MULTI2.PAS.

2. Change the **uses** declaration in line 2 to read:

   uses Graph, GrDriver, GrFont;

3. Delete lines 16-47 and 50. All fonts are stored in GrFonts—there's no need to load them from disk.

4. Compile this much shorter program to disk, creating MULTI2.EXE. Exit to DOS and type MULTI2 to run the example. Notice that switching between multiple fonts is now as fast as it was when you manually loaded the font files.

Advanced BGI Graphics

If you have a VGA 256-color display, an IBM-8514 adapter, or custom hardware, you can write BGI programs to take full advantage of these high-quality display resolutions and colors.

Two functions, InstallUserDriver and InstallUserFont, provide a way to link low-level graphics driver software to Graph unit routines. You can also write your own low-level drivers, although this subject is too involved to cover in detail here. For more information, refer to Chapter 18's discussion of InstallUserDriver and InstallUserFont.

Another procedure, SetRGBPalette, lets you program IBM-8514 256-color displays:

```
procedure SetRGBPalette(CcolorNum,
    RedValue, GreenValue, BlueValue: Integer);
```

On IBM-8514 displays, ColorNum may range from 0 to 255. The three values— RedValue, GreenValue, and BlueValue—specify the color levels to assign to the palette entry indexed by ColorNum. The first 16 such palette entries on IBM-8514 displays default to the standard EGA and VGA colors. Even though the color values are type Integer, only 6 bits of the low bytes in each value are significant.

Summary

Borland's graphics kernel automatically detects the best possible display mode for any PC graphics card or circuitry. This eases the job of programming graphics for a variety of display types, traditionally one of the most difficult aspects of writing PC graphics software.

Graphics drivers contain the machine language to implement graphics routines and other items described in the Graph unit. Drivers are stored in BGI disk files. Character fonts, which can be bit-mapped or stroked, are stored in CHR files. Normally, these files must be on disk to run graphics programs. For finished applications, follow the instructions in this chapter to combine drivers, character fonts, and your program into a single disk file.

A viewport restricts the visible viewing area of the logical coordinate grid in which programs can draw. Various Graph routines draw lines, circles, ellipses, polygons, and arcs. A host of other commands help you write programs to run correctly in various screen resolutions and colors.

Exercises

11-1.   Write a program to bounce a ball around on-screen. Your program should run correctly on any PC graphics display.

11-2.   Draw a line graph using a data set of values. Label the X and Y axes.

11-3.   (Advanced) Design procedures to save and restore graphics images in disk files.

11-4.   Write a sketching program, using the arrow keys to move a cursor around the graphics display, drawing lines.

11-5.   Add shapes to your program in exercise 11-4, drawing boxes, circles, and other patterns at the cursor.

11-6.   Use page-swapping animation techniques to display a short cartoon of your own design. (Hint: It requires a multipage graphics display.)

11-7.   (Advanced) Design a fade-in, fade-out procedure to transfer a graphics image in memory gradually to the display.

11-8.   Convert any of your answers to preceding questions into a stand-alone application. Your program should run without graphics drivers and font files on disk.

11-9.   Design your own circle procedure using only PutPixel commands.

11-10. Improve the bar chart example (Program 11-12) to display a Z axis, showing several rows of bars.

11-11. Improve Program 11-18 to display one wedge pulled out of the pie chart.

11-12. Animate your answer to exercise 11-11.

12

More About Numbers

- Integer Numbers
- Real Numbers
- Coprocessors and Emulation Routines
- Coprocessor Emulation in Units
- Reading and Writing Numbers
- Word Alignment
- Numeric Expressions
- A Horse of a Different Radix
- Hex and Decimal Conversions
- Logical Operations on Integers
- Numeric Functions
- Transcendentals
- Advanced Constant Expressions
- Round-Off Error
- Raising to a Power
- Numbers in Business
- The Comp Data Type
- Numbers at Random

12

Key Words and Identifiers

Abs, **and**, ArcTan, Byte, Comp, Cos, **div**, Double, Exp, Extended, Frac, Hi, Int, Integer, Ln, Lo, LongInt, MaxInt, MaxLongInt, **not**, **or**, Random, Randomize, RandSeed, Real, Round, **shl**, ShortInt, **shr**, Sin, Single, Sqr, Sqrt, Str, Trunc, Val, Word, **xor**

Real numbers, as you learned in Chapter 2, range from about plus or minus 2.9E–39 to 1.7E+38 (in scientific notation). While Integer values range from –32,767 to +32,768, real numbers can express much larger or smaller values and can have fractional parts as in 3.14159 and 0.0001.

Turbo Pascal offers several variations on these two fundamental numeric data types. It also has many built-in procedures and functions useful for working with numbers. This chapter explores more about numbers and shows how to make use of a math coprocessor chip if your computer has one. You'll also learn how to enable coprocessor emulation for writing extended-real-number programs that run almost identically with and without a real coprocessor.

Integer Numbers

Table 12-1 lists Turbo Pascal's integer data types. To avoid confusion from now on, the capitalized Integer refers to the Integer data type while the uncapitalized integer refers to any of the types from Table 12-1. Values in this table have commas for clarity only—in programs, you can never type commas in numbers.

Table 12-1 Integer data types.

Type	Minimum . . Maximum	Sign	Size
ShortInt	−128 . . 127	Signed	1
Byte	0 . . 255	Unsigned	1
Integer	−32,768 . . 32,767	Signed	2
Word	0 . . 65,535	Unsigned	2
LongInt	−2,147,483,648 . . 2,147,483,647	Signed	4

Note: Values in programs cannot have commas. They have been added here for clarity.

Each type in Table 12-1 can express values ranging from a minimum to a maximum. Two types, Byte and Word are *unsigned*—they can represent only positive numbers. The other three types, ShortInt, Integer, and LongInt, are *signed*—they can represent positive and negative numbers. The table also lists the size in bytes that a variable of each type occupies in memory.

All integer types can represent zero, traditionally considered to be a positive number. Because of zero, the negative and positive values for signed types ShortInt, Integer, and LongInt are not mirror images. For example, the minimum Integer value is −32,768 while the positive maximum is 32,767—*not* 32,768. *Including* zero, there are equal numbers of positive and negative values in a signed-number range. (There are 32,768 positive Integer values including zero and 32,768 negative values excluding zero.)

The built-in constant MaxInt equals the maximum Integer value. The built-in constant MaxLongInt equals the maximum LongInt value. The other types do not have similar constants. Be aware that −MaxInt and −MaxLongInt do not equal the minimum values for their data types for the reasons just explained.

Real Numbers

Table 12-2 lists Turbo Pascal's real-number data types. The table also lists the size in bytes that variables of each type occupy in memory plus the approximate maximum number of significant digits values can have.

Table 12-2 Real-number data types.

Type	Minimum . . Maximum	Size	Significant digits
Single*	1.5E–45 . . 3.4E38	4	7-8
Real	2.9E–39 . . 1.7E38	6	11-12
Double*	5.0E–324 . . 1.7E308	8	15-16
Extended*	1.9E–4951 . . 1.1 E4932	10	19-20
Comp*	$-2^{63} + 1$ . . $2^{63} - 1$	8	18-19

*Math coprocessor or emulation required.

Note: As with integers, the uncapitalized word, real, from now on stands for any of the types in Table 12-2. The capitalized Real refers only to the six-byte Real data type.

Coprocessors offer two main advantages: speed and accuracy. Numeric expression processing can run up to 200 times faster, while reducing round-off errors by increasing the range of values you can represent with standard Real numbers.

All programs can use the standard Real type. The other four types, Single, Double, Extended, and Comp require emulation routines or a coprocessor chip—an 8087, 80287, or 80387.

Coprocessors and Emulation Routines

Two settings accessed by the IDE's *Options:Compiler* command control the use of data types in Table 12-2. Selecting the command displays the *Compiler Options* dialog, in which you can select two *Numeric processing* (NP) settings that tell the compiler whether to generate code for a math coprocessor. Select *8087/80287* if you are sure the computer on which your software will run has a math coprocessor. Select *Emulation* to generate code that will work whether or not a hardware coprocessor is present.

Instead of choosing settings from the IDE's *Compiler Options* dialog, you can insert {$N+/–} and {$E+/–} directives in programs. Using the directives overrides the IDE's settings.

The {$N+} directive enables all of the data types listed in Table 12-2. If you want to use any of the real types in addition to standard Real, include the {$N+} directive in your program. The opposite setting {$N–} disables extended real types, allowing you to use only Real.

The {$E+} directive links in Turbo Pascal's coprocessor emulation routines. The emulator allows programs to use extended real data types regardless of whether a math coprocessor is present. If a coprocessor is present, the program will use it. If a coprocessor is not present, the program will use the slower but functionally identical emulator.

The two directives are typically used together. For most programs, insert the double directive {$N+,E+} at the beginning of the program to enable extended real types and to link in the emulation routines. If you are positive that a math coprocessor will be present at runtime, you may use the directive {$N+} (equivalent to {$N+,E–}) to generate fast inline coprocessor instructions. However, program compiled with these directives will not run on systems lacking a hardware coprocessor.

> **Note:** The combined directives {$N–,E+} are senseless since they disable extended real data types and link in the emulation routines, which would not be used.

Coprocessor Emulation in Units

Emulation routines are never linked into compiled units; therefore, there's never any reason to use the {$E+} directive inside a unit. If a unit uses any of the data types from Table 12-2, insert the directive {$N+} above the **unit** key word (or change NP to "8087/80287") before compiling.

In the host program, insert the directives {$N+,E–} to force the unit's code to use a numeric coprocessor. Or, to link in emulation routines, insert the directives {$N+,E+}.

Reading and Writing Numbers

As many previous examples demonstrate, programs can directly assign the results of expressions to real or integer variables, or use Read and Readln to let operators enter values from their keyboards.

Program 12-1 demonstrates a problem that often occurs when directly reading real or integer values. When you run the program, type 3.14159 or any other number and press Enter. You should see the same value formatted in scientific notation. Run the program again, but this time press a letter key such as A and then press Enter. What happens? You receive:

```
Runtime error 106: Invalid numeric format.
```

This error occurs because the Readln statement (line 8) expects a number. Typing a letter is the same as trying to assign a character or string to a number, which, of course, you cannot do.

Program 12-1: INPUTNUM.PAS

```
 1:  program InputNumbers;
 2:  var
 3:    R: Real;
 4:  begin
 5:    Writeln('Input Numbers');
 6:    Writeln;
 7:    Write('Value? ');
 8:    Readln(R);
 9:    Writeln('R = ', R);
10:    Readln
11:  end.
```

Error-Free Input

As Program 12-1 demonstrates, when reading integer or real-number variables in a Read or Readln statement, Pascal halts the program if you enter anything other than a valid number. Of course, software reviewers would hang your program from the yardarm if it halted at every typing error. To pass scrutiny, programs need error-free methods for reading numbers.

One way to avoid the problem is to read values as strings and then convert the digits from characters to numeric values with Turbo Pascal's built-in procedure, Val. Because you can type any characters into strings, this method lets people make typing mistakes without halting the program.

Val takes three parameters, a string, a real or integer variable, and an integer error code. In Program 12-2, S is the string, R is the real number variable, and E is the error code. In line 11, Val converts string S to value R, setting error code E to zero if it detects no errors.

When you run the program and enter an illegal character, the program itself detects errors and takes appropriate action—in this case, displaying the error code value or, if the error is zero, the converted number R. The same method works with integer values, too. Change the type of R from Real to Integer, and recompile. What happens if you now enter 3.14159?

The error code that Val returns (E in Program 12-2) represents the position of an illegal character in the string. You can use this information to write a general purpose numeric input procedure, demonstrated in Program 12-3.

Program 12-2: INPUTERR.PAS

```
 1:   program InputErr;
 2:   var
 3:     E: Integer;
 4:     R: Real;
 5:     S: string[20];
 6:   begin
 7:     Writeln('Input Numbers');
 8:     Writeln;
 9:     Write('Value? ');
10:     Readln(S);
11:     Val(S, R, E);
12:     if E = 0
13:       then Writeln('R = ', R)
14:       else Writeln('Error code = ', E);
15:     Readln
16:   end.
```

Procedure GetReal (lines 5-18) prompts for a real-number value. Line 12 reads your response into string variable S. When you enter an illegal character, the **if** statement in lines 14-16 writes a caret pointing to your mistake. To find the column position of the error, GetReal adds the length of the prompt string to the error code returned by Val (line 13).

Program 12-3: INPUTPOS.PAS

```
 1:   program InputPos;
 2:   var
 3:     R: Real;
 4:
 5:   procedure GetReal(Prompt: string; var R: Real);
 6:   var
 7:     Error: Integer;
 8:     S: string;
 9:   begin
10:     repeat
11:       Write(Prompt);
12:       Readln(S);
13:       Val(S, R, Error);
```

continued

Program 12-3: continued

```
14:    if Error <> 0
15:        then Writeln('^': Length(Prompt) + Error,
16:                        '-- Entry error!')
17:      until Error = 0
18:   end;
19:
20:   begin
21:     Writeln('Input Numbers');
22:     Writeln;
23:     GetReal('Value? ', R);
24:     Writeln('R = ', R);
25:     Readln
26: end.
```

Type a few illegal entries such as 3.141A5 or 123@7.2 to see how Program 12-3 responds. You can also enter values in scientific notation. Try a few values such as 7.5025E4 and −45E−3.

Pressing Enter instead of a number is an error in this version of GetReal. To return zero in this case—a reasonable response to someone deciding not to type a number—add an **if** statement between lines 12 and 13, calling Val only if the string length is greater than zero:

```
if Length(S) = 0 then
begin
   R := 0.0;
   Error := 0
end else
```

Val works equally well for any real or integer type. Try changing Real in lines 3 and 5 in Program 12-3 to any of the types in Tables 12-1 and 12-2. Some of the answers may surprise you. As you can see, different data types have subtle effects on the accuracy and representation of numbers as program variables. If you have a numeric coprocessor, insert the directive {$N+} above **program**. If you don't have a numeric coprocessor, use the directives {$N+,E+}.

Formatted Output

Procedure Str reverses what Val does, converting numbers to strings. A database program might use Str to store numeric values in disk files but convert them to strings for editing. Val could then reconvert edited numbers back into values.

Program 12-4 demonstrates Str. Enter a value followed by the number of digits and decimals that you want in the formatted result. Line 16 converts Value to string S with no formatting. Line 19 does the same thing but formats the result to the number of Digits and Decimals you specify.

The number of digits specifies the column width for the *entire* number, including the decimal point character plus all digits to the left and right. The number of decimals limits how many digits appear to the right of the decimal point, rounding values to the next highest value. The best way to understand these specifications is to run Program 12-4 and type 3.14159 (or any other value) with various numbers of decimals and digits.

Program 12-4: NUM2STR.PAS

```
 1:   program Num2String;
 2:   var
 3:     Value: Real;
 4:     Digits, Decimals: Integer;
 5:     S: string;
 6:   begin
 7:     Writeln('Number to string converter');
 8:     repeat
 9:       Writeln;
10:       Write('Value (0 to quit)? '); Readln(Value);
11:       if Value <> 0.0 then
12:       begin
13:         Write('Digits? '); Readln(Digits);
14:         Write('Decimals? '); Readln(Decimals);
15:
16:         Str(Value, S);
17:         Writeln('Unformatted result ===> ', S);
18:
19:         Str(Value: Digits: Decimals, S);
20:         Writeln('Formatted result =====> ', S);
21:         Writeln('String length ========> ', Length(S))
22:       end
23:     until Value = 0.0
24:   end.
```

If the value to be formatted has fewer digits than the formatting values Digits and Decimals, Str right-justifies the result in the string. If the value has more digits, the result occupies as much space in the string as needed.

You can also convert integer values to strings with Str, but in that case you may specify only the number of digits, not the number of decimals, as Str's parameter. To experiment, change Real in line 3 to Integer and revise line 19 to read:

```
Str(Value:Digits, S);
```

In addition to Integer and Real, Str can convert to strings any of the types in Tables 12-1 and 12-2. You might want to try some of these types before continuing.

Word Alignment

Turbo Pascal optimizes memory accesses by aligning all variables larger than 1 byte on even addresses. For example, if a 2-byte integer variable would fall on an odd address, the compiler wastes a byte of memory to ensure that the variable's address is even.

Word alignment speeds program execution because the 16-bit 8086-family processors (but not the 8088) can load 2-byte variables faster if the first address is even. The speed increase is usually worth a little wasted memory—especially in programs that use many Integer and Word variables interspersed with other multibyte arrays, records, sets, and so forth. If you prefer to save as much memory as possible, include the directive {$A–} above the **program** or **unit** headers to turn off word alignment. Be aware that this may slow your program.

With alignment on, as it normally is, multibyte records are also aligned on even address boundaries, but individual fields in such records are *not* word aligned. If you want to align Integer and Word fields inside records, you must insert your own dummy variables to make sure that preceding fields occupy an even number of bytes. Or, just list all Integer and Word fields first in the record.

Numeric Expressions

As you learned in Chapter 2, you can mix real numbers and integers in expressions. The results of mixed expressions, however, are always real numbers, which you cannot assign to integer variables. Instead, you first have to convert real-number values to integers using one of two available methods.

Function Round converts a real number to a LongInt value, rounded up or down to the nearest whole number. Function Trunc also converts real numbers to LongInt values but truncates with no rounding all digits to the right of the decimal. Figure 12-1 lists a few example rounded and truncated values.

When converting real numbers to integers, be careful to stay within the allowed integer range. This does not work:

```
{$R+}
R := 5.5E8;
I := Round(R);     { Incorrect! }
```

If range checking is on and if I is type Integer, assigning Round(R) to I when R is not in the range –32,767 to +32,768 generates:

```
Runtime error 201: Range check error.
```

```
Round(3.14159) = 3
Round(100.5  ) = 101
Round(1.99999) = 2

Trunc(3.14159) = 3
Trunc(100.5  ) = 100
Trunc(1.99999) = 1
```

Figure 12-1 Functions Round and Trunc convert real numbers to integers.

There is no simple way to prevent Turbo Pascal from stopping your program if this error occurs. The only solution is never to allow the condition to arise. You could use the following sequence to avoid the problem:

```
{$R+}
if (R >= -32767.0) and
   (R <=  32768.0)
  then I := Round(R)
  else I := 0;
```

Of course, it may not be adequate in all cases to set I to zero if R is out of range, but at least that approach avoids halting the program. Another possibility is to assign Round and Trunc to a LongInt variable. Except for very large real numbers, this will rarely generate runtime errors.

Converting integers to real numbers, on the other hand, is easier. Turbo Pascal automatically converts integer values to reals as needed. To convert an integer value, therefore, just assign it to a real-number variable. This sequence displays the value 1.234E+03 (plus trailing zeros):

```
I := 1234;
R := I;
Writeln(R);
```

A Horse of a Different Radix

A number's radix is the *base* to which the number belongs. The standard radix in Turbo Pascal is base ten decimal, but you may also write numbers in base 16, more commonly called *hexadecimal.* Literally, hexadecimal means "ten and six." The word refers to the 16 symbols in the hexadecimal number system: the ten digits, 0 to 9, plus the six letters, A to F.

Hexadecimal and integer numbers are just different forms of the *same* values. Hexadecimal $FF represents the same number of things as decimal 255. Hex numbers are just horses of a different color—or radix.

You might wonder, if hex and decimal numbers represent the same values, why use one over the other? The answer is intimately related to the fact that all PCs (indeed, most computers in existence) operate on binary numbers, having the digits 0 and 1. Any number can be expressed in binary, decimal, hexadecimal—or in any other radix. For example, these values are equivalent:

```
1234              (Decimal)
$0402             (Hexadecimal)
0100 1101 0010    (Binary)
```

And each of the following statements sets integer variable Num to 255.

```
Num := 255;
Num := $FF;
Num := 240 + $0F;
Num := $F0 + $000F;
```

Because 16 is a power of 2 and because there are 16 symbols in the hexadecimal radix, there is a direct relationship between hexadecimals and binary, or radix-2, values. Because of this relationship, most programmers use hexadecimals to express binary values. For example, this assigns to an Integer variable the binary value, 01001101:

```
Number := $4D;    { Binary 0100 1101 }
```

Rather than memorize complicated conversion formulas to change between binary and hexadecimal values, refer to Table 12-3's list of binary equivalents for the 16 hexadecimal digits 0 through F. Because of the direct relationship between four-digit binary and single-digit hexadecimals, simple substitution converts hexadecimal values to binary. For instance, from Table 12-3, these expressions are equivalent:

```
$1234  = 0001  0010  0011  0100
$ABCD  = 1010  1011  1100  1101
$8001  = 1000  0000  0000  0001
```

Each hexadecimal digit in the values on the left corresponds with a four-digit binary value on the right, taken from Table 12-3. From these examples, you can see why hexadecimal numbers are convenient for binary computer programmers. It's a lot easier to write and remember $ABCD than the equivalent binary value, 1010101111001101.

Table 12-3 Hexadecimal to binary converter.

Hex	Binary	Hex	Binary
0	0000	8	1000
1	0001	9	1001
2	0010	A	1010
3	0011	B	1011
4	0100	C	1100
5	0101	D	1101
6	0110	E	1110
7	0111	F	1111

The custom in programming is to write hex values with a leading dollar sign ($) and to always write two- or four-digit groups. For example, you would normally write $0F or $000F, not $F, even though all three forms represent the same value and are thus technically correct. Similarly, the custom is to write binary values in groups of four digits. The number 111 (7 in decimal) is correct, although it's more common to write 0111.

Turbo Pascal recognizes hexadecimal and decimal notations. It does not let you express numbers in binary. You can assign hexadecimal and decimal values to any variables of the integer types in Table 12-1.

Integers and Words in Hex

When assigning hexadecimal values to variables of Turbo Pascal's two 16-bit integer types, Integer and Word, the results may be different than you expect. As you probably know, the uppermost bit in positive Integer values is 0. An example makes this clear (with hexadecimal equivalents in parentheses):

```
32,767 = 0111 1111 1111 1111   ($7FFF)
```

The maximum positive Integer value 32,767 in binary has all 1 bits except for bit number 15. (Bits are numbered from right to left. The first bit is numbered 0.)

In negative 16-bit Integers, the leftmost bit (number 15) is 1. For example, −1 in binary is:

```
-1 = 1111 1111 1111 1111   ($FFFF)
```

And, the lowest possible Integer value is:

```
-32,768 = 1000 0000 0000 0000   ($8000)
```

Considering that Word and Integer variables are both 16-bits long, the binary values are ambiguous. Hexadecimal $8000 equals the *signed* integer value –32,768. But the same hex value also equals the *unsigned* Word value 32,768, implying (falsely) that –32,768 = +32,768! Because of this discrepancy, assignments such as the following do not compile:

```
I := $FFFF;     { ??? }
I := $8000,     { ??? }
```

Internally, Turbo Pascal stores those and other 16-bit hexadecimal values as 32-bit LongInt values. The statements fail to compile because they are really trying to do this:

```
I := $0000FFFF;   { 65,535 ??? }
I := $00008000;   { 32,768 ??? }
```

When viewed as full 32-bit values, it's easy to see why the assignments are incorrect. In both cases, the decimal equivalents (shown here as comments) are outside of the range allowed for signed Integers.

To assign negative values to Integer variables, preface the literal values with an additional four F hex digits, specifying full 32-bit signed values. For example, to fix the above statements, you can write:

```
I := $FFFFFFFF;   { I = -1 }
I := $FFFF8000;   { I = -32,768 }
```

Remember that in negative values, the leftmost bit is 1. Because the 16-bit values –1 and –32,768 are stored internally as 32-bit values, bits 16 through 31 (the uppermost four hex digits) must *all* be 1 for Turbo Pascal to consider the values to be negative and in the proper range.

A similar problem occurs with Word values. These assignments do not compile:

```
W := $FFFFFFFF;   { ??? }
W := $FFFF8000;   { ??? }
```

The two hex values are negative 32-bit long integers—and you can't assign negative values to unsigned Words. The correct assignments are:

```
W := $8000;     { 32,768 }
W := $7FFF;     { 65,535 }
```

Or, you can use the full 32-bit values:

```
W := $0000FFFF;     { W = 65,535 }
W := $00008000;     { W = 32,768; }
```

Hex and Decimal Conversions

Unfortunately, converting between hexadecimal and decimal is not as simple as converting between hexadecimal and binary—except for a Pascal program, that is.

There are many published methods for converting values from one radix to another. Rather than repeat these methods here, Program 12-5 solves the problem by taking advantage of the way Pascal stores integers in memory. It's not always a good idea to rely on such system dependencies, but neither should clever solutions be discounted just because they don't go strictly by the book. At the same time, the program demonstrates several new Turbo Pascal features.

Program 12-5: RADIX.PAS

```
 1:   program Radix;
 2:   const
 3:     Blank = ' ';      { Single blank character }
 4:   var
 5:     Number: Integer;
 6:
 7:   { Assumes 0 <= n <= 15 }
 8:   function Digit(N: Byte): Char;
 9:   begin
10:     if N < 10
11:       then Digit := Chr(Ord('0') + N)
12:       else Digit := Chr(Ord('A') + (N - 10))
13:   end;
14:
15:   procedure ConvertHex(Number: Integer);
16:   begin
17:
18:     Write('Base 16 =  ');
19:
20:     Write(Digit(Hi(Number) div 16),
21:           Digit(Hi(Number) mod 16));
22:
23:     Writeln(Digit(Lo(Number) div 16),
24:             Digit(Lo(Number) mod 16))
```

continued

401

Program 12-5: continued

```
25:
26:   end;
27:
28:   procedure ConvertBin(Number: Integer);
29:   var
30:     I: Integer;
31:   begin
32:     Write('Base 02 = ');
33:     for I := 0 to 15 do
34:     begin
35:       if I mod 4 = 0 then Write(Blank);
36:       Write(Digit(Ord(Number < 0)));
37:       Number := Number shl 1
38:     end;
39:     Writeln
40:   end;
41:
42:   begin
43:     Writeln('Radix Conversion');
44:     repeat
45:       Writeln;
46:       Write('Value (0 to quit)?  ');
47:       Readln(Number);
48:       ConvertHex(Number);
49:       ConvertBin(Number);
50:       Writeln('Base 10 =  ', Number)
51:     until Number = 0
52:   end.
```

Integers are stored in two eight-bit bytes, with the low-order byte preceding the high. In other words, the two bytes are reversed from the order you might expect. To convert a decimal value to hexadecimal, Program 12-5 separates an integer's two bytes and writes the appropriate hexadecimal digit for each four-bit part or *nybble*. The first nybble equals the byte divided by 16; the second nybble equals the byte modulo 16 (the remainder left after dividing by 16). Procedure ConvertHex uses this idea at lines 20-24, calling function Digit for each of the four nybbles in an integer.

To extract eight-bit bytes from Integer values, function Hi (lines 20-21) returns the upper eight bits while Lo (lines 23-24) returns the lower eight bits of parameter Number. Both Hi and Lo return values from 0 to 255 and ignore the sign of the original number.

Digit (lines 7-13) returns the appropriate character 0 through F for any value N from zero to 15. Values 0 through 9 return the *characters* 0 to 9 while values ten through 15 return characters A to F.

To convert to binary (see lines 28-40), the built-in operator **shl** (line 37) shifts the bits in Number 1 bit to the left each time through the **for** loop starting at line 33. Notice that **shl** is an *operator,* like plus (+) or minus (–). The number to the right indicates the number of shifts, which in this example is 1. Not shown here is the alternate operator **shr**, which shifts bits to the right.

The **shl** in line 37 successively shifts each bit in Number to the leftmost position. The program passes the ordinal value of the Boolean expression (Number < 0) to function Digit (line 36). Negative integers have their leftmost bit set equal to 1; therefore, if the value is less than zero, line 36 displays 1, otherwise, it displays 0.

As shown in line 50, converting to decimal couldn't be simpler in Turbo Pascal. To convert hexadecimal numbers you type into Readln statements, just precede your entry with a dollar sign. For example, try entering 255, $FF, –1, and $FFFF.

Logical Operations on Integers

In addition to the usual integer math operators, *, **div**, +, and –, Turbo Pascal understands six logical operators listed in Table 12-4. The table also shows an example expression and result in both hexadecimal and decimal.

Table 12-4 Logical operators.

Operator	Description	Example	Results Hex	Decimal
shl	Shift left	$555 **shl** 1	$00AA	170
shr	Shift right	$55 **shr** 2	$0015	21
not	Negate	**not** $55	$FFAA	–86
or	Logical **or**	$55 **or** $80	$00D5	213
and	Logical **and**	$55 **and** $0F	$0005	5
xor	Logical **xor**	$55 **xor** $55	$0000	0

The **shl** and **shr** operators shift integer values to the left or right. If N is an integer, then (N **shr** 4) shifts the bits in N four bits to the right. **shl** shifts in the opposite direction. Notice that the value to be shifted comes *before* the operator.

not negates an integer value, turning all 0 bits to 1 and all 1 bits to 0. Logical operators **or**, **and**, and **xor** (exclusive or) combine two integer values bit for bit (see Table 12-5). Compare Table 12-5 with Table 2-2, which shows the true and false results of applying these same operators with Boolean operands. Don't confuse these operations. Integer expressions evaluate to integer results. Boolean expressions evaluate to Boolean true and false results.

The IBM PC Keyboard Flag

Table 12-5 Integer or, and, and xor truth tables.

A	*or*	B	=	C
0		0		0
1		0		1
0		1		1
1		1		1

A	*and*	B	=	C
O		0		0
1		0		0
0		1		0
1		1		1

A	*xor*	B	=	C
0		0		0
1		0		1
0		1		1
1		1		0

The PC keyboard BIOS routines change certain bits in memory when you press special keys like CapsLock or Alt. Program 12-6 tests some of these bits by declaring an absolute byte variable at the location of the keyboard flag byte (line 16). To end the program, press Ctrl-Break. The constants at lines 4-12 relate keys to individual bits in a byte. The program uses these constants along with a logical integer operator to determine whether bits are on (1) or off (0).

To test for the presence of a bit, use a logical **and**, as shown in lines 33-36 and 39-42. **and**ing the keyboard flag byte with the appropriate constant isolates one bit, tested by procedure Display.

Program 12-6: KEYSTAT.PAS

```
 1:  program KeyStat;
 2:  uses Crt;
 3:
 4:  const
 5:     InsState    = $80;
 6:     CapsState   = $40;
 7:     NumState    = $20;
 8:     ScrollState = $10;
 9:     AltShift    = $08;
10:     CtlShift    = $04;
11:     LeftShift   = $02;
12:     RightShift  = $01;
13:  type
14:     String40 = string[40];
15:  var
16:     KbFlag : Byte Absolute $0040:$0017;
17:     OldFlag: Byte;
18:
19:  procedure Display(Message: String40; Value: Byte);
20:  begin
21:     Write(Message);
22:     if Value = 0
23:       then Writeln('Off')
24:       else Writeln('On ')   { On + 1 blank }
25:  end;
26:
27:  begin
28:     ClrScr;
29:     Writeln('Keyboard Status Byte--(Type Ctrl-Break to quit)');
30:     repeat
31:       Gotoxy(1, 4);
32:       Writeln('State Bits (Press and release)');
33:       Display('  Insert ........ ', KbFlag and InsState);
34:       Display('  Caps Lock ..... ', KbFlag and CapsState);
35:       Display('  Num Lock ...... ', KbFlag and NumState);
36:       Display('  Scroll Lock ... ', KbFlag and ScrollState);
```

continued

Program 12-6: continued

```
37:       Writeln;
38:       Writeln('Shift Bits (Press, hold, and release)');
39:       Display('  Alt .......... ', KbFlag and AltShift);
40:       Display('  Ctrl ......... ', KbFlag and CtlShift);
41:       Display('  Left Shift .... ', KbFlag and LeftShift);
42:       Display('  Right Shift.... ', KbFlag and RightShift);
43:       Gotoxy(1, 23);
44:       Write('Press above keys to change states...');
45:       OldFlag := KbFlag;
46:       repeat { Wait } until OldFlag <> KbFlag
47:     until False
48:   end.
```

Numeric Functions

Turbo Pascal has several general-purpose numeric functions for operating on real and integer numbers. Function Abs (*abs*olute value) returns the positive equivalent of negative or positive integers or real numbers. The result of Abs is the same type as its argument. In other words, the absolute value of an integer is an integer. The absolute value of a real number is real.

Function Int returns the integer portion of a real number in a form similar to the result of Trunc. But the type of Int is real, not integer. This seems contradictory until you examine the alternate function, Frac, which returns the fractional part of a real number. The two functions complement each other. Int returns all digits to the left of the decimal place while Frac returns the digits to the right of the decimal. For real-number R, this expression is true:

```
R = Int(R) + Frac(R)
```

Figure 12-2 lists a few examples of applying Abs, Int, and Frac to different values.

```
        Abs(-3.14159) = 3.14159    Int(123.456) = 123.000
        Abs(10) = 10               Int(-3.14159) = -3.00000

            Frac(123.456) = 4.5599999989E-01
              Frac(-3.14159) = -0.14159;

        Frac(-3.14159) + (Abs(Int(-3.14159))) = 2.85841
```

Figure 12-2 Examples of functions Abs, Int, and Frac.

Transcendentals

In mathematics, transcendentals are quantities for which no finite algebraic formulas exist. These include exponential, logarithmic, and trigonometric functions. Turbo Pascal has all the usual transcendentals found in most programming languages plus Sqr and Sqrt as listed in Table 12-6. You can find additional details on these functions in Chapter 18.

Table 12-6 Real-number functions.

Function	Description
Abs(n)	Absolute value of n
ArcTan(n)	Arctangent of n
Cos(n)	Cosine of n
Exp(n)	Exponential equal to e^n (e = 2.7182818285)
Frac(n)	Fractional portion of n
Int(n)	Whole number portion of n
Ln(n)	Natural logarithm of n
Sin(n)	Sine of n
Sqr(n)	Product of n * n
Sqrt(n)	Square root of n

Derived functions are easy to program from Turbo Pascal's built-ins. For example, Figure 12-3 lists functions for Tangent, Secant, CoSecant, and CoTangent, which are not provided in Turbo Pascal. These functions, along with the built-in ArcTan, Cos, and Sin, operate and return angles expressed in *radians*.

One radian is defined as any arc equal in length to the radius of a circle containing the arc. Joining the two end points of such an arc to the center of the circle creates an inner angle equal to about 57.296°. You don't have to memorize this formula, but you do have to be careful to express angles in the correct form. If your program uses integer angles from 0 to 360, you must convert values to radians.

Program 12-7 shows how to do the conversions. Function Radians (lines 6-9) converts angles to equivalent radians. Function Degrees (11-14) does the reverse, converting radians to angles. As a test, the program prints a table listing several angles converted both ways.

```
function Tangent(N: Real): Real;
begin
  Tangent := Sin(N) / Cos(N)
end;

function Secant(N: Real): Real;
begin
  Secant := 1 / Cos(N)
end;

function CoSecant(N: Real): Real;
begin
  CoSecant := 1 / Sin(N)
end;

function CoTangent(N: Real): Real;
begin
  CoTangent := 1 / Tangent(N)
end;
```

Figure 12-3 Other trigonometric functions are easily derived from those provided in Turbo Pascal.

Program 12-7: RADS2DEG.PAS

```
 1:   program RadsToDegrees;
 2:   var
 3:     Angle: Integer;
 4:     Ang, Rad: Real;
 5:
 6:   function Radians(Angle: Real): Real;
 7:   begin
 8:     Radians := Abs(Angle) * Pi / 180.0
 9:   end;
10:
11:   function Degrees(Radians: Real): Real;
12:   begin
13:     Degrees := (180.0 * Radians) / Pi
14:   end;
15:
16:   begin
```

```
17:  Angle := 0;
18:    Writeln('Angle    Radians    Degrees');
19:    Writeln('------------------------');
20:    while Angle <= 360 do
21:    begin
22:      Rad := Radians(Angle);
23:      Ang := Degrees(Rad);
24:      Writeln(Angle:5, Rad:10:3, Ang:10:3);
25:      Angle := Angle + 20
26:    end;
27:    Readln
28:  end.
```

Using the functions from Program 12-7, the following statements are true:

```
Radians(57.296) =   1.000;
Degrees(1.000) =   57.296;
Radians(180.0) =   Pi;
```

Notice that the number of radians in 180° equals Pi.

Advanced Constant Expressions

Chapter 2 explains the concept of constant expressions, first introduced in Turbo Pascal 5.0. Compiling such expressions is sometimes called *constant folding* because the expressions are reduced (folded) to a single value. Constant expressions never generate code that runs; they simply give you a way to assign fixed values based on the values of other constants. For example, you can write **const** declarations such as:

```
min = 5;
max = 29;
size = 1 + (max - min);
```

Now that you know more about numbers in Turbo Pascal, you'll be glad to learn that you can use *any* expression to the right of the equal sign. You can employ built-in operators such as **shl** and **xor**, and you can even call built-in functions Abs and Trunc. This lets you create fancy expressions that appear similar to statements:

```
size2 = Abs(size);
size3 = size shl 4;
```

The only restriction is that all values must be literal or must refer to the identifiers of other constants. Typed constants and variables are not allowed. Also, you may "call" only built-in pseudo-functions such as Abs in the previous example.

Real function calls—for example, to the built-in Pi—are not permitted. (Pi was a constant at one time in Turbo Pascal's past, but now, because extended math-coprocessor data types are available, Pi was changed to a function that automatically adjusts to an expression's numeric precision.)

Remember always that such constants do not execute at runtime. In all cases, the compiler reduces constant expressions to fixed values.

Round-Off Error

Real numbers expressed as fixed-size binary values can suffer from round-off error. Figure 12-2 illustrates this problem in the result of Frac (123.456). Although the correct answer should be 0.456, the fractional part of the value 123.456, the answer given is 4.5599999989E-01. Close, but no cigar.

The problem occurs because of lost bits during certain operations on real numbers expressed in binary, leading to insignificant but annoying errors in the result.

Scientists have long been aware of round-off error. They effectively deal with the problem by agreeing on a system of significant digits where the result of any operation cannot have more digits than the smallest number of significant digits among all operands. In other words, (1/7) may read 0.1428571 on your calculator, but it is accurate to state only that the answer lies somewhere between 0.1 and 0.2. If, however, you divide 1.0000000 by 7.0000000, then you can safely trust the answer to eight significant digits.

In accounting programs, where lost pennies are unacceptable, programs often deal with the problem of round-off errors by formatting output in Writeln statements:

```
Writeln(Frac(123.456):3:3);
```

By specifying three digits and three decimal places, the foregoing statement now gives the correct result. However, this approach works only with relatively small numbers. Because real numbers may have up to 11 or 12 significant digits in Turbo Pascal (more with a math coprocessor), results approaching or exceeding the maximum limits can suffer from round-off errors.

One solution is to install a numeric coprocessor and use the Double or Extended types instead of Real. Because more bits are used to represent numbers of these types, the values are more accurate—at least for values well within the ranges listed in Table 12-2. Also, the coprocessor does all calculations internally using the ten-byte Extended format, which improves the accuracy of all real-number calculations, not just those involving Extended variables.

If you do plan to use a numeric coprocessor, you should probably not use Turbo Pascal's six-byte Real data type. On systems with coprocessors, expressions involving Real variables cause calls to be made to time-wasting subroutines that convert Real numbers to Extended and back again. Compiled programs do not perform similar conversions for expressions that use the extended types listed in Table 12-2. Therefore, using Single, Double, and Extended types usually makes programs run faster. (We'll get to the Comp type in a moment.)

Raising to a Power

Many languages, but not Turbo Pascal, have an "exponential" operator for raising a number to a power. While it's easy to write equivalent formulas for integer powers, raising a real number to a real power is not so simply done. For example, 2 to the fourth power (often written $2 \char`^\char`^ 4$) is simply $2 * 2 * 2 * 2$, or 16. But how do you calculate $3.14159 \char`^\char`^ 2.321$?

One solution is to write a function named Power that calculates the result of raising a base by an exponent. For positive bases, the standard method is to use Turbo Pascal's exponential and logarithm functions in an expression such as

```
R := Exp(E * Ln(B));
```

where R is any real number variable, E is the exponent, and B is the positive base.

Unfortunately, this method has drawbacks. If B is less or equal to 0, executing that expression halts the program and displays

```
Runtime error 207: Invalid floating point operation.
```

The error occurs because arguments to Ln must be greater than 0. To handle the special cases of negative and zero bases raised to any power (except for two exceptions), use the Power function in Program 12-8. The function can handle any combination of base and exponent values, generating runtime error 207 for only two illegal conditions: raising 0 to a negative power, and raising a negative base to a fractional power, both of which are not permitted in mathematics.

Program 12-8: TPOWER.PAS

```
1:  {$N+,E+}
2:  program TPower;
3:  var B, E: Double;
4:
5:  function Pow(B, E: Double): Double;
6:  begin
7:    Pow := Exp(E * Ln(B))
8:  end;
```

continued

Program 12-8: continued

```
 9:
10:  function Power(B, E: Double): Double;
11:  begin
12:    if B > 0 then
13:      Power := Pow(B, E) else
14:    if B < 0 then
15:    begin
16:      if Frac(E) = 0 then
17:        if Odd(Trunc(E)) then
18:          Power := -Pow(-B, E)
19:        else
20:          Power := Pow(-B, E)
21:      else
22:        RunError(207)
23:    end else
24:    begin
25:      if E = 0 then
26:        Power := 1
27:      else if E < 1 then
28:        RunError(207)
29:      else
30:        Power := 0
31:    end
32:  end;
33:
34:  begin
35:    repeat
36:      Write('Base? '); Readln(B);
37:      Write('Exponent? '); Readln(E);
38:      Writeln(B:0:3, '^^', E:0:3, ' = ', Power(B, E))
39:    until (B = 0) and (E = 0)
40:  end.
```

Run Program 12-8 and enter 0 for the Base value. Only if you then enter a negative exponent does the program halt with an error. For negative bases, the program halts only for fractional exponents. All other values (within reasonable limits) are handled correctly. Enter 0 for both the Base and Exponent to end the program.

TPower begins with the conditional directives {$N+,E+}, which select a math coprocessor if one is present, or use Turbo Pascal's coprocessor emulation if not. In any program that declares real numbers not of type Real, you must specify {$N+} to require a math coprocessor or {$N+,E+} to select the coprocessor or emulator.

To generate a runtime error, Program 12-8 calls Turbo Pascal's RunError procedure. Passing an integer value to RunError immediately halts the program, displaying that same value as the runtime error code along with an appropriate message.

Numbers in Business

A certain amount of error is acceptable, indeed expected, in scientific calculations. But it's a different story in business. I'll never forget the customer who, when I was a part-time clerk in a computer store, vehemently insisted that his computer language (an early BASIC) had a bug. An accounting program he had written refused to account accurately for every penny. Despite my best efforts, I was unable to convince him that real numbers represented by fixed numbers of binary digits cannot be perfectly accurate for all fractional values.

In truth, a degree of inaccuracy in real-number variables is not a bug. As any mathematician will tell you, there is a difference between measuring and counting. No measurement is perfectly accurate. For example, if you measure your backyard, the result is no more accurate than the smallest spacings on your tape measure. If the tape is marked in inches and you say your yard is 175 feet, 12 1/2 inches long, you may be making a good guess, but it is still a guess. On the other hand, if you have six trees in your backyard, then you have *exactly* six trees—no more and no less.

In programming, integer values count things exactly. Real-number values represent measurements and, therefore, are accurate only to a certain number of significant digits—equivalent to the precision of a measuring tape. My poor customer's problem was that he was trying to use real-number measurements to count his pennies. You'd have no more luck balancing your checkbook with a slide rule. (Remember those?)

Dollars and Cents

In science, a mistake of a few inches in measuring the distance from the earth to the moon won't bother anyone. But in business, the loss of just one penny is enough to keep an army of grey suits sweating long past martini time. (Okay, maybe it would take two pennies.)

The problem for programmers is to choose an appropriate data type to represent dollars and cents. A common mistake is to use a Real number, assuming this is necessary to represent fractions of dollars such as $123.45. This invites all the round-off problems mentioned earlier and is generally unacceptable.

A better idea is to use an integer type and pretend there is a decimal point before the last two digits. The integer value 6578, then, equals $65.78; 256 equals $2.56 and so on. Because integers count things exactly, the program can't lose pennies due to round-off errors. The integer values represent cents, the smallest monetary division.

The Integer data type, though, is too limited for most dollar and cents values. You'll find a pretty small market for your accounting package if it can handle values no greater than $327.67!

The LongInt type is a much better choice, able to represent up to $21,474,836.47—big enough for my checkbook certainly but still miniscule in our world of trillion-dollar deficits and 300-billion-dollar defense budgets.

The Comp Data Type

For truly large counting jobs, use the Comp data type (see Table 12-2). Comp requires a math coprocessor (compile with {$N+}) or coprocessor emulation (compile with {$N+,E+}).

Comp is shorthand for *computational real,* a sort of cross-breed real and integer that's good for counting large quantities—but only up to a point. In memory, Comp variables are stored as 8-byte integers, twice the size of LongInt values. But, in expressions, Comp values are treated as reals, so they can suffer from round-off errors when individual values are very large.

Comp 64-bit variables can represent values from exactly -2^{63} to $2^{63}-1$, approximately equal to the range -9E18 to 9E18 with 18 significant digits. Assuming two decimal places, the largest Comp dollar and cents value you can represent is about 92 million, billion dollars, or exactly:

```
$92,233,720,368,547,758.09
```

Don't put too much faith in this extreme limit of the Comp data type, though. For practical use, limit your values to 18 significant digits. Internal calculations with values having 19 digits do not produce accurate results. In other words, anything under 10 million, billion dollars is okay.

When displaying Comp values, treat them as you do other real data types. Use the :0:0 formatting command in Write and Writeln statements to prevent values from displaying in scientific notation. These two Writeln statements explain the difference, showing in braces what appears on screen:

```
C:= MaxInt * MaxInt;
Writeln(C);          { 1.07367628900000E+0009 }
Writeln(C:0:0);      { 1073676289 }
```

You can also specify the number of columns. Writeln(C:9:0) right justifies Comp numbers in nine columns, with no decimal places. Using the formatting command :9:2 displays 1073676289.00. Because Comp variables, like all integer types, cannot represent fractions less than 1, the ability to display Comp values with decimal places is not that useful. You might do this, however, if your values represent whole dollar amounts but you want to display $9.00 instead of just $9.

Comp to String

As explained earlier in this chapter, Str and Val convert between values and strings, easing the job of getting numbers in and out of programs. You can use these procedures with all data types in Tables 12-1 and 12-2, including Comp.

Program 12-9 demonstrates one way to use Str and Val to help represent and display dollar and cents values in Comp variables. The program lets you type in dollar amounts, keeping a running total. Procedure StrToComp (lines 7-21) converts strings to Comp values. Procedure CompToStr (lines 23-29) converts Comp values into strings.

When running this program, type numbers as you would on a mechanical calculator. You do not have to type a decimal point. Typing 7654 is the same as typing 76.54. If you do type a decimal point, you must type two digits. Typing 15.5 equals 1.55, not 15.50 as you might expect. This happens because the procedures in Program 12-9 simply ignore the decimal point—a cheap but useful trick.

StrToComp removes any decimal points in the strings you enter at line 36. Line 18 calls Val to convert the string to a Comp value, returning 0 if you make any typing errors. CompToStr calls Str at line 25, converting raw values into strings. The **while** loop (lines 26-27) adds leading zeros so that 3, for example, comes out as 0.03. Line 28 inserts the decimal point.

Program 12-9: GOODCENT.PAS

```
 1:  {$N+,E+}
 2:  program GoodCents;
 3:  var
 4:    Total, Amount: Comp;
 5:    S: string;
 6:
 7:  procedure StrToComp(S: string; var C: Comp);
 8:  var
 9:    E: Integer;   { Val error code }
10:    P: Integer;   { Position of decimal point (if any) }
11:  begin
12:  P := Pos('.', S);
```

continued

Program 12-9: continued

```
13:    while P > 0 do
14:      begin
15:        Delete(S, P, 1);    { Remove any decimal point }
16:        P := Pos('.', S)
17:      end;
18:      Val(S, C, E);
19:      if E <> 0
20:        then C := 0    { Any errors return C = 0 }
21:    end;
22:
23:    procedure CompToStr(C: Comp; var S: string);
24:    begin
25:      Str(C:0:0, S);
26:      while Length(S) < 3 do    { Add leading zeros if needed }
27:        Insert('0', S, 1);
28:      Insert('.', S, Length(S) - 1)  { Insert decimal point }
29:    end;
30:
31:    begin
32:      Total := 0;
33:      Writeln('Count your pennies.  Press Enter to end.');
34:      repeat
35:        Write('$');
36:        Readln(S);
37:        if Length(S) > 0 then
38:        begin
39:          StrToComp(S, Amount);
40:          Total := Total + Amount;
41:          CompToStr(Total, S);
42:          Writeln('$' + S: 20)
43:        end
44:      until Length(S) = 0
45:    end.
```

Numbers at Random

The expression "random number" is popular but imprecise. There is no such thing as a random number; there are only numbers taken from random sequences. The value 1024 is random only if it is statistically unpredictable from previous values in the sequence to which 1024 belongs. Obviously, 1024 is not random if taken from the sequence:

1, 2, ..., 1023, 1024, 1025, ..., n

There are two methods for producing numbers at random in Turbo Pascal. Used with no parameters, function Random returns a real number in the range:

0.0 <= Random < 1.0

With an integer parameter, Random returns a positive integer in the range:

0 <= Random(M) <= M

In other words, Random(M) produces a random integer modulo M, equal to the remainder following a division by M, which must be an Integer value.

One property of a random sequence is a statistically even distribution. In other words, any value from a random sequence should be as likely to occur as any other. But how can you test that assumption? It is not adequate to simply count the occurrences of various randomly selected values. With that as the only test of randomness, the following sequence proves perfectly random:

1,1,1,2,2,2,3,3,3,4,4,4,5,5,5

Each value in this sequence occurs as often as any other, but the sequence is obviously not random! A better test simulates the action of a *known* series of random events and then uses statistical methods to verify the randomness of the Random function.

Rolling the Dice

Program 12-10 simulates dice rolls as a "benchmark" test of Turbo Pascal's random number generator. (A benchmark is a program that tests the performance of a computer or language.)

Line 67 calls Randomize to begin a new random sequence. Randomize seeds the random number generator, ensuring that new program runs use different random sequences. A seed is a starting value, or a value that produces a new starting value, also taken at random.

Assuming a pair of six-sided dice is on the up and up, it's easy to calculate the probability of all possible dice-roll combinations. For example, there are three ways to make 4: 3+1, 2+2, and 1+3. Because there are 36 (6*6) different pairings of two six-sided die, the probability of rolling 4 is 3/36, or 1/12.

Program 12-10 similarly calculates probabilities for dice-roll values 2 to 12, assigning the results to real-number array P (lines 61-66). Another array, Count, remembers the number of times the program rolls each value. The program compares these counts to the known probabilities. The random number generator is working if the results are more or less equal to expectations.

Line 19 simulates a dice roll. The statement Succ(Random(6)) produces a number at random in the range 1 to 6, simulating the roll of one die. The program adds the results of two such values to simulate the roll of a pair of dice. It would not be correct to simulate dice rolls with the expression 2 + Random(11) although this also produces values from 2 to 12. Because a single value at random equalizes the probability of all rolls, this would destroy the test, to say nothing of the house percentage.

Program 12-10: DICE.PAS

```
 1:   program Dice;
 2:   const
 3:     Min = 2;              { Lowest category }
 4:     Max = 12;             { Highest category }
 5:   type
 6:     RealArray = array[Min .. Max] of Real;
 7:   var
 8:     N    : LongInt;       { Number of throws }
 9:     Count: RealArray;     { Result counts }
10:     P    : RealArray;     { Probabilities }
11:
12:   procedure ThrowDice(N: LongInt);
13:   var
14:     K: Min .. Max;        { Holds value of one throw }
15:     I: LongInt;
16:   begin
17:     for I := 1 to N do
18:     begin
19:       K := Succ(Random(6)) + Succ(Random(6));
20:       Count[K] := Count[K] + 1.0
21:     end
22:   end;
23:
24:   function ChiSquare(N: Real): Real;
25:   var
26:     V: Real;
27:     I: Integer;
28:   begin
29:     V := 0;
30:     for I := Min to Max do
31:       V := V + ((Sqr(Count[I])) / P[I]);
32:     ChiSquare := ((1.0 / N) * V) - N
33:   end;
```

```
34:
35:  procedure PrintResults(N: Real);
36:  var
37:    I: Integer;
38:  begin
39:    Writeln;
40:    Writeln('Dice      Proba-     Expected    Actual  ');
41:    Writeln('Value     bility     Count       Count   ');
42:    Writeln('=====================================');
43:    for I := Min to Max do
44:      Writeln(I: 5,              ' ':4,         { Dice value }
45:              P[I]: 1: 3,        ' ':5,         { Probability }
46:              P[I] * N: 8: 0, ' ':4,           { Expected count }
47:              Count[I]: 8: 0         );         { Actual count }
48:    Writeln;
49:    Writeln('Chi Square result = ', ChiSquare(N):0:3)
50:  end;
51:
52:  procedure Initialize(var N: LongInt);
53:  var
54:    I: Integer;
55:  begin
56:    Writeln('Dice - A random number benchmark');
57:    Writeln;
58:    Write('How many throws? ');
59:    Readln(N);
60:    for I := Min to Max do Count[I] := 0.0;
61:    P[ 2] := 1.0/36;  P[ 3] := 1.0/18;
62:    P[ 4] := 1.0/12;  P[ 5] := 1.0/9;
63:    P[ 6] := 5.0/36;  P[ 7] := 1.0/6;
64:    P[ 8] := 5.0/36;  P[ 9] := 1.0/9;
65:    P[10] := 1.0/12;  P[11] := 1.0/18;
66:    P[12] := 1.0/36;
67:    Randomize
68:  end;
69:
70:  begin
71:    Initialize(N);
72:    if N > 0.0 then
73:    begin
74:      ThrowDice(N);
75:      PrintResults(N)
76:    end;
77:    Readln
78:  end.
```

The program prints a chart of the results of however many rolls you request. The more rolls the better, with 10,000 or more a minimum for accurate results. The chart shows the probability, expected count, and actual count received for each possible value, 2 to 12. Figure 12-4 lists an example chart for 50,000 rolls.

```
Dice - A random number benchmark

How many throws?  50000

Dice    Proba-  Expected  Actual
Value   bility  Count     Count
=====================================
  2     0.028    1389     1387
  3     0.056    2778     2848
  4     0.083    4167     4087
  5     0.111    5556     5467
  6     0.139    6944     6896
  7     0.167    8333     8379
  8     0.139    6944     7070
  9     0.111    5556     5539
 10     0.083    4167     4136
 11     0.056    2778     2800
 12     0.028    1389     1391

Chi Square result = 8.027
```

Figure 12-4 Example output of Program 12-10.

When you examine the chart in Figure 12-4 or from running Program 12-10, the distribution *(Actual Count)* should closely match the anticipated results *(Expected Count)*. This however, does not complete the test. To verify randomness, the program also compares the counts received against the expected probabilities using a statistical method called the Chi Square, written X^2. Function ChiSquare evaluates the formula:

$$V = \frac{1}{n} \sum_{1 \le i \le K} \left(\frac{o_i^2}{p_i} \right) - n$$

In the formula, o is the observed result, and p is the probability over the range 1 to n. Compare the result of the formula to a Chi Square distribution table, found in most elementary statistics books. (Table 12-7 shows a portion of a typical Chi Square table.) Table rows represent *degrees of freedom*, equal to one less than the number of categories in the original data. In the case of dice, there are 11 categories for the values 2 to 12. One less than that is 10, the row in which to look.

From Table 12-7, you expect the Chi Square result of Program 12-10 to fall in the range between 6.737 and 12.55 about 50% of the time. (See bottom of Figure 12-4.) A value greater than or equal to 23.21 should occur no more often than 1% of the time. To interpret the Chi Square result accurately, then, run Program 12-10 several times, at least three. A single bad result has a low statistical probability but does not necessarily indicate a faulty random number generator.

Table 12-7 Chi square distribution (sample).

v	99%	95%	75%	50%	25%	05%	01%
9	2.088	3.325	5.899	8.343	11.39	16.92	21.67
10	2.558	3.940	6.737	9.342	12.55	18.31	23.21
11	3.053	4.575	7.584	10.34	13.70	19.68	24.73

Restarting Random Sequences

When you call Randomize to begin a new random sequence, Turbo Pascal scrambles a LongInt variable, RandSeed, in the System unit. This causes new random sequences to begin at random, generating different values for each program run.

To repeat the same random sequence, assign a starting value to RandSeed. For example, you might use these statements to display ten values at random:

```
RandSeed := 100;
for I := 1 to 10 do
  Writeln(Random(MaxInt));
```

Because of the assignment to RandSeed, the **for** loop displays the same ten-number random sequence every time the program runs. Each different value you assign to RandSeed starts a different random sequence.

Repeating random sequences this way can be helpful during debugging. For example, a flight simulator is, of course, supposed to behave randomly. Controlled by random sequences, the simulated winds shift, causing changes in direction and altitude, and it wouldn't do to have the winds shift in exactly the same way during every flight!

But testing such randomly acting programs can be difficult. To repeat identical conditions, perhaps as a test of a hard-to-find bug, you could assign the same value to RandSeed—shifting the winds in a sort of instant replay fashion—and then later take out the assignment when you compile the final program.

Random numbers, and tests of randomness, are subjects that could fill books. It is time to move on before they fill this one!

Summary

Turbo Pascal has many built-in functions and procedures for converting and for manipulating numbers in various ways. Two functions, Val and Str, convert numbers and strings for error-free input. Other functions convert and process numbers in a variety of ways.

Real-number values measure things. Integer values count things.

Real-number calculations suffer from round-off errors, which can be minimized by careful programming. A math coprocessor gives several real number types that can help avoid round-off error by increasing the number of significant digits values can represent.

The 6-byte Real data type is always available, but offers only a limited range of values and suffers from round-off error in all but the simplest calculations. For better results, use the Double, Extended, and Comp types. To use these types with Turbo Pascal 5.0 and later versions, programs compiled with the directives {$N+,E-} require a math coprocessor. Use the directives {$N+,E+} to select a coprocessor automatically or to use emulation routines.

For large dollar and cents values, use either the LongInt or Comp data types. Comp requires a math coprocessor.

Turbo Pascal produces random number sequences of real numbers or integers. With random sequences, simulations of real events, such as the rolling of dice, are easy to program.

Exercises

12-1. The formula to find the hypotenuse of a right triangle is:

$$\sqrt{a^2 + b^2}$$

Write the formula into a program. It should handle input errors in a friendly way.

12-2. Write a simple program to simulate a hand-held calculator. Add programmer's utilities to convert numbers to hexadecimal and binary and to do logical operations such as shifting left (**shl**) and right (**shr**).

12-3. Using random sequences, write a game to simulate a one-armed-bandit slot machine. Keep track of the player's winnings.

12-4. As mentioned in the text, one of the many tests of randomness is to record the frequency of values in a range. Over many repetitions, all frequencies should be more or less the same. Write a program to test this assumption against the output of Turbo Pascal's Random function.

12-5. A popular radix in programming is *octal*, which has eight digits 0 to 7. Write a program to convert hexadecimal, octal, and decimal values. (Hint: Each octal digit directly represents three binary digits. See the two left columns of Table 12-3.)

12-6. Write a procedure to set and reset specific bits in a Word variable. Use logical operators in your solution.

13

Advanced Techniques

- Conditional Compilation
- Typecasting
- Mem, MemW, and MemL
- Port and PortW
- Compiling Large Programs
- Untyped Parameters
- Filling Memory
- Memory Moves
- Text File Device Drivers
- Increasing Text-File Buffer Size
- Free Declaration Ordering
- Structured Variable Constants
- Special Directory Commands

- Custom Exit Procedures
- Procedure Types
- Dealing with Heap Errors
- Dealing with the Stack
- Other Memory Concerns
- Passing Command-Line Parameters
- Inside a File Variable
- Advanced Overlay Management
- Setting the Overlay Access Code
- Extra Goodies

13

Key Words and Identifiers

> Absolute, ChDir, DosExitCode, Exec, FillChar, Halt, Mem, MemL, MemW, MkDir, Move, OvrClearBuf, OvrFileMode, OvrGetRetry, OvrLoadCount, OvrReadBuf, OvrReadFunc, OvrSetRetry, OvrTrapCount, ParamCount, ParamStr, Port, PortW, **procedure**, **function**, RmDir, SetTextBuf, SwapVectors

This chapter collects various tips, tricks, and tidbits that make Turbo Pascal special. In here you'll learn about conditional compilation, typecasting, special variables, text file device drivers, and designing custom exit procedures—plus several other juicy items.

Conditional Compilation

With a special set of compiler directives, you can write programs that compile differently based on one condition or another. This technique, called *conditional compilation,* is useful for debugging and for designing software that's easy to customize.

The process is simple. First you define various symbols, similar to other Pascal identifiers. (See figure 1-2.) Then, you tell Turbo Pascal to compile either one section or another based on whether certain symbols are defined. Defining different symbols changes which sections of code are compiled.

The commands, in the form of compiler directives, form a kind of minilanguage inside Pascal. Always keep in mind, though, that conditional compilation-commands are not Pascal statements. Like other compiler directives, these commands are merely instructions that change how the compiler operates. Table 13-1 lists the compiler directives of this minilanguage within a language.

Table 13-1 Conditional compilation directives.

Directive	Description
{$DEFINE id}	Define symbol (id)
{$UNDEF id}	Undefine symbol (id)
{$IFDEF id}	Continue normally if (id) is defined
{$IFNDEF id}	Continue normally if (id) is not defined
{$IFOPT id}	Continue normally depending on switch (id)
{$ELSE}	Compile next section if preceding **if**... fails
{$ENDIF}	Mark end of **if** and optional **else** section

In Table 13-1, *id* represents a conditional symbol. You can invent your own symbols or use one of several that are predefined. For example, this defines a symbol named Debugging:

```
{$DEFINE Debugging}
```

Having defined a symbol, you can use the directives IFDEF (if defined) and IFNDEF (if not defined) to test whether certain symbols exist. To compile two Writeln statements for a test of two program variables, you could write:

```
{$IFDEF Debugging}
   Writeln('Debugging');
   Writeln('I=', I, ' J=', J);
{$ENDIF}
```

This is not the same as a Pascal **if** statement. The two Writeln statements are compiled only if you have previously defined the Debugging symbol. If you have not used the {$DEFINE Debugging} command, the two Writeln statements *are completely ignored.* A typical program might contain hundreds of such debugging statements. After testing the program, change the DEFINE to UNDEF:

```
{$UNDEF Debugging}
```

Undefining the Debugging symbol is the same as never defining it in the first place. Now, the two Writeln statements, although still in the source code text, are not compiled. You could, of course, delete the debugging statements, but, then, you'd have to retype them if a later problem develops and you want to continue debugging. With conditional compilation, you simply define the Debugging symbol and recompile.

Be sure to understand that conditional compilation symbols like Debugging are not variables or constants. Symbols have no values. They are not true or false; they simply exist or don't exist. The conditional command {$IFDEF Debugging} does not test whether Debugging is true or false, but only whether you have previously defined the Debugging symbol.

In place of IFDEF, which tests if a symbol is defined, you can use IFNDEF, which tests if a symbol is not defined. You could use this idea to display a message identifying the program as the real McCoy or the debugging version:

```
{$IFNDEF Debugging}
  Writeln('Production version 1.00');
{$ELSE}
  Writeln('Debugging version 1.00');
{$ENDIF}
```

Notice that the {$ELSE} directive identifies an alternate Writeln statement. Only one Writeln is compiled depending on whether the program previously defines Debugging. The {$ENDIF} follows the optional {$ELSE} section.

Testing Options

As you know, Turbo Pascal has various options that you can select. For example, you can turn on numeric coprocessor data types with {$N+} or turn them off with {$N–}. Likewise, {$R+} and {$R–} turn range checking on and off.

Use the {$IFOPT id} conditional compilation directive to test the state of any option and, if the option has the value you specify, to compile the text that follows until reaching the next {$ELSE} or {$ENDIF}. For example, to compile a program with a variable Distance of type Real on plain systems but of type Extended on systems with math coprocessors, you could write the **var** section like this:

```
var
{$IFOPT N+}
  Distance: Extended;
{$ELSE}
  Distance: Real;
{$ENDIF}
```

With this declaration, changing {$N+} to {$N–}, or using the IDE's *Options:Compiler* command to enable the *8087/80287* setting, is all you have to do to compile the program on systems without coprocessors. The conditional compilation commands alter the source code for you by automatically selecting the Extended or Real types for Distance.

Predefined Symbols

In addition to defining your own symbols, you can test whether certain built-in symbols exist. Table 13-2 lists Turbo Pascal's predefined conditional symbols.

Table 13-2 Predefined conditional symbols.

Symbol	Meaning if defined
VER40	Turbo Pascal version 4.0
VER41	Turbo Pascal version 4.1
VER50	Turbo Pascal version 5.0
VER55	Turbo Pascal version 5.5
VER60	Turbo Pascal version 6.0
VERn	Turbo Pascal version n
MSDOS	MS-DOS or PC-DOS compiler version
CPU86	Computer has an 80x86-family processor
CPU87	Computer has an 80x87-family math coprocessor

Use the VERn symbol to design programs to compile under different Turbo Pascal versions where n is 40 for version 4.0, 41 for version 4.1, 50 for version 5.0, 55 for version 5.5, or 60 for version 6.0. Suppose that only version 3.9 (there is no such release number) supports a data type called Quark. Other versions require you to use Real instead. To design the program to compile correctly under both versions, you could write:

```
var
{$IFDEF VER39}
  BlackHole: Quark;
{$ELSE}
  BlackHole: Real;
{ENDIF}
```

I suppose physicists will wince at my choice of terms, but you get the idea.

The MSDOS and CPU86 symbols are defined to allow developing software for multiple operating systems and processors. Turbo Pascal for Windows, for example, defines the WINDOWS symbol and CPU86, but not MSDOS. By inserting {$IFDEF WINDOWS} and {$IFDEF MSDOS} directives into your programs, you could develop one set of source-code files that will compile differently for MS-DOS and Windows-based computers.

If and when Turbo Pascal becomes available for processors outside of the 80x86 family, you should be able to compile sections of processor-specific code by inspecting the CPU86 symbol and whatever similar symbol is defined for the other processor. Currently, the only versions of Turbo Pascal that run on non-80x86 processors are Turbo Pascal for CP/M (Z80 processor) and Turbo Pascal for the Macintosh (68000 processor). Borland no longer actively markets these two versions, however, which aren't compatible with Turbo Pascal 6.0 for MS-DOS systems.

The final symbol in Table 13-2, CPU87, is defined only if the computer has an 80x87-family math coprocessor chip. When using the CPU87 symbol, be aware that a conditional directive such as {$IFDEF CPU87} is evaluated at compile time, not when the program runs. This fact means you can use CPU87 to determine whether a coprocessor is present during compilation, but you can't use the symbol to find out if a coprocessor is available when the program runs. Program 13-1 demonstrates how to use CPU87 along with IFOPT to write programs to use a coprocessor data type automatically if a math chip is available during compilation.

The conditional directives in lines 1-5 test if the compiler is Turbo Pascal version 4.0, which does not have math-coprocessor emulation. If so, and if CPU87 tests positive in line 2, the directive {$N+} enables extended real-number data types; otherwise, {$N–} disables them. Lines 3-5 handle Turbo Pascal versions 5.0 and higher; in which cases, {$N+,E+} automatically detects and uses a coprocessor if present, or enables emulation routines if not.

Lines 11-15 use the conditional directives IFOPT, ELSE, and ENDIF to define the variable constant SpeedOfLight as type Double if {$N+} is in effect, or Real if not (version 4.0 only). Don't confuse the ELSE conditional directive with Pascal's **else** key word—the two are unrelated, though they perform equivalent tasks. A similar technique in lines 23-27 defines two variables, Miles and Seconds. Depending on the version and setting of the N+/– compiler option, lines 30-38 display one of the messages:

```
Coprocessor installed
Coprocessor not installed
Coprocessor or emulator installed
```

Remember that all these decisions are made at compile time, *not* at runtime. Conditional compilation directives generate no code—they merely tell the compiler which sections to compile and which sections to skip.

Program 13-1: LIGHT.PAS

```
1:  {$IFDEF VER40}
2:    {$IFDEF CPU87} {$N+} {$ELSE} {$N-} {$ENDIF}
3:  {$ELSE}
4:    {$N+,E+}
5:  {$ENDIF}
6:
7:  program Light;
8:
9:  const
10:
11: {$IFOPT N+}
12:   SpeedOfLight: Double = 186282.3976; { Miles per second }
13: {$ELSE}
14:   SpeedOfLight: Real = 186282.3976;
15: {$ENDIF}
16:
17:   PromptChar = ']';
18:   ProgramName = 'S p e e d   O f   L i g h t';
19:   PromptString = 'Enter number of miles';
20:
21: var
22:
23: {$IFOPT N+}
24:   Miles, Seconds: Double;
25: {$ELSE}
26:   Miles, Seconds: Real;
27: {$ENDIF}
28:
29: begin
30:   Writeln(ProgramName);
31:   Write('Coprocessor ');
32: {$IFNDEF VER40}
33:   Write('or emulator ');
34: {$ENDIF}
35: {$IFOPT N-}
36:   Write('not ');
37: {$ENDIF}
38:   Writeln('installed');
39:   Writeln;
40:   Writeln(PromptString);
41:   Writeln;
```

continued

Program 13-1: continued

```
42:    Write(PromptChar);
43:    Readln(Miles);
44:    Seconds := Miles / SpeedOfLight;
45:    Writeln('Light travels ', Miles, ' miles in ');
46:    Write(Seconds, ' seconds, or ');
47:    Writeln(Seconds / 60.0, ' minutes.');
48:    Readln
49:  end.
```

Typecasting

In assignment statements, Turbo Pascal normally requires values, expressions, and variables on opposite sides of the assignment operator := to be of the same types. *Typecasting* is a technique for breaking this rule, which you should do only when absolutely necessary. Subverting Turbo Pascal's strong type-checking abilities is potentially dangerous.

There are two different kinds of typecasting: value and variable. A value typecast transforms the *value* of an expression from one type to another. A variable typecast tells the compiler to consider a *variable* to be of a different type than originally declared. The following value typecast converts the value 66 into a character B in a Writeln statement:

```
Writeln('The letter is ', Char(66));
```

The data type identifier Char encloses the value in parentheses you want the compiler to recast as a different type, here the character B. Variable typecasts look similar, but operate differently. For example, this program fragment converts an array of four bytes into a string of three characters:

```
type
  Str3 = string[3];
var
  A: array[0 .. 3] of Byte;
begin
  A[0] := 3;
  A[1] := Byte('A');
  A[2] := Byte('B');
  A[3] := Byte('C');
  Writeln(Str3(A))
end;
```

The array and Str3 data types each occupies four bytes. The assignment to A[0] tells how many characters follow. Because array A is an array of Byte and not Char, three value typecasts assign characters as ASCII values to index positions 1, 2, and 3. Finally, the Writeln statement displays this oddly constructed array recast as type Str3, overcoming the compiler's natural reluctance to allow byte arrays in Writeln statements. (Try compiling Writeln(A) to see the error message you receive.) The variable typecast in the Writeln statement bypasses the compiler's check for proper data types, requiring you to ensure that the array in this example contains the correct values.

Sometimes the difference between value and variable typecasts is unclear. Casting a simple Byte variable to type LongInt, for example, is a value typecast because Byte variables represent values. The same is true for all scalar variables and pointers. Typecasting these types of objects is always a value, not a variable, cast.

Though obscure, the difference can be important. Turbo Pascal allows value typecasts between objects of different sizes. For example, you can write:

```
var
  Short: ShortInt;
  Long: LongInt;
begin
  Short := -123;
  Long := LongInt(Short);
end;
```

This is a *value* typecast, even though the second assignment uses the variable Short. (This particular example is for demonstration only—you could more simply assign the Short variable directly to Long.) The *value* of Short is converted to a LongInt data type. Also, the sign of Short is extended to Long. In other words, after the typecast, Long has the same value as Short.

Contrast this with the variable array typecast demonstrated earlier. In that case, the array was interpreted as a different data type—no conversion was performed. This is an important and subtle difference to understand. In general:

- A value typecast converts the value of an expression or scalar variable to a different data type. In an assignment, the two types do not have to be the same size. Values are sign-extended, meaning that negative values come out negative; positive values, positive.

- A variable typecast interprets the bytes in a variable as a different data type. In an assignment, the two types must be exactly the same size.

Typecasting Versus Free Unions

Chapter 5 explains how to use a free union record to trick the compiler into treating a variable as two or more different data types. Instead of a free union, you can accomplish the same task with a variable typecast. For example, suppose you need to access the high and low 16-bit words in a 32-bit LongInt variable. You can't use the Lo and Hi functions—they return the low and high bytes of 16-bit quantities. Instead, a variable typecast extracts the individual bytes and words in a LongInt variable.

Program 13-2 demonstrates how to do this. The program typecasts a LongInt variable into two record types: Words (lines 3-5) with two word fields, and Bytes (lines 6-8) with two byte fields. The Writeln statement displays the original value (Long), the low and high words in this value, and the four bytes in these two words. (You don't have to type the comment in line 14, which just makes typing the previous two lines easier.)

Notice the qualifiers—the periods and field names after the closing parentheses in the typecast—in lines 18-23. Only variable typecasts may have such qualifiers. A value typecast cannot have qualifiers. As you can see from this example, typecasting with record types is one way to accomplish a variable typecast (transforming one type to another) when using values.

Program 13-2: LONGBYTE.PAS

```
 1:   program LongBytes;
 2:   type
 3:     Words = record
 4:       LoWord, HiWord: Word
 5:     end;
 6:     Bytes = record
 7:       LoByte, HiByte: Byte
 8:     end;
 9:   var
10:     Long: LongInt;
11:   begin
12:     Writeln('                         LoWord          HiWord'  );
13:     Writeln('  Value  LoWord  HiWord LoByte HiByte LoByte  HiByte');
14:   (*       12345678123456781234567812345678123456781234567812345678*)
15:
16:     for Long:= -10 to 10 do
17:       Writeln(Long: 8,
18:         Words(Long).LoWord: 8,
19:         Words(Long).HiWord: 8,
20:         Bytes(Words(Long).LoWord).LoByte: 8,
21:         Bytes(Words(Long).LoWord).HiByte: 8,
```

```
22:        Bytes(Words(Long).HiWord).LoByte: 8,
23:        Bytes(Words(Long).HiWord).HiByte: 8);
24:    Readln
25:  end.
```

Typecasting Pointers

Another use for typecasting is to convert pointers of one kind of data type into another. Suppose you have a pointer to type **string** but you want the compiler to treat the variable as a byte instead, perhaps to get to the length byte in the front of all **string** types. You have these declarations:

```
type
  SPtr = ^string;
  BPtr = ^Byte;
var
  Sp: SPtr;
  Bp: BPtr;
```

You then create a string variable on the heap with New and assign a string to the variable:

```
New(Sp);
Sp^ := 'String em up';
```

The New statement creates a string variable on the heap. The second statement assigns a 12-character string to the variable. Because of Turbo Pascal's strong type-checking ability, you can't write:

```
Bp := Sp;    { ??? }
Writeln('Length of string = ', Bp^);
```

Turbo Pascal does not allow you to assign one pointer to another of a different type. To get around the problem, and address the first byte of the string, use a typecast:

```
Writeln('Length of string = ', BPtr(Sp)^);
```

The typecase recasts the string pointer Sp as a BPtr type, displaying 14, the length of the string. (You no longer need variable Bp.) The importance of this technique is that it doesn't generate any code. The typecast BPtr(Sp) is not a function call, although it appears to be. It is just an instruction to the compiler to pretend for the moment that Sp addresses a variable of type BPtr.

Mem, MemW, and MemL

Three arrays, Mem, MemW, and MemL, open all computer memory to your program. These special variables are predeclared—all you have to do is use them.

To access a single byte of memory, use Mem. For two-byte memory words, use MemW. To read and write memory as four-byte long integers, use MemL. In each case, you specify a memory address as an array index with a segment and an offset value. You can read or assign values to and from memory. For example, this statement reads the current timer value into TimerCount, a Word variable:

```
TimerCount := MemW[0000:$046C];
```

If you know BASIC, you'll recognize this as equivalent to a PEEK command. To assign a value to memory, move the array to the left of the assignment symbol (in BASIC, similar to a POKE). The next example toggles the IBM PC print-screen key on and off. After executing the statement once, the Shift-PrtSc keys no longer print the screen contents. Execute the same statement again to turn the print screen feature back on:

```
Mem[$0050:0] := Mem[$0050:0] xor 1;
```

Program 13-3 uses this idea to assign the 16-bit value, located at address 0000:$0410, to variable EquipFlag (line 16). The program uses MemW because the value is a two-byte word, containing information about devices attached to the computer. The program uses logical **and**s and shifts to decipher the information and display a configuration list.

Of course, a program of this kind assumes that the value at 0000:$0410 has the needed information. Because there is no guarantee that all computers store the same information at the same place, Program 13-3 is an example of a "system-dependent" program—one that might not run on other systems. (The program should run on most PCs and compatibles, though.)

Program 13-3: DEVICES.PAS

```
1:  program Devices;
2:  var
3:    EquipFlag: Integer;
4:
5:  procedure ShowVid(N: Integer);
6:  begin
7:    case N of
8:      1: Writeln('40x25 (Color)');
9:      2: Writeln('80x25 (Color)');
```

```
10:        3: Writeln('80x25 (Monochrome)');
11:        else Writeln('<not used>')
12:      end
13:   end;
14:
15:   begin
16:     EquipFlag := MemW[0000:$0410];
17:     Writeln;
18:     Writeln('IBM PC Devices');
19:     Writeln;
20:     Writeln('Number of printers ......... ',
21:       EquipFlag shr 14);
22:     Writeln('Game I/O attached .......... ',
23:       (EquipFlag and $1000)=1);
24:     Writeln('Number of serial ports ..... ',
25:       (EquipFlag shr 9) and $07);
26:     Writeln('Number of diskette drives .. ',
27:       ((EquipFlag and 1) * (1 + (EquipFlag shr 6) and $03)));
28:     Write(  'Initial video mode ......... ');
29:       ShowVid((EquipFlag shr 4) and $03);
30:     Writeln;
31:     Readln
32:   end.
```

Port and PortW

Two other built-in arrays, Port and PortW, access the computer's input and output ports. A port is a special channel attached to the computer processor. Accessing a device through a data port is the most direct way to communicate with hardware peripherals. You can, for example, directly read and write data stored in the controlling circuits and chips for various devices such as the video display or serial communications line.

Use Port to access eight-bit data ports. Use PortW to access 16-bit ports. To read a port, place the array identifier on the right side of an assignment statement. To write to a port, place the array on the left. The following duplicates an assembly language IN instruction and assumes you have the monochrome video display and printer adapter in your IBM PC (variable PrintStatus is type Byte):

```
PrintStatus := Port[$03BD];
```

Try using the foregoing statement in a short program, then run it with your printer on and then off. Provided you have the correct hardware in your system, you should see different values from port address $3BD. Programs could decipher this information to determine the printer's status.

To write a value to a port, reverse the process. The following commands set and clear the nonmaskable interrupt:

```
Port[$A0] := $80;  { Set }
Port[$A0] := 0;    { Clear }
```

Be especially careful when experimenting with data ports. Although I chose these examples for their relative safety, some ports activate events when you read them, not only when you write to them. You can easily turn on disk drive motors, affect your video display, destroy data in disk sectors, and experience other nasty surprises if you fiddle indiscriminately with ports.

For experimenting with ports, one relatively safe device is the PC's timer, which has special data registers at ports $40, $42, and $43. An associated chip, an 8255A Programmable Peripheral Interface (PPI) at port address $61, connects the timer with the computer's speaker to make sounds.

Program 13-4 assigns initializing values to timer registers through the Port array (lines 16-18). It then turns on PPI output bit numbers 0 and 1 (line 20), sending the output of the timer to the speaker and making it beep. Because the PPI has other purposes, it's important to preserve all bits other than the ones that control the output of the timer to the speaker. The program does this by saving the original port value (line 19) and then restoring that value at line 22. This also turns off the speaker.

You can find more information about ports and the meaning of various port values in an IBM PC Technical Reference Manual.

Program 13-4: BEEPER.PAS

```
 1:  program Beeper;
 2:  uses Crt;
 3:  const
 4:    PortB        = $61;    { 8255 address }
 5:    Timer        = $40;
 6:    TimerOut     = $42;
 7:    TimerControl = $43;
 8:  var
 9:    Ch: Char;
10:    Pitch, Duration: Integer;
11:
12:  procedure Beep(Frequency, Milliseconds: Integer);
13:  var
14:    SavePortB: Byte;
```

```
15:  begin
16:     Port[TimerControl] := $B6;              { Select timer mode }
17:     Port[TimerOut    ] := Lo(Frequency);   { Set frequency divisor }
18:     Port[TimerOut    ] := Hi(Frequency);
19:     SavePortB := Port[PortB];               { Save old PortB setting }
20:     Port[PortB] := SavePortB or $03;        { Turn on speaker }
21:     Delay(Milliseconds);                    { Wait }
22:     Port[PortB] := SavePortB                { Turn off speaker }
23:  end;
24:
25:  begin
26:     Writeln('Beeper');
27:     Pitch := $255; Duration := 75;  { Default values }
28:     repeat
29:       Writeln;
30:       Write('Pitch? '   ); Readln(Pitch);
31:       Write('Duration? '); Readln(Duration);
32:       Writeln;
33:       Writeln('   Pitch    = ', Pitch);
34:       Writeln('   Duration = ', Duration);
35:       Writeln;
36:       Write(  '   Press any key to stop...');
37:       while not Keypressed do
38:       begin
39:         Beep(Pitch, Duration);
40:         Delay(100)
41:       end;
42:       Write(Readkey);
43:       Writeln; Writeln;
44:       Write('Again? ');
45:       Ch := Readkey;
46:       Writeln(Ch)
47:     until Upcase(Ch) <> 'Y'
48:  end.
```

Compiling Large Programs

Turbo Pascal can compile huge programs with thousands of symbols. But if your system has limited free memory, it's possible for the compiler to run out of room. When this happens, follow these hints to gain more space:

- Reboot without installing memory-resident utilities, keyboard enhancers, function-key macros, and so on.

- Use the command-line TPC.EXE compiler instead of TURBO.EXE, otherwise known as the IDE (integrated development environment). All the memory that the Turbo Pascal editor and debugger use will then be available for compiling.

- If your computer has an 80286, 80386, or an 80486 processor and at least 1 megabyte of extended (not expanded) RAM, you can run the TPCX protected-mode command-line compiler, which operates similarly to TPC, but can put every scrap of available memory to work. See "Compiling in Protected Mode" later in this chapter for more information.

- Select the IDE's *Options:Linker* command and change *Link buffer* from its default *Memory* setting to *Disk*. Or you can use the /L option with the command-line compiler. Either way, the option lengthens compilation time but frees up memory normally used by the compiler during linking of compiled units—in other words, when references to various symbols in units are *resolved* into actual addresses.

- Use units to "hide" information in unit implementation sections. Organizing your program into units, and placing only the absolute minimum number of symbols in the unit interface sections, reduces the total number of symbols the compiler stores in memory.

- Run the TPUMOVER utility and remove one or more units from TURBO.TPL. Keep only the most frequently used units in TURBO.TPL.

The *Turbo Pascal User's Guide* lists a few other memory-saving tips, but the hints listed here give the best results.

Of course, you can also purchase more memory. The IDE automatically detects and uses up to 400K (increased from 64K in version 5.5) of expanded (EMS) memory for overlays and various other items. If you have other programs that use EMS RAM, check if there's a way to reserve some EMS for the IDE.

Include Files

One way to handle large programs is to divide them into editable pieces, storing program text in *include* files. An include file is just a separate disk text file that the compiler includes at some moment during compilation of another text. For example, the following line tells the compiler to include file LIBRARY.PAS, presumably a collection of procedures and functions that the program uses:

```
{$I library.pas}
```

Don't confuse this directive with {$I+} or {$I–}, which turn I/O error checking on and off. With a space after the I, the compiler expects to find a file name next. You can also use the alternate comment brackets (* and *) like this:

```
(*$I library.pas*)
```

When the compiler comes to an include directive, it reads the include file as though the text was part of the original source code. Include files themselves may include other files, up to about eight levels deep, although simple tests indicate you can nest beyond this stated maximum. (Don't be too concerned with the actual limit—nesting include files more than a few levels deep is rarely necessary.) The only restriction is that an include directive may not appear between **begin** and **end**. You can't include statements inside procedures, for example.

When the compiler exhausts the included text, it continues where it left off in the source. Of course, the included file must be on disk when you compile the parent file. If not, you receive:

```
Error 15: File not found.
```

If you don't use a file name extension, Turbo Pascal automatically adds .PAS to a file name. This directive also includes LIBRARY.PAS:

```
{$I library}
```

Using the Dos Unit Exec Procedure

Another way to segment large programs is to divide them into modules—independently running subprograms—and then write a controller to call each module in turn. The controller might be a main menu from which you select major program operations. Each operation is a separate module, which you design, compile, and test separately.

The Dos unit contains a procedure, Exec, that lets you run other programs or, to use the operating system term, processes. When a process ends, control returns to the calling program. Exec takes two string parameters:

```
procedure Exec(Path, CmdLine: string);
```

The Path string is the name of the EXE or COM program you want to run. This can be a compiled Turbo Pascal program or any other program you normally run from the DOS command line. The Path may include drive and subdirectory names as in C:\UTIL\FORMAT.

The CmdLine string holds any information you need to pass to a program. For example, if you have a program named SORT.EXE (not shown here) that takes input and output file names, then to sort NAMES.TXT to NAMES.SRT you might use Exec like this:

```
Exec('sort', 'names.txt names.srt');
```

Programs 13-5,13-6, and 13-7 show how to use Exec to design a multimodule program. To compile the complete program, save Program 13-5 as MENU.PAS and compile to MENU.EXE. Save Program 13-6 as SUB1.PAS and compile to SUB1.EXE. Finally, save Program 13-7 as SUB2.PAS and compile to SUB2.EXE. Quit Turbo Pascal and, with the three .EXE files on disk, type Menu to run the program. Press key 1 to select subprogram 1. Press key 2 to select subprogram 2. Press key 3 to quit.

Line 1 in each program uses a special compiler directive to restrict memory use. The directive takes the form:

```
{$M stacksize, heapmin, heapmax}
```

The *stacksize* value is the number of bytes, ranging from a low of 1024 to a high of 65520. Values *heapmin* and *heapmax* control the minimum and maximum heap (free memory) size available to variables created by New and GetMem. These two values must be in the range of 0 to 655360.

You must restrict the stack and heap size when running programs that call Exec because Turbo Pascal and DOS normally reserve all available memory for programs. Therefore, unless you change your main program's memory requirements, there won't be any room left to run subprograms.

If your program does not use New or GetMem, set *heapmin* and *heapmax* to zero. Setting the *stacksize* limit correctly is tricky. Every program has different stack requirements, depending largely on how many procedures call others (in other words, the overall nesting level of all procedures and functions), plus the numbers and types of parameters passed to routines and the sizes of local variables. In general, though, a stack size of about 8K should be adequate for most small to medium-sized programs. The default stack is 16K. A 32K stack is huge.

Lines 36-37 of Program 13-5 call Exec, passing the name of the subprogram to run. The first such call passes no parameters. The second passes two parameters. Notice that the two parameters are written as a *single* string (line 37).

Program 13-5: MENU.PAS

```
 1:  {$M 4000, 0, 0}       { 4K stack, no heap minimum or maximum }
 2:
 3:  program Menu;
 4:
 5:  uses Crt, Dos;
 6:
 7:  const
 8:    TheCowsComeHome = false;
 9:  var
10:    Choice: Char;
11:
```

```
12:   { Center string S at this display row }
13:   procedure Center(Row: Integer; S: string);
14:   begin
15:     GotoXY(40 - (Length(S) div 2), Row);
16:     Write(S)
17:   end;
18:
19:   procedure DisplayMenu;
20:   begin
21:     ClrScr;
22:     Center( 8, '    Main Menu');
23:     Center( 9, '-----------------');
24:     Center(10, '1 = Sub program 1');
25:     Center(11, '2 = Sub program 2');
26:     Center(12, '3 = Quit         ');
27:     Center(16, 'Which? ');
28:   end;
29:
30:   begin
31:     DisplayMenu;
32:     repeat
33:       Choice := Readkey;
34:       Writeln(Choice);
35:       case Choice of
36:         '1': Exec('sub1.exe', '');
37:         '2': Exec('sub2.exe', 'Param1 Param2');
38:         '3': Halt
39:       end;
40:       if Choice in ['1', '2']
41:         then DisplayMenu { on return from sub process }
42:     until TheCowsComeHome
43:   end.
```

Program 13-6: SUB1.PAS

```
1:   {$M 2000, 0, 0}
2:
3:   program Sub1;
4:   { Compile to SUB1.EXE }
5:
6:   uses Crt;
7:
```

continued

Program 13-6: continued

```
 8:   begin
 9:     ClrScr;
10:     Writeln('Here we are in SUB1.EXE!');
11:     Writeln;
12:     Write('Press <Enter> to return to menu...');
13:     Readln;
14:   end.
```

Program 13-7: SUB2.PAS

```
 1:   {$M 2000, 0, 0}
 2:
 3:   program Sub2;
 4:   { Compile to SUB2.EXE }
 5:
 6:   uses Crt;
 7:
 8:   var I: Integer;
 9:
10:   begin
11:     ClrScr;
12:     Writeln('Here we are in SUB2.EXE!');
13:     Writeln;
14:     Writeln('Number of params = ', ParamCount);
15:     for I := 1 to ParamCount do
16:       Writeln(I:2, ' : ', ParamStr(I));
17:     Writeln;
18:     Write('Press <Enter> to return to menu...');
19:     Readln
20:   end.
```

Exec Return Codes

Often, a subprogram needs to pass a return code back to its caller. Usually, the value indicates whether an error occurred. The usual way to do this is through the Halt procedure with an optional parameter. For example, instead of simply ending subprogram 1 (Program 13-6), insert this statement between lines 13 and 14:

```
Halt(1);
```

The main program can inspect the value passed to Halt by calling function DosExitCode in the Dos unit. The result of this function is a Word and, therefore, cannot be negative. Usually, zero means no error, although interpreting the code is up to you. To examine the return code, you might replace line 36 in Program 13-5 with:

```
'1' : begin
        Exec('sub1.exe', '');
        if DosExitCode <> O then
        begin
          GotoXY(1, 24);
          Writeln;
          Writeln('Error # ', DosExitCode);
          Readln
        end
      end;
```

Unlike the IoResult function, you may use DosExitCode more than once to receive the value passed to Halt by a subprogram.

Executing DOS Commands

You can also use Exec to issue DOS commands like DIR, COPY, and FORMAT. To do this requires starting a temporary copy of COMMAND.COM, the program that displays the DOS prompt (C:>) and executes commands. The parameter string passed to Exec is the DOS command you want COMMAND.COM to execute. Because you don't want this second copy of COMMAND.COM to install itself in memory, you must also pass option /C, telling DOS that this is not the primary command processor.

To execute simple commands, make sure your program **uses** DOS; and includes a directive such as {$M 8192,1024,1024} before the **program** header, setting the stack and heap memory sizes. Then, insert single Exec statements such as:

```
Exec('\command.com', '/C dir');
```

to start COMMAND.COM and execute a DIR command. When the command ends, the statement following Exec runs. If your program clears or writes to the display, you may want to follow Exec with a pause:

```
Writeln;
Write('Press Enter to continue...');
Readln;
```

People often move COMMAND.COM to another location, usually to a RAM drive for extra speed. Deal with this by inspecting the COMSPEC environment variable for COMMAND.COM's current location. Assuming that variable Comspec is a string, the previous command expands to:

```
Comspec := GetEnv('COMSPEC');
if Length(Comspec) = 0
  then Comspec := '\command.com';
Exec(Comspec, '/C dir');
```

Testing whether GetEnv returns a null string (indicating that COMSPEC is not defined) is probably unnecessary—COMSPEC is *always* defined. (See Chapter 9 for more information about GetEnv and environment variables.) If you are more trusting than I am, you can probably just write:

```
Exec(GetEnv('COMSPEC'), '/C dir');
```

Vector Swapping

A subtle problem can develop when using Exec. Because Turbo Pascal installs several low-level routines to handle disk errors, to check for Ctrl-Break keypresses, and to handle other critical conditions, if such events happen when a subprogram is running, then the parent program's error handlers receive the calls.

If this is not what you want, you must restore the original error handlers before calling Exec. Then, after Exec, you must replace Turbo Pascal's handlers. To accomplish these tasks, call the Dos unit SwapVectors routine before and after Exec. Doing this swaps Turbo Pascal's vectors (copied by the System unit when the program starts) with those stored in system memory at RAM addresses starting with 0000:0000.

Program 13-8 demonstrates how to use SwapVectors and Exec to return temporarily to DOS—similar to using the IDE's *File:DOS shell* command. Lines 16-18 surround Exec with calls to SwapVectors, thus restoring and then resetting interrupt vectors. Line 19 tests DosError in case the attempt to run COMMAND.COM fails—usually due to a lack of memory. Notice that line 17 passes no parameters to COMMAND.COM, thus you have to type EXIT and press Enter to return to the program.

Program 13-8: EXITTO.PAS

```
1:  {$M 8096, 1024, 1024}
2:  program ExitToDos;
3:  uses Crt, Dos;
4:  var
5:    Choice: Integer;
6:
7:  procedure RunDosCommands;
8:  var Comspec: string[80];
```

```
 9:  begin
10:     Writeln;
11:     Writeln('Type EXIT to return to program');
12:     Writeln;
13:     Comspec := GetEnv('COMSPEC');
14:     if Length(Comspec) = 0
15:       then Comspec := '\command.com';
16:     SwapVectors;
17:     Exec(Comspec, '');
18:     SwapVectors;
19:     if DosError <> 0 then
20:     begin
21:       Writeln;
22:       Writeln('*** Error: Can''t run COMMAND.COM')
23:     end
24:  end;
25:
26:  procedure DoNothing;
27:  begin
28:     Writeln;
29:     Writeln('Doing (almost) nothing');
30:     Write('Press Enter...');
31:     Readln
32:  end;
33:
34:  begin
35:     repeat
36:       ClrScr;
37:       Writeln('Test Menu');
38:       Writeln('---------');
39:       Writeln('1 - do nothing');
40:       Writeln('2 - Run DOS commands');
41:       Writeln('3 - Quit');
42:       Writeln;
43:       Write('Which? ');
44:       Readln(Choice);
45:       case Choice of
46:         1: DoNothing;
47:         2: RunDosCommands
48:       end
49:     until Choice = 3
50:  end.
```

Untyped Parameters

Procedures and functions may declare untyped variable parameters. Such parameters have identifiers but no colons and data types. For example, the following declares two untyped parameters, V1 and V2:

```
procedure Demo(var V1, V2);
```

You can declare only variable untyped parameters. To say that another way, you must pass untyped parameters by reference, not by value. You can still mix typed and untyped parameters in the same declaration, though:

```
procedure Demo(var V1, V2; Count: Integer);
```

Declared this way, Count is an Integer value parameter of the normal variety, but V1 and V2 can represent any kinds of variables. To these two untyped parameters, you can pass strings, arrays, records, or variables of any other data type. The procedure itself, though, must eventually define what V1 and V2 are. Let's say you want to treat V1 and V2 as arrays of characters. To do this, Demo makes the following declarations:

```
type
   ChArray = array[1 .. 1] of Char;
var
   Ch1: ChArray Absolute V1;
   Ch2: ChArray Absolute V2;
```

After declaring data type ChArray, two local variables Ch1 and Ch2 are given the same addresses as the parameters V1 and V2, using the Absolute identifier. Any variable passed to Demo appears inside the procedure as an array of characters, regardless of its original data type.

To demonstrate the usefulness of untyped parameters, Program 13-9 includes a procedure to erase a variable of any data type. You can use ZeroVar (line 8) to clear arrays, strings, real numbers, buffers, or any other type. (Using ZeroVar on files is allowed but not recommended.)

The test program asks for four values: a character, an integer, a real number, and a string. The procedure at lines 19-26 displays your entries before and after passing each variable to ZeroVar. Notice how function Sizeof determines the correct number of bytes for ZeroVar to clear (lines 36-39).

Program 13-9: UNTYPED.PAS

```
1:   program UnTypedParameters;
2:   var
```

```
 3:    Ch: Char;
 4:     S: string[80];
 5:     I: Integer;
 6:     R: Real;
 7:
 8:  procedure ZeroVar(var V; Count: Integer);
 9:  type
10:     Vtype = array[1 .. MaxInt] of Byte;
11:  var
12:     A: Vtype Absolute V;
13:     I: Integer;
14:  begin
15:     for I := 1 to Count do
16:       A[I] := 0
17:  end;
18:
19:  procedure Display;
20:  begin
21:     Writeln;
22:     Writeln('Ch = ', Ch, ' (ASCII ', Ord(Ch), ')');
23:     Writeln(' I = ', I);
24:     Writeln(' R = ', R);
25:     Writeln(' S = ', S, ' (LENGTH ', Length(S), ')')
26:  end;
27:
28:  begin
29:     Write('Enter a character ..... '); Readln(Ch);
30:     Write('Enter an integer ...... '); Readln(I);
31:     Write('Enter a real number ... '); Readln(R);
32:     Write('Enter a string ........ '); Readln(S);
33:     Writeln;
34:     Writeln('Before zeroing:');
35:     Display;
36:     ZeroVar(Ch, Sizeof(Ch));
37:     ZeroVar(I, Sizeof(I));
38:     ZeroVar(R, Sizeof(R));
39:     ZeroVar(S, Sizeof(S));
40:     Writeln;
41:     Writeln('After zeroing:');
42:     Display;
43:     Readln
44:  end.
```

Filling Memory

As written in Program 13-9, ZeroVar (lines 8-17) resembles another built-in procedure, FillChar. Use FillChar as in the following statement, which inserts zero bytes at every position in string S (including the length byte at S[0]):

```
FillChar(S, Sizeof(S), 0);
```

FillChar takes three parameters: the variable to fill, the variable's size in bytes, and the value or character to insert into the variable. You can also index array variables, filling at a starting point anywhere in the array. For example, this inserts five bytes equal to character A starting at index ten in array A:

```
FillChar(A[10], 5, 'A');
```

Memory Moves

Another built-in procedure moves bytes from one place to another, generally faster than doing the same operation in a loop. If you have two string variables of the same type, S1 and S2, this sets S1 equal to S2:

```
Move(S2, S1, Sizeof(S2));
```

Move takes three parameters: the source, the destination, and the number of bytes to transfer. In this example, function Sizeof tells Move to move all bytes in S2 to S1. Of course, you can do the same thing with the simple assignment:

```
S1 := S2;
```

Move shines when moving many bytes in large arrays. Assume you have this array variable:

```
var
  BigArray: array[1 .. 10000] of char;
```

To transfer 1000 characters from BigArray[1] to BigArray[100]—in other words, to move 1000 characters down 100 array positions—you could use the **for** loop:

```
for I := 1000 downto 1 do
  BigArray[I + 100] := BigArray[I];
```

Notice that you have to start at the end of the block of characters you want to move. Move does the same thing in one easy step:

```
Move(BigArray[1], BigArray[100], 1000);
```

Using Move also avoids a problem with the **for** loop approach that may at first not be obvious. Consider this **for** loop:

```
for I := 1 to 1000 do
  BigArray[I + 100] := BigArray[I];
```

The problem here is that the indexes overlap, assigning characters to positions that the **for** loop control variable hasn't come to yet. Move avoids the problem by always moving data in the correct direction to prevent overlapping when the source and destination variables are the same. For example, to move the same 1000 bytes back to index 1, simply reverse the indexes:

```
Move(BigArray[100], BigArray[1], 1000);
```

To do the same in a **for** loop, you have to be careful to index in the correct direction:

```
for I:= 1 to 1000 do
  BigArray[I] := BigArray[I + 100];
```

Text File Device Drivers

The Dos unit defines record TextRec, which you can use to attach custom routines for controlling devices. Suppose, for example, you attach a graphics plotter or a speech synthesizer to a computer port. Because Turbo Pascal has no native commands to control such devices, you can write your own controlling routines and attach them to Turbo Pascal. Together, the custom routines make up a *device driver*. By attaching a custom device driver to a program, you can use Rewrite, Reset, Write, Read, and other I/O routines to run your device.

Program 13-10 is a unit shell that you can use as a template for your own device driver designs. Line 7 lists the only public procedure in the unit, AssignDev, which you'll probably rename for different devices. The procedure is similar to Assign or to AssignCrt in the Crt unit. AssignDev prepares a text file (F) for an eventual Reset or Rewrite.

Don't try to use Program 13-10 as listed here. The procedures and functions are unfinished. Notice the {$F+} directive in line 11, which tells Turbo Pascal to compile procedures and functions as *far* routines. A *far* routine can be called from anywhere in memory, not only from the same code segment. A *near* routine must be called only from within its own code segment. Normally, Turbo Pascal compiles procedures and functions as *near* routines. Because system routines located in another segment call the device driver code, the functions must be *far*.

> **Note:** Rather than use the {$F+} directive, you can follow a procedure or function declaration with the key word **far**, which has the same effect. The **far** key word is new to Turbo Pascal 6.0, however, so if your programs must compile with earlier Turbo Pascal versions beginning with 4.0, you must use the {$F+} directive. Generally, it's easier to use the directive to compile several far routines and to use the **far** key word for designating individual far procedures and functions.

Program 13-10: UDEVICE.PAS

```
 1:  unit UDevice;
 2:
 3:  interface
 4:
 5:  uses Dos;
 6:
 7:  procedure AssignDev(var F: Text; FileName: string);
 8:
 9:  implementation
10:
11:  {$F+}   { All device functions must be FAR }
12:
13:  { Assign to functions that do nothing }
14:  function DoNothing(var F: TextRec): Integer;
15:  begin
16:     DoNothing := 0   { No error for doing nothing }
17:  end;
18:
19:  { Input from device }
20:  function DevInput(var F: TextRec): Integer;
21:  begin
22:  end;
23:
24:  { Output to device }
25:  function DevOutput(var F: TextRec): Integer;
26:  begin
27:  end;
28:
```

```
29:  { Close file }
30:  function DevClose(var F: TextRec): Integer;
31:  begin
32:  end;
33:
34:  { Called by Reset, Rewrite, Append }
35:  function DevOpen(var F: TextRec): Integer;
36:  begin
37:    with F do
38:    begin
39:      if Mode = fmInput then
40:      begin
41:        InOutFunc := @DevInput;
42:        FlushFunc := @DoNothing
43:      end else
44:      begin
45:        Mode := fmOutput;          { In case mode was fmInOut }
46:        InOutFunc := @DevOutput;
47:        FlushFunc := @DevOutput;
48:      end;
49:      CloseFunc := @DevClose
50:    end;
51:    DevOpen := 0
52:  end;
53:
54:  {$F-}  { End of local FAR functions. }
55:
56:  { Initialize file variable }
57:  procedure AssignDev;
58:  begin
59:    FillChar(F, SizeOf(F), 0);   { Zero file variable }
60:    with TextRec(F) do
61:    begin
62:      Handle   := $FFFF;
63:      Mode     := fmClosed;
64:      BufSize  := SizeOf(Buffer);
65:      BufPtr   := @Buffer;
66:      OpenFunc := @DevOpen;
67:      Name[0]  := #0                { Ignore filename }
68:    end
69:  end;
70:
71:  end.
```

Function DoNothing (lines 14-17) simply returns 0, indicating no error. When you have a routine that has no meaning for a specific device, call DoNothing. The function also shows the correct form for all device driver routines. Device driver functions receive a single variable parameter F of Dos unit type TextRec, listed in Figure 13-1. You must supply routines for these four basic I/O functions:

1. *Open*—called by Reset, Rewrite, and Append.

2. *Input* and *Output*—called by Read, Readln, Write, Writeln, Eof, Eoln, SeekEoln, and Close.

3. *Flush*—Called by Flush and after Read, Readln, Write, and Writeln.

4. *Close*—called by Close.

```
TextBuf = array[0 .. 127] of Char;
TextRec = record
  Handle: Word;
  Mode: Word;
  BufSize: word;
  Private: Word;
  BufPos: Word;
  BufEnd: Word;
  BufPtr: ^TextBuf;
  OpenFunc: Pointer;
  InOutFunc: Pointer;
  FlushFunc: Pointer;
  CloseFunc: Pointer;
  UserData: array[1 .. 16] of Byte;
  Name: array[0 .. 79] of Char;
  Buffer: TextBuf;
end;
```

Figure 13-1 The Dos unit TextBuf and TextRec data types, which you can use to write custom text file device drivers.

In each of these functions, you can examine the TextRec.Mode field to determine the correct action. Mode can be any of the values listed in Table 13-3.

Table 13-3 File mode constants.

Constant	Value	Action
fmClosed	$D7B0	File is closed
fmInput	$D7B1	Insert input into Buffer
fmOutput	$D7B2	Process characters in Buffer
fmInOut	$D7B3	File is open for read/write

In Program 13-10, the AssignDev procedure (lines 57-69) prepares the text file (F), first filling it with zero bytes (line 59) and then initializing various fields in the record. The **with** statement (lines 60-68) uses a typecast to force Turbo Pascal to consider the Text data type as a TextRec record. Normally, the insides of Text are unavailable to programs. Using a typecast gives you access to the text file's normally invisible fields.

Line 66 assigns the address of the DevOpen function to field OpenFunc. The other Pointer fields (see Figure 13-1) may be ignored at this point. The Handle $FFFF is the normal value for an unopen file. If you plan to use DOS calls for I/O, you could store the file handle here later when you open the file. Set Mode to fmClosed (line 63), marking the file unopened. Lines 64-65 prepare the address and size of the text file buffer, normally 128 bytes. You could use a longer or shorter buffer if you wish and assign its address to BufPtr.

The FileName string (see line 7) is ignored in this example. Line 67 sets the first byte of the Name character array to zero. If you need to keep track of file names, you can store them here, but you don't have to. In fact, you may as well remove the FileName parameter from AssignDev if you don't need it.

Using Text Device Drivers

An example device driver will help clarify the preceding discussion. Program 13-11 is a modified copy of the device driver shell in Program 13-10. The purpose of this device driver is to display expanded characters using the same bit patterns for normal-sized letters and symbols. Local procedure Expander (lines 12-39) writes a single large character on-screen, reading the bit pattern for the character image from ROM (line 28) and displaying large blocks (line 32) or blanks (line 33) for each pattern dot.

The AssignExp procedure prepares the device driver. We don't need a file name in this case, and, therefore, the FileName field is not included in the procedure declaration (line 7).

DevOpen (lines 66-83) tests the Mode field. The driver cannot handle input for Read and Readln and accordingly sets fields InOutFunc and FlushFunc (lines 72-73) to the DoNothing procedure. Line 76 sets Mode to fmOutput. (If Append opens the file, Mode equals fmInOut here. If you need to distinguish between Rewrite and Append, examine Mode and take appropriate action. This example treats Append and Rewrite identically.)

Line 80 assigns the address of the Close function to field CloseFunc. In this example, closing the file does nothing. In your own drivers, assign the address of a function to deinitialize a device or close a disk file. Line 82 passes an error code back as the function result.

The output routine (lines 44-59) calls procedure Expander (line 53) for each character in the text buffer. The **while** loop shows the correct way to process all buffered characters. Again, an error code is passed back as the function result (line 58).

Save Program 13-11 as UEXPAND.PAS and compile to disk, creating the unit file, UEXPAND.TPU. Following the program is an example that shows how to use the custom device driver.

Program 13-11: UEXPAND.PAS

```
 1:  unit UExpand;
 2:
 3:  interface
 4:
 5:  uses Crt, Dos;
 6:
 7:  procedure AssignExp(var F: Text);
 8:
 9:  implementation
10:
11:  { Write one expanded-size character }
12:  procedure Expander(Ch: Char);
13:  const
14:    Pattern = $FA6E;
15:    Width   = 73;      { 33 for 40-col screens }
16:  var
17:    X, Y, Segment, Offset, I, J: Word;
18:    EightBits: Byte;
19:  begin
20:    if WhereX >= Width
21:      then for I := 1 to 9 do Writeln;
22:    X := WhereX; Y := WhereY;
23:    Gotoxy(X, Y - 8);
24:    Segment := $F000;
25:    Offset  := Pattern + (Ord(Ch) * 8);
26:    for I := 0 to 7 do
27:    begin
```

```
28:    EightBits := Mem[Segment: Offset + I];
29:      for J := 0 to 7 do
30:      begin
31:        if EightBits and $80 <> 0
32:          then Write(Chr(177))
33:          else Write(' '); { 1 blank }
34:        EightBits := EightBits shl 1
35:      end;
36:      Gotoxy(X, WhereY + 1)  { cr/lf }
37:    end;
38:    Gotoxy(X + 9, Y)
39:  end;
40:
41:  {$F+}   { All device functions must be FAR }
42:
43:  { Output expanded text }
44:  function DevOutput(var F: TextRec): Integer;
45:  var
46:    K: Word;   { Text buffer index }
47:  begin
48:    with F do
49:    begin
50:      K := 0;
51:      while K < BufPos do
52:      begin
53:        Expander(BufPtr^[K]);
54:        Inc(K)
55:      end;
56:      BufPos := 0
57:    end;
58:    DevOutput := 0
59:  end;
60:
61:  function DoNothing(var F: TextRec): Integer;
62:  begin
63:    DoNothing := 0
64:  end;
65:
66:  function DevOpen(var F: TextRec): Integer;
67:  begin
68:    with F do
69:    begin
70:      if Mode = FmInput then
71:      begin
72:    InOutFunc := @DoNothing;
```

continued

Program 13-11: continued

```
73:      FlushFunc := @DoNothing
74:        end else
75:        begin
76:          Mode := fmOutput;
77:          InOutFunc := @DevOutput;
78:          FlushFunc := @DevOutput;
79:        end;
80:        CloseFunc := @DoNothing
81:      end;
82:      DevOpen := 0
83:    end;
84:
85:    {$F-}  { End of local FAR functions. }
86:
87:    procedure AssignExp;
88:    begin
89:      FillChar(F, SizeOf(F), 0);   { Zero file variable }
90:      with TextRec(F) do
91:      begin
92:        Handle   := $FFFF;
93:        Mode     := fmClosed;
94:        BufSize  := SizeOf(Buffer);
95:        BufPtr   := @Buffer;
96:        OpenFunc := @DevOpen;
97:        Name[0]  := #0
98:      end
99:    end;
100:
101:   end.
```

Using the UExpand Unit

Program 13-12 tests the device driver in Program 13-11. The program uses two units, Crt and UExpand. (You must have UEXPAND.TPU on disk to compile this example.)

Line 7 passes Text file variable ExpFile to AssignExp, the public procedure in unit UExpand. This initializes the file variable for the Rewrite statement in line 8. Then, displaying text with Write and Writeln statements (line 13) passes characters to the custom device driver, displaying headline-size characters on-screen. When you run the program, type a short string and press Enter to see the result.

Program 13-12: TESTEXPA.PAS

```
 1:  program TestExpand;
 2:  uses Crt, UExpand;
 3:  var
 4:     ExpFile: Text;
 5:     S: string;
 6:  begin
 7:     AssignExp(ExpFile);  { Initialize file variable }
 8:     Rewrite(ExpFile);
 9:     ClrScr;
10:     Write('Enter a string: ');
11:     Readln(S);
12:     GotoXY(1, 20);
13:     Write(ExpFile, S);
14:     Readln
15:  end.
```

Increasing Text-File Buffer Size

When reading and writing text files, Turbo Pascal normally uses a 128-byte buffer in memory to hold information on its way to and from disk. This minimum-size buffer saves RAM but can also make disk I/O painfully slow, especially when copying large amounts of text from one file to another. Increasing the buffer size to 256, 512, or even 1024 bytes or larger can add remarkable speed to "I/O-bound" code.

Call the built-in SetTextBuf procedure to increase a text file's I/O buffer. The procedure has no effect on files of other data types, in which case buffering is handled by DOS, not by Turbo Pascal. First, you need to declare a new buffer variable and a text file:

```
var
   Buffer: array[0 .. 511] of Byte;
   T: Text;
```

That creates a 512-byte array named Buffer. The actual format of the variable is unimportant—it doesn't have to be an array of bytes. Anything that's big enough will do. In the code, after assigning a name to text file T, attach the buffer to the file variable with:

```
Assign(T, 'filename.txt');
SetTextBuf(T, Buffer);
Reset(T);
```

Always call SetTextBuf after Assign and before Reset. If the file is already open, Close it and then call SetTextBuf. Never call SetTextBuf to attach a new buffer to an open file. Though it's technically possible to switch buffers for open files, doing so risks destroying information held in the buffer that's replaced by another.

A second way to call SetTextBuf is to add a Word parameter equal to the buffer size—useful when the buffer size is variable. (If you don't specify the buffer size, SetTextBuf uses the entire buffer space by default.) For example, suppose you have the previous variables (except Buffer) plus:

```
var
  Bp: ^Byte;    { Buffer pointer }
  Size: Word;   { Size of buffer }
```

Pointer Bp will address a variable-length buffer on the heap. Variable Size equals the number of bytes in the buffer. You can then allocate buffer space on the heap and attach that space to a text file with these commands:

```
Size := 1024;
GetMem(Bp, Size);
Assign(T, 'filename.txt');
SetTextBuf(T, Bp^, Size);
Reset(T);
```

When attaching buffer variables to a text file, don't dispose the buffer memory while the file is open. This will almost always lead to a major system crash. To avoid such troubles, follow these guidelines:

- Declare buffer variables global to the entire program. Global variables exist during the program's entire execution lifetime.

- If you must declare buffer variables local to procedures and functions, you *must* Close the text file before the routine declaring the buffer variable ends. There are no exceptions to this rule—local variables exist only while their declaring routines are active.

- Close files *before* using Dispose to recover heap memory attached to a text file. If you do this, don't forget to call SetTextBuf again if you later decide to reopen this same text file.

- Don't move buffers around in memory after calling SetTextBuf. In other words, if you assign a buffer to another variable, the open text file will still use the original buffer space. You must call SetTextBuf again to use a different buffer.

Free Declaration Ordering

In Pascal's original design, **label**, **const**, **type**, and **var** declarations must appear in that order, with only one of each section within a program, procedure, or function block. Turbo Pascal doesn't care about this rule and allows **type** sections that follow **var** declarations, or as many **const** sections as you need. You can even declare new types and variables in between procedures and functions.

Up to now, the examples in this book purposely ignored this unique feature. Programs that take advantage of free declaration ordering are not likely to compile with other Pascal compilers. By the way, Turbo Pascal also ignores the **program** header, which you see at the top of all examples in this book, except the following. Here, then, is the shortest possible Turbo Pascal program:

```
begin end.
```

Although there is no practical purpose to deleting the **program** header, there are times when reversing the normal declaration order has advantages. For a good example, refer to Program 13-13, which has a serious bug.

Program 13-13 GLOBALBU.PAS: (with errors):

```
 1:  program GlobalBug;
 2:  const
 3:    k = 100;
 4:  var
 5:    I: Integer;
 6:
 7:  procedure Display(J: Integer);
 8:  begin
 9:    if J < I then    { Incorrect!  Should be J < k! }
10:    begin
11:      Display(J + 1)
12:    end;
13:    Write(J:10)
14:  end;
15:
16:  begin
17:    Writeln('Countdown (with a bug)');
18:    Write('Enter a number from 0 to ', k, ': ');
19:    Readln(I);
20:    Display(I);
21:    Writeln;
22:    Readln
23:  end.
```

The program counts down from constant k (line 3) to any value you enter (line 19). Procedure Display (lines 7-14) recursively calls itself while (J < I). Unfortunately, this is incorrect—the expression in line 9 should be (J < k). The programmer goofed.

We've seen this common side-effect bug before. Procedure Display has no business referring to global variable I, used only in the main program (lines 19-20). To repair the problem, move lines 4-5 to *between* lines 15 and 16 and recompile. Because global variable I now comes after the buggy Display procedure, the compiler displays:

```
Error 3: Unknown identifier.
```

when it gets to line 9. If this were a real program, you'd notice your mistake, change I to k, and be rid of a nasty bug before it chews up the program's results.

Don't abuse free declaration ordering, scattering your type declarations and variables throughout the source code. But if moving a declaration clarifies your program or helps prevent bugs as in this example, then by all means use this unique Turbo Pascal feature.

Not only can declarations in Turbo Pascal be freely ordered, they may also repeat any number of times. You can, for example, have three **type** sections, six **var** blocks, and as many **const** areas as you need.

Multiple **type** and **const** sections are of limited value, except perhaps to help categorize multiple declarations in a lengthy program. Multiple **var** sections, however, may help Turbo Pascal's built-in linker to save memory. Suppose you write the following program:

```
var
  X, Y: Integer;
  Z: Integer;
begin
  X := 100;
  Y := 200
end.
```

As you can see, the program's main block assigns 100 to X and 200 to Y, but no statements refer to Integer Z. That's a common situation—perhaps Z is left over from a test and the programmer forgot to remove it. Or, perhaps this is a module that uses conditional compilation, and the statements that normally refer to Z aren't needed for this particular compilation.

Nevertheless, Turbo Pascal allocates space for Z in memory. Even though the program never uses that variable, it's still there, eating up two bytes of RAM. Waste like that can build to mountainous proportions in programs with dozens of unused variables. To minimize this sort of waste, declare the variables in separate **var** sections. The new program places Z in a **var** declaration of its own:

```
var
  X, Y: Integer;
var
  Z: Integer;
begin
  X := 100;
  Y := 200
end.
```

Because the unused Z is in its own **var** section, and because the program never refers to Z, Turbo Pascal's linker does not allocate space for the unused variable.

When using this technique, keep in mind that variable stripping occurs only on a **var**-section level. If the program never refers to any variables in a **var** section, the linker will not allocate space for those variables. But if a statement refers to even one variable in a **var** section, then the linker will allocate space to *all* variables declared in that same section, whether those variables are used or not.

Structured Variable Constants

Chapter 2 introduced simple variable constants—constants that operate as variables with preinitialized values. (Recall that Borland's Turbo Pascal references call them "typed constants.") You can also declare structured variable constants, predefining values for arrays, records, sets, or any other Pascal data type. (See Figures 13-2, 13-3, and 13-4.) Although attractive, variable constants have their advantages and disadvantages.

The greatest advantage is that variable constants operate like preinitialized variables. This saves you the step of initializing variables and, therefore, reduces the compiled program size.

variable (typed) constant declaration

Figure 13-2 Railroad diagram for a variable constant declaration. (See also Figures 13-3 and 13-4.)

The primary disadvantage is that variable constants are global to the entire program and occupy valuable memory space. A few variable constants probably won't do much harm, but don't make the mistake of declaring all your variables this way.

variable (typed) constant

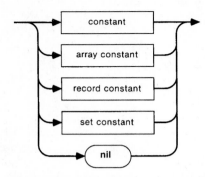

Figure 13-3 Use one of these items after the equal sign in a variable constant declaration (Figure 13-2).

array constant

record constant

set constant

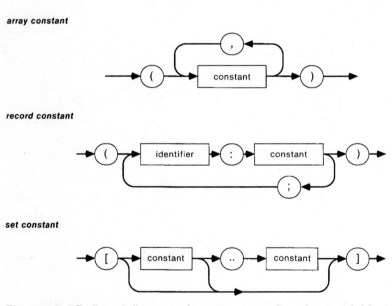

Figure 13-4 Railroad diagrams for array, record, and set variable constant declarations (Figure 13-2).

Variable Constant Arrays

A variable constant array is the same as any other array but has preinitialized elements. You can have single-dimension or multiple-dimension constant arrays.

Program 13-14 declares a constant array MonthNames, an array of 12 preset strings. Lines 16-17 print the names of the months. This works because the Turbo Pascal compiler embeds the predeclared array elements (lines 6-9) directly in the data segment. Therefore, there is no need to assign strings to the Months array—the month names are already there.

Program 13-14: MONTHNUM.PAS

```
 1:   program MonthNumbers;
 2:   type
 3:      Months = array[1 .. 12] of string[3];
 4:   const
 5:      MonthNames:
 6:         Months = ('Jan', 'Feb', 'Mar',
 7:                   'Apr', 'May', 'Jun',
 8:                   'Jul', 'Aug', 'Sep',
 9:                   'Oct', 'Nov', 'Dec');
10:   var
11:      Month: 1 .. 12;
12:   begin
13:      Writeln;
14:      Writeln( 'Month Numbers' );
15:      Writeln;
16:      for Month := 1 to 12 do
17:         Writeln(Month:2, ' : ', MonthNames[Month]);
18:      Readln
19:   end.
```

To declare multiple-dimension constant arrays, use nested parentheses. For a less confusing style, line up opening and closing parentheses as shown in Program 13-15, Chess. The program does not, of course, really play chess. It merely declares a chessboard using modern notation with ranks from 1 to 8 and *files* from a to z.

Program 13-15: CHESS.PAS

```
 1:   program Chess;
 2:   type
 3:      Piece = (Empty, WPawn, WRook, WKnight, WBishop, WQueen, WKing,
 4:                       BPawn, BRook, BKnight, BBishop, BQueen, BKing);
 5:      Ranks = 1 .. 8;
 6:   Files = (A, B, C, D, E, F, G, H);
```

continued

```
 7:  CheckerBoard = array[Ranks, Files] of Piece;
 8:
 9:  const
10:    Board:
11:    CheckerBoard =
12:    (
13:     (WRook, WKnight, WBishop, WKing,WQueen,WBishop, WKnight, WRook),
14:     (WPawn, WPawn,   WPawn,   WPawn,  WPawn,  WPawn,   WPawn,  WPawn),
15:     (Empty, Empty,   Empty,   Empty,  Empty,  Empty,  Empty, Empty),
16:     (Empty, Empty,   Empty,   Empty,  Empty,  Empty,  Empty,  Empty),
17:     (Empty, Empty,   Empty,   Empty,  Empty,  Empty,  Empty,  Empty),
18:     (Empty, Empty,   Empty,   Empty,  Empty,  Empty,  Empty,  Empty),
19:     (BPawn, BPawn,   BPawn,   BPawn,  BPawn,  BPawn,   BPawn,  BPawn),
20:     (BRook, BKnight, BBishop, BKing,  BQueen, BBishop,BKnight,BRook)
21:    );
22:
23:    PieceNames:
24:      array[Piece] of string[2] =
25:        ('..', 'wP', 'wR', 'wN', 'wB', 'wQ', 'wK',
26:               'bP', 'bR', 'bN', 'bB', 'bQ', 'bK');
27:
28:  procedure MovePiece(R1: Ranks; F1: Files;
29:                      R2: Ranks; F2: Files);
30:  begin
31:    Board[R2, F2] := Board[R1, F1];
32:    Board[R1, F1] := Empty
33:  end;
34:
35:  procedure DisplayBoard;
36:  var
37:    R: Ranks;
38:    F: Files;
39:  begin
40:    for R := 8 downto 1 do
41:    begin
42:      Writeln;
43:      Write(R, ': ');
44:      for F := A to H do
45:        Write(' ', PieceNames[Board[R, F]])
46:    end;
```

```
47:   Writeln;
48:     Writeln;
49:     Writeln('     a   b   c   d   e   f   g   h');
50:   end;
51:
52:   begin
53:     Writeln('Pawn to Q4 (d2-d4)');
54:     MovePiece(2, D, 4, D);
55:     DisplayBoard;
56:     Readln
57:   end.
```

Board is a variable constant, multidimensional array. That may sound and look complicated. But, as shown here, using a variable constant array efficiently sets up the chessboard, skipping an otherwise messy initialization step. As far as playing ability goes, the program knows one move, Pawn to Q4, or in the modern notation, 2-d to 4-d (see line 54).

You are welcome to finish Program 13-15 with no royalties due to the author.

Variable Constant Records

Variable constant records are similar to arrays but add field names and colons to predeclared values. Assume you have this record definition:

```
type
  NameRec = record
    Name: string[20];
    Age: Integer
  end;
```

You can then declare a variable constant of this structure, with fields set to these values:

```
const
  Nr: NameRec =
  (Name: 'GEORGE';
   Age: 25);
```

Variable Constant Sets

You can also have set constants with predeclared elements. Predefined character sets are especially useful when the set contents won't change during a program run. For example, you can have a set of characters named Digits declared this way:

```
type
  CharSet = set of Char;
const
  Digits: Charset = ['0' .. '9'];
```

You don't even need the type declaration. The following produces the identical results.

```
const
  Digits: set of Char = ['0' .. '9'];
```

Variable Constant Pointers

Variable constants can represent pointers, a new Turbo Pascal 6.0 feature most often used to address other constants. Suppose, for example, you are writing a database system to store records with structures something like this:

```
type
  DataRec = record
    Product: string[40];
    Company: string[40];
  end;
```

Although your database stores most records on disk, you also need to embed in the program one or more fixed records with default information. To avoid having to initialize these dummy records at runtime, create them as variable constants, writing

```
const
  fixedRec1: DataRec =
  (Product: 'Turbo Pascal 6.0';
   Company: 'Borland International');

  fixedRec2: DataRec =
  (Product: 'Mastering Turbo Pascal 6.0';
   Company: 'Hayden Book Company (SAMS)');
```

So far, so good. Constants fixedRec1 and fixedRec2 store fixed strings for the Product and Company fields in the two records. You can use these constants just like any other DataRec variables—in fact, they *are* variables that come preinitialized with the values shown here.

Later, you decide to modify your record structure, adding a Next pointer field so you can link multiple records in a list. The new definition is now:

```
type
  PDataRec = ^DataRec;
  DataRec = record
    Next: PDataRec;
    Product: string[40];
    Company: string[40];
  end;
```

The new PDataRec type addresses DataRec structures, and inside that record's design, the Next field links a DataRec variable to another record of the same type.

The trouble is, how can you link the fixed variable constant records together? In past Turbo Pascal versions, the answer was: you can't. The compilers through version 5.5 did not allow address values in variable constants. Turbo Pascal 6.0 remedies the problem by allowing you to rewrite the two preceding constant declarations as:

```
const
  fixedRec2: DataRec =
  (Next: nil;
   Product: 'Mastering Turbo Pascal 6.0';
   Company: 'Hayden Book Company (SAMS)');

  fixedRec1: DataRec =
  (Next: @fixedRec2;
   Product: 'Turbo Pascal 6.0';
   Company: 'Borland International');
```

The Next fields have the same general layout as any other variable constant record fields. The only difference is that Turbo Pascal 6.0 allows assigning values to those fields using expressions such as **nil** and @fixedRec2, which assigns the address of fixedRec2 to the Next field in fixedRec1. Using this technique, the program links fixedRec1 via Next to fixedRec2.

But there's a fly in the ointment. It's not possible to create a self reference using variable constant pointers. In other words, you can't change @fixedRec2 to @fixedRec1 in the preceding example. If you try to make this change, the compiler will display "Error 20: Variable identifier expected." Apparently, identifiers like fixedRec1 do not become valid until after the compiler processes the identifier's entire declaration; therefore, fixedRec1 is unable to refer to itself.

Special Directory Commands

Four directory commands let you work with subdirectories, which are useful for organizing the large amount of space available on a hard disk drive. (You can also use subdirectories with floppy disks, but to a lesser advantage.)

ChDir (Change Directory), MkDir (Make Directory), and RmDir (Remove Directory) take a single string parameter representing a subdirectory path name such as 'c:\util' or '\tpas'. The path name can also be a drive letter and colon ('A:'). Suppose you have a subdirectory LIB containing a library of procedures and functions. To change the current working directory, you could execute this statement:

```
ChDir('\pascal\lib');
```

You can also use ChDir to change to a different disk drive. This switches to drive B:

```
ChDir('A:');
```

Procedure MkDir creates a new subdirectory if one by that name doesn't already exist. RmDir removes a subdirectory, an operation allowed only if the directory is empty.

GetDir has a different format from the previous three commands. The procedure takes two parameters: a drive number equal to 0 for the current drive, 1 for drive A:, 2 for B:, and so on; and a string variable that GetDir sets to the current path name. To set a string variable PathName to the current directory, use these statements:

```
GetDir(0, PathName);
Writeln(PathName);
```

Program 13-16 demonstrates the four directory commands. Using the program, you can create a subdirectory, change to a new directory or drive, and remove subdirectories.

Program 13-16: SUBDIRS.PAS

```
 1:   program SubDirectories;
 2:   uses Crt;
 3:   type
 4:     MiscString = string[64];
 5:   var
 6:     Ch: Char;
 7:     PathName: MiscString;
 8:
 9:   procedure GetPath;
10:   begin
11:     Write(' what directory? '); Readln(PathName)
12:   end;
13:
```

```
14: {$I-} { I/O check off }
15: procedure ChangeDir;
16: begin
17:   Write('Change to'); GetPath;
18:   ChDir(PathName)
19: end;
20:
21: procedure MakeDir;
22: begin
23:   Write('Make'); GetPath;
24:   MkDir(PathName)
25: end;
26:
27: procedure RemoveDir;
28: begin
29:   Write('Remove'); GetPath;
30:   RmDir(PathName)
31: end;
32: {$I+} { I/O check back on }
33:
34: begin
35:   ClrScr;
36:   Writeln('Sub Directories');
37:   repeat
38:     ClrScr;
39:     GetDir(0, PathName); { 0=current drive; 1=A:, 2=B:, etc. }
40:     NormVideo;
41:     Writeln('Path is: ', PathName);
42:     Writeln; LowVideo;
43:     Write('C.hange, M.ake, R.emove, Q.uit? ');
44:     repeat
45:       Ch := Upcase(ReadKey)
46:     until Ch in ['C', 'M', 'R', 'Q'];
47:     Writeln(Ch); Writeln;
48:     case Ch of
49:       'C': ChangeDir;
50:       'M': MakeDir;
51:       'R': RemoveDir
52:     end;
53:     if Ioresult <> 0 then
54:     begin
55:       Writeln;
56: Writeln('No directory, bad path, or all files not removed');
```

continued

Program 13-16: SUBDIRS.PAS

```
57:    Write('Press return...'); Readln
58:       end
59:    until Ch = 'Q'
60: end.
```

Custom Exit Procedures

When a Turbo Pascal program ends, several normally invisible events occur. The standard Input and Output files are closed. A message is displayed if a runtime error caused the program to end prematurely. A return code is passed back to DOS (or to a parent program from a child process). And changed interrupt vectors are restored to their original values, saved earlier by Turbo Pascal runtime routines when the program started.

Linking into the Exit Chain

By following a few simple rules, you can weld your own links to the chain of events after the **end** of a Turbo Pascal program. Your custom exit procedure runs immediately before standard exit events occur, gaining control when:

- The program ends normally.

- A Halt statement was executed anywhere in the program.

- An Exit statement was executed in the program's outer block.

- A runtime error occurred.

Program 13-17 demonstrates how to write a custom exit procedure. When you run the program, it displays:

```
Welcome to ExitShell
Press <Enter> to end program...
Inside CustomExit procedure
```

The message "Inside CustomExit procedure" appears after you press Enter to end the program, proving that procedure CustomExit runs even though the program never calls it directly. To make this happen, ExitShell performs two assignments at the beginning of the program's main body:

```
SavedExitProc := ExitProc;
ExitProc := @CustomExit;
```

The first assignment saves the value of ExitProc, a Pointer variable defined in the System unit, which Turbo Pascal automatically links to every compiled program. ExitShell's global variable, SavedExitProc, holds the original ExitProc value for the program's duration. In your own programs, always save ExitProc in a similar global variable. Never assign ExitProc to a variable declared local to a procedure or function or to a dynamic variable on the heap. The saved ExitProc must be available after the program ends, and, therefore, only a global variable will do.

The second assignment sets ExitProc to the address of the custom exit procedure—CustomExit in Program 13-17. The @ operator returns the address of CustomExit. Because ExitProc points to the custom exit procedure, Turbo Pascal calls this procedure when the program ends.

Program 13-17: EXITSHEL.PAS

```
 1:  program ExitShell;
 2:
 3:  { Demonstrate how to write a custom exit procedure }
 4:
 5:  var SavedExitProc: Pointer;  { Old ExitProc value }
 6:
 7:  { Custom exit procedure }
 8:  procedure CustomExit; far;
 9:  begin
10:    Writeln('Inside CustomExit procedure');
11:    Write('Press <Enter> to leave...');
12:    Readln;
13:    ExitProc := SavedExitProc  { Restore saved ExitProc pointer }
14:  end;
15:
16:  begin
17:    SavedExitProc := ExitProc; { Save ExitProc pointer }
18:    ExitProc := @CustomExit;   { Install custom error procedure }
19:    Writeln;
20:    Writeln('Welcome to ExitShell');
21:    Write('Press <Enter> to end program...');
22:    Readln
23:  end.
```

Together, these assignments link the custom exit procedure, which has no parameters, into the exit chain. You can name the procedure anything you like.

Inside the exit procedure, assign the saved pointer back to ExitProc. This preserves the exit chain, letting other processes execute their own exit procedures after yours finishes. Except for this step, there is no limit to what you can do inside a custom exit procedure. You can read and write files, display values, use DOS functions, call other procedures and functions, and perform any other actions as part of your program's shutdown sequence.

A critical step is to declare the exit procedure *far* by ending its declaraion with **far** key word. (See CustomExit in Program 13-17.) Or, if you want your program's text to be compatible with earlier Turbo Pascal versions, you can surround the declaration with the directives {$F+} and {$F–}. Either way, Turbo Pascal will then call the exit procedure with a *far* CALL 80x86 instruction (technically called an "Inter-Segment Call"). Using **far** key word or {$F+} directive also tells Turbo Pascal to end the procedure with a complementary Inter-Segment *far* return instruction.

One of the most common mistakes is to forget to declare an exit procedure *far*. Turbo Pascal does not prevent this error, which causes an inevitable disaster from which you'll probably have to reboot to recover. If screwy things happen or if the computer hangs when your program ends, you probably forgot to include the **far** key word or to surround the custom exit procedure declaration with {$F+} and {$F–}.

Customizing a Runtime Handler

Custom exit procedures make it easy to write your own runtime error handler, perhaps displaying a more helpful message than that same ol' line:

```
Runtime error 106 at 0000:001E
```

For an example custom runtime handler, compile and run Program 13-18. As in Program 13-17, two assignments begin ErrorShell, saving ExitProc in SavedExitProc and assigning to ExitProc the address of CustomExit.

Program 13-18: ERRORSHE.PAS

```
1:  program ErrorShell;
2:
3:  { Demonstrate how to write a custom halt and
4:    runtime error handler. }
5:
6:  var
7:    SavedExitProc: Pointer; { Old ExitProc value }
8:    Num: Integer;            { Test number }
9:
```

```
10:  { Custom exit and runtime error handler }
11:  procedure CustomExit; far;
12:  begin
13:    if (ExitCode <> 0) and (ErrorAddr = nil) then
14:    begin
15:      Writeln;
16:      Writeln('Program halted!');
17:      Writeln('Exit code = ', ExitCode); { Display halt code }
18:      Write('Press <Enter> to exit...');
19:      Readln
20:    end;
21:    ExitProc := SavedExitProc  { Restore saved ExitProc pointer }
22:  end;
23:
24:  begin
25:    SavedExitProc := ExitProc; { Save ExitProc pointer }
26:    ExitProc := @CustomExit;   { Install custom error procedure }
27:    Writeln;
28:    Writeln('Welcome to ErrorShell');
29:    Writeln;
30:    Write('Enter an integer value: ');
31:    Readln(Num);
32:    Halt(Num)
33:  end.
```

Inside CustomExit, an **if** statement examines two global System unit variables, ExitCode (type Integer) and ErrorAddr (type Pointer). ExitCode holds one of three values: the integer number passed to a Halt statement, a runtime error code, or zero if the program ended normally or if an Exit statement was executed in the outer program block. ErrorAddr addresses the location of a runtime error if one occurred.

To determine the meaning of a nonzero ExitCode value, check whether ErrorAddr is **nil**. If so, then no runtime error occurred, and, therefore, ExitCode holds the value passed to a Halt statement. But if ExitCode is nonzero and if ErrorAddr is not **nil**, then a runtime error occurred. In that case, ErrAddr specifies the segment and offset address of the runtime error, and ExitCode equals the error code. (See your *Turbo Pascal Programmer's Guide* for a complete list of runtime error codes and their meanings.)

To better understand how to use ExitCode and ErrorAddr, try the following three experiments.

1. Run Program 13-18. When it asks for an integer value, press 0 and then Enter. The zero value passed to Halt is assigned to ExitCode, which CustomExit then examines. Consequently, CustomExit's **if** statement does not execute, and, therefore, the program silently ends as though it had no custom exit procedure.

2. Run Program 13-18 again, but, this time, type 100. When you press Enter, the program passes 100 to Halt, setting ExitCode to that value. Because no runtime error occurred, ErrorAddr is **nil** and CustomExit's **if** statement executes, displaying the messages:

```
Program halted!
Exit code = 100
```

3. Run Program 13-18 a third time. Type ABC and press Enter. Assigning alphabetic characters to integer variable Num causes a runtime error during the call to Readln, assigning to ErrorAddr the address of the instruction that caused the error and setting ExitCode to 106, Turbo Pascal's error code for an "Invalid numeric format." Sensing that a runtime error has occurred, CustomExit's **if** statement does not execute, instead letting Turbo Pascal display its familiar runtime error message.

As you can see from these experiments, ExitCode and ErrorAddr indicate why the program is ending. Table 13-4 lists the possible combinations of the two values. By testing ExitCode and ErrorAddr, you can write a custom error handler to take different actions before passing control back to DOS or to the parent process that activated the program.

Table 13-4 ExitCode and ErrorAddr combinations.

ExitCode	ErrorAddr	Meaning
= 0	= **nil**	Normal program end
<>0	= **nil**	Halt(N) executed; exitCode = N
<>0	<> **nil**	Runtime error occurred; ExitCode = error code; ErrorAddr= address

Trapping Runtime Errors

Because ExitCode and ErrorAddr are variables, you can change their values inside a custom error handler to trap runtime errors and handle them yourself. For example, suppose your custom exit procedure finds that ErrorAddr is not **nil**, indicating a runtime error has occurred. After taking appropriate action—perhaps displaying the ExitCode value, deallocating memory, closing files, and so on—set ErrorAddr to **nil** and ExitCode to zero, cancelling the runtime error.

To see how this works, run Program 13-19, a modified version of Program 13-18. Type ABC to force a runtime error as you did in the earlier experiment. You should see a message similar to this:

```
A small problem has developed.
Please jot down the following numbers
and call the programmer at 555-1212.

Address = 0:749
Code    = 106

Thank you for your support!
```

This certainly is more friendly than Turbo Pascal's usual runtime error message. The new exit procedure sets ErrorAddr to **nil** and ExitCode to zero, cancelling the runtime error. This way, Turbo Pascal is unaware that an error occurred. If you remove the two assignments in lines 28-29, Turbo Pascal displays its own run-time error message in addition to your custom note.

Lines 26-27 pause the program until you press Enter. Usually, you can do a similar job at any place in a program by inserting a Readln statement with no parameters. However, since a runtime error occurred during a preceding Readln at line 41, Turbo Pascal cancels all future input until the program or runtime system handles the problem. Consequently, when you enter ABC or other nonnumeric input to the program's prompt, the subsequent runtime error causes Turbo Pascal to ignore the Readln statement in the custom exit procedure.

Fixing this potential problem is easy—just reset the standard Input file as Program 13-19 does at line 26. To prove the value of this statement, remove it, recompile, and run. As you'll see, despite the Readln statement at line 27, the program no longer pauses when a runtime error occurs.

Program 13-19: ERR2.PAS

```
 1:  program ErrorShell2;
 2:
 3:  { Demonstrate how to write a custom halt and
 4:    runtime error handler. }
 5:
 6:  var
 7:     SavedExitProc: Pointer;   { Old ExitProc value }
 8:     Num: Integer;             { Test number }
 9:
10:  procedure CustomExit; far;
11:  begin
12:     if ErrorAddr <> nil then
13:     begin
14:       Writeln('-------------------------------------');
15:       Writeln('A small problem has developed.'       );
16:   Writeln('Please jot down the following numbers');
```

continued

477

Program 13-19: continued

```
17:    Writeln('and call the programmer at 555-1212.' );
18:        Writeln;
19:        Writeln('Address = ',
20:           Seg(ErrorAddr^), ':', Ofs(ErrorAddr^));
21:        Writeln('Code    = ', ExitCode);
22:        Writeln;
23:        Writeln('Thank you for your support!'        );
24:        Writeln('-----------------------------------');
25:        Write('Press <Enter> to quit...');
26:        Reset(Input);
27:        Readln;
28:        ErrorAddr := nil;    { Cancel runtime error }
29:        ExitCode := 0
30:      end;
31:      ExitProc := SavedExitProc    { Restore saved ExitProc pointer }
32:    end;
33:
34:  begin
35:      SavedExitProc := ExitProc;    { Save ExitProc pointer }
36:      ExitProc := @CustomExit;      { Install custom error procedure }
37:      Writeln;
38:      Writeln('Welcome to ErrorShell');
39:      Writeln;
40:      Write('Enter an integer value: ');
41:      Readln(Num);
42:      Halt(Num)
43:  end.
```

Units and Exit Procedures

Another use for custom exit procedures is to add automatic shutdown code to units. Each unit that a program uses can insert its own exit procedure into the chain of events that occurs when the host program ends.

This technique opens countless doors for programmers. A memory management unit might deallocate a list of master pointers stored on the heap. A database unit might close temporary files, dumping buffered data to disk. A telecommunications unit could hang up the phone. These actions are guaranteed to occur even if the program halts prematurely due to a runtime error.

Units install custom exit procedures in the same way as Programs 13-17 and 13-18 demonstrate. In this case, though, because multiple units might install several procedures into the exit chain, it's important to understand the order in which the program and various components in the units run.

As you recall from earlier chapters, a unit may have a main body, called the initialization section. The statements in this section run before the first statement in a program that uses the unit. When a program uses multiple units, the initialization sections in all units run in the same order the unit names appear in the program's **uses** declaration. After all initialization sections finish, the program's statements begin running. Then, when the program ends, any exit procedures installed by the units run in the *opposite* order of the unit declarations in **uses**.

An example helps to clarify these actions. Consider a program that begins like this:

```
program DemoExit;
uses UnitA, UnitB, UnitC;
```

The program uses three units, UnitA, UnitB, and UnitC. Figure 13-5 illustrates the order in which the unit initialization sections and exit procedures run. After Turbo Pascal completes its own startup chores, the initialization sections in UnitA, UnitB, and UnitC run (left side of Figure 13-5). Then, when the program ends— either normally, through Halt or Exit, or due to a runtime error—Turbo Pascal calls the custom exit procedures one by one, this time in the opposite order of the unit declarations (right side of Figure 13-5). In this example, Units A and C attach procedures to the exit chain. Unit B does not have an exit procedure and thus performs no actions when the program ends.

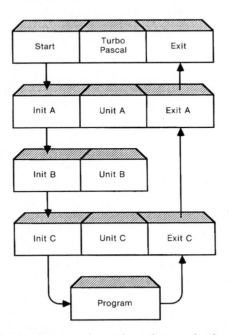

Figure 13-5 Multiple exit procedures in units run in the opposite order of the unit initialization sections.

Programs 13-20 through 13-23 correspond with Figure 13-5. To run the complete example, enter and compile each unit to a TPU (Turbo Pascal Unit) disk file. Next, enter Program 13-23. Compile and run. You should see these lines on display:

```
Inside Unit A initialization
Inside Unit B initialization
Inside Unit C initialization
Welcome to DemoExit
Inside Unit C exit procedure
Inside Unit A exit procedure
```

Note: After running this and similar programs in this chapter that do not pause to let you view their output, if you are using the IDE, press Alt-F5 to see the output screen after the editor display returns. Or, compile to disk and run the programs directly from the DOS prompt.

Several important details contribute to making this multiple-unit example work correctly. Unit A and Unit C save ExitProc in global Pointer variables, declared inside each unit's **implementation** section. You could declare SavedExitProc in the unit interfaces, but because there is no reason for statements outside the unit to use the saved pointers, it's probably best to hide SavedExitProc variables in the implementations where items are visible only to statements inside the units.

The custom exit procedures—ExitA and ExitC in Programs 13-20 and 13-22— are declared *far,* but are not listed in the **interface**. This makes the procedures private to the unit and prevents the host program (or another unit) from calling exit procedures directly, which would be a poor and possibly dangerous practice. As in Programs 13-17, 13-18, and 13-19, the exit procedures restore the saved ExitProc pointers before ending, preserving the exit chain.

Program 13-20: UNITA.PAS

```
 1:  unit UnitA;
 2:
 3:  interface
 4:
 5:  implementation
 6:
 7:  var SavedExitProc: Pointer;   { Old ExitProc pointer }
 8:
 9:  procedure ExitA; far;
10:  begin
```

```
11:  Writeln('Inside Unit A exit procedure');
12:    ExitProc := SavedExitProc
13:  end;
14:
15:  begin
16:    SavedExitProc := ExitProc;
17:    ExitProc := @ExitA;
18:    Writeln('Inside Unit A initialization')
19: end.
```

Program 13-21 UNITB.PAS

```
1: unit UnitB;
2:
3:  interface
4:
5:  implementation
6:
7:  begin
8:    Writeln('Inside Unit B initialization')
9: end.
```

Program 13-22: UNITC.PAS

```
 1: unit UnitC;
 2:
 3:  interface
 4:
 5:  implementation
 6:
 7:  var SavedExitProc: Pointer;  { Old ExitProc pointer }
 8:
 9:  procedure ExitC; far;
10:  begin
11:    Writeln('Inside Unit C exit procedure');
12:    ExitProc := SavedExitProc
13:  end;
14:
15:  begin
16:  SavedExitProc := ExitProc;
```

continued

Program 13-22: continued

```
17:  ExitProc := @ExitC;
18:    Writeln('Inside Unit C initialization')
19:  end.
```

Program 13-23: DEMOEXIT.PAS

```
1:  program DemoExit;
2:  uses Crt, UnitA, UnitB, UnitC;
3:  begin
4:    Writeln('Welcome to DemoExit')
5:  end.
```

Breaking the Exit Chain

A simple experiment demonstrates what happens if you fail to preserve the exit chain when using multiple exit procedures. Remove line 12 from the ExitC procedure in Program 13-22.

When you run the buggy program, UnitC's exit procedure runs but UnitA's does not. This happens because UnitC breaks the exit chain by failing to restore the saved ExitProc pointer; therefore, the pointer to UnitA's exit procedure is lost.

Careful readers may realize that if ExitProc addresses ExitC in UnitC and if ExitC fails to restore the previous ExitProc pointer, an infinite loop is the logical result—ExitC would end, and Turbo Pascal would repeatedly call ExitC as the next exit procedure in the chain.

Turbo Pascal prevents this runaway condition by setting ExitProc to **nil** *before* calling each exit procedure in the chain. When a program ends for one of the reasons listed earlier, a portion of the runtime code linked to the program executes the following loop, expressed here in Pascal-like pseudo-code:

```
while ExitProc <> nil do
begin
  TempProc := ExitProc;
  ExitProc := nil;
  Call procedure at tempProc
end;
Continue with Turbo Pascal's exit chores
```

Because ExitProc is **nil** when UnitC's modified ExitC procedure begins running, failing to restore ExitProc to its saved value ends the runtime loop, causing

Turbo Pascal to perform its own exit chores immediately. Knowing this technical detail about how Turbo Pascal works through the exit chain suggests a way to break the chain explicitly—just leave ExitProc unchanged. (There's no need to set ExitProc to **nil**, although doing so is harmless. ExitProc is already **nil** when a custom exit procedure begins.)

Breaking the exit chain is an advanced technique that you should employ only after careful thought. There are times when the method might come in handy, though. Suppose the first of several exit procedures discovers a fatal disk error in a database system of many related units. To prevent subsequent exit procedures from writing to disk and, therefore, displaying multiple disk error messages for the identical condition, the exit procedure could break the exit chain. The program might use an **if** statement similar to this:

```
{$I-} Close(F); {$I+}
ErrNum := IoResult;
if ErrNum <> O
   then Writeln('Fatal disk error #', ErrNum)
   else ExitProc := SavedExitProc;
```

If the Close on file F fails, the program displays an error message, leaving ExitProc unchanged (equal to **nil**) and, therefore, breaking the exit chain. Otherwise, it restores ExitProc to its saved value, continuing with the next exit procedure in line. This way, disk errors abort the program, preventing other exit procedures from gaining control.

Debugging with Exit Procedures

Program 13-24, SysDebug, shows how to use an exit procedure as a debugging device during program development. Adding SysDebug to a program's **uses** declaration displays several internal Turbo Pascal variables when the program ends. After debugging, remove SysDebug from the **uses** declaration and recompile to create the finished code file.

To use SysDebug, type in and compile Program 13-24 to disk, creating the file SYSDEBUG.TPU. Next, type in Program 13-25, SDTest. When you run SDTest, type 0, 100, or ABC—just as you did in the earlier experiments. In each case, the program ends by displaying a list of variables similar to the sample in Figure 13-6. (The listed items are discussed at various places in this book.) Notice that, because CustomExit does not reset ErrorAddr, Turbo Pascal displays the usual message if a runtime error occurs.

When writing your own units and programs, you can use similar debugging techniques. For example, suppose you have a telecommunications unit named Modem. You could write a separate unit, ModemDebug, to dump Modem's global variables after a test program run. Isolating the debugging statements in a separate unit's exit procedure makes it easy to remove the debugging when you're ready to compile the production program. Later, if problems develop, you can quickly add the debugging statements by compiling after reinserting ModemDebug in the program's **uses** declaration.

Custom exit procedures, while not difficult to create, require careful programming. In your own projects, remember to follow these four critical steps:

1. Save ExitProc in a global Pointer variable.

2. Assign to ExitProc the address of your custom exit procedure.

3. Declare the custom exit procedure with the **far** key word or surround the declaration with {$F+} and {$F–} compiler directives.

4. Inside the custom exit procedure, restore the saved ExitProc pointer from the value saved in step 1.

```
System unit and other global variables
- - - - - - - - - - - - - - - - - - - - - - - - - - - - - - - - - - - -
Memavail    = 463152 bytes
Maxavail    = 463152 bytes
PrefixSeg   = $2973
CSeg        = $298E
DSeg        = $2AC3
SSeg        = $2AED
SPtr        = $3FF4
Heaporg     = $2EED:0000
HeapPtr     = $2EED:0000
FreePtr     = $9000:0000
FreeMin     = 0
HeapError   = nil
ExitProc    = nil
ExitCode    = 106
ErrorAddr   = $0000:009E
RandSeed    = 0
FileMode    = 2
StackLimit  = 0
InoutRec    = 0
Test8087    = 0
Runtime error 106 at 0000:009E.
```

Figure 13-6 Adding sysDebug to a **uses** declaration displays several variables when the program ends, as shown in this sample output from Program 13-25 after typing ABC to force a runtime error.

Program 13-24: SYSDEBUG.PAS

```pascal
 1: unit SysDebug;
 2:
 3: { System globals debugging unit }
 4:
 5: interface
 6:
 7: implementation
 8:
 9: type String15 = string[15];   { WPointer string parameter }
10:
11: var SavedExitProc: Pointer;   { Old ExitProc value }
12:
13:
14: { Display v as a 4-digit hex string }
15: procedure WHex(V: Word);
16: const
17:   Digits: array[0 .. 15] of Char = '0123456789ABCDEF';
18: begin
19:   Write(Digits[Hi(V) div 16],
20:         Digits[Hi(V) mod 16],
21:         Digits[Lo(V) div 16],
22:         Digits[Lo(V) mod 16] )
23: end;
24:
25:
26: { Display pointer value in 0000:0000 format }
27: procedure WPointer(Description: String15; P: Pointer);
28: begin
29:   Write(Description);
30:   if P = nil then Write('nil') else
31:   begin
32:     Write('$');
33:     WHex(Seg(P^));
34:     Write(':');
35:     WHex(Ofs(P^))
36:   end;
37:   Writeln
38: end;
39:
40:
```

continued

Program 13-24: continued

```
41: { Display word value in 0000 hex format }
42: procedure WWord(Description: String15; W: Word);
43: begin
44:    Write(Description, '$');
45:    WHex(W);
46:    Writeln
47: end;
48:
49:
50: { Display system global variables at exit }
51:
52: procedure CustomExit; far;
53:
54: begin
55:    Writeln;
56:    Writeln( 'System unit and other global variables');
57:    Writeln( '------------------------------------');
58:    Writeln( 'Memavail   = ', Memavail, ' bytes');
59:    Writeln( 'Maxavail   = ', Maxavail, ' bytes');
60:    WWord(   'PrefixSeg  = ', PrefixSeg );
61:    WWord(   'CSeg       = ', CSeg       );
62:    WWord(   'DSeg       = ', DSeg       );
63:    WWord(   'SSeg       = ', SSeg       );
64:    WWord(   'SPtr       = ', SPtr       );
65:    WPointer('HeapOrg    = ', HeapOrg    );
66:    WPointer('HeapPtr    = ', HeapPtr    );
67:    WPointer('HeapEnd    = ', HeapEnd    );
68:    WPointer('FreeList   = ', FreeList   );
69:    WPointer('HeapError  = ', HeapError );
70:    WPointer('ExitProc   = ', ExitProc   );
71:    Writeln( 'ExitCode   = ', ExitCode   );
72:    WPointer('ErrorAddr  = ', ErrorAddr );
73:    Writeln( 'RandSeed   = ', RandSeed   );
74:    Writeln( 'FileMode   = ', FileMode   );
75:    Writeln( 'StackLimit = ', StackLimit);
76:    Writeln( 'InOutRes   = ', InOutRes   );
77:    Writeln( 'Test8087   = ', Test8087   );
78:
79:    ExitProc := SavedExitProc    { Restore saved ExitProc pointer }
80:
81: end;
```

```
82:
83:
84:  begin
85:      SavedExitProc := ExitProc;    { Save ExitProc pointer }
86:      ExitProc := @CustomExit       { Install custom exit procedure }
87: end.
```

Program 13-25: SDTEST.PAS

```
 1: program SDTest;
 2:
 3:  { Test SysDebug unit }
 4:
 5:  uses SysDebug;
 6:
 7:  var  Num: Integer;
 8:
 9:  begin
10:    Writeln('Welcome to SysDebug unit test');
11:    Writeln;
12:    Write('Type an exit code : ');
13:    Readln(Num);
14:    Halt(Num)
15:  end.
```

Procedure Types

The original Pascal language as designed by Niklaus Wirth (see Bibliography) allowed procedure and function parameters to refer to other procedures and functions. With this ability, programs can pass subroutines to procedures and functions the same way they pass variables of other types. Turbo Pascal 5.0 and later versions now have a similar feature called *procedure types.*

A procedure type defines the format, but not the actual code, of a procedure or function. In the case of a function, a procedure type also defines the type of data that the function returns. Just as with real procedures and functions, procedure types may also declare value and variable parameters. For example, a procedure that takes a string parameter S might be defined as a procedure type this way:

```
type
  DisplayProc = procedure(S: string);
```

DisplayProc defines a procedure type with a single string parameter S. Notice that unlike real procedures and functions, a procedure-type declaration does not have a naming identifier. Procedure types might also be parameterless:

```
type
  AnyProc = procedure;
```

Procedure-type function declarations are similar to those for procedures but use the **function** key word and return any of the usual function data types:

```
type
  RealFunc = function(N: Real): Real;
  IntegerFunc = function(var A, B, C: Integer): Integer;
  StringFunc = function: string;
```

The procedure-type functions RealFunc and IntegerFunc declare value and variable parameters. StringFunc is parameterless. As with procedure-type procedures, the function definitions do not have naming identifiers. Procedure-type functions may return the same kinds of values that regular functions return, but with one exception: Function results may not be other procedure data types.

Using Procedure Types

After declaring procedure types, you can declare *procedure variables* of those types as shown here:

```
var
  DisplayF: DisplayProc;
  RealF: RealFunc;
  StringF: StringFunc;
```

The three procedure variables, DisplayF, RealF, and StringF, are actually 32-bit pointers. That doesn't mean you have to manipulate them with pointer routines like New and Dispose—Turbo Pascal understands that procedure variables address procedures and functions elsewhere in the program. Those procedures and functions must conform to the numbers and types of parameters and function result types defined earlier by the procedure types:

```
procedure DoubleSpace(S: string); far;
begin
  Writeln;
  Writeln(S)
end;

function Cube(N: Real): Real; far;
begin
  Cube := N * N * N
end;
```

```
function Copyright: string; far;
begin
  Copyright := '(C) 1991 by Duck Hardware'
end;
```

The procedures and functions must be compiled with **far** keywords (or with the {$F+} directive in effect) because, as just explained, procedure variables that will address these routines are actually 32-bit *far* pointers with segment and offset parts. Like all pointers, procedure-type variables are not initialized when the program runs. You must perform this step by assigning the addresses of actual procedures and functions to the pointer variables:

```
DisplayF := DoubleSpace;
RealF := Cube;
StringF := Copyright;
```

That completes the setup phase of writing programs with procedure types and variables. To use the procedures and functions addressed by the procedure variables, DisplayF, RealF, and StringF, insert a variable's identifier at any place where the procedure or function identifier normally could go. For example, the following three statements all display the copyright string assigned to the Copyright function:

```
DisplayF(Copyright);
DoubleSpace(StringF);
DisplayF(StringF);
```

The first line calls procedure DoubleSpace via the procedure variable DisplayF, passing as a parameter the result of Copyright, which returns a string data type. The second line does the same, this time calling DoubleSpace directly, but passing StringF—the procedure-type variable that addresses the Copyright function. The third line performs the identical action but uses only procedure-type variables. The three different-looking but similar-acting examples demonstrate that procedure and function identifiers are fully interchangeable with procedure-type variables.

A Procedure-Type Example

Procedure types let you design programs with "hooks," to which you can assign the addresses of custom routines. A good example where this design method is useful is a program that plots the result of a numeric function. The main portion of the program sets up the display, draws X- and Y-axis lines, and plots the function as a graph.

Without procedure types, changing the plotted function requires you to rewrite the original source code. Using procedure types to pass the address of a custom function to the plot package simplifies the job—especially if the bulk of the code is precompiled as a separate unit.

Program 13-26 demonstrates how this works. Save the program as PLOTU.PAS and compile to PLOTU.TPU. As the listing shows, the unit has a simple **interface** section. Line 6 declares the procedure type PlotFunction:

```
PlotFunction = function(X: Integer): Real;
```

Line 8 uses this type in a normal procedure declaration, with a single parameter of type PlotFunction:

```
procedure PlotGraph(Pf: PlotFunction);
```

With this design, plotting new functions is a simple matter of writing the function code—which must conform to the PlotFunction data type—and passing the function name to PlotGraph. Line 70 calls the assigned function to calculate the Y coordinate for every possible X value.

An example host program that uses PlotU follows the listing for Program 13-26.

Program 13-26: PLOTU.PAS

```
 1:  unit PlotU;
 2:
 3:  interface
 4:
 5:  type
 6:     PlotFunction = function(X: Integer): Real;
 7:
 8:  procedure PlotGraph(Pf: PlotFunction);
 9:
10:
11:  implementation
12:
13:  uses
14:     Crt, Graph;
15:
16:  var
17:     GraphDriver, GraphMode: Integer;    { Graph unit variables }
18:     XMax, YMax, XMin, YMin: Integer;    { X,Y coordinate limits }
19:     XCenter, YCenter: Integer;          { Center coordinate }
20:     Scale: Integer;                     { Miscellaneous }
```

```
21:
22:  procedure DisplayAxes;
23:  { Draw X and Y axes lines with "tick" marks }
24:  var X, Y, Xf, Yf, Xd, Yd: Integer;     { See comments below }
25:  begin
26:    SetColor(LightBlue);
27:    SetLineStyle(DottedLn, 0, NormWidth);
28:    Line(XCenter, YMin, XCenter, YMax);   { Draw X axis }
29:    Line(XMin, YCenter, XMax, YCenter);   { Draw Y axis }
30:    SetColor(LightGray);
31:    SetLineStyle(SolidLn, 0, NormWidth);
32:    Xf := GetMaxX div 20;    { Tick mark at every Xf point }
33:    Xd := Xf div 3;          { Length of horizontal tick marks }
34:    Yf := GetMaxY div 20;    { Tick mark at every Yf point }
35:    Yd := Yf div 3;          { Length of vertical tick marks }
36:    for X := XMin to XMax do
37:      if (X mod Xf) = 0
38:        then Line(X, YCenter - Yd, X, YCenter + Yd);
39:    for Y := YMin to YMax do
40:      if (Y mod Yf) = 0
41:        then Line(YCenter - Xd, Y, YCenter + Xd, Y)
42:  end;
43:
44:  procedure Initialize;
45:  { Miscellaneous initializations }
46:  begin
47:    XMax := GetMaxX div 2;
48:    YMax := GetMaxY div 2;
49:    XMin := -XMax;
50:    YMin := -YMax;
51:    XCenter := 0;
52:    YCenter := 0;
53:    Scale := GetMaxX div 8;
54:    SetViewPort(XMax, YMax, GetMaxX, GetMaxY, ClipOff)
55:  end;
56:
57:  procedure YPlot(X: Integer; Y: Real);
58:  { Plot point at X,Y }
59:  begin
60:    PutPixel(X, Round(Y * Scale), White)
61:  end;
```

continued

Program 13-26: PLOTU.PAS

```
62:
63:  procedure PlotGraph(Pf: PlotFunction);
64:  { Display plot of user's function }
65:  var X: Integer;
66:  begin
67:    Initialize;
68:    DisplayAxes;
69:    for X := XMin to XMax do
70:      YPlot(X, Pf(X));
71:    repeat until Keypressed;
72:    CloseGraph
73:  end;
74:
75:  begin
76:    GraphDriver := Detect;
77:    InitGraph(GraphDriver, GraphMode, '');
78:    if GraphResult <> GrOk then
79:    begin
80:      Writeln('Error initializing graphics');
81:      Halt(1)
82:    end
83:  end.
```

Writing PlotU Host Programs

Program 13-27 demonstrates how to write a host program that calls PlotGraph in the PlotU unit (Program 13-26). Save as PLOT.PAS and compile. Lines 10-13 contain the function to plot—compiled with the required **far** key word. Notice that this function has the format required by the PlotFunction procedure—type definition (Program 13-26, line 8).

The entire main program reduces to a single statement at line 16, which calls the PlotGraph, passing the address of the function to plot. There's no need to modify the PlotU package just to plot a different mathematical function. To demonstrate how this works, change Cos in line 12 to Sin, or invent your own functions. Then, recompile PLOT.PAS and you're done.

Program 13-27: PLOT.PAS

```
 1:   program Plot;
 2:
 3:   uses PlotU;
 4:
 5:   function Radians(Angle: Integer): Real;
 6:   begin
 7:     Radians := Angle * Pi / 180.0
 8:   end;
 9:
10:   function F(X: Integer): Real; far;
11:   begin
12:     F := Cos(Radians(X))
13:   end;
14:
15:   begin
16:     PlotGraph(F)
17:   end.
```

Procedure-Type Complications

Procedure types are useful, especially when designing units such as PLOTU with hooks to which you can attach your own custom routines. But when using procedure types, you should be aware of a few subtle complications the technique introduces.

Procedures and functions addressed by procedure variables must be of your own design—for example, you can't assign the addresses of standard routines such as Writeln to procedure variables. The procedures and functions may not nest inside other routines—they must be at the global program level. Procedure variables also may not address interrupt handlers or InLine procedures and functions (see Chapter 14).

Another complication involves assignments. As explained earlier, to initialize a procedure variable, you must assign the name of an actual procedure or function to the variable:

```
StringF := Copyright;
```

That assigns the *address* of function Copyright to the StringF procedure variable. Compare this with the more traditional assignment of a function to a variable, for example, a string named S:

```
S := Copyright;
```

That assignment executes function Copyright. The function's return value is a string, which is assigned to string variable S. The difference between the two assignments is important. In the first example, Copyright does not run. In the second, it does. The dissimilar results are hidden by the similar looking statements.

Usually, Turbo Pascal generates the proper code for such assignments, so there's little need for concern. But, the compiler may not understand your intentions all the time. Suppose the program needs to call a Reinitialize procedure if the StringF procedure variable is not equal to the address of Copyright:

```
if StringF <> Copyright     { ??? }
   then ReInitialize;
```

That statement may not work correctly. Processing the expression, Turbo Pascal assumes that it should generate function calls to StringF and to Copyright, and then compare the returned strings. This makes sense—both identifiers address string functions; therefore, their results are compatible in expressions. But, we want to compare the function *addresses,* not the function *results.* The solution is to use the @ symbol to force Turbo Pascal to compare addresses:

```
if @StringF <> @Copyright
   then ReInitialize;
```

With @ signs, the *address value* of the procedure variable StringF is compared with the *address* of the Copyright function. Now the expression works correctly.

Be aware of the difference between a procedure variable's address value, and the address of a procedure. As you know, the @ operator returns the address of an identifier. But when applied to a procedure variable, @ returns the variable's *value,* which, as you know, is actually a pointer. If you need to access the address where the procedure variable is stored in memory, you must use a double @@ sign. In other words, to assign the address of the variable StringF to a pointer P, you have to write:

```
P := @@StringF;  { Assign address of StringF to P }
```

This differs from the usual method for taking the addresses of common variables, such as an integer I, which requires only a single @ sign:

```
P := @I;  { Assign address of I to P }
```

Procedure-Type Variable Constants

Variable (typed) constants may refer to procedures or functions, a technique that's useful for preparing default subroutines that other parts of a program can execute via pointers. To change the actions of such a program, all you need to do is change the addresses of the target routines—a job that even the program itself could accomplish.

The format of a procedure-type constant is similar to any other variable constant declaration. Because that constant refers to a procedure or function, that routine must come *before* the constant's declaration. Here's a sample:

```
type
  WelcomeProc = procedure;

procedure PWelcome; far;
begin
  Writeln('Welcome to My Program 1.0!')
end;

const
  Welcome: WelcomeProc = PWelcome;

begin
  Welcome;
  Write('Press <Enter> to end...');
  Readln
end.
```

The program begins by associating type WelcomeProc with a plain procedure. Next comes a procedure in that same form, using the **far** key word, equivalent to surrounding the declaration with {$F+} and {$F−}. There's nothing special about the procedure. The only rule is that it must be **far**.

With the WelcomeProc procedure type and PWelcome procedure in place, a **const** declaration creates a variable constant named Welcome of type WelcomeProc. To that constant the program assigns PWelcome, in effect causing Welcome to *point* to the procedure's code. The program can then call PWelcome either directly or by using the variable constant Welcome as shown in the main block's first line.

Dealing with Heap Errors

When using New or GetMem to allocate memory for variables on the heap, if enough memory is not available, the program halts with the unfriendly message:

```
Runtime error 203: Heap overflow error.
```

To prevent programs from ending when out of memory, you can install your own heap error function, as Program 13-28 demonstrates. Function HeapErrorTrap (lines 8-11) takes a Word parameter size and returns type Integer. The function must be declared with the **far** key word or the compiler directive {$F+} because it will be called from a different code segment.

Line 18 assigns the address of HeapErrorTrap to the System unit HeapError variable. This informs System to call the custom function instead of halting if New or GetMem cannot handle a request to allocate memory. When this happens, parameter Size equals the number of requested bytes. The custom heap error function can then return one of three values listed in Table 13-5. Remove line 18 and run the program to see the effect of not using a custom heap error handler.

Table 13-5 Heap error function values.

Value	Action
0	Halt program with runtime error
1	Have New and GetMem return **nil**
2	Retry same New or GetMem

Usually, return 1 to force New and GetMem to return a **nil** pointer instead of halting the program. You can test for this condition, as the **repeat** loop demonstrates in Program 13-28, lines 19-21. If the custom heap error handler returns 2, Turbo Pascal retries the New or GetMem statement that caused the failure. If you write programming to compact the heap after an out-of-memory failure—no small task, which we'll have to leave unimplemented here—then you could return 2 to retry memory allocation requests. Finally, you could return 0, which forces a runtime error to occur, the default condition in the absence of a custom heap error handler.

Program 13-28: HEAPOF.PAS

```
 1:  program HeapOfTrouble;
 2:  type
 3:    Atype = array[1 .. 10000] of Real;
 4:  var
 5:    P: ^Atype;
 6:
 7:
 8:  function HeapErrorTrap(Size: Word): Integer; far;
 9:  begin
10:    HeapErrorTrap := 1    { Forces New, GetMem to return nil }
11:  end;
12:
13:
14:  begin
15:    Writeln;
16:    Writeln('Memory at start  = ', Memavail);
17:    Writeln('Size of variable = ', Sizeof(Atype));
18:    HeapError := @HeapErrorTrap;
19:    repeat
20:      New(P)
21:    until P = nil;
```

```
22:  Writeln('Memory at end  = ', Memavail);
23:    Write('Press <Enter> to end...');
24:    Readln
25:  end.
```

Dealing with the Stack

As you learned in Chapter 7, New and GetMem allocate memory space for variables on the heap. Local variables in procedures and functions are created on the stack when a statement calls the routines that declare the variables. If there isn't enough memory on the stack to hold the variables, the program halts with:

```
Runtime error 202: Stack overflow error.
```

Unlike the heap overflow error discussed in the previous section, there is no way to recover from a stack overflow—it's already too late by the time you discover the problem. The only cure is prevention, using the {$M} compiler directive to change the amount of stack space reserved for your program.

To detect stack overflow errors, Turbo Pascal inserts code to test the stack and heap at the start of each procedure and function. These checks take only a small amount of time—but they do take *some* time. To squeeze every ounce of power out of a program, you can turn off stack error checking by inserting this compiler directive at the start of your program:

```
{$S-}   { Turn off stack error checks }
```

Turning off stack error checking this way is extremely dangerous. If there is not enough stack space to hold local variables when you call procedures and functions, your program will ignore this condition and merrily overwrite whatever other variables or code are in its way. The usual result is a system crash, erased disk files, data destruction, and a loss of hair—yours. Never turn off stack error checking unless you are 100% positive that a stack overflow cannot occur.

Other Memory Concerns

The System unit defines several pointers that keep track of allocated and free memory on the heap. You can examine (and possibly change) the values of these pointers to investigate and modify the heap's parameters.

Appendix B diagrams the heap, and explains more about how the heap manager works. Refer to that diagram as you read the following descriptions of the heap manager's pointers.

HeapOrg points to the start of the heap, immediately above the stack and any overlay buffer (see "Advanced Overlay Management" later in this chapter.)

HeapPtr points to the current top of the heap, which moves to higher addresses each time you call New and GetMem. That is, unless those routines find an unused block of memory within the current region defined by HeapOrg and HeapPtr.

HeapEnd points to the end of the heap, usually at the address of the last available byte in a PC's conventional 640K of RAM.

FreeList points to the first of any free memory blocks previously disposed. The heap manager links all such memory blocks (and also combines adjacent blocks) to make disposed memory available for future calls to New and GetMem. If FreeList equals HeapPtr, no free blocks are available.

FreeZero is a dummy pointer that is always **nil**. In memory, FreeZero follows FreeList, creating a two-pointer structure with the same format as a TFreeRec free-list record used to manage blocks of available heap memory. (TFreeRec is described next). To simplify some of the low-level programming for combining multiple free blocks, the heap manager addresses FreeList and FreeZero as though this pair of pointers formed a TFreeRec record in which FreeList identifies the next free block and FreeZero represents the size of that block. Since FreeZero is always **nil** (represented as the address value 0000:0000), this dummy block's size is also always 0. FreeZero has no practical use in applications; it's strictly for the heap manager's private consumption.

The heap manager rounds the size of every newly allocated block up to the next multiple of 8, neatly aligning memory blocks in memory and also guaranteeing that at least eight bytes will be available in every block. When a program disposes a memory block, the heap manager links that block onto the free list, configuring the first eight bytes of the block to conform with these pointer and record types:

```
PFreeRec = ^TFreeRec;
TFreeRec = record
  Next: PFreeRec;
  Size: Pointer
end;
```

TFreeRec's Next field addresses the next free block on the disposed-memory list. Although TFreeRec declares the Size field as a Pointer, this field is actually a special 32-bit value with the high-order word equal to the number of 16-byte *paragraphs* and the low-order word equal to the number of additional bytes in every free block. Multiplying the high-order word by 16 and adding to that product the low-order word computes the size of a free block in bytes.

Even though every disposed block begins with a TFreeRec header, that space is not wasted when the block is in use. All bytes in allocated blocks are available to your program. The heap manager adds the TFreeRec linkage information only for disposed blocks stored on the free list.

> **Note:** Since the heap manager rounds the size of every allocated block up to the next multiple of 8, small variables on the heap can waste RAM. To avoid such waste, do not store small variables on the heap. Or, if you do need to create small dynamic variables, allocate heap memory for an array of those values rather than just one at a time. For example, to store six integers on the heap, it's far more efficient to allocate space for an **array** [0 .. 5] **of** Integer than it is to allocate space individually for six two-byte Integers. The array occupies 16 bytes (the next highest multiple of 8 after 12 (6 * 2). The individual integers would each occupy eight bytes (the smallest possible heap block), using 48 bytes and wasting 36.

Passing Command-Line Parameters

When you compile a program to a disk EXE file, you execute the program by typing its name. At the same time, you can type extra commands or other parameters following the program name. For example, if you have the program, SORT, and you want to sort a text file, NAMES.TXT you might type:

```
A>sort names.txt
```

Program 13-29 demonstrates how a program picks up extra parameters like NAMES.TXT from the command line. The program creates one long text file out of a number of other files. You can use it to combine several small programs into a single file, perhaps for uploading to a bulletin board or time-sharing network.

If you type no parameters, the program prints out instructions. Line 58 senses how many parameters there are by testing the built-in function, ParamCount. If there are no parameters, the **if** statement calls procedure Instruct; otherwise, it calls Process. To print instructions, compile the program to an EXE file and run from DOS by typing COMBINE.

To give parameters to the program, enter the name of the output file followed by as many other text files as you want to combine. If you have files named SUB1.PAS and SUB2.PAS, the following combines them into a single file, SUBS.PAS:

```
C>combine subs.pas sub1.pas sub2.pas
```

The program reads your parameters with procedure ParamStr, as shown in lines 31 and 45. ParamStr takes an integer value indicating which parameter you want. To display the second parameter, you could use the Writeln statement:

```
Writeln(ParamStr(2));
```

If you're running DOS 3.0 or a later version, you can find out the program's path name by examining ParamStr(0). You can then use Dos unit routines to store the path to the program's location, giving you a way to read and write miscellaneous program files there even if people change directories:

```
PathName := FExpand(ParamStr(0));
Writeln('Program name = ', PathName);
FSplit(PathName, Dir, Name, Ext);
Writeln('Directory = ', Dir);
```

While debugging a program that recognizes parameters, use the IDE's *Run:Parameters* command to simulate parameter passing. This avoids compiling to an EXE file, exiting the IDE, and running your program just to test minor corrections.

Program 13-29: COMBINE.PAS

```
 1:   program Combine;
 2:   uses Crt;
 3:
 4:   procedure Instruct;
 5:   begin
 6:     Writeln;
 7:     Writeln('Combine <output> <input1> <input2> ... <inputn>');
 8:     Writeln; Writeln('  A>combine new.txt texta.pas textb.pas');
 9:     Writeln;
10:     Writeln('The above combines TextA.Pas and TextB.Pas into a new');
11:     Writeln('file, New.Txt. If New.Txt exists, you are asked for');
12:     Writeln('permission to overwrite it.');
13:     Writeln
14:   end;
15:
16:   function FileExists(var F: Text): Boolean;
17:   begin
18:   {$I-} Reset(F); Close(F); {$I+}
19:     FileExists := (IoResult = 0)
20:   end;
21:
22:   procedure Process;
23:   var
24:     Ch       : Char;
25:     Fname    : string[64];
26:     I        : Integer;
27:     Infile,
```

```
28:    OutFile: Text;
29:    S: string[132];
30:  begin
31:    Fname := ParamStr(1);
32:    if Length(Fname) > 0 then
33:    begin
34:      Assign(OutFile, Fname);
35:      if FileExists(OutFile) then
36:      begin
37:        Write(Fname, ' exists.  Overwrite it? ');
38:        Ch := ReadKey;
39:        Writeln(Ch);
40:        if Upcase(Ch) <> 'Y' then Halt
41:      end;
42:      Rewrite(OutFile);
43:      for I := 2 to ParamCount do
44:      begin
45:        Fname := ParamStr(I);
46:        Assign(InFile, Fname); Reset(Infile);
47:        while not Eof(InFile) do
48:        begin
49:          Readln(Infile, S); Writeln(OutFile, S)
50:        end;
51:        Close(Infile)
52:      end;
53:      Close(OutFile)
54:    end
55:  end;
56:
57:  begin
58:    if ParamCount <= 0 then Instruct else Process
59:  end.
```

Inside a File Variable

All file variables contain hidden details that Turbo Pascal normally reserves for its own use. With typecasting and the help of the Dos unit FileRec data type, you can access these details. FileRec is defined as:

```
FileRec = record
  Handle: Word;
  Mode: Word;
  RecSize: Word;
  Private: array[1 .. 26] of Byte;
  UserData: array[1 .. 16] of Byte;
  Name: array[0 .. 79] of Char
end;
```

To use this record, insert a **uses** Dos; declaration in your program. Then, typecast any file variable to type FileRec. For example, Program 13-30 displays the record size for a file of type Real.

The statements before the Writeln in line 7 assign a name and open the file variable before accessing FileRec fields. The variable typecast in line 7 shows how to gain access to the normally hidden fields inside a file variable. Here, the program simply displays the file's record size.

Program 13-30: SHOWFILE.PAS

```
 1:  program ShowFileSize;
 2:  uses Dos;
 3:  var F: file of Real;
 4:  begin
 5:    Assign(F, 'TEST.$$$');  { Must open file first }
 6:    Rewrite(F);
 7:    Writeln('Record size = ', FileRec(F).RecSize);
 8:    Close(F);
 9:    Erase(F);
10:    Readln
11:  end.
```

You can use the same method to access other fields, too. Handle is the handle or reference value that DOS returns for file I/O operations. Turbo Pascal calls these DOS routines and stores the DOS handle in the Handle field. The Mode field can be one of the values from Table 13-3. The RecSize field equals the size of file data elements in bytes.

Although Turbo Pascal does not seem to use the Private array, don't store any values here. Future compiler releases may use this field. You may store any data you want in the 16-byte UserData array, though. If you need more than 16 bytes, store a pointer in UserData to your other variables.

The final field, Name, stores the file name originally passed to Assign. This field is an ASCIIZ string ending in a null character (ASCII 0), not a Pascal string data type.

Advanced Overlay Management

Turbo Pascal 5.5 and 6.0 add several advanced features to the Overlay unit, first introduced in version 5.0. Most of the time, the information in Chapter 10 is all you need to write overlay programs—overlays are fully compatible in both compiler versions. If you're developing commercial software, though, you'll want to be sure that overlays are working at top efficiency by carefully considering the options discussed here.

Overlay Initializations

As you know, units may have an initialization section, comparable to a program's main block. The initialization code appears between **begin** and **end** at the end of the unit text:

```
unit AnyUnit;
interface
  { Public declarations }
implementation
  { Private declarations }
begin
  { Perform unit initializations }
end.
```

In a host program that **uses** AnyUnit, unit initialization statements run before the host's first statement executes, which leads to sticky problems when the units are overlays. As explained in Chapter 10, you must call OverInit to initialize the Overlay unit *before* any overlays can be loaded. But, the overlays must be loaded in order to execute their initialization sections before the program has a chance to call OverInit.

One way to resolve this confusion, and ensure that overlay initializations perform in the correct order at the right times, is to call OverInit from the initialization section of another unit and then list that unit in a **uses** declaration ahead of all overlays that have their own initialization blocks. Program 13-31 lists a sample unit that you can use for this purpose.

To use the unit, change PROGNAME.OVR in line 10 to the name of your program's overlay file. Compile the unit to OVRSTART.TPU and include a **uses** declaration in your main program similar to this:

```
uses Overlay, Crt, OvrStartup, OvrUnitA, OvrUnitB, OvrUnitC;

{$O OvrUnitA}
{$O OvrUnitB}
{$O OvrUnitC}
```

In this example, overlay units OvrUnitA, OvrUnitB, and OvrUnitC have initialization sections that must run ahead of the main program's first statement. Inserting the OvrStartup unit ahead of the overlays calls OvrInit (line 10), allowing the overlays to be loaded into memory before executing their initialization code.

Program 13-31: OVRSTART.PAS

```
 1:  unit OvrStartup;
 2:
 3:  interface
 4:
 5:  implementation
 6:
 7:  uses Overlay;
 8:
 9:  begin
10:    OvrInit('PROGNAME.OVR');
11:    if OvrResult <> OvrOk then
12:    begin
13:      Writeln('Overlay error');
14:      Halt(1)
15:    end;
16:    OvrInitEMS
17:  end.
```

Overlay Unit Complications

Although the previous section solves the problem of having to call OvrInit before executing overlay initialization sections, there are two good reasons to avoid such situations:

- Before running the overlay initialization code, the overlay units must be loaded from disk. With many units, this can slow program startup to a crawl.

- Even though the initialization sections run only once, the initialization code is loaded into memory along with the rest of the unit, wasting RAM and time.

For these reasons, some programmers prefer to stuff initialization statements into yet another overlay unit and eliminate initialization sections from other overlays. When combined with the OvrStartup unit (Program 13-31), this reduces startup chores to loading a single overlay and running all initializations.

Optimizing the Overlay Buffer

As Chapter 10 explains, you can call OvrGetBuf to find out the size of the overlay buffer, the memory area where overlay units are stored. OvrSetBuf can increase the buffer size to allow multiple units to fit together in this memory space, improving performance by reducing disk reads. (Remember, though, if enough EMS RAM is available, there's no advantage to increasing the overlay buffer size.)

Turbo Pascal 5.5 and 6.0 manage the overlay buffer in an effort to keep the most frequently used code in memory for the longest time. In most programs, the new algorithm—called the *probation-reprieve* method—can reduce the number of times overlays are loaded from disk, often without having to increase the overlay buffer size.

The method works by putting units "on probation" when the unit's code falls within an adjustable *probation area,* usually equal to about a third of the total overlay buffer space. During this time, if any statements call the unit's procedures or functions, when it comes time to load a new overlay into the buffer, the overlay loader "reprieves" the unit that was placed on probation. Instead of moving that unit out to make room in the buffer, the loader releases a less frequently used unit. The reprieved unit then stays in the buffer until the next time more space is needed. As a result, units that work harder tend to stay in RAM longer—and the program runs faster.

Enabling Probation-Reprieve

Switching on the probation-reprieve method is easy—just set the probation area size, normally 0 (off), to any positive value. If you don't do this, the version 5.5 and 6.0 overlay memory managers work as they do in Turbo Pascal 5.0. To enable probation-reprieve buffer management, call OvrSetRetry, passing a value somewhere between one half and a third the size of the full overlay buffer:

```
OvrInit('PROGNAME.OVR');
if OvrResult <> OvrOk then Halt(1);
OvrSetBuf(sizeOfBuffer);
OvrSetRetry(sizeOfBuffer div 3);
```

Usually, you'll call OvrSetBuf before OvrSetRetry to increase the overlay buffer size, in this example, using a previously declared constant sizeOfBuffer. To find out the current probation-area size, call OvrGetRetry:

```
Writeln('Probation area size = ', OvrGetRetry);
```

If you don't like the idea of setting a fixed buffer size, you can increase the default buffer size by adding to OvrGetBuf. To set the probation area to a third of the adjusted size, you can use the statements

```
OvrSetBuf(OvrGetBuf * 2);      { Double default buffer size }
OvrSetRetry(OvrGetBuf div 3); { Set probation area }
```

Calculating the best probation-area size is not always easy. Although Borland recommends a size of a third to one half of the total buffer space, each set of overlays has a unique configuration that results in the most code in memory for the longest times.

To find the best values for your programs, use Turbo Debugger (or the built-in debugger) to monitor two Overlay unit variables, OvrLoadCount and OvrTrapCount. Or, just display the two values in Writeln statements. The variables collect statistics that can help you to pick the best probation-area size:

- OvrLoadCount measures the number of times units are loaded from disk. Aim for the lowest possible value, indicating that units are staying in memory longer. You can usually reduce a high OvrLoadCount by increasing the overlay buffer size with OvrSetBuf.

- OvrTrapCount counts two items: the number of times units are loaded from disk, and the number of times units are accessed while on probation. Each count represents one interception by the Overlay manager of a call to a unit that is either not in Memory or is on probation. If OvrTrapCount increases at nearly the same rate as OvrLoadCount, then the probation-reprieve scheme is not working well—try increasing the probation-area size by calling OvrSetRetry. You might also need a larger overlay buffer. If OvrTrapCount increases at a greater rate than OvrLoadCount, then more units are being reprieved—a good sign that you're headed in the right direction. If OvrTrapCount increases while OvrLoadCount advances slowly or not at all, you've probably hit the ideal configuration. You might even try *reducing* the buffer and probation sizes to minimize memory use.

How the Probation-Reprieve Method Works

Fine-tuning the overlay buffer for peak performance requires a good understanding of how the Overlay unit manages memory. For test purposes, assume there are three overlay units of identical size—A, B, and C—plus a main program that loads the overlays in this order:

```
A B A C A B B C B A B
```

Figures 13-7 through 13-9 show how the size of the overlay buffer and the amount of probation space affect the performance of this test program. (I prepared the diagrams by hand while examining the overlay buffer contents with a program not listed here. The figures are snapshots of the actual overlay buffer in memory.) The vertical blocks (numbered below and to the left) represent the overlay buffer. The shaded areas represent unused memory. Above the buffers are the values of

OvrTrapCount listed on top of OvrLoadCount for each step. Uppercase letters along the bottom show the progression of calls to overlay routines.

The first test (see Figure 13-7) uses the default buffer size, which is just a little larger than the largest unit. The buffer is always aligned to offsets 0000 at 16-byte "paragraphs" in memory; so there's usually a little waste at the end. The test shows that ten disk reads are required for 11 calls to overlay routines. Obviously, because the buffer can hold only one overlay at a time, the overlay loader has to release the buffer space to load another unit. The only savings in this test comes at step 7 (numbered at the bottom of the bar), which calls a routine in unit B. Because B is already in the buffer from step 6, no disk read occurs (shown by the dashes above step number 7).

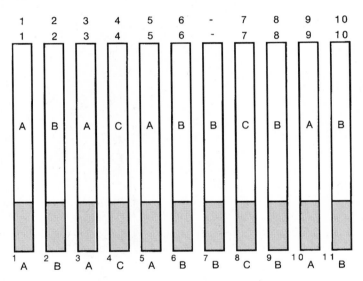

Figure 13-7 Overlay test using the default buffer size.

The next test doubles the overlay buffer size, but does not switch on probation-reprieve memory management (see Figure 13-8). Now, two overlays can fit into the buffer together, which should reduce disk reads.

At step 1, unit A is loaded, after which the program calls a routine in B at step 2. Because there's plenty of unused space available, the overlay loader places B after A. As a result, step 3 does not require a disk read—A is already in the buffer. Likewise, step 9 saves another disk read because B is already in the buffer from as far back as step 6.

Only eight disk reads are now required for the 11 steps, a savings of two disk operations from the previous default-buffer test. Increasing the buffer size decreases OvrLoadCount (the bottom of the two numbers on top of the bars). But, OvrTrapCount still rises at the same rate as OvrLoadCount, indicating that further optimizations are possible.

If you examine Figure 13-8 closely, you'll see another indication that overlay buffer management isn't working as well as it could. Step 4 loads unit C, replacing unit A in the buffer. Step 5 then calls A, forcing the overlay loader to reload A, thus wasting time. It would have been better to release B at step 4, not A.

Figure 13-9 shows the final test, optimized with probation-reprieve memory management, which can detect conditions that may cause inefficient overlays. The buffer size is the same as in the previous test, but the probation area is set to a third of the total buffer. For the purposes of deciding which overlays to place on probation, the overlay loader considers the total buffer to be circular. The probation area includes the free space in the buffer plus extra space extending in the diagrams down and around to the top. For example, at step 1, A is in the probation area. At step 8, overlay B is on probation.

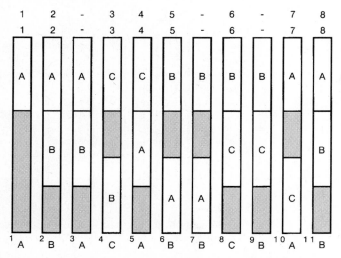

Figure 13-8 Overlay test with double the default buffer size.

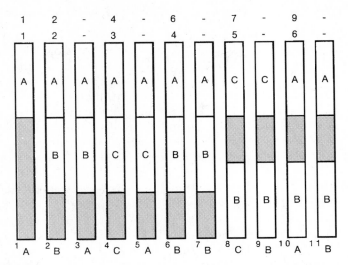

Figure 13-9 Overlay test with probation-reprieve buffer management.

Steps 1-3 are the same as in the previous test. But, at step 3, because A is on probation, the call to one of A's routines causes the overlay loader to give A a reprieve. This means that, when step 4 calls C, the loader throws out the less frequently used unit B; therefore, step 5 does not require another disk read because A is already in memory.

Notice the values on top. Only six disk reads are needed to complete the sequence, a significant savings over the ten disk reads in the first test (Figure 13-7) and the eight in the second experiment (Figure 13-8). Also, OvrTrapCount reaches a final value of 9 and increases more rapidly than OvrLoadCount—a sign of increased reprieval activity.

From examining these tests, you might think that a more simple "least recently used" algorithm (often labeled LRU) would do just as well as the probation-reprieve method. In other words, just count all calls to routines in overlays and, when more space is needed, throw out the units with the lowest LRU counts. That certainly would work, but would require an increment operation for each call to routines in overlays plus space for the LRU values. The probation-reprieve method—which is a little more difficult to use and understand—offers the same benefits in most cases without sacrificing space or performance. The results seem to be especially good in real-life programs with dozens of overlays competing for the same buffer space.

Clearing the Overlay Buffer

Call OvrClearBuf to empty the overlay buffer. After this, any calls to overlay unit procedures and functions force the Overlay unit to load an overlay from disk or from EMS RAM.

Normally, you don't need to call OvrClearBuf. One of the goals of good overlay-buffer management is to keep as much code in memory as possible, not to increase the number of disk reads. You might want to call OvrClearBuf during debugging as a worst-case test of program performance, though.

A more practical use for OvrClearBuf is to provide some space to store something else in the overlay buffer—for example, saved text behind a pop-up window. Two System unit variable (typed) constants locate the overlay buffer's starting and ending segment addresses at the base of the heap. After calling OvrClearBuf, you may use the bytes from OvrHeapOrg:0000 up to but not including the byte at OvrHeapEnd:0000.

Of course, when using the overlay buffer for your own purposes this way, you must not call any routines in overlay units until you're finished with the borrowed space.

Setting the Overlay Access Code

Another new variable in the Turbo Pascal 5.5 and 6.0 Overlay unit, OvrFileMode, sets the mode value given to DOS when overlays are loaded from disk. Normally, the mode value is 0 (read-only access).

On single-user PCs, the default value rarely if ever needs changing. But on multiple-user systems, such as networks, a different mode value might be needed to allow two or more terminals to open the same overlay .OVR file, perhaps stored on a common file-server disk that all users share. Some networks insist that shared files be opened with read-only status, preventing two or more users from accidentally updating the same data. Even though programs never have any good reason to write data to overlay files, the network software doesn't know that and may prohibit Turbo Pascal overlay code from running on multiple-network terminals.

Table 13-6 lists various bit combinations that make up file-access mode values for DOS 2.0 and 3.0 (plus in-between and later versions). DOS 2.0 recognizes only bits 0-2; other bits are reserved and should be 0. Only three file modes are available: read-only, write-only, and read/write.

Table 13-6 File access modes.

DOS 2.0 (and later versions)

7 6 5 4 3 (reserved)	2 1 0 (access mode)	Hex value
0 0 0 0 0	0 0 0 (Read-only)	$00
	0 0 1 (Write-only)	$01
	0 1 0 (Read/Write)	$02

DOS 3.0 (and later versions)

7 (inherit)	6 5 4 (denials)	3 (reserved)	Hex value
0 (On)	0 0 0 (Compatibility)	0	$00
1 (Off)			$80
	0 0 1 (Deny read/write)		$10
	0 1 0 (Deny write)		$20
	0 1 1 (Deny read)		$30
	1 0 0 (Deny nothing)		$40

DOS 3.0 and later versions use the full byte except bit 3, which should be 0. Bits 0-2 are the same as in DOS 2.0. Bit 7 determines if child processes (subprograms called by another program) inherit open files from their parents. Bits 4-6 select various "denials." If these three bits are 0, then the value defaults to the compatible bit patterns for DOS 2.0. The other listed settings deny read/write, write, and read-only accesses. When bit 6 is 1 and the other two bits are 0, no denials are recognized.

It's difficult to suggest one correct value for all networks. Some people report that $42 works (deny nothing, enable read/write). Others say $40, $C0, and $A0 are the correct values. You'll just have to experiment. If you think your code will run on a network, you'd be wise to add a global variable that users can change to try out different file-access modes in case problems develop.

Intercepting Overlay Requests

Another new Turbo Pascal 5.5 and 6.0 Overlay unit feature lets you intercept calls to the routines that load overlay code from disk. Two declarations in the Overlay unit let you hook custom code into the overlay's loader.

```
type
   OvrReadFunc = function(OvrSeg: Word): Integer;
var
   OvrReadBuf: OvrReadFunc;
```

OvrReadFunc is a procedure-type function that takes one Word parameter and returns type Integer. OvrReadBuf is a procedure variable of type OvrReadFunc.

When loading overlay units from disk, the overlay loader calls the function addressed by OvrReadBuf. A function result of 0 indicates a successful load; a nonzero result indicates an error, causing the overlay manager to generate a runtime error number 209. The OvrSeg parameter identifies which of several overlay units to load. Usually, you'll pass this value along to the standard loader after your custom code finishes—the OvrSeg value hasn't any other practical use.

Many possible uses come to mind for hooking custom code to the overlay loader. You might use this advanced feature:

- to prevent overlay runtime errors from halting programs, usually caused by a missing overlay file

- to prompt users to insert a diskette containing the overlay file—especially useful on a floppy-disk-only system

- to debug overlays by intercepting calls to the overlay loader

Hooking In an Overlay Function

In addition to performing its own duties, a custom overlay function must call the stock overlay loader. To provide a place to save the address of the loader for later use, create a global variable of type OvrReadFunc:

```
var
   StockOvrLoader: OvrReadFunc;   { Original loader address }
```

Next, write a custom function with the format of OvrReadFunc. As with all procedures and functions addressed by procedure variables, compile the function with the **far** key word or the {$F+} directive. The function name can be anything you want. Here's a simple example that prompts for a diskette named OVERLAYS:

```
{$I-}  { Disable I/O error checks }
function OvrPrompter(OvrSeg: Word): Integer; far;
var
  F: file;              { For checking if overlay file exists }
  Result: Integer;   { Stock loader result code }
begin
  repeat
    Assign(F, 'PROGNAME.OVR');
```

```
  repeat
    Write('Insert diskette OVERLAYS and press Enter...');
    Readln;
    Reset(F)
  until IoResult = 0;   { 0 = PROGNAME.OVR found on disk }
    Close(F);
    Result := StockOvrLoader(OvrSeg)  { Call stock loader }
  until Result = 0;
  OvrPrompter := Result    { Pass 0 result code back to caller }
end;
{$I+}  { Enable I/O error checks }
```

The inner **repeat** loop cycles until Reset successfully opens file PROGNAME.OVR, indicating that the correct diskette is in place. After this, the function calls the stock overlay loader via the StockOvrLoader procedure variable, passing the OvrSeg parameter, which tells the loader which overlay to retrieve. The outer **repeat** loop cycles until the result of this code equals 0, indicating that the overlay has been successfully loaded. Only then is the result (always 0) passed back to the overlay manager through the OvrPrompter function identifier.

To enable the custom OvrPrompter function, the main program's initialization code must save the stock loader's address and assign the custom function's address to OvrReadBuf, the procedure variable declared in the Overlay unit:

```
StockOvrLoader := OvrReadBuf;   { Save original loader address }
OvrReadBuf := OvrPrompter;      { Hook in new loader function }
```

Now, every time a call is intercepted to an overlay unit that's not in the overlay buffer, the custom function runs.

Extra Goodies

Here are a few extra Turbo Pascal 6.0 features that you'll find useful on occasion.

Compiling in Protected Mode

As long as you are not running another protected mode program such as DesqView or Windows 3.0 in 386-Enhanced mode, you may be able to use the protected mode compiler TPCX.EXE to take advantage of extended memory on your computer.

Supplied with Professional versions of Turbo Pascal 6.0, TPCX is based on a *DOS extender,* which allows programs to run in protected mode and to use extended memory above the usual 1-megabyte high water mark. To use the extended TPCX compiler, your computer must have:

- An 80286, 80386, 80486 or compatible processor

- At least 1 megabyte of extended memory

- No other protected mode software currently running

Even if your system meets these minimum requirements, you should use TPCX only if you need to compile large programs that cause the IDE and TPC compilers to run out of memory. TPCX runs more slowly than TPC—the plain-vanilla command-line compiler that works on all PCs. For this reason, when compiling from the DOS prompt, it's best to use TPC until you run out of memory. Only then should you consider using TPCX.

Aside from running in protected mode and being able to use all available extended memory, TPCX offers the same capabilities and generates the same code as the IDE and TPC compilers. You gain no new features by using TPCX; you gain only additional memory for compiling large programs.

Note: You can't use TPCX to create your own protected-mode applications. TPCX is a protected-mode application, but it can't create similar protected-mode programs.

TPCX supports the XMS and VCPI memory management protocols, which means you should be able to install a VCPI-compatible memory manager and still be able to run TPCX. If TPCX detects a VCPI manager, it will use that program's features to switch into protected mode and to access extended memory.

If running a VCPI manager and TPCX does not appear to win back any additional memory, you may have to configure your memory manager to supply *expanded* rather than *extended* memory to the compiler. Any other incompatibilities between your memory manager and TPCX might be easier to pinpoint by following these suggestions:

- Boot to a "clean" system—that is, to a system configuration that does not use a VCPI memory manager.

- Run the TPCXINST utility to configure TPCX for your system.

- Type TPCX with no parameters. You should see a list of command-line options—the same list you see when running TPC.

- Try compiling a program. If you get this far, you can be reasonably certain that TPCX is working correctly.

- Boot again to a system configuration that installs your memory manager, preferably using only default or minimum settings.

- Try using TPCX again. If this test fails, make sure you are using the most recent version of your memory manager.

- If TPCX seems healthy, try adding back your former memory manager options one by one until you find an optimum configuration or run into trouble, at which point you may have to compromise between the ideal settings for your system and a set of parameters that work with TPCX.

Generating 80286 Instructions

Specify the /$G+ option when compiling from the DOS prompt to generate 80286-compatible instructions for compiled programs. Or, when using the IDE, use the *Options:Compiler* command to switch on *286 instructions.* To do the same directly in a program's source code, insert the directive {$G+}.

Whichever technique you use to generate 80286-compatible instructions, programs compiled with this setting will run only on systems with an 80286, 80386, 80486, or an equivalent processor. These processors provide Enter and Leave machine-code instructions that simplify startup and shutdown code in subroutines. Turbo Pascal can use these instructions instead of the usual front and back "ends" of compiled procedures and functions, and as a result, increase program performance. Turbo Pascal also uses the 80286 PUSH *immediate,* extended IMUL, SHL *immediate,* and SHR *immediate* instructions, all of which can contribute extra speed to programs in some situations.

The only drawback to using 80286 instructions is that your programs will no longer run on older 8088- or 8086-based computers. That fact means your code will not work with the millions of plain PCs and XTs still running on desktops throughout the world. Don't use this technique, then, unless you are 100% certain that your programs won't run on computers using pre-80286 processors.

Alternatively, you might consider distributing two versions of your programs, one compiled with 80286 instructions and one without. Users can then select between the two versions. You don't have to maintain two sets of program files, just recompile the identical source text with and without the /$G option (or equivalent setting).

Using the Extended Syntax Option

A new and somewhat controversial Turbo Pascal 6.0 feature allows you to call functions as though they were procedures. This technique can save time and memory by eliminating temporary variables to which you assign unneeded function results. For example, suppose you write a function declared as

```
function CopyData(Source, Dest: Pointer; Size: LongInt): LongInt;
```

The hypothetical CopyData function copies Size bytes from a Source location to a Destination, both passed to the function as pointers. After performing its duties, CopyData returns a LongInt value equal to the number of bytes copied. (It doesn't matter how the function works; only the function result enters into the discussion here.) To call CopyData, you might write declarations and statements such as these:

```
var
  BytesCopied: LongInt;
  Source, Dest: BufferRec;  { Not shown }
begin
  ...
  BytesCopied := CopyData(@Source, @Dest, Sizeof(Source));
  if BytesCopied <= 0 then
    Error { Call error routine }
end;
```

Assigning the value of CopyData to BytesCopied gives the program a way to detect the number of copied bytes. In this imaginary example, if that value is less or equal to 0, the **if** statement calls an Error procedure.

But what if you don't care to examine CopyData's function result? This is a common situation with functions that perform actions in addition to returning counts, error codes, and other values that may have meanings only in some but not all circumstances. In previous versions of Turbo Pascal, calling such functions required using a temporary variable, which many programmers appropriately call Junk. With its temporary variable, the code might look like this:

```
var
  Junk: LongInt; { Holds unused function result }
begin
  ...
  Junk := CopyData(@Source, @Dest, Sizeof(Source));
  ...
end;
```

That kind of solution works, but it's messy. Also, in a program with hundreds of similar situations, typing all those temporary variables wastes time and memory. A better solution is to use Turbo Pascal 6.0's new *extended syntax option,* enabled in one of three ways:

- In the IDE, use the *Options:Compiler* command to select *Extended syntax* in the *Syntax options* section.

- When using the TPC or TPCX command-line compilers, specify the /$X+ option.

- Insert the directive {$X+} at the beginning of a source code text file.

With any one of these techniques, extended syntax enables you to write the preceding fragment without a temporary variable:

```
{$X+}
begin
  ...
  CopyData(@Source, @Dest, Sizeof(Source));
  ...
end;
```

The CopyData statement now looks just like a procedure call, and it is except for one fact: After the function returns, rather than store the function's result in a memory location, the compiler simply throws the result away.

You'll find extended syntax so useful you'll probably want to leave this option permanently enabled. Be aware, however, that you may call extended syntax only with functions defined in a program or unit module. In other words, you may not call the System unit's built-in functions as procedures. This means you can't write:

```
{$X+}
var
  N: Integer;
begin
  Odd(N); { ??? }
  ...
end;
```

Even though the first line enables Turbo Pascal's extended syntax option, the Odd(N) statement won't compile. Function Odd is built into Turbo Pascal and is therefore unaffected by the extended syntax setting. The statement also makes no sense because the only reason for using the Odd function is to determine whether an integer argument is odd. If you are going to throw the function result away, you may as well not call the function in the first place.

Note: The reason you can't use extended syntax with built-in functions is because those functions compile directly into machine language instructions; they do not result in a subroutine call. For example, the statement C := Chr(65) assigns the ASCII value 65 to a Char variable C. But even though the expression to the right of the assignment symbol looks like a function call, it isn't. To carry out the statement, the compiler generates a single machine-language instruction that stuffs the value 65 into C's location in memory. For that reason, it's impossible to call a function like Chr as a procedure since there is no Chr subroutine in Turbo Pascal!

Far and Near Procedure Directives

As you've seen elsewhere in this book, it's often necessary to select between two memory models: near and far. In the *near* model, calls to procedures and functions require only 16-bit offset address values that locate those routines within a 64K (maximum size) segment. In the *far* model, calls to procedures and functions use full 32-bit segment and offset addresses, permitting those calls to be made from any location—in the same segment or from any other.

For all procedures and functions in units, Turbo Pascal automatically forces public declarations (those in **interface** sections) to use the far model. Obviously, since a unit's code is stored in a separate code segment, that unit's procedures and functions must be far; otherwise, it would not be possible to call the routines from other modules. Local unit procedures and functions, however, use the near model since only other routines in that unit's same code segment can call the local subroutines.

As you've seen in this chapter, when you need to select a specific memory model, you may surround one or more procedures and functions with the {$F+} and {$F–} directives. {$F+} switches on far-code generation; {$F–} switches it off. Rather than use these switches, Turbo Pascal 6.0 now includes true procedural directives named **near** and **far**, which you may attach to any procedure or function declaration. Here are a few samples:

```
procedure DoSomething; far;
procedure WriteTheseValues(X, Y: Integer); near;
function Verified(S: string): Boolean; far;
function Factorial(N: Integer): Real; far;
function UserQuits: Boolean; near;
```

Adding the **far** or **near** key words after the declarations tells the compiler which memory model to use for each routine. Other routines are unaffected, as is the current status of any {$F+} or {$F–} directives.

You may use **near** and **far** anywhere a procedure or function might be declared. However, you may *not* use these key words in a unit's interface section where all procedure and function declarations are always far by default.

Summary

Conditional compilation lets you create programs that compile differently based on the presence or absence of symbols that you define in compiler directives. You can use conditional compilation to customize programs, to write code to run with and without a math coprocessor, and to create programs that compile correctly under different compiler versions.

Variable and value typecasting methods convert data types from one form to another. Variable typecasts must involve variables of equal size. One use for variable typecasts is to access fields in file variables, normally hidden from view.

Mem, MemW, MemL, Port, and PortW are special built-in arrays that make it easy to read and write bytes and words in memory or in I/O ports.

Include files help you to write large programs. You can also use the Dos unit Exec procedure to divide large programs into separate pieces.

Writing your own text file device drivers lets you customize Read, Readln, Write, Writeln, Reset, and Rewrite statements.

Turbo Pascal allows **label**, **type**, **const**, and **var** declarations to appear in any order, even between procedures and functions. Using this technique can make programs incompatible with other Pascal compilers but is useful in some circumstances and can help prevent side-effect errors.

Variable constants (or typed constants, as the Turbo Pascal Reference Manual calls them) can be structured, letting you define preinitialized arrays, records, and sets.

Turbo Pascal comes with a variety of special commands and variables to use subdirectories, fill and move memory, retrieve command-line parameters, add custom exit procedures to programs, read DOS environment variables, and deal with out-of-memory errors.

Procedure types and procedure-type variables let you pass the addresses of procedures and functions as parameters to other routines. This lets you design code with "hooks," to which you can attach custom code at runtime.

Turbo Pascal 5.5 and 6.0 add several enhancements to the Overlay unit introduced in version 5.0. The enhancements, which include a memory-management technique called probation-reprieve, help to keep frequently used overlays in memory for a longer time, thus improving program speed.

Exercises

13-1. The byte at address $F000:$FFFE indicates the computer model. $FF=IBM PC; $FE = PC/XT; $FD = PCjr; and $FC = PC/AT. Write a program to display your computer type. Use the Mem array.

13-2. Take all programs from any chapter (except Chapter 1) and design a menu program that lets you select which program you want. Each program should then return to the menu when it is finished, letting you select another. Use the Dos unit Exec procedure.

13-3. Rewrite Program 13-15 without using a constant variable array for Board. Investigate efficient methods for initializing the array.

13-4. Using a design similar to Program 13-15, write a program, Checkers, that sets up a checkerboard and lets two people take turns playing.

13-5.   Using conditional compilation, write a program that uses the custom beeper in Program 13-4 or the standard method, using a Write(Chr(7)) statement. It should be possible to change the program by modifying one symbol definition.

13-6.   Write a program to inspect a range of memory bytes in the computer.

13-7.   Write a DOS menu program to let people see directories, change to new subdirectories, delete files, and run other programs. It should be possible to select commands with function or single-letter keys.

13-8.   (Advanced) Design a custom text file device driver to select printer modes. Write an AssignPrn procedure to select among various possibilities, perhaps AssignPrn(F, CompressedText), and so on.

13-9.   Test the speed advantages of using FillChar and Move instead of **for** loops to fill and move memory.

13-10. (Advanced) Design a custom exit procedure to dump sections of memory to a disk file when a program ends with an error. (In the "old" days of computing, this was called a *core dump*.)

13-11. (Advanced) Modify your answer to exercise 13-10 to write the core dump to the disk file or device specified by a DOS environment variable. For example, you should be able to SET DUMP = PRN to print the core dump or SET DUMP=E:\CORE.DAT to send output to a disk file on a RAM or other disk drive.

14

Pascal Meets Assembly Language

- Assembly Versus Machine Language
- Three Machine Language Methods
- Why Use Assembly Language?
- Data Type Formats
- Anatomy of a Pascal Procedure
- Anatomy of a Pascal Function
- Inline Statements
- Inline Procedures and Functions
- Parameters and Inline Routines
- Using the Built-in Assembler
- External Procedures and Functions
- Programming Interrupts
- Adding Assembly Language to Units

14

Key Words and Identifiers

asm, **assembler**, External, **function**, InLine, Interrupt

Adding assembly language to Pascal programs is devil's work. If you're not careful, you can give birth to an uncontrollable monster that runs wild, destroying every memory byte in its way. Like the Wolf Man, a Pascal program with embedded assembly language can act normally for a while but then become a most unfriendly beast after only innocent provocation from an unwary computer operator.

> **Suggestion:** If the moon is full, come back to this chapter another day. And don't forget your garlic necklace.

Assembly Versus Machine Language

The term *machine language* refers to the actual bytes that a computer processor interprets as instructions. *Assembly language* is a mnemonic system for writing machine language programs in text form. An assembler is a program that converts assembly language text into machine language, or *object code*. A linker is a program that combines multiple object-code modules and performs other tasks to create the finished, executable code.

If you have no experience with assembly language, you might have trouble understanding some of the material in this chapter. I assume that you know about bits, bytes, words, addresses, segments, and registers, and that you have at least a fundamental knowledge of machine language instructions such as MOV and XOR. I'll explain some of these terms as we go along, but if you're already lost, you might want to read an assembly language tutorial before continuing.

Past Turbo Pascal compilers included only primitive support for mixing machine language and Pascal programs. Sophisticated assembly language meant using a stand-alone assembler such as Turbo Assembler (TASM) or the Microsoft Macro Assembler (MASM).

Turbo Pascal 6.0 adds another choice, a built-in assembler, known informally as BASM, that lets you insert assembly language instructions directly in your programs. For *most* assembly language work, BASM is the best choice. Although BASM isn't on the same high level as TASM or MASM, and although BASM offers fewer features than a stand-alone assembler, the new built-in assembler is more than adequate for writing critical procedures, functions, and embedded statements in assembly language.

This chapter covers all methods for inserting assembly language into Turbo Pascal 6.0 programs. Even though most programmers will use BASM, there are still times when the older methods are useful, and you should at least be familiar with them—especially since existing programs may use these techniques.

Note: You'll find more information about adding assembly language to Turbo Pascal programs—plus a tutorial on writing stand-alone Turbo Assembler programs in "Ideal mode"—in my book, *Mastering Turbo Assembler,* 1989, Howard W. Sams.

Three Machine Language Methods

Regardless of which assembler you have, Turbo Pascal can attach machine language instructions to programs in four ways:

1. Inline statements

2. Inline procedures and functions

3. Built-in assembly language (BASM) instructions

4. External routines

An *inline statement* directly injects machine language into a program's blood stream. You can insert any byte values at any place in a program, code entire procedures and functions in machine language, or insert machine instructions between other Pascal commands with inline statements.

An *inline procedure or function* operates like an assembly language macro, which translates words like PRINT or INKEY into frequently used machine language sequences. Macros are to programmers what shorthand symbols are to a stenographer. Turbo Pascal's inline procedures and functions are similar to an assembler's macros, expanding procedure and function identifiers into machine language instructions instead of making subroutine calls.

A *built-in assembly language* instruction talks directly to the processor. By writing BASM statements, you take over the compiler's usual job of converting high-level Pascal statements into machine code. In essence, with BASM, *you* become the compiler, and you are responsible for generating the individual processor commands that perform the tasks you need. Unlike inline statements, procedures, and functions, BASM statements are written in mnemonic form—one step above pure hexadecimal, and therefore easier to understand and use. Programming in BASM isn't simple, but it's not as cryptic as writing code directly in hex would be.

An *external routine* is a procedure or function that you write in assembly language, assemble to an object code file with your favorite assembler, and then link into Pascal. This method is particularly useful for replacing tested Pascal routines with optimized assembly language.

Why Use Assembly Language?

If adding assembly language to Pascal is so dangerous, why do it? Usually, the answer involves speed. In the hands of an expert willing to use every trick in the microprocessor book, an assembly language program can beat the clock on any compiler's output, even that of top-rated compilers like Turbo Pascal.

Another reason to use assembly language is to manipulate computer hardware, modems, and plotters directly and to do other jobs difficult to accomplish in pure Pascal. Because Turbo Pascal has many hardware-specific facilities—for example, Mem and Port arrays, logical operators, and explicit addressing techniques—using assembly language for this reason is usually unnecessary.

A third reason for adding assembly language is to save memory. You might be able to save a few bytes by storing variables in processor registers, packing multiple values into bytes and words, and calling subroutines in the ROM BIOS. Memory and disk space, though, are inexpensive when compared to the time it takes to save a few bytes. Also, Turbo Pascal's smart linker already keeps program size to a minimum by excluding unneeded runtime routines.

Probably, then, the best reason to mix assembly language and Pascal is to increase program speed. But don't get caught in the speed trap of thinking that the more of your code you convert to assembly language, the faster your program will run. Frederick P. Brooks, Jr. in *The Mythical Man-Month* estimates that all speed problems can be solved by translating from 1 to 5% of a program into machine language. Other studies confirm this assumption, showing that typical programs spend most of their time executing a small percentage of their code. Identifying that critical code and converting it to optimized assembly language often drastically improves a program's operating speed. Converting the other 90 to 95% of a program most often has a negligible effect on speed.

Data Type Formats

Successful assembly language programming requires intimate knowledge of how Turbo Pascal stores variables in memory. You must know how many bytes a LongInt variable occupies, how to access fields in records, and how to calculate array indexes. You can no longer rely on the compiler to take care of such details for you.

This section describes Turbo Pascal's army of data formats, organized into four divisions (Pascal identifiers are capitalized):

1. *Ordinal types*—Boolean, Char, enumerated, and subranges.

2. *Integer types*—ShortInt, Byte, Integer, Word, and LongInt.

3. *Real types*—Single, Real, Double, Extended, and Comp.

4. *Structured types*—pointers, arrays, records, sets, strings, and files.

Figure 14-1 illustrates an imaginary data type to help you better understand the data format diagrams in Figures 14-2 through 14-5. The pretend data type in Figure 14-1 occupies 32 bits with two parts, A and B, each 16 bits long. Bits in part B are numbered from 0 to 15. Bits in part A are numbered from 16 to 31. The most significant bit (MSB) is to the left. The least significant bit is to the right (LSB). In memory, lower addresses are to the right; higher addresses, to the left. In other words, the two bytes are swapped in memory with B physically coming before A.

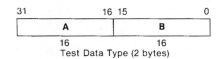

Figure 14-1 Test data type.

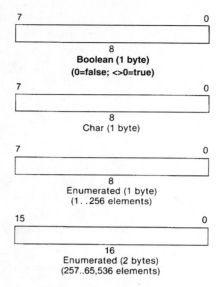

Figure 14-2 Ordinal types.

Ordinal Types

Figure 14-2 diagrams Turbo Pascal's three basic ordinal data types: Boolean, Char, and enumerated values. Enumerated types with from one to 256 elements occupy one byte. Enumerated types with more than 256 elements occupy two bytes.

Integer Types

Figure 14-3 diagrams Turbo Pascal's five integer data types. Subranges (not shown) occupy the smallest possible space. A subrange of –5 .. 120, for example, would be encoded as a ShortInt value. The S represents the sign bit, which if equal to 1, indicates a negative number in twos-complement form.

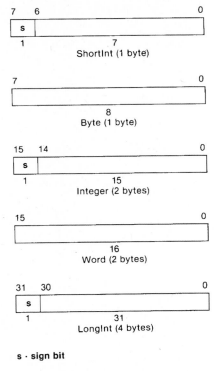

Figure 14-3 Integer types.

Real Types

Figure 14-4 diagrams Turbo Pascal's Real data type plus the four math coprocessor types: Single, Double, Extended, and Comp. For more information about how to use these types in assembly language programming, refer to a math coprocessor technical reference.

Structured Types

Figure 14-5 diagrams Turbo Pascal's structured data types: pointers, sets, arrays, records, and strings. Except for pointers, which occupy four bytes, the byte sizes of structured types vary. Use the Sizeof function to calculate the size of specific variables.

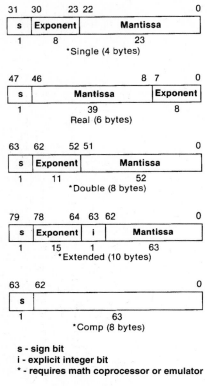

Figure 14-4 Real types.

Arrays are stored with the first element first in memory, followed by the elements with the rightmost array index incrementing first. Record fields are stored in declaration order. Strings begin with a length byte followed by one to 255 character bytes. Strings are not terminated with a null character (ASCII 0) as they are in some languages, such as C and C++.

Files are not diagrammed here. Refer to the Dos unit types FileRec and TextRec in the DOS.INT (unit interface) file in Turbo Pascal's DOC directory for details.

Anatomy of a Pascal Procedure

When it comes to learning how to add machine language to Pascal programs, there's no better teacher than the compiler itself, which, after all, is an expert machine language encoder. A good way to begin, then, is with a look inside a typical Turbo Pascal procedure.

Program 14-1 is a simple test program with one procedure, Count, at lines 3-12. The main body calls Count, which counts from 1 to 10 in a **repeat** loop.

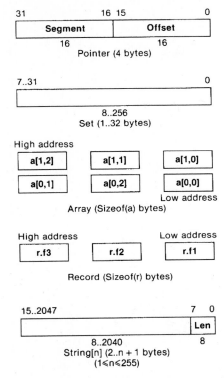

Figure 14-5 Structured types.

Program 14-1: PROCANAT.PAS

```
1:   program ProcAnatomy;
2:
3:   procedure Count;
4:   var
5:     I: Integer;
6:   begin
7:     I := 0;
8:     repeat
9:       I := I + 1;
10:      Writeln(I)
11:    until I = 10
12:  end;
13:
14:  begin
15:    Count
16:  end.
```

I compiled this program to a disk EXE code file and then disassembled the results to produce the listing in Figure 14-6. The figure shows the compiled machine language that Turbo Pascal generates for Program 14.1. For reference, the Pascal statements are mixed with the associated machine language. Read the comments to the right of most lines for a play-by-play description of how the code operates.

```
 1:    program ProcAnatomy;
 2:
 3:    procedure Count;
 4:    var
 5:      I: Integer;
20A9:0000 55            PUSH  BP             ; Push BP register onto stack
20A9:0001 89E5          MOV   BP,SP          ; Set BP equal to stack pointer
20A9:0003 B80200        MOV   AX,0002        ; Check that stack has 2 bytes,
20A9:0006 9AAD02AF20    CALL  SYSTEM:02AD    ;   enough space for var I
20A9:000B 83EC02        SUB   SP,+02         ; Reserve two bytes on stack
                                             ;   for integer variable I
 6:    begin
 7:      I := 0;
20A9:000E 31C0          XOR   AX,AX          ; Set register AX to 0000
20A9:0010 8946FE        MOV   [BP-02],AX     ; Store AX in variable I
 8:      repeat
 9:        I := I + 1;
20A9:0013 8B46FE        MOV   AX,[BP-02]     ; Load current I value into AX
20A9:0016 40            INC   AX             ; Add 1 to AX (I := I + 1)
20A9:0017 8946FE        MOV   [BP-02],AX     ; Store new value back in I
10:        Writeln(I)
20A9:001A BF0001        MOV   DI,0100        ; All this just to write
20A9:001D 1E            PUSH  DS             ;   the value of I plus
20A9:001E 57            PUSH  DI             ;   a carriage return!
20A9:001F 8B46FE        MOV   AX,[BP-02]
20A9:0022 99            CWD
20A9:0023 52            PUSH  DX
20A9:0024 50            PUSH  AX
20A9:0025 31C0          XOR   AX,AX
20A9:0027 50            PUSH  AX
20A9:0028 9A2508AF20    CALL  SYSTEM:0825
20A9:002D 9A8B07AF20    CALL  SYSTEM:078B
20A9:0032 9A7702AF20    CALL  SYSTEM:0277    ; End of Writeln(I) statement
11:        until I = 10
20A9:0037 837EFE0A      CMP   Word Ptr [BP-02],+0A ; Compare I with 10
20A9:003B 75D6          JNZ   0013           ; Jump to :0013 if I <> 10
12:    end;                                  ; Prepare to exit Count
20A9:003D 89EC          MOV   SP,BP          ; Restore old stack pointer
20A9:003F 5D            POP   BP             ; Restore saved BP register
20A9:0040 C3            RET                  ; Return to caller
13:
14:    begin
20A9:0041 9A0000AF20    CALL  SYSTEM:0        ; Call startup routines
20A9:0046 89E5          MOV   BP,SP          ; Prepare BP register
15:        Count
20A9:0048 E8B5FF        CALL  COUNT          ; Call Count procedure
16:  end.
20A9:004B 89EC          MOV   SP,BP          ; Restore stack pointer from BP
20A9:004D 31C0          XOR   AX,AX          ; Get ready to end program
20A9:004F 9AF301AF20    CALL  SYSTEM:01F3    ; Call shutdown routines
```

Figure 14-6 Program 14-1 disassembled into machine language.

If you have the stand-alone Turbo Debugger program, you can view a similar disassembly on your display. (Turbo Pascal's built-in debugger lacks the ability to show you a compiled program's assembled machine code.) After saving Program 14-1 as PROCANAT.PAS, enter these commands to compile and load the result into Turbo Debugger:

```
tpc /v procanat
td procanat
```

You should see the program source code in Turbo Debugger's main window. Press F7 once to execute the program's startup code. Then, press Alt-V C to open the CPU window, and press F5 to expand the window to full screen. This display, which is very useful for learning how the compiler works, shows you the compiled machine language below the associated Pascal statements—nearly identical to Figure 14-6, but with some addresses changed. (The figure shows Turbo Pascal 4.0's output, and you might notice a few minor differences with version 6.0's.)

Procedure Entry Duties

Several important details are clear from Figure 14-6. At the beginning of Count, these two instructions prepare register BP (Base Pointer):

```
PUSH  BP
MOV   BP,SP
```

The PUSH instruction saves the current BP value by pushing BP onto the stack. The MOV instruction moves the value of the stack pointer SP register into BP, thus making the two registers address the same location in memory relative to the stack segment register SS.

These two instructions are at the beginning of all procedures. The reason for equating SP and BP is to prepare for addressing variables on the stack. These variables might be parameters, or they might be variables declared local to the procedure. In this example, there is one local variable, integer I. The next three instructions prepare space on the stack to hold the variable:

```
MOV   AX,0002
CALL  SYSTEM:02AD
SUB   SP,+02
```

The first two instructions call a system routine that checks whether there is enough stack space for the variable—two bytes here. As shown here, the routine is located in the SYSTEM segment at offset 02AD. But it is foolhardy to assume that this address will remain unchanged in future compiler versions. Therefore, in your own machine code, you should never call system routines at explicit addresses.

The second instruction reserves local variable space by subtracting 2 from the current stack pointer SP. As you recall from earlier chapters, local variables are created on the stack when procedures and functions run. The SUB instruction performs this magic, reserving uninitialized stack memory for local variables.

By the way, if you turn off stack error checking with the {$S–} compiler directive, Turbo Pascal generates only the SUB instruction and does not check whether enough stack space is available for local variables.

The rest of the Count procedure down to line 12 (**end**;) executes the statements inside the procedure. You should be able to follow most of this code by reading the comments to the right. (Don't be too concerned with understanding every detail.)

Procedure Exit Duties

The end of a procedure executes three instructions, returning to the machine language instruction following the one that called the procedure:

```
MOV   SP,BP
POP   BP
RET
```

The MOV instruction assigns BP to SP. This restores the stack pointer to its original value before allocating space on the stack for local variables. Recall that BP was equated to SP's value at the start of the procedure. Therefore, as long as no other instructions or subroutines change BP, this is the fastest method to restore the stack pointer before ending the procedure. The second instruction pops BP from the stack restoring BP to the value it had at the procedure start. Finally, a RET instruction continues the program at the instruction following the call to Count.

Register Use in Procedures

In your own machine language procedures, you may freely use, and you do not have to preserve, registers AX, BX, CX, DX, DI, and SI. You may change the stack and base pointers SP and BP as described earlier, but you must restore both of these registers before executing RET. You must preserve the data segment register DS, the stack segment register SS, and the code segment register CS. You may use the extra segment register ES for your own purposes. (There's no guarantee that other code will leave ES untouched, though. Always initialize ES before use.) You may also change the processor flags.

Anatomy of a Pascal Function

Functions in machine language are similar, but not identical, to procedures. Again, studying a disassembled example is a great way to learn the ropes before writing your own machine language functions. Program 14-2 assigns the squares of values 1 to 10 to a ten-integer array (lines 11-12), calling function MySquare (lines 5-8) for the square of integer parameter N.

Program 14-2: FUNCANAT.PAS

```
 1:  program FuncAnatomy;
 2:  var
 3:    I: Integer;
 4:    A: array[1 .. 10] of Integer;
 5:
 6:  function MySquare(N: Integer): Integer;
 7:  begin
 8:    MySquare := N * N
 9:  end;
10:
11:  begin
12:    for I := 1 to 10 do
13:      A[I] := MySquare(I)
14:  end.
```

Figure 14-7 lists the machine language that Turbo Pascal generates for Program 14-2. As in the previous example, the Pascal statements are followed by the associated machine language instructions. Read the comments to the right of most lines for a play-by-play description of how the code operates.

Function Entry Duties

Although the first five machine language instructions in Figure 14-7 are identical to the instructions in Figure 14-6, there is a subtle difference between the startup code for functions and procedures. Procedures reserve stack space for local variables by subtracting a value from the stack pointer register SP. In this example, though, function MySquare has no local variables. Yet, the code still subtracts 2 from SP, reserving two bytes on the stack.

The reason for this action is to reserve space for the function result. In this case, the function is type Integer and, therefore, two bytes are needed to hold the value. If there were any local variables in the function, additional stack space would be reserved for both the variables and the function result.

The guts of the MySquare function first load parameter N into register AX, multiply N * N with an IMUL (Integer Multiply) instruction, and save the result in the space reserved on the stack for the function result.

```
 1:   program FuncAnatomy;
 2:   var
 3:     I: Integer;
 4:     A: array[1 .. 10] of Integer;
 5:
 6:   function MySquare(N: Integer): Integer;
 7:   begin
2E5E:0000 55              PUSH BP                ; Push BP register onto stack
2E5E:0001 89E5            MOV  BP,SP             ; Set BP equal to stack pointer
2E5E:0003 B80200          MOV  AX,0002           ; Check that stack has 2 bytes,
2E5E:0006 9AAD02642E      CALL SYSTEM:02AD       ;  enough for function result
2E5E:000B 83EC02          SUB  SP,+02            ; Reserve two stack bytes for
                                                 ;  intermediate function result
 8:     MySquare := N  * N
2E5E:000E 8B4604          MOV  AX,[ BP+04]    ; Load parameter N into  AX
2E5E:0011 F76E04          IMUL Word Ptr [BP+04] ;  Multiply N * N
2E5E:0014 8946FE          MOV  [BP-02],AX     ;  Store result in stack
2E5E:0017 8B46FE          MOV  AX,[BP-02]     ;  Load result into  AX
2E5E:001A 89EC            MOV  SP,BP          ;  Restore old stack pointer
2E5E:001C 5D              POP  BP             ;  Restore saved  BP register
2E5E:001D C20200          RET  0002           ;  Return to caller, releasing
                                              ;  parameter space on stack
 9:   end;
10:
11:   begin
2E5E:0020 9A0000642E      CALL SYSTEM:0       ; Call startup routines
2E5E:0025 89E5            MOV  BP,SP          ; Prepare BP register
12:       for I:= 1 to 10 do
2E5E:0027 C70600000100    MOV  Word Ptr [0000],0001 ; Initialize for loop
2E5E:002D E804            JMP  @+13 (0033)    ;  Jump to begin <for> loop
2E5E:00ZF FF060000        INC  Word Ptr [0000] ;  Increment control variable
13:       A[I] := MySquare(I)
2E5E:0033 FF360000        PUSH [0000]         ; Pass I by value to MySquare
2E5E:0037 E8C6FF          CALL MYSQUARE       ; Call MySquare function
2E5E:003A 8B3E0000        MOV  DI,[0000]      ; Calculate array index offset
2E5E:003E D1E7            SHL  DI,1           ; in register DI
2E5E:0040 8985000         MOV  [DI+0000],AX   ; Store function result in  A[I]
2E5E:0044 833E00000A      CMP  Word Ptr [0000],+0A ; Test control variable
2E5E:0049 75E4            JNZ  @+0F (002F)    ; Continue or end <for> loop
14:   end.
2E5E:004B 89EC            MOV  SP,BP          ; Restore stack pointer from  BP
2E5E:004D 31C0            XOR  AX,AX          ; Get ready to end program
2E5E:004F 9AF301642E      CALL SYSTEM:01F3    ; Call shutdown routines
```

Figure 14-7 Program 14-2 disassembled into machine language.

Function Exit Duties

The MySquare function's exit instructions following line 9 (**end**;) in Figure 14-7 are similar, but not identical, to the instructions that end procedure Count in Figure

14-6. The first job is to load register AX with the intermediate function result, currently stored on the stack. This is done by executing:

```
MOV AX,[BP-02]
```

Remember that BP is equated with the stack pointer on entry to the function and, therefore, used here to locate the function space starting two bytes lower than BP. (We'll get to the details of parameter addressing later in this chapter.)

Ordinal and integer functions—those that return data types diagrammed in Figures 14-2 and 14-3—return their results in register AX. Look at the code under the array assignment in line 13. About halfway down, AX is stored in the array following the CALL instruction to MySquare.

Ordinal and integer values that occupy single bytes are returned in AL—the least significant half of AX. Refer to Table 14-1 for details on the register assignments for other function result types.

Table 14-1 Function result registers.

Function type	Register(s)
Boolean	AL
Char	AL
Enumerated (8-bit)	AL
Enumerated (16-bit)	AX
ShortInt	AL
Byte	AL
Integer	AX
Word	AX
LongInt	DX = high, AX = low words
Single	See note 1
Double	See note 1
Real	DX=high, BX=mid, AX=low words
Extended	See note 1
Comp	See note 1
Pointer	DX = segment, AX = offset
String	See note 2

1. These function types are returned in the math coprocessor top-of-stack register.

2. String functions receive a pointer to a temporary work space created by the caller to the function. The function stores characters at this address, returning the pointer undisturbed on the stack.

Register Use in Functions

The same rules and restrictions for register use in procedures apply to functions. The only exception is that you must return function results in registers as detailed in Table 14-1.

Parameters and Variables

Inside machine language routines, you'll often need to store and retrieve values in Pascal variables. Of course, in Pascal, you simply use the variable's identifier and let the compiler decide where in memory to store values. In machine language, you are responsible for knowing where to find your variables.

> **Note**: Later in this chapter, you'll learn how to refer to Pascal variables by name. It's still a good idea, however, to learn how Pascal addresses variables.

As you learned in the previous sections, local variables are stored in temporary stack space created after calling the procedure or function that declared the variables. Callers to procedures and functions push parameters onto the stack. Other variables are stored in the program's data segment.

Figure 14-8 illustrates the stack during a call to a typical procedure. Function calls are similar, but they allocate extra space to hold the function result, as explained earlier. The boxes in the illustration each represent one byte with higher memory addresses at the top. The stack expands toward lower addresses. The organization of variables and other items on the stack during a procedure or function call is known as a *stack frame*.

The notes on the right side of Figure 18 show the location of SP and BP at various times during the procedure call. The notes on the left side show the locations of variables relative to register BP. The diagram corresponds with a procedure declared as:

```
procedure Typical(Param: Word);
var V1, V2: Word;
```

This hypothetical procedure has a single Word parameter (Param) and two local Word variables (V1 and V2). In machine language, the caller to this procedure executes the instructions

```
PUSH  AX       ;  Push one-word parameter
CALL  TYPICAL  ;  Call procedure
```

Figure 14-8 Snapshot of a stack frame during a typical procedure.

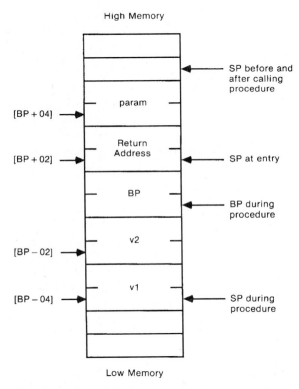

This assumes that the parameter to be passed to Typical is presently in AX. When Typical begins running, SP addresses the *return address*—the location following the CALL instruction. On the stack, the parameter is above the return address. As Figure 14-6 shows, Typical first executes these instructions:

```
PUSH  BP
MOV   BP,SP
SUB   SP,+04
```

Referring to Figure 14-8, the PUSH instruction stores the current value of BP on the stack, just below the return address. The MOV instruction sets BP equal to SP ("BP during procedure" in the figure). The SUB instruction then subtracts four from SP, reserving four bytes for the two local Word variables, V1 and V2. SP now addresses the first byte of V1. (A real program would also call Turbo Pascal's stack overflow checker unless you turn off stack checking with {$S–}.)

Local Variables

Use BP minus an offset value to locate local variables on the stack. In Figure 14-8, V1 is at [BP-04] and V2 is at [BP-02]. Variables declared first in the local **var** section are *farthest* away from BP. To assign the value 8 to V2, you could use the assembly language instruction:

```
MOV  Word Ptr [BP-02],8
```

Figure 14-8 shows the stack for two-byte variables. To locate a variable of a different size, subtract the variable's byte size plus the total byte sizes of all variables declared *after* the one you need. A stack frame diagram like Figure 14-8 helps avoid confusion.

Value Parameters

Use BP also to locate value parameters passed to a procedure or function. As Figure 14-8 shows, value parameters are stored above the return address. In this sample, the single two-byte Param is at [BP+04]—four bytes higher than the location that BP addresses after being initialized at the procedure start. To assign the value 8 to Param, you could write:

```
MOV  Word Ptr [BP+04],8
```

Figure 14-8 illustrates a common *near* procedure call. Calls to *far* routines—those declared in a unit's interface section, for example—push a four-byte return address. The first parameter above the return address in *far* routines, then, is at [BP+06].

Parameters are pushed in the order they appear inside the procedure or function parentheses. The first parameter is *farthest* away—at a higher address—from BP. The last declared parameter is just above the return address.

When a procedure or function ends—except for string functions as noted in Table 14-1—the parameter stack space must be removed. To do this, the procedure illustrated in Figure 14-8 ends with these instructions:

```
MOV  SP,BP
POP  BP
RET  0002
```

The MOV instruction deallocates the stack space occupied by local variables V1 and V2, resetting SP to the location in the figure reading "BP during procedure." The POP instruction then restores the original value of BP from the stack, making SP again point to the location "SP at entry."

The RET instruction specifies the optional parameter 0002, telling the processor first to remove the return address from the stack, inserting this address in the instruction pointer register IP, and then adding 2 to SP. Doing this deallocates the two bytes occupied by Param, returning SP to the value it had before calling the procedure.

Variable Parameters

Variable parameters are passed to procedures and functions as full 32-bit addresses. In Figure 14-8, if Param was a **var** parameter, then [BP+04] would locate the four-byte address of Param on the stack. To use such addresses, programs typically employ the LES instruction and DI register like this:

```
LES  DI,[BP+04]
MOV  Word Ptr ES:[DI],8
```

The LES instruction loads the register combination ES:DI with the data at [BP+04]. The MOV instruction then uses this address to assign 8 to the variable. This is more complicated (and time-consuming) than referencing value parameters and local variables, which you can directly address on the stack.

Global Variables

Turbo Pascal lumps all global variables, including globals declared in units, into a single data segment. DS:0000 locates the first byte of this data space. Consider a program that declares three global integer variables:

```
program Globals;
var G1, G2, G3: Integer;
```

To initialize the three variables to 8, you could write:

```
MOV Word Ptr [0000],8   ; G1 := 8;
MOV Word Ptr [0002],8   ; G2 := 8;
MOV Word Ptr [0004],8   ; G3 := 8;
```

Of course, the actual addresses, expressed as offsets from the base location addressed by segment register DS, might be different than 0000, 0002, and 0004. Global variables are stored in declaration order, with the last declared variable at a higher offset relative to DS. Variable (typed) constants are also stored in the data segment but, unlike plain variables, begin with preinitialized values. Plain constants are stored in the code stream as needed. String constants, which are not duplicated even if used multiple times, are also stored in the code segment.

Static Links

Accessing local variables and parameters from within nested procedures and functions is tricky. Consider these procedures:

```
procedure Outer(A, B: Integer);
var
  I, J: Word;
  procedure Inner;
  begin
    { Inner statements }
  end;
begin
  Inner;
  { Outer statements }
end;
```

Procedure Outer can access parameters A and B plus local variables I and J, as described earlier, relative to BP. However when Inner runs, BP is again initialized for Inner's own stack frame; therefore, the locations of the two parameters and local variables are no longer directly available as offsets from BP.

To solve this dilemma, Turbo Pascal creates a *static link* to variables and parameters from within nested blocks (procedures and functions). The static link tells nested routines how to find an outer routine's variables and parameters. To create the static link in this example, Outer pushes the current BP value onto the stack just before calling Inner. Suppose Outer assigns 5 to local variable I and then calls Inner. The code would be:

```
MOV  Word Ptr [BP-04],5   ; I := 5
PUSH BP                   ;  Create static link
CALL INNER                ;  Call inner procedure
```

The assignment to I uses BP minus an offset value, similar to the arrangement in Figure 14-8. The PUSH instruction passes BP on the stack immediately before calling Inner. This is the static link value that Inner uses to locate Outer's parameters and local variables. If Inner had any parameters, Outer would push their values before BP.

When Inner begins running, the stack appears similar to Figure 14-8, but with no parameters or local variables. In this case, Param equals the static link value of BP, located at [BP+04]. This locates the static link for *near* procedures and functions.

When the outer procedure or function is *far,* the return address of a nested procedure or function's stack is a four-byte value.

With the static link available on the stack, locating the outer routine's parameters and variables is now possible. For example, these instructions inside Inner assign 3 to Outer's parameter A:

```
MOV  DI,[BP+04]           ;  Get static link
MOV  Word Ptr SS:[DI+06],3   ;  A := 3
```

The first MOV instruction retrieves the static link—the BP value pushed on the stack before calling Inner—assigning this value to register DI. The second MOV instruction uses DI as an alternate base pointer with the segment override SS:, telling the processor to locate data in the stack segment. The offset (06) is the same value that Outer would use directly with BP to assign 3 to A:

```
MOV  Word Ptr [BP+06],3
```

Inline Statements

Inline statements inject bytes directly into Turbo Pascal's code stream. You can insert bytes anywhere inside a procedure or function block or in a main program body. You can also code inline statements in private or public unit routines or in a unit's initialization section. Inline statements can go anywhere Turbo Pascal normally allows other kinds of statements.

An inline statement begins with the identifier InLine followed by a list of byte and word values in parentheses. Separate multiple values with slashes (/). Values that evaluate to eight-bit data types generate one byte of code or data. Values that evaluate to 16-bit data types generate two bytes of code or data. Here's a simple one-byte inline example that disables interrupts:

```
InLine($FA);   { CLI  ;  Clear interrupt flag }
```

The $FA byte is the machine language for the CLI instruction, "Clear Interrupt Flag." This enables interrupts:

```
InLine($FB);   { STI  ;  Set interrupt flag }
```

The $FB byte represents the STI instruction, "Set Interrupt Flag." You could insert either of these inline statements anywhere in your program to enable and disable interrupts—two jobs that have no direct equivalents in Turbo Pascal. The compiler inserts the $FA and $FB machine language instruction bytes directly into the code file.

Notice the comments to the right of these two inline examples. It's a good idea to document your machine language statements carefully, listing the assembly language text and additional descriptions to explain exactly what each instruction means.

Replacing Pascal with Inline Statements

One use for inline statements is to optimize the code that Turbo Pascal generates. As an example, let's recode function MySquare in Program 14-2 using an inline statement.

Examine the machine language for line 8 in Figure 14-7, the disassembly of Program 12. Assigning AX to [BP–02]—the stack space reserved for the intermediate function result—is immediately followed by an assignment to AX of this very same value! Obviously, if AX already equals the function result, there's no need to store AX in the intermediate space. Pascal returns Integer function values in AX anyway (see Table 14-1); therefore, the two MOV instructions at 2E5E:0014 and 2E5E:0017 are superfluous. In this example, we can do better than the compiler by recoding the multiplication in line.

The reason for this apparent inefficiency, by the way, is that Turbo Pascal is a *one-pass* compiler. The compiler evaluates each statement, generating the appropriate machine language before going on to the next statement. When Turbo Pascal compiles the multiplication in line 8 (Figure 14-7), it doesn't know this is the last statement in the function until reaching the **end** key word, and by then it's too late to avoid storing AX in the intermediate function result space. If there were other statements after the multiplication, then it would be necessary to store the intermediate function result at [BP–02], retrieving this value just before ending the function. The compiler simply can't make the appropriate decision in this case, a good example of why high-level language compilers like Turbo Pascal are not as expert as competent assembly language programmers.

Having spotted the inefficiency in Program 14-2, we can recode function MySquare with an inline statement. Program 14-3 lists the final result. The inline statement simply duplicates the instructions from the disassembly in Figure 14-7, skipping the unnecessary assignment to the function value's intermediate stack space.

Program 14-3: INLINEFN.PAS

```
1:   program InlineFunction;
2:   var
3:     I: Integer;
4:     A: array[1 .. 10] of Integer;
5:
6:   function MySquare(N: Integer): Integer;
7:   begin
8:   (* MySquare := N * N *)
9:
```

```
10:     inline( $8B/ $46/ $04/    { MOV  AX,[BP+04] ; load N into AX }
11:             $F7/ $6E/ $04/    { IMUL Word Ptr [BP+04]  ; AX<-N*N }
12:             $89/ $EC/         { MOV  SP,BP       ; restore SP }
13:             $5D/              { POP  BP          ; restore BP }
14:             $C2/ $02/ $00 );  { RET  0002        ; return, deallocate N }
15:
16:   end;
17:
18:   begin
19:     for I := 1 to 10 do
20:       A[I] := MySquare(I);
21:     for I := 1 to 10 do
22:       Writeln('A[', I:2, '] = ', A[I]:2);
23:     Readln
24:   end.
```

There are a couple of important details in Program 14-3. First, the original Pascal statement is commented out (line 8), creating a reference to what the inline statement accomplishes. Besides documenting the code, this comment also helps programmers transfer the program to different computers—perhaps a Macintosh using a 68000 processor, which can't execute the same inline code. To transfer or *port* the program to the Macintosh, a programmer could remove the inline statements and enable the original Pascal, perhaps later writing 68000 inline instructions after debugging the program.

Notice that lines 12-14 in Program 14-3 duplicate the exit code in the original function (Figure 14-7). Such duplicate code is usually unnecessary because Turbo Pascal adds its own startup and exit code for the function. However, to avoid loading AX from the function result's stack space (at address 2E5E:0017 in the figure), the inline statement must end the procedure itself.

I hope you are getting the idea by now that mixing machine language and Pascal is no piece of cake and comes with no guarantee of improved efficiency. In this example, we've managed to cut two MOV instructions—an important improvement that might be critical in a tight situation but, in most cases, probably will have little practical effect. We've saved no space, trading the six bytes saved by discarding two MOVs with a six-byte duplication of the function's exit code. This just proves that adding machine code to Pascal programs is tricky business. Be sure the payoff is worth the effort before going to all this trouble!

Using Identifiers in Inline Statements

In place of the literal [BP+04] references in Program 14-3 (lines 10-11), you can use parameter and variable identifiers in inline statements. When you do this, Turbo Pascal replaces the identifiers with the *offset* value representing the location of the variable in the appropriate segment. For example, you can rewrite lines 10-11 like this:

```
InLine($8B/ $86/ N/   { MOV  AX,N  ;  Load N into AX }
        $F7/ $AE/ N/   { IMUL N     ;  AX <- N * N }
```

Notice that the original $46 is now $86 and the $6E is $AE, changing the MOV and IMUL instructions to use 16-bit instead of eight-bit offsets. Turbo Pascal replaces parameter N with the full 16-bit offset value ($0004), generating this code for these two instructions:

```
8B860400   MOV  AX, Word Ptr [BP+0004]
F7AE0400   IMUL Word Ptr [BP+0004]
```

This illustrates a serious danger when using identifiers in inline statements. You must be absolutely certain that the machine language instructions are able to handle the 16-bit offset values that the compiler inserts in place of identifiers.

Often, however, default 16-bit values are not acceptable. To force Turbo Pascal to insert eight-bit bytes, even though a value or identifier evaluates to a 16-bit word, use the < and > operators. The less-than sign (<) extracts the least significant byte. The greater-than sign (>) extracts the most significant byte. To return to using eight-bit offsets, while specifying parameter identifier N, rewrite lines 10-11 this way:

```
InLine($8B/ $46/ <N/   { MOV  AX,N  ;  Load N into AX }
        $F7/ $6E/ <N/   { IMUL N     ;  AX <- N * N }
```

Now, we can again use the eight-bit offset forms of MOV and IMUL. The <N designation tells the compiler to insert the least significant byte of the 16-bit offset 0004 (the offset address of N), acceptable in this example because the most significant byte is zero. Of course, if the parameter is more than 255 ($FF) bytes away from BP, then you have to use a 16-bit offset.

You may conclude from these notes that using identifiers in inline statements is too much trouble. But there's a good reason to use <N instead of the literal $04 offsets in Program 14-3, lines 10-11. As now written, the program assumes that Turbo Pascal will always organize the stack according to the illustration in Figure 14-8—a potentially dangerous assumption. For instance, if you add an {$F+} directive at line 5, the compiler will generate code for function MySquare as a *far* routine. *If you are following along, change the $04 bytes in Program 14-3, lines 10-11, to <N before running the modified program with MySquare declared far!* Calls to MySquare then push a four-byte return address on the stack causing parameters to begin at [BP+06] instead of [BP+04]. Obviously, the literal $04 inline offset values will no longer work. (See Figure 14-8.)

By specifying <N instead of literal values, the compiler generates the correct offsets for both *far* and *near* routines. Such subtle differences are important to

understand, especially when rewriting as inline statements procedures and functions in units, which are *far* by default. You must be certain to use the appropriate data forms for your machine language instructions. The compiler offers no safeguards against errors.

Inline Procedures and Functions

An inline procedure or function is similar to an inline statement. As you have learned, an inline statement is just like any other statement. An inline procedure or function, though, is a kind of shorthand that represents short, machine language sequences. A few examples help explain how this works:

```
procedure ClrInt; InLine($FA);
procedure SetInt; InLine($FB);
```

An inline procedure starts with the key word **procedure** followed by the procedure name and a semicolon. After that comes an inline declaration, with exactly the same form as an inline statement. In this case, though, Turbo Pascal does not insert the inline code directly into the code stream. This happens later when you write ClrInt or SetInt:

```
ClrInt;   { Clear Interrupts }
Writeln('Interrupts are off');
SetInt;   { Enable interrupts }
Writeln('Interrupts are on');
```

In place of ClrInt, the compiler inserts the inline byte, $FA, representing the machine language CLI (Clear Interrupt Flag) instruction. In place of SetInt, the compiler inserts $FB, the machine language STI (Set Interrupt Flag) instruction. From the Pascal text, it appears that calls are made to the ClrInt and SetInt procedures, but this is not the case. The procedure identifiers operate similarly to assembly language macros, as mentioned earlier, directly expanding to the inline bytes the identifiers represent.

You can also code inline functions. For example, this function returns the value of the system timer, stored at 0000:046C - 0000:046F:

```
function Timer: LongInt;
InLine(
  $31/  $C0/                { XOR AX,AX        ;  Zero AX }
  $8E/  $C0/                { MOV  ES,AX       ;  Set ES to 0000 }
  $BF/  $6C/  $04/          { MOV  DI,046C     ; DI = offset }
  $26/  $8B/  $05/          { MOV  AX,ES:[DI]  ;  Low word }
  $26/  $8B/  $55/  $02 );  { MOV  DX,ES:[DI+02] ;  High word }
```

Use this inline function, which returns a LongInt value in registers AX:DX (see Table 14-1), as you do any Pascal function. For example, you could display Timer values in a **for** loop:

```
var
  I: Integer;
begin
  for I:= 1 to 100 do
    Writeln(Timer);
end.
```

When Turbo Pascal compiles this loop, it does not call a function subroutine named Timer. Instead, it inserts the inline Timer function's code directly into the code stream. As a result, the program avoids all the overhead normally associated with calling subroutines—all the stack details described earlier, the CALL and RET instructions, and so on. The inline code works like a function without this overhead and, therefore, improves the speed of the loop.

Another advantage to using inline functions is that the compiler does not reserve space for the function value on the stack as it does for a real function.

Parameters and Inline Routines

You may pass variable and value parameters to inline procedures and functions. The parameters are pushed onto the stack just as they are for normal procedure and function calls. In this case, your inline code is responsible for removing the parameters from the stack.

Suppose you need a function to square a 16-bit Word value, which you pass to the function by value, returning a LongInt result. You could code the function in Pascal:

```
function LongSqr(N: Word): LongInt;
begin
  LongSqr := LongInt(N) * N
end;
```

The typecast expression LongInt(N) is necessary to force a long integer result in the multiplication. The equivalent inline function pops the Word parameter N from the stack into register AX, multiplying AX by AX, leaving the result in DX:AX:

```
function LongSqr(N: Word): LongInt;
  InLine($58/        { POP AX  ;  Pop N into AX  }
         $F7/ $E0);  { MUL AX  ; DX:AX <- AX * AX }
```

This three-byte function is neat and efficient. Table 14-1 specifies that the DX:AX register pair returns LongInt function results. Perhaps by coincidence, or perhaps by design, the MUL instruction leaves the result of the multiplication in the proper registers

Short inline procedures and functions like LongSqr are useful for optimizing code that, if written in Pascal, waste time preparing the stack, referencing variables relative to BP, storing function results in intermediate stack variables, and calling system routines. This observation does not hold true for all procedures and functions, though, and you should use inline routines only for short code that must run as fast as possible.

Using the Built-in Assembler

If you know how to program in assembly language, you'll probably find Turbo Pascal 6.0's new built-in assembler to be the best choice for adding machine code to Pascal. Officially dubbed the "Turbo Pascal Inline Assembler," programmers have nicknamed the new built-in assembler BASM.

Like TASM, BASM is a mnemonic assembler, capable of translating assembly language instructions such as MOV and JMP into binary machine code. With BASM, you can insert assembly language mnemonics directly into Pascal programs. You don't need to convert instructions into hex, and you don't need to purchase a stand-alone assembler. With a few exceptions explained later, BASM understands most of the same opcodes, operands, and directives as TASM and MASM.

This isn't the time or place to teach assembly language programming, and if you don't know your way around TASM or MASM, you may find several unexplained terms in the following descriptions. If so, you'll need to study assembly language and then return to this chapter later. But even if you are just learning how to program in assembly, you'll find BASM to be a great learning tool, especially if you are comfortable with Pascal. Because you can selectively insert BASM instructions into Pascal programs, you can build Pascal shells that take care of various startup, shutdown, display, and other chores while you concentrate on relatively small BASM procedures and functions.

In fact, ease of use is one of BASM's primary advantages. With BASM, it's possible to introduce mnemonic assembly language instructions directly into Pascal programs at any place where those instructions will do the most good. You can do the same with inline statements, but with BASM, you skip the tedious and error-prone job of calculating hexadecimal bytes and words.

Writing asm Statement Blocks

Every BASM instruction must appear inside an *asm statement block*. This block looks like any other in Pascal—a **repeat** or **while** statement for example—but begins with the key word **asm** and ends with **end**. Here's a sample:

```
asm
   MOV  AL,'A'          { Set AX to the character 'A' }
   PUSH AX              { Push AX onto stack }
   CALL Subroutine     { Call a subroutine }
   POP  AX             { Pop AX from stack }
end;
```

The actual instructions in that fragment are just for demonstration. Concentrate for the moment on the form of the **asm** block rather than the contents. First comes the **asm** key word, a new reserved word in Turbo Pascal 6.0. Next are the assembly language instructions, which use a syntax similar to that of stand-alone TASM and MASM assemblers. As you can see, assembly language instructions may refer to literal values such as the character 'A', registers such as AL and AX, and labels such as Subroutine. Text elements like these make BASM much easier to use than inline hex values.

BASM comments must be in Pascal style, that is, delimited with braces { and } or the double-symbol alternates (* and *). Unlike stand-alone assembly language, BASM does not recognize a semicolon as a comment marker. In stand-alone TASM or MASM programs, you can write:

```
MOV  AL, 'A'  ; BASM rejects this TASM/MASM-style comment
```

In BASM, the semicolon is a statement separator, just as semicolons always are in Pascal. For that reason, you can't write comments in this familiar form. Instead, you have to store comments in Pascal style as the preceding examples illustrate.

In an **asm** statement block, after the last assembly language instruction, the key word **end** tells the compiler to return to compiling Pascal statements. In between **asm** and **end**, the compiler turns all processing duties over to BASM.

You may insert as many **asm** blocks as needed in a program, but only within areas that would normally generate code—inside procedures, functions, and main blocks for instance. Pascal statements and **asm** blocks can mingle inside procedures and functions, and programs can drop in and out of assembly language as often as required. You can't insert **asm** statement blocks in **type** or **const** declarations, and you can't nest multiple **asm** blocks insider one another. But there's no limit on the number of **asm** blocks you can insert into a program.

Note: Because **asm** is a new reserved word, if you have any variables, procedures, or other identifiers named *asm*, you'll have to rename them.

Because individual assembly language instructions have narrowly defined jobs to perform, it often takes many such instructions to accomplish even the simplest tasks. As a result, assembly language listings tend to stretch for page after page, which can obscure meaning. To reduce the length of your BASM statements, you can string multiple instructions on single lines separating instructions with semicolons. For example, you could write the earlier example like this:

```
asm
  MOV AL,'A'; PUSH AX; CALL Subroutine; POP AX
end;
```

Although there's nothing technically wrong with such statements, they are difficult to read. They also complicate editing and debugging. For these reasons, it's usually best to insert BASM instructions on separate lines.

There are a few times, however, when multiple-instruction BASM statements lend extra clarity to code. For instance, many assembly language subroutines PUSH registers onto the stack, and then later POP those same registers from the stack to restore their original values. Rather than write such common PUSH and POP sequences over and over on separate lines, you may as well string them together in an **asm** block like this:

```
asm
  PUSH AX; PUSH BX; PUSH CX; PUSH DX
{ ... Other instructions }
  POP  DX; POP  CX; POP  BX; POP  AX
end;
```

Embedded asm Statements

BASM's **asm** blocks give you the means to drop in and out of assembly language and Pascal at will. You can mix Pascal statements with assembly language or write entire BASM procedures and functions.

When embedding **asm** blocks among Pascal statements, you'll often need to refer to data elements declared in Pascal. At such times, you need to consider carefully the format of that data. Program 14-4, BASMWELC.PAS, demonstrates a typical case.

Program 14-4: BASMWELC.PAS

```
 1:  program BasmWelcome;
 2:  const
 3:    Message: string[17] = 'Welcome to BASM!$';
 4:  begin
 5:    Writeln(Message);
 6:    asm
 7:      MOV AH,9
 8:      MOV DX,OFFSET Message + 1
 9:      INT 21h
10:    end;
11:    Readln
12:  end.
```

When you enter and run BASMWELC, you'll see two lines on screen:

```
Welcome to BASM!$
Welcome to BASM!
```

The first line ends with a dollar sign; the second doesn't. If you examine the program's source code, you'll see the reason for this discrepancy. A Writeln statement displays the first line, using the variable constant Message declared in the program's global **const** section. An **asm** block writes the second line, in this case, by calling the DOS string-output routine, function number 9, via the software interrupt instruction INT 21h.

The Writeln statement is, of course, pure Pascal. As you know, Pascal strings begin with a length byte that indicates how many significant characters follow. For this statement, the dollar sign is just another character, and therefore Writeln displays that character along with the welcome message.

For DOS function 9, however, a dollar sign is the string's terminator. DOS doesn't know how to display length-byte strings, and for that reason, the Message must end with a dollar sign to tell DOS where to stop displaying characters. In the **asm** block, after assigning the DOS function number 9 to register AH, a MOV instruction assigns to register DX the offset address of the variable constant Message. Adding 1 to this offset value skips the string's hidden length byte, causing DX to address Message's first character. Passing that address to interrupt 21h then displays the string, but not the dollar sign.

As this small example shows, even the simplest BASM statements frequently require careful planning and intimate knowledge of data formats, DOS function requirements, and similar low-level details. On the other hand, if you examine the machine code that Turbo Pascal generates for the seemingly simple Writeln statement, you'll see that despite appearances, Writeln's associated machine code is far more complex than the three-instruction **asm** block shown here. Such tradeoffs may make a difference in your program's use of time and memory, but then again, they may not. There's no guarantee that a little assembly language will improve a section of code. That's your job.

Pure asm Procedures and Functions

Rather than embed **asm** blocks among Pascal statements, you can also write "pure" BASM procedures and functions. To take advantage of this special feature, add the key word **assembler** after the procedure or function declaration, replace the routine's initial **begin** key word with **asm**, and then insert your assembly language statements. For example, rather than write

```
procedure AnyRoutine;
begin
  asm
```

```
   { Assembly language instructions }
 end;
end;
```

you can do away with the extra **begin** and **end** by writing

```
procedure AnyRoutine; assembler;
asm
  { Assembly language instructions }
end;
```

Since the **asm** block occupies the entire procedure (it could also be a function), you may not use Pascal statements along with BASM instructions in pure **asm** procedures and function. To mix Pascal and BASM, you must code AnyRoutine as in the latter example, creating a common Pascal **begin** and **end** statement block with embedded **asm** blocks inside. The pure **asm** procedure or function may contain only assembly language instructions and does not have a Pascal statement block.

Except for this difference, all other parts of a pure **asm** procedure or function remain the same as they are in Pascal. You may declare parameters, constants, labels, types, and variables just as you do when not using BASM.

Program 14-5, BASMFN.PAS, shows the same MySquare function from Program 14-3 converted to a pure **asm** function.

Program 14-5: BASMFN.PAS

```
 1:   program BasmFn;
 2:   var
 3:     I: Integer;
 4:     A: array[1 .. 10] of Integer;
 5:
 6:   function MySquare(N: Integer): Integer; assembler;
 7:   asm
 8:     MOV   AX,N              { Load N into AX }
 9:     IMUL  Word Ptr [BP+04]  { AX <- N * N }
10:     MOV   SP,BP             { Restore SP }
11:     POP   BP               { Restore BP }
12:     RET   0002             { Return, deallocate  N }
13:   end;
14:
15:   begin
16:     for I := 1 to 10 do
17:       A[I] := MySquare(I);
18:     for I := 1 to 10 do
```

```
19:      Writeln('A[', I:2, '] = ', A[I]:2);
20:    Readln
21:  end.
```

When writing pure **asm** functions, the **assembler** key word follows the function data type—Integer for the MySquare function in Program 14-5 (line 6). Note how the function refers to the Integer parameter N, assigning that value directly to register AX. Generally, you may refer to parameters and variables by name, although as the next section outlines, when using Pascal data in **asm** blocks, you need to keep on your toes to avoid stumbling over various addressing details that Pascal normally takes care of for you.

Using Data and Variables

BASM statements can refer to Pascal parameters and variables, or an **asm** block can create its own data. Each of these two methods for using data and variables in BASM statements has advantages and disadvantages.

You may declare data directly in **asm** blocks using the directives DB, DW, or DD. The three directives allocate space for variables directly in the current code segment (not in the data segment). The directives have the same meanings and purposes as they do in stand-alone assembly language:

- DB defines one or more 8-bit bytes

- DW defines one or more 16-bit words

- DD defines one or more 32-bit double words

To "define" means to "allocate space for." Remember always that DB, DW, and DD define space at their current location, inserting one or more bytes, words, or double words into the code stream. For that reason, you may need to insert a jump instruction to skip over data elements. If you don't take this step, your program might attempt to execute your data as instructions, a dangerous condition that's almost certain to cause your program to fail.

Program 14-6 shows how to use DB to embed a copyright notice into a compiled .EXE file.

Program 14-6: NOTICE.PAS

```
1:  program Notice;
2:
3:  var
4:    I: Integer;
5:
```

```
 6:   procedure Copyright; assembler;
 7:   asm
 8:     JMP @@1
 9:     DB  13,10,' 1991 by Tom Swan. All rights reserved.'
10:   @@1:
11:   end;
12:
13:   begin
14:     Copyright;
15:     Writeln('Welcome to my program');
16:     Writeln('I will now count to 10');
17:     for I := 1 to 10 do
18:       Writeln(I);
19:     Write('Press <Enter> to quit...');
20:     Readln
21:   end.
```

Compile NOTICE.PAS to create NOTICE.EXE, then use a text-file lister program to examine the compiled code. (The README.COM program supplied with Turbo Pascal will do nicely.) As you can see, the **asm** block's string, allocated by DB, shows up clearly at the beginning of the file. The JMP statement inside the block jumps over the string to prevent it from being executed as instructions. (@@1 is a local label, explained in the next section.)

Jumping over the string data in Copyright is necessary because the main program calls the Copyright procedure, thus preventing Turbo Pascal's smart linker from eliminating the procedure, which it would do if no statement referred to Copyright. (In this case, the linker is too smart for the program's own good!) The carriage return and line feed control codes (13 and 10) that preface the copyright notice ensure that the notice will begin on a new line when examined by README.COM or a similar utility.

Use the other two directives, DW and DD, as you use DB. End hexadecimal values with the letter h (in upper- or lowercase). For example, to insert byte, word, and double word values in hex, you can write

```
asm
  DB  0Eh
  DW  0FF09h
  DD  00FF00A7h
end;
```

Hex values must begin with a digit from 0 to 9 in addition to ending with h. FF09h is an identifier; 0FF09h is a hexadecimal value. The easiest way to satisfy these rules is to begin all hexadecimal values with leading 0s. Most of the time, you'll use DB and DW to create byte and word values, and DD to store 32-bit address values.

An **asm** block's instructions may also refer to global and local variables, as well as to any parameters passed to procedures and functions. Global variables are stored in the global data segment and addressed as offsets from the current value of segment register DS. Program 14-7 illustrates how to refer to global data in **asm** blocks.

Program 14-7: BASMGLOB.PAS

```
 1:  program BASMGlob;
 2:
 3:  var
 4:    S:  string;     { Global string variable }
 5:
 6:  procedure ShowString; assembler;
 7:  asm
 8:    MOV  AH, 9            { Select DOS function 9 }
 9:    MOV  DX, OFFSET S + 1 { Address string past length byte }
10:    INT  21h             { Call DOS to display string at DS:DX }
11:  end;
12:
13:  procedure ShowParam(S: string); assembler;
14:  asm
15:    MOV  AH, 9           { Select DOS function 9 }
16:    PUSH DS              { Save DS on stack }
17:    LDS  DX, S           { Load string address into DS:DX }
18:    INC  DX              { Increment DX to skip length byte }
19:    INT  21h             { Call DOS to display string at DS:DX }
20:    POP  DS              { Restore saved DS from stack }
21:  end;
22:
23:  begin
24:    S := 'A Pascal and DOS string $';
25:    ShowString;
26:    Writeln;
27:    ShowParam(S);
28:    Writeln;
29:    Readln
30:  end.
```

BASMGLOB.PAS defines a global **string** variable S, which two BASM procedures display in two different ways. After the main program assigns a string to S, the first procedure, ShowString, displays S much like the way BASMWELC.PAS does (see Program 14-4). First, the **asm** block assigns function number 9 to AH. Then it assigns the offset address of the global variable to DX, adding one to that value to skip the string's length byte. Finally, INT 21h executes the DOS function identified by AH, displaying the dollar-sign-terminated string.

As you can see from ShowString, global variables such as S evaluate to their addresses. The expression OFFSET S + 1 tells BASM to take the offset portion of S's address and add one to that value. If you need the segment portion of an address, replace OFFSET with SEG (*not* SEGMENT).

It's important to realize that expressions like OFFSET S + 1 are constants, and like all constants, are evaluated at compile time, not when the program runs. Remember, you are programming in assembly language. If you write X + Y * 2, BASM must be able to "fold" that expression into a constant value. Unlike the Pascal compiler, BASM does not generate instructions to evaluate expressions at runtime. After all, that's one reason for using high-level languages like Pascal. If you need a BASM expression evaluator, you'll have to write one. Or, a better solution is to switch back to Pascal, store an expression result in a variable, then use that result in an **asm** block.

The second BASM procedure in BASMGLOB.PAS shows how to address parameters passed to a procedure. (You can treat function parameters in the same way.) Since the compiler stores all such parameters on the stack, the **asm** block needs to take additional steps in order to pass the address of S to DOS function 9. After assigning 9 to AH, the program pushes the current value of DS onto the stack. This is important since Pascal requires DS to address the program's data segment. If a program were to change DS, that program would lose track of its global data. After saving DS, LDS loads DS:DX with the address of S. But because Pascal passes strings by address—even when those strings are declared as value parameters (without **var**)—the LDS instruction loads the passed *address value* from the stack into DS:DX. The next step increments that address's offset to skip the string's length byte, and then calls DOS function 9 by executing DOS interrupt 21h. When that's done, POP DS restores the original DS segment register previously saved on the stack.

BASMGLOB.PAS demonstrates an important principle in assembly language programming: Always know where your variables are! You can refer to variables and parameters by name, but those names simply represent addresses, and it's up to you to use those addresses in sensible ways.

Global variables are the easiest to use since Turbo Pascal stores them all in the program's data segment. The same is true of variable (typed) constants. Most of the time, you can simply refer to these data elements by name.

Like parameters, local variables are stored on the stack in space that's allocated when a statement calls the declaring procedure or function. Because the stack stores all local variables and parameters, **asm** blocks need to address those variables in reference to the stack segment register SS.

BASM simplifies such concerns by converting references to local variables into equivalent offsets from register BP. As explained earlier in this chapter, programs refer to stack variables by using expressions such as [BP+4] and [BP−8]. Pascal procedures and functions automatically prepare BP for this purpose, a fact that BASM knows and will use to the best possible advantage.

An example shows how to access local variables from inside an **asm** block. Program 14-8, BASMLOC.PAS, counts from 0 to 9, a simple job carried out with an **asm** statement that increments a local variable.

Program 14-8: BASMLOC.PAS

```
 1:   program BASMLoc;
 2:
 3:   procedure Local;
 4:   var
 5:     Count: Word;
 6:   begin
 7:     Count := 0;
 8:     while Count < 10 do
 9:     begin
10:       writeln('Count = ', Count);
11:       asm
12:         INC Count
13:       end
14:     end
15:   end;
16:
17:   begin
18:     Local;
19:     Readln
20:   end.
```

Procedure Local declares a local Word variable Count, displayed in a Pascal **while** statement that cycles as long as Count's value is less than 10. A single-instruction **asm** statement (lines 11-13) increments count, executing the assembly language mnemonic INC.

Although this code looks simple, and would execute just as well with a Pascal Inc(Count) statement, there's more to the assembly language instruction INC Count than is obvious from the text. In place of Count, BASM generates a machine language INC operand as though you had written:

```
INC WORD PTR [BP-02]
```

You can insert that line in place of INC Count and the program will operate exactly as it did before. Obviously, however, it's a lot easier to write INC Count than to calculate the location of Count in reference to BP and use a WORD PTR expression to increment the 16-bit value at that address.

Except for arrays and strings, you can address value parameters in exactly the same way as you do local variables. In fact, except for their locations in reference to

BP, there isn't any technical difference between local variables and value parameters passed to procedures and functions. Both forms of data are stored temporarily on the stack, and in **asm** blocks, you can refer to both forms simply by using their identifiers.

Variable parameters are not so easy to address. When a program passes an argument to a variable parameter, Turbo Pascal pushes that variable's 32-bit address onto the stack. In the procedure or function, you need to take extra steps in order to pick up that address, and in that way, locate the actual data which might be stored anywhere in memory.

Program 14-9, BASMVARP.PAS, demonstrates the difference between addressing value and variable parameters from asm blocks. Run the program and enter word values to the two prompts. The program will then display two equal numbers, the results of combining your two words into 32-bit LongInt values. The first value comes from a function that returns a LongInt value. The second comes from a procedure that stores a similar LongInt value into a variable parameter.

Program 14-9: BASMVARP.PAS

```
 1:  program BASMVarP;
 2:
 3:  function MakeLong1(WLo, WHi: Word): LongInt; assembler;
 4:  asm
 5:    MOV DX,WHi    { Assign high order value to DX }
 6:    MOV AX,WLo    { Assign low order value to AX }
 7:  end;
 8:
 9:  procedure MakeLong2(WLo, WHi: Word; var L: LongInt); assembler;
10:  asm
11:    MOV DX,WHi             { Same as in MakeLong1 }
12:    MOV AX,WLo             { "    "    "    "     }
13:    LES BX,L               { Address var L with ES:BX }
14:    MOV [ES:BX],AX         { Copy low order word to variable }
15:    MOV [ES:BX + 02],DX    { Copy high order word to variable }
16:  end;
17:
18:  procedure GetLowHigh(var WLo, WHi: Word);
19:  begin
20:    Write('WLo? ');
21:    Readln(WLo);
22:    Write('WHi? ');
23:    Readln(WHi)
24:  end;
25:
```

continued

Program 14-9: continued

```
26:  var
27:    WLo, WHi: Word;
28:    L: LongInt;
29:
30:  begin
31:    GetLowHigh(WLo, WHi);
32:    L := MakeLong1(WLo, WHi);
33:    Writeln('After MakeLong1 L = ', L);
34:    L := 0;
35:    MakeLong2(WLo, WHi, L);
36:    Writeln('After MakeLong2 L = ', L);
37:    Readln
38:  end.
```

BASMVARP.PAS's MakeLong1 function accepts two variable parameters, WLo and WHi. It combines those two words into a LongInt value, returned as the function result. As the listing shows, the entire process takes only two assembly language instructions (see lines 5-6). Since LongInt function values are passed in registers AX and DX, assigning the two value parameters to those registers both creates the LongInt result and returns that same value.

The MakeLong2 procedure takes a different course. Because this is a procedure, it can't return values. Instead, to pass back the LongInt equivalent of WLo and WHi, the procedure stores the combined value of those two words in a variable parameter L.

As in MakeLong1, MakeLong2 begins by assigning the parameter words to AX and DX. After those steps, an LES instruction finds the address of the variable parameter L. All variable parameters are passed by address. The LES instruction copies an address into the ES segment register and another named register, here BX. In the sample listing, the instruction LES BX,L transfers the 4-byte address of L from the stack to the two registers ES:BX. Together, the register pair ES:BX serves as a pointer to the passed parameter. Two subsequent MOV instructions then copy AX and DX to the low- and high-order words of that parameter.

Function Results

In functions with **asm** blocks, you need to make sure that function results are passed to their callers in the correct registers. This rule is easiest to satisfy in pure **asm** functions like MakeLong in Program 14-9. To the beginning of pure functions (and procedures), BASM adds only these two instructions:

```
PUSH BP
MOV  BP,SP
```

If the routine declares any local variables, BASM also executes:

```
SUB   SP,Size
```

where Size equals the number of bytes required by all local variables. At the end of the routine, BASM inserts the instructions

```
MOV   SP,BP
POP   BP
RET
```

If there are any parameters, BASM adds the size in bytes to the RET instruction, removing those parameters from the stack.

As these overhead instructions show, in pure **asm** functions, it's up to you to store the correct values in registers in order to pass function results back to their callers. The same is *not* true when embedding **asm** blocks inside functions. In other words, for functions that use this form

```
function AnyFunction(K: Integer): Word;
begin
  ...
  asm
    { assembly language instructions }
  end
  ...
end;
```

the function result is treated as a hidden local variable. Normally, to access that variable, you write Pascal statements to assign values to the function identifier, as in this sample

```
AnyFunction := 100;
```

Such a statement passes the value 100 back as AnyFunction's result. You can't write such statements inside an embedded **asm** block; therefore, to give you a way to assign the function result, BASM provides a special symbol named @Result. Treat @Result as a pointer to a location on the stack where you can store a function's value. For example, inside an **asm** block, to assign 100 to @Result, you can write:

```
asm
  MOV   AX,100
  MOV   @Result,AX
end;
```

Or, you can simply write

```
asm
  MOV   @Result,100
end;
```

The reason for storing a function's result in @Result is because Turbo Pascal normally adds instructions at the end of a function to copy the temporary result value from the stack into the proper registers. In other words, when AnyFunction ends, it executes the equivalent of this instruction:

```
MOV  AX,@Result
```

Before this instruction, if you stored the function's result in AX, the MOV instruction would destroy that value.

Another key difference between pure assembly language routines and those with embedded **asm** blocks concerns the stack frame. In pure assembly language routines, if there are no parameters and no local variables, BASM does not generate any stack frame instructions, only a RET instruction. When you need peak efficiency, parameterless procedures and functions without local variables give you the least possible overhead. Only inline procedures and functions are more streamlined.

Labels and Jumps

Earlier, you saw examples of JMP instructions that referenced the local label @@1:. Local labels in BASM must begin with an @ sign. (In my programs, I use double at-sign symbols @@ to match Turbo Assembler's local-label style.)

Most labels in BASM statements should be local. You can use named labels such as @Here and @@There, but many programmers prefer to use numbers like @@10 and @99, at least for short hops where it's easy to see a jump and its destination on the same page. Local labels must be unique within the same **asm** block, but you may reuse the same local labels in other **asm** blocks.

Standard named labels are more difficult to use than local labels. Even in an **asm** block, you must declare all named labels in advance. For example, to call a subroutine inside an **asm** block, you can write something like this

```
function Return100: Word;
label
  Subroutine, TheEnd;
begin
  asm
    CALL Subroutine
    JMP  TheEnd
Subroutine:
    MOV @Result,100
    RET
  end;
TheEnd:
end;
```

Function Return100 take a torturous route to return the value 100, demonstrating how inconvenient it is to use named labels in **asm** blocks. First, a **label** section declares two labels, Subroutine and TheEnd. Inside the function's body, an **asm** block calls a local subroutine, identified by the Subroutine: label. (All labels, local and otherwise, must end with colons where those labels mark locations in the program's code.) The JMP instruction uses another label, required to jump over the internal subroutine.

By the way, although not recommended, since labels like Subroutine and TheEnd are declared in advance, Pascal **goto** statements may jump to those labels. It's possible, for instance, to insert a label inside an **asm** block and then execute a **goto** statement to jump to that location. You can even have two or more **asm** blocks jumping among each other. Jumping into fire is an equally attractive proposition, so if you use these techniques, don't be surprised if you get burned.

One other note concerning jumps: BASM automatically selects the most efficient conditional and unconditional jump instruction forms. For example, if you write

```
JNE   @@10   { Short distances only }
```

BASM will assemble that instruction unchanged as long as the distance from JNE's location to the target label @@10 is within −128 to +127 bytes backward or forward. If the target label is farther away, BASM translates conditional jumps such as JNE into something like this:

```
JE    @@XX
JMP   @@10   { Capable of reaching longer distances }
@@XX:
```

I used @@XX just for illustration; there isn't any such label in the final result. The effect is to skip the unconditional JMP instruction if the opposite condition holds. Together, the negated unconditional JNE and JMP perform the identical job as the original jump, but can "hit" targets farther away.

BASM takes similar steps to optimize unconditional JMP instructions. If you write

```
JMP   @@10
```

and if the label @@10 refers to an address that's within −128 to +127 bytes away, BASM inserts the shortest possible JMP instruction code, taking only 2 bytes of space. If the target is farther away, BASM uses a 3-byte JMP.

You can override these jump optimizations by prefacing labels with NEAR PTR and FAR PTR. For example, to force a FAR jump to a nearby label, you can write

```
JMP   FAR PTR @@10
```

In that case, even if label @@10 is within −128 to +127 bytes away, BASM will assemble a 3-byte JMP instruction. It's rare that you'll need to override jump optimizations this way, but you might do so if you need to maintain an exact number of bytes in an **asm** section, or if you are writing self-modifying code that will insert other addresses into a JMP instruction at runtime.

Other BASM Concerns

BASM does not support a few features that are popular among TASM and MASM programmers. However, most of these features have Pascal counterparts that perform similar jobs. Others are more suitable for a stand-alone assembler. BASM's missing features are:

- *EQU declarations.* In stand-alone assembly language, EQU associates an identifier with a constant value. In BASM code, use Pascal **const** declarations instead.

- *PROC statements.* Declare BASM procedures and functions exactly as you do in Pascal. There's no need for a separate PROC directive, which in stand-alone assembly language, marks the beginning of a subroutine procedure.

- *STRUC declarations.* Pascal records take the place of assembly language STRUCs. Use dot notation (for example, MyRec.MyField) to find the offset addresses of specific fields.

- *SEGMENT key word.* You may not define segments in BASM code. All BASM instructions must operate within Turbo Pascal's segmented memory model. If you need to create your own segments, you must use a stand-alone assembler.

- *MACRO key word.* There aren't any counterparts to assembly language macros in BASM. If you need to use macros, you'll have to write external modules for TASM or MASM as described later in this chapter.

There are a few other miscellaneous details that may be important to some programmers. Keep the following facts about BASM in mind.

@Code and @Data Symbols

The symbol @Code refers to the current code segment. @Data represents the current data segment. Preface either of these symbols with the SEG operator as in the instructions

```
MOV AX, SEG @Code
MOV BX, SEG @Data
```

The first instruction moves the code segment value into AX. The second moves the data segment value into BX. In the compiled program, BASM translates the instructions into commands similar to these

```
MOV AX, 0542Dh
MOV BX, 053D8h
```

In other words, @Code and @Data are *not* aliases for the code and data segment registers CS and DS. Rather, the symbols @Code and @Data refer to the literal segment address values that are in effect at this place in the program. If you need the actual segment register values, you can write

```
MOV AX, CS
MOV BX, DS
```

Opcodes and Coprocessors

BASM supports 80286 instructions, but only when compiling with the {$G+} option enabled. It's your responsibility to ensure that any 80286 instructions will be executed only on hardware with a suitable processor—an 80286, 80386, 80486 or compatible model.

BASM also supports all 8087 and 80287 math coprocessor instructions, but only when compiling with the {$N+} option enabled. To use 80287 instructions, insert the double directive {$G+, N+} at the beginning of your module.

Return Types

BASM selects the correct RET instruction to conform with the current near or far model. Normally, in a procedure or function, you do not have to supply an explicit RET. However, if you want to return from inside an **asm** block, you may do so provided you are careful to clean up the stack. For example, you can write a procedure using the form

```
function EarlyReturn(N: Integer): Integer;
begin
  Writeln('Inside EarlyReturn. N = ', N);
  asm
    MOV   AX,4321   { Assign function result to AX }
    MOV   SP,BP     { Restore stack pointer }
    POP   BP        { Restore BP register }
    RET   2         { Return and deallocate param }
  end;
  EarlyReturn := N  { Never executed! }
end;
```

Function EarlyReturn does what its name suggests. Despite the fact that the final Pascal statement assigns the value of parameter N to the function identifier, this function always returns the value 4321 assigned to AX inside an **asm** statement block. To prevent the function from executing its final statement—a trick that might prove useful when you need to provide a fast exit from a function or procedure—MOV and POP instructions restore the stack and base pointer registers SP and BP, after which RET returns to the function's caller. The 2 after the RET instruction deallocates the two bytes of stack space that store the Integer value parameter N.

If a far-mode option {$F+} is in effect, or if the current procedure or function uses the **far** key word, BASM assembles a *far* return instruction RETF. If near-mode is in effect, BASM translates RET to RETN. You may also use RETF or RETN explicitly to override BASM's automatic selection of return types, but then you are also responsible for ensuring that other statements make the proper near or far calls to the routine.

Debugging BASM Instructions

Turbo Pascal 6.0's built-in debugger, and also Turbo Debugger 2.01 (and later versions) are BASM aware. This fact means you can single step through an **asm** block's instructions, examine registers as though they were variables, and use other debugger features on assembly language code.

You don't have to perform any special tricks to prepare for debugging **asm** statements. Just compile your program with the necessary switches (/v if you are using one of the command-line compilers), and load the result into Turbo Debugger. For debugging from Turbo Pascal 6.0's IDE, select the *Options:Compiler* command, and switch on the two settings, *Debug information* and *Local symbols*, in the *Compiler Options* dialog's *Debugging* section. These settings tell the compiler to generate debugging information along with local symbols (turn this option off to conserve memory). Also use the *Options:Debugger* command and switch on the *Debugger* dialog's *Integrated* option under the *Debugging* header. You can then use the Debug menu's commands to examine your BASM instructions along with Pascal statements.

External Procedures and Functions

The fourth and final method for mixing assembly language and Pascal requires an assembler—either Turbo Assembler (TASM) 1.0 or later or the Microsoft Macro Assembler (MASM) 4.0 or later.

In this method, you write external assembly language procedures and functions in separate text files, assemble the text to object code files, and link the results into a Pascal program. This approach offers many advantages over inline techniques, some of which you can also gain by using BASM. For example:

- You can use the many features found in your assembler for declaring data structures.

- You can use assembly language macros.

- You can jump to labeled instructions.

- You can work on your assembly language modules apart from the Pascal program.

- You can use your assembler's listing abilities to document your assembly language modules.

An External Shell

Program 14-10, SHELL.ASM, is a shell that you can use as a starting place for your own external procedures and functions. Lines and portions of lines beginning with semicolons are comments, which the assembler ignores. Insert any data declarations into the DATA segment where marked by the comment. Unlike with previous version of Turbo Pascal, version 6.0 can now link in initialized data from assembled object-code files.

The CODE key word identifies what follows as a code memory segment. The WORD alignment specified in the segment directive could also be BYTE, although Turbo Pascal's linker always aligns segments on word boundaries regardless of the setting you specify.

The ASSUME directive tells the assembler to assume that register CS is based at this segment. The PUBLIC directive exports symbols in the external listing to the Turbo Pascal linker. For every procedure and function in the external listing—and you can have as many as you want—add the routine's name to the PUBLIC directive. If you declare a procedure MyStuff and a function AddThings, you would write:

```
PUBLIC MyStuff, AddThings
```

The dummy procedure in Program 14-10 starts with a PROC directive, identifying Identifier as Near. If this routine will be linked to a Pascal procedure or function declared *far* (with the **far** key word or the {$F+} compiler directive) or to a routine declared in a unit's interface section, then you must change Near to Far. It's your responsibility to declare *near* and *far* routines—you'll get no help in this regard from the assembler or compiler.

The dummy Identifier routine contains the usual entry and exit code plus a few instructions that might be unnecessary in some cases. For example, if you don't change the stack pointer SP, there's no reason to restore SP's value from BP before the procedure ends. The equate (EQU) assigns to symbol Params the addressing details of a parameter located at [BP+04] on the stack. This step is optional but recommended.

The end of the dummy Identifier procedure ends with an ENDP directive, matching the previous PROC. All PROCs must have a corresponding ENDP, or you'll receive an error from the assembler.

Finally, the last two lines tell the assembler this is the end of the code segment (ENDS) and the end of the entire text file (END).

Program 14-10: SHELL.ASM

```
 1:  ;-- Turbo Pascal shell for external procedures and functions
 2:  ;-- For Turbo Assembler (TASM) or Microsoft Macro Assembler (MASM)
 3:
 4:  DATA     SEGMENT WORD PUBLIC
 5:
 6:  ;-- Insert any external data declarations here
 7:
 8:  DATA      ENDS
 9:
10:  CODE     SEGMENT WORD PUBLIC
11:
12:          ASSUME  CS:CODE,DS:DATA
13:
14:          PUBLIC  Identifier
15:
16:  ;----------------------------------------------------------------
17:  ; procedure Identifier(Params);
18:  ; function Identifier(Params): type;
19:  ;----------------------------------------------------------------
20:
21:  Identifier      PROC    Near    ; may be Far or Near
22:
23:  Params          EQU     (Word Ptr [BP+04]) ; declare parameters
24:
25:          PUSH    BP              ; save bp
26:          MOV     BP,SP           ; address parameters with bp
27:
28:  ;-- insert code here
29:
30:          MOV     SP,BP           ; restore stack pointer
31:          POP     BP              ; restore bp register
32:          RET                     ; return to caller
33:
34:  Identifier      ENDP            ; end of routine
35:
36:  CODE     ENDS            ; end of CODE segment
37:
38:          END             ; end of text
```

Declaring External Data Segments

You can declare a data segment to hold variables for use by external routines. The segment must be named DATA. You can assume that register PS addresses this segment, which the linker combines with global variables declared in the Pascal program. To declare global data in the assembly language module, use a segment declaration such as this:

```
DATA      SEGMENT WORD PUBLIC
count     dw     5
message   db     "This is a string",0
index     db     ?
DATA      ENDS
```

This segment declares three variables, a 16-bit count, a string message ending in a null character, and an uninitialized byte index. These items are mixed with other Pascal globals in the program's data segment. To find the variables, tell the assembler that DS addresses the data segment. To do this, begin the code segment this way:

```
CODE      SEGMENT WORD PUBLIC
          ASSUME CS:CODE, DS:DATA
```

Inside the code segment, to initialize the index variable to $2000, you could write:

```
MOV  index,2000h
```

Because you told the assembler to assume that DS addresses the data segment and because Turbo Pascal initialized DS for you, there's no need to assign the segment address to DS.

For other variables, you can reserve space on the stack just as Pascal procedures and functions do for local variables. Study Figures 14-6 and 14-7 for hints on how to do this.

An External Example

Program 14-11 contains two external functions and two external procedures for accessing an asynchronous serial I/O line, perhaps attached to another computer. To save space, the four routines are simplified and do no error checking, but they still are useful for writing programs to transfer information over a serial line. The comments in the listing describe the commands, for which there isn't room to fully explain here. (This is, after all, a Pascal tutorial, not an assembly language primer!)

Use the Turbo Pascal IDE's editor—or a programmer's text editor—to enter and save Program 14-11 as COMM.ASM. Then, if you have TASM, assemble the code with this DOS command:

```
tasm comm
```

To assemble with MASM, use the command:

```
masm comm;
```

The semicolon tells MASM not to prompt for various optional file names. To see the prompts, enter the same command without a semicolon. Turbo Assembler never displays such prompts.

After assembling, you'll have an object code file named COMM.OBJ containing the assembled code in a form ready for linking to a Turbo Pascal program.

Program 14-11: COMM.ASM

```
 1:  ;-- Communications externals for Turbo Pascal
 2:  ;-- For Turbo Assembler (TASM) or Microsoft Macro Assembler (MASM)
 3:
 4:  DATA      SEGMENT WORD PUBLIC
 5:
 6:  ThePort          dw      ?          ; comm port number
 7:
 8:  DATA      ENDS                      ; end of DATA segment
 9:
10:  CODE      SEGMENT WORD PUBLIC
11:
12:           ASSUME  CS:CODE,DS:DATA
13:
14:           PUBLIC  CommInit, CharReady, GetByte, SendByte
15:
16:  ;------------------------------------------------------------
17:  ; procedure CommInit(Port: Word; Params: Byte);
18:  ;------------------------------------------------------------
19:
20:  CommInit        PROC    Near
21:
22:  port            EQU     (Word Ptr [BP+06])
23:  params          EQU     (Byte Ptr [BP+04])
24:
25:           PUSH    BP              ; save bp
26:           MOV     BP,SP           ; address parameters with bp
27:           MOV     DX,PORT         ; move port number into dx
28:           MOV     ThePort,DX      ; save port number for later
29:           MOV     AL,PARAMS       ; get parameters
```

```
30:            MOV     AH,0            ; select BIOS init function
31:            INT     14H             ; call BIOS RS232-IO
32:            POP     BP              ; restore bp register
33:            RET     10              ; return and deallocate params
34:
35: CommInit       ENDP                ; end of CommInit
36:
37: ;------------------------------------------------------------------
38: ; function CharReady: Boolean;
39: ;------------------------------------------------------------------
40:
41: CharReady      PROC    Near
42:
43:            MOV     DX,ThePort      ; get Comm port number
44:            MOV     AH,3            ; select BIOS status
45:            INT     14H             ; call BIOS RS232-IO
46:            XCHG    AH,AL           ; move ah to al
47:            AND     AX,01H          ; return result in bit 0
48:            RET                     ; return to caller
49:
50: CharReady      ENDP                ; end of CharReady
51:
52: ;------------------------------------------------------------------
53: ; function GetByte: Char;
54: ;------------------------------------------------------------------
55:
56: GetByte        PROC    Near
57:
58:            MOV     DX,ThePort      ; get Comm port number
59:            MOV     AH,2            ; select BIOS receive
60:            INT     14H             ; call BIOS RS232-IO
61:            RET                     ; return to caller
62:
63: GetByte        ENDP                ; end of GetByte
64:
65: ;------------------------------------------------------------------
66: ; procedure SendByte(TheByte: Byte);
67: ;------------------------------------------------------------------
68:
69: SendByte       PROC    Near
70:
71: TheByte        EQU     Byte Ptr [BP+04]
72:
```

```
73:            PUSH    BP              ; save bp
74:            MOV     BP,SP           ; address parameters with bp
75:            MOV     AL,TheByte      ; get the byte to send
76:            MOV     DX,ThePort      ; get Comm port number
77:            MOV     AH,1            ; select BIOS send
78:            INT     14H             ; call BIOS RS232-IO
79:            POP     BP              ; restore bp register
80:            RET     2               ; return and deallocate param
81:
82: SendByte           ENDP           ; end of SendByte
83:
84: CODE    ENDS               ; end of CODE segment
85:
86:         END                ; end of text
```

Linking Externals to Pascal

Linking external routines to Pascal programs requires two steps. First, tell the compiler the name and location of the object code file containing the routines. Second, tell the compiler the format of each routine. Lines 5-13 in Program 14-12 demonstrate how to do this.

Line 5 uses the compiler directive {$L COMM.OBJ}, telling Turbo Pascal to link the routines in the file COMM.OBJ. You do not have to specify the OBJ extension. After this step, lines 7-13 tell the compiler about the routines in the object code file.

Notice that these declarations list the procedures and functions with **external** key words in place of the usual blocks. The word **external** tells the compiler that the actual instruction codes for these routines are external to the program. Compile the program to disk or memory as you normally do. You don't have to perform any special tasks to link in the assembled object code.

Use these external routines just as you do any other Pascal procedures and functions. For example, line 53 calls the external CommInit to initialize serial communications.

While demonstrating how to write external procedures and functions, Program 14-12 is a useful utility for transferring text to other computers and devices such as serial printers that understand a simple I/O protocol called XON-XOFF. Make sure the remote device is ready to receive text and then run the program. Supply the name of a text file to transfer. If you have trouble, press Esc to quit. You might have to adjust the parameters to CommInit to match the configuration of the remote device.

Note: When debugging mixed Pascal and assembly language code with the stand-alone Turbo Debugger, calls to external routines are treated as indivisible statements. In other words, pressing F7 to step into the code of an external procedure or function does not show you the individual assembly language instructions as you might expect. One alternative is to switch to the CPU screen by pressing Alt-V C just before pressing F7 at a call to an external routine. This doesn't show you the original assembly language source code statements, but it does show the external routine's disassembled machine code. You can then press F7 again to execute the original assembly language instructions. Another alternative is to use BASM. As explained earlier in this chapter, Turbo Debugger can step through BASM statements.

Program 14-12: SENDTEXT.PAS

```
 1:    program SendText;
 2:
 3:    uses Crt;
 4:
 5:    {$L comm.obj}    { Link the following routines in COMM.OBJ }
 6:
 7:    procedure CommInit(Port: Word; Params: Byte); external;
 8:
 9:    function CharReady: Boolean; external;
10:
11:    function GetByte: Byte; external;
12:
13:    procedure SendByte(TheByte: Byte); external;
14:
15:    const
16:
17:       Baud110    = $00;      { Baud rate settings }
18:       Baud150    = $20;
19:       Baud300    = $40;
20:       Baud600    = $60;
21:       Baud1200   = $80;
22:       Baud2400   = $A0;
23:       Baud4800   = $C0;
24:       Baud9600   = $E0;
25:
```

```
26:    Noparity   = $00;    { Parity settings }
27:    Oddparity  = $08;
28:    Evenparity = $18;
29:
30:    Onestop    = $00;    { Stop bits settings }
31:    Twostop    = $04;
32:
33:    Len7       = $02;    { Byte length settings }
34:    Len8       = $03;
35:
36:    XON        = ^Q;     { Flow-control characters }
37:    XOFF       = ^S;
38:
39: var
40:
41:    Ch: Char;
42:    F: file of Char;
43:    FileName:  string;
44:    I: Integer;
45:
46: procedure CheckKeyboard;
47: begin
48:    if Keypressed then
49:       if ReadKey = Chr(27) then Halt
50: end;
51:
52: begin
53:    CommInit(0, Baud9600+Noparity+Onestop+Len8);
54:    Write('Send what file? ');
55:    Readln(FileName);
56:    Assign(F, FileName);
57:    Reset(F);
58:    Writeln('Press Esc to stop sending');
59:    while not Eof(F) do
60:    begin
61:      if CharReady then
62:      begin
63:        Ch := Chr(GetByte);
64:        if Ch = XOFF then
65:        repeat
66:          CheckKeyboard;
67:          if CharReady then Ch := Chr(GetByte)
68:        until Ch = XON
69:      end;
```

```
70:       CheckKeyboard;
71:       Read(F, Ch);
72:       SendByte(Ord(Ch))
73:    end;
74:    Close(F)
75: end.
```

Programming Interrupts

As the next example shows, you can also write your own interrupt procedures. Usually, but not always, you'll code the interrupt in assembly language. If you prefer to use Pascal, do so with care. Because interrupts might be activated at any time and from any place, you cannot use Pascal commands that call DOS or BIOS routines, most of which are not reentrant—meaning that, if an interrupted routine is called via mutual recursion by the interrupt handler, problems are almost bound to occur.

To write an interrupt handler, also called an *interrupt service routine,* declare a special Pascal procedure like this:

```
procedure Service(Flags,CS,IP,AX,BX,CX,DX,SI,DI,DS,ES,BP: Word);
  interrupt;
```

The parameters are phony, having the sole purpose of allowing Pascal statements to return values in processor registers. For example, to return a value in register AX, you could write:

```
AX := $1000;     { MOV AX,1000h }
```

If you don't need to reference registers or flags, you may optionally leave them out of the parameter list, cutting from Flags to BP. In other words, if you need to use CX, then you must declare CX plus all the registers following as in this sample:

```
procedure Service(CX,DX,SI,DI,DS,ES,BP: Word);
  interrupt;
```

The key word **interrupt** identifies the procedure as an interrupt service routine. When the Service routine is called, registers AX, BX, CX, DX, SI, DI, DS, ES, and BP are pushed onto the stack. BP and SP are initialized as in a normal procedure for referencing local variables. All registers are pushed onto the stack even if you do not declare the phony register parameters. Also, register DS is initialized to the global data segment, a necessary action because the interrupted process may have changed DS. Therefore, you may reference global variables inside your interrupt service procedure without having to reinitialize DS.

An Example Interrupt Routine

As an example of writing interrupt service routines in Pascal, Program 14-13 displays an independently running timer in the upper-right corner of the display. Before typing and running the program, be aware that installing interrupts in memory can affect the operation of your computer. Line 68 prevents you from breaking out of the program by not allowing you to type the break character, Ctrl- C or Ctrl-Break. This feature lets the program remove the interrupt from memory before ending. Not resetting the interrupt would leave the interrupt vector pointing to procedure ShowTime (lines 12-39), a dangerous practice that is certain to lead to serious problems.

Because of the sensitive nature of Program 14-13, be sure to save it to disk before running it. If you make any typing errors in the **asm** statement, you may have to reboot your computer, losing the in-memory program text.

The interrupt service routine, ShowTime in lines 12-39, does not have any Pascal statements and, therefore, declares no register parameters. The program prepares interrupt number $1C to display the time of day in the top-right corner of your screen. Use the appropriate value in line 6 for your computer. $B000 is for monochrome displays. $B800 is for color displays and the PCjr (80-column modes only).

The program operates by taking advantage of the IBM PC timer circuits, which execute interrupt number $1C hexadecimal 18.2 times per second. Because the program changes the interrupt $1C vector to the service routine's address, ShowTime runs at this same frequency independently of the other program parts. To demonstrate this independence, an example of *concurrent processing,* procedure DoWhateverYouWant at lines 47-60 lets you enter strings, which the procedure then writes 40 times. This arbitrary action demonstrates that the procedure and the clock interrupt, cycling at 18.2 times per second, run concurrently.

To set up this action, InitInterrupt calls Dos unit routines GetIntVec and SetIntVec at lines 43-44 to initialize interrupt $1C to the address of the ShowTime interrupt service routine, saving the current interrupt vector in a pointer variable for later restoring. Notice how line 44 uses the @ operator to pass the address of the service routine to SetIntVec.

Procedure DeInitInterrupt (lines 62-65) reverses the process, restoring interrupt $1C to whatever routine the vector previously addressed. After deinitializing, the program may safely end with no worry of accidentally leaving the independently executing interrupt routine in memory.

The **asm** statement at lines 13-39 decodes the IBM PC timer values located at addresses $0000:046C to $0000:046F. These actions display each digit of time in reversed video by simply poking the appropriate characters directly into video display memory (see lines 26, 28, 36, and 38). The comments to the right of the assembly language statements explain how the procedure works.

Program 14-13: TIMER.PAS

```pascal
 1:  program Timer;
 2:
 3:  uses Crt, Dos;
 4:
 5:  const
 6:    DispSeg = $B800;        { Use $B000 for Monochrome display }
 7:
 8:  var
 9:    OldVector: Pointer;  { Holds original interrupt $1C vector }
10:
11:  { WARNING: Never directly call this procedure! }
12:  procedure ShowTime; interrupt; assembler;
13:  asm
14:    xor ax,ax                 { ax<-0000                }
15:    mov ds,ax
16:    mov ax,[$046d]            { get timer div 256       }
17:    mov bx,DispSeg            { bx=display addr         }
18:    mov ds,bx                 { ds=display addr         }
19:    mov word ptr [$009a],$0f07c { display '¦'           }
20:    mov bh,$70                { attribute=reversed      }
21:    push ax                   { save timer value        }
22:    xchg ah,al                { ah=timer hi mod 256     }
23:    aam                       { make unpacked bcd       }
24:    or ax,$3030               { convert to ascii        }
25:    mov bl,ah
26:    mov [$0096],bx            { display 1st hr digit }
27:    mov bl,al
28:    mov [$0098],bx            { display 2nd hr digit }
29:    pop ax                    { restore timer value  }
30:    mov cx,$0f06              { calc ax / 4.26       }
31:    mul ch                    {   ax<-ax * 15        }
32:    shr ax,cl                 {   ax<-ax / 64        }
33:    aam
34:    or  ax,$3030
35:    mov bl,ah
36:    mov [$009C],bx            { display 1st min dig. }
37:    mov bl,al
38:    mov [$009e],bx            { display 2nd min dig. }
39:  end;
40:
```

continued

Program 14-13: continued

```
41:   procedure InitInterrupt;
42:   begin
43:     GetIntVec($1C, OldVector);   { Save old interrupt $1C vector }
44:     SetIntVec($1C, @ShowTime)    { Set new interrupt $1C vector }
45:   end;
46:
47:   procedure DoWhateverYouWant;
48:   var
49:     I: Integer;
50:     S:  string [80];
51:   begin
52:     repeat
53:       Write('Enter a string (RET to quit): ');
54:       Readln(S);
55:       for I := 1 to 40 do
56:         Write(S);
57:       Writeln;
58:       Writeln
59:     until Length(S) = 0
60:   end;
61:
62:   procedure DeInitInterrupt;
63:   begin
64:     SetIntVec($1C, OldVector)
65:   end;
66:
67:   begin
68:     CheckBreak := false;   { Must not end program with ^C! }
69:     InitInterrupt;
70:     DoWhateverYouWant;
71:     DeInitInterrupt        { Required before ending program. }
72:   end.
```

Adding Assembly Language to Units

You can use any of the techniques discussed so far to optimize units with assembly language. The following notes will help:

- You may declare inline procedures and functions in a unit's public interface. These routines are then available to host programs, just as though the host declared them directly. Unlike regular procedure and functions declarations, inline routines do not require completed bodies in the unit's implementation.

- Inline procedures and functions may also be declared in a unit's private implementation. Like other declarations in this section, private inline routines are not available to host programs.

- Inline statements must go in the unit's implementation, as do all code-generating statements. You can't insert inline statements in a unit's interface.

- A unit's implementation may include BASM **asm** statement blocks in procedures, functions, and in the unit's initialization section.

- External routines may be public or private. Declare such routines in the unit's interface as though you were going to write their bodies in Pascal. In the unit's interface, declare the same routines with **external** key words in place of their statement bodies.

- In the .ASM file, public external routines must be *far*. Private externals must be *near*. Neglect this rule and your code is certain to crash.

As explained earlier, optimizing critical procedures and functions is one of the best ways to increase runtime performance. Adding assembly language to units makes it easy to keep two versions of your important routines—one version optimized with assembly language and the other written purely in Pascal. If you suspect a bug in your assembly language code, a quick substitution with the original (and, of course, fully tested) Pascal routines will confirm your suspicions.

Because a unit hides the details of its implementation—only the interface's declarations are visible to the outside world—host programs (and host-program programmers) do not have to know whether the actual code is written in Pascal or assembly language. As a real-life example, consider the standard Turbo Pascal Dos, Crt, and Graph units. Some of these units' routines were written in assembly language; others, in Pascal—facts that you don't need to know when using the units.

To demonstrate how to optimize units with assembly language, Program 14-14 incorporates Program 14-11's, communication routines into a Pascal unit. You'll have to make a few changes to earlier programs before using this unit. Follow these steps:

- Copy Program 14-11, COMM.ASM, to a new file named COMMF.ASM. Load this file into your editor and change Near to Far (four times). In CommInit change port address [BP+06] to [BP+08]. Change Params address [BP+04] to [BP+06]. In SendByte, change theByte address [BP+04] to [BP+06].

- Assemble COMMF.ASM with the command "tasm commf" or "masm commf;" depending on which assembler you have. This creates the file COMMF.OBJ.

- Save Program 14-14 as COMMU.PAS and compile to COMMU.TPU.

- To test the new unit, copy Program 14-12, SENDTEXT.PAS, to a new file named SEND2.PAS. Edit this file and delete lines 5-13. Also, change line 3 to:

```
uses Crt, CommU;
```

After completing these steps, you need only the COMMU.TPU file to compile SEND2.PAS and other host programs that use the assembly language communications routines. You don't need the .ASM or .OBJ files. You also don't need the COMMU.PAS file. (If this were a commercial program, you'd want to supply a .DOC or .INT file listing COMMU's interface.)

Notice that Program 14-14's interface and the modified host program show no sign that COMMU's routines are actually written as external assembly language routines. Organizing the unit as illustrated here hides the dirty implementation details from view.

Program 14-14: COMMU.PAS

```
 1: unit CommU;        { Communications unit }
 2:
 3: interface
 4:
 5: { Initialize a comm port with parameters. Set Port to a comm port
 6: number. COM1: = 0, COM2: = 1, COM3 = 2, and COM4 = 3. Set Params to a
 7: combination of baud rate, parity, stop bits, and byte length values.
 8: For example, Params might be baud9600 + noparity + onestop + len8.
 9: You may add or use logical OR operators to combine values. See
10: SENDTEXT.PAS for an example. }
11:
12: procedure CommInit(Port: Word; Params: Byte);
13:
14: { Returns true if a character is waiting to be read. Returns false
15: if no character is waiting. After CharReady returns true, call
16: GetByte to retrieve the waiting character. }
17:
18: function CharReady: Boolean;
```

```
19:
20:   { Returns a byte (or character) from the comm port. Usually, you
21:   should call CharReady, and if that function returns true, immediately
22:   call GetByte to retrieve the waiting character. }
23:
24:   function GetByte: Byte;
25:
26:   { Send a byte (or character) to the comm port. }
27:
28:   procedure SendByte(TheByte: Byte);
29:
30:   implementation
31:
32:   {$L commf.obj}      { Link the following far routines from COMMF.OBJ }
33:
34:   procedure  CommInit(Port: Word; Params: Byte); external;
35:
36:   function CharReady: Boolean; external;
37:
38:   function GetByte: Byte; external;
39:
40:   procedure SendByte(TheByte: Byte); external;
41:
42:   end.
```

Summary

Converting critical routines into machine language can improve the performance of a Pascal program. Turbo Pascal provides four ways to add machine language to programs: inline statements, inline procedures and functions, **asm** statement blocks, and external routines.

When adding machine language to Pascal, it's your responsibility to know how to locate variables in memory, prepare a stack frame, and preserve registers. You also must know the storage details of variables—details that the compiler normally handles.

Turbo Pascal lets you write your own interrupt service routines either in Pascal or in machine language.

Exercises

14-1. Convert Program 14-12 to receive text transmitted from a remote computer.

14-2. (Advanced) Add error checking to the external routines in COMM.ASM (Program 14-11).

14-3. (Advanced) Code your own interrupt procedure to sound an alarm at a certain time.

14-4. (Advanced) Optimize a Pascal program of your choice by identifying and converting critical routines to assembly language. Use inline statements, inline procedures and functions, asm statements, or external modules. Run time-trials to prove that your efforts are worth the trouble.

14-5. (Advanced) Convert MySquare in Program 14-3 to an inline function. What is the advantage of this method over the one in the listing?

15

Object-Oriented Programming

- Objectives
- Turbo Pascal's OOP Extensions
- Programming with Turbo Pascal Objects
- Inheritance
- Virtual Methods
- Dynamic Objects
- Objects and Variable (Typed) Constants
- Private Object Declarations
- SizeOf and TypeOf
- Glossary of OOP Terms

15

Objectives

Every once in a while, a new computing concept blows in like a summer breeze on a sultry morning. Structured programming comes to mind. BASIC deserves a place in the sun, as do Pascal, the IBM PC, and the Apple II. Now there's something new in the air; something called *object-oriented programming,* which goes by the almost comical acronym, OOP.

This chapter explores Turbo Pascal 6.0's OOP extensions and puts a practical face on what to many programmers is a mysterious stranger with unknown intentions. Who needs OOP and why? What are OOP's advantages and disadvantages? Those are good questions and you should be skeptical. OOP is new. OOP is different. And, who knows, after the dust from this new wind settles, all the hOOPla may not have been warranted.

While learning about OOP, keep in mind that everything in this chapter is completely optional. No other chapters, except the material on Turbo Vision in chapters 16-17, require you to know OOP techniques. Most Turbo Pascal programs (and most programmers) do not use OOP, although that soon may change.

To understand the information in this chapter, you should first read chapters 1 through 7 and be able to do the exercises. A good understanding of pointers and heap memory management is especially helpful. Also, be aware that Turbo Pascal OOP extensions are experimental, and they may be further enhanced in future compiler versions. It's even conceivable that OOP will die out for lack of interest.

But I doubt that will happen. More likely, OOP will be accepted for its real value—a concept that helps programmers solve increasingly complex problems posed by modern personal computers and new advances in operating systems, especially in the area of graphical interfaces. We're fast approaching the time when OOP will be an essential programming tool, and those who learn OOP now will be in a position to control the future of programming.

That is, of course, until the next new breeze drifts ashore.

A Brief History of OOP

OOP's roots began in the late 1960s with a language called Simula 67, which traces its own beginnings to Algol. Simula was designed for writing simulations—still an excellent purpose for OOP techniques. Since then, other OOP languages have appeared with an array of names that reads like the back wall of an ice cream shop: Smalltalk, LOOPS, Flavors, Object Pascal (for the Macintosh), Neon (also for the Mac), Objective C, C++, and Actor (for Microsoft Windows). As you can see, OOP concepts have been around for some time and the OOP field isn't exactly barren.

Why, then, is OOP coming into the forefront now? One reason is the complexity of software that PC programmers are writing. Software source code is becoming longer and more difficult to modify. Time is becoming more expensive, and market competition is ever more fierce. OOP promises to help programmers and software companies become more productive. But whether that promise pans out remains to be seen.

Perhaps programmers have been slow to adopt OOP because none of the current OOP languages implements object-oriented concepts in exactly the same way. Add to this confusion Turbo Pascal's unique OOP extensions—borrowed in part from C++ and Object Pascal—and it's easy to see that there's little consensus among designers about the best way to implement OOP languages.

Don't be dismayed by this apparent jumble. Keep in mind that OOP *concepts* are what matter the most—not the forms. Learn the concepts, and you'll have no trouble with the details. In this department, Turbo Pascal OOP extensions are among the easiest to get to know.

What OOP Can and Can't Do

To understand what OOP can and can't do, you need to learn two new terms: *encapsulation* and *inheritance*. (There are many other new terms and phrases that go with OOP, some of which can be confusing at first. I'll introduce the more important terms as the OOP story unfolds. The Glossary of OOP Terms at the end of this chapter explains these terms and more.)

Encapsulation refers to the binding of data and executable code, which are stored separately in procedural languages such as non-OOP Pascal and C. In OOP, an *object* is a data structure, similar to a Pascal **record**, that contains variables and related processes, called *methods.* Instead of writing procedures and functions that act upon data, in OOP you create objects that know how to perform actions on themselves.

Inheritance refers to the ability of new objects to inherit the characteristics—data and methods—of other objects. Similar to the way non-OOP Pascal lets you structure large programs into many small procedures and functions that make up the grand whole, OOP lets you easily create new objects by extending those that already exist. In this way, OOP simplifies building new programs from existing program libraries, usually without having to make extensive modifications to programming that already works.

With OOP, instead of reinventing the wheel every time you start a new program, you simply choose a set of objects that approximate the data and methods you need, and then extend those objects to finish the job. At least, that's the theory. Accomplishing this ideal in practice requires patience and careful programming, especially if you're just learning OOP's ropes.

Turbo Pascal's OOP Extensions

Turbo Pascal's OOP extensions add five new reserved key words, listed in Table 15-1. Three other new identifiers are Fail (a new built-in procedure), Self (a pointer to an object), and TypeOf (a new standard function). You'll meet these new items again later on.

Table 15-1 Turbo Pascal OOP reserved words.

Reserved word	Meaning
constructor	Prefaces an object's constructor methods
destructor	Prefaces an object's destructor methods
object	Begins object definitions
private	Marks an object's private section
virtual	Designates virtual method definitions

Except for these eight new identifiers (the five in the table plus Fail, Self, and TypeOf), everything else about OOP is standard Turbo Pascal. You can use **if** and **while** statements, assign values to variables, and perform other actions just as before. Everything you already know about procedures, functions, parameters, variables, pointers, and other Pascal elements holds true. You can mix OOP and standard Pascal at will. These facts let you pick up OOP concepts in your own good time without having to learn a new language from scratch. When converting programs to use OOP techniques, you can revise existing code in small chunks, rather than face a complete rewrite—never an enjoyable task.

By the way, Turbo Pascal OOP extensions resemble those in C++ and, to a lesser degree, Object Pascal for the Macintosh. See the Bibliography for references that describe these languages.

> **Note:** Appendix A includes syntax (railroad) diagrams for Turbo Pascal's new object-oriented extensions.

Programming with Turbo Pascal Objects

An *object type*—called a *class* in some other OOP languages—defines an object's contents. Object types are similar to Pascal record definitions such as:

```
DateRec = record
  Month: Byte;
  Day: Byte;
  Year: Word;
end;
```

The three data fields Month, Day, and Year are grouped by DateRec's definition, allowing programs to create multipart variables:

```
var
  Today: DateRec;
```

The Today **record** is a variable of type DateRec with two Byte fields and one Word field. To assign values to the individual fields in Today, programs execute statements such as:

```
Today.Month := 6;
Today.Day := 6;
Today.Year := 1989;
```

Or, you can use a **with** statement to simplify the program text:

```
with today do
begin
  Month := 6;
  Day := 6;
  Year := 1989;
end;
```

If this were a real program, at this point, you'd probably begin writing a few procedures to display the date, to let people enter new dates from the keyboard, to advance a DateRec variable to the next day, to determine if a year is a leap year, and so on. To perform these operations, you'd then feed DateRec variables to your procedures. In essence, that's the standard programming approach in procedural languages like Pascal and C.

Object Data Fields

An OOP solution to the same problem also defines a new data structure, but this time using the **object** key word in place of **record**:

```
DateObj = object
  Month: Byte;
  Day: Byte;
  Year: Word;
  procedure Init(MM, DD, YY: Word);
  function StringDate: string;
end;
```

As before, three data fields Month, Day, and Year store values representing a unique date. Some OOP languages call these fields *instance variables*. Unlike a Pascal record, **procedure** and **function** headers define the format of two routines Init and StringDate in addition to the object's data fields. These routines are the object's *methods*—the actions that the DateObj object knows how to perform. Usually, methods do something with an object's data fields, in this example assigning parameters MM, DD, and YY to Month, Day, and Year, and returning the date as a **string**. (The code for these functions comes later.) As explained earlier, merging data and code this way is called encapsulation. The object type DateObj encapsulates variables and methods in one handy package.

Remember that the object declaration is just that—a data-type declaration. An object type is a *design* for an object, not the object itself. An object type occupies no space and contains no code. It merely describes the form of an object—just as a **record** data-type definition describes the form of **record** variables to be created later.

An example that fleshes out the DateObj object type helps explain more about Turbo Pascal OOP. Compile Program 15-1 as you normally do. You don't need to change any settings or use special option letters to switch on OOP extensions. Turbo Pascal is always OOP-ready.

Program 15-1: DATEOBJ.PAS

```
1:   program DateObjects;
2:
3:   type
4:     DateObj = object
5:       Month: Byte;
6:       Day: Byte;
7:       Year: Word;
8:       procedure Init(MM, DD, YY: Word);
9:       function StringDate: string;
10:    end;
11:
12:  var
13:    Today: DateObj;
14:
15:  procedure DateObj.Init(MM, DD, YY: Word);
16:  begin
17:    Month := MM;
18:    Day := DD;
19:    Year := YY
20:  end;
21:
22:  function DateObj.StringDate: string;
23:  var
24:    MStr, DStr, YStr: string[10];
25:  begin
26:    Str(Month, MStr);      { Convert month to string }
27:    Str(Day, DStr);        { Convert day to string }
28:    Str(Year, YStr);       { Convert year to string }
29:    StringDate := MStr + '/' + DStr + '/' + YStr
30:  end;
31:
32:  begin
33:    Today.Init(12, 20, 1989);
34:    Writeln('The date is: ', Today.StringDate);
35:    Readln
36:  end.
```

Object Methods

Lines 12-13 in Program 15-1 declare a variable Today of type DateObj. In OOP parlance, a variable of an object data type is called an *object instance*. The object type is *instantiated* in the variable—just a fancy way of saying that memory space is allocated for a variable of the object type. As you know, you can create many variables of any Pascal data types, for instance, a series of Integers:

```
var
   I, J, K: Integer;
```

Similarly, you can declare many instances of object types:

```
var
   Today, Yesterday, Tomorrow: DateObj;
```

The three object instances Today, Yesterday, and Tomorrow each has its own copies of the data fields declared in DateObj. But there's a major difference between objects and records: Multiple instances of object types *share the same methods.* In Program 15-1, those methods are completed at lines 15-30, appearing much like normal Pascal procedures and functions. Dot notation identifies the routines as object methods. For example, examine line 15:

```
procedure DateObj.Init(MM, DD, YY: Word);
```

Method Init is joined by dot notation to DateObj, telling the compiler that Init is a method belonging to DateObj. This special format lets you write a non-OOP procedure named Init without conflict, although the resulting confusion of naming common procedures and methods similarly is unappealing. Try not to use the same identifiers for methods and other Pascal procedures and functions.

Figure 15-1 illustrates how multiple-object instances (variables) of the same object type have separate copies of the object's data fields but share the same method implementations. This is an important concept to learn.

The method implementations (lines 15-30) contain Pascal statements that perform the actions for the DateObj object type. Init assigns its three parameters to the appropriate object data fields. Most objects contain similar methods to assign new values to an object's instance variables. DateObj uses Turbo Pascal's built-in Str procedure and three temporary string variables (lines 23-24) to convert the date field values to strings, which are joined together with slashes at line 29 and passed back as the StringDate function result.

Lines 33 and 34 call the object methods, assigning date values to Today and displaying the result. Again, dot notation tells the compiler that this is an object method:

```
Today.Init(12, 20, 1989);
```

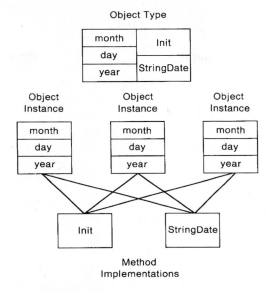

Figure 15-1 Multiple-object instances have separate copies of an object type's data fields but share the same method implementations.

In technical OOP talk, such statements are said to pass the *message* Init to the object instance Today, in effect giving Today a command to initialize itself. Strictly speaking, the statement does *not* call a procedure named Init, although, of course, the compiled machine code does in fact perform a subroutine call to Init's address. If this description seems arbitrary and confusing, don't dwell on it. The distinction between passing messages to objects and calling procedures and functions is less important in Turbo Pascal OOP than it is in some other OOP languages.

A few more observations about Program 15-1 explain other key OOP concepts:

- An object type such as DateObj at lines 4-10 is similar to a unit's interface section, where global functions, procedures, and variables are declared. The method implementations (lines 15-30) are analogous to a unit's implementation section, where the details of the unit's design are hidden from the rest of the program. Like units, objects hide their messy coding details, insulating programmers from becoming mired in too many low-level details.

- Inside a method's implementation, an implied **with** statement makes the object's data fields available to statements. Line 17 assigns MM to Month, a field in DateObj. An object's data fields are readily available inside the object's method implementations. Because of this requirement, identifiers in method parameter lists—for example, MM, DD, and YY in line 8—must be different from any data fields in the object, such as Month, Day, and Year at lines 5-7. Using the same name for a data field and a method parameter is a common mistake that causes a "Duplicate identifier" compiler error.

- You may access data fields in object instances directly outside of a method's implementation, too. For example, there's nothing to prevent you from writing:

```
Today.Month := 10;
```

This may seem natural, but there's a good reason for not accessing object data fields directly this way—a reason that will become clear later on. Direct access to object fields is always allowed, but is best avoided.

Inheritance

So far, you may be thinking there's not much point to OOP. After all, it would be easy to write a non-OOP version of Program 15-1. OOP's advantages become clearer when you see how new object definitions can inherit the characteristics of other objects. As mentioned earlier, inheritance is one of OOP's major contributions to programming.

Ancestors and Descendants

An object that inherits the characteristics of another object is called a *descendant object*. The object from which the inherited features come is called the *ancestor object*. An important rule to memorize is that descendant objects can have only one immediate ancestor, as Figure 15-2 illustrates. Conversely, ancestor objects can have an unlimited number of descendants. This relationship is called *single inheritance*. Some OOP languages allow *multiple inheritance*, where a descendant object may have more than one parent. This is not possible in Turbo Pascal—at least not yet. In the figure, the dashed line shows what would be an illegal multiple ancestor relation for the bottom object.

The importance of multiple inheritance is a hotly debated topic in OOP circles—and the outcome of this debate is still uncertain.

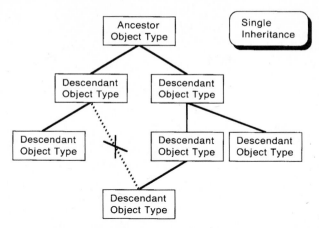

Figure 15-2 Single inheritance allows objects to have many descendants but only one immediate ancestor. Multiple inheritance (represented by the dashed line) is not allowed in Turbo Pascal.

Inherited Data Fields

To create a new object that inherits the characteristics of another object, define a new object type with the ancestor object type name in parentheses. For example, suppose you now need to represent the time *and* the date. If you've done a lot of Pascal programming, you'd probably attempt to define a new date type like this:

```
TimeRec = record
  Hour: Byte;
  Minute: Byte;
  Second: Byte;
  TheDate: DateObj;
end;
```

Turbo Pascal's OOP extensions allow a much better way to accomplish inheritance: Define a new object type that inherits the characteristics of DateObj:

```
TimeObj = object(DateObj)
  Hour: Byte;
  Minute: Byte;
  Second: Byte;
  procedure Init(MM, DD, YY, HH, MI, SS: Word);
  function StringTime: string;
end;
```

The new object type, TimeObj, declares three data fields Hour, Minute, and Second, representing a certain time. Two methods initialize the object (Init) and return the time as a string (StringTime).

591

Because TimeObj is descended from DateObj, the new object contains all features in its ancestor. Every TimeObj instance has Hour, Minute, and Second fields *plus* Month, Day, and Year fields from DateObj. Descendant objects always inherit all data fields from their ancestors.

Inherited Methods

In addition to inheriting data fields, the new TimeObj object type inherits its ancestor's methods. Every TimeObj instance "knows" how to perform a StringTime function—defined by the TimeObj object type—and a StringDate function—defined by the ancestor DateObj.

All TimeObj instances also have an Init procedure, and this brings up another important OOP concept. Because TimeObj's Init function has the same name as its ancestor Init from DateObj, the descendant's method definition *overrides* the ancestor method. This fact doesn't mean that the ancestor method disappears. It's still there, beneath the surface of the descendant's replacement method. As you recall, DateObj's Init method is declared as:

```
procedure Init(MM, DD, YY: Word);
```

The new TimeObj Init method is declared as:

```
procedure Init(MM, DD, YY, HH, MI, SS: Word);
```

The overriding Init lists all the parameters of the ancestor Init, and it adds three new parameters, representing the hour, minute, and seconds for initializing a TimeObj object instance. This is a typical OOP setup. The overriding procedures and functions—especially those that initialize object data fields—add new parameters to those in ancestor methods.

> **Note:** Only methods may be overridden in descendant objects. Data fields may never be overridden; therefore, in a descendant object, new data fields must have identifiers that are unique not only in the object declaration, but among all ancestors from which the object descends.

Program 15-2 lists the final result, duplicating all of Program 15-1 and extending DateObj with the TimeObj object type at lines 12-18. Line 22 declares Appointment as a TimeObj instance.

Study the new method implementations. TimeObj.Init at lines 41-47 assigns the three new parameters to the descendant object's data fields, initializing the time. Look closely at line 43. The statement:

```
DateObj.Init(MM, DD, YY);
```

calls the ancestor's Init method, passing the other three parameters to initialize the inherited date fields. Prefacing Init with the DateObj object type identifier and a period tells the compiler which of the identically named Inits to use. Although this example has only two object types, another program might have several objects, each descended from another, and each with its own Init method. TimeObj's Init method implementation could directly assign the date values to the inherited date fields. But it's easier just to call the ancestor's method, which is already programmed to perform that task.

Lines 49-60 implement a non-OOP procedure to convert values to strings with leading zeros. Lines 62-72 implement the StringTime method, similar to the StringDate method explained earlier.

Finally, examine lines 77-80. First, a single statement initializes the entire object—assigning date and time values. A Writeln statement then displays the date and time. Line 80 proves that Appointment has a StringDate method, inherited from the object's DateObj ancestor.

Program 15-2: DATEOBJ2.PAS

```
 1:  program DateObjects2;
 2:
 3:  type
 4:    DateObj = object
 5:      Month: Byte;
 6:      Day: Byte;
 7:      Year: Word;
 8:      procedure Init(Mm, Dd, Yy: Word);
 9:      function StringDate: string;
10:    end;
11:
12:    TimeObj = object(DateObj)
13:      Hour: Byte;
14:      Minute: Byte;
15:      Second: Byte;
16:      procedure Init(Mm, Dd, Yy, Hh, Mi, Ss: Word);
17:      function StringTime: string;
18:    end;
19:
20:  var
21:    Today: DateObj;
22:    Appointment: TimeObj;
23:
```

continued

Program 15-2: continued

```
24:   procedure DateObj.Init(Mm, Dd, Yy: Word);
25:   begin
26:     Month := Mm;
27:     Day := Dd;
28:     Year := Yy
29:   end;
30:
31:   function DateObj.StringDate: string;
32:   var
33:     MStr, DStr, YStr: string[10];
34:   begin
35:     Str(Month, MStr);      { Convert month to string }
36:     Str(Day, DStr);        { Convert day to string }
37:     Str(Year, YStr);       { Convert year to string }
38:     StringDate := MStr + '/' + DStr + '/' + YStr
39:   end;
40:
41:   procedure TimeObj.Init(Mm, Dd, Yy, Hh, Mi, Ss: Word);
42:   begin
43:     DateObj.Init(Mm, Dd, Yy);
44:     Hour := Hh;
45:     Minute := Mi;
46:     Second := Ss
47:   end;
48:
49:   procedure Convert(N: Word; var S: string; Len: Word);
50:   { Convert n to string s of length n, inserting leading 0s }
51:   var P: Integer;
52:   begin
53:     Str(N:Len, S);      { Do raw number to string conversion }
54:     P := Pos(' ', S);
55:     while P > 0 do
56:     begin
57:       S[P] := '0';
58:       P := Pos(' ', S)
59:     end
60:   end;
61:
62:   function TimeObj.StringTime: string;
63:   var
```

```
64:    HStr, MStr, SStr: string[10];
65:  begin
66:  {$V-} { Turn off string length checks }
67:    Convert(Hour, HStr, 2);      { Convert hour to string }
68:    Convert(Minute, MStr, 2);    { Convert minute to string }
69:    Convert(Second, SStr, 2);    { Convert second to string }
70:  {$V+} { Turn string length checks on }
71:    StringTime := HStr + ':' + MStr + ':' + SStr
72:  end;
73:
74:  begin
75:    Today.Init(12, 20, 1989);
76:    Writeln('The date is: ', Today.StringDate);
77:    Appointment.Init(12, 24, 1989, 17, 15, 00);
78:    Writeln('The appointment is at: ',
79:      Appointment.StringTime, ' on ',
80:      Appointment.StringDate);
81:    Readln
82:  end.
```

Turbo Pascal's Smart Linker

One of OOP's possible drawbacks is the fact that new objects inherit everything from their ancestors. But what if you don't need all that the ancestor has to share? You might be tempted in such cases to start over, designing new object types from scratch to avoid wasting memory.

Avoid this temptation. While you can't prevent objects from inheriting ancestor data fields, you can freely extend object methods without worrying about introducing methods that won't ever be used. Turbo Pascal's "smart" linker strips out methods that are never called. If a program never refers to a method, the code for that method is not included in the compiled result. There is no penalty for adding methods that are never used. They take up space only in the program text.

Virtual Methods

The methods in object types such as DateObj and TimeObj (see Program 15-2, lines 8-9 and 16-17) are *static methods.* A static method header in an object definition is identical in form to a procedure or function header in a unit's interface section.

Virtual methods add the **virtual** key word to the end of the method definition. For example, to convert Init and StringDate in Program 15-2 to virtual methods, change lines 8 and 9 to:

```
procedure Init(MM, DD, YY: Word); virtual;
function StringDate: string; virtual;
```

Don't make this change just yet. Virtual methods require special initialization to avoid an almost certain system crash. To understand why this is so, you need to learn the purpose of virtual methods plus another new term, *polymorphism*.

Note: Unlike static methods, unused virtual methods are not stripped by Turbo Pascal's smart linker.

Polymorphism

Virtual methods let you create *polymorphic objects*—literally object instances that can assume different forms when the program runs. A polymorphic object instance might take on the form of itself or any of its descendants.

For example, an object type's root ancestor might be named Vehicle with descendants TwoWheelers and FourWheelers from which Cart, Bicycle, and Automobile are descended. All such objects share some of the same characteristics—the ability to go, to stop, to accelerate, and so on. Suppose you create an object instance of type Automobile:

```
var MyWheels: Automobile;
```

You then want to tell the object to stop. Because there's a world of difference in the way you stop a cart, a bicycle, and an automobile, each object type defines its own Stop method, overriding its ancestor's method. To stop any object takes only a simple statement:

```
MyWheels.Stop;
```

But now a complication sets in. Suppose also that the root ancestor object Vehicle defines a data field Velocity and another method called SlowDown. The implementation for SlowDown might be something like this:

```
procedure Vehicle.SlowDown;
begin
  if Velocity > 0
    then Velocity := Velocity - 1;
  if Velocity = 0
    then Stop
end;
```

All objects descending from Vehicle slow down in exactly the same way. (At least they do for our purposes.) Because descendant objects inherit the methods of their ancestors, it's perfectly legal to write:

```
MyWheels.SlowDown
```

If this causes Velocity to reach 0, the **if** statement in SlowDown calls the Stop method.

But which Stop method?

Obviously, we want SlowDown to use the Stop method that applies to an Automobile. Unfortunately, this is not what happens. Because SlowDown is implemented as a method in the root ancestor Vehicle, the compiler generates code to call Vehicle.Stop, not Automobile.Stop.

Fixing this problem is easy—just make Stop virtual. By doing this, you are telling the compiler that the actual Stop method to use isn't known until the SlowDown method executes. At that time, you want the code to examine the type of object that's slowing down and, if the velocity reaches 0, to call the appropriate Stop method that applies to this type of Vehicle.

A more general explanation illustrates this problem, which virtual methods neatly solve. Program 15-3 defines two objects, Object1 and Object2 at lines 4-11. Object1 defines two methods, MethodA and MethodB. A descendant object inherits these methods but replaces MethodA with its own version.

Examine the method implementations. Each MethodA simply displays a message so we know which method is running. Object1's MethodB does the same, but also calls MethodA.

Two object instances, Item1 of type Object1 and Item2 of type Object2, are declared at lines 13-15. The main body of the program (lines 34-35) calls MethodB, displaying:

```
Inside Object1's MethodA
Inside MethodB
Inside Object1's MethodA
Inside MethodB
```

But this is not correct. When Item2 activates MethodB inherited from Object1, we want the statement at line 24 to call the new MethodA that Object2 defines as a replacement for the ancestor's method. Figure 15-3 illustrates the problem. MethodB's implementation is hard wired during compilation to MethodA in Object1, a process called *early binding*. Object2's replacement MethodA can never be called by MethodB. The solution, as you'll see in the next program, is to convert MethodA to a virtual method.

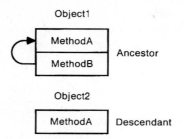

Object1

MethodA
MethodB

Ancestor

Object2

MethodA

Descendant

Figure 15-3 MethodB is tightly bound to Object1's MethodA, preventing it from calling Object2's replacement MethodA.

Program 15-3: STATIC.PAS

```
 1:   program StaticTrouble;
 2:
 3:   type
 4:     Object1 = object
 5:        procedure MethodA;
 6:        procedure MethodB;
 7:     end;
 8:
 9:     object2 = object(Object1)
10:        procedure MethodA;
11:     end;
12:
13:   var
14:     Item1: Object1;
15:     Item2: object2;
16:
17:   procedure Object1.MethodA;
18:   begin
19:     Writeln('Inside Object1''s MethodA')
20:   end;
21:
22:   procedure Object1.MethodB;
23:   begin
24:     MethodA;
25:     Writeln('Inside MethodB')
26:   end;
27:
```

```
28:  procedure object2.MethodA;
29:  begin
30:    Writeln('Inside Object2''s MethodA')
31:  end;
32:
33:  begin
34:    Item1.MethodB;
35:    Item2.MethodB;
36:    Readln
37:  end.
```

Constructors

Object types that define virtual methods require a special method called a *constructor*. The purpose of a constructor is similar to that of the Init method in Program 15-1. Object constructors are syntactically identical to procedure methods but use the key word **constructor** in place of **procedure**. A constructor may have parameters, but it doesn't have to. Constructors can be inherited just like other methods and can be replaced by new methods defined in descendants.

Every object that defines one or more virtual methods *must* have a constructor. If you don't define a constructor method in an object with virtual procedures and functions, the program will fail to operate. There are no exceptions to this rule.

A constructor performs two services. It can initialize data fields in the object instance—just as Init does in Program 15-1. And it always initializes an object's *Virtual Method Table* (VMT), which is stored in the program's global data segment (see Appendix B's memory map).

A VMT stores two kinds of information—the size of the object and a set of pointers to the object type's methods. The method pointers in the VMT allow an object instance to use inherited methods in ancestor objects that in turn use replacement methods in the descendant. The constructor links the object instance to its VMT, allowing the object to locate its methods. This linkage occurs at run time, a process called *late binding*.

> **Note:** Turbo Pascal creates a VMT for object *types* defined in a program. Multiple object *instances* (variables) of the same type share a single VMT. The VMT is stored in the program's data segment along with other global variables. VMT's are not stored in object instances.

Figure 15-4 shows the new arrangement after making MethodA virtual. MethodB in Object1 now locates MethodA by consulting the VMT rather than calling the method directly, as it did in Figure 15-3. There still is only one copy of MethodB's code in memory. But, because Object2 inherits MethodB from Object1, and because MethodB now consults the object's VMT for virtual method calls, MethodB now calls the replacement MethodA in Object2 while still calling the original MethodA in Object1 as before.

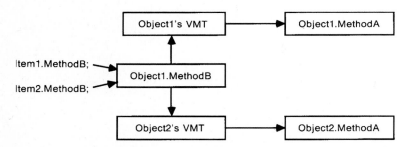

Figure 15-4 Objects consult the VMT for the addresses of *virtual* methods.

Program 15-4 puts these observations to the test. The program is nearly identical to Program 15-3, but adds constructor Init to Object1 at line 7. Also, the key word **virtual** is added to the two MethodA definitions at lines 8 and 13. This tells the compiler to generate code that consults the VMT for every call to MethodA. The actual MethodA that runs depends on the type of the object instance.

Another change is at lines 20-23, listing the Init constructor's implementation. In this example, the constructor is empty. In practice, a constructor usually performs various initialization duties, assigns values to variables, prepares pointers, and so forth. But, despite appearances, the seemingly empty constructor is not a do-nothing shell. It still performs the vital (if invisible) service of initializing an object instance to address the correct VMT for this object type.

The final change is at lines 42-43, which activate the Init constructor for each object instance (variable). Object2 inherits the constructor from Object1, just as it inherits the other methods. Init must be called for each object instance. If you have 100 object instances of the same object type, this rule means that you have to call the Init constructor 100 times—once per object instance.

Because of these changes, running the program now correctly displays:

```
Inside Object1's MethodA
Inside MethodB
Inside Object2's MethodA
Inside MethodB
```

Note: Run Program 15-4 under control of the built-in or stand-alone Turbo Debugger. Press F7 repeatedly to execute statements one at a time. Notice that when MethodB first calls MethodA, it uses the version for Object1 (line 25 in the listing). The second time, it calls MethodA for Object2 (line 36). You are seeing virtual methods in action.

Program 15-4: VIRTUAL.PAS

```
1:  {$R+}    { Check for uninitialized objects }
2:
3:  program VirtualPleasure;
4:
5:  type
6:    Object1 = object
7:      constructor Init;
8:      procedure MethodA; virtual;
9:      procedure MethodB;
10:   end;
11:
12:   object2 = object(Object1)
13:     procedure MethodA; virtual;
14:   end;
15:
16: var
17:   Item1: Object1;
18:   Item2: object2;
19:
20: constructor Object1.Init;
21: begin
22:   { Initializes object's VMT }
23: end;
24:
25: procedure Object1.MethodA;
26: begin
27:   Writeln('Inside Object1''s MethodA')
28: end;
29:
30: procedure Object1.MethodB;
31: begin
32:   MethodA;
```

continued

Program 15-4: continued

```
33:    Writeln('Inside MethodB')
34:  end;
35:
36:  procedure object2.MethodA;
37:  begin
38:    Writeln('Inside Object2''s MethodA')
39:  end;
40:
41:  begin
42:    Item1.Init;
43:    Item2.Init;
44:    Item1.MethodB;
45:    Item2.MethodB;
46:    Readln
47:  end.
```

Catching Constructor Errors

The two most important rules to remember about constructors are:

- Every object with one or more virtual methods must define (or inherit) a constructor method, even if that constructor has no direct duties to perform.

- The program must call the constructor for each object instance (variable) of that object type.

Failing to obey either rule is catastrophic. You have to remember the first rule yourself. Switching on the {$R+} switch (normally used to check **array** index and integer subranges) lets Turbo Pascal help you to remember the second.

Line 1 of Program 15-4 demonstrates how the {$R+} switch works. To see what happens if you forget to call an object instance's constructor, change line 43 to:

```
(* Item2.Init; *)
```

In other words, turn the statement into a comment. Recompile and run. You should receive error 210, "Object not initialized." If you also delete line 1, the program will crash when it tries to call the object's methods without first linking the object to its VMT. (You don't have to try this. If you do, be prepared to reboot.)

Checking for object VMT errors takes time and space. The compiler must generate subroutine calls around *every* use of all virtual methods. For this reason, after testing your program, be sure to reset the R switch to its normal state {$R–}, or to remove the switch altogether.

Assigning Objects

You can, of course, assign one object instance to another of a compatible type. But in objects with virtual methods, the results may be unexpected. For example, if you have the object type:

```
ObjectType = object
   X, Y: Word;
   constructor init(XX, YY: Word);
   { ... virtual methods }
end;
```

And if you define two variables of type ObjectType:

```
var Obj1, Obj2: ObjectType;
```

You might be tempted to initialize Obj1 and assign it to Obj2 like this:

```
Obj1.Init(4, 3);
Obj2 := Obj1;           { ??? }
```

Such assignments are dangerous. Because ObjectType declares virtual methods, its constructor must be called for every object in order to link the object instance with the appropriate VMT, locating the addresses of the object's methods. To satisfy this requirement, the previous assignment must be followed by:

```
Obj2.Init(4, 3);
```

Even though you already initialized Obj1 and assigned it to Obj2, you still *must* call Obj2's Init constructor. If you don't do this, Obj2's pointer to its VMT will not be set up, and calls to Obj2 methods will fail. Remember always to call each object instance's constructor, even after copying one object to another.

You may wonder why assignment statements don't copy VMT pointers along with everything else in objects. The reason is that ancestor object instances may be assigned to instances of their descendants, which begin with a copy of the ancestor's fields. Descendant objects have their own VMTs unique from ancestor VMTs, and copying the ancestor's VMT pointer to a descendant's VMT pointer would be a serious error.

Virtual Methods and Constructors

As you've seen, virtual methods allow precompiled code (procedures and functions inherited from ancestor objects) to call new methods in descendant objects. Imagine the possibilities this opens. If you purchase a toolkit from a software supplier, even if you don't have the original source code, you can write new methods and have the existing routines in the toolkit call your custom code! For this reason, it's wise to make most methods virtual. If you make them static, you may prevent people (and yourself) from extending existing code later.

A few other notes will help you to use virtual methods and constructors effectively:

- Make methods virtual by adding the **virtual** key word to the end of the method definition in the object type. This is the only place the **virtual** key word may appear.

- Methods that override ancestor virtual methods must be virtual, and they must have identical names and parameter lists. Overriden static methods and constructors may have different parameter lists.

- Make sure each object type that uses virtual methods defines or inherits at least one constructor method.

- Never forget to call a constructor for each object instance of any object type that defines virtual methods.

- Constructors can *never* be virtual. If a constructor initializes the VMT, which holds the addresses of an object type's virtual methods, you'd be unable to use a virtual constructor because the VMT wouldn't be initialized before the constructor ran at least one time!

- Objects may have multiple constructors, a useful technique when objects must be initialized in different ways depending on other circumstances. In such cases, you must call only one of an object's many constructors to ensure that the VMT link is initialized. You don't have to call every constructor defined in the object type.

- Calling a constructor more than once is perfectly okay. The VMT is initialized only on the first such use. But, be aware that constructors often allocate memory on the heap for other variables. Unless you do something to recover that memory, calling constructors in succession could cause the heap to be come permanently fragmented.

Dynamic Objects

Until now, example object instances have been plain Pascal variables, declared in the program's var section. A more popular OOP strategy is to declare pointers to object types and allocate space for object instances at runtime. A few observations explain why this OOP technique is vital:

- A single pointer may address object instances of its own object base type or of object instances of *any descendant type*.

- The reverse is not true: A pointer to an object instance may not address an instance of an ancestor object type.

- The object's constructor simplifies memory management by cooperating with an extended form of New to allocate space for object instances on the heap.

- The object can also define a *destructor*. Along with constructors, destructors simplify memory management by cooperating with an extended form of Dispose to delete object instances from the heap.

The first two of these points may seem odd at first. A pointer to an object type may address object instances of that type or any of its descendants. For example, using the earlier analogy, a pointer to type Vehicle might address a Cart, a Bicycle, or an Automobile, all of which descend from objects FourWheelers and TwoWheelers. Figure 15-5 illustrates this concept, which bends Pascal's normally strict type-checking rules. Shaded boxes represent inherited characteristics in descendant objects. Each descendant adds its own features (data fields and methods), shown as the unshaded box at the bottom of each new object type. Descendant objects inherit the data fields of their ancestors; therefore, a pointer to Vehicle can safely manipulate the inherited Vehicle and FourWheelers data at the top of a Cart object instance. But the reverse is not true. A pointer to a Bicycle object must not attempt to treat that object as though it were a Cart—there are no Bicycle and TwoWheeler fields in a Cart object instance, and writing to those nonexistent fields could overwrite other data in memory, causing a serious bug.

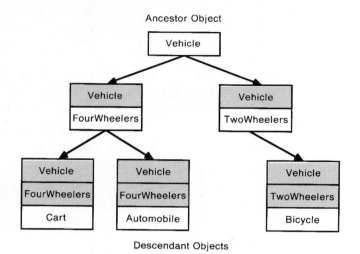

Figure 15-5 Pointers to objects are fully compatible with descendants of those objects.

Can you see the importance of this idea and how it relates to virtual methods? If you write code with pointers to objects that metamorphosize (change form) at runtime, then the object instances themselves *must* be able to decide which methods are the correct ones to use. There's no way you can predict which polymorphic object a pointer will actually address at runtime. As explained before, virtual methods allow this freedom by looking up method addresses in the object's VMT. Pointers to such objects take full advantage of OOP polymorphism—the ability of objects to assume different forms when the program runs.

An excellent example of dynamic objects and polymorphism is a simple linked list. Your Turbo Pascal User's Guide contains a similar example, defining a Node object that contains two pointers: one to the next node and one to the variable-length data stored in memory. If you have that book handy, a diagram of this structure appears on page 116. In Turbo Pascal 5.5's OOP Guide (included with 6.0.'s User's Guide), the diagram appears on page 55.

This is a typical setup. A different, and perhaps more purely polymorphic, approach lets the nodes metamorphosize, taking whatever form is needed to store integers, real numbers, and strings on the same list. The objects themselves take care of what is usually a messy job of managing memory and pointers—without the need for nonpolymorphic Node objects linked together. The next sections put this idea to work.

Constructors and Destructors

Program 15-5 implements two simple objects that can manage linked lists containing any data types. Line 11 introduces a new key word, **destructor**. Destructors typically perform cleanup chores for objects created in heap memory. Often, such objects themselves contain pointers to other data, and the destructor disposes this memory in preparation for releasing the memory occupied by the object instance.

Like a constructor, a destructor is identical to a procedure method except that **destructor** replaces **procedure**. Destructors are almost always virtual, allowing future code to inherit an ancestor object's definitions and redefine the destructor's duties, perhaps disposing new data fields and performing other jobs. Destructors may be static, however, in cases where such enhancements are unnecessary.

Destructors are usually named Done, although you can choose a different name if you want. Unlike constructors, objects that define virtual methods do not require destructors. Also, an object may define multiple destructors, useful when objects need different disposal techniques depending on other circumstances.

Lines 34-36 implement the Item object's Done destructor. In this example, there are no statements in the destructor implementation. Even so, the destructor contains machine code that simplifies memory management, as explained after the listing.

Compile Program 15-5 to create LISTU.TPU. The program is in the form of a unit, with the object type definitions in the interface section and the methods hidden neatly away in the implementation.

> **Note:** Some people recommend defining only one destructor per object type, as this more closely mirrors the way languages such as C++ operate. Future Turbo Pascal versions may take advantage of this arrangement, automatically calling an object's designed destructor when the program disposes object instances or when those instances are no longer within the scope of currently active procedures and functions. That's pure guesswork, however, and you are certainly free to define multiple destructors in object types. But if you want to gamble on my crystal ball, or if you plan to port your Pascal programs to C++, limit your objects to one destructor with *no* parameters.

Program 15-5: LISTU.PAS

```
1:   unit ListU;
2:
3:   interface
```

continued

Program 15-5: continued

```
 4:
 5:  type
 6:
 7:    ItemPtr = ^Item;
 8:    Item = object
 9:      Next: ItemPtr;
10:      constructor Init;
11:      destructor Done; virtual;
12:      procedure Print; virtual;
13:    end;
14:
15:    List = object
16:      Root: ItemPtr;
17:      constructor Init;
18:      procedure InsertItem(N: ItemPtr);
19:      procedure DisposeList;
20:      procedure PrintList;
21:    end;
22:
23:
24:  implementation
25:
26:
27:  { Item }
28:
29:  constructor Item.Init;
30:  begin
31:    Next := nil
32:  end;
33:
34:  destructor Item.Done;
35:  begin
36:  end;
37:
38:  procedure Item.Print;
39:  begin
40:    Writeln    { Start new display line }
41:  end;
42:
43:
```

```
44:   { List }
45:
46:   constructor List.Init;
47:   begin
48:     Root := nil
49:   end;
50:
51:   procedure List.InsertItem(N: ItemPtr);
52:   begin
53:     N^.Next := Root;
54:     Root := N
55:   end;
56:
57:   procedure List.PrintList;
58:   var Ip: ItemPtr;
59:   begin
60:     Ip := Root;
61:     while (Ip <> nil) do
62:     begin
63:       Ip^.Print;
64:       Ip := Ip^.Next
65:     end
66:   end;
67:
68:   procedure List.DisposeList;
69:   var Ip: ItemPtr;
70:   begin
71:     while Root <> nil do
72:     begin
73:       Ip := Root;
74:       Root := Ip^.Next;
75:       Dispose(Ip, Done)
76:     end
77:   end;
78:
79:   end.
```

Extended New and Dispose

As you recall from Chapter 7, the standard procedure New allocates space on the heap for a variable addressed by a pointer. You can use the standard New to create object instances on the heap. For example, if Op is a pointer to a Cart object type, you could write:

```
New(Op);
```

But you now are faced with finishing the initialization of your object instance, calling the **constructor** to set up the link to the object's VMT:

```
Op^.Init;
```

There's an easier way to perform both of these steps with one statement. New allows you to pass the name of the object's constructor as a second parameter:

```
New(Op, Init);
```

This allocates space on the heap for the object instance, calls the constructor, and initializes the VMT (if necessary). You'll almost always create new dynamic objects this way.

You can also use New as a function that returns a pointer to an instance of the object data type. (This form of New also works with other Pascal data types.) If OpTypePtr is a pointer type to an object type named OpType with a constructor named Init, and Op is of type OpTypePtr, this statement allocates heap space for the object instance and assigns the pointer to Op:

```
Op := New(OpTypePtr, Init);
```

The effect is no different from the earlier example, so you'll rarely use New this way. New's real value as a function comes when passing the address of newly allocated objects to other methods, leading to statements such as:

```
Variable.Insert(New(OpTypePtr, Init('String', 14, 3.14159)));
```

Get used to this sort of code, which is commonplace in OOP. In this hypothetical example, New allocates space for an object instance of type OpType, calling the object's constructor Init with three parameters and passing the result (an OpTypePtr pointer) to Variable.Insert (not shown), a method that requires a pointer to an instance of type OpTypePtr as a parameter.

The familiar Dispose procedure is also extended, taking a pointer to an object instance as its first parameter and the name of a destructor as the second:

```
Dispose(Op, Done);
```

Using Dispose this way calls the Done destructor (presumably defined in OpType) and disposes the memory occupied by the object instance addressed by Op. Unlike New, Dispose can't be used as a function.

Dispose truly comes into its own when polymorphic objects are involved. Most often, descendant objects redefine what a virtual destructor Done accomplishes. Depending on what type of object a pointer addresses, Dispose must be able to call the appropriate destructor—a fact that can't be known until runtime.

Program 15-5 demonstrates this use of Dispose at line 75 inside the List object's DisposeList method. This code releases the memory occupied by listed items—

which might contain any kind of data. Because the code is written before the list items are defined, it's impossible for DisposeList to know ahead of time what kind of data will be stored in the list.

> **Note:** I hope that last sentence makes a little light go on in your head. Think about this. How is it possible to program a method that disposes a list of items when we haven't even decided what or even how big those items will be? But that's exactly what OOP is all about—the ability to write code for the unforeseen future. DisposeList is a *finished* method. It is not a shell. It will not require modification to handle new kinds of data later. This is polymorphism at work—providing future programs with the ability to create objects of new forms, which existing code such as DisposeList will be able to handle with ease.

Now, let's throw some data into a list and see what happens. Program 15-6 uses ListU and creates three new object types at lines 7-27. IntObj stores integers. RealObj stores real numbers. StrObj stores strings. Each of these objects is a direct descendant of Item (see Program 15-5, lines 8-13). Consequently, each of the new object types inherits a Next field of type ItemPtr plus three methods.

IntObj and RealObj update two of those methods, Init and Print. Because these object types require no special handling for disposal, they simply inherit Item's destructor. The new object types add a single field each—an integer (line 9) and a real number (line 16). Thanks to polymorphism, a pointer to Item can address IntObj and RealObj object instances.

Line 23 in StrObj defines a pointer to a **string**. The new object could define a string variable directly, but the pointer allows variable-length strings to occupy only as much heap space as needed. Because this requires custom code to allocate space for strings on the heap, StrObj replaces the Done destructor with a new version that cleans up this additional memory.

Compile and run Program 15-6. (You must first compile Program 15-5 to create the compiled unit file LISTU.TPU.)

Program 15-6: **LISTDEMO.PAS**

```
1:    program ListDemo;
2:
3:    uses ListU;
4:
5:    type
6:
7:      IntObjPtr = ^IntObj;
```

continued

```
 8:    IntObj = object(Item)
 9:      I: Integer;
10:      constructor Init(II: Integer);
11:      procedure Print; virtual;
12:    end;
13:
14:    RealObjPtr = ^RealObj;
15:    RealObj = object(Item)
16:      R: Real;
17:      constructor Init(RR: Real);
18:      procedure Print; virtual;
19:    end;
20:
21:    StrObjPtr = ^StrObj;
22:    StrObj = object(Item)
23:      S: ^string;
24:      constructor Init(SS: string);
25:      destructor Done; virtual;
26:      procedure Print; virtual;
27:    end;
28:
29:
30: var
31:
32:    ItemList: List;
33:
34:
35: { IntObj }
36:
37: constructor IntObj.Init(II: Integer);
38: begin
39:    Item.Init;
40:    I := II
41: end;
42:
43: procedure IntObj.Print;
44: begin
45:    Item.Print;
46:    Write('Integer = ', I)
47: end;
```

```
48:
49:
50:   { RealObj }
51:
52:   constructor RealObj.Init(RR: Real);
53:   begin
54:     Item.Init;
55:     R := RR
56:   end;
57:
58:   procedure RealObj.Print;
59:   begin
60:     Item.Print;
61:     Write('Real = ', R)
62:   end;
63:
64:
65:   { StrObj }
66:
67:   constructor StrObj.Init(SS: string);
68:   begin
69:     Item.Init;
70:     GetMem(S, Length(SS) + 1);
71:     S^ := SS
72:   end;
73:
74:   destructor StrObj.Done;
75:   begin
76:     FreeMem(S, Length(S^) + 1);
77:     Item.Done
78:   end;
79:
80:   procedure StrObj.Print;
81:   begin
82:     Item.Print;
83:     Write('String = ', S^);
84:   end;
85:
86:
87:   begin
88:     ItemList.Init;
89:     Writeln('Memory before insertions = ', MemAvail);
90:     ItemList.InsertItem(New(RealObjPtr, Init(123.456)));
```

continued

Program 15-6: continued

```
 91:    ItemList.InsertItem(New(IntObjPtr, Init(451)));
 92:    ItemList.InsertItem(New(StrObjPTr, Init('Fahrenheit')));
 93:    Writeln('Memory after insertions  = ', MemAvail);
 94:    ItemList.PrintList;
 95:    ItemList.DisposeList;
 96:    Writeln;
 97:    Writeln;
 98:    Writeln('Memory after disposal     = ', MemAvail);
 99:    Writeln;
100:    Readln
101:    end.
```

How the ListDemo Works

The best way to understand how the previous two programs work, and how polymorphism allows the appropriate methods to recognize objects of different forms, is to run the code under control of Turbo Debugger. If you're using the integrated version, just press F7 to step through the program one statement at a time. If you're using the stand-alone debugger, execute the DOS commands:

```
tpc /b /v listdemo
td listdemo
```

This assumes you've named the text file LISTDEMO.PAS. The /b switch rebuilds the program (compiling LISTU.PAS to LISTU.TPU). The /v switch adds debugging information to the result.

Figure 15-6 illustrates the structure that Programs 15-5 and 15-6 create in memory. A list head named ItemList begins the list, with a field Root addressing the first listed object. Each of the three objects on the list—of types RealObj, IntObj, and StrObj—inherits Item's properties, including a Next pointer to the next listed item. Each object defines its own data field, R, I, and S. Notice that S is a pointer to a string for which space is allocated separately. The other two objects store their data directly.

After compiling Program 15-6 (and loading into Turbo Debugger if you're using the stand-alone model), press F7 to single step through the code. As the program progresses, InsertItem adds new object instances to the list, adjusting the Root and Next pointers. Parameter N (see line 51 in Program 15-5) addresses an ItemPtr. Remember, because of polymorphism, N might actually address any Item descendant.

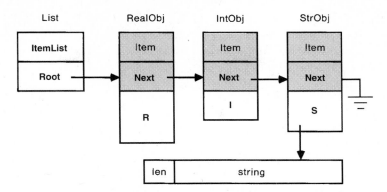

Figure 15-6 A list of polymorphic objects that take on new forms at runtime.

After creating the list, the program calls PrintList (lines 57-66 in Program 15-5). There, a **while** loop cycles, starting by setting a local ItemPtr variable Ip to Root and progressing from Next pointer to Next pointer. Line 63 activates the Print method. (OOP purists would say such statements "pass a Print message to the object instance at Ip.") Exactly which Print method runs depends on the object type addressed by Ip. As you'll see when you step through this code, the program magically runs the IntObj, RealObj, and StrObj print methods to display the correct data for each listed object. In effect, *the objects themselves do the printing.*

Similarly, DisposeList at lines 68-77 in Program 15-5 removes individual objects from the heap, calling the extended Dispose at line 75 and passing the virtual destructor named Done. RealObj and IntObj objects inherit Item's stock Done, which doesn't execute any statements. StrObj objects call the replacement Done in program 15-6 lines 74-78, where FreeMem disposes the separately stored string space (see Figure 15-6) before passing control to Item.Done, completing the disposal.

As you can see from these experiments, Programs 15-5 and 15-6 make good use of polymorphism, allowing lower-level programming in PrintList and DisposeList to acquire new abilities—merely by defining new objects, not by revising the code. Master this concept, and you'll move to the front of the OOP pack in no time.

The Self Pseudo-Variable

You might wonder how object methods are able to refer to data fields inside object instances. For example, line 61 in Program 15-6 displays the value of real number R, a field in the RealObj object type. But the actual object instance is stored in heap memory, and the exact location of this variable may change each time the program runs. How does the Write statement know where R is?

Object methods know the location of the associated object instances through a normally invisible pointer named Self—a pseudo-variable that you can't change. Self acts as a **var** parameter of the object type. Knowing this, you can rewrite line 61 this way:

```
Write('Real = ', Self.R);
```

Most of the time you won't need to do this. But, if there was another variable named R within the scope of that statement, you could use Self to specify which R to use—the variable or the field in the object instance.

Self is passed as a 32-bit pointer on the stack to every object method, whether or not the method declares other parameters. A neat trick is to add Self to Turbo Debugger's Watch window (press Ctrl-F7 and type SELF), letting you inspect the address and data to which Self points. The debugger shows the object data type that Self addresses as the code executes various methods.

Dealing With Memory Errors

Lines 67-72 in Program 15-6 neglect the always present possibility that enough memory won't be available to hold a new string. Simple programs such as this one can get away with ignoring this error—a memory shortage will halt the program when GetMem at line 70 executes.

Such Stone Age error handling won't do for a finished product, though. As explained in Chapter 16, you can install a custom HeapFunc function to trap out-of-memory conditions. Instead of halting the program, GetMem and New return **nil** pointers if the amount of memory you request isn't available. Other statements can then take whatever action is necessary.

When using a custom HeapFunc function in conjunction with OOP constructors, a subtle problem sneaks in through the back door. Because programs usually call constructors via the extended form of New, as lines 90-93 in Program 15-6 demonstrate, Turbo Pascal must reserve heap memory for the object instance that's being constructed *before* the constructor code runs. Inside the object constructor, if a call to GetMem or New falls, the program has to be careful to dispose the space that's been allocated to the object instance.

To make this happen, use the standard procedure Fail, which has no parameters. Fail immediately exits the constructor, disposing all memory allocated to the object instance. You can't use Fail anywhere else—only inside a constructor's implementation.

Program 15-7 demonstrates the correct way to use Fail. The program uses LISTU.TPU (Program 15-5) and is similar to Program 15-6. To save space, only StrObj is defined at lines 8-13.

The custom HeapFunc function appears at lines 22-28. The function must be compiled with the {$F+} switch in effect, allowing the function to be called from other code segments. Also, HeapFunc may not be nested inside any other procedure or function. Returning a function result of 1 causes New and GetMem to return **nil** pointers instead of halting the program when out of memory. Line 60 installs the new heap error function by assigning HeapFunc's address to the special System variable HeapError.

Closely examine StrObj's Init constructor and Done destructor at lines 33-50, comparing these with the previous versions in Program 15-6, lines 67-78. The new code tests whether GetMem sets pointer S to **nil** (Program 15-7, line 37). If so, the program is out of memory, and the **if** statement calls Fail at line 40 to deallocate the object instance that the constructor is constructing.

Notice that line 39 calls the Done destructor for the object that's under construction. This ensures that all deallocation steps are performed in case of errors during an object's construction, and it's usually wise to call the object's destructor this way before executing Fail. As a consequence, lines 47-48 must test whether S is **nil** before calling FreeMem. Careful memory management requires that Done (and other destructors) be prepared to clean up partially constructed object instances.

Because of these changes, the main program must now initialize and insert new object instances differently than before (see lines 63-68). First, New attempts to create and initialize a new object, assigning the object instance's address to pointer Sp. If this fails, because of the custom HeapFunc, Sp will be **nil**; otherwise, ItemList.Insert inserts the new object onto the list.

Program 15-7: LISTFAIL

```
1:   program ListFailDemo;
2:
3:   uses ListU;
4:
5:   type
6:
7:     StrObjPtr = ^StrObj;
8:     StrObj = object(Item)
9:       S: ^string;
10:       constructor Init(SS: string);
11:       destructor Done; virtual;
12:       procedure Print; virtual;
```

continued

Program 15-7: continued

```
13:    end; { StrObj }
14:
15:
16:  var
17:
18:    ItemList: List;
19:    Sp: StrObjPtr;
20:
21:
22:  {$F+}     { Switch on "far" code generation }
23:  function HeapFunc(Size: Word): Integer;
24:  { Allow New and GetMem to return Nil when out of memory }
25:  begin
26:    HeapFunc := 1
27:  end; { HeapFunc }
28:  {$F-}     { Switch off "far" code generation }
29:
30:
31:  { StrObj }
32:
33:  constructor StrObj.Init(SS: string);
34:  begin
35:    Item.Init;
36:    GetMem(S, Length(SS) + 1);
37:    if S = nil then
38:    begin            { Out of memory! }
39:      Done;              { Deallocate string object s pointer }
40:      Fail               { Exit and dispose object instance }
41:    end else
42:      S^ := SS     { Assign string to heap space }
```

```
43:  end;
44:
45:  destructor StrObj.Done;
46:  begin
47:  if S <> nil
48:      then FreeMem(S, Length(S^) + 1);
49:    Item.Done
50:  end;
51:
52:  procedure StrObj.Print;
53:  begin
54:    Item.Print;
55:    Write('String = ', S^)
56:  end;
57:
58:
59:  begin
60:    HeapError := @HeapFunc;     { Install custom heap function }
61:    ItemList.Init;
62:    Writeln('Memory before insertions = ', MemAvail);
63:    New(Sp, Init('This is the first string'));
64:    if Sp <> nil then ItemList.InsertItem(Sp);
65:    New(Sp, Init('This is the second string'));
66:    if Sp <> nil then ItemList.InsertItem(Sp);
67:    New(Sp, Init('This is the last string'));
68:    if Sp <> nil then ItemList.InsertItem(Sp);
69:    Writeln('Memory after insertions  = ', MemAvail);
70:    ItemList.PrintList;
71:    ItemList.DisposeList;
72:    Writeln;
73:    Writeln;
74:    Writeln('Memory after disposal    = ', MemAvail);
75:    Writeln;
76:    Readln
77:  end.
```

Boolean-Function Constructors

It is unfortunate that, while fixing one problem, Program 15-7 has introduced another that may not be obvious. To understand the danger, consider what happens if you create a static object of type StrObj. (The phrase *static object* refers to an object instance declared in a Pascal **var** section. A *dynamic object* is one that is addressed by a pointer.)

For an experiment, add a new variable at line 20 in Program 15-7:

```
StringObject: StrObj;
```

Variable StringObject is a static object—an object instance declared as a plain Pascal variable. Next, delete lines 61-75, replacing the main program body with:

```
StringObject.Init('This is a test string');
StringObject.Print;
StringObject.Done;
```

When you compile and run the modified program, the first statement initializes the static StringObject instance, assigning to it the string "This is a test string." The Print method then displays the string, and Done cleans up the object before the program ends, disposing the memory space occupied by the string characters.

Figure 15-7 illustrates how the static object appears in memory. Field S addresses a dynamic string variable on the heap. When the Done method executes, this memory is disposed by FreeMem at line 48. Because the object is a static variable in the data segment, it is *not* disposed. Like all global variables, StringObject remains in the data segment at all times. And, as for other common variables, New and Dispose can't manage static objects. New and Dispose operate only with pointers to dynamic variables.

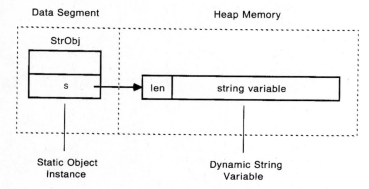

Figure 15-7 A static object in the data segment addressing a dynamic string variable on the heap.

And that's the problem. After creating a static object, if the program attempts to link that object onto a List object, the static variable will become part of that list. This is easy to do with OOP! A list of polymorphic instances can contain dynamic objects in heap memory, global static objects in the program's data segment, and local variables on the stack. Figure 15-8 illustrates how such a setup might appear, threading together many objects stored in various memory segments. Obviously, managing this structure takes careful programming.

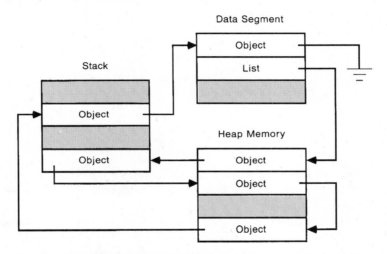

Figure 15-8 Polymorphic objects in various memory locations, all linked to a common list.

Consider what happens when the list is disposed of by the List object's DisposeList method (Program 15-5, lines 68-77). Line 75 calls Dispose, activating the object instance's Done destructor. But Dispose can operate only on pointers to dynamic variables on the heap. At line 75, ItemPtr Ip might address a static object in the data segment, causing Dispose to fail when it attempts to release this memory.

Obviously, DisposeList must be revised to deal with objects that weren't created by New. Or does it? Remember that new objects inherit everything from their ancestors. A better plan is to create a new list object type and *replace the DisposeList method with fresh code that handles static object instances.* To make this change, copy Program 15-7 to a new file named STATIC.PAS. Define a new object type named StaticList, descended from List in LISTU.TPU. Add this new definition between lines 14 and 15:

```
StaticList = object(List)
  procedure DisposeList;
end;
```

Everything else in List remains the same. All the methods work as before. We don't even have to think about them. All we want is to replace the DisposeList method. Add the implementation for that method between lines 57 and 58:

```
procedure StaticList.DisposeList;
var
  Ip: ItemPtr;
begin
  while Root <> nil do
  begin
    Ip := Root;
    Root := Ip^.Next;
    If (Seg(Ip^) <> DSeg) and (Seg(Ip^) <> SSeg)
      then Dispose(Ip, Done)
      else Ip^.Done
  end
end;
```

Compare this method with Program 15-5, lines 68-77. The code is nearly the same, but checks Ip's segment address, comparing this with DSeg (data segment) and SSeg (stack segment) values. If Ip's segment doesn't match either of these, it must be addressing a variable on the heap. (It's practically impossible to store object instances in a code segment, so the program ignores this possibility.) Dispose is then called to dispose the dynamic object. But if the object is not on the heap, the **else** clause runs the Done destructor as before, cleaning up any other variables and pointers that this object might very well contain.

The program also needs a static variable. Add this line between lines 19 and 20:

```
MyString: StrObj;   { A "static" object instance }
```

Also change ItemList's type at line 18 to:

```
ItemList: StaticList;
```

Finally, add a statement between lines 68 and 69 to initialize the static MyString object and insert it onto the list:

```
if MyString.Init('Initializing a static object instance!')
  then ItemList.InsertItem(@MyString);
```

Notice that the constructor Init is used here as a Boolean function, a special allowance that Turbo Pascal makes specifically to handle the situation where static objects contain pointers to dynamic variables (which could be other objects, of course). If the constructor returns via Fail, then Init returns False; otherwise, it returns True. Notice that ItemList's method InsertItem is used as before, but this time, because MyString is a static object, the @ operator is used to pass the address of MyString to the method, which expects to receive a pointer to an Item or to any of its descendants.

When you run the modified program, you'll see that the static object's string displays along with the others, proving that the new list now includes objects in the heap and in the global data segment.

There's an even more important observation to make. You've made a major change to the LISTU.TPU unit, replacing the DisposeList method with a new implementation. And you did this without modifying the original unit. If LISTU.TPU were a commercial toolkit for which the source code was not available, you still could have made this change. Everything else in the program operates as it did before—but the original List object is extended to handle static as well as dynamic object instances. This is one of the great benefits of OOP—the ability to add new methods and information to existing code without revising statements that already work.

Objects and Variable (Typed) Constants

When you need a preinitialized object instance, you can declare a variable constant (also known as a typed constant) of any object type. For example, using DateObj from Program 15-1, the following declares a variable constant initialized to July 4, 1976:

```
const
  CelebrationDate: DateObj =
    (Month: 7; Day: 4; Year: 1976);
```

CelebrationDate is the variable constant's identifier, which you can use just like any other object variable. The colon (:) tells Turbo Pascal that a data type follows (DateObj here). After the equal sign comes a series of expressions inside parentheses. Each expression begins with a field name (Month, Day, Year) followed by a colon and an initial value. Semicolons separate multiple fields. This is the same format used to declare variable constant records. (See Chapter 13.)

You may assign initial values only to object data fields. You can't refer to an object's methods in the constant declaration—only in program statements. For example, this displays CelebrationDate:

```
Writeln('Party day = ', CelebrationDate.StringDate);
```

The next program explains a few other details about variable constant objects. Program 15-8 is similar to Program 15-1, but adds a variable constant at lines 14-16 and uses the Dos unit's GetDate routine (see line 41) to determine today's date. This information is passed to the Today object's Init constructor (line 42). Lines 43-44 then display Today and the preinitialized variable constant VersionDate.

Lines 10-11 declare Init as a constructor and StringDate as a virtual function. As you recall, objects with virtual methods must have at least one constructor, which the program must call in order to initialize the object's pointer to its VMT. If you forget this step, the object won't be able to find its methods, and the program is almost certain to crash.

That rule is a little different for preinitialized variable constant objects. As line 42 shows, Init must be called for Today, a simple object variable. But the constructor does not have to be called for VersionDate. In fact, doing so would overwrite the data field values in the object, negating the purpose of declaring preinitialized variable constants. For this reason, Turbo Pascal automatically initializes the object's VMT pointer—you do not have to call a variable constant's constructor method, even if the object declares virtual methods.

Program 15-8: OOPCONST.PAS

```
1:   program OOPConstants;
2:
3:   uses Crt, Dos;
4:
5:   type
6:     DateObj = object
7:       Month: Byte;
8:       Day: Byte;
9:       Year: Word;
10:        constructor Init(MM, DD, YY: Word);
11:        function StringDate: string; virtual;
12:     end;
13:
14:  const
15:     VersionDate: DateObj =
16:        (Month: 4; Day: 3; Year: 1988);
17:
18:  var
19:     Today: DateObj;
20:     Year, Month, Day, DayOfWeek: Word;
21:
22:  constructor DateObj.Init(MM, DD, YY: Word);
23:  begin
24:     Month := MM;
25:     Day  := DD;
26:     Year := YY
27:  end;
28:
29:  function DateObj.StringDate: string;
30:  var
31:     MStr, DStr, YStr: string[10];
32:  begin
```

```
33:     Str(Month, MStr);
34:     Str(Day, DStr);
35:     Str(Year, YStr);
36:     StringDate := MStr + '/' + DStr + '/' + YStr
37:   end;
38:
39:
40:   begin
41:     GetDate(Year, Month, Day, DayOfWeek);
42:     Today.Init(Month, Day, Year);
43:     Writeln('Today   = ', Today.StringDate);
44:     Writeln('Version = ', VersionDate.StringDate);
45:     Readln
46:   end.
```

Private Object Declarations

All declarations in objects are normally public—that is, any statement can reach into an object and use any of its fields and methods. For example, given this object:

```
AnyObject = object
  AField: Word;
  constructor Init;
  destructor Done;
  procedure Method;
end;
```

After declaring a variable of type AnyObject like this:

```
var
  AnInstance: AnyObject;
```

statements are free to refer to the data field, constructor, destructor, and procedure in AnyObject. These statements, for example, are perfectly legal:

```
AnInstance.Init;
Writeln(AnInstance.AField);
AnInstance.Method;
AnInstance.Done;
```

Such freedom is often helpful, but at times you'll want to prevent unauthorized access to an object's contents. Usually, you'll take that action to prevent statements from modifying an object's data fields, as this statement attempts to do:

```
AnInstance.AField := 1234;
```

There's nothing technically wrong with such assignments, but directly changing a data field in an object goes against the OOP grain. A more generally acceptable technique is to define a method that assigns values to fields. Future object descendants then can inherit and override that method, giving you a high degree of control over what portions of a program have access to specific data elements. If a data-related bug develops, rather than waste time hunting at random for the cause, you can limit your search to the objects and methods that have legitimate access to that data.

Turbo Pascal 6.0 allows you to declare data fields, constructors, destructors, static methods, and virtual methods to be private to the module (a program or unit) that declares an object. Inside any object's declaration, all declarations following a **private** key word are accessible only to statements inside that object's module. For instance, to make AField and Method private to AnyObject, you can rewrite that object as

```
AnyObject = object
  constructor Init;
  destructor Done;
private
  AField: Word;
  procedure Method;
end;
```

Private declarations—in this case, AField and Method—must come at the end of the object. All declarations above **private** remain public.

With this new AnyObject declaration, the preceding four statements are still legal, but the following two

```
Writeln(AnInstance.AField);
AnInstance.Method;
```

will compile only if the statements appear in the same program or unit module that declares AnyObject.

Private declarations are not private to an object, but to that object's module. Any statement anywhere in a program or unit may always access all fields in objects declared in that same module. Outside of the unit's module, statements may not access private object declarations.

SizeOf and TypeOf

You've seen Sizeof before—it's the function that calculates the size of a variable or data type. Sizeof returns type Word, and you can use it anywhere a Word argument makes sense, as in this fragment which displays the size of an array and its contents:

```
var
  A: array[1 .. 10] of Integer;
begin
  Writeln('Sizeof(Integer) = ', Sizeof(Integer));
  Writeln('Sizeof(Array  ) = ', Sizeof(A))
end.
```

Running this short program reports the size of an Integer to be 2 bytes and the size of an array of 10 integers to be 20 bytes.

Sizeof also works with object types and instances. Given the object declarations in the preceding section for AnyObject and AnInstance, these statements display the sizes of those items:

```
Writeln('Sizeof(AnyObject)  = ', Sizeof(AnyObject));
Writeln('Sizeof(AnInstance) = ', Sizeof(AnInstance));
```

The first statement displays the size of the object type AnyObject in bytes. The second displays the same size, but passes the object instance AnInstance to Sizeof. There's a potential bug lurking here, however, because Sizeof consults an object's VMT to determine that object's size; therefore, before executing Sizeof(AnInstance), another statement must have executed:

```
AnInstance.Init;
```

Calling an object's constructor (if it has one) initializes that object's VMT. Sizeof reads the object's size from the VMT, which must have been initialized before calling Sizeof.

The reason Sizeof looks at an object's VMT is to handle cases where a pointer addresses an object type. Since that pointer might address an object or any of its descendants, Sizeof must calculate an object's size at runtime. For instance, if you write:

```
var
  P: PAnyObject;
```

where PAnyObject is a type declared as ^AnyObject, you can initialize an instance of AnyObject, assign its address to P, and find the size of that instance with the statements:

```
New(P, Init);
Writeln('Sizeof(P^) = ', Sizeof(P^));
```

In other words, Sizeof is polymorphic—capable of determining from a pointer an addressed object's type at runtime, and also capable of calculating that object's size.

A similar function, TypeOf, returns a pointer to an object's VMT. Use TypeOf as demonstrated here:

```
var
  PVmt: Pointer;
begin
  PVmt := TypeOf(AnInstance)
end.
```

TypeOf returns an untyped 32-bit pointer. To the function, pass an object instance, in this case, the global identifier AnInstance. The returned pointer addresses the object's VMT.

You probably won't have much use for TypeOf just yet. In chapter 17, you'll meet TypeOf again. There, you'll learn how TypeOf plays a role in streams, a technique for reading and writing object data in disk files.

Summary

Object-Oriented Programming, or OOP, is Turbo Pascal's newest addition. OOP concepts, which have been in existence for years, promise to help programmers deal with increasingly complex requirements in writing programs for more sophisticated hardware and operating systems. Whether OOP catches on or passes as just another fad remains to be seen. The subject is enjoying heightened attention, and most signs suggest that OOP is here to stay.

In Turbo Pascal OOP, an object is similar to a record but uses the **object** key word in place of **record**. Object type declarations contain both data fields and methods—procedures and functions that the object knows how to perform. This combination of data and code is known as encapsulation, one of OOP's most important contributions to programming.

Objects may inherit the characteristics of other objects, another important OOP concept. In Turbo Pascal, as in most OOP languages, descendant objects may have many descendants, but only a single ancestor (which might be descended from a more distant ancestor object). This is called single inheritance. A few OOP languages, but not Turbo Pascal, implement multiple inheritance, where one object may be descended from more than one parent.

Polymorphism refers to the ability of object instances to assume new forms at runtime. With OOP, it's possible to write code that uses object methods without knowing ahead of time the exact type of the object instance defining those methods. Polymorphism allows existing programs to be extended, often without requiring modifications to source code that already works.

Turbo Pascal OOP extensions include five new reserved key words— **constructor**, **destructor**, **object**, **private**, and **virtual**—and three new key identifiers: Fail, Self, and TypeOf. Except for these uniquely OOP items, everything else about Turbo Pascal programming remains the same.

The addresses of static methods (those defined without the **virtual** key word) are known at compile time—a concept called early binding. Because static method addresses are hard wired into the code, calls to static methods are slightly faster than calls to virtual methods, which require the program to consult the object's VMT for method addresses, a process called late binding, which occurs at runtime.

Virtual methods are advantageous because they can be replaced by new objects and used by code that was compiled before the new object is defined. Static methods cannot be replaced this way.

Extended forms of New and Dispose simplify memory management of dynamic objects created in heap memory. Object constructors and destructors cooperate with New and Dispose to allocate space for object instances and to dispose of that memory after the objects are no longer needed.

Use the **private** key word to create private declarations in objects. Such declarations are available only to the module (program or unit) in which the object data type is declared.

Exercises

15-1. Create an object that represents a computer's diskette drive. What data fields might such an object need? What methods does it need to know how to perform?

15-2. What does a constructor do?

15-3. What does a destructor do?

15-4. How may constructors and destructors may an object type define?

15-5. What are the main differences between static and virtual methods?

15-6. Write an OOP simulation of a lunar lander, a computer game that's available on most bulletin boards and time-sharing systems. Use objects to simulate the lander's engine, fuel supply, and guidance systems.

Glossary of OOP Terms

Dozens of new terms and phrases, many of which are more confusing than helpful, have stalled the acceptance of OOP. The following glossary describes object-oriented terms that have appeared in many different sources. Turbo Pascal doesn't use or even require you to understand all these terms. In fact, the Turbo Pascal User's and Programmer's Guides specifically avoid many of the more confusing entries. But, because some of you will want to examine other OOP languages (particularly C++), I've included terms that apply to those languages, too. All the following terms and phrases have appeared somewhere in print.

Abstract class   An object definition that is never instantiated—in other words, an object type used only as the basis for defining other objects, never to declare object instance variables. A good example of an abstract class is a location on a computer screen. Probably, you'd never need an actual variable of type Location. But you might need a variable of an object descended from the abstract Location class, perhaps a character at a certain spot on the display.

Ancestor   An object from which another object is descended. Ancestor objects may have any number of descendants, but a descendant object may have only one immediate ancestor, a concept known as *single inheritance.* Some OOP languages, but not Turbo Pascal, allow *multiple inheritance,* where descendant objects may have more than one immediate ancestor.

Class   A synonym for an "object type" in Turbo Pascal. A class defines the data fields and method headers of a single object, which might be descended from another object class.

Constructor   A special method, prefaced in Turbo Pascal with the key word **constructor**, and usually called as the second parameter in the extended New standard procedure. All objects that define one or more virtual methods must have at least one constructor, which initializes the object's VMT, containing the addresses of those virtual methods. Programs must call at least one of those constructor methods for each object instance of such types. Failure to follow this rule will almost certainly cause the program to crash. When called via New, constructors automatically allocate memory for an instance of the object type; otherwise, they operate as common procedure methods. Usually, constructors also allocate memory space for variables addressed by pointer fields in objects. If such allocations fail, use Fail to exit the constructor and dispose of the object's allocated space. Objects may define multiple constructors. Constructor methods are always static, never virtual.

Descendant   Inherits all the data fields and methods from its immediate ancestor, which may have inherited properties from its own ancestor. An object may have any number of descendants, but in Turbo Pascal (as in most OOP languages), only one immediate ancestor.

Destructor   A special method, prefaced in Turbo Pascal with the key word **destructor**, and usually called as the second parameter in the extended Dispose standard procedure. When called via Dispose, destructors dispose of the memory occupied by dynamic object instances; otherwise, destructors operate as common procedure methods. Usually, a destructor's duties include disposing of memory allocated to pointer fields defined in the object. Because descendant objects may add additional such fields, destructors should be virtual, allowing the new objects to add statements to dispose of the additional variables. Destructors may be static in rare circumstances, though. An object may define more than one destructor.

Dynamic object   An object instance for which space is allocated in heap memory, addressed by a pointer to the object type. See also *Static* object. The word "dynamic" refers to the fact that such object instances are created and destroyed by New and Dispose statements dynamically at runtime.

Early binding   The addresses of static methods (those without a **virtual** key word) are hard wired (bound) into the program during compilation, in other words, early in the game. The phrase "early binding" describes this process. Because of early binding, calls to static methods run a tiny bit faster than calls to virtual methods.

Encapsulation   Object types combine (encapsulate) definitions for data fields (as in Pascal records) and also definitions for methods—procedures and functions that describe operations an object can perform.

Fail   A new Pascal standard procedure for use only inside an object's constructor method. Executing Fail causes the constructor to end (similar to the way Exit works). When the constructor was called by the extended New procedure, Fail executes code that removes the heap memory allocated to the object, presumably because of another memory allocation problem, usually when attempting to reserve heap space for a pointer field. When the constructor was called directly (most often for a static object declared as a variable), Fail causes the constructor identifier to return False. (Constructors can be used as procedures or as Boolean functions.)

Inheritance   Objects can inherit the properties (data fields and methods) of other objects. Inheritance is one of OOP's prime features. See also *Ancestor.*

Instance   A variable of an object type, similar to the way an integer variable is an "instance" of type Integer. An object instance may be a plain variable declared in a Pascal **var** section, or it may be addressed by a pointer to the object type. Also called an object instance.

Late binding   The addresses of virtual methods are stored in the object type's VMT. An object instance's constructor method links the object instance with the proper VMT in the data segment, allowing the object to locate its method code in memory. This linkage is performed when the object is initialized by a constructor at runtime, a process known as late binding. Because virtual method addresses are stored in the VMT, an additional lookup operation is needed for each virtual method activation. For this reason, virtual method calls run more slowly than calls to static methods. See also *Early* binding.

Message   OOP purists never say that a program "calls" an object's methods. Instead, they say that statements "pass messages" (method names) to objects, telling objects to perform operations on themselves. In pure OOP, one doesn't initialize objects; one passes an object a message to initialize itself. One doesn't print an object's data; one gives an object a message to print what it contains.

In practice (and especially in Turbo Pascal), such semantic jargon is best learned and forgotten. True, in some OOP languages, the notion of passing messages is important—but mostly because those languages were designed to emphasize this importance in the first place. The concept of message passing isn't as vital to OOP as some would have you believe. Procedures and functions still run just as they do in non-OOP Pascal—whether you "call" them or pass them as "messages" to objects.

Method   A procedure or function definition in an object type (a class in standard OOP lingo). Methods describe the operations that objects know how to perform.

Method implementation   Contains the actual statements that flesh out an object type's definition. The implementation of a method is shared by all object instances of the object type. Statements in object methods are the same as in non-OOP procedures and functions.

Multiple inheritance   See *Ancestor*

Object instance   See *Instance*

Object type   An *object* type (also called a class) defines an object's data fields and methods. An object type is a definition for an object, not the object itself. Programs can declare object instances (variables) of object types, and they can declare pointers to objects, just as they can declare pointers to other data types.

Overloading   Turbo Pascal ignores this important OOP concept, which refers to the ability for object methods to have the same names but different parameter lists. An example of overloading is the familiar Pascal WriteLn procedure, which can have no parameters or many of different kinds. Even with OOP, however, it's not possible to write similar Pascal procedures of your own.

OOP languages such as C++ allow "operator loading," actually just an extension of the idea that methods can have identical names but different forms in the same object definition. Operator overloading allows you to define new data types and write numerical C++ expressions such as X = X * Y. With operator overloading, X might be an **array** object, and the expression might be performing a complex **array** multiplication. Accomplishing this requires overloading the = and * operators, allowing the compiler to generate code that implements the expression.

Turbo Pascal does not (yet?) allow operator overloading. The term is so frequently used in OOP circles, though, that you should be aware of what it means.

Overide   Methods in descendant objects can override methods of the same names in their ancestors. In Turbo Pascal, overriding is automatic—just give the new method the same name as the old. In some other OOP languages, overriding methods might need a special key word.

Overridden static objects and constructors may have different parameter lists in the descendant object definitions. Overridden virtual methods must have the same names and parameter lists.

Paradigm   ("Para-dime") This word actually refers to a Marx Brothers joke where Chico says, "I sell you a paradigm for a quarter," and Harpo buys several. Honk. Honk.

Okay, there is a serious meaning. In general, a paradigm is a conceptual model. In programming, a paradigm is a conceptual model for building computer programs. An important paradigm in computer science history is the concept of structured programming. OOP is a relatively new paradigm—a new conceptual model for programmers to use for writing code.

Polymorphism   One of OOP's most important concepts, polymorphism refers to the ability of objects to assume different forms but still be type-compatible with existing code. A good example of a polymorphic object is a graphics shape. A location on a graphics screen might be the ancestor of a visible pixel, which might be the ancestor of a square, from which a three-dimensional box is descended, and so on. The objects are polymorphic in the sense that a pointer to a location might actually address a pixel, a square, or a box. Program statements can perform operations (pass messages to) polymorphic objects without knowing in advance the actual form of the object. In OOP, you can tell a polymorphic graphics object to move to a new location without having to hard wire statements that know how to process specific object types. At runtime, the object instance itself decides how to handle the message, moving its shape by whatever means are necessary.

Self   Every object method implementation receives a normally invisible 32-bit pointer that addresses the object instance (variable) in memory. This pointer is named Self, which acts like a **var** parameter of the object's type. You can't assign new values to Self. Self assumes the data type of the object that defined the method; therefore, you don't have to use a caret (^) to dereference the pointer as you do with common Pascal pointers. If the object contains a data field named Count, Self.Count refers to the object instance's data field.

Normally there's no need to use Self this way—you can simply use Count as though you had declared it as a variable in the method implementation. Use Self only to resolve identifier conflicts—for example, with a global variable that's also named Count. (In C++, Self is called *this*.)

Single inheritance   See *Ancestor*

Static method   All methods in Turbo Pascal object type definitions are static by default. Virtual methods require the **virtual** key word. Other methods are static. Constructors are always static.

Static method addresses are calculated at runtime; therefore, calls to such methods are faster than calls to virtual methods. Also, the smart linker can remove unused static methods from compiled code. See also *Early binding* and *Late binding*.

Static object   An object instance declared as a Pascal variable in a **var** section is a static object. The term is slightly misleading because object instances declared local to procedures and functions are temporarily allocated space on the stack, just as for other local variables. (Usually the word "static" refers only to global variables.) See also *Dynamic object*.

Virtual method   Use the key word **virtual** to define a virtual method inside an object type definition. A virtual method may be a procedure or function, and it may or may not have parameters. Constructors may not be virtual methods. Destructors may be virtual. They probably should be virtual in most cases.

The addresses for virtual methods are stored in the object type's VMT; therefore, calls to virtual methods require an additional lookup operation to load this address. The addresses of static methods are known at compile time, and for this reason, static method calls operate a little faster than virtual method calls.

Virtual methods are usually preferred in OOP because existing code can use overridden virtual methods in object descendants. Static methods can't be used this way. If an ancestor object method A calls another method B in that object, and if a descendant object replaces B with a new method, method A will still call the original B unless B is virtual.

Virtual method table **(VMT)** There is one VMT per object type definition in the program. No matter how many object instances (variables) there are of that type, there is still only one VMT. All VMTs are stored in the program's global data segment in the program's .EXE disk file.

Only objects that define one or more virtual methods and constructors have VMTs. The constructors in such objects link object instances to the correct VMTs, allowing the object instances to locate their methods. Failing to initialize objects with virtual methods by calling at least one constructor almost always leads to a system crash. Use the {$R+} switch to detect this condition. VMTs also store the sizes of object instances, a fact that New and Dispose use to allocate and dispose memory space for objects.

Introducing Turbo Vision

- Getting Started with Turbo Vision
- Turbo Vision's Units
- Configuring the Compiler
- Event-Driven Programming
- A Shell for All Desktops
- Menu Bars and Status Lines
- Windows
- Views
- Color Palettes
- Window and View Options

16

Key Words and Identifiers

TApplication, TDesktop, TFrame, TMenuBar, TObject, TPoint, TProgram, TRect, TStatusLine, TView, TWindow

If you have read this book from the beginning, you might recall chapter 1's opening words: "The best way to master a programming language is to enter programs and make them run on a computer." In this chapter, that same introduction deserves repeating because, as many programmers have discovered, learning how to use *Turbo Vision* might seem like learning how to program all over again. This chapter explains Turbo Vision's basics, and presents the fundamental information you should have to begin using this sophisticated object-oriented library included with Turbo Pascal 6.0.

Getting Started with Turbo Vision

What is Turbo Vision? Why should you learn how to use it? Answering the first question is easy: Turbo Vision is a package of objects and other items supplied with Turbo Pascal for constructing complex software interfaces with pull-down menus, overlapping windows, dialog boxes, and similar features that are fast becoming standard equipment for modern commercial programs. In fact, the interface for Turbo Pascal's own integrated development environment (IDE) is written entirely in Turbo Vision. If you want your program's interface to look and feel like Turbo Pascal's, Turbo Vision is the ideal choice.

Note: If you are not familiar with objects and object-oriented programming in Turbo Pascal, you'll need to read chapter 15 before continuing. Programming in Turbo Vision requires a thorough understanding of Turbo Pascal's object-oriented extensions.

Answering the second question—why should you learn how to use Turbo Vision—is more difficult. Some programmers will find Turbo Vision to be the ideal environment for their applications. Others might discover that Turbo Vision leads to a dead end—it's definitely not for everyone. If you are writing graphics software, for example, you can probably skip this and the next chapter. Turbo Vision is designed to work in text mode only, and its primary purpose is to provide a clean way to implement text-based user interfaces powered by *event-driven technology*—a term you'll explore later in more detail.

While digging into this chapter and the next, which explores more Turbo Vision subjects, keep in mind that Turbo Vision is a highly sophisticated library of objects, procedures, functions, and data structures. A couple of chapters cannot possibly cover all Turbo Vision has to offer—after all, the 400-page *Turbo Vision Guide* supplied with Turbo Pascal is nearly half the size of this book! The goal of this chapter and the next, then, is not to replace Borland's documentation, but to present enough of the basics so you can decide whether Turbo Vision is appropriate for your projects.

Note: For more information about Turbo Vision, in addition to the printed *Turbo Vision Guide*, remember to consult Turbo Pascal's on-line Help system, which includes facts and tips on all Turbo Vision objects, procedures, functions, and data structures.

Turbo Vision's Units

Table 16-1 lists Turbo Vision's 14 units. The unit names are in the leftmost column. Use these names minus the .TPU file extensions in your program's **uses** declaration. The middle column lists the units that each unit uses. Starred names in this column are used privately in the unit's implementation section; names without stars are used publicly in the unit's interface. The right column briefly describes the purpose of each unit.

Table 16-1 Turbo Vision's Units.

Unit	Uses	Purpose
app.tpu	Objects, Drivers, Memory, HistList, Views, Menus	Basic Turbo Vision application support. Declares TProgram and TApplication objects (among others). All Turbo Vision programs use this unit.
buffers.tpu	Objects*	Used by the Editors unit to create a fixed memory area in the heap. See file BUFFERS.DOC in your TURBO\DOC directory for information on this unit.
colorsel.tpu	Objects, Drivers, Views, Dialogs	Adds custom color selector to programs, similar to the IDE's custom-color commands.
dialogs.tpu	Objects, Drivers, Views, HistList*	Basic unit for constructing and using dialog boxes and controls such as buttons and check boxes.
drivers.tpu	Objects	Low-level event drivers and declarations. Declares the essential TEvent record.
editors.tpu	Drivers, Objects, Views, Memory*, Buffers*, Dos*	Contains a high-level object for adding text editors to applications. Provides most the same functions available in the IDE's editor.
histlist.tpu	Objects*	Used for adding history lists to input boxes, such as the previously entered file names listed in the IDE's File:Open dialog.
memory.tpu	none	Low-level memory allocations and support routines.
menus.tpu	Objects, Drivers, Views	Basic pull-down menu support unit. Any Turbo Vision program with a menu bar uses this unit.
msgbox.tpu	Objects, Drivers*, Views*, Dialogs*, App*	Handy, but optional, unit for creating message-box dialogs—to display error messages, for example.

Unit	Uses	Purpose
objects.tpu	none	Low level objects needed by most other Turbo Vision units. All Turbo Vision applications include this unit. You also might find this unit to be useful for non-Turbo Vision programs.
stddlg.tpu	Objects, Drivers, Views, Dialogs, Dos, App*, Memory*, HistList*, MsgBox*	Standard file-dialog unit with objects for constructing file-open and file-save dialogs similar to those used by the IDE's *File* menu *Open, Save,* and *Save as* commands.
textview.tpu	Objects, Drivers, Views, Dos	Objects for constructing read-only views of text information. Useful for adding text-file listing capabilities to Turbo Vision applications.
views.tpu	Objects, Drivers, Memory	Basic view object unit. In Turbo Vision, what you see in a window is called a view, and any application that displays information in windows uses this unit.

* Used privately in unit's implementation. Unmarked units are used publicly in the unit's interface.

Configuring the Compiler

Before you can compile Turbo Vision programs, you might have to tailor the IDE or the command-line compiler's configuration. When you installed Turbo Pascal, if you accepted the default directories and other settings, you can probably use your current settings. But if you installed your system with custom parameters, or if you have rearranged your files and directories after installing them, consult this section for help in preparing your system for Turbo Vision programming.

You may compile Turbo Vision programs with the IDE or the command-line compiler. The following notes explain how to configure each environment. However, even if you prefer using the command-line compiler, for this chapter, you might want to switch to the IDE. Because the IDE's interface was written in Turbo Vision, it offers an excellent guide to the features available to your own code. The best way to learn about what Turbo Vision can do is to use it, and the best example of a Turbo Vision application is Turbo Pascal's IDE.

Configuring the IDE

If you are using the IDE, read this section for tips on configuring the environment for compiling Turbo Vision code. If you are using the command-line compiler, skip to "Configuring the Command-Line Compiler."

- When compiling units, be sure to set *Compile:Destination* to *Disk*. That setting will create .TPU files containing the compiled unit code that other programs will be able to use without your having to recompile those same units.

- Use the *Options:Compiler* command to turn on *Extended syntax* (an X should appear inside that labeled box.) Turbo Vision programs typically make use of Turbo Pascal 6.0's new ability to call functions as though they were procedures—in other words, ignoring a function's return value to use a function for performing an action. Turning on Extended syntax enables this feature. Or, you can type the embedded options, {$X+} or (*$X+*), at the beginning of a program listing.

- If you experience out-of-memory errors, check whether *Options:Memory sizes* is set to *Stack size* = 16384, *Low heap limit* = 0, and *High heap limit* = 655360. Other values also may work, and it is impossible to give values that suit every situation. Just be sure to give Turbo Vision a sizeable stack and heap.

- Depending on the amount of memory in your computer and the amounts allocated to TSRs and device drivers, you might have to use the *Options:Linker* command to set *Link buffer* to *Disk*. This setting causes Turbo Pascal's linker to store unit symbol tables on disk rather than entirely in memory. Change this setting to *Disk* only if necessary, as it might slow linking.

- Finally, you must be sure to list the directories where you store Turbo Vision's units. Use the *Options:Directories* command and be sure that the *Unit directories* line includes the following directories separated with semicolons and no spaces:

  ```
  C:\TP;C:\TP\TVISION;C:\TP\TVDEMOS
  ```

You can add other directories to this list, but it must contain at least the three shown here. Of course, if you have installed Turbo Pascal using a different directory structure or a drive other than C:\TP, you might have to adjust these settings to match your installation's path names. (The default installation directory is C:\TURBO, but I use C:\TP, which is shorter.)

When compiling programs, press F9 to compile units; Ctrl-F9 to compile and run programs. Other Run and Compile menu commands also will work, of course, but these two are probably easiest to use for the sample listings in this chapter and the next.

Configuring the Command-Line Compiler

The best way to configure the command-line compiler for Turbo Vision programming is to create a text file named TPC.CFG containing the lines:

```
/$X+
/UC:\TP;C:\TP\TVISION;C:\TP\TVDEMOS
```

Store this file in the same directory where you will store the sample listings from this chapter. The first line selects Turbo Pascal's extended syntax option, allowing programs to call functions as though they were procedures—that is, to ignore a function's return value. The second line tells the compiler where to find various Turbo Vision units, and it might include other directories (or a base path name other than C:\TP) in addition to the three directories listed here.

To compile a unit or program with the command-line compiler, use the /m (make) option to compile all out-of-date modules. For example, to compile a program named MYPROG, you could enter the command:

```
tpc /m myprog
```

or you could add /m to TPC.CFG.

Note: If you experience trouble compiling the programs in this chapter, especially if you receive "Error 122: Invalid variable reference," be sure Turbo Pascal's extended syntax option is on. Or, add the declaration, {$X+}, to the beginning of each listing, overriding the compiler's default setting.

Event-Driven Programming

Turbo Vision is not like other Turbo Pascal programming libraries you might have used or heard about. To use Borland's term, Turbo Vision is an *application framework*, a library of objects and subroutines powered by event-driven technology.

Event-driven programs are fundamentally different from conventional ones. In a conventional program, you might invent a procedure to get a keypress, perhaps to execute a command when somebody presses a certain key. You could write the procedure as:

```
procedure GetCommand(var C: Char);
begin
  Write('Menu: A, B, C: ');
  repeat
    C := UpCase(ReadKey)
  until C in ['A', 'B', 'C'];
  Writeln
end;
```

A program that **uses** the Crt unit (which defines the ReadKey function) could call this procedure to prompt for a menu-command letter A, B, or C. While waiting for a keypress, the GetCommand procedure captures the program's entire attention, and nothing else may happen until the program's user types one of those three keys.

There is nothing wrong with this technique, and for simple programming jobs, procedures like GetCommand are easy to write and maintain. But that same procedure does not work so well in a more sophisticated environment where users can select on-screen items with a mouse or with keyboard commands, and where other processes compete for shares of the computer's time. Imagine, for example, a program where one section is printing some text, another is displaying the time, and another is sorting a database file. Obviously, the current version of GetCommand would not allow those other processes to continue while the procedure waits for a command.

To fix the problem, you might attempt to rewrite the procedure like this:

```
procedure GetCommand(var C: Char);
begin
  Write('Menu: A, B, C: ');
  C := #0;
  repeat
    UpdateThings;
    if Keypressed then
      C := UpCase(ReadKey)
```

```
   until C in ['A', 'B', 'C'];
   Writeln
end;
```

Presumably, another procedure UpdateThings carries out other processes that are supposed to continue while the program waits for a keypress. To ensure the **repeat** loop continues to call UpdateThings, it is now necessary to check the Keypressed function to determine whether a key has been pressed; otherwise, the call to ReadKey would pause the program's action, thus preventing the loop from looping and also preventing UpdateThings from updating its "things" (whatever they are).

The proposed solution seems reasonable, but consider what would happen if one of the updated processes also takes a length of time to finish. How can that process allow GetCommand to operate? The answer is: It probably can't, and it's bottlenecks like this that make conventional programming techniques inappropriate for interactive environments where many processes run in parallel, or seemingly so.

Event-driven programming neatly solves this kind of problem. In an event-driven program, procedures and functions do not wait for actions such as keypresses to occur. Instead, the program's subroutines respond to events such as keypresses or mouse clicks as they happen. Rather than write a subroutine to get a keypress, for example, in an event-driven environment, you write code that responds directly to keyboard events. An event-driven program is exactly what its name suggests: a program driven by external events that might come along in any order and at any time.

Objects are natural building blocks for event-driven programs. As you learned in chapter 15, objects encapsulate code and data, providing independent packages that can mirror objects in the real world. In a Turbo Vision program, you use and write objects that know how to respond to events represented as messages. For example, a message might tell an object that a mouse button has been clicked. The object can then respond to that event, perhaps selecting a button on-screen to activate a program option. Best of all, you can write the object and its code independently of the events to which the object responds, a fact that becomes extremely important in a program that might be called on to respond to thousands of events. Turbo Vision takes care of the low-level details that generate messages corresponding to external events. All you have to do is create the necessary objects to respond to those events as they occur.

A Shell for All Desktops

Program 16-1, DESK.PAS, demonstrates several key principles of event-driven programming, and it shows the general layout of a Turbo Vision application. You can use the program as a starting place, or a shell for your own programs. The shell uses five units: Objects, Drivers, Views, Menus, and App. To compile Desk, TP must be able to find the .TPU files for those units, so before compiling, be sure to specify the necessary unit path names as explained earlier.

Program 16-1: DESK.PAS

```pascal
 1:  program Desk;
 2:
 3:  uses Objects, Drivers, Views, Menus, App;
 4:
 5:  type
 6:    PTheApp = ^TheApp;
 7:    TheApp = object(TApplication)
 8:      procedure InitMenuBar; virtual;
 9:      procedure InitStatusLine; virtual;
10:    end;
11:
12:  { Initialize application's pull-down menus }
13:  procedure TheApp.InitMenuBar;
14:  var R: TRect;
15:  begin
16:    GetExtent(R);
17:    R.B.Y := R.A.Y + 1;
18:    MenuBar := New(PMenuBar, Init(R, NewMenu(
19:      NewSubMenu('~F~ile', hcNoContext, NewMenu(
20:        NewItem('E~x~it', 'Alt-X', kbAltX, cmQuit, hcNoContext,
21:        nil)),
22:      nil))
23:    ))
24:  end;
25:
26:  { Initialize application's status line }
27:  procedure TheApp.InitStatusLine;
28:  var R: TRect;
29:  begin
30:    GetExtent(R);
31:    R.A.Y := R.B.Y - 1;
32:    StatusLine := New(PStatusLine, Init(R,
33:      NewStatusDef(0, $FFFF,
34:        NewStatusKey('', kbF10, cmMenu,
35:        NewStatusKey('~Alt-X~ Exit', kbAltX, cmQuit,
36:        nil)),
```

```
37:      nil)
38:    ))
39:  end;
40:
41:  var
42:    Application: TheApp;
43:
44:  begin
45:    Application.Init;
46:    Application.Run;
47:    Application.Done
48:  end.
```

When you run Desk, you see a menu bar at top with a single command named File (Figure 16-1). Open that menu by clicking on it with a mouse, or if you prefer, using the keyboard (or you don't have a mouse) press Alt-F (or F10 and the down arrow). To quit Desk and return to the DOS prompt, select the menu's Exit command, or press Alt-X.

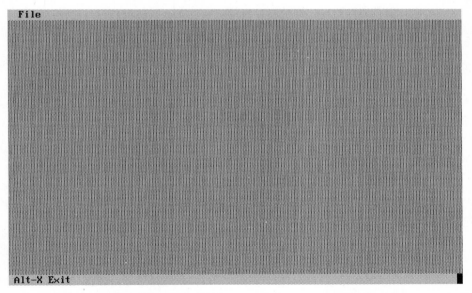

Figure 16-1 DESK.PAS displays Turbo Vision's blank desktop.

At the bottom of DESK's display, you also see a status line that lists currently active commands. This line reminds you that you can press Alt-X to quit. If you have a mouse, you also can click on the status line's labels to execute the displayed commands.

To create this bare-bones desktop display, Desk declares a pointer PTheApp bound to an object data type named TheApp. That object inherits the properties (fields and methods) from TApplication, the foundation on which all Turbo Vision programs are built.

Turbo Vision's TApplication object, defined in the App unit, activates a program's desktop containing menus, a status line, windows, dialogs, and other items. In most Turbo Vision programs, you declare a custom object like TheApp that inherits TApplication's properties. The custom object is your program's gateway to all Turbo Vision's territory.

In your TApplication descendant, at a minimum, you must provide replacements for two inherited virtual methods: InitMenuBar and InitStatusLine. You also need a pointer to your new object. The bare minimum design is:

```
PTheApp = ^TheApp;
TheApp = object(TApplication)
  procedure InitMenuBar; virtual;
  procedure InitStatusLine; virtual;
end;
```

PTheApp is a pointer to TheApp, which descends from TApplication. The Desk program doesn't use PTheApp, but it is typical to declare the pointer and its associated object data type together.

TheApp inherits a wealth of methods and fields from TApplication and its ancestors, TProgram, TGroup, TView, and TObject. The full Turbo Vision hierarchy is complex and is stuffed with thousands of details, and it would be an overwhelming task to study all these many facts at once. Stick to the forest for the moment. Later, you'll look at some of the trees.

The two essential TApplication methods are InitMenuBar and InitStatusLine, which every Turbo Vision program of any significance will probably override. InitMenuBar prepares the program's menu bar shown at the top of the desktop. InitStatusLine prepares the status line shown at the display's bottom. You'll learn more about these procedures later—for now, just be aware these methods are where the menu bar and status line receive their initializations.

Desk also shows a key Turbo Vision design goal: a short main block. Look at the end of the program listing. There, a single global variable named Application of type TheApp executes three methods inherited from TApplication: Init, Run, and Done. (Actually, Init and Done trace back to TObject. Run originates in TProgram.) These three methods are the ABCs of every Turbo Vision application. Init prepares a slew of internal variables and brings the desktop to life. Run starts your application's ball rolling. Done cleans up before the program ends.

Notice that Application is defined just before the program's main block, proving that no statement except for the three below call any methods directly in Application. The entire program operates under the control of the event-driven engine that powers the Turbo Vision library.

Menu Bars and Status Lines

The Desk program displays a blank desktop, a simple menu bar, and a status line—three ingredients that most, if not all, Turbo Vision programs share. Because pulldown menus are one of the most common features of modern user interfaces, they make good starting places for learning more about how Turbo Vision works. Status lines are closely related to menus, so you can tackle both at once.

Designing Menus

All Turbo Vision applications initialize their pull-down menus in a replacement of the TApplication method InitMenuBar. You should never call this method directly; Turbo Vision does that when it initializes the program.

In Desk's TApplication object, TheApp, InitMenuBar declares a local variable R of type TRect, which defines a rectangle on-screen. Declared in the Objects unit, TRect is composed of two fields, A and B, of type TPoint, another object in the Objects unit. A TPoint object has two fields, X and Y, representing a coordinate, or point, on screen. TPoint is an unusual object because it has no ancestor and declares no methods. The Objects unit declares TPoint as:

```
TPoint = object
  X, Y: Integer;
end;
```

As you can see, TPoint resembles a record with two data fields X and Y, which pinpoint a coordinate on-screen. Unlike a record, however, you can create a new object that inherits TPoint, thus building on its meager base. TRect does not inherit TPoint that way; instead, it owns two TPoint instances. Skipping method declarations (which you can look up in your Turbo Vision Guide or using the IDE's on-line help), TRect is declared as:

```
TRect = object
  A, B: TPoint;
  ...
end;
```

This is an example of the runtime relationship between objects that occurs often in Turbo Vision. All TRect instances own two TPoint objects, A and B. Together, these points define the upper-left and lower-right corners of a rectangle—marking the boundaries of a window, for example. In addition to its two TPoint objects, TRect has several methods you can use to manipulate rectangles for a variety of purposes. You'll see some of these methods in action in later examples.

Most Turbo Vision programs use TRect objects just about everywhere, often by calling a method GetExtent (inherited from TView) to get the extent (limits) of an object's boundaries. In Desk, InitMenuBar calls GetExtent to get the size of the application's display, then sets R.B.Y to R.A.Y + 1, thus reducing the height of the rectangle to one row at the top.

Next, InitMenuBar calls New to create an instance of a TMenuBar object, assigning the address of that instance to a PMenuView pointer field named MenuBar declared as a variable (typed) constant in the App unit. The nested New statement is a bit daunting:

```
MenuBar := New(PMenuBar, Init(R, NewMenu(
  NewSubMenu('~F~ile', hcNoContext, NewMenu(
    NewItem('E~x~it', 'Alt-X', kbAltX, cmQuit, hcNoContext,
    nil)),
  nil))
))
```

Take this one step at a time and you'll see that what seems to be a jumble of elements is only a collection of relatively simple parts. New creates an object of type TMenuBar (declared in unit Menus), using the pointer type PMenuBar as the first argument. In Turbo Vision, object type identifiers that begin with P represent pointers to object types that begin with T in place of the P. You can tell at a glance that PMenuBar is the pointer type for an object named TMenuBar. Just replace P with T to get the object name—you don't have to memorize the names or look them up.

After specifying PMenuBar as the type of object to create, New calls TMenuBar's Init constructor, passing as the first argument the TRect object R, initialized a moment earlier. Init's second argument is the result of NewMenu, a function (not a method) declared in the Menus unit. NewMenu also calls NewSubMenu, which in turn calls NewMenu again, which in turn calls NewItem for each menu command. What a jumble! And this is only a small sample. The full menu listing in a major program might continue for a page or two on a printout.

You'll understand this construction better by examining the declaration for TMenuBar.Init—the constructor called by New when creating a new menu bar. Init is declared in TMenuBar as:

```
constructor Init(var Bounds: TRect; AMenu: PMenu);
```

The first argument is a TRect object, describing the location of the menu bar. The second argument is a pointer to a menu object of type TMenu. (Remember, PMenu is the pointer type for TMenu). Function NewMenu is declared as:

```
function NewMenu(Items: PMenuItem): PMenu;
```

Because NewMenu's result is a value of type PMenu, the function's value can be passed to the Init constructor's second argument. NewMenu's own argument, Items, is a pointer to a TMenuItem object. To this constructor, you can pass the result of another function, NewSubMenu, declared as:

```
function NewSubMenu(Name: TMenuStr; AHelpCtx: Word; SubMenu: PMenu;
  Next: PMenuItem): PMenuItem;
```

And the final function in the mix is NewItem, declared as:

```
function NewItem(Name, Param: TMenuStr; KeyCode: Word; Command: Word;
  AHelpCtx: Word; Next: PMenuItem): PMenuItem;
```

TMenuBar's Init constructor and the three functions NewMenu, NewSubMenu, and NewItem are designed to nest inside each other. Taking the last function (NewItem) first, a typical setup is:

```
NewItem('E~x~it', 'Alt-X', kbAltX, cmQuit, hcNoContext, nil)
```

First comes the menu-command name as a string, 'E~x~it' in this sample. The tilde characters (~) surrounding the letter x designate that letter as a hot key, which users can press along with Alt to select the command. Pressing Alt-X, then, selects the Exit command. To display that fact in the menu, the second string shows the hot key assignment. The third argument, kbAltX, is one of several Word constants that represent specific key combinations, in this case Alt-X.

You can find a complete list of kbXXXX constants in your documentation and on-line help. After the key constant comes the symbol cmQuit—the value that is associated with this command. Programs need this value to know when a certain command has been selected. Here, cmQuit is tied to the Exit command. The next to last argument is hcNoContext. If you wanted to add on-line help for this command, you would use a value here to represent that help's context, in other words, its identifying number. When not implementing on-line help, use the constant hcNoContext, as shown here.

> **Note:** There isn't enough room in this chapter to explain how to create on-line help windows in Turbo Vision applications, but the process is fully spelled out in Turbo Pascal's references. A help "context" is just a value that you can use to identify entries in a program's on-line help file. Programs that don't implement on-line help, such as the listings in this chapter, use the hcNoContext constant rather than specify context values.

The final argument in this sample NewItem function call is **nil**. Look back at NewItem's function declaration. As you can see, the last argument (Next) is type PMenuItem, the same type that the function returns. This means functions can be nested by inserting another call to NewItem as the final argument in any NewItem function call. For example, to add three commands to a menu, you can write:

```
NewItem('~O~pen', 'Alt-O', kbAltO, cmOpen, hcNoContext,
NewItem('~C~lose', 'Alt-C', kbAltC, cmClose, hcNoContext,
NewItem('~Q~uit', 'Alt-Q', kbAltQ, cmQuit, hcNoContext, nil)))
```

The second NewItem function call nests inside the first. The third nests inside the second. The final function call ends with **nil** and as many parentheses as there are NewItems. The expression looks like three distinct function statements, but it is really one statement with nested parts. The entire expression returns type PMenuItem, the data type expected by function NewSubMenu, and therefore, capable of being nested inside that function with a statement such as this:

```
MenuBar := New(PMenuBar, Init(R, NewMenu(
  NewSubMenu('~M~enu', hcNoContext, NewMenu(
    NewItem('~O~pen', 'Alt-O', kbAltO, cmOpen, hcNoContext,
    NewItem('~C~lose', 'Alt-C', kbAltC, cmClose, hcNoContext,
    NewItem('E~x~it', 'Alt-X', kbAltX, cmQuit, hcNoContext,
    nil)))),
  nil))
))
```

These are the same three NewItem function calls from earlier, but this time passed to function NewMenu as the final argument of NewSubMenu. The result is to create one pull-down menu named Menu (with the hot key M) and having three commands, Open, Close, and Exit (with hot keys O, C, and X).

Newcomers to Turbo Vision and experts alike find all the parentheses in such statements to be confusing. A useful trick is to indent the expressions as shown here, typing one closing parenthesis for each preceding NewItem plus one extra. There are three NewItem functions in this sample, so the expression ends with four closing parentheses. Don't forget the comma after the last parenthesis—these are nested statements passed to function arguments. Therefore, they are separated by commas, not semicolons, as are stand-alone statements.

The final **nil** and two closing parentheses terminate the NewSubMenu function, telling it there are no more menus to be added. Again, a simple counting trick tells you how many parentheses to use—one for each NewSubMenu plus one extra. There is only one NewSubMenu call in this sample, so you must have two parentheses. The two additional closing parentheses on the final line of the statement match the first two opening parentheses in the call to New. If you follow the parentheses conventions suggested here, all MenuBar statements will end with two closing parentheses.

Carrying these concepts further, you can add additional menus to an application's menu bar by nesting additional calls to NewSubMenu and NewItem as Program 16-2, NESTED.PAS, demonstrates. The program displays three menus, File, Edit, and Window, each with a series of commands. Run the program and examine the menus while you study the InitMenuBar method in the listing. Notice how the indentation levels match the menu structure—a stylistic trick that makes the creation of complex menus easy. Also count the closing parentheses that end each indentation level—there is always one more parenthesis than function calls (except for the required two closing parentheses at the end).

Program 16-2: NESTED.PAS

```
 1:  program Nested;
 2:
 3:  uses Objects, Drivers, Views, Menus, App;
 4:
 5:  const
 6:    cmOpen = 100;
 7:    cmClose = 101;
 8:
 9:  type
10:    PTheApp = ^TheApp;
11:    TheApp = object(TApplication)
12:      procedure InitMenuBar; virtual;
13:      procedure InitStatusLine; virtual;
14:    end;
15:
16:  { Initialize application's pull-down menus }
17:  procedure TheApp.InitMenuBar;
18:  var R: TRect;
19:  begin
20:    GetExtent(R);
21:    R.B.Y := R.A.Y + 1;
22:    MenuBar := New(PMenuBar, Init(R, NewMenu(
23:      NewSubMenu('~F~ile', hcNoContext, NewMenu(
24:        NewItem('~O~pen' , 'Alt-O', kbAltO, cmOpen,  hcNoContext,
25:        NewItem('~C~lose', 'Alt-C', kbAltC, cmClose, hcNoContext,
26:        NewItem('E~x~it' , 'Alt-X', kbAltX, cmQuit,  hcNoContext,
27:        nil))))),
```

continued

```
28:        NewSubMenu('~E~dit', hcNoContext, NewMenu(
29:          NewItem('Cut'    , '', kbNoKey, cmCut,    hcNoContext,
30:          NewItem('Copy'   , '', kbNoKey, cmCopy,   hcNoContext,
31:          NewItem('Paste'  , '', kbNoKey, cmPaste, hcNoContext,
32:          NewItem('Clear'  , '', kbNoKey, cmClear, hcNoContext,
33:          nil))))),
34:        NewSubMenu('~W~indow', hcNoContext, NewMenu(
35:          NewItem('Cascade', '', kbNoKey, cmCascade, hcNoContext,
36:          NewItem('Tile',    '', kbNoKey, cmTile,    hcNoContext,
37:          nil))),
38:        nil))))
39:      ))
40:    end;
41:
42:    { Initialize application's status line }
43:    procedure TheApp.InitStatusLine;
44:    var R: TRect;
45:    begin
46:      GetExtent(R);
47:      R.A.Y := R.B.Y - 1;
48:      StatusLine := New(PStatusLine, Init(R,
49:        NewStatusDef(0, $FFFF,
50:          NewStatusKey('', kbF10, cmMenu,
51:          NewStatusKey('~Alt-X~ Exit', kbAltX, cmQuit,
52:          nil)),
53:        nil)
54:      ))
55:    end;
56:
57:    var
58:      Application: TheApp;
59:
60:    begin
61:      Application.Init;
62:      Application.Run;
63:      Application.Done
64:    end.
```

Designing the Status Line

At the other end of the Turbo Vision desktop is the status line. Like the menu bar, the status line is initialized in a virtual method; in this case, InitStatusLine, inherited by TApplication from TProgram.

The format for a status-line method is similar to that used by InitMenuBar (see Program 16-2, NESTED.PAS, for an example). As when initializing a menu, GetExtent loads a TRect object with the boundaries assigned to the application. The upper TPoint (R.A) is then adjusted to shrink the line to one row at the bottom of the screen. You could move the status line to mid-screen by adding this line after the assignment to R.A.Y:

```
R.Move(0, -10);
```

That command subtracts 10 from the Y component of the rectangle, moving it upward. Of course, you wouldn't do this in a real application, but the change will help you to understand how the TRect method Move works. For another twist, swap the statement below GetExtent in InitMenuBar and InitStatusLine. Now, the menu should be at the bottom of the display and the status line should be at top. This just shows that Turbo Vision will do your bidding. Your program doesn't have to look and act like Turbo Pascal unless you want it to.

After adjusting the TRect object R, InitStatusLine calls New to create an instance of TStatusLine, assigning the address of this instance to the App unit's PStatusLine variable (typed) constant pointer, StatusLine. The nested call to New calls NewStatusDef. The zero and $FFFF arguments specify a range of help contexts that can be used to display on-line help. There isn't any such help in the Nested program (or in any of the sample listings in this chapter), but it does not hurt to specify the maximum range anyway.

Each nested call to NewStatusKey that follows inserts a hot-key command into the status line. The first such command inserts an invisible entry for key F10, identified by the constant kbF10, and attached to the cmMenu command. (Like cmQuit, cmMenu is another built-in Turbo Vision command constant.) The invisible entry lets you press F10 to open menus. If you do not want that to happen, remove the line and subtract one of the parentheses after the first **nil** below.

When counting parentheses in InitStatusLine, use the same tips given earlier for InitMenuBar, but reduce the number of parentheses after the two **nil**s by one on each line.

Responding to Commands

After designing your program's menu bar and optional status line, the next step is to program the actions to respond to selected commands. Because a Turbo Vision application is event driven, and because the selection of a command is an event, programs respond to menu commands by implementing a virtual method designed to receive events in the form of TEvent messages. That method is HandleEvent, inherited by your program's TApplication descendant object.

In general, responding to events such as menu commands is simple. First, add a HandleEvent method to your TApplication object. Then, inside the implementation of your method, inspect the fields in the TEvent record passed by Turbo Vision to the method. If you detect that one of your program commands has been selected, you can then call an appropriate subroutine (which might be a procedure, a function, or a method in an object). In that way, your code carries out commands while Turbo Vision does most of the work of displaying menus, enabling a mouse, intercepting hot keys, and so on.

Program 16-3, ONEWIND.PAS, shows the basic techniques used by Turbo Vision applications to respond to menu commands. Enter, compile, and run the program, then press F3 or use the pull-down menu's Open command a number of times to display a series of windows at random on the desktop. If you have a mouse, you can also move the windows, resize them, zoom them, and perform other operations that are probably old hat if you have some experience with Turbo Pascal's IDE. (The next listing, Program 16-4, shows how to enable keyboard window commands for mouseless computers.) Figure 16-2 shows the program's display with several windows open.

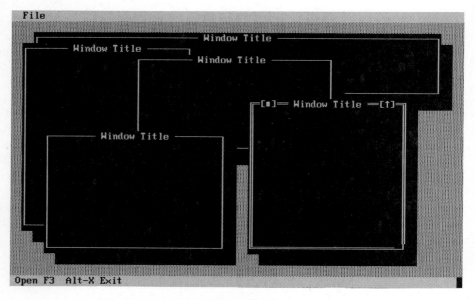

Figure 16-2 ONEWIND.PAS and its windows.

Program 16-3: ONEWIND.PAS

```pascal
1:   program OneWind;
2:
3:   uses Objects, Drivers, Views, Menus, App;
4:
5:   const
6:     cmOpen = 100;
7:
8:   type
9:     PTheApp = ^TheApp;
10:    TheApp = object(TApplication)
11:      procedure HandleEvent(var Event: TEvent); virtual;
12:      procedure InitMenuBar; virtual;
13:      procedure InitStatusLine; virtual;
14:    end;
15:
16:  function Rand(Low, High: Integer): Integer;
17:  begin
18:    Rand := Low + Random(High - Low + 1)
19:  end;
20:
21:  { Randomize coordinates in R. Assumes R.A.X = R.A.Y = 0. }
22:  procedure RandomRect(var R: TRect);
23:  var
24:    X, Y, Xd2, Yd2: Integer;
25:  begin
26:    with R do
27:    begin
28:      X := B.X;
29:      Y := B.Y;
30:      Xd2 := (B.X div 2) - 8;
31:      Yd2 := (B.Y div 2) - 6;
32:      Assign(Rand(0, Xd2), Rand(0, Yd2),
33:        Rand(Xd2 + 16, X), Rand(Yd2 + 12, Y))
34:    end
35:  end;
36:
37:  { Open a window }
38:  procedure OpenWindow;
39:  var
```

continued

Program 16-3: continued

```
40:    R: TRect;
41:    W: PWindow;
42:  begin
43:    Desktop^.GetExtent(R);
44:    RandomRect(R);
45:    New(W, Init(R, 'Window Title', 0));
46:    DeskTop^.Insert(W)
47:  end;
48:
49:  { Respond to an event message }
50:  procedure TheApp.HandleEvent(var Event: TEvent);
51:  begin
52:    TApplication.HandleEvent(Event);
53:    if Event.What = evCommand then
54:    begin
55:      case Event.Command of
56:        cmOpen:   OpenWindow;
57:        { Insert other commands here }
58:      else
59:        Exit
60:      end;
61:      ClearEvent(Event)
62:    end
63:  end;
64:
65:  { Initialize application's pull-down menus }
66:  procedure TheApp.InitMenuBar;
67:  var R: TRect;
68:  begin
69:    GetExtent(R);
70:    R.B.Y := R.A.Y + 1;
71:    MenuBar := New(PMenuBar, Init(R, NewMenu(
72:      NewSubMenu('~F~ile', hcNoContext, NewMenu(
73:        NewItem('~O~pen', 'F3',    kbF3,   cmOpen, hcNoContext,
74:        NewItem('E~x~it', 'Alt-X', kbAltX, cmQuit, hcNoContext,
75:        nil))),
76:      nil))
77:    ))
78:  end;
79:
```

```
 80:  { Initialize application's status line }
 81:  procedure TheApp.InitStatusLine;
 82:  var R: TRect;
 83:  begin
 84:    GetExtent(R);
 85:    R.A.Y := R.B.Y - 1;
 86:    StatusLine := New(PStatusLine, Init(R,
 87:      NewStatusDef(0, $FFFF,
 88:        NewStatusKey('', kbF10, cmMenu,
 89:        NewStatusKey('~Open~ F3',    kbF3,   cmOpen,
 90:        NewStatusKey('~Alt-X~ Exit', kbAltX, cmQuit,
 91:        nil))),
 92:      nil)
 93:    ))
 94:  end;
 95:
 96:
 97:  var
 98:    WindApp: TheApp;
 99:
100:  begin
101:    WindApp.Init;
102:    WindApp.Run;
103:    WindApp.Done
104:  end.
```

OneWind is similar to Desk (Program 16-1), but adds one new virtual method to TheApp object, HandleEvent, declared as:

```
procedure HandleEvent(var Event: TEvent); virtual;
```

This method receives all application messages in the form of a TEvent record named Event. Most often, you have to know about only one of TEvent's many fields, one named What of type Word. Turbo Vision sets What to a constant value that describes the type of event received by HandleEvent. Inside the method, you examine What to determine whether you have to respond to this message—if not, you can ignore the message.

Despite the key role HandleEvent plays in a Turbo Vision application, the method is generally easy to write. Think of HandleEvent as a kind of dispatcher whose job it is to recognize events as they occur, and then either direct those event messages to another location, or call a subroutine (a procedure, function, or method) that responds to a specific event.

The sample HandleEvent method in OneWind demonstrates how to respond to menu-command events, generated when users select commands from the program's menu or status line (or when they press a command's hot key). Regardless of the event's origin, the first job in every HandleEvent is to call the ancestor method (see line 52), with the statement:

```
TApplication.HandleEvent(Event);
```

Never forget this all-important statement! It gives Turbo Vision the opportunity to deal with, among other things, keyboard events that select windows and shut down the program. After calling the ancestor method, you may inspect Event.What to determine the kind of event just received. Usually, you write a combination **if** and **case** statement to detect menu commands and respond to them, using code like this:

```
if Event.What = evCommand then
begin
  case Event.Command of
    { Respond to commands here }
  else
    Exit
  end;
  ClearEvent(Event);
  ...
end;
```

Constant evCommand is one of several evXXXX constants that describe the nature of an event. If Event.What equals evCommand, then the event was generated by the selection of a menu command. At times, TEvent's What field may hold more than one event at a time, with each evXXXX value encoded as a single bit set to 1 inside What. For this reason, you may want to replace

```
if Event.What = evCommand then
```

with the statement

```
if (Event.What and evCommand) = evCommand then
```

The expression uses a logical **and** operator to mask all bits in Event.What, except for the one bit that represents evCommand. If the result of the expression equals evCommand, then that bit was set; otherwise, the bit was not set and the event is not a command.

You can use similar expressions to test for other events. If Event.What contains the evMouseDown bit, for instance, then a mouse button has been pressed. See your *Turbo Vision Guide* for a list of other event constants.

If the event is a command, the next step is to find out which command was selected. Do that by inspecting another TEvent Word field named Command. For all evCommand events, this field is set to the command's value—the same value you assigned to the command when you designed the application's menu bar and status line. In OneWind, for example, if Event.Command equals cmOpen, then the application can assume the File menu's Open command (identified by constant cmOpen) has been selected. A simple **case** statement intercepts this command and calls OpenWindow to open a window on-screen:

```
case Event.Command of
  cmOpen: OpenWindow;
else
  Exit
end;
```

After inspecting Event.Command and calling an appropriate procedure to handle the program's command events, the **case** statement calls Exit to end HandleEvent for any unrecognized commands. This is not strictly necessary, but in a large HandleEvent method, calling Exit this way ends the procedure cleanly for unprocessed commands—those for which you have not yet completed the programming, for example.

The final step in every HandleEvent method executes the statement:

```
ClearEvent(Event);
```

which sets the Event.What field to the constant evNothing, thus erasing this event message's identifying information. ClearEvent, a method declared in the TView object (one of TApplication's distant ancestors), also sets the Event's InfoPtr to @Self, representing the address of the TView or descendant object instance for which HandleEvent was called. These conventions simply give other event-handlers in a program (there are not any in this small example) the means to ignore events that have already been handled. If you don't clear an event after dealing with it, you might discover that more than one HandleEvent method will respond to the same event. In some other cases, you might want to construct programs that do exactly that, in which case you would not call ClearEvent.

Now that you know how to handle events, you can begin to write programs that respond to menu commands, often by opening windows and displaying information in them. OneWind shows the basic techniques required for opening and displaying windows. In the next part, you take a closer look at these requirements.

Windows

When you run OneWind (Program 16-3), every time you press F3, another window appears on-screen at a random location and size. You are seeing samples of Turbo Vision's basic windows, which typically have three major components:

- A TWindow object instance.

- A TFrame object instance.

- A TView object instance.

A TWindow object instance is an invisible container that holds a window's parts and pieces together. Inside every TWindow instance is a field named Frame of type PFrame, a pointer to a TFrame object instance. When you see a window's border, you are actually seeing its frame, managed by a TFrame object. A TView object instance is typically responsible for a window's contents. If a TWindow is a sheet of glass, a TView instance is what you see when you look through the pane.

The following sections explain how to use the TWindow object, to which Turbo Vision attaches a frame. Later, you will learn how to attach TView instances to windows. (OneWind's windows do not have TView instances.)

The TWindow Object

A TWindow object is nearly a finished product. It can respond to mouse and keyboard events, it can open, close, move, and resize its borders, zoom to full screen, and zoom back to original size. When somebody moves or closes a window, the desktop automatically restores any uncovered windows below.

To add a window to a program, create a new object based on TWindow. Then, perhaps in response to a menu command, execute these steps:

- Create a TRect instance that defines the window's boundaries.

- Call New to allocate heap space for a TWindow object. To that object's constructor, pass the TRect you just initialized, the window's title string, and the window number (zero if the window is not numbered).

- Insert the new window into the TDeskTop object addressed by the global DeskTop pointer.

You can implement those three steps in a common procedure or inside an object's method. Usually, programs open windows in a TApplication method. But for demonstration, OneWind uses a conventional Pascal procedure OpenWindow (see lines 38-47 in Program 16-3).

> **Note:** Remember always that Turbo Pascal is a hybrid OOP language. In your Turbo Vision programs, you can mix and match conventional programming and objects as in OneWind. Just because Turbo Vision is object oriented does not mean you have to use objects for every aspect of your code.

OpenWindow initializes the TRect instance R by calling GetExtent for the TDeskTop object addressed by DeskTop. GetExtent sets its TPoint parameter R's fields to the same values that outline the desktop's boundaries. After that step, another conventional procedure, RandomRect, adjusts the values in R to restrict the new window's rectangle to fit within the desktop's borders. You also could use other TRect methods, such as Assign and Move, to specify a window's size and location.

After defining the window's boundaries, OpenWindow calls New to allocate heap space for a TWindow instance, executing the statement:

```
New(W, Init(R, 'Window Title', 0));
```

Local variable W is a pointer of type PWindow—in other words, a pointer to an object of type TWindow. That object's Init constructor requires three parameters: a TRect object, a string for the window's title, and an integer representing the window's number. If you don't want the window to have a title, use a null string (") for the second argument. If you want to select multiple windows by pressing Alt and a digit key, you may replace the third Init parameter with a window number from 1 to 9. (A listing later in this chapter, Program 16-4, demonstrates how to identify windows by number.) Use zero as shown here if you don't want to assign a number to the window.

After creating the TWindow instance (line 45) and assigning its address to the pointer variable W, the final step is to insert the window into the desktop, usually by executing:

```
DeskTop^.Insert(W);
```

which establishes the desktop as window W's owner. DeskTop is a variable (typed) constant of type PDeskTop (a pointer to a TDeskTop object instance) defined in the App unit. Typically, the desktop, itself a TView descendant, owns all an application's major windows, a fact that automates typical window operations such as zooming, moving, hiding, and others. You don't have to write code to handle such actions; all you have to do is create a TWindow object and insert it into the desktop. Turbo Vision does the rest.

Changing a Window's Title

One of TFrame's duties is to display a window's caption, a string addressed by the Title field in the TWindow object instance that owns the frame. You may change a window's title by assigning a new string to the Title field and calling the TFrame's Draw method to update the display. First, however, you have to dispose of an existing title if there is one, by executing the statement:

```
if Title <> nil then
  DisposeStr(Title);
```

Outside of a TWindow object method, to change a window's title, you first need a PWindow pointer to the window. If that pointer is named MyWindow, then to change the window title, you would write:

```
if MyWindow^.Title <> nil then
  DisposeStr(MyWindow^.Title);
```

The window's Title pointer may be **nil**, in which case the frame has no title. If Title is not **nil**, call DisposeStr to dispose the PString variable addressed by the Title pointer. After this step, you may assign a new string to Title. If, for example, you want the title to match the current directory, you can write:

```
Title := NewStr(FExpand('.'));
```

copying the result of the Dos unit's FExpand function to a new string allocated on the heap and then assigning the address of that string to Title (or you could use MyWindow^.Title). By the way, using FExpand with a single period in quotations is a useful trick for obtaining the current directory as a string.

You may not assign a string variable or constant directly to a window frame's title. The Title field is a pointer, and it must address a string stored on the heap because, at some point, Turbo Vision may dispose of that string by calling DisposeStr. To assign a literal string as the new title, therefore, you must create that string as a variable on the heap, using a technique such as this:

```
Title := NewStr('New Window Title');
```

These steps alone, however, are not enough to change the frame's visible title. In addition to modifying the string that Title addresses, you also have to call TFrame.Draw, updating the frame and, consequently, displaying the new title string. To call the Draw method, execute the statement:

```
Frame^.Draw;
```

which calls Draw for the instance identified by the Frame PFrame pointer in the TWindow object. (Outside of a TWindow method, you'd need to refer to the window via a pointer—MyWindow^.Frame, for example.) Because all such objects have TFrames by default, you probably do not have to check whether Frame is **nil**. However, for extra safety, you might want to change the preceding line to:

```
if Frame <> nil then
  Frame^.Draw;
```

As you can see from these examples, there is a strong bond between a TWindow object and a TFrame. Because TFrame uses the Title pointer in TWindow, a TFrame object must be owned by a TWindow instance. The TFrame object reaches back into its TWindow owner where TFrame's Draw method expects to find Title and other fields, and therefore only a TWindow may own a TFrame.

Creating a Standard Window Menu

Program 16-4, WINDMENU.PAS, expands the ONEWIND.PAS listing (Program 16-3) into a multiwindow shell you can use as a starting place for many Turbo Vision applications. The program keeps track of window numbers, enables and disables menu commands at appropriate times, and implements a standard Window menu with commands such as Zoom, Tile, Cascade, and others that operate identically to those same commands in the IDE's Window menu.

Program 16-4: WINDMENU.PAS

```
1:   program WindMenu;
2:
3:   uses Objects, Drivers, Views, Menus, App;
4:
5:   const
6:     noTitle     = 'Untitled';    { Title for untitled windows }
7:     maxWindows  = 12;            { Maximum number of windows open }
8:     cmOpen      = 100;           { Open-command number }
9:
10:  const
11:    numWindows: Integer = 0;
12:    windowNums: set of 1 .. maxWindows = [];
13:
14:  type
15:    PTheApp = ^TheApp;
16:    TheApp = object(TApplication)
17:      constructor Init;
18:      procedure HandleEvent(var Event: TEvent); virtual;
19:      procedure Idle; virtual;
20:      procedure InitMenuBar; virtual;
21:      procedure InitStatusLine; virtual;
22:      procedure OpenWindow(WTitle: string);
23:    end;
24:
25:    PTheWindow = ^TheWindow;
26:    TheWindow = object(TWindow)
27:      constructor Init(WTitle: string);
28:      procedure Close; virtual;
29:      function GetWindowNumber: Integer;
30:      procedure PutWindowNumber;
```

continued

Program 16-4: continued

```
31:    end;
32:
33:   { Construct a new application }
34:   constructor TheApp.Init;
35:   begin
36:     TApplication.Init;
37:     if ParamCount > 0 then
38:       OpenWindow(ParamStr(1))
39:   end;
40:
41:   { Act on events that belong to your application }
42:   procedure TheApp.HandleEvent(var Event: TEvent);
43:
44:     procedure TileWindows;
45:     var R: TRect;
46:     begin
47:       GetExtent(R);
48:       R.Grow(0, -1);
49:       R.Move(0, -1);
50:       Desktop^.Tile(R)
51:     end;
52:
53:     procedure CascadeWindows;
54:     var R: TRect;
55:     begin
56:       GetExtent(R);
57:       R.Grow(0, -1);
58:       R.Move(0, -1);
59:       Desktop^.Cascade(R)
60:     end;
61:
62:   begin
63:     TApplication.HandleEvent(Event);
64:     if Event.What = evCommand then
65:     begin
66:       case Event.Command of
67:         cmOpen:    OpenWindow(noTitle);
68:         cmTile:    TileWindows;
69:         cmCascade: CascadeWindows;
70:       else
```

```
71:        Exit
72:      end;
73:      ClearEvent(Event)
74:    end
75:  end;
76:
77:  { Perform various commands when event queue is empty }
78:  procedure TheApp.Idle;
79:
80:  { Return true if view addressed by P is tileable }
81:    function IsTileable(P: PView): Boolean; far;
82:    begin
83:      IsTileable := P^.Options and ofTileable <> 0
84:    end;
85:
86:  begin
87:    TApplication.Idle;
88:    if Desktop^.FirstThat(@IsTileable) <> nil then
89:      EnableCommands([cmTile, cmCascade])
90:    else
91:      DisableCommands([cmTile, cmCascade])
92:  end;
93:
94:  { Initialize application's pull-down menus }
95:  procedure TheApp.InitMenuBar;
96:  var R: TRect;
97:  begin
98:    GetExtent(R);
99:    R.B.Y := R.A.Y + 1;
100:   MenuBar := New(PMenuBar, Init(R, NewMenu(
101:     NewSubMenu('~F~ile', hcNoContext, NewMenu(
102:       NewItem('~O~pen', 'F3', kbF3, cmOpen, hcNoContext,
103:       NewLine(
104:       NewItem('E~x~it', 'Alt-X', kbAltX, cmQuit, hcNoContext,
105:       nil)))),
106:     NewSubMenu('~W~indow', hcNoContext, NewMenu(
107:       NewItem('~S~ize/Move','Ctrl-F5', kbCtrlF5, cmResize,
108:         hcNoContext,
109:       NewItem('~Z~oom', 'F5', kbF5, cmZoom, hcNoContext,
110:       NewItem('~T~ile', '', kbNoKey, cmTile, hcNoContext,
111:       NewItem('C~a~scade', '', kbNoKey, cmCascade, hcNoContext,
112:       NewItem('~N~ext', 'F6', kbF6, cmNext, hcNoContext,
```

continued

Program 16-4: continued

```
113:        NewItem('~P~revious', 'Shift-F6', kbShiftF6, cmPrev,
114:          hcNoContext,
115:        NewItem('~C~lose', 'Alt-F3', kbAltF3, cmClose, hcNoContext,
116:        nil)))))))),
117:      nil)))
118:    ))
119: end;
120:
121: { Initialize application's status line }
122: procedure TheApp.InitStatusLine;
123: var R: TRect;
124: begin
125:   GetExtent(R);
126:   R.A.Y := R.B.Y - 1;
127:   StatusLine := New(PStatusLine, Init(R,
128:     NewStatusDef(0, $FFFF,
129:       NewStatusKey('', kbF10, cmMenu,
130:       NewStatusKey('~Alt-X~ Exit', kbAltX, cmQuit,
131:       NewStatusKey('~F3~-Open', kbF3, cmOpen,
132:       NewStatusKey('~F5~-Zoom', kbF5, cmZoom,
133:       NewStatusKey('~F6~-Next', kbF6, cmNext,
134:       nil))))),
135:     nil)
136:    ))
137: end;
138:
139: { Open a new window }
140: procedure TheApp.OpenWindow(WTitle: string);
141: var W: PTheWindow;
142: begin
143:   New(W, Init(WTitle));
144:   DeskTop^.Insert(W)
145: end;
146:
147: { Initialize a new instance of type TheWindow }
148: constructor TheWindow.Init(WTitle: string);
149: var R: TRect;
150: begin
151:   Desktop^.GetExtent(R);
152:   R.Assign(numWindows, numWindows, R.B.X, R.B.Y);
153:   inc(numWindows);
```

```
154:      TWindow.Init(R, WTitle, GetWindowNumber);
155:      Options := Options or ofTileable;
156:      if numWindows >= maxWindows then
157:        DisableCommands([cmOpen])
158:    end;
159:
160:    { Clean up when a window is closed }
161:    procedure TheWindow.Close;
162:    begin
163:      TWindow.Close;
164:      PutWindowNumber;
165:      dec(numWindows);
166:      EnableCommands([cmOpen])
167:    end;
168:
169:    { Get a window number for a new window to use }
170:    function TheWindow.GetWindowNumber: Integer;
171:    var I: Integer;
172:    begin
173:      for I := 1 to maxWindows do
174:        if not (I in windowNums) then
175:        begin
176:          GetWindowNumber := I;
177:          windowNums := windowNums + [I];
178:          exit
179:        end;
180:      GetWindowNumber := wnNoNumber
181:    end;
182:
183:    { Make window's number available for future windows }
184:    procedure TheWindow.PutWindowNumber;
185:    begin
186:      if (1 <= Number) and (Number <= maxWindows) then
187:        windowNums := windowNums - [Number]
188:    end;
189:
190:    var
191:      Application: TheApp;
192:
193:    begin
194:      Application.Init;
195:      Application.Run;
196:      Application.Done
197:    end.
```

Before digging too deeply into the code, compile the listing and take the program for a test drive. Examine WINDMENU's two menus: File and Window. In the File menu are two commands: Open and Exit. These and other commands have associated hot keys F3 and Alt-X, which you can press to select their related commands without opening the menu. For instance, you can open a new window by pressing F3, or by opening the File menu and selecting the Open command.

Although Turbo Vision imposes no limit on the number of open windows, WINDMENU restricts the program to 12 windows open at once. You can change constant maxWindows (line 7) to increase or decrease this number. However, due to the way WindMenu keeps track of window numbers in a Pascal set variable, the upper limit for maxWindows is 255. (It's hard to imagine a program that would have more windows than 255, so this limit should not be too severe.)

Notice that WindMenu's status line shows the two commands from the File menu along with two more, F5-Zoom and F6-Next. These two commands, which you also find in the Window menu, are initially disabled. You can select them, but they don't do anything. In general, it's a good idea to disable inactive commands. That way, users always know what options are available. See "Enabling and Disabling Commands" in the next section for instructions about how to do the same in your own programs.

Press Alt-W or click on Window in the menu bar to open the Window menu. When you open a new window by pressing F3, the menu's commands are enabled. After closing all windows, the commands are again disabled.

You also can supply a file-name argument when you start WindMenu from DOS. For example, type WINDMENU MYFILE.PAS. The program doesn't open any disk files, it just displays whatever you type as the first window's title, so you can type any string for the argument. This demonstrates how you might construct a program to open a file initially, or just to display the blank desktop if no file is specified on the command line. In TheApp's constructor (lines 34-39), if ParamCount is greater than zero, the program calls OpenWindow, passing ParamStr(1) as the window's title. If ParamCount is zero, then no window is opened initially.

Enabling and Disabling Commands

Every TApplication object inherits two methods, EnableCommands and DisableCommands. Use these methods to activate and deactivate commands in menus. The methods are defined in the TView object—the data type behind just about every visible Turbo Vision object, and one of TApplication's ancestors.

After a program disables a menu command, you cannot select that command, although you can still see the command's dimmed letters in the menu. By showing disabled commands this way, the program tells you what commands are currently unavailable and prevents those same commands from being selected at inappropriate times.

To disable specific commands, pass the command constants as a set to DisableCommands. To enable a set of commands, pass their constants to EnableCommands. For example, to deactivate the Tile and Cascade menu commands, represented by the predefined constants cmTile and cmCascade, you can execute this statement from inside any method in a TApplication or derived object:

```
EnableCommands([cmTile, cmCascade]);
```

Disable commands similarly. To disable the cmCascade command, for example, you can execute the statement:

```
DisableCommands([cmCascade]);
```

Because sets can store values from 0 to 255, commands identified by numbers only in that range can be enabled and disabled. You can assign any integer values to commands, but you can enable and disable only those with values from 0 to 255. Though Turbo Vision reserves values 0 to 99 for its own use, you may use the predefined constants associated with these values to identify commands in your programs. For example, the predefined constant cmQuit equals 1, cmZoom equals 5, and so forth. You may use these constants for your own commands, but you should not attempt to redefine their meanings. For custom commands, you may use values starting with 100. (Look up the complete set of predefined command constants under cmXXXX in your Turbo Vision Guide.)

When and where to enable and disable specific commands are often difficult questions. At times you'll want to call EnableCommands and DisableCommands in response to a specific operation. For instance, if you are designing a program that can open only one file at a time, you might want to call DisableCommands after a file is opened. Then, after the program closes the file, you can re-enable the menu command to allow a new file to be opened.

That simple plan might not work so well in a complex program with dozens of interactive commands, and in such cases, it is difficult to keep track of which menu commands should be enabled or disabled at specific times. Rather than call EnableCommands and DisableCommands in various places, therefore, it is often better to enable and disable all your menu's commands at once based on the program's current state. The following section demonstrates one good way to implement this plan.

Coasting In Idle

Most Turbo Vision programs spend a great deal of time waiting for events to happen. During moments of relative inactivity—for example, in between keypresses or mouse button clicks—Turbo Vision calls a virtual method named Idle, declared in the TProgram object. TApplication descends from TProgram, so Idle is available to your own program's TApplication descendant.

Technically, Turbo Vision calls Idle when no events are waiting to be processed. The Idle method gives you a hook that you can use to snag a slice of time away from Turbo Vision when nothing else of importance is going on. An Idle procedure is a good place to update a clock, display debugging information, or perform tasks that seem as though they were running in the background of other more prominent tasks.

An excellent use for Idle is to enable and disable menu commands based on the application's current status—the approach taken by WindMenu, Program 16-4. To add new commands to Idle, the program declares the method in its TApplication descendant, TheApp (lines 15-23). Because the method is virtual, existing code inside Turbo Vision calls the new method for instances of TheApp. You don't have to take any other actions to inform Turbo Vision that it should call the new method. It does so automatically. All you have to do is create a replacement method in your program's TApplication descendant object.

Because Idle is called in between events, including the selection of menu commands, Idle is an ideal place to enable and disable commands in pull-down menus. In WindMenu, for example, the Idle method (lines 78-92) first calls TApplication.Idle—an important step that gives the ancestor TApplication method the opportunity to perform its own chores. In this case, those chores include disabling and enabling standard window-menu commands other than Tile and Cascade. WindMenu has to handle only those two commands itself.

To fulfill that requirement, an **if** statement in the overridden Idle method calls FirstThat, which returns a pointer to the first window in the desktop. To FirstThat, the program passes the expression @IsTileable—in other words, the address of the local subfunction named IsTileable (lines 81-84). FirstThat calls IsTileable (which could have a different name) to determine whether a specific condition is true for all the views attached to TheApp. In this case, the program wants to know whether at least one window can be tiled. If there aren't any windows open, IsTileable returns false, and the program disables the Tile and Cascade commands.

Cascading and Tiling Windows

With the menu commands properly disabled or enabled, the next step in implementing cascading and tiling of multiple windows is to respond to a Tile or Cascade command using two TDeskTop methods. Not too coincidentally, these methods are named Tile and Cascade.

In WINDMENU's HandleEvent method, when Event.Command equals cmTile, the program calls a local procedure TileWindows (see line 68). Similarly, when Event.Command equals cmCascade, the program calls CascadeWindows. These two subprocedures are nearly identical. Each declares a TRect variable R and each executes the three statements:

```
GetExtent(R);
R.Grow(0, -1);
R.Move(0, -1);
```

GetExtent sets R to the application's boundaries, providing the coordinates in which Turbo Vision will tile or cascade the desktop's windows. After obtaining the full extent of these boundaries, R.Grow and R.Move are used to adjust the values in R to leave room at the top and bottom for the menu bar and status line. If you did not adjust R this way, Turbo Vision tiles or cascades windows on top of these lines, obscuring them from view.

After preparing the R object, TileWindows executes the statement:

```
Desktop^.Tile(R);
```

calling the Tile method in the global Desktop variable defined in the App unit. Passing R to Tile gives that method the boundaries in which to redisplay in tiled fashion every window the desktop owns. Similarly, CascadeWindows executes:

```
Desktop^.Cascade(R);
```

to display the desktop's windows that are cascaded like a fanned deck of cards.

Tracking Window Numbers

If you've run Turbo Vision's supplied demonstration programs, you might have noticed a problem. After opening several windows, if you close one or two, those window's numbers are not reused. With a little extra effort, you can fix this problem by keeping track of window numbers that are in use, and assign unused numbers to newly opened windows.

This plan makes it possible to select most windows by pressing Alt and a digit key from 1 to 9. You can select other windows by pressing F6 or by using the mouse, but you can activate only the first nine with Alt.

To demonstrate one way to keep track of window numbers, WindMenu defines a variable (typed) constant windowNums as a set of values from one to maxWindows (see line 12). Initially, the set is empty, making all numbers available. Another variable constant, numWindows at line 11, stores the total number of open windows.

Most Turbo Vision programs create custom window objects from the basic TWindow data type. WindMenu's custom object is named TheWindow (lines 26-31). In TheWindow are two methods GetWindowNumber and PutWindowNumber that use WindMenu's typed constants to keep track of used and unused window numbers.

You can see this mechanism in action after you run the program and open a new window. At that time, the Init constructor in TheWindow object runs. The constructor's statements are similar to those you saw earlier in OneWind, Program

16-3. This time, however, rather than specify zero for the window's number (see line 45 in ONEWIND.PAS), WindMenu increments constant numWindows (line 153) and calls method GetWindowNumber (line 154) to obtain a fresh number for the new window.

Also notice how the Init constructor sets the ofTileable bit in the Options word. If the constructor did not set this bit, the window would be skipped for the Tile and Cascade commands—a fact that might come in handy if you want to create windows that do not change size or shape and have others that are tiled and cascaded normally. The Options word contains other bits that select various window options—see "Window and View Options" later in this chapter.

A final **if** statement in TheWindow's constructor calls DisableCommands to deactivate the File Menu's Open command. You could perform this step in the application's Idle method, but in this case, it's reasonable to disable the Open command in TheWindow's constructor when numWindows equals maxWindows. When you open 12 windows, this is the statement that dims the File:Open command.

When a window closes, the TWindow destructor calls a virtual TWindow procedure Close (lines 161-167). WindMenu replaces Close with its own version for two reasons: to add closed window numbers back to the pool of numbers that are used for new windows, and to enable the File:Open command. Obviously, if even one window closes, then the maximum number of windows cannot be open—so it makes sense to enable the Open command at this time. TheWindow.Close calls TWindow.Close to erase the window from view.

Views

A Turbo Vision window without a view is like a real window with one-way glass facing the wrong way. A window's view is responsible for that window's visible content. Without a view, a Turbo Vision window displays only a blank, uninteresting background.

In this section, you learn how to attach views to windows. You also discover how to add text to windows—a job nearly every program will have to do. And, you investigate how Turbo Vision selects colors for items on-screen.

Adding Views to Windows

Adding views to windows is similar to adding windows to the desktop. First, create an object instance, typically a descendant of TView. Then, insert the TView instance into the TWindow object that is to own the view. Even though it's attached to a window, a TView instance operates independently of any other object instance, and it can take any necessary steps to display information on-screen. Because the view is owned by a window, however, that view can follow the window if it moves, and it can easily respond to other window-related actions such as a change in the window's size.

To add views to your programs, you typically create a new object descendant of TView, one of the lowest objects in Turbo Vision's hierarchy. Start by including the Views unit in a uses statement like this:

```
uses Views;
```

Next, create a view object, and attach it to a program's window. In keeping with Turbo Vision's style rules, the complete definition consists of a pointer to the new object plus the object itself:

```
PTheView = ^TheView;
TheView = object(TView)
  TextArray: array[0 .. 4] of string[40];
  constructor Init(var Bounds: TRect);
  procedure Draw; virtual;
end;
```

PTheView is a pointer to a new object named TheView. That object inherits all the capabilities of TView—literally a bumper crop of view-object fields and methods. To TheView's rich inheritance, the sample object adds an array of strings, which gives the view some data to display. The two other items in TheView replace TView's Init constructor and Draw method. There are many other methods you can use in views (look them up in Borland's *Turbo Vision Guide*). However, you usually replace at least Init and Draw as shown here.

As in most objects, the view's Init constructor initializes instances of the object data type, and the constructor is a good place to take steps for preparing data to display in a window. For example, the constructor might store some text in the object's string array like this:

```
constructor TheView.Init(var Bounds: TRect);
begin
  TView.Init(Bounds);
  TextArray[0] := 'Good night, good night!';
  TextArray[1] := 'Parting is such sweet sorrow,';
  TextArray[2] := 'That I shall say good night';
  TextArray[3] := 'Till it be morrow.';
  TextArray[4] := '    -- Romeo and Juliet II, ii';
end;
```

If there is a method that carries more than its fair share of a Turbo Vision program's weight, it is a view's Draw method, the second replacement method in TheView. Practically every visible character on display is handled by one or another Draw method. In this simple example, Draw displays the text stored in the object's string array:

```
procedure TheView.Draw;
var
  Y: Integer;
begin
  TView.Draw;
  for Y := 0 to 4 do
    WriteStr(1, Y + 4, TextArray[Y], 1)
end;
```

The first statement in Draw calls the ancestor's method, giving that method the opportunity to draw its own data. Don't skip this step without good reason—to completely replace an ancestor Draw method's output, for example. Usually, you want the ancestor method to perform its duties to which you add new output in the replacement procedure.

The **for** loop in the new Draw method calls procedure WriteStr to display text in the view. WriteStr is one of four routines that TView objects provide for writing text: WriteBuf, WriteChar, WriteLine, and WriteStr. In general, when you have to display some text in a view, use one of these four procedures.

Inexperienced Turbo Vision programmers might be tempted to use Write and Writeln statements to display text in views. Don't do that. The special requirements of an event-driven environment make Write and Writeln obsolete for Turbo Vision applications. (You may still use the standard procedures to write data to files, however. You just can't use them to display text on-screen.)

Writing Text in Windows

Although Program 16-5, DISPLAY.PAS, doesn't do too much, it demonstrates the basic requirements for displaying text in views. Compile and run the program. As you can see, it displays some text in its window and lets you end the program by pressing Alt-X or selecting that label from the status line.

Program 16-5: DISPLAY.PAS

```
1:  program Display;
2:
3:  uses Objects, Views, App;
```

```
 4:
 5:  type
 6:    TheApp = object(TApplication)
 7:      constructor Init;
 8:    end;
 9:
10:    PTheWindow = ^TheWindow;
11:    TheWindow = object(TWindow)
12:      constructor Init;
13:    end;
14:
15:    PTheView = ^TheView;
16:    TheView = object(TView)
17:      TextArray: array[0 .. 4] of string[40];
18:      constructor Init(var Bounds: TRect);
19:      procedure Draw; virtual;
20:    end;
21:
22:  constructor TheApp.Init;
23:  var
24:    W: PTheWindow;
25:  begin
26:    TApplication.Init;
27:    New(W, Init);
28:    DeskTop^.Insert(W)
29:  end;
30:
31:  constructor TheWindow.Init;
32:  var
33:    R: TRect;
34:    V: PTheView;
35:  begin
36:    Desktop^.GetExtent(R);
37:    TWindow.Init(R, 'Test Window', 0);
38:    GetClipRect(R);
39:    R.Grow(-1, -1);
40:    V := New(PTheView, Init(R));
41:    Insert(V)
42:  end;
43:
44:  constructor TheView.Init(var Bounds: TRect);
45:  begin
```

continued

Program 16-5: continued

```
46:      TView.Init(Bounds);
47:      GrowMode := gfGrowHiX + gfGrowHiY;
48:      TextArray[0] := 'Good night, good night!';
49:      TextArray[1] := 'Parting is such sweet sorrow,';
50:      TextArray[2] := 'That I shall say good night';
51:      TextArray[3] := 'Till it be morrow.';
52:      TextArray[4] := '    -- Romeo and Juliet II, ii';
53:  end;
54:
55:  procedure TheView.Draw;
56:  var
57:      Y : Integer;
58:  begin
59:      TView.Draw;
60:      for Y := 0 to 4 do
61:        WriteStr(1, Y + 4, TextArray[Y], 1)
62:  end;
63:
64:  var
65:      Application: TheApp;
66:
67:  begin
68:      Application.Init;
69:      Application.Run;
70:      Application.Done
71:  end.
```

The program declares three objects. TheApp, a descendant of TApplication, is simple, having only a single method, constructor Init. TheWindow, a descendant of TWindow, is equally simple. It too has only a constructor method. TheView, which inherits the properties of TView, is repeated from earlier. This object's TextArray stores some data to display in a window, and declares two methods: a constructor Init and a virtual Draw method for displaying the view's information.

When line 27 creates a new instance of TheWindow, assigning that object instance's address to local variable W, the window's constructor runs. At that time, several actions take place (see lines 36-41). First, the program obtains the boundaries of the desktop, passing those values in a TRect object R to the TWindow ancestor's constructor. Lines 38-39 adjust R to fit snugly inside the window, executing the statements:

```
GetClipRect(R);
R.Grow(-1, -1);
```

Calling GetClipRect assigns the window's clipping boundaries to a local TRect variable R. To further restrict output to the area inside the window frame, the program calls R.Grow to reduce the vertical and horizontal limits by one character on both sides and on the top and bottom.

The clipping boundary defines the no-man's land beyond which output routines are prohibited from treading. In graphics, the term *clipping* refers to the process of chopping lines and other shapes at well marked borders, thus preventing shapes from overwriting others that have to be protected. In Turbo Vision, clipping restricts text to a specified rectangle, so programs can send output to their views without concern that text in one view will interfere with text in another. In fact, clipping is one of the fundamental forces behind Turbo Vision's windowing capabilities. Without clipping, it would be extremely difficult to write code that keeps a view's contents from going astray.

After the program adjusts the rectangle R's values, line 40 creates an instance of TheView and assigns its address to a local PTheView pointer V. To associate the new view with the window, the program calls the inherited TWindow method Insert at line 41, passing the view's address. It is not necessary to retain a pointer to the view object instance—just insert it into the window and forget about it. The window keeps track of its view (or views). Later, when the window closes, it will automatically dispose of any inserted views.

Lines 44-53 show the steps taken to initialize the new view object instance. When line 40 creates an instance of TheView, New calls TheView.Init. TheView.Init then calls the ancestor constructor (line 46), sets the view's GrowMode variable (line 47), and assigns some text data to the TextArray instance variable. Setting GrowMode to gfGrowHiX + gfGrowHiY ensures that when the window's size changes, the associated view will adjust itself automatically to fit within the window's new borders.

The view's Draw method (lines 55-62) is responsible for displaying the view object's data. The first step in most Draw methods is to call the ancestor's method, here TView.Draw at line 59. After that step, which gives the ancestor the opportunity to execute its own output statements, the view can call WriteStr or another of the four output procedures listed earlier to display text in the window. WriteStr, a method defined in TView, is defined as:

```
procedure WriteStr(X, Y: Integer; Str: string; Color: Byte);
```

Set X and Y to the location inside the view where the string Str should appear. The upper left corner of a view is located at coordinate (0,0). Set the Color value to the color index of the view's palette, selecting a color for the text. Try changing the second 1 to 2 or 3, for example, at line 61.

Color palettes, and color index values, are among Turbo Vision's least understood techniques. You'll take a closer look at color palettes in a moment. First, however, there are a couple of stock views, called gadgets, that can add value to any Turbo Vision program.

Using Turbo Vision's Gadgets

A TView object's Draw method is the most common way to display text in views. Other good examples of this technique are demonstrated in GADGETS.PAS, a unit that is provided with Turbo Pascal. Tapping into this unit lets you display a free-running clock and the amount of free heap space available in memory.

Program 16-6, HEAPTIME.PAS, shows how to attach these gadgets to Turbo Vision applications. When you run the program, you see a bare desktop with the time in the upper right and the amount of free heap space in the lower right.

Program 16-6: HEAPTIME.PAS

```pascal
1:   program HeapTime;
2:
3:   uses Objects, App, Gadgets;
4:
5:   type
6:     PTheApp = ^TheApp;
7:     TheApp = object(TApplication)
8:       Clock: PClockView;
9:       Heap: PHeapView;
10:      constructor Init;
11:      procedure Idle; virtual;
12:    end;
13:
14:  constructor TheApp.Init;
15:  var
16:    R: TRect;
17:  begin
18:    TApplication.Init;
19:    GetExtent(R);
20:    R.A.X := R.B.X - 9; R.B.Y := R.A.Y + 1;
21:    Clock := New(PClockView, Init(R));
22:    Insert(Clock);
23:    GetExtent(R);
24:    R.A.X := R.B.X - 9; R.A.Y := R.B.Y - 1;
```

```
25:    Heap := New(PHeapView, Init(R));
26:    Insert(Heap)
27: end;
28:
29: procedure TheApp.Idle;
30: begin
31:    TApplication.Idle;
32:    Clock^.Update;
33:    Heap^.Update
34: end;
35:
36: var
37:    Application: TheApp;
38:
39: begin
40:    Application.Init;
41:    Application.Run;
42:    Application.Done
43: end.
```

Although HEAPTIME.PAS doesn't have any windows or a menu, you can use it as a guide to adding clock and heap views to your own, more complex, programs. Begin by adding the Gadgets unit to a **uses** declaration (see line 3). Then, to your TApplication descendant object, add the two fields:

```
Clock: PClockView;
Heap: PHeapView;
```

Clock, a pointer of type PClockView, will address an object instance of type TClockView. Similarly, Heap, a pointer of type PHeapView, will address an instance of type THeapView. Inserting these views into the application causes them to show up automatically when the program runs.

Lines 19-22 show how to insert the clock view. Lines 23-26 demonstrate similar steps for the heap value. You can copy these lines to your own application's constructor. You also can modify the locations of the views by changing the values assigned to the TRect variable R's fields.

To continually update the time and heap, TheApp.Idle, which you learned about earlier, calls Update methods for the two views (see lines 32-33). Because Idle runs only when nothing else of importance is going on, these actions do not interfere with a program's normal activity.

If you want to know more about how the clock and heap gadgets work, examine the GADGETS.PAS file provided with Turbo Pascal. As you'll see, the two objects are TView descendants. Notice how the objects' Draw methods call WriteLine to display the time and heap space.

Color Palettes

The first rule in learning how to use Turbo Vision color palettes is to stop thinking of colors as visible hues. A color value in Turbo Vision is merely an index into a table—or to use the fancier term, a palette—that determines the actual color you see on-screen. In Turbo Vision, you never specify colors such as Red, White, or Blue for a program's output. You instead specify index values that tell Turbo Vision to make one item's color like another's.

Color Mapping

By making a few modifications to DISPLAY.PAS, Program 16-5, you gain a clearer picture of how Turbo Vision maps color palette index values to visible colors. Copy DISPLAY.PAS to a new file named CDISPLAY.PAS, and load the copy into the Turbo Pascal editor.

> **Note:** The following descriptions of palettes assume you are using a color monitor. If your computer has a monochrome display, you will not be able to see all the effects mentioned here.

Next, change line 61 in the original DISPLAY.PAS to the following

```
WriteStr(1, Y + 4, TextArray[Y], Y + 1)
```

In other words, rather than specify a color value of 1, pass Y + 1 to WriteStr, selecting color values 1 through 5 for each execution of the loop. When you run the modified program, the text lines in the window are now painted in different colors, except for the last two lines, which are the same (for reasons that will become clear later).

Consider the first execution of the loop when the program passes 1 for WriteStr's color value. When displaying characters, Turbo Vision maps (translates) that value into another value stored in a palette string, which might be declared as:

```
MyColors = #3#8#9;
```

The constants #3, #8, and #9 are Turbo Pascal's way of representing characters as ASCII values—a convenient way to string a series of byte values, in this case color indexes. You also could write similar strings in hexadecimal:

```
MyHexColors = #$70#$71#$0F;
```

Don't put quotations around such strings. The following is not correct:

```
MyColors = '#3#8#9';    { ??? }
```

That's a six-character string composed of the ASCII values for the characters shown in quotations. Without quotes, the expression #3#8#9 is a three-character string composed of ASCII values 3, 8, and 9.

The reason for storing color index values in strings this way is to take advantage of Turbo Pascal's ability to index individual bytes in strings. For example, if B is a Byte variable, this expression

```
B := MyColors[2];
```

sets B equal to the second value in the MyColors string. Using the earlier value #3#8#9 assigned to MyColors, after the assignment, B will equal 8. In a sense, the index value 2 in that assignment is remapped, or translated, to the value 8. And that is exactly how color mapping works in Turbo Vision. Index values like the 2 in the previous expression are used as indexes into arrays of other color index values to map one value to another.

Changing Color Mappings

Another modification to CDISPLAY.PAS explains how you can alter the mapping, and therefore, change the colors of text in windows. First, add a new declaration to object TheView, just after TextArray between lines 17 and 18 in the original DISPLAY.PAS listing:

```
function GetPalette: PPalette; virtual;
```

Function GetPalette is inherited from TView, but simply returns **nil** unless you override it as you are doing here. Implement the function like this:

```
function TheView.GetPalette: PPalette;
const
  CTheView = #1#2#3#4#5;
  PTheView: string[Length(CTheView)] = CTheView;
begin
  GetPalette := @PTheView
end;
```

Constant CTheView is this descendant view's color palette. Similar to the earlier examples, the value assigned to the constant is a string of five byte values, in this case the values 1 through 5. PTheView is a variable (typed) constant string to which the program assigns CTheView. Notice the use of the Length function to allocate just enough space to hold the constant.

The function's body performs only one job—it returns the address of the typed constant PTheView. When a statement calls GetPalette, it will receive the address of the view's palette.

Run the modified CDISPLAY program. As you can see, despite the changes you just made, the colors on-screen are the same as they were previously. The reason there is no change is because the values in the new palette string #1#2#3#4#5 are the same as the index values used to extract those values. For example, CTheView[2] equals 2 and CTheView[4] equals 4. There's no change of colors because there's no remapping of one color index to another.

Now, modify the constant assigned to CTheView. For example, you could reverse the index values, changing the declaration to:

```
CTheView = #5#4#3#2#1;
```

As you might expect, reversing the palette mappings reverses the colors of the text lines in the window. But as you can see if you ran the modified program, the change also affected the view's background color, which uses the color palette index value 1. Next, try this:

```
CTheView = #1#3#2#1#2;
```

Now the background returns to its default color of Blue because the first color palette index #1 in effect performs no remapping of that value to another (CTheView[1] equals 1). Also try this faulty declaration:

```
CTheView = #4;   { ??? }
```

When you run this modification, you see that the background of the window's view has changed to cyan, because the first (and only) color palette index value translates the background color index (always 1) to 4, and thus alters its colors. (Never mind which color that is—the fact that the color changes as a result of the remapping is all that matters.)

You probably have noticed another problem with this new palette. All the text except for the first line is now an annoying flashing white on red background. This is a common Turbo Vision palette error that happens when a program uses color index values for which no mappings are provided. In this case, WriteStr specifies color index values 1 through 5, but the GetPalette function provides a mapping for only the first index. The others end up flashing red, an indication that the program has used more index values than provided for.

Suppose you want all the text lines to appear normally, but you want the last line to be highlighted. This does the trick:

```
CTheView = #2#2#2#2#4;
```

In effect, this remapping says "make color index values 1 through 4 the same as the default value of 2, but change color index value 5 to 4." In other words, CTheView[1] through CTheView[4] equal 2. CTheView[5] equals 4. The index values are the "colors" you can use in your program's WriteStr and similar statements. The values in the palette are the mappings that tell Turbo Vision to make your colors look like those.

Understanding Color Palettes

If you have made the modifications to DISPLAY.PAS outlined in the preceding section, you still might have lingering doubts about how colors actually become visible. At some point, of course, color index values have to be translated to color attributes that will be stored in the PC's video memory buffer and therefore show up as visible colors (or monochrome attributes) on-screen.

To understand how that process works, you should keep in mind that all color index mappings occur at runtime. When one object instance owns another—as a TWindow object may own a TView—that relationship, not the inheritance of one object by another, is what determines the final colorful outcome.

Figure 16-3 shows how color mapping works in Turbo Vision. At the bottom of the figure is the palette returned by TheView's replacement GetPalette function. (If you have made the changes suggested earlier, assign the string #1#3#5#6#7 to CTheView in CDISPLAY.PAS to make the program match the figure.)

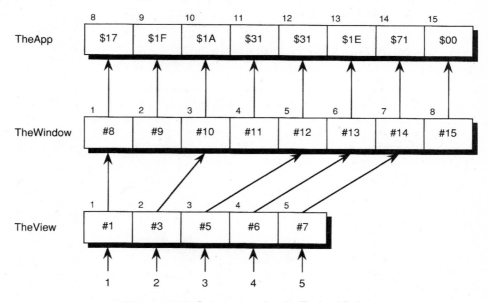

Figure 16-3 Color mapping in Turbo Vision.

The index values 1, 2, 3, 4, and 5 shown at the bottom of Figure 16-3 are the values that you can use in WriteStr and similar output statements. To map these indexes to visible colors, Turbo Vision begins with the current object instance, in this case, TheView. For example, suppose you specify the color index value 3. That value is remapped to 5, the third entry in TheView's palette. (The palette index values are shown in small digits on top of the boxes for reference.)

Because TheView is owned by TheWindow, a TWindow descendant, another level of color index remapping occurs. Turbo Vision takes the current index 5 (mapped from the original 3), and uses it to index the palette in the object's immediate owner. Because that object (TheWindow) does not provide a replacement GetPalette, it uses the inherited one from TWindow shown in the figure. As you can see, color index values 1 through 8 are remapped to indexes 8 through 15. So, the 5 now becomes translated into 12—the value stored at the fifth location in TheWindow's palette.

TheWindow is inserted into the global DeskTop, which does not have a palette and, therefore, stops the remapping process. At this stage, Turbo Vision takes the final remapped index (12 in this case) and uses that value as an index into one of three 63-byte real-color palettes CColor, CBlackWhite, and CMonochrome defined in the App unit and returned by TProgram's GetPalette method.

A portion of this final palette is shown at the top of Figure 16-3. The values stored in the array are the actual color attributes that are stored in the PC's video buffer. To complete the example, the final color index 12 is mapped to the color attribute $31 hexadecimal and used to color the display.

Selecting Default Colors

The preceding section assumes you have a color display, and even though color monitors are becoming increasingly popular, not all CRTs are color. You still have to provide the means to configure your programs for black and white (also called gray scale) and monochrome displays.

When a Turbo Vision application begins, the TApplication Init constructor calls TProgram.Init as its last duty. In addition to other tasks, Init in turn calls InitScreen, a virtual method defined in TProgram. Among other duties, InitScreen inspects the current ScreenMode variable (defined in the Drivers unit), and sets another global variable AppPalette in the App unit to one of the three constants: apColor, apBlackWhite, or apMonochrome.

In most cases, Turbo Vision detects the current screen type and sets AppPalette accordingly. However, you still have to give users the option of selecting an alternate configuration in case the autodetection fails, or to allow people to configure a laptop's gray-scale display. To do that, you can declare a TApplication object like this:

```
TheApp = object(TApplication)
  { other fields and methods }
  procedure InitScreen; virtual;
end;
```

and implement InitScreen as shown here:

```
procedure TheApp.InitScreen;
begin
  TApplication.InitScreen;
  AppPalette := apBlackWhite;
end;
```

Inside the replacement InitScreen method, call TApplication.InitScreen. Then, change AppPalette to one of the three constants apColor, apBlackWhite, or apMonochrome. To see how this works, add the declarations and method to DISPLAY.PAS (or to the modified CDISPLAY.PAS if you created it.) When you run the program, its display will be in black and white—suitable for use on an LCD display as typically found in portable and laptop computers.

Window and View Options

Now that you know how to create windows and views, you might want to select various options available in these objects. This section explains options for TWindow objects and then, after that, for TView objects.

TWindow Options

Every TWindow object and descendant has a Byte field named Flags. In that field, four bits control whether the window can move, grow, close, and zoom. By setting or clearing these bits in your window's constructor, you can alter its start-up characteristics.

Turbo Vision defines four constants that you can use to modify a window's Flags field. Table 16-2 lists these constants and their values.

Table 16-2 TWindow Flags options.

Constant	Value	Description
wfMove	$01	When set (1), window can move. When cleared (0), window's position remains fixed in place.
wfGrow	$02	When set (1), window is allowed to grow and shrink in size, and a resize button is displayed in the window frame's bottom-right corner. When cleared (0), window's size may not be changed and no resize button is displayed.
wfClose	$04	When set (1), window has a close button at top left and may be closed, either by clicking the button or pressing Alt-F3. When cleared, window may not be closed and does not have a close button.
wfZoom	$08	When set (1), window has a set of zoom buttons at top right and may be zoomed to full screen or back to normal size. When cleared (0), window may not be zoomed and does not have zoom buttons.

The four flag values may be combined or used separately to affect one or more window options. Use logical **or** operators to create a multioption value. For example, the expression (wfMove **or** wfZoom) would set those two flags. Or, you can add the constants. The expression (wfGrow + wfClose + wfZoom) would set those three flags, and so on.

To clear a flag, use the **and** and **not** operators. For instance, to create a window that can't move, grow, close, or zoom, you can clear all four bits in the Flags field. To experiment with this technique, make a copy of the DISPLAY.PAS program listed earlier in this chapter (Program 16-5). In TheWindow's constructor, between lines 37 and 38 following the call to the ancestor constructor, add this statement:

```
Flags := Flags and (not (wfMove + wfGrow + wfClose + wfZoom));
```

You also could replace the plus signs with logical **or** operators—either of the two forms works equally well. However, if you want to insert one or more constants into an existing Flags value, always use logical **or** expressions, not addition. For example, this expression:

```
Flags := Flags or wfMove;
```

correctly sets the wfMove bit in Flags, regardless of the field's current value. But this expression:

```
Flags := Flags + wfMove;  { ??? }
```

is probably an error, because the wfMove bit might already be set in Flags, in which case that bit plus the new one would be added, causing a carry to occur and affecting other bits in the final value. (If these expressions are not clear, you might want to review the discussion on Boolean logic in chapters 2 and 12.)

To clear a single bit value, use an expression such as

```
Flags := Flags and not wfMove;
```

The negation of wfMove results in a value with a single bit set to zero and all others equal to one. **And**ing that value with Flags clears that single bit (sets it to zero).

TView Options

Like TWindow objects, TViews have a field that you can use to select a variety of options, each represented by a single bit that can be on (1) or off (0). Because TWindow is a descendant of TView, all TWindow objects (and their descendants) also share the same options as plain TViews.

TView declares an Options Word field with 11 settings, associated with constants beginning with "of." For example, the constant ofSelectable determines whether a view selects itself automatically when a mouse pointer is clicked in the view's space. If you do not want that action to occur, you can turn it off by executing:

```
Options := Options and not ofSelectable;
```

You also can test whether specific options are set. For instance, Program 16-4, WINDMENU.PAS, examines the Options field to determine whether the view is able to be tiled, executing this statement at line 83:

```
IsTileable := P^.Options and ofTileable <> 0
```

The function result IsTileable will be true only if the view's ofTileable bit is set in the Options field addressed by the PView pointer P.

In that same program, line 155 sets the ofTileable bit in the window's constructor, thus ensuring that each new window can be tiled and cascaded. To prevent that action from occurring, you can change the statement to:

```
Options := Options and not ofTileable;
```

As with TWindow Flags values, use logical **or** to set bit values; use **and** and **not** to clear them.

The Turbo Vision Guide lists all TView Options and describes what they do. To find them, look up ofXXXX in the guide.

Summary

Turbo Vision is a highly sophisticated object-oriented library for writing Turbo Pascal programs with pull-down menus, overlapping windows, dialog boxes, and other elements of modern user interfaces. Turbo Pascal's own IDE is the best example of what Turbo Vision can do—the entire IDE interface was written using Turbo Vision's tools.

Behind the scenes, Turbo Vision is powered by event-driven technology. An event-driven program is driven by events that are passed to a program as messages, and representing external activities such as mouse button clicks and keypresses. Event-driven programs respond to actions as they occur rather than request actions from users, as is typically done in conventional programming.

A Turbo Vision program's desktop is based on the TApplication object, which prepares the program's menu bar and status line. Menu commands are typically handled by the application's HandleEvent method.

In most cases, programs insert a TWindow object into the desktop. Windows are usually composed of three object instances, of types TWindow, TFrame, and TView. TWindows are invisible. TFrames control the window's border. TViews are responsible for a windows contents. Users can select among multiple windows by pressing Alt and a digit key from 1 to 9. Windows also can be tiled and cascaded— two operations provided by the global Desktop object, instance.

Use WriteStr, WriteBuf, WriteChar, or WriteLine to write text in window views. You should not use the standard Write and Writeln procedures to display text in Turbo Vision windows.

Colors in Turbo Vision programs are represented by color palette index values, not by display attributes. To map a color index to a visible hue, Turbo Vision translates the current view's color index to that of the palette in the view's owner. Eventually, after running out of owners, Turbo Vision translates a color index to a display attribute, using one of three low-level palettes defined in the App unit.

Various options are available for TWindow and TView objects. Generally, options are represented by single bit flags, which you can set and reset using Boolean expressions.

Exercises

16-1. Explain how an event-driven program differs from a conventional one.

16-2. Add a new menu and commands to DESK.PAS (Program 16-1). The commands do not have to perform any actions.

16-3. Write dummy procedures for your menu in exercise 16-2. Add a HandleEvent method to the programs TApplication descendant object, and call your procedures from the method's implementation. Use Turbo Pascal's built-in debugger to prove that, when you select a command, the associated dummy procedure is called.

16-4. Write a program that opens a window and displays the first 10 lines from a text file. If you name the program TEN.PAS, you should be able to enter the DOS command TEN MYFILE.TXT to display MYFILE.TXT's first 10 lines.

16-5. Add a free-running clock and heap display to your answer for exercise 16-4.

16-6. (Advanced) Revise your program in exercise 16-4 to display multiple windows for one or more files entered at the command-line prompt.

16-7. In HEAPTIME.PAS (Program 16-6), modify the colors of the clock and heap views. (Hint: Create new objects that inherit the TClockView and THeapView objects, then add your own GetPalette function.)

Turbo Vision Tools

- Conversational Dialogs
- Working with Dialogs and Controls
- Collectibles
- List Boxes
- Stream Basics

17

Key Words and Identifiers

NewSItem, RegisterType, TBufStream, TButton, TCheckBoxes, TCluster, TCollection, TDialog, TDosStream, TEmsStream, TInputLine, TLabel, TListBox, TObject, TRadioButtons, TRect, TSortedCollection, TStaticText, TStream, TStreamRec, TStringCollection, TView

Now that you have explored some of Turbo Vision's basics, you're ready to begin applying your knowledge to more sophisticated applications. In this chapter you explore three of Turbo Vision's most useful interface tools: dialogs, collections, and streams.

Conversational Dialogs

For helping people communicate with programs, one of the primary tools in Turbo Vision's chest is the *dialog box*. For fun, and to provide a platform for experimenting with the techniques that follow, you'll enter and run an order-entry program for a fictitious pizza parlor. The program uses a dialog box to prompt for order information. Later, you'll construct a similar dialog box for a more practical utility that prompts for runtime options.

By grouping options into a dialog box, your program's users can concentrate on using your software rather than wasting time figuring out what the program's options are and how to select them. Dialog boxes are more or less required in modern commercial applications. It's the rare program that doesn't have at least one dialog box.

Message Dialogs

The most basic of dialogs is a message box, which displays a brief message and waits for a response. In the simplest case, the dialog contains only the message text and a single button, usually labeled Ok. After reading the message, you can select the Ok button to close the dialog window.

The MsgBox unit supplied with Turbo Pascal provides standard dialogs for displaying messages. To create a message dialog requires two variables: a pointer Dialog of type PDialog and a rectangle R of type TRect. The pointer addresses an object of type TDialog stored on the heap. The rectangle specifies the size and position of the dialog's window. Programs almost never declare descendant objects of type TDialog. Instead, they create a standard TDialog object and feed it various items for display. Because it is rarely used to create descendant objects, TDialog is known as a *terminal object*.

Here's a sample dialog procedure, which a program might call in response to a menu selection:

```
function TestDialog: Word;
var
  Dialog: PDialog; { Pointer to TDialog }
  R: TRect;        { Size and position }
begin
  R.Assign(0, 0, 64, 15);
  Dialog := New(PDialog, Init(R, 'Test'));
  with Dialog^ do
  begin
   Options := Options or ofCentered;
   R.Assign(45, 12, 55, 14);
   Insert(New(PButton, Init(R, 'O~k~', cmOK, bfDefault)));
  end;
  Desktop^.ExecView(Dialog);
  Dispose(Dialog, Done)
end;
```

The function first assigns to the TRect variable R four values that represent the X and Y coordinates of the dialog's upper-left and lower-right corners. Because this dialog will be centered on the desktop, the first two values are 0; the last two values represent the dialog's width and height. In this example, the dialog will be 64 characters wide and 15 characters high when it is displayed.

The second statement calls New to create the dialog object on the heap and assign the object's address to the Dialog pointer variable. New calls TDialog.Init, passing the TRect variable R and a string for the dialog's title. If you don't want the dialog to have a title, pass a null string for the second argument. TDialog descends from TWindow. Therefore, every dialog box is actually a window in disguise. Unlike common windows, however, dialogs are colored differently (gray rather than blue on color monitors for example), are not resizeable, lack zoom buttons, and do not have window numbers that you can select by pressing Alt and a digit key.

The **with** statement in TestDialog applies to the statements between the inner **begin** and **end**. In that section, bit ofCentered is set in the dialog's Options field, which causes the dialog's owner (usually the desktop) to center the dialog window on-screen. To display the dialog in another position, delete this assignment and adjust R's values as you wish.

Before activating the dialog, which at this stage is a bare window, you need to insert at least one button so that people can close the dialog box. Using the same TRect variable R, first assign the size and location of the button. Then call the dialog's Insert method along with New to insert an object of type PButton into the dialog.

```
R.Assign(45, 12, 55, 14);
Insert(New(PButton, Init(R, 'O~k~', cmOK, bfDefault)));
```

There's no need to save the PButton pointer. Just insert the object into the dialog and forget about it. As the button's owner, the dialog takes care of displaying the button and disposing the button object when the dialog closes.

PButton is a pointer to type TButton, another terminal object almost never used as a descendant object's ancestor. To create a button, New calls TButton's Init constructor, passing four values:

- A TRect variable

- A string to use for the button's label

- A command to be generated when the button is clicked

- Either bfDefault or bfNormal

The first two values specify the button's location, size, and label. Use tilde characters to assign an Alt hot key to the button. In this example, 'O~k~' specifies Alt-K as the button's hot key. The button's command should usually be cmOk, cmCancel, cmYes, or cmNo. When selected, each of these commands closes the dialog. The fourth argument indicates which button is the default, selected by pressing Enter. Only one button can be identified by bfDefault. Use bfNormal for all other buttons inserted into a dialog.

You have now created an entire dialog. All that remains is to display the dialog window so that people can see and use its contents. Fortunately, this step is the simplest of all. Just call the Desktop's ExecView method, then dispose of the TDialog object.

```
Desktop^.ExecView(Dialog);
Dispose(Dialog, Done);
```

ExecView handles all keyboard and mouse commands. To ensure that dialogs can be closed, ExecView translates Esc keypresses into cmCancel commands. You can also close dialogs by clicking the window's close button, pressing Alt-F3, or selecting the label "Alt-F3" from the desktop's status line.

When ExecView finishes, it closes the dialog. At that point, unless you plan to call ExecView again for the same dialog, you should call Dispose to remove the dialog object and all associated controls from the heap.

About this Program

In programs with pulldown menus, programmers typically place a copyright or a personal notice inside a dialog called an *About box.* For a quick and dirty About box, use the AboutProgram procedure in unit DIAG.PAS (see Program 17-1). After compiling the listing, add Diag (short for Dialogs) to your program's **uses** declaration. You can then call AboutProgram to display an About box with an Ok button and three lines of text (see Figure 17-1).

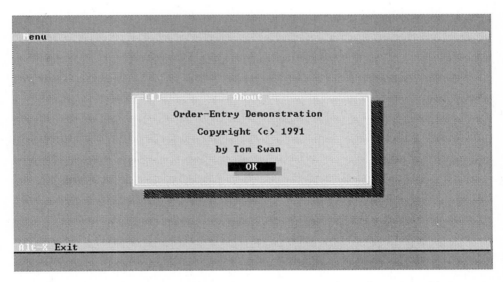

Figure 17-1 AboutProgram in DIAG.PAS displays an About box as in this screen sample from another program in this chapter.

Program 17-1: DIAG.PAS

```pascal
 1:  unit Diag;
 2:
 3:  interface
 4:
 5:  uses Crt, Objects, Views, App, Dialogs;
 6:
 7:  procedure AboutProgram(ProgramTitle: string);
 8:  function Yes(Prompt: string): Boolean;
 9:  procedure ErrorMessage(ErrNumber: Integer; ErrMessage: string);
10:
11:
12:  implementation
13:
14:  { Display "About Program" dialog box }
15:  procedure AboutProgram(ProgramTitle: string);
16:  var
17:    AboutPtr: PDialog;
18:    R: TRect;
19:  begin
20:    R.Assign(0, 0, 40, 11);
21:    AboutPtr := New(PDialog, Init(R, 'About'));
22:    if (AboutPtr <> nil) then with AboutPtr^ do
23:    begin
24:      Options := Options or ofCentered;
25:      R.Grow(-1, -1);
26:      Insert(New(PStaticText, Init(R,
27:        #13^C + ProgramTitle + #13 +
28:        #13^C'Copyright (c)  1991'#13 +
29:        #13^C'by Tom Swan'
30:      )));
31:      R.Assign(15, 8, 25, 10);
32:      Insert(New(PButton, Init(R, 'O~K', cmOk, bfDefault)));
33:      Desktop^.ExecView(AboutPtr);
34:      Dispose(AboutPtr, Done)
35:    end
36:  end;
37:
38:  { Prompt user for Yes or No answer. Returns true for Yes }
39:  function Yes(Prompt: string): Boolean;
40:  var
41:    YNDiag: PDialog;
```

```
42:     R: TRect;
43:   begin
44:     R.Assign(0, 0, 60, 7);
45:     YNDiag := New(PDialog, Init(R, 'Please answer Yes or No'));
46:     if (YNDiag <> nil) then with YNDiag^ do
47:     begin
48:       Options := Options or ofCentered;
49:       R.Grow(-1, -2);
50:       Insert(New(PStaticText, Init(R, ^C + Prompt)));
51:       R.Assign(35, 4, 43, 6);
52:       Insert(New(PButton, Init(R, '~N~o', cmNo, bfNormal)));
53:       R.Assign(17, 4, 26, 6);
54:       Insert(New(PButton, Init(R, '~Y~es', cmYes, bfDefault)));
55:       Yes := Desktop^.ExecView(YNDiag) = cmYes;
56:       Dispose(YNDiag, Done)
57:     end
58:   end;
59:
60:   { Display error message }
61:   procedure ErrorMessage(ErrNumber: Integer; ErrMessage: string);
62:   var
63:     ErrDiag: PDialog;
64:     R: TRect;
65:     ENS: string[6];  { Error-number string }
66:   begin
67:     Str(ErrNumber, ENS);
68:     R.Assign(0, 0, 60, 7);
69:     ErrDiag := New(PDialog, Init(R, 'Error #' + ENS));
70:     if (ErrDiag <> nil) then with ErrDiag^ do
71:     begin
72:       Options := Options or ofCentered;
73:       R.Grow(-1, -2);
74:       Insert(New(PStaticText, Init(R, ^C + ErrMessage)));
75:       R.Assign(20, 4, 40, 6);
76:       Insert(New(PButton, Init(R, '~O~k', cmOK, bfNormal)));
77:       Sound(440);
78:       Delay(200);
79:       NoSound;
80:       Desktop^.ExecView(ErrDiag);
81:       Dispose(ErrDiag, Done)
82:     end
83:   end;
84:
85:   end.
```

To customize AboutProgram, change the copyright notice and other information at lines 27-29. Then, in response to a menu command (or at any other time), call AboutProgram, which passes the name of your program as an argument.

```
AboutProgram('IncredibleCalc');
```

AboutProgram's statements are nearly the same as outlined earlier. The only new feature is the way the dialog displays text by executing

```
R.Grow(-1, -1);
Insert(New(PStaticText, Init(R,
  #13^C + ProgramTitle + #13 +
  #13^C'Copyright  1991'#13 +
  #13^C'by Tom Swan'
)));
```

R.Grow adjusts the dialog's rectangle to nest inside the window's borders. Insert then calls New to create an object of type TStaticText, addressed by a pointer of type PStaticText. To that object's constructor, the program passes R and a string. Despite appearances, the three lines beginning with #13 form *one* string. Into this strange-looking construction, #13 embeds a carriage return control code to begin a new line. Similarly, ^C instructs TStaticText to center the line within the specified rectangle. The result, which is far less complex in the compiled code than the statements suggest, is three lines of text neatly centered in the dialog's window.

A similar procedure in Diag displays an error message. To ErrorMessage, pass an error code and brief message to display. Other than sounding a short tone by calling the standard Sound, Delay, and NoSound procedures, the code in ErrorMessage is identical to AboutProgram's.

Interactive Dialogs

Diag's only function, Yes, is similar to AboutProgram and ErrorMessage; however, it displays two buttons, which are labeled Yes and No. Yes is an interactive dialog—it displays values and returns a response. To use Yes, pass your prompt as a string argument and then inspect the function's result, which will be true only if the Yes button was chosen to end the dialog. For example, to prompt whether to quit the program, you can use the statement:

```
if Yes('Quit program now?')
  then { end the program }
```

The only significant difference between Yes and the two other Diag routines is the way Yes calls ExecView near the end of the function.

```
Yes := Desktop^.ExecView(YNDiag) = cmYes;
```

ExecView returns a Word value equal to the command issued by selecting a button to close the dialog. In this case, the command value cmYes is compared to the value that ExecView returns. Only if the values match does Yes return true.

Adding Controls to Dialogs

In addition to TStaticText and TButton objects, many dialogs contain four other types of controls: check boxes, radio buttons, input boxes, and labels. Using these few items, you can create sophisticated dialogs that let people select a variety of program options.

Two of the most popular controls are check boxes and radio buttons, called *clusters* because of the way they are usually grouped into sets, and because the associated Turbo Vision objects TCheckBoxes and TRadioButtons both descend from TCluster. To see examples of these cluster objects in action, run ORDERS.PAS (see Program 17-2), a fictitious pizza parlor order-entry program. Select the Menu:Order command to bring up the Order dialog (Figure 17-2), which displays three clusters: Toppings, Size, and Style. Toppings is a cluster of five check boxes. The other two clusters are radio buttons, so called because they resemble the buttons on a car radio where only one button can be punched at a time.

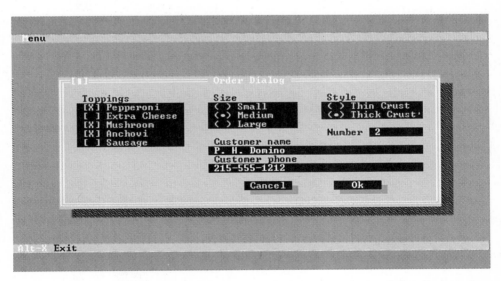

Figure 17-2 The Order dialog displays clusters of check boxes and radio buttons.

Program 17-2: ORDERS.PAS

```pascal
1:   program Orders;
2:
3:   uses Objects, Drivers, Views, Menus, App, Dialogs, Diag;
4:
5:   const
6:     cmAbout = 100;   { About-program command number }
7:     cmSave  = 101;   { Save command number (not implemented) }
8:     cmOrder = 102;   { Order-entry command number }
9:
10:  type
11:
12:    { Order record to match order-entry dialog box }
13:    OrderInfoRec = record
14:      OToppings: Word;        { Toppings check boxes }
15:      OSize: Word;            { Size radio buttons }
16:      OStyle: Word;           { Style radio buttons }
17:      ONumber: string[4];     { Number input box }
18:      OName: string[64];      { Customer name input box }
19:      OPhone: string[64];     { Customer phone input box }
20:    end;
21:
22:    { Application object }
23:    PTheApp = ^TheApp;
24:    TheApp = object(TApplication)
25:      constructor Init;
26:      procedure HandleEvent(var Event: TEvent); virtual;
27:      procedure InitMenuBar; virtual;
28:    end;
29:
30:  var
31:
32:    Order: OrderInfoRec;   { Global order (represents data base) }
33:
34:  { Initialize global Order variable }
35:  procedure NewOrder;
36:  begin
37:    with Order do
38:    begin
39:      OToppings := 0;       { Change settings to affect initial }
40:      OSize := 0;           {   contents of order-entry dialog }
41:      OStyle := 0;
```

```
42:        ONumber := '';
43:        OName := '';
44:        OPhone := ''
45:      end
46:  end;
47:
48:  { Construct application object }
49:  constructor TheApp.Init;
50:  begin
51:    TApplication.Init;      { Call ancestor constructor }
52:    NewOrder                { Initialize order variable }
53:  end;
54:
55:  { Respond to various events }
56:  procedure TheApp.HandleEvent(var Event: TEvent);
57:  var
58:    Result: Boolean;
59:
60:    { Create and execute order-entry dialog }
61:    function OrderDialog: Word;
62:    var
63:      Dialog: PDialog;      { Pointer to TDialog object }
64:      V: PView;            { For creating various controls }
65:      R: TRect;            { For specifying various rectangles }
66:      C: Word;             { Holds result of dialog execution }
67:    begin
68:      { Create the dialog object }
69:      R.Assign(0, 0, 64, 15);
70:      Dialog := New(PDialog, Init(R, 'Order Dialog'));
71:      with Dialog^ do
72:      begin
73:
74:       Options := Options or ofCentered;  { Center dialog window }
75:
76:        { Create Toppings check boxes }
77:        R.Assign(3, 3, 21, 8);
78:        V := New(PCheckBoxes, Init(R,
79:          NewSItem('Pepperoni',
80:          NewSItem('Extra Cheese',
81:          NewSItem('Mushroom',
82:          NewSItem('Anchovy',
83:          NewSItem('Sausage',
84:          nil)))))
```

continued

Program 17-2: continued

```
 85:        ));
 86:        Insert(V);
 87:        R.Assign(3, 2, 21, 3);
 88:        Insert(New(PLabel, Init(R, 'Toppings', V)));
 89:
 90:        { Create Size radio buttons }
 91:        R.Assign(25, 3, 40, 6);
 92:        V := New(PRadioButtons, Init(R,
 93:          NewSItem('Small',
 94:          NewSItem('Medium',
 95:          NewSItem('Large',
 96:          nil)))
 97:        ));
 98:        Insert(V);
 99:        R.Assign(25, 2, 40, 3);
100:        Insert(New(PLabel, Init(R, 'Size', V)));
101:
102:        { Create Style radio buttons }
103:        R.Assign(44, 3, 61, 5);
104:        V := New(PRadioButtons, Init(R,
105:          NewSItem('Thin Crust',
106:          NewSItem('Thick Crust',
107:          nil))
108:        ));
109:        Insert(V);
110:        R.Assign(44, 2, 61, 3);
111:        Insert(New(PLabel, Init(R, 'Style', V)));
112:
113:        { Create Number, Name, Phone input boxes }
114:        R.Assign(52, 6, 61, 7);
115:        V := New(PInputLine, Init(R, 4));
116:        Insert(V);
117:        R.Assign(44, 6, 51, 7);
118:        Insert(New(PLabel, Init(R, 'Number', V)));
119:        R.Assign(25, 8, 61, 9);
120:        V := New(PInputLine, Init(R, 64));
121:        Insert(V);
122:        R.Assign(25, 7, 61, 8);
123:        Insert(New(PLabel, Init(R, 'Customer name', V)));
124:        R.Assign(25, 10, 61, 11);
125:        V := New(PInputLine, Init(R, 64));
```

```
126:         Insert(V);
127:         R.Assign(25, 9, 61, 10);
128:         Insert(New(PLabel, Init(R, 'Customer phone', V)));
129:
130:         { Create Cancel and Ok buttons }
131:         R.Assign(30, 12, 40, 14);
132:         Insert(New(PButton, Init(R, 'Cancel', cmCancel, bfNormal)));
133:         R.Assign(45, 12, 55, 14);
134:         Insert(New(PButton, Init(R, 'O~k~', cmOK, bfDefault)));
135:
136:       end;
137:
138:       { Perform dialog }
139:       Dialog^.SetData(Order);
140:       C := Desktop^.ExecView(Dialog);
141:       if C <> cmCancel then Dialog^.GetData(Order);
142:       Dispose(Dialog, Done);
143:       OrderDialog := C        { So caller can inspect result }
144:
145:     end;
146:
147:   begin {TheApp.HandleEvent}
148:     if (Event.What = evCommand) and (Event.Command = cmQuit) then
149:       if not Yes('Quit now?') then ClearEvent(Event);
150:     TApplication.HandleEvent(Event);
151:     if Event.What = evCommand then
152:     begin
153:       case Event.Command of
154:         cmAbout: AboutProgram('Order-Entry Demonstration');
155:         cmSave:  ErrorMessage(999, 'Feature not implemented');
156:         cmOrder: if OrderDialog <> cmCancel
157:                     then {save Order}
158:                     else NewOrder;
159:       else
160:         Exit
161:       end;
162:       ClearEvent(Event)
163:     end
164:   end;
165:
166:   procedure TheApp.InitMenuBar;
167:   var R: TRect;
168:   begin
```

continued

Program 17-2: continued

```
169:    GetExtent(R);
170:    R.B.Y := R.A.Y + 1;
171:    MenuBar := New(PMenuBar, Init(R, NewMenu(
172:      NewSubMenu('~M~enu', hcNoContext, NewMenu(
173:        NewItem('~A~bout', '', kbNoKey, cmAbout, hcNoContext,
174:        NewItem('~S~ave', '', kbNoKey, cmSave, hcNoContext,
175:        NewItem('~O~rder', '', kbNoKey, cmOrder, hcNoContext,
176:        NewLine(
177:        NewItem('E~x~it', 'Alt-X', kbAltX, cmQuit, hcNoContext,
178:        nil)))))),
179:      nil))
180:    ))
181:  end;
182:
183:  var
184:    Application: TheApp;
185:
186:  begin
187:    Application.Init;
188:    Application.Run;
189:    Application.Done
190:  end.
```

Function OrderDialog in Orders creates the Toppings cluster by executing the statements

```
R.Assign(3, 3, 21, 8);
V := New(PCheckBoxes, Init(R,
  NewSItem('Pepperoni',
  NewSItem('Extra Cheese',
  NewSItem('Mushroom',
  NewSItem('Anchovy',
  NewSItem('Sausage',
  nil)))))
));
Insert(V);
R.Assign(3, 2, 21, 3);
Insert(New(PLabel, Init(R, 'Toppings', V)));
```

Similar to the way buttons are added to dialogs, first a TRect variable R is assigned the location and size of the cluster. Then New creates an object of type TCheckBoxes (addressed by a PCheckBoxes pointer) on the heap. The result of New is stored in a local TView variable V, used later. To the TCheckBoxes constructor, the program passes R plus a set of strings created by NewSItem, a function in the Dialogs unit. You can specify up to 16 strings, one per check box. If you need more than 16 check boxes, create another PCheckBoxes object for the dialog. Check box clusters are stored in 16-bit Word variables that use one bit per box, thus limiting check boxes to 16 per set. However, there's no limit on the number of check box clusters you can create.

After calling New, insert the cluster into the dialog. Then, to give the cluster a label, assign new coordinate values to R. Into the dialog insert an object of type TLabel addressed by a PLabel pointer. Notice that this object's constructor requires a PView pointer as its last argument. That pointer is the address of the cluster to which the label applies. The label is associated with the cluster so that people can select the label with a mouse or by pressing Tab, and then use the cursor keys and Spacebar to highlight and modify the cluster's items.

Radio buttons are equally simple to construct. Start by assigning coordinates to a TRect object, then call New to allocate space for a TRadioButtons cluster. Keep the value returned by New in a PView variable (a pointer to an object instance of type TView), and call NewSItem to create a string for each button. Insert the saved address into the dialog, then create and insert a label for the cluster. Here's how Orders creates the Size radio buttons in the order-entry dialog:

```
R.Assign(25, 3, 40, 6);
V := New(PRadioButtons, Init(R,
  NewSItem('Small',
  NewSItem('Medium',
  NewSItem('Large',
  nil)))
));
Insert(V);
R.Assign(25, 2, 40, 3);
Insert(New(PLabel, Init(R, 'Size', V)));
```

It's even simpler to create input boxes like the Number, Customer name, and Customer phone fields in Orders. For example, to prepare the Customer name field, the program executes

```
R.Assign(25, 8, 61, 9);
V := New(PInputLine, Init(R, 64));
Insert(V);
R.Assign(25, 7, 61, 8);
Insert(New(PLabel, Init(R, 'Customer name', V)));
```

Once again, a TRect object R specifies the control's size and position. Then New creates the object on the heap, this time, of type TInputLine addressed by a PInputLine pointer. To the constructor, the program passes R and a maximum length value 64. To store the result of the input box in a string variable, it's best to use a maximum length no larger than 255.

After inserting the new TInputLine object into the dialog, a TLabel is created and associated with the control, similar to the way labels were attached to the check box and radio button clusters earlier.

In your own dialogs, you can insert as many buttons, check boxes, radio buttons, static text items, and input boxes as you need. As the next section explains, setting your controls to specific values and extracting new values after the dialog closes requires only a few more lines of code.

Working with Dialogs and Controls

Any pizza parlor worth its weight in pepperoni couldn't afford to toss out orders. Similarly, any Turbo Vision program that uses dialogs needs to insert, extract, and save information entered with a dialog's buttons, check boxes, and input controls.

In this section, you'll learn how to communicate with a dialog's controls. You'll also investigate a sample program that shows how to use Turbo Vision's file and message dialogs. The program, TABS.PAS, is a useful utility that can insert, remove, and convert the spacing of embedded tabs in text files.

Instructions for using the program follow the three listings. Program 17-3 is the main TABS.PAS program file. Program 17-4, TABSOPT.PAS, creates the program's options dialog. Program 17-5, TABSUNIT.PAS, provides miscellaneous support routines. Enter the three files. Then, with TABS.PAS in the foremost window, use the Compile:Make command to compile the entire program. Or, use the /M option with the command-line compiler to compile TABS.PAS and its two units.

Program 17-3: TABS.PAS

```
1:   program Tabs;
2:
3:   uses Dos, Objects, Drivers, Views, Menus, App, Dialogs, StdDlg,
4:        MsgBox, Diag, TabsOpt, TabsUnit;
5:
6:   const
7:
8:     cmAbout        = 100;    { Menu-command constants }
9:     cmHelp         = 101;
```

```
10:     cmFileSelect      = 110;
11:     cmFileChangeDir    = 111;
12:     cmFileExit         = cmQuit;
13:     cmOptionsSettings  = 112;
14:     cmOptionsReset     = 113;
15:     cmOptionsSave      = 114;
16:     cmOptionsRetrieve  = 115;
17:     systemMenuChar     = #240;    { ASCII Triple-bar symbol }
18:
19:  type
20:
21:     { Application object }
22:     PTabApp = ^TabApp;
23:     TabApp = object(TApplication)
24:       constructor Init;
25:       procedure HandleEvent(var Event: TEvent); virtual;
26:       procedure InitMenuBar; virtual;
27:       procedure InitStatusLine; virtual;
28:       procedure ProcessFile(var FileName: PathStr);
29:     end;
30:
31:  { Construct application object }
32:  constructor TabApp.Init;
33:  begin
34:     TApplication.Init;    { Call ancestor constructor }
35:     InitTabOptions;       { Initialize global TabOptions variable }
36:     DoOptionsRetrieve     { Read options from TABS.CFG if present }
37:  end;
38:
39:  { Respond to events; execute program's commands }
40:  procedure TabApp.HandleEvent(var Event: TEvent);
41:  var
42:     Result: Boolean;
43:
44:     procedure DoOptionsSettings;
45:     begin
46:       if GetTabOptions <> cmCancel then
47:         if TabOptions.OMisc and optAutoSave <> 0
48:           then DoOptionsSave
49:     end;
50:
```

continued

Program 17-3: continued

```
51:    procedure DoOptionsReset;
52:    begin
53:      if Yes('Reset options to default settings?')
54:        then InitTabOptions
55:    end;
56:
57:    procedure DoFileSelect;
58:    var
59:      D: PFileDialog;
60:      FileName: PathStr;
61:    begin
62:      D := New(PFileDialog, Init('*.*', 'Select a File',
63:        '~N~ame', fdOpenButton, 100));
64:      if ValidView <> nil then
65:      begin
66:        if Desktop^.ExecView <> cmCancel then
67:        begin
68:          D^.GetFileName(FileName);
69:          ProcessFile(FileName)
70:        end;
71:        Dispose(D, Done)
72:      end
73:    end;
74:
75:    procedure DoFileChangeDir;
76:    var
77:      D: PChDirDialog;
78:    begin
79:      D := New(PChDirDialog, Init(cdNormal, 101));
80:      if ValidView <> nil then begin
81:        DeskTop^.ExecView;
82:        Dispose(D, Done)
83:      end
84:    end;
85:
86:  begin {TabApp.HandleEvent}
87:    TApplication.HandleEvent(Event);
88:    if Event.What = evCommand then
89:    begin
90:      case Event.Command of
```

```
 91:          cmAbout: AboutProgram('Tab Insert/Remove/Convert Utility');
 92:          cmHelp          : ErrorMessage(999, 'Help unavailable!');
 93:          cmFileSelect    : DoFileSelect;
 94:          cmFileChangeDir  : DoFileChangeDir;
 95:          cmOptionsSettings : DoOptionsSettings;
 96:          cmOptionsReset   : DoOptionsReset;
 97:          cmOptionsSave    : DoOptionsSave;
 98:          cmOptionsRetrieve : DoOptionsRetrieve;
 99:        else
100:          Exit
101:        end;
102:        ClearEvent(Event)
103:      end
104:  end;
105:
106:  { Initialize application's menu bar }
107:  procedure TabApp.InitMenuBar;
108:  var R: TRect;
109:  begin
110:     GetExtent(R);
111:     R.B.Y := R.A.Y + 1;
112:     MenuBar := New(PMenuBar, Init(R, NewMenu(
113:      NewSubMenu(systemMenuChar, hcNoContext, NewMenu(
114:       NewItem('~A~bout Tabs...', '', kbNoKey, cmAbout, hcNoContext,
115:       NewItem('~H~elp', 'F1', kbF1, cmHelp, hcNoContext,
116:       nil))),
117:      NewSubMenu('~F~ile', hcNoContext, NewMenu(
118:       NewItem('~S~elect...', 'F3', kbF3, cmFileSelect, hcNoContext,
119:       NewItem('~C~hange dir...', '', kbNoKey, cmFileChangeDir, hcNoContext,
120:       NewLine(
121:       NewItem('E~x~it', 'Alt-X', kbAltX, cmQuit, hcNoContext,
122:       nil))))),
123:      NewSubMenu('~O~ptions', hcNoContext, NewMenu(
124:       NewItem('Se~t~tings...', '', kbNoKey, cmOptionsSettings, hcNoContext,
125:       NewItem('R~e~set', '', kbNoKey, cmOptionsReset, hcNoContext,
126:       NewLine(
127:       NewItem('~S~ave options...', '', kbNoKey, cmOptionsSave, hcNoContext,
128:       NewItem('~R~etrieve options...', '', kbNoKey, cmOptionsRetrieve, hcNoContext,
129:       nil)))))),
130:      nil))))
131:    ))
132:  end;
```

continued

```
133:
134:   { Initialize application's status line }
135:   procedure TabApp.InitStatusLine;
136:   var R: TRect;
137:   begin
138:     GetExtent(R);
139:     R.A.Y := R.B.Y - 1;
140:     StatusLine := New(PStatusLine, Init(R,
141:       NewStatusDef(0, $FFFF,
142:         NewStatusKey('', kbF10, cmMenu,
143:         NewStatusKey('~F1~ Help', kbF1, cmHelp,
144:         NewStatusKey('~F3~ Select', kbF3, cmFileSelect,
145:         NewStatusKey('~Alt-X~ Exit', kbAltX, cmQuit,
146:         nil)))),
147:       nil)
148:     ))
149:   end;
150:
151:   { Process one file identified by FileName }
152:   procedure TabApp.ProcessFile(var FileName: PathStr);
153:   begin
154:     with TabOptions do
155:     case OOperation of
156:       OptInsert:
157:         begin
158:           if Yes('Insert tabs into ' + FileName + '?') then
159:             if ProcessTabs(FileName, true, OMisc and optBackup <> 0) then
160:               MessageBox('Tabs inserted into ' + FileName,
161:                 nil, mfInformation or mfOkButton)
162:         end;
163:       OptRemove:
164:         begin
165:           if Yes('Remove tabs from ' + FileName + '?') then
166:             if ProcessTabs(FileName, false, OMisc and optBackup <> 0) then
167:               MessageBox('Tabs removed from ' + FileName,
168:                 nil, mfInformation or mfOkButton)
169:         end;
170:       OptConvert:
171:         begin
172:           if Yes('Convert tabs in ' + FileName + '?') then
```

```
173:              if ProcessTabs(FileName, false, OMisc and optBackup <> 0) then
174:                if ProcessTabs(FileName, true, false) then
175:                  MessageBox('Tabs converted in ' + FileName,
176:                    nil, mfInformation or mfOkButton)
177:            end
178:        end
179:    end;
180:
181:    var
182:      Application: TabApp;
183:
184:    begin
185:      Application.Init;
186:      Application.Run;
187:      Application.Done
188:    end.
```

Program 17-4: TABSOPT.PAS

```
 1:   unit TabsOpt;
 2:
 3:   interface
 4:
 5:   uses Dos, Objects, Views, Dialogs, App;
 6:
 7:   const
 8:
 9:     optInsert      = 0;       { Options radio-button values }
10:     optRemove      = 1;
11:     optConvert     = 2;
12:     optBackup      = $01;     { Options misc. check boxes }
13:     optAutosave    = $02;
14:     optStrip       = $04;
15:     optUpper       = $08;
16:     slenConfig     = 65;      { Options input-string lengths }
17:     slenTabs       = 2;
18:     slenBakExt     = 3;
19:
20:    type
21:
```

continued

```
22:    { Options record to hold contents of Options dialog box }
23:    OptionsRec = record
24:      OOperation: Word;           { Operation radio button }
25:      OMisc: Word;                { Miscellaneous check boxes }
26:      OConfig: string[slenConfig]; { Configuration path }
27:      OInTab: string[slenTabs];    { Input tab size }
28:      OOutTab: string[slenTabs];   { Output tab size }
29:      OBakExt: string[slenBakExt]; { Backup extension }
30:    end;
31:
32:  var
33:
34:    TabOptions: OptionsRec;      { Global options }
35:
36:  procedure InitTabOptions;
37:  function TabsDialog: PDialog;
38:  function GetTabOptions: Word;
39:  procedure DoOptionsSave;
40:  procedure DoOptionsRetrieve;
41:
42:  implementation
43:
44:  { Initialize global TabOptions defaults }
45:  procedure InitTabOptions;
46:  var
47:    D: DirStr;
48:    N: NameStr;
49:    E: ExtStr;
50:  begin
51:    FSplit(ParamStr(0), D, N, E); { Parse home directory path }
52:    N := 'TABS';                  { Change name to TABS }
53:    E := '.CFG';                  { Change extension to CFG }
54:    with TabOptions do
55:    begin
56:      OOperation := optConvert;
57:      OMisc      := optBackup or optAutosave;
58:      OConfig    := D + N + E;
59:      OInTab     := '8';
60:      OOutTab    := '8';
61:      OBakExt    := 'BAK'
```

```
62:      end
63:   end;
64:
65:   { Perform Tabs options dialog }
66:   function TabsDialog: PDialog;
67:   var
68:      Dialog: PDialog;      { Pointer to TDialog object }
69:      V: PView;            { For creating various controls }
70:      R: TRect;            { For specifying various rectangles }
71:   begin
72:      R.Assign(0, 0, 57, 15);
73:      Dialog := New(PDialog, Init(R, 'Options Dialog'));
74:      if Dialog <> nil then with Dialog^ do
75:      begin
76:       Options := Options or ofCentered;  { Center dialog window }
77:
78:       { Operation radio buttons }
79:       R.Assign(2, 3, 16, 6);
80:       V := New(PRadioButtons, Init(R,
81:         NewSItem('Insert',
82:         NewSItem('Remove',
83:         NewSItem('Convert',
84:         nil)))
85:       ));
86:       Insert(V);
87:       R.Assign(2, 2, 12, 3);
88:       Insert(New(PLabel, Init(R, 'O~p~eration', V)));
89:
90:       { Miscellaneous check boxes }
91:       R.Assign(20, 3, 55, 7);
92:       V := New(PCheckBoxes, Init(R,
93:         NewSItem('Backup original file',
94:         NewSItem('Autosave configuration',
95:         NewSItem('Strip 8th bit',
96:         NewSItem('Convert to uppercase',
97:         nil))))
98:       ));
99:       Insert(V);
100:      R.Assign(20, 2, 34, 3);
101:      Insert(New(PLabel, Init(R, '~M~iscellaneous', V)));
102:
103:      { Input boxes }
```

continued

Program 17-4: continued

```
104:        R.Assign(17, 8, 55, 9);
105:     V := New(PInputLine, Init(R, slenConfig));
106:     Insert(V);
107:     R.Assign(2, 8, 15, 9);
108:     Insert(New(PLabel, Init(R, '~C~onfig file:', V)));
109:     R.Assign(20, 10, 25, 11);
110:     V := New(PInputLine, Init(R, slenTabs));
111:     Insert(V);
112:     R.Assign(2, 10, 19, 11);
113:     Insert(New(PLabel, Init(R, '~I~nput tab size:', V)));
114:     R.Assign(20, 12, 25, 13);
115:     V := New(PInputLine, Init(R, slenTabs));
116:     Insert(V);
117:     R.Assign(2, 12, 19, 13);
118:     Insert(New(PLabel, Init(R, '~O~utput tab size:', V)));
119:     R.Assign(49, 10, 55, 11);
120:     V := New(PInputLine, Init(R, slenBakExt));
121:     Insert(V);
122:     R.Assign(29, 10, 49, 11);
123:     Insert(New(PLabel, Init(R, '~B~ackup extension:', V)));
124:
125:     { Buttons }
126:     R.Assign(29, 12, 39, 14);
127:     Insert(New(PButton, Init(R, 'Cancel', cmCancel, bfNormal)));
128:     R.Assign(43, 12, 53, 14);
129:     Insert(New(PButton, Init(R, 'O~k~', cmOK, bfDefault)));
130:   end;
131:   TabsDialog := Dialog   { Pass address of dialog to caller }
132: end;
133:
134: { Create and execute Options dialog }
135: function GetTabOptions: Word;
136: var
137:   Dialog: PDialog;     { Pointer to TDialog object }
138:   C: Word;             { Holds result of dialog execution }
139: begin
140:   Dialog := TabsDialog;        { Make Options dialog }
141:   if Dialog <> nil then
142:   begin
143:     Dialog^.SetData(TabOptions);
```

```
144:        C := Desktop^.ExecView(Dialog);
145:        if C <> cmCancel then Dialog^.GetData(TabOptions);
146:        Dispose(Dialog, Done);
147:        GetTabOptions := C        { Return result to caller }
148:      end
149: end;
150:
151: {$I-}
152: procedure DoOptionsSave;
153: var
154:    F: file of OptionsRec;
155: begin
156:    Assign(F, TabOptions.OConfig);
157:    Rewrite(F);
158:    Write(F, TabOptions);
159:    Close(F);
160:    if IoResult <> 0 then {ignore error} ;
161: end;
162:
163: procedure DoOptionsRetrieve;
164: var
165:    F: file of OptionsRec;
166: begin
167:    Assign(F, TabOptions.OConfig);
168:    Reset(F);
169:    if Ioresult = 0 then
170:    begin
171:      Read(F, TabOptions);
172:      Close(F)
173:    end
174: end;
175: {$I+}
176:
177: end.
```

Program 17-5: TABSUNIT.PAS

```
1: unit TabsUnit;
2:
3: interface
4:
```

continued

Program 17-5: continued

```
 5:  uses Dos, Diag, TabsOpt;
 6:
 7:  function ProcessTabs(var FileName: PathStr;
 8:    Inserting, BackingUp: Boolean): Boolean;
 9:
10:  implementation
11:
12:  const
13:
14:    tabChar   = #9;
15:    blankChar = #32;
16:
17:  var
18:
19:    InFile, OutFile: Text;
20:    InName, OutName, BakName: PathStr;
21:
22:  function FileExists(var FileName: PathStr): Boolean;
23:  var
24:    F: file;
25:  begin
26:    Assign(F, FileName);
27:    {$I-}
28:    Reset(F);
29:    Close(F);
30:    {$I+}
31:    FileExists := IoResult = 0
32:  end;
33:
34:  function OpenFiles(var FileName: PathStr): Boolean;
35:  var
36:    D: DirStr;
37:    N: NameStr;
38:    E: ExtStr;
39:  begin
40:    OpenFiles := false;
41:    InName := FileName;
42:    FSplit(FileName, D, N, E);
43:    OutName := D + N + '.$$$';
44:    BakName := D + N + '.' + TabOptions.OBakExt;
```

```
45:     Assign(InFile, FileName);
46:     Assign(OutFile, OutName);
47:     {$I-} Reset(InFile); {$I+}
48:     if IoResult <> 0 then Exit;
49:     {$I-} Rewrite(OutFile); {$I+}
50:     if IoResult <> 0 then
51:     begin
52:       Close(Infile);
53:       Exit
54:     end;
55:     OpenFiles := true
56:   end;
57:
58:   procedure ExpandLine(var Line: string);
59:   var
60:     I, TabWidth, Ignore: Integer;
61:     C: Char;
62:     NewLine: string;
63:   begin
64:     Val(TabOptions.OInTab, TabWidth, Ignore);
65:     if TabWidth < 2 then TabWidth := 2;
66:     NewLine := '';
67:     for I := 1 to Length(Line) do
68:     begin
69:       C := Line[I];
70:       if C = tabChar
71:       then
72:         repeat
73:           NewLine := NewLine + blankChar
74:         until (Length(NewLine) mod TabWidth) = 0
75:       else
76:         NewLine := NewLine + C
77:     end;
78:     Line := NewLine
79:   end;
80:
81:   procedure CompressLine(var Line: string);
82:   var
83:     C: Char;
84:     Col, TabCol, TabWidth, Ignore: Integer;
85:     EndOfLine: Boolean;
86:     NewLine: string;
```

continued

```
87:
88:    function NextChar(var C: Char): Char;
89:    begin
90:      C := Line[Succ(TabCol)];
91:      NextChar := C;
92:      EndOfLine := C = #0
93:    end;
94:
95:  begin
96:    Val(TabOptions.OOutTab, TabWidth, Ignore);
97:    if TabWidth < 2 then TabWidth := 2;
98:    NewLine := '';
99:    Line := Line + #0;
100:   Col := 0;
101:   repeat
102:     TabCol := Col;
103:     while NextChar = blankChar do
104:     begin
105:       Inc(TabCol);
106:       if TabCol mod TabWidth = 0 then
107:       begin
108:         NewLine := NewLine + tabChar;
109:         Col := TabCol
110:       end
111:     end;
112:     while (Col < TabCol) do
113:     begin
114:       NewLine := NewLine + blankChar;
115:       Inc(Col)
116:     end;
117:     if not EndOfLine then
118:     begin
119:       NewLine := NewLine + C;
120:       Inc(Col)
121:     end
122:   until EndOfLine;
123:   Line := NewLine
124: end;
125:
126: procedure StripLine(var Line: string);
```

```
127:   var
128:     I: Integer;
129:   begin
130:     for I := 1 to Length(Line) do
131:       Line[I] := Chr(Ord(Line[I]) and $7F)
132:   end;
133:
134:   procedure UpperLine(var Line: string);
135:   var
136:     I: Integer;
137:   begin
138:     for I := 1 to Length(Line) do
139:       Line[I] := UpCase(Line[I])
140:   end;
141:
142:   function ErrorDetected: Boolean;
143:   var
144:     Result: Integer;
145:   begin
146:     Result := IoResult;
147:     if Result <> 0 then
148:     begin
149:       ErrorMessage(Result, 'I/O Error');
150:       ErrorDetected := true;
151:       Close(InFile);
152:       Close(OutFile)
153:     end else
154:       ErrorDetected := false
155:   end;
156:
157:   procedure CloseFiles(BackingUp: Boolean);
158:   var
159:     BakFile: file;
160:   begin
161:     Close(InFile);
162:     Close(OutFile);
163:     if BackingUp then
164:     begin
165:       if FileExists(BakName) then
166:       begin
167:         Assign(BakFile, BakName);  { Prepare to create backup }
168:         Erase(BakFile)             { Delete old backup if any }
```

continued

```
169:      end;
170:      Rename(InFile, BakName)      { Original file —> file.bak }
171:    end else
172:    begin
173:      Assign(InFile, InName);      { Prepare to delete original }
174:      Erase(InFile)                { Delete file }
175:    end;
176:    Rename(OutFile, InName)        { Rename temp file —> original }
177:  end;
178:
179:  { Insert tabs if Inserting = true; else remove tabs from file }
180:  function ProcessTabs(var FileName: PathStr;
181:    Inserting, BackingUp: Boolean): Boolean;
182:  var
183:    Line: string;
184:  begin
185:    ProcessTabs := false;
186:    if OpenFiles(FileName) then
187:    begin
188:      while not eof(InFile) do
189:      begin
190:        {$I-} Readln(InFile, Line); {$I+}
191:        if ErrorDetected then Exit;
192:        if Inserting then CompressLine(Line) else ExpandLine(Line);
193:        if TabOptions.OMisc and OptStrip <> 0 then StripLine(Line);
194:        if TabOptions.OMisc and OptUpper <> 0 then UpperLine(Line);
195:        {$I-} Writeln(OutFile, Line); {$I+}
196:        if ErrorDetected then Exit
197:      end;
198:      CloseFiles(BackingUp);
199:      ProcessTabs := true
200:    end else
201:      ErrorMessage(0, 'Error opening files')
202:  end;
203:
204:  end.
```

Using Tabs

You can probably figure out how to use Tabs on your own, so this section describes only its key features. Use the Settings command in the Options menu to bring up the options dialog. Select the Insert radio button to translate blanks to tabs. Choose Remove to convert tabs to spaces. Use Convert to translate tabs from one format to another. Set the Input tab size to the spacing used by the file from which you want to remove tabs. Set the Output tab size to the desired spacing when inserting tabs into files. Set both tab-size values when converting one tab format to another.

The Convert operation is tailor-made for converting files with nonstandard tabs. For instance, to convert eight-space tabs to four-space tabs, set Input tab size to 8 (the current tab spacing) and Output tab size to 4 (the desired spacing). After selecting the Ok button to close the options dialog, open a file and select Yes from the resulting prompt box. Tabs converts the file's tabs, keeping all lines in their relative positions. If the Backup option is on, Tabs also saves a backup copy of the original text.

The other options should be obvious. You can choose whether to save the options dialog settings in a file named TABS.CFG (or another name entered into the Config file field). You also can choose whether to strip the eighth bit from all characters (which is useful for translating WordStar-formatted text to plain ASCII). You can choose whether to convert text to all uppercase, perhaps to prepare for sending a file via modem to a computer that can't handle upper- and lowercase letters. You can also specify a different backup file-name extension.

> **Warning:** Until you become familiar with Tabs, keep extra backup copies of processed files. It's possible to obliterate a file's formatting if you specify the wrong tab sizes, especially when using the program's Convert operation. Also, because Tabs reads text a line at a time into a Turbo Pascal string, processing files with long lines can cause a loss of information. Always check the final results carefully before discarding your backup files. Also, since Tabs uses the temporary extension .$$$, you should not use that same extension for your own file names.

Storing a Dialog's Settings

Tabs displays a dialog box for selecting options, such as how many spaces to insert for each tab, and whether to save a backup copy of the original file (see Figure 17-3). Presenting all options in one dialog box lets people view current settings at a glance and select new options easily.

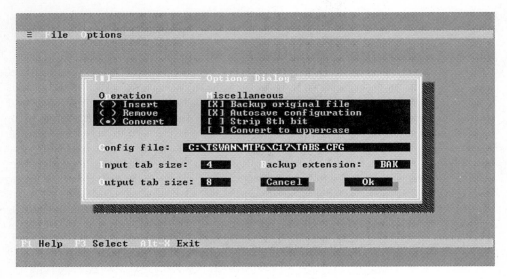

Figure 17-3 Options dialog from Tabs.

Despite its simple appearance, a dialog box is a highly sophisticated structure. Because a dialog is internally complex, it can consume plenty of memory, making dialogs impractical for permanent data storage. To conserve memory, it's best to store a dialog's contents separately in a variable designed for that purpose, rather than using the dialog itself for storage. Tabs stores its options in a Pascal record defined in TabsOpt as

```
OptionsRec = record
  OOperation: Word;
  OMisc: Word;
  OConfig: string[slenConfig];
  OInTab: string[slenTabs];
  OOutTab: string[slenTabs];
  OBakExt: string[slenBakExt];
end;
```

Field names begin with a capital O to identify them as options. The first field, OOperation, is a 16-bit word that represents the value of the dialog's radio button group. Only one button in a radio group can be selected at a time, meaning that OOperation will have one of the following values defined as constants in TabsOpt:

```
optInsert = 0;
optRemove = 1;
optConvert = 2;
```

To detect which radio button is on, a program statement could compare OOperation with one of those constants. For example, in Tabs, a **case** statement similar to this abbreviated version

```
case TabOptions.OOperation of
  OptInsert:  { perform tab insertion };
  OptRemove:  { perform tab removal };
  OptConvert: { perform tab conversion };
end;
```

chooses the correct program operation based on which radio button is currently selected. (Comments in this sample take the place of real statements.) TabOptions is a global OptionsRec variable, modified by the Options dialog. Although it's probably best to restrict the use of global variables in programs, in this case, because many different parts of the program need to examine the current settings, a global variable is justified.

The second OptionsRec field, OMisc, is also a Word, but stores the dialog's four miscellaneous check boxes (see Figure 17-3). Unlike radio buttons, each check box is represented by a single bit, requiring logical expressions to extract and insert individual settings. To make that job easier, TabsOpt defines the four constants

```
optBackup   = $01;
optAutosave = $02;
optStrip    = $04;
optUpper    = $08;
```

These constants are called *masks*. Because each value has a single bit set to one—for example, $04 in binary is 0000 0100—using a logical **and** to combine a mask with OMisc gives 0 only if the corresponding bit equals 0, meaning the check box is not selected. Therefore, to test whether the optAutosave option is selected, you can write

```
if TabOptions.OMisc and optAutosave <> 0
  then { perform Autosave operation }
```

To preset any option, use a logical **or** expression, such as

```
TabOptions.OMisc := TabOptions.OMisc or optStrip;
```

To turn a check box off, use **and not**.

```
TabOptions.OMisc := TabOptions.OMisc and not optStrip;
```

You saw similar logical expressions in chapter 16 for selecting TWindow and TView options.

The remaining fields in OptionsRec are four string variables. These values hold the configuration file name (OConfig), the input-tab spacing (OInTab), the output-tab spacing (OOutTab), and the backup extension name (OBakExt). There's nothing special about these fields—you can use them exactly as you would other string variables.

Reading and Writing Dialog Data

In TabsOpt, function TabsDialog fills the options dialog with radio buttons, check boxes, and input fields. Each control has a corresponding field in OptionsRec—a requirement that's vital to the program's health. Any discrepancies between the dialog and its record will cause serious bugs. For example, if the record has too few fields, or if the fields inserted into the dialog and declared in the record are in different orders, transfers of data between the dialog and record might copy values to the wrong fields.

Another function in TabsOpt, GetTabOptions, creates and activates the dialog box, then retrieves any modified information. Just before displaying the dialog, the function passes to the dialog's SetData method the current value of TabOptions. The single statement

```
Dialog^.SetData(TabOptions);
```

initializes the entire dialog by transferring the bytes in TabOptions directly to the dialog's controls. For that reason, records like TabOptions are called *transfer buffers*. After activating the dialog by calling ExecView, unless the Cancel button was selected, the program calls GetData like this:

```
C := Desktop^.ExecView(Dialog);
if C <> cmCancel
  then Dialog^.GetData(TabOptions);
```

to retrieve the possibly modified control values. ExecView passes back a value stored here in a Word C that represents the button selected to end the dialog. If that value does not equal cmCancel (a predefined Turbo Vision constant), the program calls GetData to copy the current control values back to TabOptions.

Other Dialogs in Tabs

When you run Tabs, you may be surprised to discover that every operation in the program is performed in a dialog box. Of course, that same scheme won't work for every application, but it's useful to realize that it's possible to construct entire Turbo Vision programs using only dialogs.

In Tabs' system menu, the two commands About Tabs and Help display dialogs using procedures AboutProgram and ErrorMessage from the Diag unit (Program 17-1). You might want to try your hand at completing the unfinished Help command.

The first two commands in the File menu use two of Turbo Vision's most useful dialog objects. TFileDialog opens the familiar file dialog from which you can select files in the current or other directories. TChDirDialog displays a tree diagram of directories on any disk drive and lets you change to a new directory. These are the same file and directory dialogs used in Turbo Pascal's IDE.

Procedure DoFileSelect in Tabs shows how to use TFileDialog. After calling New to instantiate the object, and calling ValidView to check whether the dialog view is valid, the procedure executes

```
if Desktop^.ExecView <> cmCancel then
begin
  D^.GetFileName(FileName);
  ProcessFile(FileName)
end;
```

D addresses the TFileDialog object, a descendant of TDialog and an exception to the rule that TDialog rarely needs descendants. A file dialog is a highly sophisticated, interactive window, and its special requirements require special handling. You can find TFileDialog's source code in file STDDLG.PAS, which is supplied with Turbo Pascal.

After displaying the dialog, if ExecView does not return cmCancel, the program calls GetFileName to extract the selected file. To process that file, another statement passes the file's name to TabApp.ProcessFile.

Using TChDirDialog to change directories is even easier. Just call New to create the object instance, use ValidView to make sure that instance is ready for action, and execute DeskTop^.ExecView, passing the PChDirDialog pointer as an argument. See procedure DoFileChangeDir in Tabs for an example. In this case, you can ignore ExecView's result. TChDirDialog is completely self-contained, and it returns no useful information.

For variety, the program also uses the MessageBox procedure from unit MsgBox, which contains other handy dialogs. You can find the unit's source code in the MSGBOX.PAS file supplied with Turbo Pascal. Tabs calls MessageBox to display a confirmation box after a file has been successfully processed. (See TabApp.ProcessFile near the end of Tabs.) MessageBox requires three arguments: a string containing the text of the message to be displayed, a pointer to a list of string-formatting parameters, and a Word value that selects various options. MSGBOX.PAS explains these elements in detail.

Collectibles

Turbo Vision is not just another pretty interface; it's a storehouse of objects, data structures, and other items that can simplify common programming chores. One of the most useful of Turbo Vision's low-level objects is TCollection, a capable pack rat that can store collections of other objects, strings, or just about any other sort of information you want to keep.

Of course, you can always use arrays or lists to store data. But those traditional Pascal data structures often require a good bit of low-level programming, which may impose unattractive restrictions on an application. For instance, if you don't know how many items will be stored in an array, you may need to write extra programing to create dynamic arrays that grow or shrink at runtime. Or, you may need to store items in a linked list, thus giving up the advantages and speed of array indexing.

There's nothing wrong with these common solutions to the problem of storing a varying amount of information in memory. However, with Turbo Vision's TCollection object, there's no need to go to all the trouble of writing code to support dynamic arrays and lists.

TCollection Roots

TCollection's immediate ancestor is TObject, the mother of all Turbo Vision objects, and the lowest object on the totem pole. Most of the time, you won't need to dig so deeply into Turbo Vision's insides. Instead, you can safely concentrate on higher-level objects such as TApplication and TView and let Turbo Vision keep its inner secrets to itself.

On the other hand, the more you know about Turbo Vision, the better prepared you are to write your own applications and to fix them if something should go wrong. Before getting into TCollection, then, let's take a close look at TObject. You can find TObject's declaration in OBJECTS.INT, which is located in the \TP\DOC directory. The complete declaration begins with PObject, a pointer to TObject, followed by the object declaration

```
PObject = ^TObject;
TObject = object
  constructor Init;
  procedure Free;
  destructor Done; virtual;
end;
```

TObject declares only three methods: a constructor named Init, a procedure Free, and a virtual destructor Done. All objects that inherit the properties of TObject inherit these same three methods, which perform these vital functions:

- **Init** is responsible for constructing TObject instances. In most cases, Init includes statements that initialize a descendant object's data fields. You might think of Init as a kind of object-making machine. As a constructor, Init's job is to build new objects and to ensure their proper initialization.

- **Free** disposes the memory allocated by Init for a dynamic object. For objects created through calls to New, you can call Free to dispose of those objects. Free also calls the Done destructor.

- **Done** destroys an object, performing the reverse job of the Init constructor. If a descendant's Init constructor allocated heap space to any pointer fields, the Done destructor is a good place to dispose of that space.

Caution: TObject.Init zeroes all data fields in all descendant objects, a quirk that many programmers believe should not have been added to Turbo Vision. In classic object-oriented programming, ancestor objects should have no knowledge of their descendants. Because that's not the case in Turbo Vision, you must *never* allow TObject.Init to be called after you have initialized any object data fields; otherwise, the method will wipe out your initialized values! Perhaps Borland will get rid of this questionable feature in a future release, but in the meantime, don't let this quirk turn into a nasty bug in your code.

TObject is an *abstract object*. This means you should never declare or create an instance of type TObject. You should instead create or use a descendant of TObject in which you declare additional methods and possibly override TObject's three methods, Init, Free, and Done. One such immediate descendant is TCollection, an object that can store just about any kind of data you can throw in its direction.

Creating Collections

TCollection and its three descendants TSortedCollection, TStringCollection, and TResourceCollection, combine the best features of arrays and lists. Like arrays, a TCollection can be indexed to reference items by number. Like lists, TCollections expand and shrink as needed to hold collected items, thus conserving memory.

To create a TCollection, first define a pointer of type PCollection. The pointer can be a global or local variable, or it can be a data field in an object. Next, call New to allocate space for the collection object. For example, to create a collection of 250 items, you can write

```
var
  CP: PCollection;
begin
  CP := New(TCollection, Init(250, 50));
end;
```

CP is a pointer to a TCollection object, allocated on the heap by New. The statement calls TCollection's Init constructor, passing two values to Init's Limit and Delta parameters. Limit specifies the number of items to store in the collection. Delta is used to expand the collection's capacity when new items are inserted into a full collection. In that event, TCollection increases the collection by an additional Delta items. After inserting 250 items into the collection, for instance, adding another would cause the structure to expand its capacity by 50 to hold up to 300 items.

Internally, TCollection creates an array of four-byte pointers. The number of pointers in the array equals the Limit value passed to TCollection.Init. Each pointer in the array addresses the actual data in memory, creating an efficient structure that can store variable-sized data (a set of strings, for example) in the smallest possible space.

Choosing good Limit and Delta values takes a lot of practice, much thought, and a bit of luck. As a general rule, make Limit as large as possible—each increment takes only four additional bytes, so a little waste won't matter much. Pick a Delta value of 20 percent or 25 percent of Limit. Choose a value of 10 percent or 15 percent if Limit is very large. Except for highly volatile collections that expand and contract frequently, which might benefit from large Delta values, these guidelines should help you to select Limit and Delta values that give the best mix of storage capacity and performance.

Hint: Set Delta to 0 to create a fixed-sized collection. Such an object will be able to store no more items than the number specified by Limit.

Using Collections

After creating a collection, you can use it to hold objects and other data. Usually, the items you insert should be descendants of TObject, because some TCollection methods call your object's Done destructor. Making your objects descendants of TObject guarantees that they are compatible with all TCollection methods.

First, create your object and, as usual, a pointer to that same object. Here's a sample TObject descendant from a listing you'll see in full later:

```
POneRec = ^TOneRec;
```

```
TOneRec = object(TObject)
  RecNum: LongInt;
  Field1: PString;
  Field2: PString;
  constructor Init(RN: LongInt; Data1, Data2: string);
  destructor Done; virtual;
end;
```

The three fields in TOneRec—RecNum, Field1, and Field2—store the object's information. Used this way, TOneRec resembles a Pascal record. However, for the most efficient use of memory, Field1 and Field2 are declared as string pointers, using the PString data type, which the Objects unit declares as

```
PString = ^string;
```

The reason for using a pointer to a string instead of a string variable is to allow the program to allocate heap space for variable-length strings. The Field1 and Field2 pointers address those strings, which take up only as much room as needed to store their characters.

There are two main disadvantages with this approach to storing strings in memory. One, because PString is a pointer to a string, the compiler considers the addressed string to be 255 characters long, which may or may not be true. Two, some standard routines such as Concat and Insert can cause a string to expand beyond its allocated memory, thus overwriting whatever is stored after the end of the string. If that happens, the resulting bug will be difficult to find because it will be dependent on the data fed to the program. When using string pointers, it's a good idea to avoid using routines that change a string's length. If you do need to use such a routine, the safest approach is to copy the string into a 255-character string variable, perform the operation, then reallocate new heap space to store the result.

In addition to the fields in TOneRec, the object provides replacements for TObject's Init constructor and Done destructor. In any object that will be stored in a collection, you must override Init. You need to override Done only if you allocate any heap space that needs to be disposed before an object instance is destroyed.

After creating a TObject descendant, use TCollection.Insert to insert instances of your objects into the collection. Suppose, for example, you want to insert a record numbered 123 that has two string fields, 'Seattle' and 'Washington'. To create the record and insert it into a TCollection addressed by CP, you could execute the statement

```
CP^.Insert(New(POneRec, Init(123, 'Seattle', 'Washington')));
```

If that seems complicated, take it one step at a time. CP^.Insert's single parameter is declared as Item:Pointer; therefore, you can insert any addressable data item into a collection. In this case, the address of the inserted item is returned by

New, which allocates heap space for a TOneRec instance, addressed by POneRec, as defined earlier. To initialize the object instance, the statement calls TOneRec's Init constructor, passing the initial values, which are assigned to the new object's data fields with the statements

```
RecNum := RN;
Field1 := NewStr(Data1);
Field2 := NewStr(Data2);
```

The first statement in the constructor assigns RN (equal to 123 in this example) to the RecNum field in the new TOneRec instance. The second and third statements call NewStr, a PString function declared in the Objects unit. NewStr allocates just enough heap space to store a string's characters. In this example, the constructor uses NewStr to allocate space for the two strings Data1 and Data2, assigning the addresses of those strings to Field1 and Field2. The result is a record that occupies only as much space as needed, with not one byte wasted.

NewStr's cousin procedure is DisposeStr, which operates like Dispose, but should be used only to dispose strings allocated by NewStr. The sample program in the next section demonstrates how to use DisposeStr.

Sorted Collections

Program 17-6, TDB.PAS, creates a TCollection using the descendant object TSortedCollection. Enter and run the test program, and when prompted, type names or other information into the records, each of which has two fields. Press Enter after entering a few values (you can't save the records, so don't bother to enter any important information). You can then enter search information to locate specific records.

Program 17-6: TDB.PAS

```
 1:    program Tdb;
 2:
 3:    uses Crt, Dos, Objects;
 4:
 5:    type
 6:       POneRec = ^TOneRec;
 7:       TOneRec = object(TObject)
 8:          RecNum: LongInt;
 9:          Field1: PString;
10:          Field2: PString;
11:          constructor Init(RN: LongInt; Data1, Data2: string);
```

```
12:        destructor Done; virtual;
13:      end;
14:
15:      PDBCollection = ^TDBCollection;
16:      TDBCollection = object(TSortedCollection)
17:        function Compare(Key1, Key2: Pointer): Integer; virtual;
18:        function KeyOf(Item: Pointer): Pointer; virtual;
19:      end;
20:
21:    procedure ShowOneRec(P: POneRec);
22:    begin
23:      Writeln;
24:      Writeln(';;;;;;;;;;;'); { Separator }
25:      with P^ do
26:      begin
27:        Writeln('     #: ', RecNum);
28:        Writeln('FIELD1: ', Field1^);
29:        Writeln('FIELD2: ', Field2^)
30:      end
31:    end;
32:
33:    function GetRecords(DB: PCollection): LongInt;
34:    var
35:      N: LongInt;
36:      F1, F2: string;   { Input strings }
37:
38:      function GetOneRec: Boolean;
39:      begin
40:        GetOneRec := false;
41:        Writeln;
42:        Writeln('Entering record #', N);
43:        Writeln('Press <Enter> to quit.');
44:        Write('Field1? '); Readln(F1);
45:        if Length(F1) = 0 then Exit;
46:        Write('Field2? '); Readln(F2);
47:        GetOneRec := true
48:      end;
49:
50:    begin
51:      N := 1;
52:      while GetOneRec do
53:        begin
```

continued

Program 17-6: continued

```
54:       DB^.Insert(New(POneRec, Init(N, F1, F2)));
55:       Inc(N)
56:     end;
57:     GetRecords := N - 1
58:   end;
59:
60:   procedure PrintRecords(DB: PCollection);
61:
62:     procedure PrintOneRecord(P: POneRec); far;
63:     begin
64:       ShowOneRec(P)
65:     end;
66:
67:   begin
68:     DB^.ForEach(@PrintOneRecord)
69:   end;
70:
71:   procedure SearchRecords(DB: PCollection);
72:   var
73:     Result: POneRec;
74:     Key: string;
75:
76:     function Quitting: Boolean;
77:     begin
78:       Write('Search again? ');
79:       Quitting := UpCase(ReadKey) <> 'Y';
80:       Writeln
81:     end;
82:
83:     function MatchesKey(P: POneRec): Boolean; far;
84:     begin
85:       MatchesKey := Pos(Key, P^.Field1^) = 1
86:     end;
87:
88:   begin
89:     Writeln; Writeln('Search for records');
90:     repeat
91:       Write('Search for? ');
92:       Readln(Key);
93:       Result := DB^.FirstThat(@MatchesKey);
```

```
 94:       if Result <> nil then
 95:         ShowOneRec(Result)
 96:       else
 97:         Writeln('***Error: Record not found')
 98:     until Quitting
 99:   end;
100:
101:   { TOneRec }
102:
103:   constructor TOneRec.Init(RN: LongInt; Data1, Data2: string);
104:   begin
105:     RecNum := RN;
106:     Field1 := NewStr(Data1);
107:     Field2 := NewStr(Data2)
108:   end;
109:
110:   destructor TOneRec.Done;
111:   begin
112:     DisposeStr(Field1);
113:     DisposeStr(Field2)
114:   end;
115:
116:   { TDBCollection }
117:
118:   function TDBCollection.Compare(Key1, Key2: Pointer): Integer;
119:   begin
120:     if PString(Key1)^ < PString(Key2)^ then
121:       Compare := -1
122:     else if PString(Key1)^ > PString(Key2)^ then
123:       Compare := +1
124:     else
125:       Compare := 0
126:   end;
127:
128:   function TDBCollection.KeyOf(Item: Pointer): Pointer;
129:   begin
130:     KeyOf := POneRec(Item)^.Field1  { Or Field2 }
131:   end;
132:
133:   var
134:     Database: PSortedCollection;
135:       N: LongInt;
```

continued

Program 17-6: continued

```
136:
137:  begin
138:    Database := New(PDBCollection, Init(100, 25));
139:    if Database = nil then
140:    begin
141:      Writeln('***Error creating TCollection');
142:      Exit
143:    end;
144:    N := GetRecords(Database);
145:    Writeln;
146:    Writeln(N, ' records entered');
147:    if N > 0 then
148:    begin
149:      PrintRecords(Database);
150:      SearchRecords(Database)
151:    end
152:  end.
```

Because TSortedCollection is a direct descendant of TCollection, it has all the capabilities of its ancestor. However, TSortedCollection's Insert method maintains items in sorted order. To accomplish that, the TDBCollection object (lines 16-19) overrides two of TSortedCollection's methods, Compare and KeyOf. In TDB Collection at line 130, KeyOf executes the statement

```
KeyOf := POneRec(Item)^.Field1
```

As a result of this assignment, KeyOf returns a Pointer to the identifying data or *key* for this object. Usually, the key is simply the address of a field in the object, in this case the string pointer Field1. The typecast expression POneRec(Item) informs the compiler that Item addresses a TOneRec object. It's up to you to make sure that Item actually addresses the object you specify. Typecasts subvert Turbo Pascal's type checking rules. A simple mistake in typecasting can turn into a whopping bug if you're not careful.

To specify the second field as the collection's key, you could replace Field1 with Field2. To make the object's key equal to its record number, replace the statement in KeyOf with

```
KeyOf := @POneRec(Item)^.RecNum
```

The @ sign is needed in this example to form the address of RecNum. Because Field1 and Field2 are pointers, @ is not needed to assign those fields to the function result. (If you try this change, you'll also have to modify the program's MatchesKey function at line 83 to search for record numbers.)

If you don't override KeyOf, the default function returns the address of an entire object. Unless you want the complete object to serve as a key, however, you must override KeyOf and return the address of an appropriate data field. That address is then used in the Compare function to determine whether one object is less than, equal to, or greater than another.

In a TSortedCollection, the meaning of comparisons between objects is completely up to you. A collection can be sorted alphabetically on a certain string field, or it can be ordered in another way. To determine your collection's sorting order, provide a Compare function, which compares two object keys. In TDBCollection, the Compare function at lines 118-126 contains the statements

```
if PString(Key1)^ < PString(Key2)^ then
  Compare := -1
else if PString(Key1)^ > PString(Key2)^ then
  Compare := +1
else
  Compare := 0
```

A Compare function receives two Pointer parameters, Key1 and Key2. As in the KeyOf method, the program needs to typecast these pointers so the compiler knows what sort of data they address. In this case, because KeyOf returns a pointer to a string, the Key1 and Key2 parameters are cast to PStrings with the expressions PString(Key1) and PString(Key2). If your KeyOf function returned a pointer to a different data type, you would use that type as the cast in Compare.

Compare must return one of three integer values: −1 if Key1 is less than Key2, 0 if the two keys are equal, or +1 if Key1 is greater than Key2. You are free to perform the comparison in any way you like, but you should try to keep Compare running as fast as possible. The Compare function will be called frequently to keep your collection in sorted order. A little time spent optimizing Compare goes a long way toward keeping your program running at top speed.

> **Hint:** To sort in reverse, simply swap −1 and +1. In other words, if you want your objects to be sorted alphabetically from Z to A, return +1 if Key1 is less than Key2, and −1 if Key1 is greater than Key2.

Browsing Collections

Most collections perform some operations for some or for all objects. The usual approach, demonstrated in Tdb, is to use TCollection's ForEach and FirstThat functions to browse and search a collection.

Each of these functions uses a technique known as a *callback routine*. A callback routine is a procedure or function that is called by another routine to which you pass the address of the routine to be called. Callback routines are also called *hooks* because they provide the means to hook custom code onto programs.

Procedure PrintRecords in Tdb (see lines 60-69) shows the classic method for performing an operation on all objects in a collection. To the procedure the program passes a pointer DB to a TCollection. It doesn't matter that the collection is a derived TSortedCollection object. Through the magic of polymorphism—the ability of statements to determine at runtime the nature of an addressed object—the procedure works correctly despite the fact that DB addresses a different object from the one passed as an argument.

> **Note:** See Chapter 15 for an explanation of the term polymorphism and its importance in object-oriented programming.

The subprocedure PrintOneRecord is the callback procedure. The declaration ends with the key word **far**. You could also compile the program using the {$F+} switch. The procedure must be local to its host—a callback procedure may not be global. These restrictions are necessary because a local procedure's stack frame is set up differently from a global procedure's, and methods like ForEach expect the stack to be configured correctly.

Inside PrintOneRecord, a single statement browses an entire collection. Executing

```
DB^.ForEach(@PrintOneRecord)
```

starts the ball rolling. For every item in the collection addressed by DB, ForEach calls PrintOneRecord, which is passed to ForEach by address with the @ operator. The callback procedure receives a pointer to each item in turn. That pointer can be declared as type POneRec here, because that's the kind of object stored in this sample collection. The parameter also can be declared as a pointer to an ancestor object from which a collection's items descend. In either case, you can be sure that your callback procedure will receive a pointer to each collected object. What you do with that pointer is up to you. PrintOneRecord calls ShowOneRec to display each item in the database. It could just as well print those records, perform some operation on selected fields, copy records to a disk file, and so on.

A similar method browses a collection looking for a matching key, giving your TCollection objects the means to perform searches. Method FirstThat returns a pointer to the first object that satisfies a condition. Assuming Result is a POneRec pointer, procedure SearchRecords calls FirstThat with the statement

```
Result := DB^.FirstThat(@MatchesKey);
```

The callback function here is MatchesKey, passed by address to the FirstThat method for the collection addressed by DB. MatchesKey, which you could rename, is expected to return a Boolean true or false value, indicating whether a selected object satisfies a search condition of your making. If Result equals **nil** after calling FirstThat, then no matching object was found. Otherwise, Result addresses the first matching object in the collection.

Like PrintOneRecord, MatchesKey receives a pointer to an individual record in the collection. The statement

```
MatchesKey := Pos(Key, P^.Field1^) = 1
```

calls the standard Pos string function to determine whether the current search argument (Key) is located at the beginning of the first field in the examined object. The search argument in this example is stored in a local variable declared in the SearchRecords procedure.

A corresponding method LastThat (not shown in the sample program) also searches a collection, but starts with the last object. As its name suggests, LastThat locates the last object for which your callback function returns true. Use LastThat similarly to FirstThat.

Odds and Ends

Most of TCollection's methods, and those in descendant objects such as TSortedCollection and TStringCollection, have obvious purposes, but are described only briefly in the Turbo Vision Guide. Following are a few notes that will help you use these methods in your own collections:

- Use the At method as though you were indexing an array. For example, if A is an array and C is a TCollection pointer, the expression A[5] is equivalent to C^.At(5). However, be aware that At returns a Pointer, and therefore, you probably have to use a typecast expression to tell the compiler what type of data the pointer addresses. These expressions tend to be cryptic and, if you're not comfortable with typecasting, difficult to write. For instance, to display the string addressed by Field1 in the third TOneRec (see Program 17-6), assuming DB addresses the TSortedCollection object, you could use the statement

```
Writeln(POneRec(DB^.At(2))^.Field1^);
```

You have to specify 2 to access the third item because the first item is numbered 0.

- Other "At" methods work similarly. AtDelete deletes an object at a specified index. AtInsert inserts an item into a certain position. Other objects are shuffled as necessary to accommodate deletions and insertions. AtPut replaces a specified object with another. These routines are roughly analogous to array assignments and to loops that move array items up and down.

- When you know an item's address, call IndexOf(Item) to find its index. You can then use that index value in other TCollection methods that accept an Integer "Index" argument. Unlike arrays, however, indexes are *not* the fastest means to look up items in a collection. To perform an indexed operation, TCollection has to translate an index into a pointer; therefore, referring to items via pointers is preferable.

- Methods Free, FreeAll, and FreeItem expect collected items to be descendants of TObject, specifically for calling that object's Done destructor, or the replacement destructor in a descendant of TObject. If you store other data or objects in a collection, you must override FreeItem and perform whatever cleanup duties are necessary. In this case, do *not* call TCollection.FreeItem. You must completely replace the inherited method in order to prevent it from attempting to call TObject.Done.

- You can call AtDelete, Delete, and DeleteAll to delete items from a collection, but when those items are objects, you should probably call Free, FreeAll, or FreeItem instead. The "Free" methods ensure proper disposal of TObject descendants. The "Delete" methods are more appropriate for collections of non-TObject instances.

- To dispose of an entire collection, execute the statement Dispose(P, Done), where P is a pointer to a TCollection or descendant instance. Calling a collection's Done destructor also disposes of all objects in the collection by calling TCollection.FreeAll. You do not have to empty your collections before disposal.

- If you are sure you will make no more insertions into a collection, you can shrink a TCollection object to its minimum size, thus deleting space allocated to hold future objects. To minimize a collection addressed by a PCollection pointer P, execute the statement

```
P^.SetLimit(P^.Count);
```

String Collections

TStringCollection is made to order for storing lists of strings. Because the object descends from TSortedCollection, strings are automatically sorted into alphabetic order. To create a string collection, first declare a pointer to a TSortedCollection or TStringCollection instance, and initialize the list the same way you create any TCollection object.

```
var
  P: PStringCollection;
begin
  P := New(PStringCollection, Init(100, 10));
  ...
end;
```

P's data type could be PStringCollection or PSortedCollection (or it could even be PCollection) because, as you may recall from Chapter 15, a pointer may address an object instance or any descendant of that instance's data type. In this program fragment, the string collection addressed by P is big enough to hold 100 strings, and will increase by 10 items at a time if the collection grows beyond its initial limit. It's important to realize that creating a string collection this way does not reserve space for storing characters in memory. The new collection has the *potential* to hold up to 100 strings (and possibly more), but you still need to include programming to verify that there's enough heap space available for storing the actual string data.

After creating the string collection, you can insert strings into it using TSortedCollection's Insert procedure. Probably the best plan is to create new strings on the heap and pass the string addresses to Insert. For example, to insert three strings into the TStringCollection addressed by P, you can write

```
P^.Insert(NewStr('Borland'));
P^.Insert(NewStr('Zortech'));
P^.Insert(NewStr('Microsoft'));
```

Of course, in most cases, you can read strings from a disk file or perhaps from the keyboard into a string variable. If that variable is S, you can insert it into the collection with the statement

```
P^.Insert(NewStr(S));
```

TStringCollection is a high-level object, and in many cases it can be used directly as in these samples. TStringCollection's Compare function is written in assembly language and is capable of comparing two strings very quickly. However, the function does not take case into account. For that reason, if you store mixed case keys in your string collection, you may have to take one of three actions to sort the collection alphabetically:

- Store only capitalized, all uppercase, or all lowercase strings in the collection. If you can enforce this rule during data entry, you'll eliminate the need to worry about sorting mixed-case data.

- Create a descendant object of TSortedCollection and replace the Compare function with one that ignores case.

- Add a caseless key field to your objects.

The first option is the best, but it may not always be possible. If you can ensure that all key fields use consistent case, there is no need to write special programming to take upper- and lowercase letters into account. The second option is the least desirable, but it works. A Compare function that converts the same key over and over to upper- or lowercase can greatly degrade a large collection's performance.

The final option is best when the first is impossible and the second is impractical. Adding an all upper- or lowercase key field to a record is a typical method for allowing mixed-case data in collections but eliminating the need to consider case for the purposes of sorting and searching. However, this option also means you can no longer use a TStringCollection object to store your data. That object is capable of storing *only* string data addressed by pointers. To store other kinds of data such as multifield records, you need to use a TSortedCollection object as explained earlier.

Another potential problem with TStringCollection concerns duplicated entries. A TStringCollection inherits a Boolean Duplicates field from TSortedCollection. If you need to store duplicated strings in a collection, you must set this variable to true. When Duplicates is false (the default setting), the collection rejects duplicate strings.

A TStringCollection Sorter

Program 17-7, TSORT.PAS, demonstrates how to use TStringCollection to sort strings in a text file. All characters in the file, including spaces, are significant. The program also shows that not all Turbo Vision programs need to be based on a desktop event-driven model. It's also possible to use TCollection objects in conventional Turbo Pascal programs. Run TSort and enter the name of a text file with 255-character or smaller lines to sort alphabetically. Also enter an output file name, which will be overwritten without warning, so type carefully. The program reads the input text into a sorted string collection and writes the results to the output file.

Program 17-7: TSORT.PAS

```pascal
1:   program TSort;
2:
3:   uses Dos, Objects;
4:
5:   var
6:     Inf, Outf: Text;
7:     InFileName, OutFileName: PathStr;
8:     Lines: PStringCollection;
9:
10:  procedure OpenFiles;
11:  begin
12:    Write('Input File to sort? ');
13:    Readln(InFileName);
14:    if Length(InFileName) = 0 then Halt;
15:    Assign(Inf, InFileName);
16:    Reset(Inf);
17:    Write('Write to what file? ');
18:    Readln(OutFileName);
19:    Assign(Outf, OutFileName);
20:    Rewrite(Outf)
21:  end;
22:
23:  procedure ReadFile;
24:  var
25:    S: string;
26:  begin
27:    while not eof(Inf) do
28:    begin
29:      Readln(Inf, S);
30:      if Length(S) > 0 then
31:        Lines^.Insert(NewStr(S))
32:    end
33:  end;
34:
35:  procedure WriteFile;
36:
37:    procedure WriteLine(P: PString); far;
38:    begin
39:      Writeln(Outf, P^)
40:    end;
```

continued

Program 17-7: continued

```
41:
42:  begin
43:    Lines^.ForEach(@WriteLine)
44:  end;
45:
46:  begin
47:    Lines := New(PStringCollection, Init(250, 50));
48:    Lines^.Duplicates := true;
49:    if Lines = nil then
50:    begin
51:      Writeln('***Error creating TStringCollection');
52:      Exit
53:    end;
54:    OpenFiles;
55:    ReadFile;
56:    WriteFile;
57:    Close(Inf);
58:    Close(Outf);
59:    Dispose(Lines, Done)
60:  end.
```

Variable Lines (see line 8) is a pointer to a TStringCollection instance, created by New and initialized to hold up to 250 lines of text. The Duplicates field is set to true at line 48. Remove this statement if you will be sorting files with no duplications.

Procedure ReadFile reads each line from the text file into a string variable S, which is then inserted into the TStringCollection with the statement:

```
Lines^.Insert(NewStr(S))
```

NewStr allocates just enough heap space to hold a copy of string S's characters, thus conserving memory by eliminating the wasted space typically found in string variables. Calling insert and passing the address of a string is all you need to do to add new strings to the collection. The newly added strings will be stored in alphabetical order.

Procedure WriteFile calls the collection's ForEach routine to write each line from the collection to disk. A local callback procedure, WriteLine, performs the output duty, handled in this case by a simple Writeln statement.

The final statement in TSort is unnecessary in this small example, but is included to point out that in most cases you should dispose your TStringCollection objects (and other TCollection descendants). This is all you need to do in order to clean the heap of an entire collection. You don't need to dispose the individual items stored in the collection. They are disposed by the collection's Done destructor.

TSort Modifications

TSort does not ignore the difference between upper- and lowercase letters. If that won't work for your application, you can take one of the steps mentioned earlier to ignore case. Assuming it's not possible to convert the file to a consistent case, here's one way to modify TSort's TStringCollection object to ignore case for input strings.

First add the following type declaration, creating a descendant object named TNoCaseC (the C stands for Collection):

```
type
  PNoCaseC = ^TNoCaseC;
  TNoCaseC = object(TStringCollection)
    function Compare(Key1, Key2: Pointer): Integer; virtual;
  end;
```

Next, add the function implementation above procedure OpenFiles.

```
function ToUpperStr(P: PString): string;
var
  I: Integer;
  S: string;
begin
  for I := 1 to Length(P^) do
    S[I] := UpCase(P^[I]);
  S[0] := P^[0];
  ToUpperStr := S
end;
```

Also add the Compare method's implementation.

```
function TNoCaseC.Compare(Key1, Key2: Pointer): Integer;
var
  S1, S2: string;
begin
  S1 := ToUpperStr(PString(Key1));
  S2 := ToUpperStr(PString(Key2));
  if S1 < S2 then Compare := -1 else
  if S1 > S2 then Compare := +1 else
                  Compare := 0
end;
```

Finally, change the first statement in TSort's main block to the following (in other words, change PStringCollection to PNoCaseC):

```
Lines := New(PNoCaseC, Init(250, 50));
```

Now when you compile and run the modified program, it ignores case while sorting. Unfortunately, the program runs far more slowly than before, because the replacement Compare function now converts every compared string to uppercase. This works, but when speed matters, one of the other alternative solutions mentioned earlier would be preferable.

List Boxes

TCollection container objects, which are useful for storing all kinds of data, become even more powerful when combined with another object, TListBox. One of Turbo Vision's most highly evolved tools, the TListBox object automatically enables a vertical scroll bar, recognizes the mouse and keyboard, and lets you select items listed in a window.

Using TListBox

TListBox is a descendant of TListViewer, a general-purpose object for creating scrollable views in windows. Remember that in Turbo Vision programming, a window is invisible. To put something inside that window, you need to attach a view, usually by inserting an instance of an object descended from TView. TListViewer and TListBox are descendants of TView. You use them just like you do other views.

However, programs rarely if ever use TListBox directly. Instead, they create a descendant object that inherits TListBox's properties and adds a replacement GetText method. The list box uses GetText to display whatever is stored in the list.

In addition to GetText, you can supply a SelectItem method for selecting individual listed items. You also need to write a constructor for initializing a TCollection instance, which supplies raw data to the list box. In addition to these elements, you may want to override GetPalette as well to provide color mapping for the view.

Program 17-8, TVLIST.PAS, shows how to use the TListBox object. When you run the program, you'll see a few strings in a window that can't be closed. Use the mouse or cursor keys to highlight a string and either double click the left mouse button or press the Spacebar. You'll then see a message box confirming the choice you made.

Program 17-8: TVLIST.PAS.

```
 1:  program TVList;
 2:
 3:  uses Objects, Dialogs, Views, App, MsgBox;
 4:
 5:  type
 6:
 7:    PListApp = ^TListApp;
 8:    TListApp = object(TApplication)
 9:      constructor Init;
10:    end;
11:
12:    PPickView = ^TPickView;
13:    TPickView = object(TListBox)
14:      TheList: PStringCollection;
15:      constructor Init(var Bounds: TRect; ANumCols: Word;
16:        AScrollBar: PScrollBar);
17:      destructor Done; virtual;
18:      function GetPalette: PPalette; virtual;
19:      function GetText(Item: Integer; Maxlen: Integer): string; virtual;
20:      procedure SelectItem(Item: Integer); virtual;
21:    end;
22:
23:    PPickWin = ^TPickWin;
24:    TPickWin = object(TWindow)
25:      constructor Init(Bounds: TRect);
26:    end;
27:
28:  constructor TListApp.Init;
29:  var
30:    R: TRect;
31:  begin
32:    TApplication.Init;
33:    Desktop^.GetExtent(R);
34:    Desktop^.Insert(New(PPickWin, Init(R)))
35:  end;
36:
37:  constructor TPickView.Init(var Bounds: TRect; ANumCols: Word;
38:    AScrollBar: PScrollBar);
39:  begin TListBox.Init(Bounds, ANumCols, AScrollBar);
40:    GrowMode := gfGrowHiX + gfGrowHiY;
```

continued

Program 17-8: continued

```
41:    TheList := New(PStringCollection, Init(50, 25));
42:    TheList^.Insert(NewStr('Banana'));
43:    TheList^.Insert(NewStr('Apple'));
44:    TheList^.Insert(NewStr('Peach'));
45:    TheList^.Insert(NewStr('Cherry'));
46:    TheList^.Insert(NewStr('Grapefruit'));
47:    NewList(TheList)
48: end;
49:
50: destructor TPickView.Done;
51: begin
52:    if List <> nil then Dispose(List, Done);
53:    TListBox.Done
54: end;
55:
56: function TPickView.GetPalette: PPalette;
57: const
58:    CTheView = #2#3#4;
59:    PTheView: string[Length(CTheView)] = CTheView;
60: begin
61:    GetPalette := @PTheView
62: end;
63:
64: function TPickView.GetText(Item: Integer; Maxlen: Integer): string;
65: begin
66:    GetText := PString(TheList^.At(Item))^;
67: end;
68:
69: procedure TPickView.SelectItem(Item: Integer);
70: begin
71:    MessageBox(GetText(Item, 40), nil, mfInformation + mfOkButton)
72: end;
73:
74: constructor TPickWin.Init(Bounds: TRect);
75: var
76:    R: TRect;
77: begin
78:    TWindow.Init(Bounds, 'List Demo', 0);
79:    Flags := wfMove + wfGrow + wfZoom;
```

```
80:      GetExtent(R);
81:       R.Grow(-1,  -1);
82:      Insert(New(PPickView, Init(R, 1,
83:       StandardScrollBar(sbVertical + sbHandleKeyboard)))))
84:  end;
85:
86:  var
87:
88:      ListApp: TListApp;
89:
90:  begin
91:    ListApp.Init;
92:    ListApp.Run;
93:    ListApp.Done
94:  end.
```

To add list box views to your program's windows, you need to declare two objects similar to TPickView (a descendant of TListBox) and TPickWin (a descendant of TWindow) as demonstrated in TVList (lines 12-26).

In your TWindow object, you need to provide a constructor named Init containing programming similar to the statements at lines 74-84. As usual, the first job is to call the ancestor constructor, initializing the inherited portions of the object. Because the sample program has no menu, and, therefore, no way to open new windows, the constructor modifies the inherited TWindow.Flags field to create a window that can't be closed. The flag settings wfMove + wfGrow + wfZoom specify a window that can be moved, resized, and zoomed to full screen and back. However, because the wfClose flag is left out of the mix, the window's frame will not have a close button. This is a useful technique when all you need is one window. However, be aware that after inserting such a window into the desktop, the window will stay there until the program ends.

The rest of TPickWin's constructor prepares a TRect variable R, used to insert the program's TListBox view into the window. Programs almost always create list box views this way. To the object's Init constructor, pass the view's rectangle (R in this sample), the number of columns (1), and either **nil** for no scroll bar or, as shown here, the result of the StandardScrollBar function. Because TListBox objects can have only vertical scroll bars, you must pass the sbVertical flag to StandardScrollBar. Usually, you should also add in sbHandleKeyboard to enable keyboard commands for controlling the list. (Mouse support comes free of charge.)

Writing TListBox Views

A TListBox is empty until you provide it some data in the form of a TCollection. A TListBox can be used with any TCollection object or a descendant, such as TSortedCollection or TStringCollection.

The TListBox constructor—TPickView.Init in the sample TVList program—first calls TListBox.Init (line 40), passing the three parameters received from the object's creator. The constructor then creates a collection of items to be inserted into the list box. In this case, the collection is addressed by a PStringCollection pointer field named TheList, initialized by New to make a string collection large enough to hold at least 50 items. Of course, you can create lists of nearly any size—TListBox works with a few items or thousands of items.

After creating the collection list, the program calls Insert to add five sample strings to the string collection. Because TStringCollecton is a descendant of TSortedCollection, the strings are maintained in alphabetical order. You must pass only dynamic strings to TStringCollection.Insert, because when the collection is disposed, it calls StrDispose to dispose listed strings.

With the TStringCollection initialized, the final step in TPickView.Init is to call the TListBox method NewList, passing the collection pointer TheList as an argument. NewList first disposes any list currently associated with the list box, then attaches the new list by assigning the passed pointer to TListBox.List, a field of type PCollection. You can access this field later, or as in the sample listing, you can keep a pointer such as TheList in your object's descendant. After the program calls NewList, both of these pointers address the same collection.

The GetText Function

For displaying every listed item, TListBox calls GetText, which should return a string as you want it to appear in the list box view. TListBox passes two parameters to GetText: Item and MaxLen. Item is an integer index of the item that the list box needs. MaxLen represents the maximum length of the string that GetText should return. If you are sure that listed strings are not longer than can be displayed in the view, you can ignore the MaxLen parameter. However, if even one string longer than MaxLen is ever returned, the results will be unpredictable.

Usually, you should call the collection's At method to find the address of the item that the list box requires. You can then recast the item to a string, or perform some other action to return the item in string form. The sample program's GetText method executes the statement

```
GetText :=  PString(TheList^.At(Item))^;
```

At(Item) returns the indicated item from the collection addressed by TheList. (You could also use the inherited List field here in place of TheList.) The result of the expression TheList ^ .At(Item) is recast to type PString, because in this case the items stored in the TStringCollection are string pointers. The result of this expression is then dereferenced to pass the required string back as GetText's function result.

In non-string list boxes, you may have to include programming to create a string for display. In that case, you'd first call List ^ .At(Item) to locate the indicated item in your collection. You could use the result of that method to access various fields, which you could then convert to strings for passing back as the function result. For example, in a collection of integer values, you could assign to GetText a string converted from an integer by the standard Str procedure.

Selecting Listed Items

In addition to GetText, most of the time you should also add a replacement for SelectItem, which the list box calls when an item is selected in the view's window.

SelectItem receives a single integer parameter equal to the index of the selected item. The first item in a list is numbered 0, the second is 1, the third is 2, and so on. As in GetText, you can call List ^ .At(Item) to find the selected item in your TCollection object.

In cases where you need to return a selected item in string form, you also can call the GetText method directly as demonstrated in TVList at line 71 in SelectItem. When the list box calls SelectItem, the method passes the result of GetText, which is limited to 40 characters, to MessageBox. As a result of this action, when you select one of the demo's sample strings, a message box dialog pops up to confirm your choice. (To select items, double click any line with a mouse, or highlight a line and press the Spacebar.)

Changing Lists

Changing horses in the middle of a stream may not be wise. However, you will often need to change collections at some point in the midst of a list box's actions. To do so, first dispose of the old collection by executing

```
NewList(nil);
```

Passing **nil** to TListBox.NewList causes the list box to dispose of its current collection by calling Dispose(List, Done). The collection and all of its items, no matter how many, are all disposed by this one statement. If the list has no collection, the statement has no effect. After this step, you can allocate a new collection and call NewList again to attach the collection to the list box.

You also can combine these steps with a single call to NewList, which always disposes a current collection before attaching a new one. It's possible to replace an existing collection and attach a new one with a statement such as

```
NewList(New(PC, Init(100, 10)));
```

where PC is a pointer type to a TCollection object.

Modifying Lists

After attaching a collection to a TListBox object, you can call the collection's methods to insert new items, delete old ones, and perform other jobs. Even though the list box owns the collection, you can use the object as you can any independent collection.

There's one catch, however. If the number of items in a collection ever changes, you need to inform the TListBox of that change. The best way to accomplish this is to execute the statement

```
SetRange(N);
```

where N is the new number of the item in the collection. SetRange is inherited by TListBox from TListViewer. Calling the method assigns N to the TListViewer's Range field and adjusts the scroll bar if one is attached.

Don't forget this important step. If the number of items in an attached collection changes and you don't call SetRange to inform TListBox of the change, the inherited Range field will be out of synch with the collection's similar Count field. In cases where the number of items has been reduced, this can lead to a crash when the list box attempts to access collected items that aren't there.

Inside a TListBox method, you can resynch the Range and Count fields with the statement

```
SetRange(List^.Count);
```

Disposing List Boxes

TListBox lacks a defined destructor, and for that reason you must not allow a TListBox object with an active collection to be destroyed *unless* you store a pointer to that collection as TVList does in TheList (see line 14). When a TListBox object is disposed, it does not dispose of any current collection addressed by its List field.

This is not a bug, but a realization by Turbo Vision's designers that you may not want TListBox to dispose of a currently attached list. For example, you may want to maintain several collections and call NewList as described earlier to list them in the same TListBox view. After the TListBox object is disposed, you could then dispose of your collections by calling their Done destructors, usually in a Dispose statement.

At other times, to keep memory clear of old collections, you may need to provide a Done destructor in your TListBox object. The destructor in TVList should work for all collections, no matter what their types. First, Dispose is called to destroy the current list if List is not **nil**. Then, TListBox.Done is called to complete the destruction of the list box. These steps ensure that an attached collection and all its items are properly disposed.

Scrolling Text Views

By making a simple change, you can convert TVList into a general-purpose data-file lister. Just replace TPickView's constructor with the following:

```
constructor TPickView.Init(var Bounds: TRect; ANumCols: Word;
  AScrollBar: PScrollBar);
var
  S: string;
  F: Text;
begin
  TListBox.Init(Bounds, ANumCols, AScrollBar);
  TheList := New(PStringCollection, Init(50, 25));
  Assign(F, 'DATA.TXT');
  Reset(F);
  while not Eof(F) do
  begin
    Readln(F, S);
    if length(S) > 0 then
      TheList^.Insert(NewStr(S))
  end;
  Close(F);
  NewList(TheList)
end;
```

You also have to supply a DATA.TXT file containing some text to display. (For test purposes, you might want to copy TVList to DATA.TXT to provide this file.) Rather than insert literal strings into the list as in the original code, the modified program opens the file and reads its lines into a local string variable, which is then passed to NewStr and TheList^.Insert.

As you can see when you run this program, the text lines are sorted and duplicates are removed. Because TStringCollection descends from TSortedCollection, to list an unsorted collection of strings, you need to base your list's collection on TCollection and write your own string-handling code into your object. You probably also want to add menu commands to open other files for listing rather than loading DATA.TXT directly in the constructor.

Stream Basics

The usual methods for reading and writing disk files don't work with polymorphic objects, which can assume different forms and sizes at runtime. A file of an object base type might contain instances of that object type and any of its descendants. To handle this situation, Turbo Vision implements *streams,* a technique that you can use to read and write object data in disk files.

Strictly speaking, streams are not part of Turbo Vision. They are low-level objects declared in the Objects unit, which also declares the TObject data type, the ancestor for all Turbo Vision objects. All objects in a stream must be descended from TObject, and therefore the relationship between streams and Turbo Vision is strong, but not airtight. You can use streams in Turbo Vision programs, but you can also use them in other Pascal programs as well.

An OOP Database

If you've ever used a commercial database system, you probably know one of the major problems with software that stores fixed-size records in files. Such an arrangement ignores the fact that information in the real world rarely fits neatly into a one-size-takes-all cubbyhole. For example, in a name-and-address database, you may want to store different information about your personal entries than you would for your business contacts.

With the help of OOP and streams, doing exactly that is easy. To demonstrate how to use streams to store object data in files, the next three programs implement a polymorphic database—admittedly lacking many features that a full-fledged program would need, but capable enough to demonstrate the highlights of using streams to read and write polymorphic objects in disk files.

The first step is to create an object that defines the fixed information—in other words, the fields that all database entries share. Because other programs need this information, Program 17-9 is in the form of a unit. Save the program as ADDRU.PAS and compile to disk, creating ADDRU.TPU.

Program 17-9: ADDRU.PAS

```
1:  unit AddrU;
2:
3:  interface
4:
5:  uses Objects;
6:
```

```
 7:  type
 8:
 9:    NameStr = string[30];
10:    AddressStr = string[30];
11:    CityStZipStr = string[30];
12:    PhoneStr = string[12];
13:
14:    AddrObjPtr = ^AddrObj;
15:    AddrObj = object(TObject)
16:      Name: NameStr;
17:      Address: AddressStr;
18:      CityStZip: CityStZipStr;
19:      Phone: PhoneStr;
20:      constructor Init(Na: NameStr; Ad: AddressStr;
21:        Csz: CityStZipStr; Ph: PhoneStr);
22:      constructor Load(var S: TStream);
23:      procedure Store(var S: TStream);
24:      procedure Display; virtual;
25:    end;
26:
27:    AddrCollection = object(TCollection)
28:      procedure DisplayList; virtual;
29:    end;
30:
31:  const
32:
33:    RAddrObj: TStreamRec = (
34:      ObjType: 100;
35:      VmtLink: Ofs(TypeOf(AddrObj)^);
36:      Load: @AddrObj.Load;
37:      Store: @AddrObj.Store
38:    );
39:
40:  procedure RegisterAddrUObjects;
41:
42:  implementation
43:
44:  { AddrObj }
45:
46:  constructor AddrObj.Init(Na: NameStr; Ad: AddressStr;
47:    Csz: CityStZipStr; Ph: PhoneStr);
48:  begin
```

continued

```
49:    Name := Na;
50:    Address := Ad;
51:    CityStZip := Csz;
52:    Phone := Ph
53:  end;
54:
55:  constructor AddrObj.Load(var S: TStream);
56:  begin
57:    S.Read(Name, SizeOf(NameStr));
58:    S.Read(Address, Sizeof(AddressStr));
59:    S.Read(CityStZip, SizeOf(CityStZipStr));
60:    S.Read(Phone, SizeOf(PhoneStr))
61:  end;
62:
63:  procedure AddrObj.Store(var S: TStream);
64:  begin
65:    S.Write(Name, SizeOf(NameStr));
66:    S.Write(Address, SizeOf(AddressStr));
67:    S.Write(CityStZip, SizeOf(CityStZipStr));
68:    S.Write(Phone, SizeOf(PhoneStr))
69:  end;
70:
71:  procedure AddrObj.Display;
72:  begin
73:    Writeln;
74:    Writeln(';;;;;;;;;;;;;');
75:    Writeln(Name);
76:    Writeln(Address);
77:    Writeln(CityStZip);
78:    Writeln(Phone)
79:  end;
80:
81:  { AddrCollection }
82:
83:  procedure AddrCollection.DisplayList;
84:    procedure DisplayItem(Item: AddrObjPtr); far;
85:    begin
86:      Item^.Display
87:    end;
88:  begin
```

```
89:    ForEach(@DisplayItem)
90:  end;
91:
92:  procedure RegisterAddrUObjects;
93:  begin
94:    RegisterType(RAddrObj)
95:  end;
96:
97:  end.
```

Lines 9-12 in AddrU declare four string types. If you want, you can change the lengths of these strings. Lines 14-25 declare the AddrObj object type and a pointer to that type, AddrObjPtr. In this object are four data fields of the string types declared earlier. Every database object therefore has a set of Name, Address, CityStZip, and Phone fields.

There are four methods in AddrObj. The first two of these are constructors named Init and Load. There are two ways that programs create AddrObj instances, thus the object declaration needs two constructors—one to create new object instances in memory (Init) and one to load objects saved in disk files (Load).

Constructor Init's parameters are assigned directly to the four data fields, initializing the object with four new strings (see lines 49-52).

Constructor Load's parameter is a single variable of type TStream. All objects that use streams must have a similar constructor named Load. Examine lines 57-60. The four statements there read the object's four fields—presumably from a disk file currently managed by the stream identified by Load's parameter. The Stream.Read method is declared as

```
TStream.Read(var Buf; Count: Word); virtual;
```

The first parameter is the identifier of the variable stored on disk, usually a field in the object type. The second parameter represents the size of this data in bytes. The method is virtual and can be replaced in a descendant TStream object, although you probably won't need to do that. The Objects unit provides three such descendants ready to go: TDosStream for simple file handling, TBufStream for buffered file reads and writes (probably the best choice for most object files), and TEmsStream, which gives programs the means to read and write data in EMS (expanded) memory.

Lines 65-68 implement the Store method for the AddrObj. These statements are similar in form to those in AddrObj.Load, but call the stream's Write method to write data to disk.

For most streamable objects, write Load and Store methods similar to those shown here. In your own code, be sure to read and write your object data fields in exactly the same order. The order of data in streams is critical, and you must load fields in the same order those fields are written to disk.

The final AddrObj method is Display (see lines 71-79). This method simply displays the contents of the object for test purposes and is not required for using streams.

In addition to the fundamental AddrObj object, the program needs a way to store names and addresses in memory. For that, a TCollection object is the perfect solution. AddrU creates a suitable collection at lines 27-29. The program uses most of the TCollection object as it is supplied by Turbo Vision, adding only a DisplayList method for displaying the collected names and addresses. Lines 83-90 show the method's implementation, which calls ForEach and DisplayItem (which in turn calls the item's Display method) for every record in the collection.

Registration

Every streamable object must ultimately descend from TObject, and must declare Load and Store methods as demonstrated in AddrU.

So that streams can distinguish one object from another, streamable objects must also be *registered* at runtime. That's "registered" as in registering to vote. To let streams know about the objects you will store in disk files, your program must register those objects.

Registering streamable objects requires you to take two key steps. First create a TStreamRec record containing information about a streamable object. Then call the RegisterType procedure declared in the Objects unit, passing the TStreamRec record as an argument.

AddrU demonstrates these essential steps. Lines 33-38 define a variable (typed) constant record of type TStreamRec like this:

```
RAddrObj: TStreamRec = (
  ObjType: 100;
  VmtLink: Ofs(TypeOf(AddrObj)^);
  Load: @AddrObj.Load;
  Store: @AddrObj.Store
);
```

Prefacing AddrObj with R for the TStreamRec name helps remind you that RAddrObj is the registration record for the AddrObj object. Of course, you can name your TStreamRec records anything you like.

Each TStreamRec record must have four fields. To the first, ObjType, assign a value from 100 to 65535. Turbo Vision reserves values 0 to 99, so don't use those for your own object type values. (To a stream, the ObjType identifier 0 represents a **nil** object containing no data.)

Note: Page 158 of Borland's Turbo Vision Guide states that registration numbers "0 through 99" are reserved. Page 381 of that same guide states that "0 through 999" are reserved and that programmers should therefore use values beginning with 1000. A search through Turbo Vision's source code proves that no object currently uses a registration value higher than 74, so it's probably safe to begin your own values with 100 as suggested here.

The ObjType value *must* be unique for all objects stored in a stream. It's up to you to enforce this rule. If you assign the same value to two or more TSreamRec ObjType fields, the stream will not be able to distinguish among the different types of object data in a disk file, leading to all sorts of nasty surprises.

Hint: You might want to start a global database of your streamable object names and ObjType values. If you follow this plan and never reuse an ObjType value, you will be able to read and write *any* of your streamable objects in any disk file, now and forevermore, without risk of conflict.

The second field in a TSreamRec record is VmtLink, to which you must assign the offset address of your streamable object's Virtual Method Table (VMT). Streams use this information along with the ObjType field to link the correct objects in disk files with the object's VMT in memory. In your own programs, use the same format shown here, but replace AddrObj with your own object type name. Remember, the object must be a descendant of TObject, and thus, is assured of having a VMT, which is a requirement of streamable objects.

The second and third TStreamRec fields are named Load and Store. To these two pointer fields assign the addresses of your object's Load and Store methods. The addresses provide the stream with the means to call your object's methods to read and write object data in disk files.

After creating a TStreamRec record for each streamable object, pass those records to the RegisterType procedure in the Objects unit. It's probably best to create a common procedure such as RegisterAddrUObjects (see lines 40 and 92-95), which other programs can then call to register the unit's objects. Before using any streams, a program should call every "RegisterXXX" procedure in every unit containing streamable objects. This mirrors the organization of Turbo Vision's units, which declare similar registration procedures. For example, APP.PAS declares RegisterApp. To read and write App's objects in streams, a program would call RegisterApp in the application's constructor or as part of the program's early initialization chores.

That completes the basic steps for creating a streamable object. For your own objects, use AddrU as a guide. As you'll see in a moment, providing Load and Store methods is all you need to do to prepare for reading and writing objects in disk files.

Building Streamable Objects

The primary advantage of streams is their capability of reading and writing different objects in the same file without getting mixed up. Streams "know" what kinds of objects are stored in files because you were careful to register your objects using a unique ObjType value in the object's TStreamRec record.

Inside the object data file, the stream stores the ObjType value along with the size of the object's data in bytes. Then, when reading that same file, the stream retrieves the ObjType value, uses it to associate a newly loaded object with the correct VMT in memory, and loads the correct number of bytes from disk.

To demonstrate how streams can read and write different types of objects in the same file, and to add another piece to the OOP database example that AddrU started, Program 17-10, PERSONU.PAS, declares two other object data types: Personal and Business, each a descendant of AddrObj. Compile the listing to create PERSONU.TPU in the same directory that stores ADDRU.TPU.

Program 17-10: PERSONU.PAS

```
 1:  unit PersonU;
 2:
 3:  interface
 4:
 5:  uses Objects, AddrU;
 6:
 7:  type
 8:
 9:    PersonalPtr = ^Personal;
10:    Personal = object(AddrObj)
11:      Age: Integer;
12:      HomePhone: PhoneStr;
13:      constructor Init(Na: NameStr; Ad: AddressStr;
14:        Csz: CityStZipStr; Ph: PhoneStr;
15:        Ag: Integer; Hp: PhoneStr);
16:      constructor Load(var S: TStream);
17:      procedure Store(var S: TStream);
18:      procedure Display; virtual;
19:    end;
```

```
20:
21:        BusinessPtr = ^Business;
22:     Business = object(AddrObj)
23:        Balance: Real;
24:        Contact: NameStr;
25:        constructor Init(Na: NameStr; Ad: AddressStr;
26:           Csz: CityStZipStr; Ph: PhoneStr;
27:           Ba: Real; Co: NameStr);
28:        constructor Load(var S: TStream);
29:        procedure Store(var S: TStream);
30:        procedure Display; virtual;
31:     end;
32:
33:  const
34:
35:     RPersonal: TStreamRec = (
36:        ObjType: 101;
37:        VmtLink: Ofs(TypeOf(Personal)^);
38:        Load: @Personal.Load;
39:        Store: @Personal.Store
40:     );
41:
42:     RBusiness: TStreamRec = (
43:        ObjType: 102;
44:        VmtLink: Ofs(TypeOf(Business)^);
45:        Load: @Business.Load;
46:        Store: @Business.Store
47:     );
48:
49:  procedure RegisterPersonUObjects;
50:
51:  implementation
52:
53:  { Personal }
54:
55:  constructor Personal.Init(Na: NameStr; Ad: AddressStr;
56:     Csz: CityStZipStr; Ph: PhoneStr;
57:     Ag: Integer; Hp: PhoneStr);
58:  begin
59:     AddrObj.Init(Na, Ad, Csz, Ph);
60:     Age := Ag;
61:     HomePhone := Hp
```

continued

Program 17-10: continued

```
 62:    end;
 63:
 64:   constructor Personal.Load(var S: TStream);
 65:   begin
 66:     AddrObj.Load(S);
 67:     S.Read(Age, SizeOf(Integer));
 68:     S.Read(HomePhone, SizeOf(PhoneStr))
 69:   end;
 70:
 71:   procedure Personal.Store(var S: TStream);
 72:   begin
 73:     AddrObj.Store(S);
 74:     S.Write(Age, SizeOf(Integer));
 75:     S.Write(HomePhone, SizeOf(PhoneStr))
 76:   end;
 77:
 78:   procedure Personal.Display;
 79:   begin
 80:     AddrObj.Display;
 81:     Writeln('Age = ', Age);
 82:     Writeln('Home phone = ', HomePhone)
 83:   end;
 84:
 85:   { Business }
 86:
 87:   constructor Business.Init(Na: NameStr; Ad: AddressStr;
 88:     Csz: CityStZipStr; Ph: PhoneStr;
 89:     Ba: Real; Co: NameStr);
 90:   begin
 91:     AddrObj.Init(Na, Ad, Csz, Ph);
 92:     Balance := Ba;
 93:     Contact := Co
 94:   end;
 95:
 96:   constructor Business.Load(var S: TStream);
 97:   begin
 98:     AddrObj.Load(S);
 99:     S.Read(Balance, SizeOf(Real));
100:     S.Read(Contact, SizeOf(NameStr))
101:   end;
```

```
102:
103:    procedure Business.Store(var S: TStream);
104:    begin
105:       AddrObj.Store(S);
106:       S.Write(Balance, SizeOf(Real));
107:       S.Write(Contact, SizeOf(NameStr))
108:    end;
109:
110:    procedure Business.Display;
111:    begin
112:       AddrObj.Display;
113:       Writeln('Balance = $', Balance:0:2);
114:       Writeln('Contact = ', Contact)
115:    end;
116:
117:    procedure RegisterPersonUObjects;
118:    begin
119:       RegisterType(RPersonal);
120:       RegisterType(RBusiness)
121:    end;
122:
123:    end.
```

Although PERSONU.PAS is longer than ADDRU.PAS, if you examine the code closely, you see that the two units are very much alike. The Personal and Business object types (lines 10-19 and 22-31) are descended from AddrObj. Consequently, every instance of these new types has Name, Address, and other data fields declared in AddrObj. All the new objects Personal and Business have to do is declare additional fields specific to their needs: Age and HomePhone in Personal; and Balance and Contact in Business.

In addition, the Init constructors in the two objects add new parameters to initialize the inherited and new fields. Pay special attention to the constructor implementations at lines 55-62 and 87-94. In each case, the constructors call the ancestor AddrObj.Init constructor to initialize the inherited fields. The new Init parameters are assigned to the object's unique fields. In this way, the extended constructors completely initialize object instances.

The other constructor and two methods in Personal and Business—Load, Store, and Display—are similar in scope and design to those methods of the same names in AddrObj. Notice how Personal.Load calls the ancestor AddrObj.Load method before reading the object's unique fields with S.Read, executing the three statements

```
AddrObj.Load(S);
S.Read(Age,   SizeOf(Integer));
S.Read(HomePhone, SizeOf(PhoneStr))
```

Calling AddrObj.Load reads the ancestor data from disk, regardless of what that data contains. The object trusts its ancestor to take care of its own duties, executing new S.Read statements only for the new fields added to Personal. A future descendant of Personal could do the same, calling Personal.Load before calling S.Read to read new data fields. This is a vital concept in OOP and Turbo Pascal streams. New objects build on other objects, adding as little as possible to enhance what's already there.

The Personal.Store method (lines 71-76) uses a similar technique, first calling AddrObj.Store to write the ancestor's data fields, and then calling S.Write to write the fields that are unique to Personal. As explained for AddrObj, it's critical that Load and Store read and write the same fields in the same order.

Personal.Display (lines 78-83) also calls its ancestor's Display method before displaying the two new fields in the Personal object.

The Load, Store, and Display methods in the Business object are nearly identical to those in Personal, but of course, they read, write, and display data unique to the Business object.

Also similar to AddrU's declarations are the TStreamRec records at lines 35-47. Note the unique values used for the ObjType fields—101 for Personal and 102 for Business. AddrObj, you recall, uses an ObjType field value of 100. Because these three objects are stored in the same disk file, they must have unique ObjType values. The other fields are initialized as explained previously, assigning the object VMT, Load, and Store addresses.

Finally in PersonU, a common procedure named RegisterPersonUObjects (lines 49 and 117-121) calls RegisterType for each of the two TStreamRec records. A program that uses the PersonU unit must call RegisterPersonUObjects to register the unit's streamable objects before reading and writing them in disk files.

Gently Down the Stream

Armed with three streamable objects: AddrObj, Personal, and Business, a program can create object instances, store those instances in disk files using a stream, and read those same instances from disk back into memory.

Program 17-11, ADDRESS.PAS, completes the sample database program, and demonstrates how to use a stream to read and write streamable objects. Compile and run the program, and read the on-screen messages which inform you what the program is doing at each step. Press Enter after every message to create a few test records in memory. Write those records to a file named ADDR.XXX, read the records back, and then dispose of them before ending.

Program 17-11: ADDRESS.PAS

```
 1: program Address;
 2:
 3: uses Crt, Objects, AddrU, PersonU;
 4:
 5: var
 6:
 7:   AddrList: AddrCollection;
 8:   AddrFile: TBufStream;
 9:
10: { Display a message and pause until Enter key is pressed }
11:
12: procedure Message(S: string);
13: begin
14:   Writeln;
15:   Write('---- Press <Enter> to ', S);
16:   Readln
17: end;
18:
19: { Insert records into collection. Simulates data entry }
20:
21: procedure InsertRecords;
22: begin
23:   AddrList.Insert
24:   (New
25:     (PersonalPtr, Init    { create new personal object }
26:       (
27:         'A. Friend',              { name }
28:         '47 Western Way',         { address }
29:         'Our Town, PA 19876',     { city state zip }
30:         '212-515-1212',           { daytime phone }
31:         35,                       { age in years }
32:         '000-1212'                { home phone }
33:       )
34:     )
35:   );
36:   AddrList.Insert
37:   (New
38:     (BusinessPtr, Init     { create new business object }
39:       (
40:         'Cookies Incorporated', { name }
```

continued

Program 17-11: continued

```
41:          '100 Park Place',        { address }
42:          'New York, NY 10010',    { city state zip }
43:          '717-555-1212',          { company phone }
44:          3549.79,                 { balance }
45:          'Mr. T. F. Cookie'       { contact }
46:        )
47:      )
48:    );
49:    AddrList.Insert
50:    (New
51:      (PersonalPtr, Init      { create new personal object }
52:        (
53:          'E. Z. Pickins',         { name }
54:          '23 Easy Street',        { address }
55:          'Anyplace, TX 77665',    { city state zip }
56:          '800-555-1212',          { daytime phone }
57:          62,                      { age in years }
58:          '(unlisted)'             { home phone }
59:        )
60:      )
61:    );
62:  end;
63:
64:  begin
65:    ClrScr;
66:    Writeln('Streamable Objects Demonstration');
67:    Message('register streamable objects');
68:    RegisterAddrUObjects;
69:    RegisterPersonUObjects;
70:    Message('create list in memory');
71:    AddrList.Init(50, 10);
72:    InsertRecords;
73:    Message('display list in memory');
74:    AddrList.DisplayList;
75:    Message('write list to disk');
76:    AddrFile.Init('ADDR.XXX', stCreate, 1024);
77:    AddrList.Store(AddrFile);
78:    AddrFile.Done;
79:    Message('delete list from memory');
80:    AddrLIst.FreeAll;
```

```
81:     Message('display empty list');
82:     AddrList.DisplayList;
83:     Message('read list from disk');
84:     AddrFile.Init('ADDR.XXX', stOpen, 1024);
85:     AddrList.Load(AddrFile);
86:     AddrFile.Done;
87:     Message('display list in memory');
88:     AddrList.DisplayList;
89:     Message('delete list from memory');
90:     AddrList.FreeAll;
91:     AddrList.Done;
92:     Message('end program')
93:   end.
```

Address declares two global variables. AddrList is an object of type AddrCollection, the descendant of TCollection, declared in AddrU. This object stores a few sample records in memory. You could store them in an array or by other means, but a collection is a convenient structure for keeping track of variable-sized, polymorphic objects. AddrFile is declared of type TBufStream. This is the stream object that manages reading and writing object data in a file.

So that you don't have to enter records each time you run the program, procedure InsertRecords inserts some sample data into the AddrList collection. After this procedure finishes, the collection stores two Personal objects and one Business object.

Before writing those objects to a stream, the main program calls the Register procedures in AddrU and PersonU (lines 68-69), registering the streamable objects in those units for use with streams. Lacking this step, the stream would not recognize the objects, and it would not be able to read and write them.

Lines 71-72 create the sample collection and fill it with sample data. Then, after line 74 displays the list in memory, lines 76-78 store the entire collection in a file named ADDR.XXX. The following three statements demonstrate how to create and write most kinds of stream files:

```
AddrFile.Init('ADDR.XXX', stCreate, 1024);
AddrList.Store(AddrFile);
AddrFile.Done;
```

To create a new stream file, call the stream object's Init constructor as shown here, passing the file name, the constant stCreate, and a buffer size. For objects of type TDosStream, omit the buffer size. For objects of type TEmsStream, pass a minimum size value to Init. Other than these startup differences, you can use streams of all three types in similar ways.

Constant stCreate is one of four you can use to initialize a stream. Table 17-1 describes the four constants. (Your Turbo Vision Guide lists other "stXXXX" constants used for identifying stream errors, which is not covered here.)

Table 17-1 Stream initialization constants.

Constant	Value	Description
stCreate	$3C00	Create a new stream file.
stOpen	$3D02	Open an existing stream file for reading and writing.
stOpenRead	$3D00	Open an existing stream file for reading only (not writing).
stOpenWrite	$3D01	Open an existing stream file for writing only (not reading).

To write data to a stream, call a streamable object's Store method, passing the initialized stream as a parameter. In this sample, the program calls AddrList.Store, a method provided by TCollection for writing lists of information to a stream. The collection's Store method calls each of the Store methods in the collected object instances, thus in this example, writing the Personal and Business objects to disk.

After writing data to a stream, close it by calling the stream object's Done destructor (see line 78). For streams, the Done destructor is analogous to Turbo Pascal's Close procedure, which closes open files.

Reading data from a stream takes similar steps. As before, call the stream's Init constructor to initialize the stream object and open the disk file. Then, instead of calling Store, call Load for one or more streamable objects. Finally, call the stream's Done destructor to deinitialize the object and close the file. Here are the statements that read the data you wrote to disk a moment ago:

```
AddrFile.Init('ADDR.XXX', stOpen, 1024);
AddrList.Load(AddrFile);
AddrFile.Done;
```

In place of stCreate, stOpen specifies to the stream that it should open an existing file. Loading the collection object AddrList automatically loads every object instance previously stored in the collection. You don't need a loop or other programming to read individual objects from disk.

Summary

Dialogs are Turbo Vision's main tools for communicating with program users. Dialogs can display text, prompt for information, and present a number of controls for selecting program options. Control types include buttons, input boxes, static text items, radio buttons, and check boxes, among others. The TDialog object makes it easy to create and use dialogs in Turbo Vision programs.

Turbo Vision provides the TCollection object for storing lists of objects of just about any type. Most objects stored in TCollections, however, should be descended from TObject. Descendants of TCollection give you the means to create sorted collections (TSortedCollection) and to collect strings (TStringCollection).

Streams are provided in the Objects unit. You can use streams in Turbo Vision or in conventional Pascal OOP programs to read and write object data in disk files. With streams, you can store different types of objects in the same file without conflicts.

Exercises

17-1. Convert the AboutProgram procedure in the Diag unit (Program 17-1) to display your own name. Write a program to test your About dialog box.

17-2. Write a program to test the other two Diag unit procedures, Yes and ErrorMessage.

17-3. Using Orders (Program 17-2) as a guide, write a program to prompt users for personal information, as might be stored in a database. For example, your dialog box might include spaces for a name and address, age, education, sex, and so on. Use a combination of input fields, buttons, and check boxes in your program.

17-4. Add a transfer-buffer record to your answer to exercise 17-3, and verify that the program correctly stores the dialog's data in the record.

17-5. Complete the Help command in the Tabs program.

17-6. Create a TCollection descendant object that can store an unsorted collection of strings. Your object should also be able to store null (zero-length) strings.

17-7. Write a text file "README" program, using your string collection object from exercise 17-5. (Hint: Use TVList, Program 17-8, as a starting place, but substitute your own TCollection descendant for the TStringCollection instance variable, addressed by TheList in object TPickView.)

17-8. Write a program to read the current disk directory into a TListBox object.

17-9. Modify your answer to exercise 17-7 to display disk subdirectories, and to let users select a directory and make it the current one.

17-10. Create a hierarchy of objects, descended from TObject, for a music collection. Make your objects streamable. Write a test program that stores object instances in a disk file, then reads them back.

17-11. Use a dialog box to let users enter new music records into your program from exercise 17-10.

18

Turbo Pascal Encyclopedia

- Using the Encyclopedia
- Abs
- Addr
- Append
- Arc
- ArcTan
- Assign
- AssignCrt
- Bar
- Bar3d
- BlockRead
- BlockWrite
- ChDir
- Chr
- Circle
- ClearDevice
- ClearViewPort
- Close
- CloseGraph
- ClrEol
- ClrScr
- Concat
- Copy
- Cos
- CSeg
- Dec
- Delay
- Delete
- DelLine
- DetectGraph
- DiskFree
- DiskSize
- Dispose
- DosExitCode
- DosVersion
- DrawPoly

- DSeg
- Ellipse
- EnvCount
- EnvStr
- Eof
- Eoln
- Erase
- Exec
- Exit
- Exp
- Fail
- FExpand
- FilePos
- FileSize
- FillChar
- FillEllipse
- FillPoly
- FindFirst
- FindNext
- FloodFill
- Flush
- Frac
- FreeMem
- FSearch

- FSplit
- GetArcCoords
- GetAspectRatio
- GetBkColor
- GetCBreak
- GetColor
- GetDate
- GetDefaultPalette
- GetDir
- GetDriverName
- GetEnv
- GetFAttr
- GetFillPattern
- GetFillSettings
- GetFTime
- GetGraphMode
- GetImage
- GetIntVec
- GetLineSettings
- GetMaxColor
- GetMaxMode
- GetMaxX
- GetMaxY
- GetMem

- GetModeName
- GetModeRange
- GetPalette
- GetPaletteSize
- GetPixel
- GetTextSettings
- GetTime
- GetVerify
- GetViewSettings
- GetX
- GetY
- GotoXY
- GraphDefaults
- GraphErrorMsg
- GraphResult
- Halt
- HeapFunc
- Hi
- HighVideo
- ImageSize
- Inc
- InitGraph
- InLine
- Insert
- InsLine
- InstallUserDriver
- InstallUserFont
- Int
- Intr
- IoResult
- Keep
- Keypressed
- Length
- Line
- LineRel
- LineTo
- Ln
- Lo
- LowVideo
- Mark
- MaxAvail
- MemAvail
- MkDir
- Move
- MoveRel
- MoveTo
- MsDos
- New

- NormVideo
- NoSound
- Odd
- Ofs
- Ord
- OutText
- OutTextXY
- OvrClearBuf
- OvrGetBuf
- OvrGetRetry
- OvrInit
- OvrInitEMS
- OvrReadFunc
- OvrSetBuf
- OvrSetRetry
- PackTime
- ParamCount
- ParamStr
- Pi
- PieSlice
- Pos
- Pred
- Ptr
- PutImage
- PutPixel

- Random
- Randomize
- Read
- ReadKey
- ReadLn
- Rectangle
- RegisterBGIDriver
- RegisterBGIFont
- Release
- Rename
- Reset
- RestoreCrtMode
- Rewrite
- RmDir
- Round
- RunError
- Sector
- Seek
- SeekEof
- SeekEoln
- Seg
- SetActivePage
- SetAllPalette
- SetAspectRatio
- SetBkCol

- SetCBreak
- SetColor
- SetDate
- SetFAttr
- SetFillPattern
- SetFillStyle
- SetFTime
- SetGraphBufSize
- SetGraphMode
- SetIntVec
- SetLineStyle
- SetPalette
- SetRGBPalette
- SetTextBuf
- SetTextJustify
- SetTextStyle
- SetTime
- SetUserCharSize
- SetVerify
- SetViewPort
- SetVisualPage
- SetWriteMode
- Sin
- SizeOf
- Sound
- SPtr
- Sqr
- Sqrt
- SSeg
- Str
- Succ
- Swap
- SwapVectors
- TextBackground
- TextColor
- TextHeight
- TextMode
- TextWidth
- Trunc
- Truncate
- TypeOf
- UnpackTime
- UpCase
- Val
- WhereX
- WhereY
- Window
- Write
- Writeln

This chapter is an alphabetical reference to all Turbo Pascal standard procedures and functions. Each routine is described in a separate section, which has five parts, listing a routine's syntax, location, description, "see also" references, and a programming example. The sections are:

1. ***Syntax.*** Using a form similar to a typical Pascal declaration, this section lists the procedure or function name, the function data type, and any parameters. For example, the syntax for function Chr is:

```
function Chr(N: Byte): Char;
```

This tells you that Chr takes a single Byte parameter (N) and returns the Char data type. If you were to write your own Chr function, you'd declare it in the form listed here.

Occasionally, the syntax breaks with standard Pascal style. For example, Writeln, which takes a variable number of parameters or none at all, cannot be written in Pascal. Function Abs, which returns a data type equal to the type of its argument, is another example. For these and other nonstandard declarations, refer to Table 18-1 for a description of various symbols and notations you'll encounter from time to time.

2. ***Location.*** Most Turbo Pascal procedures and functions are stored in units. Native routines and those in the System unit, which automatically envelops every program, are listed as belonging to System. Other routines are located in other units. To use a procedure or function, insert the unit name in a **uses** declaration. You can omit or include the System unit as you wish. See Chapters 9 and 10 for more information about using units.

3. ***Description.*** This section describes how to use the procedure or function. If you need more help after reading the brief overview here, check the index for references to pages with additional details. Also check the table of contents and key-word list at the beginning of each chapter.

4. ***See also***. Refers to related procedures and functions. Not all entries have this function.

5. ***Example.*** The programming example shows how to use the procedure or function in a real program. Each example is a complete program, ready to type and run. I tried to choose examples that demonstrate key features and problems. However, in order to keep this chapter within a reasonable size, programs are often simplistic. Even so, running the examples on your computer should answer many of your questions. Unlike other programs in this book, the examples here have no line numbers.

Table 18-1 Encyclopedia symbols and notations

Symbol	Description
¦	*Or*—as in Byte¦Integer (Byte or Integer)
[<item>]	The square-bracketed <item> is optional
...	A continuing sequence of one or more items
<ident>	Identifier
<type>	Any type except <file>
<ordinal>	<integer>¦Char¦Boolean¦<enumerated type>
<enumerated type>	(<ident>, <ident>, ..., <ident>)
<number>	<integer>¦<real>
<integer>	<signed integer>¦<unsigned integer>
<signed integer>	ShortInt¦Integer¦LongInt
<unsigned integer>	Byte¦Word
<real>	Real¦<IEEE real>
<IEEE real>	Single¦Double¦Extended¦Comp
<pointer>	Pointer¦<typed pointer>
<typed pointer>	^<type>¦<file>
<file>	<text file>¦<untyped file>¦<typed file>
<untyped file>	**file**
<typed file>	**file of** <type>
<text file>	Text¦**file of** Char
<string>	<string variable>¦<string constant>
<string variable>	<typed string>¦**string**
<typed string>	**string**[N] where 0 < N <= 255
<proc>	**procedure** or **function**
<constructor>	Object **constructor** method
<destructor>	Object **destructor** method
<pointer type>	Pointer data type

Using the Encyclopedia

If you purchased the listings on disk (see the last page inside the back cover for an order form), programs are stored in files named X*id*.PAS, in which *id* is the procedure or function name. For example, the listing for the Pred function is stored in XPRED.PAS. See the README file on your disk for a few oddball cases for which names are changed or abbreviated.

If you did not purchase the disks, you might want to follow a similar file-naming convention when you are typing the examples. By saving the listings on disk, you'll build a library of tests for every Turbo Pascal procedure and function. When you upgrade your compiler to new versions, these programs are a useful way to test changes and improvements.

A few parameter names differ in spelling and capitalization from the names used in the Turbo Pascal manuals and in the unit interface .INT text files on your master disks. In all cases, these changes are for clarity and have no effect on the operation and use of the procedures and functions. Where the Turbo Pascal manuals and the .INT text files disagree, I relied on the .INT files and the Turbo Pascal runtime library source code (RTL, available separately from Borland) as the ultimate authorities.

Note: Graph unit examples require driver files and, in some cases, character font files on disk, as Chapter 11 explains. These programs also require you to have appropriate graphics hardware.

Abs

Syntax
```
function Abs(N: <number>): <number>;
```

Location
System

Description
Abs returns the absolute (unsigned) value of N. The function result is of the same type as its parameter, which can be of any numerical type. For example, Abs(–5) returns 5, Abs(–100.25) returns 100.25, and Abs(3.141) returns 3.141.

See also

Round, Trunc

Example

```
program XAbs;
var I : Integer; R : Real; L : Longint;
begin
  for I := -10 to 10 do
    Writeln('I=', I, ' Abs(I)=', Abs(I));
  R := -2567;
  Writeln('R=', R, ' Abs(R)=', Abs(R));
```

```
L := -Maxlongint;
Writeln('L=', L, ' abs(L)=', Abs(L))
end.
```

Addr

Syntax
```
function Addr(Id: <ident>): Pointer;
```

Location
System

Description
Addr returns the memory address of Id, which can be any variable, procedure, or function identifier. The function result is a 32-bit pointer containing two 16-bit values that represent the segment and offset where Id exists in memory.

You can use the result of Addr anywhere you could use a pointer of any type with one exception: You cannot directly dereference Addr with a following caret (^). As the example shows, to dereference the pointer, you must first assign the result of Addr to a pointer variable and then dereference the variable.

If Id is an array, it can have an index (as in Id[5]) to find the address of a specific array element. You also can specify fields in records to find their addresses. If Id is a record, then Addr(Id.Name) locates the address of the Name field in Id.

The @ operator is a convenient shorthand for Addr. When using @, you do not have to surround Id with parentheses. The shorthand character produces the same result as the function.

See also
Ofs, Ptr, Seg

Example
```
program XAddr;
var
  P, Q: Pointer;
  R: record A, B: Integer end;

  procedure P1;
  begin
    Writeln('Inside p1')
  end;

begin
  P := Addr(P1);     { Assign address of procedure p1 to p }
  Q := @P1;          { Same as above statement }
```

```
if P <> Q
  then Writeln('P <> Q!')  { This should never appear }
  else Writeln('P1 is at ', Seg(P^), ':', Ofs(P^));
R.A := 10; R.B := 20;  { Assign values to a record }
P := Addr(R.A);        { P points to R.A in memory }
Q := @R.B;             { Q points to R.B in memory }
Writeln('A=', Integer(P^));   { Display R.A value }
Writeln('B=', Integer(Q^))    { Display R.B value }
end.
```

Append

Syntax
```
procedure Append(var F: Text);
```

Location
System

Description
Append opens text file F, preparing the file to accept new lines at its current end. The only legal operations on a file opened with Append are Write(F) and Writeln(F). Before using Append, Assign a file name to file variable F.

See also
Assign, Close, Reset, Rewrite, Write, Writeln

Example
```
program XAppend;
var Tf: Text;
begin
  Assign(Tf, 'TEST.TXT');
  Rewrite(Tf);
  Writeln(Tf, 'This is line #1');
  Close(Tf);
  Append(Tf);
  Writeln(Tf, 'This is line #2');
  Close(Tf)
end.
```

Arc

Syntax
```
procedure Arc(X, Y: Integer; StAngle, EndAngle, Radius: Word);
```

Location
Graph

Description
Arc draws a semicircle anchored at coordinate (X,Y) in the color passed to SetColor. Words StAngle and EndAngle are the end points of the arc. You can imagine these points as being on the tips of lines that are equal in length to Radius, extending from the center of a circle on which the arc lies.

The example draws a pseudo-three-dimensional tube out of arcs by varying the position of the arc while increasing its size and length.

See also
Circle, Ellipse, GetArcCoords, GetAspectRatio, PieSlice, Sector, SetAspectRatio

Example
```pascal
program XArc;
uses Crt, Graph;
var
  GraphDriver, GraphMode, X, Y: Integer;
  MaxX: Word;
begin
  DetectGraph(GraphDriver, GraphMode);
  InitGraph(GraphDriver, GraphMode, 'c:\tp\bgi');
  MaxX := GetMaxX;
  Y := 10;
  for X := 25 to MaxX - 75 do
  begin
    SetColor(X mod 16);
    Arc(X, Y, Y mod 360, X mod 360, X div 10);
    Y := Y + (X mod 2)
  end;
  repeat until Keypressed;
  CloseGraph
end.
```

ArcTan

Syntax
```pascal
function ArcTan(R: <real>): <real>;
```

Location
System

Description
ArcTan returns the arctangent in radians of angle R, also expressed in radians. To convert angles to radians, use the Radians function listed in the example.

See also

Cos, Sin

Example

```
program XArcTan;
var Angle: Integer;

  function Radians(Angle: Integer): Real;
  begin
    Radians := Abs(Angle mod 360) * Pi / 180.0
  end;

begin
  Angle := 0;
  while (Angle < 360) do
  begin
    Writeln('Angle=', Angle:3, ' Arctan in radians=',
      ArcTan(Radians(Angle)):8:3);
    Angle := Angle + 15
  end
end.
```

Assign

Syntax

```
procedure Assign(var F: <file>; Filename: <string>);
```

Location

System

Description

Before using Reset or Rewrite on file variable F, assign a file name with this procedure. The Filename string, which can be from zero to 79 characters long, can refer to a disk file with or without a path (as in C:\UTIL\TEST.TXT), or it can refer to a device such as CON (console) or PRN (printer).

If filename is null (the string length equals zero) and if file F is a text file, resetting F directs input through the standard input file. Rewriting F with a null Filename directs output through the standard output file.

The example shows how to use Assign in two ways. File Tf is a text file, directed to standard Output. File Temp is a plain file, used here to determine whether file TURBO.EXE is on disk. Because Tf is directed through standard Output, you can redirect the result of the program to another file instead of to the console. Compile the program to XASSIGN.EXE and type these commands. The result of running the program goes into file TEST.TXT, which the second command then displays.

```
XASSIGN>TEST.TXT
TYPE TEST.TXT
```

See also
Append, Close, Reset, Rewrite

Example
```
program XAssign;
var
  Temp: file;
  Tf: Text;
begin
  Assign(Tf, '');              { Assign null string to tf }
  Rewrite(Tf);                 { Direct tf to standard output }
  Write(Tf, 'TURBO.EXE is ');  { Write to standard output }
  Assign(Temp, 'TURBO.EXE');   { Assign file name to temp }
   {$I-} Reset(Temp); {$I+}    { Test if file exists }
  if IoResult <> 0             {  it does only if ioresult = 0 }
    then Write(Tf, 'not ')
    else Close(Temp);
  Writeln(Tf, 'here!');
  Close(Tf)
end.
```

AssignCrt

Syntax
```
procedure AssignCrt(var F: Text);
```

Location
Crt

Description
AssignCrt associates any text file variable with the Crt unit's direct-video output routines. After rewriting the file assigned to the Crt, Write and Writeln output statements that use the file display text on-screen as fast as possible. Read and Readln input statements are also redirected, although the effects of AssignCrt on input are not as apparent.

This can be useful in programs that write to the standard Output file. To display a message on the screen (perhaps an error message or prompt), and *not* redirect that message to the current output file, use AssignCrt to assign a file to the CRT. Using this file ensures that the output is displayed via fast direct-video routines, even if standard Output is redirected elsewhere.

The example demonstrates how to do this. File Crtf is assigned to the CRT. File Outf is assigned to standard Output (by using a null file name in the Assign statement). Compile the program to XASSIGNC.EXE and type XASSIGNC>TEST.TXT, redirecting output to a disk text file. The first string is displayed on-screen; the second is directed to a text file named TEST.TXT.

See also
Assign, Close, Rewrite

Example
```
program XAssignCrt;
uses Crt;
var
  Crtf, Outf: Text;
begin
  ClrScr;
  AssignCrt(Crtf);     { Assign crtf to CRT output }
  Rewrite(Crtf);
  Assign(Outf, '');    { Assign outf to standard output }
  Rewrite(Outf);
  Writeln(Crtf, 'This line goes directly to the CRT');
  Writeln(Outf);
  Writeln(Outf, 'This line goes to standard output');
  Close(Crtf); Close(Outf)
end.
```

Bar

Syntax
```
procedure Bar(X1, Y1, X2, Y2: Integer);
```

Location
Graph

Description
Bar draws a filled rectangle with corners at (X1, Y1) and (X2, Y2). Use SetFillStyle to prepare the color and pattern used to fill the bar. The example displays a blue vertical bar near the center of the screen.

See also
Bar3D, SetFillStyle, SetFillPattern, SetLineStyle

Example
```
program XBar;
uses Crt, Graph;
var
  GraphDriver, GraphMode: Integer;
```

```
  X1, Y1, X2, Y2: Integer;
begin
  GraphDriver := Detect;
  InitGraph(GraphDriver, GraphMode, 'c:\tp\bgi');
  X1 := GetMaxX div 2;      { Center screen }
  Y1 := GetMaxY div 4;      { Lower mid screen }
  X2 := X1 + 25;            { Width of bar }
  Y2 := Y1 * 2;             { Height of bar }
  SetFillStyle(1, 3);       { Pattern, Color }
  Bar(X1, Y1, X2, Y2);      { Draw filled bar }
  repeat until Keypressed;
  CloseGraph
end.
```

Bar3d

Syntax
```
procedure Bar3D(X1, Y1, X2, Y2: Integer; Depth: Word; Top: Boolean);
```

Location
Graph

Description
Bar3D draws a filled pseudo-three-dimensional rectangle. The example is similar to the program for Bar. The new program also displays a blue bar in the center of the screen. However, this time the bar has an outlined top and side, giving the illusion of depth.

Parameters (X1, Y1) and (X2, Y2) define the upper-left and lower-right corners of the face of the bar. Set Depth to higher values to increase the illusion of depth. Set Top to true to draw the top of the bar. Set Top to false not to draw the top, and perhaps to stack another bar on top of this one.

See also
Bar, SetFillPattern, SetFillStyle, SetLineStyle

Example
```
program XBar3D;
uses Crt, Graph;
var
  GraphDriver, GraphMode: Integer;
  X1, Y1, X2, Y2, Depth: Integer;
  Top: Boolean;
begin
  GraphDriver := Detect;
  InitGraph(GraphDriver, GraphMode, 'c:\tp\bgi');
```

```
X1 := GetMaxX div 2;      { Center screen }
Y1 := GetMaxY div 4;      { Lower mid screen }
X2 := X1 + 25;            { Width of bar }
Y2 := Y1 * 2;             { Height of bar }
Depth := 10;              { Depth of illusion }
Top := true;              { Draw top on bar }
SetFillStyle(1, 3);       { Pattern, Color }
Bar3D(X1, Y1, X2, Y2, Depth, Top);   { Draw filled 3D bar }
repeat until Keypressed;
CloseGraph
end.
```

BlockRead

Syntax
```
procedure BlockRead(var F: File; var V: <type>; N: Word [; Result: Word]);
```

Location
System

Description
BlockRead reads N 128-byte blocks of untyped file F directly into variable V, which is usually an array. (Use Reset with an optional parameter to change from 128 to a different block byte size.) Whatever V's type is, it's your responsibility to ensure that V can hold as many bytes as BlockRead requests from the file.

BlockRead sets the optional Result parameter equal to the number of blocks actually read from file F. Use this value to determine whether the BlockRead was successful. You also can use the result to know how many blocks were read from a file of unknown size. For example, this reads from zero to 10 blocks of a test file:

```
var
  A: array[1 .. 10] of array[0 .. 127] of Byte
  Result: Integer;
begin
  Assign(F, 'TEST.DAT');
  Reset(F);
  BlockRead(F, A, 10, Result);
  Writeln(Result, ' blocks loaded')
end;
```

The following example shows how to load the first 128 bytes of a file TEST.DAT into a 256-byte array. When you run the program, you'll see that this fills only half of the array. Change the Reset statement to Reset(F, 256) to fill the array completely.

See also
Assign, BlockWrite, Reset

Example
```pascal
program XBlockRead;
var
  F: file;
  A: array[0 .. 255] of Byte;
  I, Result: Integer;
begin
  FillChar(A, Sizeof(A), 0);   { Fill array with zeros }
  Assign(F, 'TEST.DAT');       { Assign file name to f }
  Reset(F);                    { Open for 128-byte block reads }
  BlockRead(F, A, 1, Result);  { Read 128 bytes into array }
  if Result = 1                         { Check if result=num blocks }
    then Writeln('Successful read')     { If so, read successful }
    else Writeln('Disk read error');    { Else read unsuccessful }
  for I := 0 to 255 do Write(A[I]:4);   { Display array contents }
  Writeln;
  Close(F)
end.
```

BlockWrite

Syntax
```pascal
procedure BlockWrite(var F: File; var V: <type>; N: Word [; Result: Word]);
```

Location
System

Description
BlockWrite writes N 128-byte blocks to untyped file F, starting from the first byte of variable V. (Use Rewrite with an optional parameter to change from 128 to a different block byte size.) It's your responsibility to ensure that the number of blocks BlockWrite writes corresponds with the size of V.

The optional Result parameter equals the number of blocks actually written to file F. You can use this value as a verification of BlockWrite's success.

The example creates a file, TEST.DAT, containing 256 bytes with successive values from 0 to 255. After running the program, use the BlockRead example to read the contents of TEST.DAT.

See also
Assign, BlockRead, Rewrite

Example
```pascal
program XBlockWrite;
```

```
var
  F: file;
  A: array[0 .. 255] of Byte;
  I, Result: Integer;
begin
  for I := 0 to 255 do    { Fill array with values from 0 to 255 }
    A[I] := I;
  Assign(F, 'TEST.DAT');        { Assign file name to f }
  Rewrite(F, 256);             { Open for 256-byte block writes }
  BlockWrite(F, A, 1, Result); { Write 256 bytes from array }
  if Result = 1                    { Check if result=num blocks }
    then Writeln('Successful write')  { If so, write successful }
    else Writeln('Disk write error'); { Else write unsuccessful }
  Close(F)
end.
```

ChDir

Syntax
```
procedure ChDir(Path: <string>);
```

Location
System

Description
ChDir changes the current subdirectory or drive letter to the Path string. Check IoResult after ChDir to determine if the change was successful. The example prompts for a new path name, changing the current directory if the path exists, or displaying an error message if it does not. This is similar to the way the DOS CHDIR and CD commands work.

See also
GetDir, MkDir, RmDir

Example
```
program XChDir;
var
  Path: string[64];
begin
  Write('New path? ');
  Readln(Path);
  {$I-} ChDir(Path); {$I+}
  if IoResult <> 0
    then Writeln(Path, ' does not exist')
end.
```

Chr

Syntax
```
function Chr(N: Byte): Char;
```

Location
System

Description
Chr returns the character with ASCII value N. If a variable is not in the range 0. .255, the character returned equals N modulo 256. In other words, if I is an Integer equal to 256, Chr(I) produces the same result as Chr(0). The example displays the alphabet by cycling I through the ASCII values for the letters A through Z.

See also
Ord

Example
```
program XChr;
var
  I: Byte;
begin
  Writeln('A programmer''s ABCs:');
  for I := 65 to 90 do
    Write(Chr(I));
  Writeln
end.
```

Circle

Syntax
```
procedure Circle(X, Y: Integer; Radius: Word);
```

Location
Graph

Description
Circle draws an unfilled circle with its center at coordinate (X, Y). The Radius equals the radius of the circle in pixels adjusted for the display's aspect ratio. Use SetColor to change the color of the circle.

The example draws a bull's-eye by increasing the radius until the circle fills about half of the display.

See also
Arc, Ellipse, GetArcCoords, PieSlice, Sector, SetAspectRatio

Example
```
program XCircle;
uses Crt, Graph;
var
  GraphDriver, GraphMode: Integer;
  Radius, XMax, YMax, Color: Integer;
begin
  GraphDriver := Detect;
  InitGraph(GraphDriver, GraphMode, 'c:\tp\bgi');
  XMax := GetMaxX;
  YMax := GetMaxY;
  Radius := 10;
  Color := 0;
  while Radius < (XMax div 4) do
  begin
    SetColor(Color mod 16);   { Set drawing color }
    Circle(XMax div 2, YMax div 2, Radius);  { x, y, radius }
    Radius := Radius + 5;      { Increase circle size }
    Color := Color + 1         { Change colors }
  end;
  repeat until Keypressed;
  CloseGraph
end.
```

ClearDevice

Syntax
```
procedure ClearDevice;
```

Location
Graph

Description
Call ClearDevice to erase the graphics screen (or to reset another graphics device).
When erasing the display, ClearDevice resets the current point (CP) to (0, 0) in the
upper-left corner.

Run the example and press Enter to clear the screen with ClearDevice. Notice
that this changes CP to (0, 0), the starting point for the first random line drawn in
the **repeat** loop. Press Esc to quit.

See also
ClearViewPort, CloseGraph, GraphDefaults, SetGraphMode

Example
```
program XClearDevice;
uses Crt, Graph;
```

```
var
  GraphDriver, GraphMode: Integer;
  CMax, XMax, YMax: Integer;
  Done : Boolean; Ch: Char;
begin
  Writeln('Press <Esc> to halt; <Enter> to clear device');
  Write('Press <Enter> now to begin...');
  Readln;
  GraphDriver := Detect;
  InitGraph(GraphDriver, GraphMode, 'c:\tp\bgi');
  XMax := GetMaxX;
  YMax := GetMaxY;
  CMax := GetMaxColor;
  Done := False;
  repeat
    SetColor(Random(CMax));
    LineTo(Random(XMax), Random(YMax));
    if Keypressed then
    begin
      Ch := ReadKey;
      if Ch = Chr(13) then ClearDevice
      else Done := (Ch = Chr(27))
    end
  until Done;
  CloseGraph
end.
```

ClearViewPort

Syntax
```
procedure ClearViewPort;
```

Location
Graph

Description
ClearViewPort erases the viewport to the current background color (which is set by SetBkColor) and resets the current point (CP) to (0, 0) in the upper-left corner of the viewport window.

In general, when clearing the entire screen, use the faster ClearDevice instead of ClearViewPort. Use ClearViewPort only to clear windows that are not open to the entire display.

See also
ClearDevice, GetViewSettings, SetViewPort

Example
```pascal
program XClearViewPort;
uses Crt, Graph;
const
  Message = 'Press Enter to ClearViewPort...';
var
  GraphDriver, GraphMode: Integer;
  XMax, YMax: Integer;
begin
  GraphDriver := Detect;
  InitGraph(GraphDriver, GraphMode, 'c:\tp\bgi');
  XMax := GetMaxX;
  YMax := GetMaxY;
  SetColor(Yellow);
  Line(0, 0, XMax div 2, YMax div 2);
  OutTextXY(0, YMax - TextHeight(Message), Message);
  repeat until ReadKey = CHR(13);
  ClearViewPort;
  OutText('<-- CP is here');
  OutTextXY(0, YMax-TextHeight('M'), 'Press Enter to quit');
  repeat until ReadKey = CHR(13);
  CloseGraph
end.
```

Close

Syntax
```pascal
procedure Close(var F: <file>);
```

Location
System

Description
Close cancels all input or output to file F and writes to disk any modified data held in memory. To avoid losing data, after writing to a file, always Close the file variable before ending your program.

The example opens text file Tf to XCLOSE.PAS. After reading and displaying the lines from the file, the program closes Tf. Because it is an error to close a file that is already closed, or a file that never was opened, the second Close produces

```
Runtime error 103: File not open.
```

This differs from earlier versions of Turbo Pascal, which allowed you to close a closed file.

See also
Append, Assign, IoResult, Reset, Rewrite

Example
```
program XClose;
var
  Tf: Text;
  S: string;
begin
  Assign(Tf, 'XCLOSE.PAS');  { Open this text file }
  Reset(Tf);
  while not Eof(Tf) do
  begin
    Readln(Tf, S);
    Writeln(S)    { Display text from file }
  end;
  Close(Tf);  { Close tf when done using the file }
  Writeln;
  Writeln('File is closed');
  Close(Tf)    { This produces runtime error 103 }
end.
```

CloseGraph

Syntax
```
procedure CloseGraph;
```

Location
Graph

Description
CloseGraph reverses what InitGraph does, removing the graphics driver from memory and returning the display to a text mode. Use CloseGraph when your program is completely finished displaying graphics.

The example displays a red circle and waits for you to press Enter. It then calls CloseGraph to remove the graphics driver from memory before displaying the message, "End of program."

See also
DetectGraph, GetGraphMode, InitGraph, RestoreCrtMode, SetGraphMode

Example

```
program XCloseGraph;
uses Graph;
var
  GraphDriver, GraphMode: Integer;
begin
  GraphDriver := Detect;
  InitGraph(GraphDriver, GraphMode, 'c:\tp\bgi');
  SetColor(4);              { Set drawing color }
  Circle(175, 85, 100);    { x, y, radius }
  Readln;                  { Pause }
  CloseGraph;              { End graphics display }
  Writeln('End of program')
end.
```

ClrEol

Syntax

```
procedure ClrEol;
```

Location

Crt

Description

ClrEol clears the display from the cursor position to the end of the line, or to the rightmost border of the current window. After clearing, the cursor returns to its original position.

The example fills the screen with x characters and then uses ClrEol to clear a space for you to enter your name. Clearing areas on the screen to let people type something in them is a typical use for the procedure.

See also

ClrScr, TextBackground, Window

Example

```
program XClrEol;
uses Crt;
var
  I, J: Integer;
  S: string;
begin
  for I := 1 to 24 do
    for J := 1 to 80 do
      Write('x');
```

```
    Gotoxy(10, 10);
    Write('Enter your name: ');
    ClrEol;
    Readln(S)
end.
```

ClrScr

Syntax
```
procedure ClrScr;
```

Location
Crt

Description
ClrScr erases the entire display or current window and places the cursor at the home position in the upper-left corner.

The example first calls ClrScr to erase the display and return the cursor to the home position. It then fills the screen with x characters and asks you to press Enter to end the program. The last two statements show a typical way to end programs, calling ClrScr and repositioning the cursor so that the DOS prompt appears on the bottom line of a blank screen.

See also
ClrEol, TextBackground, Window

Example
```
program XClrScr;
uses Crt;
var
  I, J: Integer;
begin
  ClrScr;              { Erase display and "home" the cursor }
  for I := 1 to 24 do      { Fill screen with x characters }
    for J := 1 to 80 do
      Write('x');
  Writeln;
  Write('Press <Enter> to end program...');
  Readln;
  ClrScr;              { Erase display }
  GotoXY(1, 25)    { Position cursor on bottom line }
end.
```

Concat

Syntax
```
function Concat(S1, S2, ... , Sn: <string>): string;
```

Location
System

Description
Concat concatenates, or joins, strings S1, S2, ..., Sn—which can be string variables, literal strings, or single characters—into a single string. Programs can assign the resulting string to a string variable or pass the result (by value only) as a parameter to another function or procedure.

Assigning the result of Concat to a string variable does not produce an error if the result is longer than the declared variable length. Concat automatically clips the result to fit in the variable.

Instead of using Concat, you can join strings with plus signs. There are two good reasons for using Concat, though. First, many other Pascal compilers have a Concat function but few allow the plus sign alternative. Second, Concat makes it obvious that you are adding strings together. A string expression such as A + B + C might appear to be adding values when it is actually concatenating strings, which could lead to confusion when you or someone else reads the program.

See also
Copy, Delete, Insert, Length, Pos

Example
```
program XConcat;
var
  S, S1, S2, S3, S4: string;
begin
  S1 := 'what goes ';
  S2 := 'up ';
  S3 := 'must come ';
  S4 := 'down ';
  Writeln(Concat(S1, S2, S3, S4));
  S := Concat(S1, S4, S3, S2);
  Writeln(S);
  S := S4 + S3 + S1 + S2;
  Writeln(S)
end.
```

Copy

Syntax
```
function Copy(S: <string>; Index, Len: Integer): string;
```

Location
System

Description
Copy returns a string containing Len characters from string S, beginning at character S[Index]. If there are fewer than Len characters from S[Index] to the end of the string, Copy returns only as many characters as it can.

See also
Concat, Delete, Insert, Length, Pos

Example
```pascal
program XCopy;
var
  S: string;
begin
  S := 'Mastering Turbo Pascal';
  Writeln(Copy(S, 6, 4));    { writes ring }
  S := Copy(S, 17, 6);
  Writeln(S)                 { writes Pascal }
end.
```

Cos

Syntax
```
function Cos(R: <real>): <real>;
```

Location
System

Description
Cos returns the cosine of R in radians. Use the function in the example to convert angles to radians.

See also
ArcTan, Sin

Example
```pascal
program XCos;
  var Angle: Integer;
```

```
function Radians(Angle : Integer) : Real;
begin
  Radians := Abs(Angle mod 360) * Pi / 180.0
end;

begin
  Angle := 0;
  while (Angle < 360) do
  begin
    Writeln('Angle=', Angle:3, ' Cos in radians=',
      Cos(Radians(Angle)):8:3);
    Angle := Angle + 15
  end
end.
```

CSeg

Syntax
```
function CSeg: Word;
```

Location
System

Description
CSeg returns the value of the code segment register CS equal to the segment address of the currently executing code. Remember that programs and units have their own code segments. Therefore, CSeg can be different depending on which section of the program is running.

The example displays the first 16 bytes from the program's own code segment. It does this by assigning to byte pointer P the value of CSeg as the segment address plus integer I as the offset. The Write statement then displays the byte values in decimal from addresses CS:0000 to CS:000F.

Because the actual address of the code segment is not known until the program runs, CSeg cannot be used in Absolute declarations.

See also
DSeg, Ptr, Seg, SSeg

Example
```
program XCSeg;
var
  P: ^Byte;
  I: Integer;
```

```
begin
  for I := 0 to 15 do
  begin
    P := Ptr(CSeg, I);
    Write(P^:4)
  end;
  Writeln
end.
```

Dec

Syntax

```
procedure Dec(var N: <ordinal> [; Count: LongInt]);
```

Location
System

Description
Dec subtracts one (or an optional Count) from an integer, character, Boolean, or enumerated variable. Given an integer variable N, the following statements are logically identical:

```
N := N - 1;     { Subtract 1 from N }
Dec(N);         { Subtract 1 from N }
```

Using Dec is faster than using the equivalent expression because of the way Turbo Pascal compiles the two statements. The expression, $N := N - 1$, compiles to the assembly language commands

```
MOV AX, [0000]      ; N := N - 1
DEC AX
MOV [0000],AX
```

In other words, the variable at N's address, represented here by 0000, is first moved into a register (AX). The register is decremented by one, and the result is stored back in the variable in memory. With Dec, Turbo Pascal reduces these three commands to one faster instruction, which is

```
DEC Word Ptr[0000]   ; N := N - 1
```

In Turbo Pascal 6.0, Dec can decrement typed pointers. For example, suppose you have a pointer P that addresses an array A of type-AnyRec records. The statements

```
P := @A[1];  { P addresses record at A[1] }
Dec(P);      { P addresses record at A[0] }
```

assign the address of A[1] (the second record in the array) to P, then decrement P to address the first record at A[0]. For statements like Dec(P), Turbo Pascal subtracts

N from the pointer P, where N equals Sizeof(P ^)—in other words, the size in bytes of the type addressed by P. Similarly, the expression Dec(P, 4) reduces P by (Sizeof(P ^) * 4) bytes.

See also
Inc, Pred, Succ

Example
```
program XDec;
var
  I: Integer;
begin
  I := 10;
  while I > 0 do
  begin
    Writeln(I);
    Dec(I)
  end
end.
```

Delay

Syntax
```
procedure Delay(MS: Word);
```

Location
Crt

Description
Delay pauses the program for approximately MS milliseconds (0.001 second). Delay(1000) pauses for about one second. The value of MS can range from 0 (no delay) to 65535 (about 65.5 seconds).

The accuracy of the delay depends on the accuracy of the computer's internal clock, which on most systems is no better than about $\pm$ 0.12 second. Because of this, delays of less than $\frac{1}{4}$ second (Delay(250)) are probably unreliable.

The example uses Delay to count off 10 seconds. Because Delay is initialized by a software timing loop, delays are independent of computer processor speed.

See also
GetTime, SetTime

Example
```
program XDelay;
uses Crt;
var
  I: Integer;
```

```
begin
  Write('Press return to begin...');
  Readln;
  for I := 1 to 10 do
  begin
    Delay(1000);
    Write(I:4)
  end;
  Writeln
end.
```

Delete

Syntax
```
procedure Delete(var S: <string variable>; Index, Len: Integer);
```

Location
System

Description
Delete removes Len characters from string S, starting at Index. If there are fewer than Len characters from Index to the end of the string, Delete chops off the string's end.

See also
Concat, Copy, Insert, Length, Pos

Example
```
program XDelete;
var
  S: string;
begin
  S := 'Mastering Turbo Pascal';
  Delete(S, 1, 16);               { s='Pascal' }
  Writeln(S);
  Delete(S, Pos('s', S), 3);  { s='Pal' }
  Writeln(S);
  Delete(S, 2, 128);              { s='P' }
  Writeln(S)
end.
```

DelLine

Syntax
```
procedure DelLine;
```

Location
Crt

Description
Call DelLine to delete one text line at the cursor location in the current window, moving up any lines below and blanking the bottom line of the display. After deleting a line, the cursor position does not change.

The example displays 24 numbered lines and positions the cursor on line 10. Press the Enter key to delete 10 lines and notice how the lines below move up.

See also
InsLine, Window

Example
```
program XDelLine;
uses Crt;
var
  I: Integer;
  Ch: Char;
begin
  ClrScr;
  for I := 1 to 24 do
    Writeln('This is line number ', I);
  GotoXY(1, 10);
  for I := 1 to 10 do
  begin
    Ch := Readkey;    { Pause for any keypress }
    DelLine            { Delete line at cursor }
  end
end.
```

DetectGraph

Syntax
```
procedure DetectGraph(var GraphDriver, GraphMode: Integer);
```

Location
Graph

Description

Call DetectGraph to determine whether the computer supports graphics and, if so, which GraphDriver is appropriate to use. As the example demonstrates, pass the results returned by DetectGraph to InitGraph, selecting a graphics display appropriate for this system. You also have the option of changing GraphMode to select a different mode for this driver.

If function GraphResult does not equal grOK after calling InitGraph, it is either not possible to display graphics on this system or one or more of Turbo Pascal's graphics driver files are missing (see Chapter 11).

The example shows how to write graphics programs that work on most systems, selecting a graphics mode and drawing a circle, or writing the message "No graphics available" if the computer cannot display graphics.

See also

CloseGraph, GraphResult, InitGraph

Example

```
program XDetectGraph;
uses Crt, Graph;
var
  GraphDriver, GraphMode: Integer;
  XMax, YMax: Word;
begin
  DetectGraph(GraphDriver, GraphMode);
  InitGraph(GraphDriver, GraphMode, 'c:\tp\bgi');
  if GraphResult <> GrOK then
    Writeln('No graphics available')
  else begin      { Draw a circle }
    XMax := GetMaxX;
    YMax := GetMaxY;
    SetColor(3);
    Circle(XMax div 2, YMax div 2, XMax div 4);
    repeat until Keypressed;
    CloseGraph
  end
end.
```

DiskFree

Syntax

```
function DiskFree(Drive: Byte): LongInt;
```

Location

Dos

Description

DiskFree tells you how many bytes are available on a disk in a drive. The disk can be a floppy disk, a hard drive, a RAM disk, or any other type of drive.

The Drive parameter selects a disk drive according to this scheme: 0 equals the current drive, 1 equals drive A:, 2 equals drive B:, and so on. If DiskFree does not recognize a Drive value, it returns −1.

Use DiskFree to determine if files will fit on a disk. For example, a copy program might call DiskFree and, if there is not enough room available to transfer a file from another drive, ask for a blank disk.

Compile the example to FREE.EXE and type FREE at the DOS prompt to find out how much space remains on the current disk. Type FREE d, in which d is a drive letter (A, B, C, and so on), to find out how much space remains on a different drive.

See also
DiskSize

Example

```pascal
program XDiskFree;
uses Dos;
var
  Drive: Byte;
  S: string;
begin
  if ParamCount = 0 then
    Drive := 0   { Use current drive if none other specified }
  else begin
    S := ParamStr(1);
    Drive := 1 + Ord(UpCase(S[1])) - Ord('A')
  end;
  Writeln(DiskFree(Drive), ' bytes free')
end.
```

DiskSize

Syntax
```pascal
function DiskSize(Drive: Byte): LongInt;
```

Location
Dos

Description

DiskSize returns the total number of bytes on a disk drive, including both occupied space and free space. Set parameter Drive to 0 for the current drive, 1 for drive A:, 2 for drive B:, and so on. DiskSize returns −1 if it does not recognize the Drive parameter you specify.

The example shows how to use DiskSize along with DiskFree to report the total size of a disk, the number of available bytes, and the number of bytes occupied by files. Compile the program to DISKSIZE.EXE and type DISKSIZE for a report of the current drive. Type DISKSIZE d, in which d is a drive letter (A, B, C, and so on), for a report of a different drive.

See also
DiskFree

Example

```pascal
program XDiskSize;
uses Dos;
var
  Drive: Byte;
  S: string;
  TotalSize, FreeBytes: LongInt;
begin
  if ParamCount = 0 then
    Drive := 0   { Use current drive if none other specified }
  else begin
    S := ParamStr(1);
    Drive := 1 + Ord(UpCase(S[1])) - Ord('A')
  end;
  TotalSize := DiskSize(Drive);
  FreeBytes := DiskFree(Drive);
  Writeln('Bytes on disk  = ', TotalSize:8);
  Writeln('Bytes free     = ', FreeBytes:8);
  Writeln('Bytes occupied = ', TotalSize - FreeBytes:8)
end.
```

Dispose

Syntax

```pascal
procedure Dispose(P: <pointer>);
procedure Dispose(P: <pointer>, D: <destructor>);
```

Location
System

Description
Dispose deallocates memory occupied by the variable that is addressed by P. Other dynamic variables on the heap are undisturbed. The deallocated space will be used, if possible, for future variables created by New.

Turbo Pascal attempts to minimize the number of separate disposed memory blocks by combining adjacent disposed bytes. If you dispose two variables that are physically next to each other, the heap manager combines their bytes into a single block.

An extended form of Dispose handles cleanup chores for dynamic objects addressed by pointers (see the second syntax definition). Such objects most often have *destructor* methods that perform various duties just before disposing the space occupied by objects. For example, a destructor might unlink an object from a list of other objects, or it might transfer the information in an object to another variable.

The primary purpose of the extended Dispose is to call an object's destructor and to dispose of the correct amount of memory occupied by an object instance. If an object named OType is addressed by a pointer OPtr, and if that object has a destructor named AllDone, a single statement calls AllDone and disposes the object's memory.

```
Dispose(OPtr, AllDone);
```

When called this way, Dispose will call the AllDone destructor for the object instance addressed by OPtr. The destructor can then take other actions to dispose variables that belong to an object before that object is itself disposed.

See Chapter 15 for more information on object-oriented programming concepts. The example shows the more traditional way to call Dispose. First, the program displays how much free memory is available on the heap. Next, it creates a dynamic string variable and displays how much memory remains. The program then calls Dispose to dispose the variable, thus reclaiming the space it occupied. Finally, a Writeln statement shows the amount of free space now available, which, due to the Dispose statement, should be equal to the value reported when the program began.

See also
FreeMem, GetMem, Mark, New, Release

Example
```
program XDispose;
var
  P: ^string;
begin
  Writeln('Memory at start of program = ', Memavail);
  New(P);          { Create a string variable on the heap }
  P^ := 'This string is on the heap.';  { Assign string }
  Writeln(P^);   { Display string }
  Writeln('Memory before dispose = ', Memavail);
  Dispose(P);    { Reclaim used heap space }
  Writeln('Memory after dispose  = ', Memavail)
end.
```

DosExitCode

Syntax
```
function DosExitCode: Word;
```

Location
Dos

Description
DosExitCode retrieves the value passed to a parent program from a child process that was started by Exec. If you end a child process with Halt(N), you can retrieve N with DosExitCode.

The function result is composed of two byte values. The low-order byte represents the value passed to Halt by a child process. The high-order byte is 0 if the child process terminated normally, 1 if a user pressed Ctrl-C to end the program, 2 if a device error forced the program to end, or 3 if Keep ended a program that is to remain resident in memory. Use the Lo function to extract DosExitCode's low-order byte; use the Hi function to extract the high-order byte.

Compile the first example program to disk. Then compile and run the second example program, which calls the first. Enter a test value, which will be passed to Halt and examined by the second program.

> **Note:** Running the example programs and pressing Ctrl-C to end XExitTest returns 255 in the high-order value of DosExitCode, not the value described in Turbo Pascal's documentation. Apparently, DosExitCode's return result isn't entirely trustworthy.

See also
Exec, Exit, Hi, Keep, Lo

Example
```
{$M 1024, 0, 0}
program XExitTest;
var
  N: Word;
begin
  Write('Halt with what value? ');
  Readln(N);
  Halt(N)
end.

{$M 1024, 0, 0 }
program XDosExitCode;
uses Dos;
```

```
var
  Code: Word;
begin
  Exec('xExitTest.EXE', '');
  Writeln;
  Writeln('Back in xDosExitCode');
  Code := DosExitCode;
  Writeln('DosExitCode = ', Code);
  Writeln('High byte  = ', Hi(Code));
  Writeln('Low byte   = ', Lo(Code))
end.
```

DosVersion

Syntax
```
function DosVersion: Word;
```

Location
Dos

Description
Call DosVersion for the current DOS version number. The function returns the result as a 16-bit word with the major version number in the low byte and the minor revision number in the high byte. The second Writeln statement in the example displays the current DOS version with the help of the Lo and Hi functions, which extract the individual bytes from the full word value.

See also
Hi, Lo, MsDos

Example
```
program XDosVersion;
uses Crt, Dos;
var
  Version: Word;
begin
  Version := DosVersion;
  Writeln('DosVersion value = ', Version);
  Writeln('DOS version is ',
    Lo(Version), '.', Hi(Version))
end.
```

DrawPoly

Syntax
```
procedure DrawPoly(NumPoints: Word; var PolyPoints);
```

Location
Graph

Description
Use DrawPoly to connect a series of coordinates stored in an array of PointType records. This is faster and easier than using separate Line or LineTo commands to do the same thing.

Parameter NumPoints should equal the number of PointType records stored in PolyPoints. Because PolyPoints is not typed, the array can be as large as needed.

The example shows how to use DrawPoly. Array PolyPoints holds the coordinates of three points on a triangle in the center of the display. We need four array records to close the triangle, drawing each of the three sides and returning to the starting place. After preparing the array, DrawPoly connects the dots. Change the 4 to 3 in DrawPoly to see why you need four array records instead of three array records to draw a triangle.

See also
FillPoly, SetColor, SetLineStyle, SetWriteMode

Example
```
program XDrawPoly;
uses Crt, Graph;
var
  GraphDriver, GraphMode: Integer;
  XMax, YMax, XMaxD4, YMaxD4: Word;
  PolyPoints: array[1 .. 4] of PointType;
begin
  DetectGraph(GraphDriver, GraphMode);
  InitGraph(GraphDriver, GraphMode, 'c:\tp\bgi');
  XMax := GetMaxX;
  YMax := GetMaxY;
  XMaxD4 := XMax div 4;
  YMaxD4 := YMax div 4;
  PolyPoints[1].X := XMaxD4;
  PolyPoints[1].Y := YMaxD4;
  PolyPoints[2].X := XMax - XMaxD4;
  PolyPoints[2].Y := YMaxD4;
  PolyPoints[3].X := XMax div 2;
  PolyPoints[3].Y := YMax - YMaxD4;
  PolyPoints[4] := PolyPoints[1];
  SetColor(12);
```

```
    DrawPoly(4, PolyPoints);    { Connect coordinates }
    repeat until Keypressed;
    CloseGraph
  end.
```

DSeg

Syntax
```
function DSeg: Word;
```

Location
System

Description
DSeg returns the value of the data segment register DS. This equals the segment address where program and unit global variables are stored in memory. Programs can have only one data segment totaling a maximum of 65,520 bytes. The example uses DSeg to assign addresses to pointer P, displaying the first 16 bytes of the program's data segment.

Because the actual address of the data segment is not known until the program runs, DSeg cannot be used in Absolute declarations.

See also
CSeg, Ptr, Seg, SSeg

Example
```
program XDSeg;
var
  P: ^Byte;
  I: Integer;
begin
  for I := 0 to 15 do
  begin
    P := Ptr(DSeg, I);
    Write(P^:4)
  end;
  Writeln
end.
```

Ellipse

Syntax
procedure Ellipse(X, Y: Integer; StAngle, EndAngle: Word; XRadius, YRadius: Word);

Location
Graph

Description
Ellipse draws a full or partial oval or circular outline. Set StAngle to 0 and EndAngle to 360 to display a closed outline. Set the two variables to other values in the range of 0 to 360 to draw arcs. Parameters X and Y anchor the center of the oval to this coordinate on the display. Words XRadius and YRadius specify the width and height of the oval.

When XRadius equals YRadius, unless your display's aspect ratio is 1.0, Ellipse might not draw a perfectly round circle as you would expect. Lopsided circles are typically caused by pixels that are not perfectly square, but the problem might also be due to an improperly adjusted display. See GetAspectRatio for more information about a display's aspect ratio. See SetAspectRatio for instructions about changing the Graph unit's aspect ratio to account for a display's irregularities.

The example draws successive and overlapping ovals in various colors. The first Ellipse varies the XRadius parameter. The second varies YRadius.

See also
Arc, Circle, FillEllipse, GetAspectRatio, PieSlice, Sector, SetAspectRatio

Example
```
program XEllipse;
uses Crt, Graph;
var
  GraphDriver, GraphMode: Integer;
  XMax, YMax, Radius: Integer;
begin
  GraphDriver := Detect;
  InitGraph(GraphDriver, GraphMode, 'c:\tp\bgi');
  XMax := GetMaxX;
  YMax := GetMaxY;
  Radius := 10;
  while Radius < YMax div 2 do
  begin
    SetColor(1 + Abs(Random(MaxColors)));
    Ellipse(XMax div 2, YMax div 2,
      0, 360, Radius, 50);
    Ellipse(XMax div 2, YMax div 2,
      0, 360, 50, Radius);
```

```
      Radius := Radius + 10
    end;
    repeat until Keypressed;
    CloseGraph
  end.
```

EnvCount

Syntax
```
function EnvCount: Integer;
```

Location
Dos

Description
Call EnvCount for the number of strings in the DOS environment, which stores RAM variables such as PATH and PROMPT. To set an environment variable, use the SET command. For example, typing SET TMP=\E: sets the TMP environment variable equal to the string \E:. Most people place such commands in their AUTOEXEC.BAT file to enable various settings at boot time. (See the EnvStr function for more information about reading environment variables.)

The sample displays current environment variables and calculates the total amount of space occupied, adding to this the number of strings to account for the null (ASCII 0) separators between variables, plus 1 for the extra null at the end of the DOS environment block.

See also
EnvStr, FSearch, GetEnv

Example
```
program XEnvCount;
uses Crt, Dos;
var
  I, NumStrings: Integer;
  TotalSize: LongInt;
begin
  NumStrings := EnvCount;
  TotalSize := 0;
  for I := 1 to NumStrings do
  begin
    Writeln(EnvStr(I));
    TotalSize := TotalSize + Length(EnvStr(I))
  end;
  Writeln;
```

```
            TotalSize := 1 + TotalSize + NumStrings;
            Writeln(Totalsize, ' byte(s) in ', NumStrings, ' variables')
        end.
```

EnvStr

Syntax
```
function EnvStr(Index: Integer): string;
```

Location
Dos

Description
Call EnvStr with Index equal to an environment variable's position in the DOS environment block. If the value of Index is not within the range of 1 .. EnvCount, EnvStr returns a null (zero-length) string.

Programs can use EnvStr along with EnvCount to search for a particular environment variable that is initialized by the DOS SET command. The example program demonstrates this by searching for and displaying the setting of the PATH variable (if found).

See also
EnvCount, FSearch, GetEnv

Example
```
program XEnvStr;
uses Crt, Dos;
var
  I: Integer;
  Found: Boolean;
begin
  Found := False;
  while (I <= EnvCount) and (not Found) do
  begin
    if Pos('PATH', EnvStr(I)) = 1
      then Found := True
      else Inc(I)
  end;
  if not Found then
    Writeln('No PATH variable found')
  else begin
    Writeln('Value of PATH is:');
    Writeln(Copy(EnvStr(I), 6, 255))
  end
end.
```

Eof

Syntax

```
function Eof(var F: <file>): Boolean;
```

Location
System

Description
Eof returns true after a Read or Readln statement reads the last element of data in a file. In the special case of a disk text file, Eof is true when reaching a Ctrl-Z (ASCII 26) character. This fact is important only when you are processing text files, as the example demonstrates.

See also
Eoln, SeekEof

Example

```
program XEof;
var
  Tf: Text;
  Ch: Char;
begin
  Assign(Tf, 'XEOF.PAS');
  Reset(Tf);
  while not Eof(Tf) do
  begin
    Read(Tf, Ch);
    Write(Ch)
  end;
  Close(Tf)
end.
```

Eoln

Syntax

```
function Eoln(var F: Text): Boolean;
```

Location
System

Description
Eoln returns true when it reaches the end of a line in a text file (F). Use Eoln when processing text one character at a time in programs that need to know where the ends of lines are.

The example is the same as the example for Eof. This time, the program uses Eoln to add an extra blank line, resulting in double-spaced text.

See also
Eof, SeekEoln

Example
```pascal
program XEoln;
var
  Tf: Text;
  Ch: Char;
begin
  Assign(Tf, 'XEOLN.PAS');
  Reset(Tf);
  while not Eof(Tf) do
  begin
    if Eoln(Tf)
      then Writeln;  { Add extra blank line }
    Read(Tf, Ch);
    Write(Ch)
  end;
  Close(Tf)
end.
```

Erase

Syntax
```pascal
procedure Erase(var F: <file>);
```

Location
System

Description
Erase permanently erases file F from the disk directory. Before erasing, use Assign to give F a name. If the file is open, close it before erasing. Erasing an open file is a poor programming practice and can cause bugs. File F can be any type of file, but it is usually untyped.

The example erases its own backup file, XERASE.BAK, or displays an error message if the file does not exist. Notice how {$I–} and {$I+} surround Erase to allow the program to check IoResult *after* erasing. If the result is zero, then the file was successfully erased. Otherwise, an error occurred—probably because the file does not exist.

See also
Assign, IoResult, Rename

Example

```
program XErase;
const FileName = 'XERASE.BAK';
var
  F: file;
begin
  Write(FileName);
  Assign(F, 'XERASE.BAK');
   {$I-} Erase(F); {$I+}
  if IoResult = 0
    then Writeln(' erased')
    else Writeln(' does not exist')
end.
```

Exec

Syntax

```
procedure Exec(Path, CmdLine: string);
```

Location

Dos

Description

A program calls Exec to load and run another program, which is called a child process. The original program—the parent—is suspended while the child runs.

The first string parameter, Path, specifies the path and file name of the child process to run. The second string parameter, CmdLine, contains a command to pass to the child program, similar to an argument you type on the DOS command line.

Before using Exec, you must allow enough memory for the child process. The best way to do this is to use the {$M} directive at the start of the program. The example sets three memory parameters—the stack, minimum heap value, and maximum heap value—to 1024 bytes. This limits the amount of space reserved for the parent program, leaving room for the child process.

One of the most common uses for Exec is to perform DOS commands from inside a Turbo Pascal program. As the example shows, Exec makes it easy to display directories by starting COMMAND.COM as a child process and passing it a command such as DIR *.*. The /C in the CmdLine string tells DOS that this is a second copy of COMMAND.COM.

Another use for Exec is to divide a large program into pieces and then call each piece as a child process under the control of a parent. This gives the illusion that a single monster program is running, when in fact the beast is composed of many smaller demons.

See also
DosExitCode, Halt, SwapVectors

Example
```
{$M 1024, 0, 0}
program XExec;
uses Dos;
begin
  Writeln('Press return for directory...');
  Readln;
  Exec(GetEnv('COMSPEC'), '/C DIR *.*');
  Writeln;
  Writeln('Back from exec...');
end.
```

Exit

Syntax
```
procedure Exit;
```

Location
System

Description
Exit leaves the current block. If the block is nested inside other blocks, the next outer block begins running at the statement following the one that activated the block that contains Exit. If a procedure or function exits, the next statement to run is the one following the statement that called the procedure or function. If the main program exits, the program ends immediately.

The example uses two Exit statements. The first Exit ends the program after displaying a message if you do not type a file name, as in XEXIT XEXIT.PAS. The second Exit ends the program if the file you name isn't on disk.

When exiting a program, it's possible to have Turbo Pascal automatically call a custom routine as part of the sequence of events that occurs before returning to DOS. See Chapter 13 for details.

See also
Halt

Example
```
program XExit;
var
  Tf: Text;
  S: string;
begin
```

```
    if ParamCount = 0 then
    begin
      Writeln('Type XEXIT <file> to list a text file');
      Exit
    end;
    Assign(Tf, ParamStr(1));
    {$I-} Reset(Tf); {$I+}
    if IoResult <> 0 then
    begin
      Writeln('Cannot find ', ParamStr(1));
      Exit
    end;
    while not Eof(Tf) do
    begin
      Readln(Tf, S);
      Writeln(S)
    end;
    Close(Tf)
  end.
```

Exp

Syntax
```
  function Exp(R: <real>): <real>;
```

Location
System

Description
Exp returns the exponential of R, equal to *e* raised to the power of R. The value of *e* is 2.7182818285, the base of the natural logarithms.

  The example demonstrates how to use Exp to calculate the return on an investment compounded "continuously," as some banks advertise. The program works because when R is the interest rate, *eR* equals the yearly amount of the investment per dollar, compounded continuously. (Ref: Knuth, D. E., *Fundamental Algorithms. The Art of Computer Programming,* Volume 1, Second Edition. Reading, Mass.: Addison-Wesley, 1968, p. 23.)

See also
Ln

Example
```
  program XExp;
  var
```

```
    Amount, Investment, Rate: Real;
    Years: Integer;
begin
  Write('Amount invested yearly?');
  Readln(Amount);
  Write('Interest rate? (e.g. 0.09 = 9%) ');
  Readln(Rate);
  Write('How many years? ');
  Readln(Years);
  Investment := 0;
  while Years > 0 do
  begin
    Investment := (Investment + Amount) * Exp(Rate);
    Years := Years - 1
  end;
  Writeln('Investment at end of period = $', Investment:0:2)
end.
```

Fail

Syntax
```
procedure Fail;
```

Location
System

Description
Use Fail to exit an object's constructor method, usually when GetMem or New return **nil**, which indicates an out-of-memory error. For this to work, you must install a HeapFunc function. (See HeapFunc in this chapter.)

If New created the object instance on the heap, Fail deallocates the object's memory space. If the object instance is a plain Pascal variable, Fail does not have this effect. In most cases, just before calling Fail, you should call the object's destructor (if it has one) to clean up any partially allocated variables addressed by pointer data fields in the object. This is a typical OOP strategy, but it isn't strictly required.

When constructors are used as Boolean functions, Fail causes the function to return false. If the constructor ends normally (without calling Fail), the constructor returns true.

See also
Dispose, HeapFunc, New

Example

> **Note:** For a complete object-oriented example, see Program 15-7, ListFailDemo. The constructor implementation Init from that program is repeated here, showing how to use Fail.

```
constructor StrObj.Init(SS: string);
begin
  Item.Init;
  GetMem(S, Length(SS) + 1);
  if S = nil then
  begin          { Out of memory! }
    Done;        { Deal locate string object s pointer }
    Fail         { Exit and dispose object instance }
  end else
    S^ := SS;    { Assign string to heap space }
end;
```

FExpand

Syntax
```
function FExpand(Path: PathStr): PathStr;
```

Location
Dos

Description
Function FExpand returns a PathStr string expanded to include the drive letter and any subdirectories for another PathStr, usually a file name. The Dos unit defines PathStr as **string**[79].

The function is particularly useful in programs that let people change directories (perhaps by executing ChDir). Because the current directory may change, the program needs to know the complete path name to various files.

The example program displays the current directory, expanding all file names to include disk drive letters and subdirectory names.

See also
FindFirst, FindNext, FSearch, FSplit

Example
```
program XFExpand;
uses Dos;
var
  Sr: SearchRec;
```

```
begin
  Writeln;
  FindFirst('*.*', 0, Sr);
  while DosError = 0 do
  begin
    Writeln(FExpand(Sr.Name));
    FindNext(Sr)
  end;
  Writeln
end.
```

FilePos

Syntax
```
function FilePos(var F: <untyped file>¦<typed file>): LongInt;
```

Location
System

Description
FilePos returns the current file pointer position, or record number, of open file F. The file may not be type Text. It can be a file of Char.

FilePos equals the LongInt number of the record that will be affected by the next read or write. On an untyped file, FilePos returns the number of the next 128-byte block or other size disk block to be processed. On a typed file, FilePos returns the number of the next file element to be processed. After resetting a file, FilePos always returns 0, the record number of the first element in all files.

One use for FilePos is to back up one or more records from the current position. For example, suppose a program reads ten records out of a file. To back up to record number 9, use the statement

```
Seek(F, FilePos(F) - 2);
```

To read the same record again, Seek to FilePos(F) – 1. To advance to a certain record beyond the current one, add a positive integer to FilePos in a similar Seek statement. The example demonstrates this idea by creating a file of 100 integers, seeking to 50, and then backing up to 40.

See also
FileSize, Reset, Seek

Example
```
program XFilePos;
var
  F: file of Integer;
  I: Integer;
```

```
begin
  Assign(F, 'TEST.DAT');
  Rewrite(F);
  for I := 1 to 100 do
    Write(F, I);
  Seek(F, 49);
  Read(F, I);
  Writeln('Should equal 50 -- ', I);
  Seek(F, FilePos(F) - 11);
  Read(F, I);
  Writeln('Should equal 40 -- ', I);
  Close(F)
end.
```

FileSize

Syntax
```
function FileSize(var F: <untyped file>¦<typed file>): LongInt;
```

Location
System

Description
Use FileSize to determine how many records there are in file F. The file may not be type Text. On an untyped file, FileSize returns the number of 128-byte blocks or other size disk blocks in the file. On a typed file, FileSize returns the number of records the file contains.

   The example shows how to use FileSize to prepare for appending new records to the end of an existing file. The program writes 100 integers to disk, closes and reopens the file, appends another 100 integers, and displays the results. This works because the first component of all files is numbered zero. Seeking FileSize(f), therefore, positions the file pointer just after the last record or to an empty file's beginning.

See also
FilePos, IoResult

Example
```
program XFileSize;
var
  F: file of Integer;
  I: Integer;
begin
  Assign(F, 'TEST.DAT');
  Rewrite(F);
```

```
    for I := 1 to 100 do        { Create 100-integer file }
      Write(F, I);
    Close(F);                    { Close file }
    Reset(F);                    { Reopen file }
    Seek(F, FileSize(F));        { Prepare to append records }
    for I := 1 to 100 do         { Append another 100 integers }
      Write(F, I);
    Reset(F);                    { Display file contents }
    while not Eof(F) do
    begin
      Read(F, I);
      Write(I:4)
    end;
    Close(F)
  end.
```

FillChar

Syntax
```
procedure FillChar(var V; N: Word; C: <ordinal>);
```

Location
System

Description
FillChar fills N bytes of variable V of any type with bytes or characters C. If V is an array, it can be indexed to indicate where to begin filling; otherwise, the starting point is the first byte of V. Technically, V can be a file variable, although filling files with values is a poor and perhaps dangerous practice.

Turbo Pascal does not check whether you fill too many bytes. Filling beyond the size of your variable overwrites portions of memory, which probably destroys data, your program, or both. Use the Sizeof function as shown in the example to avoid this problem.

One use for FillChar is to zero an array—in other words, to fill an array with zero bytes. The example shows how to do this to an array of 100 integers. The second FillChar fills the same array with the value 2, setting all of the two-byte integer array values to 514. This seemingly odd result occurs because FillChar operates on bytes, not on integers or any other data type. Assigning 2 to each of the two bytes that make up an integer gives the integer the value 514. Therefore, filling an integer array with 2s effectively assigns 514 to every integer in the array.

See also
Move

Example

```
program XFillChar;
var
  A: array[1 .. 100] of Integer;
  I: Integer;
begin
  FillChar(A, Sizeof(A), 0);
  Writeln('After filling with 0:');
  Writeln;
  for I := 1 to 100 do
    Write(A[I]:4);
  Writeln;
  FillChar(A, Sizeof(A), 2);
  Writeln;
  Writeln('After filling with 2:');
  Writeln;
  for I := 1 to 100 do
    Write(A[I]:4);
  Writeln
end.
```

FillEllipse

Syntax

```
procedure FillEllipse(X, Y: Integer; XRadius, YRadius: Word);
```

Location

Graph

Description

Similar to Ellipse, FillEllipse draws a filled ellipse with the center at (X, Y), with the width equal to (XRadius * 2) and the height equal to (YRadius * 2). Unlike Ellipse, FillEllipse can't draw partial ovals (arcs).

Call SetColor to change the outline color of a filled ellipse. Call SetFillPattern or SetFillStyle to change fill patterns and colors as the example demonstrates.

See also

Arc, Circle, Ellipse, GetAspectRatio, PieSlice, Sector, SetAspectRatio, SetFillStyle

Example

```
program XFillEllipse;
uses Crt, Graph;
var
  GraphDriver, GraphMode: Integer;
  X, Direction, Count, XMax, YMax: Integer;
```

```
begin
  GraphDriver := Detect;
  InitGraph(GraphDriver, GraphMode, 'c:\tp\bgi');
  XMax := GetMaxX;
  YMax := GetMaxY;
  X := 20;
  Direction := 1;
  Count := 5;
  Randomize;
  SetColor(White);
  repeat
    if (X > XMax-50) or(X <= 0) then
    begin
      Direction := Direction * -1;
      Count := Count + 5
    end;
    SetFillStyle(Random(12), 1 + Abs(Random(MaxColors)));
    FillEllipse(X, YMax div 2,
      Count + Random(XMax div 6),
      Count + Random(YMax div 4));
    X := X + (50 * Direction)
  until Keypressed;
  CloseGraph
end.
```

FillPoly

Syntax
```
procedure Fillpoly(NumPoints: Word; var PolyPoints);
```

Location
Graph

Description
After creating a polygon—an array of coordinate points—call FillPoly to fill the enclosed shape with a certain pattern and color. Parameter NumPoints specifies how many (X, Y) coordinates are in array PolyPoints.

   The example creates polygons of 13 points selected at random. It draws the polygon outline with DrawPoly and then fills the shape with FillPoly. The result resembles Japanese origami, the art of folding paper into birds and other animals and figures. Press any key to stop the demonstration.

See also
DrawPoly, GetFillSettings, GetLineSettings, GraphResult, SetFillPattern, SetFillStyle, SetLineStyle

Example

```pascal
program XFillPoly;
uses Crt, Graph;
const
  NumPoints = 13;
  Pat: FillPatternType =
    ($11, $22, $44, $88, $11, $22, $44, $88);
var
  GraphDriver, GraphMode: Integer;
  XMax, YMax, I: Integer;
  PolyPoints: array[1 .. NumPoints] of PointType;
begin
  GraphDriver := Detect;
  InitGraph(GraphDriver, GraphMode, 'c:\tp\bgi');
  XMax := GetMaxX;
  YMax := GetMaxY;
  Randomize;
  repeat
    ClearViewPort;
    for I := 1 to NumPoints do    { Create random polygon }
    begin
      PolyPoints[I].X := ABS(Random(XMax));
      PolyPoints[I].Y := ABS(Random(YMax))
    end;
    PolyPoints[NumPoints] := PolyPoints[1];  { Complete shape }
    SetColor(1 + Random(MaxColors));
    DrawPoly(NumPoints, PolyPoints);    { Connect the dots }
    SetFillPattern(Pat, 1 + Random(MaxColors));
    FillPoly(NumPoints, PolyPoints);    { Fill polygon }
    Delay(1500)    { Pause between screens }
  until Keypressed;
  CloseGraph
end.
```

FindFirst

Syntax
```pascal
procedure FindFirst(Path: string; Attr: Word; var SR: SearchRec);
```

Location
Dos

Description
FindFirst locates the first file name entry in a disk directory matching various attributes. See FindNext for details on how to use this procedure.

See also
FindNext

Example
See the example for FindNext.

FindNext

Syntax
```
procedure FindNext(var SR: SearchRec);
```

Location
Dos

Description
FindNext and FindFirst locate file name entries in disk directories. The example explains the proper way to use the two procedures to display a listing of the files on disk.

The first step is to call FindFirst, passing a string, an attribute value, and a SearchRec variable (SR here). The string can be anything you normally would type after a DOS DIR command. For example, 'C:\TPAS*.PAS' locates all the files ending in PAS in the TPAS subdirectory on drive C:. The integer attribute can be zero or any of the following:

```
ReadOnly   =   $01
Hidden     =   $02
SysFile    =   $04
VolumeID   =   $08
Directory  =   $10
Archive    =   $20
AnyFile    =   $3F
```

A zero attribute locates all normal files on disk—the same files that a DOS DIR command displays. A nonzero attribute locates only files with matching attributes. The special value $3F finds all files regardless of their attributes.

You can combine attributes for special purposes. For example, Archive + ReadOnly locates only files with both the archive and read-only bits turned on in their attribute values.

Both FindFirst and FindNext fill a SearchRec record with the result of searching the disk directory. This record is defined in the Turbo Pascal Dos unit as

```
SearchRec = record
  Fill: array[1 .. 21] of Byte;
  Attr: Byte;
  Time: Longint;
  Size: Longint;
  Name: string[12];
end;
```

DOS initializes the Fill array when you call FindFirst and then uses the array contents for each subsequent call to FindNext. Field Attr is the attribute byte for this file entry. The Time represents the date and time the file was most recently changed. The Size equals the size of the file in bytes. Finally, the Name string is the name of the file, with an extension if there is one.

Notice how the example examines DosError, an integer variable in the Dos unit. If DosError is not zero after either FindFirst or FindNext, all entries have been located and the directory search can end.

See also
FindFirst

Example
```
program XFind;
uses Dos;
const
  Blank = ' ';    { One blank character }
var
  Sr: SearchRec;
begin
  Writeln;
  FindFirst('*.*', 0, Sr);
  while DosError = 0 do
  begin
    with Sr do
      Write(Name, Blank:16 - Length(Name));
    FindNext(Sr)
  end;
  Writeln
end.
```

FloodFill

Syntax
```
procedure FloodFill(X, Y: Integer; Border: Word);
```

Location

Graph

Description

FloodFill paints an enclosed shape with the color and pattern set by SetFillStyle or SetFillPattern. Assign to parameters X and Y the coordinate values of any pixel inside the shape. This location is called the seed—the place where filling begins. Assign to Border the current color value (0 to 15) of the shape's outline.

If the shape's outline is broken, the paint will leak into the areas around the shape. If the outline is a different color than Border specifies, FloodFill will ignore the shape's outline.

The example draws an oval inside a box. Press Enter to fill the space around the ellipse with light cyan. Press Enter again to fill the oval with red. Notice how SetFillPattern tells the graphics kernel to use the constant named Pat, making a kind of herringbone brush for painting rather than a solid color, which is the normal fill pattern.

See also

FillPoly, SetFillPattern, SetFillStyle

Example

```
program XFloodFill;
uses Crt, Graph;
const
  Pat: FillPatternType =
    ($11, $22, $44, $88, $88, $44, $22, $11);
  OutlineColor = Yellow;
var
  GraphDriver, GraphMode: Integer;
  Cx, Cy, XMaxD4, YMaxD4, XMax, YMax: Integer;

  procedure Box(X1, Y1, X2, Y2 : Integer);
  begin
    MoveTo(X1, Y1);
    LineTo(X2, Y1); LineTo(X2, Y2);
    LineTo(X1, Y2); LineTo(X1, Y1)
  end;

begin
  GraphDriver := Detect;
  InitGraph(GraphDriver, GraphMode, 'c:\tp\bgi');
  XMax := GetMaxX;
  YMax := GetMaxY;
  XMaxD4 := XMax div 4;
  YMaxD4 := YMax div 4;
  Cx := XMax div 2;
  Cy := YMax div 2;
```

```
  SetColor(OutlineColor);
  Box(XMaxD4, YMaxD4, XMax - XMaxD4, YMax - YMaxD4);
  Ellipse(Cx, Cy, 0, 360, XMaxD4 div 2, YMaxD4 div 2);
{ Fill space around the ellipse }
  Readln;
  SetFillPattern(Pat, LightCyan);
  FloodFill(XMaxD4 + 1, YMaxD4 + 1, OutlineColor);
{ Fill space inside the ellipse }
  Readln;
  SetFillPattern(Pat, Red);
  FloodFill(Cx, Cy, OutlineColor);
  repeat until Keypressed;
  CloseGraph
end.
```

Flush

Syntax
```
procedure Flush(var F: Text);
```

Location
System

Description
Flush writes buffered sectors from open text file F to disk. When you write information to disk files, Turbo Pascal and DOS save the information in memory buffers. Only when these buffers become full does DOS send the information on its way to disk. Flushing the file writes to disk all the characters temporarily held in memory.

See also
Append, Rewrite

Example
```
program XFlush;
var
  F: Text;
  Ch: Char;
begin
  Assign(F, 'TEST.TXT');
  Rewrite(F);
  for Ch := 'A' to 'Z' do  { Data saved in disk buffer }
    Write(F, Ch);
  Flush(F)        { Data safe if power should fail }
end.
```

Frac

Syntax
```
function Frac(R: <real>): <real>;
```

Location
System

Description
Frac returns the value of real number R minus its whole number part. For example, Frac(Pi) equals 0.14159.

See also
Int, Round

Example
```
program XFrac;
var
  R: Real;
  I: Integer;
begin
  for I := 1 to 20 do
  begin
    R := Random + Random * 100;
    Writeln('R=', R:8:4, '  Frac(R)=', Frac(R):7:4)
  end
end.
```

FreeMem

Syntax
```
procedure FreeMem(var P: <pointer>; Len: Word);
```

Location
System

Description
FreeMem deallocates Len heap bytes addressed by P. It assumes that P addresses a variable containing at least Len bytes. Deallocating more than that number of bytes could cause serious bugs.

Usually, employ FreeMem after reserving memory on the heap with GetMem. After using the reserved memory, call FreeMem to make the bytes available for other uses. This is similar to the way Dispose deallocates variables created on the heap, although with FreeMem it's up to you to specify the number of bytes to free.

See also
Dispose, GetMem, New

Example
```
program XFreeMem;
var
  P: ^Real;
begin
  Writeln('MemAvail before GetMem  : ', MemAvail);
  GetMem(P, 10);  { More than enough room }
  Writeln('MemAvail after GetMem   : ', MemAvail);
  P^ := Pi;
  Writeln('Value on heap=', P^);
  Writeln('MemAvail before FreeMem : ', MemAvail);
  FreeMem(P, 10); { Deallocate p^ }
  Writeln('MemAvail after FreeMem  : ', MemAvail)
end.
```

FSearch

Syntax
```
function FSearch(Path: PathStr; DirList: string): PathStr;
```

Location
Dos

Description
FSearch searches a list of directories specified by DirList for a file name in Path. The most common use of FSearch is to search multiple directories for a specific file. For example, if the current PATH environment variable is C:\TP;C:\TD;C:\DOS, passing that string to FSearch with path equal to TPC.CFG locates that file if it exists in any of the listed directories.

The example uses GetEnv to retrieve the current value of the PATH environment variable, passing this value to FSearch to look for TPC.CFG among all PATH directories.

Be aware that the result of FSearch locates only the first occurrence of a file. It does not locate multiple copies of files with the same names.

See also
FExpand, FSplit, GetEnv

Example
```
program XFSearch;
uses Crt, Dos;
const
```

```
        CONFIG = 'TPC.CFG';
    var
      FileName: PathStr;
    begin
      FileName := FSearch(CONFIG, GetEnv('PATH'));
      if Length(FileName) > 0
        then Writeln(FExpand(FileName))
        else Writeln(CONFIG, ' not found')
    end.
```

FSplit

Syntax
```
    procedure FSplit(Path: PathStr; var Dir: DirStr;
      var Name: NameStr; var Ext: ExtStr);
```

Location
Dos

Description
In programs that keep track of file names, it's often necessary to separate a path specification like C:\TP\MYPROG.PAS into its various parts. FSplit makes this easy to do. Pass the original path name in the first parameter, path. The results are returned in the other parameters—the directory name in dir, the file name in name, and the file extension in ext. The Dos unit defines the data types for these parameters.

Run the example program and enter the name of any file in the current directory. (XFSPLIT.PAS is a good choice if you saved the program by that name.) The program calls FExpand to expand the plain file name before calling FSplit to extract the various parts for display.

Notice that the example carefully checks whether the file exists before calling FExpand. This is necessary because FExpand merely assumes that the specified file exists in the current directory.

See also
FExpand, FindFirst, FindNext, FSearch

Example
```
    program XFSplit;
    uses Crt, Dos;
    var
      Path: PathStr;
      Dir: DirStr;
      Name: NameStr;
      Ext: ExtStr;
      F: file;
```

```
begin
  Write('Enter a file name: ');
  Readln(Path);
  Assign(F, Path);
  {$I-} Reset(F); {$I+}
  if IoResult <> 0 then
    Writeln('File not found')
  else begin
    Path := FExpand(Path);
    FSplit(Path, Dir, Name, Ext);
    Writeln('Path : ', Path);
    Writeln('Dir  : ', Dir);
    Writeln('Name : ', Name);
    Writeln('Ext  : ', Ext)
  end
end.
```

GetArcCoords

Syntax
```
procedure GetArcCoords(var ArcCoords: ArcCoordsType);
```

Location
Graph

Description
Immediately after drawing a semicircle with Arc, call GetArcCoords for the (X, Y) coordinates of the arc's center and two end points. The procedure takes a variable of type ArcCoordsType defined in Graph as

```
ArcCoordsType = record
  X, Y: Integer;
  XStart, YStart: Integer;
  XEnd, YEnd: Integer
end;
```

Coordinate (X, Y) is the center of the circle of which the arc is a part. (XStart, YStart) equals the starting point, and (XEnd, YEnd) equals the ending point of the arc.

The example marks the three coordinates with Xs of different colors: red for the center, blue for the start, and green for the end points.

See also
Arc, Circle, Ellipse, PieSlice, Sector

Example

```
program XGetArcCoords;
uses Crt, Graph;
var
  GraphDriver, GraphMode: Integer;
  XMax, YMax: Integer;
  ArcCoords: ArcCoordsType;

  procedure DrawX(X, Y : Integer);
  begin
    Line(X - 5, Y, X + 5, Y);
    Line(X, Y - 5, X, Y + 5)
  end;

begin
  GraphDriver := Detect;
  InitGraph(GraphDriver, GraphMode, 'c:\tp\bgi');
  XMax := GetMaxX;
  YMax := GetMaxY;
  SetColor(Yellow);
  Arc(XMax div 2, YMax div 2, 45, 135, YMax div 4);
  GetArcCoords(ArcCoords);
  with ArcCoords do
  begin
    SetColor(Red); DrawX(X, Y);
    SetColor(Blue); DrawX(XStart, YStart);
    SetColor(Green); DrawX(XEnd, YEnd)
  end;
  repeat until Keypressed;
  CloseGraph
end.
```

GetAspectRatio

Syntax
```
procedure GetAspectRatio(var XAsp, YAsp: Word);
```

Location
Graph

Description
Because individual display dots (pixels) are not perfectly square, horizontal and vertical lines of the same number of pixels can appear to be different lengths. The

aspect ratio of a graphics device, usually the display, accounts for this difference, allowing you to draw perfectly square boxes and round circles.

The example shows how to use GetAspectRatio. The procedure returns two Word values, XAsp and YAsp. Dividing floating point equivalents of XAsp by YAsp calculates the real number ratio. This result tells how many pixels to draw horizontally to equal the visual length of a vertical line a certain number of pixels long.

After these calculations, the example sets YLen to 100, the length of the vertical lines the program eventually will draw. This value divided by the aspect ratio equals XLen, the number of pixels to draw horizontal lines. Finally, the program uses XLen and YLen to display a yellow box. Because the program accounts for the display's aspect ratio, the box is perfectly square—or as nearly perfect as possible.

For an experiment, set ratio to 1.0 instead of to the result of the floating point division. When you run the modified program, the box probably will not be square.

See also
Arc, Circle, Ellipse, GetMaxX, GetMaxY, SetAspectRatio

Example

```
program XGetAspectRatio;
uses Crt, Graph;
var
  GraphDriver, GraphMode: Integer;
  XLen, YLen, XMax, YMax: Integer;
  XAsp, YAsp: Word;
  Ratio: Real;

  function Float(N: LongInt): Real;
  begin
    Float := N
  end;

begin
  GraphDriver := Detect;
  InitGraph(GraphDriver, GraphMode, 'c:\tp\bgi');
  XMax := GetMaxX;
  YMax := GetMaxY;
  GetAspectRatio(XAsp, YAsp);
  Ratio := Float(XAsp) / Float(YAsp);
  SetColor(Yellow);
  Xlen := Trunc(100.0 / Ratio);    { Adjust xlen }
  Ylen := 100;
  Line(0, 0, Xlen, 0);                    { Draw box }
  Line(Xlen, 0, Xlen, Ylen);
  Line(Xlen, Ylen, 0, Ylen);
  Line(0, Ylen, 0, 0);
```

```
    repeat until Keypressed;
    CloseGraph
end.
```

GetBkColor

Syntax
```
function GetBkColor: Word;
```

Location
Graph

Description
GetBkColor returns the color value of the graphics background. When a graphics program starts, the background color normally is black. Use SetBkColor to change the background color.

    The example shows one way to use GetBkColor. Drawing a filled bar in a color equal to GetBkColor plus one guarantees that the pattern is never the same color as the background. Drawings done in the background color are invisible. In your own programs, whenever the color of the background might change, use a similar technique to make sure that objects you draw over various background colors are visible.

See also
GetColor, GetPalette, SetAllPalette, SetBkColor, SetColor, SetPalette, SetRGBPalette

Example
```
program XGetBkColor;
uses Crt, Graph;
var
  GraphDriver, GraphMode: Integer;
  XMax, YMax, XMaxD4, YMaxD4: Integer;
begin
  GraphDriver := Detect;
  InitGraph(GraphDriver, GraphMode, 'c:\tp\bgi');
  XMax := GetMaxX;
  YMax := GetMaxY;
  XMaxD4 := XMax div 4;
  YMaxD4 := YMax div 4;
  while not Keypressed do
  begin
    SetBkColor(Random(MaxColors));
    SetFillStyle(XHatchFill, GetBkColor + 1);
    Bar(XMaxD4, YMaxD4, XMax - XMaxD4, YMax - YMaxD4);
```

```
        Delay(1000)
      end;
      CloseGraph
    end.
```

GetCBreak

Syntax
```
  procedure GetCBreak(var Break: Boolean);
```

Location
Dos

Description
Execute GetCBreak to determine the current state of the DOS Ctrl-Break switch. Pass a Boolean variable (CtrlBreak in the example program) to GetCBreak. You can then examine the switch by inspecting the variable or toggle the setting on and off (see the SetCBreak procedure).

When Ctrl-Break checking is on, pressing the Ctrl-Break keys immediately ends a program at the next DOS system call. When Ctrl-Break checking is off, pressing these keys ends the program only during console and auxiliary (serial communications) I/O and printer output. (Normally, Ctrl-Break checking should be off. Turn it on only for debugging purposes.)

See also
SetCBreak

Example
```
  program XGetCBreak;
  uses Crt, Dos;
  var
    CtrlBreak: Boolean;
  begin
    GetCBreak(CtrlBreak);
    Writeln('Control-Break checking is: ', CtrlBreak);
  end.
```

GetColor

Syntax
```
  function GetColor: Word;
```

Location
Graph

Description

Use GetColor to discover the current drawing color. Normally, the drawing color is white (15), unless you changed colors by calling procedure SetColor.

The example is similar to the program for GetBkColor. This time the drawing color varies at random, creating rectangle outlines of various hues. To ensure visible outlines, the program changes the background color to GetColor + 1.

See also

GetBkColor, GetPalette, SetAllPalette, SetColor, SetPalette, SetRGBPalette

Example

```
program XGetColor;
uses Crt, Graph;
var
  GraphDriver, GraphMode: Integer;
  XMax, YMax, XMaxD4, YMaxD4: Integer;
begin
  GraphDriver := Detect;
  InitGraph(GraphDriver, GraphMode, 'c:\tp\bgi');
  XMax := GetMaxX;
  YMax := GetMaxY;
  XMaxD4 := XMax div 4;
  YMaxD4 := YMax div 4;
  while not Keypressed do
  begin
    SetLineStyle(SolidLn, SolidFill, ThickWidth);
    SetColor(1 + Random(MaxColors));
    Rectangle(XMaxD4, YMaxD4, XMax - XMaxD4, YMax - YMaxD4);
    SetBkColor(GetColor + 1);
    Delay(1000)
  end;
  CloseGraph
end.
```

GetDate

Syntax

```
procedure GetDate(var Year, Month, Day, DayOfWeek: Word);
```

Location

Dos

Description

GetDate reads the current system date, which is correct only if your computer has a hardware clock or if you set the date manually after booting.

After calling GetDate, Year equals the current year, for example 1989 or 2001, requiring no correction. The month is a value from 1 (January) to 12 (December). The day equals the day of the month. DayOfWeek equals 0 for Sunday, 1 for Monday, and so on, up to 6 for Saturday.

By using GetDate's values as indexes to variable string array constants, the example displays the date in the form: Tue 20-Oct-1987.

See also
GetTime, SetDate, SetTime

Example

```
program XGetDate;
uses Dos;
const
  days: array[0 .. 6] of string[3] =
    ('Sun', 'Mon', 'Tue', 'Wed', 'Thu', 'Fri', 'Sat');
  months: array[1 .. 12] of string[3] =
    ('Jan', 'Feb', 'Mar', 'Apr', 'May', 'Jun', 'Jul',
     'Aug', 'Sep', 'Oct', 'Nov', 'Dec');
var
  Year, Month, Day, Dayofweek: Word;
begin
  GetDate(Year, Month, Day, Dayofweek);
  Writeln(Days[Dayofweek], ' ', Day,
    '-', Months[Month], '-', Year)
end.
```

GetDefaultPalette

Syntax
```
procedure GetDefaultPalette(var Palette: PaletteType);
```

Location
Graph

Description
After calling InitGraph, the Graph unit initializes a default palette record of type PaletteType. This record has two fields, Size of type Byte, equal to the number of palette entries, and Colors, an array of ShortInt values. The value at Colors[0] represents the background color. The values at Colors[1 .. Size −1] represent all available pixel colors.

Use GetDefaultPalette to make a copy of the default palette saved by the Graph unit. After doing this, you can modify the palette values, perhaps calling SetAllPalette to change colors instantly on the screen. You can restore the saved palette later. The example shows how to do this, displaying an animated globe that reminds me of those hanging crepe paper decorations you see at parties.

See also

GetPalette, SetAllPalette, SetPalette, SetRGBPalette

Example

```pascal
program XGetDefaultPalette;
uses Crt, Graph;
var
  GraphDriver, GraphMode: Integer;
  I, J, XMax, YMax: Integer;
  NewPalette, SavedPalette: PaletteType;
begin
  GraphDriver := Detect;
  InitGraph(GraphDriver, GraphMode, 'c:\tp\bgi');
  XMax := GetMaxX;
  YMax := GetMaxY;
  I := 1;
  J := 1;
  GetDefaultPalette(SavedPalette);
  NewPalette := SavedPalette;
  while I < YMax div 2 do
  begin
    Delay(100);
    SetColor(1 + (J mod(NewPalette.Size - 1)));
    Ellipse(XMax div 2, YMax div 2, 0, 360, I, YMax div 3);
    Inc(I, 4);
    Inc(J)
  end;
  while not Keypressed do with NewPalette do
  begin
    Delay(100);
    J := Colors[Size - 1];
    for I := Size - 1 downto 1 do
      Colors[I] := Colors[I - 1];
    Colors[1] := J;
    SetAllPalette(NewPalette)
  end;
  SetAllPalette(SavedPalette);
  CloseGraph
end.
```

GetDir

Syntax
```
procedure GetDir(Drive: Byte; var Path: string);
```

Location
System

Description
GetDir returns path equal to the current directory in Drive. Drive 0 represents the current disk drive and directory—the one that typing the DOS DIR command would list. Drive 1 stands for drive A:, 2 for B:, 3 for C:, and so on.

The example displays the current path on the current drive and on drive A:. Insert a formatted diskette into drive A: before running this program.

See also
ChDir, DiskFree, DiskSize, GetEnv, MkDir, RmDir

Example
```
program XGetDir;
var
  S: string;
begin
  GetDir(0, S);
  Writeln('Current path ........... ', S);
  GetDir(1, S);
  Writeln('Path on drive A: ....... ', S)
end.
```

GetDriverName

Syntax
```
function GetDriverName: string;
```

Location
Graph

Description
To display the name of the current graphics driver, first call InitGraph as you normally do to initialize graphics, then call the string function GetDriverName. The example program demonstrates how the function works, assigning its result to a string variable S, which is displayed before the program ends.

See also
GetModeName, InitGraph

Example

```
program XGetDriverName;
uses Crt, Graph;
var
  GraphDriver, GraphMode: Integer;
  S: string;
begin
  GraphDriver := Detect;
  InitGraph(GraphDriver, GraphMode, 'c:\tp\bgi');
  if GraphResult <> GrOk then
    Writeln('No graphics')
  else begin
    S := GetDriverName;
    CloseGraph;
    Writeln('Graphics driver is: ', S)
  end
end.
```

GetEnv

Syntax

```
function GetEnv(EnvVar: string): string;
```

Location

Dos

Description

Function GetEnv returns a string equal to the value of the environment variable
EnvVar. To use the function, pass EnvVar equal to the name of the environment
variable you want to inspect—for example, PATH or TMP—as in the example, which
sets string path to the value of the COMSPEC environment variable. The example
then uses this information to change to the directory that contains COMMAND.COM,
which is probably C:\ or A:\.

See also

EnvCount, EnvStr

Example

```
program XGetEnv;
uses Crt, Dos;
var
  Path: PathStr;
  Dir: DirStr;
  Name: NameStr;
  Ext: ExtStr;
```

```
begin
  Writeln('Changing to COMMAND.COM directory...');
  Path := GetEnv('COMSPEC');
  FSplit(Path, Dir, Name, Ext);
  if (Length(Dir) > 3) and (Dir[Length(Dir)] = '\') then
    Delete(Dir, Length(Dir), 1);
  ChDir(Dir);
  GetDir(0, Dir);
  Writeln('Directory is ', Dir)
end.
```

GetFAttr

Syntax
```
procedure GetFAttr(var F; var Attr: Word);
```

Location
Dos

Description
GetFAttr returns the attribute value stored along with file names in disk directories. By examining the attribute, you can find out if a file name is a subdirectory, if it was recently backed up, if it is a system or hidden file, or combinations of these and other attributes.

Before using GetFAttr, assign a file name to any file variable. Then pass the file variable (F) and a Word variable (Attr) to GetFAttr. The file does not have to be open. When GetFAttr ends, Attr will equal the attribute of the file.

The example shows how to use GetFAttr along with one of several constants defined in the Dos unit. **And**ing Attr with one or more constants makes it easy to tell if this file has specific attributes. In addition to Archive, you can use the attributes: readOnly, hidden, sysFile, volumeID, and directory. For example, use an **if** statement like this to identify a read-only, hidden file:

```
if Attr and (readOnly + hidden)
  then { File has read-only, hidden attributes }
```

See also
GetFTime, SetFAttr, SetFTime

Example
```
program XGetFAttr;
uses Dos;
var
  F: file;
  Attr: Word;
  Name: string;
```

```
begin
  Write('File name? ');
  Readln(Name);
  if Length(Name) > 0 then
  begin
    Assign(F, Name);
    GetFAttr(F, Attr);
    if DosError <> 0 then
      Writeln('Error reading file')
    else begin
      Writeln('Attribute = ', Attr);
      if Attr and Archive = 0
        then Writeln('File is backed up')
        else Writeln('File is not backed up')
    end
  end
end.
```

GetFillPattern

Syntax
```
procedure GetFillPattern(var FillPattern: FillPatternType);
```

Location
Graph

Description
After changing fill patterns with SetFillPattern, call GetFillPattern to preserve the fill pattern array. The procedure takes a variable defined in Graph as

```
FillPatternType = array[1 .. 8] of Byte;
```

Use GetFillPattern to preserve the current fill pattern when changing to a new setting. Then pass the saved array to SetFillPattern to restore the original pattern. The example displays the default pattern contents, which are an array of eight bytes equal to 255, or $FF in hexadecimal.

See also
GetFillSettings, SetFillPattern, SetFillStyle

Example
```
program XGetFillPattern;
uses Crt, Graph;
var
  GraphDriver, GraphMode: Integer;
  Pattern: FillPatternType;
```

```
  I: Byte;
begin
  GraphDriver := Detect;
  InitGraph(GraphDriver, GraphMode, 'c:\tp\bgi');
  GetFillPattern(Pattern);
  CloseGraph;
  Writeln('Fill pattern:');
  for I := 1 to 8 do
    Writeln('Pattern[', I, '] = ', Pattern[I])
end.
```

GetFillSettings

Syntax
```
procedure GetFillSettings(var FillInfo: FillSettingsType);
```

Location
Graph

Description
Call GetFillSettings to find out the current line-drawing pattern and color. Pass a FillSettingsType record to GetFillSettings. This record has the structure

```
FillSettingsType = record
  Pattern: Word;
  Color: Word
end;
```

See also
FillPoly, GetFillPattern, SetFillPattern, SetFillStyle

Example
```
program XGetFillSettings;
uses Crt, Graph;
var
  GraphDriver, GraphMode: Integer;
  Fst: FillSettingsType;
begin
  GraphDriver := Detect;
  InitGraph(GraphDriver, GraphMode, 'c:\tp\bgi');
  GetFillSettings(Fst);
  CloseGraph;
  with Fst do
  begin
    Writeln('Pattern = ', Pattern);
```

```
          Writeln('Color   = ', Color)
       end
    end.
```

GetFTime

Syntax
```
procedure GetFTime(var F; var Time: LongInt);
```

Location
Dos

Description
Call GetFTime for any open file (F) to set Time to the encoded date and time the file
was created or most recently closed. Unlike GetFAttr, GetFTime requires the file to
be open.

See also
PackTime, SetFAttr, SetFTime, UnpackTime

Example
```
program XGetFTime;
uses Dos;
type
  Str2 = string[2];
var
  F: file;
  Name: string;
  Time: LongInt;
  DateNtime: DateTime;

  function D2(N: Integer): Str2;
  var
    S: Str2;
  begin
    Str(N:2, S);
    if N < 10 then S[1] := '0';
    D2 := S
  end;

begin
  Write('File name? ');
  Readln(Name);
  if Length(Name) > 0 then
```

```
begin
  Assign(F, Name);
  Reset(F);
  GetFTime(F, Time);
  if DosError <> 0 then
    Writeln('Error reading file')
  else begin
    Writeln('Time value = ', Time);
    UnpackTime(Time, Datentime);
    with Datentime do
      Writeln(
        'Date = ', D2(Month), '/', D2(Day), '/', Year,
        ' Time = ', D2(Hour), ':', D2(Min), '.', D2(Sec))
  end;
  Close(F)
end
end.
```

GetGraphMode

Syntax
```
function GetGraphMode: Integer;
```

Location
Graph

Description
GetGraphMode returns a value representing the computer's video graphics mode. You can use this value to switch back to graphics after switching to a text display.

The example first initializes graphics in the usual way, draws a box, displays a message, and waits for you to press Enter. It then switches to a text display by calling RestoreCrtMode. Just before the switch, the program calls GetGraphMode, saving the current graphics mode in OldMode. After you again press Enter, the program restores the original graphics display by passing OldMode to SetGraphMode.

When you run the program the first time, the box color is light magenta. When the program returns to the original graphics display, though, the box is white. This demonstrates that switching to a previous graphics mode reinitializes drawing colors and does not preserve any objects on display.

See also
DetectGraph, RestoreCrtMode, SetGraphMode

Example
```
program XGetGraphMode;
```

```
uses Graph;
var
  GraphDriver, GraphMode: Integer;
  Oldmode: Integer;
begin
  GraphDriver := Detect;
  InitGraph(GraphDriver, GraphMode, 'c:\tp\bgi');
  SetColor(LightMagenta);
  Rectangle(100, 100, 150, 150);
  Writeln('This is the graphics page');
  Write('Press <Enter>...');
  Readln;
  Oldmode := GetGraphMode;
  RestoreCrtMode;
  Writeln('This is on the text page');
  Write('Press <Enter>...');
  Readln;
  SetGraphMode(Oldmode);
  Rectangle(100, 100, 150, 150);
  Writeln('Back on the graphics page');
  Write('Press <Enter>...');
  Readln;
  CloseGraph
end.
```

GetImage

Syntax
```
procedure GetImage(X1, Y1, X2, Y2: Integer; var BitMap);
```

Location
Graph

Description
GetImage copies a portion of the graphics screen into a variable, usually an array of bytes. The captured image's upper-left corner is at coordinate (X1, Y1) and its lower-right corner is at (X2, Y2). The pixels from this image are copied into the BitMap variable along with width and height information.

It is important to understand that pixels and not bits are copied by GetImage. Because the number of memory bits that a pixel occupies depends on the graphics mode, you cannot precalculate image sizes in bits unless you are writing a program for a fixed video mode.

Most of the time, call ImageSize to reserve enough memory for an image, storing the pixels on the heap as the example shows. Pointer Image addresses an array of an unknown number of bytes. The program calls GetMem to reserve ImageSize bytes on the heap. If this works (Image is not **nil**), the program saves a portion of the display in the reserved heap space. Finally, the program replicates the saved image by calling PutImage, filling the screen with an interesting plaid pattern.

See also
ImageSize, PutImage

Example

```
program XGetImage;
uses Crt, Graph;
const
  X1 = 100; Y1 = 100; X2 = 227; Y2 = 163;
type
  ByteArray = array[0 .. 0] of Byte;
  ByteArrayPtr = ^ByteArray;
var
  GraphDriver, GraphMode: Integer;
  XMax, YMax: Integer;
  X, Y, XSize, YSize, I: Integer;
  Image: ByteArrayPtr;
begin
  GraphDriver := Detect;
  InitGraph(GraphDriver, GraphMode, 'c:\tp\bgi');
  XMax := GetMaxX;
  YMax := GetMaxY;
  Randomize;
  for I := 1 to 100 do
  begin  { Draw a few lines at random }
    SetColor(1 + Random(MaxColors));
    LineTo(Random(XMax), Random(YMax))
  end;
  GetMem(Image, ImageSize(X1, Y1, X2, Y2));  { Reserve memory }
  if Image <> nil then
  begin
    GetImage(X1, Y1, X2, Y2, Image^);  { Copy display image }
    ClearViewPort;
    XSize := Succ(X2 - X1);
    YSize := Succ(Y2 - Y1);
    X := 0;
    while X < XMax do
    begin
      Y := 0;
      while Y < YMax do
      begin
        PutImage(X, Y, Image^, NormalPut);  { Replicate image }
```

```
            Y := Y + YSize
        end;
        X := X + XSize
      end
    end;
    repeat until Keypressed;
    CloseGraph
end.
```

GetIntVec

Syntax
```
procedure GetIntVec(IntNo: Byte; var Vector: Pointer);
```

Location
Dos

Description
GetIntVec assigns to a pointer variable the address of a hardware or software interrupt, called a *vector.* The example sets CharPtr to the address of interrupt $1F. It then displays the first 130 bytes stored at that location. In this case, the data is not an interrupt routine but the bit patterns that make up part of the graphics character set stored in ROM.

See also
SetIntVec

Example
```
program XGetIntVec;
uses Dos;
type
  ByteArray = array[0 .. 0] of Byte;
var
  CharPtr: Pointer;
  I: Integer;
begin
  GetIntVec($1F, CharPtr);  { Get address of interrupt $1F }
  for I := 1 to 130 do
    Write(ByteArray(CharPtr^) [I]:8);
  Writeln
end.
```

GetLineSettings

Syntax
```
procedure GetLineSettings(var LineInfo: LineSettingsType);
```

Location
Graph

Description
Call GetLineSettings to assign to fields in a LineSettingsType record the current line drawing style, pattern, and thickness. These are either the default values or the values most recently passed to SetLineStyle.

The example displays the line settings for the computer's default graphics display.

See also
SetLineStyle

Example
```
program XGetLineSettings;
uses Graph;
var
  GraphDriver, GraphMode: Integer;
  LineInfo: LineSettingsType;
begin
  GraphDriver := Detect;
  InitGraph(GraphDriver, GraphMode, 'c:\tp\bgi');
  GetLineSettings(LineInfo);
  with LineInfo do
  begin
    Writeln('Default line settings');
    Writeln('Line Style = ', LineStyle);
    Writeln('Pattern    = ', Pattern);
    Writeln('Thickness  = ', Thickness);
    Writeln;
    Write('Press Enter...');
    Readln
  end;
  CloseGraph
end.
```

GetMaxColor

Syntax
```
function GetMaxColor: Word;
```

Location
Graph

Description
The range 0 .. GetMaxColor includes all the color values you can pass to SetColor in the current graphics mode. GetMaxColor + 1 equals the total number of colors available, including the background color number, 0.

The example fills the screen (except the background) with horizontal and vertical lines in all possible colors. The more colors your system has, the better this program looks.

See also
GetColor, SetColor

Example
```pascal
program XGetMaxColor;
uses Crt, Graph;
var
  GraphDriver, GraphMode: Integer;
  X, Y, XMax, YMax, Color: Integer;
begin
  GraphDriver := Detect;
  InitGraph(GraphDriver, GraphMode, 'c:\tp\bgi');
  XMax := GetMaxX;
  YMax := GetMaxY;
  X := 0;
  Y := 0;
  Rectangle(0, 0, XMax, YMax);
  for Color := 1 to GetMaxColor do
  begin
    SetColor(Color);
    Line(X, 0, X, YMax);
    Line(0, Y, XMax, Y);
    X := X + (XMax div GetMaxColor);
    Y := Y + (YMax div GetMaxColor)
  end;
  repeat until Keypressed;
  CloseGraph
end.
```

GetMaxMode

Syntax
```
function GetMaxMode: Integer;
```

Location
Graph

Description
Similar to GetModeRange, GetMaxMode returns the maximum number you can pass to SetGraphMode, selecting different display options for a certain adapter card and graphics driver. GetModeRange works only for standard BGI drivers. GetMaxMode works for all drivers, even those from other vendors. Because GetMaxMode interrogates the driver itself for its maximum mode number, it's probably best to call this function instead of GetModeRange. The example displays a brief list of statistics, including the maximum mode number for the default graphics driver.

See also
GetModeRange, SetGraphMode

Example
```
program XGetMaxMode;
uses Graph;
var
  GraphDriver, GraphMode: Integer;
  XMax, YMax, MaxMode: Integer;
  Driver: string;
begin
  GraphDriver := Detect;
  InitGraph(GraphDriver, GraphMode, 'c:\tp\bgi');
  if GraphResult <> GrOk then
    Writeln('No graphics')
  else begin
    XMax := GetMaxX;
    YMax := GetMaxY;
    MaxMode := GetMaxMode;
    Driver := GetDriverName;
    CloseGraph;
    Writeln('Default driver is ', Driver);
    Writeln('x Max = ', XMax);
    Writeln('y Max = ', YMax);
    Writeln('Maximum mode = ', MaxMode)
  end
end.
```

GetMaxX

Syntax
```
function GetMaxX: Integer;
```

Location
Graph

Description
After calling InitGraph to initialize a graphics display, GetMaxX returns the maximum horizontal screen coordinate value. For example, in a display of 640 horizontal by 350 vertical pixels, GetMaxX returns 639. This is one less than the number of horizontal pixels because the minimum coordinate value is always 0.

See also
GetMaxY, GetX, GetY

Example
See the example for GetMaxY.

GetMaxY

Syntax
```
function GetMaxY: Integer;
```

Location
Graph

Description
After calling InitGraph to initialize a graphics display, GetMaxY returns the maximum vertical screen coordinate value. For example, in a display of 640 horizontal by 350 vertical pixels, GetMaxY returns 349. This is one less than the number of vertical pixels because the minimum coordinate value is always 0.

Most often you will use GetMaxX and GetMaxY together as in the example. Instead of using constants for display coordinate limits, call these functions to discover the maximum X and Y coordinate values your program can use. This way you can write programs that work correctly regardless of the display's resolution.

See also
GetMaxX, GetX, GetY

Example
```
program XGetMaxXY;
uses Crt, Graph;
var
  GraphDriver, GraphMode: Integer;
  XMax, YMax, XMin, YMin: Integer;
```

```
begin
  GraphDriver := Detect;
  InitGraph(GraphDriver, GraphMode, 'c:\tp\bgi');
  XMax := GetMaxX;
  YMax := GetMaxY;
  XMin := 0;
  YMin := 0;
  while (XMax > 0) and(YMax > 0) do
  begin
    SetColor(1 + Random(MaxColors));
    Line(XMin, YMin, XMax, YMin);
    Line(XMax, YMin, XMax, YMax);
    Line(XMax, YMax, XMin, YMax);
    Line(XMin, YMax, XMin, YMin);
    XMax := XMax - 1; YMax := YMax - 1;
    XMin := XMin + 1; YMin := YMin + 1
  end;
  repeat until Keypressed;
  CloseGraph
end.
```

GetMem

Syntax
```
procedure GetMem(var P: <pointer>; N: Word);
```

Location
System

Description
GetMem reserves N bytes of memory on the heap and assigns the address of the first byte of that memory to P. GetMem is similar to New, except it lets you specify the number of bytes to reserve, up to 65,520 bytes for each call to GetMem.

As the example shows, GetMem can allocate space for record variants, which New does not allow in Turbo Pascal. Reserving space for only the integer field of a free union record takes two bytes. Reserving space for this same record by using New would take six bytes, the size of the record's real number field. This is equivalent to the statement, New(P, B), which many Pascal compilers, but not Turbo, recognize as a command to reserve memory only for field B.

See also
Dispose, FreeMem, HeapFunc, Mark, New, Release

Example
```
program XGetMem;
```

```
type
  Rec = record
    case Integer of
      1: (A: Real);
      2: (B: Integer)
    end;
var
  P: ^Rec;
begin
  Writeln('Memory before GetMem=', Memavail);
  GetMem(P, 2);
  Writeln('Memory after GetMem =', Memavail);
  P^.B := MaxInt;
  Writeln(P^.B, ' takes ', Sizeof(P^.B), ' bytes of storage.');
  Freemem(P, 2);
  Writeln('Memory after FreeMem=', Memavail)
end.
```

GetModeName

Syntax

```
function GetModeName(GraphMode: Integer ): string;
```

Location
Graph

Description

Most graphics drivers support two or more display modes, referenced by number (see GetMaxMode and SetGraphMode for example). These modes also have names, returned by the string function GetModeName. The function supports standard BGI drivers as well as those from other vendors.

Instead of hardwiring graphics mode names into your programs, always use GetModeName, perhaps in a menu that lets people select among available modes. This way your program will be compatible with future modifications and drivers. The example displays the current graphics driver name and all possible modes.

See also
GetDriverName, GetMaxMode, GetModeRange

Example

```
program XGetModeName;
uses Graph;
var
  GraphDriver, GraphMode, I: Integer;
```

```
begin
  GraphDriver := Detect;
  InitGraph(GraphDriver, GraphMode, 'c:\tp\bgi');
  if GraphResult <> GrOk then
    Writeln('No graphics')
  else begin
    Writeln('Graphics driver is: ', GetDriverName);
    for I := 0 to GetMaxMode do
      Writeln('Mode ', I, ' : ', GetModeName(I));
    Writeln;
    Write('Press Enter...');
    Readln;
    CloseGraph
  end
end.
```

GetModeRange

Syntax

```
procedure GetModeRange(GraphDriver: Integer; var LoMode, HiMode: Integer);
```

Location

Graph

Description

Pass any graphics driver to GetModeRange to set two variables, LoMode and HiMode, to the minimum graphics mode values you can then pass to InitGraph. GetModeRange tells you how many different display modes are available for a particular driver. The example displays a table of mode ranges for all Turbo Pascal graphics drivers.

See also

GetGraphMode, InitGraph, SetGraphMode

Example

```
program XGetModeRange;
uses Graph;
const
  ModeNames: array[1 .. 10] of string[8] =
    ('CGA     ', 'MCGA    ', 'EGA     ', 'EGA64   ',
     'EGAMono ', 'RESERVED', 'HercMono', 'Att400  ',
     'VGA     ', 'PC3270  ');
```

```
var
  GraphDriver, LoMode, HiMode: Integer;
begin
  Writeln('Graphics Driver Mode Ranges');
  Writeln;
  for GraphDriver := 1 to 10 do
  begin
    GetModeRange(GraphDriver, LoMode, HiMode);
    Writeln(ModeNames[GraphDriver], ' = ',
      LoMode:2, ' ..', HiMode:2)
  end
end.
```

GetPalette

Syntax
```
procedure GetPalette(var Palette: PaletteType);
```

Location
Graph

Description
To read the current color palette, call GetPalette with a variable of type PaletteType
defined as

```
PaletteType = record
  Size: Byte;
  Colors: array[0 .. MaxColors] of ShortInt
end;
```

Field Size equals the number of entries in the colors array. The example
displays the current palette settings for the default graphics mode, listing the color
number (equal to the Palette.Colors array index) and the value stored in the array.
The example draws a bar in the specified color. Notice that to change bar colors, the
program passes the Colors array *index*—not the arrayed value—to SetFillStyle.

See also
GetDefaultPalette, GetPaletteSize, SetAllPalette, SetPalette, SetRGBPalette

Example
```
program XGetPalette;
uses Crt, Graph;
var
  GraphDriver, GraphMode: Integer;
  H, I, XMax: Integer;
  Palette: PaletteType;
  S: string;
```

```
begin
  GraphDriver := Detect;
  InitGraph(GraphDriver, GraphMode, 'c:\tp\bgi');
  XMax := GetMaxX;
  GetPalette(Palette);
  H := TextHeight('M') + 8;
  for I := 0 to Palette.Size - 1 do
  begin
    Str(I:2, S);
    MoveTo(0, I * H);
    OutText('Color #'+S+' = ');
    Str(Palette.Colors[I]:3, S);
    OutText(S+' :: ');
    SetFillStyle(SolidFill, I);
    Bar(GetX, GetY, XMax, GetY + 4)
  end;
  repeat until Keypressed;
  CloseGraph
end.
```

GetPaletteSize

Syntax
```
function GetPaletteSize: Integer;
```

Location
Graph

Description
GetPaletteSize returns the size of the Colors field in a palette record, equal to the Size field. Calling this function is easier than (and has the same effect as) reading the current palette with GetPalette or GetDefaultPalette and inspecting the Size field. The example demonstrates how to use GetPaletteSize along with GetMaxColor to randomize palette colors, which produces a "shimmering pick-up sticks" effect—at least that's what it looks like to me.

See also
GetDefaultPalette, GetMaxColor, GetPalette, SetPalette, SetRGBPalette

Example
```
program XGetPaletteSize;
uses Crt, Graph;
var
  GraphDriver, GraphMode: Integer;
  I, XMax, YMax: Integer;
```

```
begin
  GraphDriver := Detect;
  InitGraph(GraphDriver, GraphMode, 'c:\tp\bgi');
  XMax := GetMaxX;
  YMax := GetMaxY;
  for I := 1 to 100 do
  begin
    SetColor(1 + Random(GetMaxColor - 1));
    Line(Abs(Random(XMax)),
         Abs(Random(YMax)),
         Abs(Random(XMax)),
         Abs(Random(YMax)))
  end;
  while not Keypressed do
  begin
    if I >= GetPaletteSize then I := 1 else Inc(I);
    Delay(10);
    SetPalette(I, 1 + Random(GetMaxColor - 1))
  end;
  CloseGraph
end.
```

GetPixel

Syntax
```
function GetPixel(X, Y: Integer): Word;
```

Location
Graph

Description
GetPixel returns the color value of the pixel at coordinate (X, Y). Use the procedure as a kind of sensor to check for borders of objects on display.

The example displays a series of boxes and then cycles variables X and Y through every possible coordinate value. Before displaying randomly colored dots, GetPixel checks for the color of the boxes. Whenever the program locates a box edge, it toggles variable PenDown—a simple algorithm for filling about half of the box areas on the screen. The result is a confetti-colored set of outlined boxes.

See also
GetImage, PutImage, PutPixel

Example
```
program XGetPixel;
uses Crt, Graph;
```

```
const
  BorderColor = Red;
var
  GraphDriver, GraphMode: Integer;
  I, XMax, YMax, X, Y: Integer;
  PenDown: Boolean;

  procedure Box(X1, Y1, X2, Y2 : Word);
  begin
    SetColor(BorderColor);
    Line(X1, Y1, X2, Y1);
    Line(X2, Y1, X2, Y2);
    Line(X2, Y2, X1, Y2);
    Line(X1, Y2, X1, Y1)
  end;

begin
  GraphDriver := Detect;
  InitGraph(GraphDriver, GraphMode, 'c:\tp\bgi');
  XMax := GetMaxX;
  YMax := GetMaxY;
  Randomize;
  for I := 1 to 15 do
    Box(Random(XMax), Random(YMax),
        Random(XMax), Random(YMax));
  for X := 0 to XMax do
  begin
    PenDown := FALSE;
    for Y := 0 to YMax do
      if (GetPixel(X, Y) = BorderColor) and
         (GetPixel(X + 1, Y) = BorderColor) then
        PenDown := not PenDown
      else if PenDown then
        PutPixel(X, Y, Random(MaxColors))
  end;
  repeat until Keypressed;
  CloseGraph
end.
```

GetTextSettings

Syntax

```
procedure GetTextSettings(var TextInfo: TextSettingsType);
```

Location
Graph

Description
GetTextSettings returns a record containing five fields that describe the current graphics text settings. These settings affect the appearance of text displayed by OutText and OutTextXY. The TextSettingsType record has the following structure:

```
TextSettingsType = record
  Font: Word;          { Font number }
  Direction: Word;     { Horizontal or vertical direction }
  CharSize: Word;      { Relative size}
  Horiz: Word;         { Horizontal justification }
  Vert: Word           { Vertical justification }
end;
```

See also
SetTextJustify, SetTextStyle, TextHeight, TextWidth

Example
```
program XGetTextSettings;
uses Graph;
var
  GraphDriver, GraphMode: Integer;
  TsRec: TextSettingsType;
begin
  GraphDriver := Detect;
  InitGraph(GraphDriver, GraphMode, 'c:\tp\bgi');
  GetTextSettings(TsRec);
  with TsRec do
  begin
    Writeln('Font ........ ', Font);
    Writeln('Direction .... ', Direction);
    Writeln('CharSize ..... ', CharSize);
    Writeln('Horiz ........ ', Horiz);
    Writeln('Vert ......... ', Vert)
  end;
  Readln;
  CloseGraph
end.
```

GetTime

Syntax
```
procedure GetTime(var Hour, Minute, Second, Sec100: Word);
```

Location
Dos

Description
Call GetTime to read the current time of day. The procedure returns four Word variables equal to the hour, minute, second, and hundredths of a second. Because most PC clocks are driven by somewhat imprecise interrupts, the hundredths value is not very accurate. Don't trust it for less than about $\frac{1}{4}$ second. The hour is a 24-hour value. As the example shows, to display 12-hour time, subtract 12 from the hour if it is greater than 12.

See also
GetDate, SetDate, SetTime, UnpackTime

Example
```
program XGetTime;
uses Dos;
var
  Hour, Minute, Second, Sec100: Word;

  function D2(N: Word): Word;
  begin
    if N < 10 then
      Write('0');
    D2 := N
  end;

begin
  GetTime(Hour, Minute, Second, Sec100);
  if Hour > 12 then
    Hour := Hour-12;
  Writeln('The time is ',
    D2(Hour), ':', D2(Minute), ':', D2(Second))
end.
```

GetVerify

Syntax
```
procedure GetVerify(var Verify: Boolean);
```

Location
Dos

Description
When the DOS *verify* switch is true, disk writes are followed by automatic disk reads to verify that data written to disk probably was stored correctly. When the verify switch is false, disk writes are not followed by disk reads. Because write-verification slows disk I/O considerably, most people leave this switch off.

    Call function GetVerify to inspect the state of the DOS verify switch. You can change the switch setting from DOS by typing "verify ON" or "verify OFF." Or, from inside a program, use the SetVerify procedure.

See also
SetVerify

Example
```
program XGetVerify;
uses Dos;
var
  Verify: Boolean;
begin
  GetVerify(Verify);
  Writeln('Verify switch is: ', Verify)
end.
```

GetViewSettings

Syntax
```
procedure GetViewSettings(var ViewPort: ViewPortType);
```

Location
Graph

Description
To read the current viewport settings, call GetViewSettings with a variable of type ViewPortType, defined as

```
ViewPortType = record
  X1, Y1, X2, Y2: Integer;
  Clip: Boolean
end;
```

GetViewSettings fills in the record fields with the minimum (X1, Y1) and maximum (X2, Y2) display coordinates. It also sets Clip true if clipping is on or false if clipping is off. The example uses this information to outline the display and to show the current clipping value.

See also
SetViewPort

Example
```pascal
program XGetViewSettings;
uses Crt, Graph;
var
  GraphDriver, GraphMode: Integer;
  Viewport: ViewPortType;
begin
  GraphDriver := Detect;
  InitGraph(GraphDriver, GraphMode, 'c:\tp\bgi');
  GetViewSettings(Viewport);
  with Viewport do
  begin
    Rectangle(X1, Y1, X2, Y2);
    MoveTo(10, Y2 div 2);
    OutText('Clipping = ');
    if Clip
      then OutText('TRUE')
      else OutText('FALSE')
  end;
  repeat until Keypressed;
  CloseGraph
end.
```

GetX

Syntax
```pascal
function GetX: Integer;
```

Location
Graph

Description
GetX returns the internal X (horizontal) coordinate value affected by MoveTo, LineTo, LineRel, MoveRel, and OutText statements. See GetY for additional details.

See also
GetMaxX, GetMaxY, GetY

Example
See example for GetY.

GetY

Syntax
```
function GetY: Integer;
```

Location
Graph

Description
GetY returns the internal Y (vertical) coordinate value affected by MoveTo, LineTo, LineRel, MoveRel, and OutText statements. Along with GetX, the function lets you pinpoint where drawing will next appear—except in graphics routines such as Circle that let you specify other X and Y coordinates.

The example demonstrates several subtleties of coordinate positioning in the Turbo Pascal graphics kernel. First, the program displays a blue dot at the center of the screen. It then shows the current GetX and GetY values, which both remain equal to their initialized zero values. This proves that PutPixel does not affect the internally saved (X,Y) coordinate. In the next step, the program calls MoveTo to position the graphics coordinate to mid-screen. As you can see when you run the program, this and the OutText statement change the internally saved (X,Y) graphics coordinate.

See also
GetMaxX, GetMaxY, GetX

Example
```
program XGetXY;
uses Graph;
var
  GraphDriver, GraphMode: Integer;
begin
  GraphDriver := Detect;
  InitGraph(GraphDriver, GraphMode, 'c:\tp\bgi');
  PutPixel(GetMaxX div 2, GetMaxY div 2, Blue);
  Writeln('GetX=', GetX, '  GetY=', GetY);
  MoveTo(GetMaxX div 2, GetMaxY div 2);
  OutText('Testing GetX and GetY');
  Writeln('GetX=', GetX, '  GetY=', GetY);
  Readln;
  CloseGraph
end.
```

GotoXY

Syntax
```
procedure GotoXY(X, Y: Byte);
```

Location
Crt

Description
GotoXY positions the cursor at display coordinate (X,Y). The upper-left corner of the display, or "home" position, has the coordinate (1,1). In an 80-column by 25-line display, the bottom-right corner has the coordinate (80,25).

    The example shows how to use GotoXY to center a message on the display. Extract function Center for your own programs. (I borrowed the message from signs along the Pennsylvania Turnpike, in case you're interested.)

    By the way, some people say "Go-toxy," whereas others pronounce it "Goto-XY." It's your choice.

See also
WhereX, WhereY, Window

Example
```
program XGotoXY;
uses Crt;
const
  Wait = 3000;

  procedure Center(Message : string);
  begin
    GotoXY(1, 12);
    ClrEol;
    GotoXY(40 - (Length(Message) div 2), 12);
    Write(Message)
  end;

begin
  ClrScr;
  Delay(Wait);
  Center('You can drive'); Delay(Wait);
  Center('a mile a minute'); Delay(Wait);
  Center('but there''s no'); Delay(Wait);
  Center('future in it.'); Delay(Wait)
end.
```

GraphDefaults

Syntax
```
procedure GraphDefaults;
```

Location
Graph

Description
Call GraphDefaults to restore all graphics settings, the current point (CP), the viewport, and other parameters, to the values these items have immediately following a call to InitGraph. GraphDefaults does not clear the screen, however. To do that, follow GraphDefaults with ClearDevice. (You could also use the slower ClearViewPort. However, because GraphDefaults opens the viewport to full screen, ClearDevice is faster.)

Run the example to see a restricted view of random circles in the upper-left corner of your screen. Press the space bar to call GraphDefaults, opening the window to full screen but not clearing the display. Press Esc to end the demonstration.

See also
ClearDevice, InitGraph

Example
```
program XGraphDefaults;
uses Crt, Graph;
var
  GraphDriver, GraphMode: Integer;
  Done : Boolean; Ch: Char;
begin
  GraphDriver := Detect;
  InitGraph(GraphDriver, GraphMode, 'c:\tp\bgi');
  SetViewPort(10, 10, 110, 110, True);
  Done := false;
  repeat
    SetColor(1 + Random(GetMaxColor));
    Circle(Random(GetMaxX), Random(GetMaxY), Random(25));
    if Keypressed then
    begin
      Ch := ReadKey;
      if Ch = Chr(32) then
      begin
        Write(Chr(7));
        GraphDefaults
      end else
        Done := (Ch = Chr(27))
```

```
      end
    until Done;
    CloseGraph
  end.
```

GraphErrorMsg

Syntax
```
function GraphErrorMsg(ErrorCode: Integer): string;
```

Location
Graph

Description
GraphErrorMsg returns a string that describes a graphics error. You can pass error
code values to GraphErrorMsg or pass the result of function GraphResult.

The example displays error messages for values 0 down to –15. The value 0
indicates no error.

See also
DetectGraph, GraphResult, InitGraph

Example
```
program XGraphErrorMsg;
uses Graph;
var
  GraphDriver, GraphMode, I: Integer;
begin
  GraphDriver := Detect;
  InitGraph(GraphDriver, GraphMode, 'c:\tp\bgi');
  Writeln('Graphics Error Messages');
  Writeln;
  for I := 0 downto -15 do
    Writeln(I:3, ' : ', GraphErrorMsg(I));
  Readln;
  CloseGraph
end.
```

GraphResult

Syntax
```
function GraphResult: Integer;
```

Location
Graph

Description
Certain graphics operations return error codes through the GraphResult function. See Table 11-3 for a list of error codes and their meanings.

The example calls SetTextStyle with a font number you can enter when the program begins. Try numbers one and two. Then enter a bad number such as 4000, for which there is no corresponding character-font file on disk. Checking GraphResult in this situation prevents OutText from displaying a message when the font selection fails.

See also
GraphErrorMsg

Example
```pascal
program XGraphResult;
uses Graph;
var
  GraphDriver, GraphMode: Integer;
  FontNumber: Integer;
begin
  Write('Font number? ');
  Readln(FontNumber);
  GraphDriver := Detect;
  InitGraph(GraphDriver, GraphMode, 'c:\tp\bgi');
  SetColor(LightBlue);
  SetTextStyle(FontNumber, 0, 4);
  if GraphResult = GrOK
    then OutText('Font selected')
    else Writeln('Error in SetTextStyle');
  Readln;
  CloseGraph
end.
```

Halt

Syntax
```pascal
procedure Halt[(N: Word)];
```

Location
System

Description

Halt immediately ends the program, returning to the Turbo Pascal integrated editor or to DOS if the program was compiled to disk and run from the command line. You may halt a program at any place in its execution.

There are two ways to call Halt. The first passes no parameter. The second passes an integer value representing an error code. Zero means no error. Any other value indicates a problem. Batch files can check the Halt code through the ERRORLEVEL command. A program can check the Halt code of a subprogram (called a child process) through the DosExitCode function.

The example demonstrates this second use of Halt. First, type and compile to disk XHALTB.PAS, creating XHALTB.EXE. Next, type and run XHALT.PAS, either in memory or from disk. XHALT calls XHALTB with an Exec statement, running XHALTB as a child process, which ends with a Halt(3) statement. The parent program (XHALT) then continues where it stopped, displaying the Halt error code held by DosExitCode.

See also

DosExitCode, Exec, Exit, RunError

Example

```
XHALTB.PAS

{$M 2000,1000,1000}
program XHaltB;
begin
  Write('Inside HALTB.  Press <Enter>...');
  Readln;
  Halt(3);
  Writeln('This line is not displayed')
end.

XHALT.PAS

{$M 2000,1000,1000}
program XHalt;
uses Dos;
begin
  Writeln('Running HALT');
  Exec('XHALTB.EXE', '');
  Writeln('Back from HALTB');
  Writeln('DOSExitCode=', DOSExitCode)
end.
```

HeapFunc

Syntax

```
function HeapFunc(Size: Word): Integer; far;
```

Location
none

Description

HeapFunc is not a function you can call. It is a design for a function you create, then tell Turbo Pascal to call when a heap error occurs.

The example explains how HeapFunc works. Most important is the **far** keyword after the function declaration. (You could instead surround the function's header with the equivalent directives {$F+} and {$F–}.) If you forget to make HeapFunc far, the program is sure to crash and all the king's programmers won't be able to repair the damage to memory.

Inside the custom HeapFunc (see the example), a simple assignment returns 1 as the function result. Doing this changes the way New and GetMem operate. Normally, these two procedures cause a runtime error to occur when you try to allocate variables too large to fit in the available memory on the heap. By assigning the address of HeapFunc to the System unit HeapError pointer, though, rather than a runtime error, New and GetMem now return **nil** if there is not enough memory.

Run the example, which creates large arrays on the heap until running out of space. You should see the message, "Out of Memory," proving that New returned **nil**. Now, remove the assignment to HeapError and run the program again. This time, you receive a runtime error, halting the program at New.

See also
New, GetMem

Example

```pascal
program XHeapFunc;
uses Crt;
type
  BigArray = array[1 .. 10000] of Integer;
var
  P: ^BigArray;

  function HeapFunc(Size : Word) : Integer; far;
  begin
    HeapFunc := 1
  end;

begin
  HeapError := @HeapFunc;
  repeat
```

```
      if Keypressed then Halt;  { For safety }
      Writeln('Memory = ', Memavail);
      New(P);
      if P = nil then
      begin
        Writeln('Out of memory');
        Halt
      end
    until False
end.
```

Hi

Syntax
```
function Hi(N: <integer>): Byte;
```

Location
System

Description
Hi returns the high, or most significant, byte of the Word or Integer value N. The result is always in the range 0 to 255.

See also
Lo, Swap

Example
```
program XHi;
var
  I: Word;
begin
  I := 0;
  while I < MaxInt do
  begin
    Writeln('I=', I:5, '  High byte=', Hi(I):3);
    I := I + (MaxInt div 10)
  end
end.
```

HighVideo

Syntax
```
procedure HighVideo;
```

Location
Crt

Description
HighVideo sets the high intensity bit of a display character. After calling HighVideo, characters displayed through Write and Writeln statements seem brighter or a different color from normal. Depending on the display mode in effect, though, HighVideo may not change text the way you always expect. For that reason, it is a good idea to test what HighVideo does before assuming anything about the results.

The example displays a reference of text in 16 colors before and after calling HighVideo. On monochrome monitors, you see different text attributes rather than colors.

See also
LowVideo, NormVideo, TextBackground, TextColor

Example

```
program XHighVideo;
uses Crt;
var
  Color: Integer;
begin
  ClrScr;
  Writeln('HighVideo Color Text Demonstration');
  Writeln('----------------------------------');
  for Color := 0 to 15 do
  begin
    NormVideo;
    Write('Color=', Color:2);
    TextColor(Color);
    Write('   Normal video    ');
    HighVideo;
    Writeln('High video')
  end
end.
```

ImageSize

Syntax
```
function Imagesize(X1, Y1, X2, Y2: Integer): Word;
```

Location
Graph

Description
Use ImageSize to determine the number of bytes a bitmap image occupies. The image is a rectangle with its upper-left corner at (X1,Y1) and its lower-right corner at (X2,Y2). ImageSize accurately tells you how many bytes it takes for a variable to hold the video buffer bytes that make up the image plus width and height information, regardless of the display mode you are using.

The example shows how to create an array of bytes and reserve ImageSize bytes on the heap, assigning a pointer (image) to this memory. Before doing this, the program fills the screen with 30,000 randomly colored pixels. GetImage then captures the image, which a **for** loop displays using the Sin function for a three-dimensional effect.

See also
GetImage, PutImage

Example
```pascal
program XImageSize;
uses Crt, Graph;
const
  X1 = 100; Y1 = 100; X2 = 227; Y2 = 163;
type
  ByteArray = array[0 .. 0] of Byte;
  ByteArrayPtr = ^ByteArray;
var
  GraphDriver, GraphMode: Integer;
  XMax, YMax, X, Y, I: Integer;
  Image: ByteArrayPtr;

  function Radians(Angle: Word): Real;
  begin
    Radians := Abs(Angle mod 360) * Pi / 180.0
  end;

begin
  GraphDriver := Detect;
  InitGraph(GraphDriver, GraphMode, 'c:\tp\bgi');
  XMax := GetMaxX;
  YMax := GetMaxY;
  Randomize;
  for I := 1 to 30000 do
    PutPixel(Random(XMax), Random(YMax), Random(MaxColors));
  GetMem(Image, ImageSize(X1, Y1, X2, Y2));  { Reserve memory }
  if Image <> nil then
  begin
    GetImage(X1, Y1, X2, Y2, Image^);  { Copy display image }
```

```
      ClearViewPort;
      Y := 0;
      for X := 0 to XMax - (X2 - X1) do
      begin
        PutImage(X, 100 + Trunc(Sin(Radians(Y)) * 50.0),
          Image^, NormalPut);
        Y := Y + 1
      end
    end;
    repeat until Keypressed;
    CloseGraph
  end.
```

Inc

Syntax
```
procedure Inc(var N: <ordinal> [; Count: LongInt]);
```

Location
System

Description
Inc increments an ordinal variable N either by one or by an optional Count. The variable may be any integer, character, Boolean, or enumerated data type. The procedure is equivalent to the expression:

```
N := Succ(N);
```

This expression is inferior because, rather than add one to N and then assign the result back to N, Turbo Pascal generates a machine language instruction for Inc that directly increments variables.

In Turbo Pascal 6.0, Inc can increment typed pointers. For example, suppose you have a pointer P that addresses an array A of type-AnyRec records. The statements

```
P := @A[0];   { P addresses record at A[0] }
Inc(P);       { P addresses record at A[1] }
```

assign the address of A[0] (the first record in the array) to P, then increment P to address the second record at A[1]. For statements like Inc(P), Turbo Pascal advances the pointer P by N bytes, where N equals Sizeof(P $^\wedge$)—in other words, the size in bytes of the type addressed by P. Similarly, the expression Inc(P, 4) increments P by (Sizeof(P $^\wedge$) * 4) bytes.

The example shows how to use Inc to count from 1 to 10 and to display the alphabet.

See also
Dec, Pred, Succ

Example

```pascal
program XInc;
var
  N: Integer;
  Ch: Char;
begin
  N := 0;
  while N < 20 do        { Count to 20 by 2s }
  begin
    Inc(N, 2);
    Writeln(N)
  end;
  Writeln;
  Ch := 'A';
  while Ch <= 'Z' do     { Display the alphabet }
  begin
    Write(Ch);
    Inc(Ch)
  end;
  Writeln
end.
```

InitGraph

Syntax

```pascal
procedure InitGraph(var GraphDriver: Integer;
  var GraphMode: Integer; PathToDriver: string);
```

Location
Graph

Description
Call InitGraph to initialize the display to any graphics mode. Before calling InitGraph, set GraphDriver and GraphMode to the graphics hardware and mode you want to use. See Table 11-2 for a list of possible values. Initializing nonexistent graphics modes can lock the computer, forcing you to reboot. Assign to string PathToDriver the directory path where you store Turbo Pascal's graphics driver files (those ending in .BGI).

To have the graphics kernel automatically select the best possible graphics mode, set GraphDriver to the constant, Detect.

After calling InitGraph, use the GraphResult function to check for errors. If GraphResult equals grOk, then you can assume the graphics display is initialized and ready for drawing.

The example shows the correct way to use InitGraph to initialize a graphics display. If no errors occur, the program displays a few details about the display and draws some colored circles to prove you can mix graphics and text on the same screen.

See also
CloseGraph, DetectGraph, GraphDefaults, GraphResult, GraphResult, SetGraphMode

Example

```
program XInitGraph;
uses Graph;
var
  GraphDriver, GraphMode: Integer;
  I, XMax, YMax: Integer;
begin
  Write('Default display.  Press <Enter>...');
  Readln;
  GraphDriver := Detect;
  InitGraph(GraphDriver, GraphMode, 'c:\tp\bgi');
  if GraphResult = GrOk then
  begin
    XMax := GetMaxX;
    YMax := GetMaxY;
    Writeln('Graphics display');
    Writeln('----------------');
    Writeln('Graph driver = ', GraphDriver);
    Writeln('Graph mode   = ', GraphMode);
    Writeln('Maximum x coordinate = ', XMax);
    Writeln('Maximum y coordinate = ', YMax);
    for I := 1 to 50 do
    begin
      SetColor(Random(MaxColors));
      Circle(Random(XMax), Random(YMax), Random(50))
    end;
    Readln;
    CloseGraph
  end
end.
```

InLine

Syntax
```
InLine(c1/ c2/ c3/ .../ cn: Byte¦Word);
```

Location
System

Description
InLine statements inject machine language instructions and data directly into a Pascal program. Because InLine is not itself a procedure or function, but rather a special technique for adding machine code to Pascal programs, its syntax is different from most other routines in this chapter.

There are two ways to write an InLine statement. The first looks like any other Pascal statement. The second resembles an assembly language macro. The example demonstrates both forms. Procedure WriteAChar contains an InLine statement with machine language instructions to send a single character to the standard DOS output file, usually the display. In this case, the values inside the InLine statement run every time the program calls WriteAChar.

Procedure DirectWrite shows how to use the second InLine form. In this case, the InLine statement follows the procedure declaration. In the program's main body, Turbo Pascal inserts the InLine bytes in place of DirectWrite.

There are several rules to follow when designing machine language code in InLine statements. These are:

- Values in the range 0 to 255 cause one byte to be inserted. Values greater than 255 cause two bytes to be inserted.

- Identifiers generate offset values, which are up to you to use properly. In the example, Ch is replaced by its offset on the stack (because the variable is a parameter and all parameters are stored on the stack). If Ch were a global variable, then the offset generated would be relative to the data segment in which Ch is stored.

- To force Turbo Pascal to generate the least significant byte of a two-byte value, preface the value or constant identifier with <. To generate the most significant byte, preface the value with >.

- Remember that variable identifiers are replaced by the offset address of the variable—not their values. In other words, referencing an integer Num does not insert the value of Num into the program code. It inserts Num's address.

- Because InLine routines like DirectWrite in the example are macros and not real Pascal procedures or functions, you cannot take their addresses with @ or pass their identifiers to Addr, Ofs, and Seg.

- Notice in the example that the first InLine statement references Ch as a variable on the stack at location [BP + Ch]. In the second case, the InLine statement pops this same variable from the stack. The first case doesn't do this because procedure WriteAChar is responsible for removing its local variables from the stack. The second case is not a procedure call, but a macro expansion, and, therefore, DirectWrite must, itself, remove any parameters from the stack.

- Use InLine statements only where they make a real difference or where they perform operations impossible or awkward to do in Pascal. It is a good idea to program entirely in Pascal and, after testing the program, convert key routines to assembly language. It is generally not a good idea to program with InLine statements from the start. If you are doing that, then why bother using a Pascal compiler?

Note: Because Turbo Pascal 6.0 now includes a built-in assembler (see Chapter 14), there are few good reasons to use InLine statements. InLine procedures and functions are, however, still useful.

See also
Intr, MsDos

Example

```
program XInLine;
uses Crt;
const
  CR = #13; LF = #10;  { Carriage return & line feed characters }
var
  Ch: Char;

  procedure WriteAChar(Ch: Char);
  begin
    inline(
      $B4/$02/        { MOV AH, 02     ; DOS output function }
      $8A/$56/<Ch/    { MOV DL, [BP+ch] ; DL = char    }
      $CD/$21)        { INT 21h        ; Call DOS     }
  end; { WriteAChar }

  procedure DirectWrite(Ch: Char); inline(
    $B4/$02/          { MOV AH, 02     ; DOS output function }
    $5A/              { POP DX         ; Pop ch into DL }
    $CD/$21);         { INT 21h        ; Call DOS }
```

```
begin
  ClrScr;
  WriteAChar(CR); WriteAChar(LF);
  for Ch := 'A' to 'Z' do
    WriteAChar(Ch);
  DirectWrite(CR); DirectWrite(LF);
  for Ch := 'A' to 'Z' do
    DirectWrite(Ch)
end.
```

Insert

Syntax
```
procedure Insert(Source: string; var Destination: string; Index: Byte);
```

Location
System

Description
Insert inserts the Source string, which may be literal or a variable, into the Destination string starting at Destination's Index character. If the insertion causes the string to become longer than its maximum declared length, no error results, but characters pushed beyond the end of the string are irretrievably lost.

The procedure is good for adding all sorts of items to strings. For instance, the example contains a function, Dollars, which accepts a Word value N and returns a string formatted with a dollar sign and decimal place.

See also
Concat, Copy, Delete, Length, Pos

Example
```
program XInsert;
var
  N: Integer;

  function Dollars(N: Word) : string;
  var
    S: string;
  begin
    Str(N:5, S);
    while Length(S) < 3 do
      Insert('0', S, 1);
    Insert('.', S, Length(S) - 1);
    Dollars := '$' + S
```

```
  end;

begin
  Randomize;
  for N := 1 to 25 do
    Writeln(Dollars(Random(MaxInt)))
end.
```

InsLine

Syntax
```
procedure InsLine;
```

Location
Crt

Description
InsLine inserts a blank line at the cursor's position in the current text display window, causing any lines below to move down one line and pushing the bottom line irretrievably off the display. After a line is inserted, the cursor position does not change. The example uses InsLine to simulate the insertion of text into a word processor.

See also
DelLine, TextBackground, Window

Example
```
program XInsLine;
uses Crt;
var
  I: Integer;
begin
  ClrScr;
  GotoXY(1, 1);
  Writeln('Blasting Turbo Rascal');
  Writeln('by Tom Duck');
  GotoXY(1, 2);
  for I := 1 to 8 do begin
    Delay(500);
    InsLine
  end;
  GotoXY(1, 2);
  Writeln('Fourth edition');
  Writeln('for version 6.0');
```

```
    GotoXY(1, 4);
    for I := 1 to 6 do begin
      Delay(500);
      DelLine
    end
  end.
```

InstallUserDriver

Syntax
```
function InstallUserDriver(Name: string;
  AutoDetectPtr: Pointer): Integer;
```

Location
Graph

Description
Call InstallUserDriver to load a custom graphics driver, which you might have received from the manufacturer of a graphics card that supports special modes, possibly in addition to the usual CGA, EGA, and VGA displays. Suppose this driver is named 3DG.BGI. To force the Graph unit to use the driver, execute the commands:

```
graphDriver := InstallUserDriver('3DG.BGI', nil);
if graphDriver = GrError then Halt;
InitGraph(GraphDriver, GraphMode, 'c:\tp\bgi');
if GraphResult = GrOk then
begin
  { Insert graphics commands here }
  CloseGraph
end;
```

When used this way, InstallUserDriver takes two parameters: the name of the driver and a **nil** pointer, which defeats an optional auto-detection scheme. InstallUserDriver returns an Integer value. If this value equals grError, then the BGI device table is full and the program should halt. Unless you are loading several custom drivers simultaneously, you will rarely see this error. If the program does not detect an error, it can then pass the InstallUserDriver result to InitGraph, which calls low-level routines in the new driver to initialize graphics. If GraphResult equals grOk after this step, all Graph unit commands use the new driver's low-level graphics routines.

More advanced graphics drivers and video hardware allow InitGraph to detect their presence automatically. To enable this feature, you need to write a detection function, similar to Detect3DG in the example. The function must be far—compiled with {$F+} in effect or by using the **far** keyword in the function header—and it should return grError if it fails to detect the custom driver or hardware; otherwise, the function should return a mode number representing the default graphics configuration. (The example function is a dummy that always returns an error.)

Next, call InstallUserDriver as the example demonstrates, passing the address of the custom detection function as the second parameter (@Detect3DG). This causes the Graph unit to link Detect3DG into the built-in detection logic for common modes such as CGA, EGA, and VGA displays. If InstallUserDriver does not return grError, then pass the constant detect to InitGraph as most graphics programs normally do. InitGraph then calls Detect3DG. If the custom function returns a positive value or zero, InitGraph loads and initializes the custom driver. If the custom function returns grError (as it always does in the example), then InitGraph proceeds with its normal auto-detection duties. This process lets you write graphics programs that work with custom hardware or software drivers, but still work correctly on more common systems.

Notice that InitGraph calls the auto-detection Detect3DG function, even though you pass the function address to InstallUserDriver.

See also
InitGraph, InstallUserFont, RegisterBGIDriver, RegisterBGIFont

Example

```
program XInstallUserDriver;
uses Graph;
var
  UserDriver, GraphDriver, GraphMode: Integer;
  XMax, YMax: Integer;

  function Detect3DG: Integer; far;
  const
    DriverFound = False; { Dummy value }
    DefaultMode = 3;     { Default }
  begin
    if DriverFound
      then Detect3DG := DefaultMode
      else Detect3DG := GrError
  end;

begin
  UserDriver := InstallUserDriver('3DG.BGI', @Detect3DG);
  if UserDriver = GrError then
  begin
    Writeln('Graphics-driver table is full');
    Halt(1)
  end;
```

```
{---- Method #1 (pass userDriver to InitGraph): }
(* GraphDriver := userDriver; *)
{---- Method #2 (let InitGraph auto-detect driver): }
  GraphDriver := Detect;
  InitGraph(GraphDriver, GraphMode, 'c:\tp\bgi');  { Calls Detect3DG! }
  if GraphResult <> GrOk then
    Writeln('Error initializing graphics')
  else begin
    XMax := GetMaxX;
    YMax := GetMaxY;
    Ellipse(XMax div 2, YMax div 2, 0, 360, XMax div 6, 50);
    Readln;
    CloseGraph
  end
end.
```

InstallUserFont

Syntax
```
function InstallUserFont(FontFileName: string): Integer;
```

Location
Graph

Description
The BGI Graph unit comes with several standard fonts. InstallUserFont loads other font files, perhaps purchased from a software company or supplied with a special video card. The example shows the correct way to use the function. Pass the name of the font disk file to InstallUserFont, which returns a number that you can later pass to SetTextStyle. Calling GraphResult after InstallUserFont does not detect font-loading errors. Instead, examine GraphResult after calling SetTextStyle with the font number returned by InstallUserFont. If an error occurs at this time, you can select a different font as the example demonstrates.

See also
InstallUserDriver, RegisterBGIDriver, RegisterBGIFont

Example
```
program XInstallUserFont;
uses Crt, Graph;
var
  UserFont, GraphDriver, GraphMode: Integer;
  X, Y, Size: Integer;
  SizeStr: string[2];
begin
```

```
      UserFont := InstallUserFont('3DG.CHR');
      GraphDriver := Detect;
      InitGraph(GraphDriver, GraphMode, 'c:\tp\bgi');
      if GraphResult <> GrOk then
        Writeln('Error initializing graphics')
      else begin
        SetTextStyle(UserFont, HorizDir, 2);
        if GraphResult <> GrOk
          then UserFont := SansSerifFont;
        X := 0;
        Y := 0;
        for Size := 1 to 7 do
        begin
          SetTextStyle(UserFont, HorizDir, Size);
          Y := 4 + Y + TextHeight('M');
          Str(Size, SizeStr);
          OutTextXY(X, Y, 'Testing font size=' + SizeStr)
        end;
        repeat until Keypressed;
        CloseGraph
      end
end.
```

Int

Syntax
```
function Int(R: <real>): <real>;
```

Location
System

Description
Int returns the integer part of real number R, equal to the value of R minus its fractional part. For example, Int(3.141) = 3.0 and Int(65538.2) = 65538.0.

Despite its name, the function returns a real number, not an integer. The example shows this clearly, displaying:

```
Pi = 3.1415926536E+00     Int(Pi) = 3.0000000000E+00
```

See also
Frac, Round, Trunc

Example
```
program XInt;
```

```
begin
  Writeln('Pi=', Pi, '   Int(Pi)=', Int(Pi))
end.
```

Intr

Syntax
```
procedure Intr(IntNo: Byte; var Regs: Registers);
```

Location
Dos

Description
Intr calls the software interrupt specified by IntNo, passing the register values in record Regs.

The example shows how to use Intr to change the cursor from its usual underline shape to a fat block. Consult a DOS or PC technical reference for a list of interrupt numbers and their meanings.

See also
MsDos

Example
```
program XIntr;
uses Dos;
var
  Reg: Registers;
begin
  with Reg do
  begin
    Ah := 1;     { Set cursor type }
    Ch := 0;
    Cl := 7
  end;
  Intr($10, Reg)
end.
```

IoResult

Syntax
```
function IoResult: Word;
```

Location
System

Description
IoResult returns the Input/Output (I/O) error code result if Input/Output error checking is turned off with the compiler option {$I–}. IoResult has the intended side effect of resetting Turbo Pascal's internal error code and is valid only on its first use following the Input/Output operation.

Error codes match those returned by DOS. See a DOS technical reference or your Turbo Pascal Manual for a list of error codes and their meanings.

The example lists a handy function, FileExists, that uses IoResult to test whether a certain file exists on disk. Press Enter to end the program.

See also
Read, Readln, Reset, Rewrite, Write, Writeln

Example
```pascal
program XIoResult;
var
  FileName: string;

  function FileExists(Fname: string): Boolean;
  var
    F: file;
  begin
    Assign(F, Fname);
    {$I-} Reset(F); {$I+}
    FileExists := (Ioresult = 0)
  end;

begin
  Writeln('File check');
  repeat
    Write('Name? ');
    Readln(FileName);
    if Length(FileName) > 0 then
      if FileExists(FileName)
        then Writeln('file exists')
        else Writeln('file does not exist')
  until Length(FileName) = 0
end.
```

Keep

Syntax
```
procedure Keep(ExitCode: Word);
```

Location
Dos

Description
Keep causes a program or child process to terminate and stay resident (TSR) in memory. The entire program stays, including all memory allocated to it; therefore, be sure to use the {$M} directive to reduce reserved memory to the absolute minimum before using Keep.

The example shows how to use Keep to install an interrupt in memory. Procedure Crawl is a simple routine that counts up to 30,000 before ending. By attaching this routine to interrupt vector $1C, the PC ROM BIOS timer calls the new routine once for every hardware timer tick—about 18.2 times per second. This slows the computer to a crawl!

Compile the example to a disk code file KEEP.EXE. *Do not run this program from inside the integrated Turbo Pascal editor!* Quit Turbo Pascal and type KEEP to install the program in memory. Try executing commands such as DIR and TYPE, which now run as fast as ants stuck in honey.

You might use the example to debug programs that run too fast, slowing actions to a crawl. Reboot to restore your computer to full speed.

See also
DosExitCode, Exec, Exit, Halt

Example
```
{ !!!!!!!!!!!!!!!!!!!!!!!!!!!!!!!!!!!!!!!!!!!!!!!!!!!!!!!!!!!!!!!
  WARNING: This program stays resident until you reboot.  Do not
  run more than once without rebooting.  DO NOT RUN FROM INSIDE
  INTEGRATED TURBO PASCAL EDITOR.
  !!!!!!!!!!!!!!!!!!!!!!!!!!!!!!!!!!!!!!!!!!!!!!!!!!!!!!!!!!!!!! }

{$M 1024, 0, 0}   { Use minimum amount of memory }
{$N-,S-}          { No coprocessor, no stack overflow checking }
program XKeep;
uses Dos;

  procedure Crawl(Flags, CS, IP, AX, BX, CX, DX, SI, DI, DS, ES, BP:
Word);
    interrupt;
  var
```

```
    K: Word;
  begin
    for K := 1 to 30000 do {wait}
  end;

begin
  SetIntVec($1C, @Crawl);  { Install timer interrupt }
  Keep(0)  { Terminate, stay resident }
end.
```

Keypressed

Syntax
```
function Keypressed: Boolean;
```

Location
Crt

Description
Keypressed returns true if a character is waiting to be read from the keyboard.

The most common use for Keypressed is to read a character only *after* someone types something. This allows the program to continue if no characters are waiting. One example where this technique might be useful is in a game where certain keys move figures on-screen. With Keypressed, the game action continues until a key is pressed. You might find the following statements inside the program:

```
if Keypressed then
  case ReadKey of
    'U': Up;
    'D': Down
  end;
```

Another use for Keypressed is to clear the keyboard input buffer. This buffer fills with characters that you type while other program events are occurring. The example shows how to empty the buffer by calling Readkey while Keypressed returns true. By doing this, you can force people to give programs instructions at critical points, preventing them from answering Yes to questions they have not yet seen.

See also
ReadKey

Example
```
program XKeypressed;
uses Crt;
```

```
var
  I: Integer;

  procedure Pause;
  var
    Ch: Char;
  begin
    Write('Press Space to continue...');
    while Keypressed do        { Throw away buffered typing }
      Ch := ReadKey;
    repeat
      if Keypressed then
        if ReadKey = CHR(32)  { Wait for Space character }
          then Exit
    until False
  end;

begin
  for I := 1 to 50 do
  begin
    Delay(50);
    Writeln('Start typing now');
  end;
  Writeln;
  Pause;
  Writeln('Ending program')
end.
```

Length

Syntax

```
function Length(S: <string>): Integer;
```

Location
System

Description
Length returns the length of string S, which may be variable, literal, or constant. The length of the string is equal to the number of characters it contains, not the declared string length. A zero-length string is called a *null string*.

The example shows how to use Length to center text on display. You can use Center in your own programs to center messages, program titles, and so on.

See also
Concat, Copy, Delete, Insert, Pos

Example
```pascal
program XLength;
uses Crt;

  procedure Center(S: string);
  begin
    Writeln(S:40 + (Length(S) div 2))
  end;

begin
  ClrScr;
  Center('Welcome to');
  Writeln;
  Center('** Monster Spreadsheet **');
  Writeln;
  Center('"The program that ate Wallstreet"');
  Writeln;
  Center('written by ByteMan');
  GotoXY(1, 25);
  Readln
end.
```

Line

Syntax
```pascal
procedure Line(X1, Y1, X2, Y2: Integer);
```

Location
Graph

Description
Use Line to draw lines of various styles and colors, connecting the two coordinates
(X1, Y1) and (X2, Y2). Call SetColor before Line to change the line's color. Use
SetLineStyle to change the thickness and style of the line.

See also
LineRel, LineTo, MoveTo, SetColor, SetLineStyle

Example
```pascal
program XLine;
uses Crt, Graph;
var
  GraphDriver, GraphMode: Integer;
```

```
    XMin, YMin, XMax, YMax: Integer;
  begin
    GraphDriver := Detect;
    InitGraph(GraphDriver, GraphMode, 'c:\tp\bgi');
    XMax := GetMaxX;
    YMax := GetMaxY;
    XMin := 0;
    YMin := 0;
    while (XMin < XMax) or (YMin < YMax) do
    begin
      Delay(50);
      SetColor(Random(MaxColors));
      Line(XMin, YMin, XMax, YMin);
      Line(XMin, YMax, XMax, YMax);
      Inc(XMin);
      Inc(YMin);
      Dec(XMax);
      Dec(YMax)
    end;
    repeat until Keypressed;
    CloseGraph
  end.
```

LineRel

Syntax
```
  procedure LineRel(Dx, Dy: Integer);
```

Location
Graph

Description
Call LineRel (Line Relative) to draw a line from the current coordinate (X, Y) to (X + Dx, Y + Dy). Because LineRel takes only two parameters, it is faster than Line, which takes four. Use LineRel to write programs that draw figures the same way at any starting location.

The example displays a series of boxes in various colors for an animated display. The four calls to LineRel draw boxes with only two variables, XMax and XMin.

See also
Line, LineTo, MoveRel, MoveTo, SetLineStyle

Example
```
  program XLineRel;
```

```
uses Crt, Graph;
var
  GraphDriver, GraphMode: Integer;
  XMax, YMax : Integer; Color: Word;
begin
  GraphDriver := Detect;
  InitGraph(GraphDriver, GraphMode, 'c:\tp\bgi');
  Randomize;
  while not Keypressed do
  begin
    XMax := GetMaxX;
    YMax := GetMaxY;
    MoveTo(0, 0);
    Color := 1 + Random(MaxColors);
    while XMax > 1 do
    begin
      SetColor(Random(Color));
      LineRel(XMax, 0);
      LineRel(0, YMax);
      LineRel(-XMax, 0);
      LineRel(0, -YMax);
      Dec(XMax, 2);
      Dec(YMax, 2);
      MoveTo(Succ(GetX), Succ(GetY))
    end
  end;
  CloseGraph
end.
```

LineTo

Syntax
```
procedure LineTo(X, Y: Integer);
```

Location
Graph

Description
Use LineTo to draw lines starting from the current coordinate to (X,Y). After LineTo, the current coordinate changes to (X,Y); therefore, you can use this procedure to draw continuing lines where each starting point is the end point of the last. Use MoveTo to preset the current coordinate before drawing with LineTo.

The example draws lines at random in a recursive procedure Lines that also erases each line it draws in a pulsating pattern. Reduce TimeDelay to speed up the action and change MaxLines to draw different numbers of lines.

See also
Line, LineRel, MoveRel, MoveTo, SetLineStyle

Example

```
program XLineTo;
uses Crt, Graph;
const
  MaxLines = 125;
  TimeDelay = 50;
var
  GraphDriver, GraphMode: Integer;
  XMax, YMax: Integer;

  procedure Lines(N: Integer);
  var X1, Y1, X2, Y2: Integer;
  begin
    Delay(TimeDelay);
    if N < MaxLines then
    begin
      X1 := GetX;
      Y1 := GetY;
      SetColor(1 + Random(MaxColors));
      X2 := Random(XMax);
      Y2 := Random(YMax);
      LineTo(X2, Y2);
      Lines(N + 1)
    end;
    Delay(TimeDelay);
    SetColor(Black);
    Line(X1, Y1, X2, Y2)
  end;

begin
  GraphDriver := Detect;
  InitGraph(GraphDriver, GraphMode, 'c:\tp\bgi');
  XMax := GetMaxX;
  YMax := GetMaxY;
  while not Keypressed do
    Lines(1);
  CloseGraph
end.
```

Ln

Syntax
```
function Ln(R: <real>): <real>;
```

Location
System

Description
Ln returns the natural logarithm of real number R. Ln(R) = $\log_e R$ where base $e = 2.7182818285$. If R is zero or negative, a runtime error 207 (Invalid floating point operation) is generated, halting the program.

See also
Exp

Example
```
program XLn;
var
  R: Real;
begin
  Writeln('Ln demonstration');
  Writeln('Type 0 to quit');
  Writeln;
  repeat
    Write('Value? ');
    Readln(R);
    if R > 0.0
      then Writeln('Ln = ', Ln(R))
  until R <= 0.0
end.
```

Lo

Syntax
```
function Lo(I: <integer>): Byte;
```

Location
System

Description
Lo returns the low, or least significant, byte of the Word or Integer value I. The result is always in the range 0 to 255.

See also
Hi, Swap

Example

```
program XLo;
var
  N: Integer;
begin
  N := 1;
  while N > 0 do
  begin
    N := N shl 1;
    Writeln('N=', N:6,
        ' high byte=', Hi(N):6,
        ' low byte=', Lo(N):6);
  end
end.
```

LowVideo

Syntax

```
procedure LowVideo;
```

Location

Crt

Description

LowVideo clears the high-intensity bit of a display character. After calling LowVideo, characters displayed through Write and Writeln statements seem dimmer or a different color than after calling HighVideo. LowVideo clears the high-intensity bit of character bytes stored in the video display buffer.

Depending on the display mode in effect, though, LowVideo may not change text the way you always expect. For that reason, it's a good idea to test what LowVideo does before assuming anything about the results.

The example displays a reference of text in 16 colors before and after calling LowVideo. On monochrome monitors, you see different text attributes rather than colors.

See also

HiVideo, NormVideo, TextBackground, TextColor

Example

```
program XLowVideo;
uses Crt;
var
  Color: Integer;
begin
```

```
      ClrScr;
      Writeln('LowVideo Color Text Demonstration');
      Writeln('---------------------------------');
      for Color := 0 to 15 do
      begin
        HighVideo;
        Write('Color=', Color:2);
        TextColor(Color);
        Write('   High video   ');
        LowVideo;
        Writeln('Low video')
      end
    end.
```

Mark

Syntax
```
procedure Mark(var P: Pointer);
```

Location
System

Description
Mark records the current address of the Pascal heap top, setting P equal to that value. After calling Mark, you can restore the heap to its original size by passing P to Release. Although P may be any pointer variable, it is usually an untyped Pointer variable.

   The example displays the amount of available memory before calling New to allocate space for an array of real numbers on the heap. After filling and displaying the array's contents, the program calls Release with the pointer (heap) initialized by Mark. As you can see when you run the program, this reclaims the memory the array previously occupied.

See also
Dispose, FreeMem, GetMem, New, Release

Example
```
program XMark;
type
  Items = array[1 .. 100] of Real;
var
  Heap: Pointer;
  I: Integer;
  A: ^Items;
```

```
begin
  Mark(Heap);
  Writeln('Memory before new    = ', Memavail);
  New(A);
  Writeln('Memory after new     = ', Memavail);
  for I := 1 to 100 do
    A^[I] := Random;
  for I := 1 to 100 do
    Write(A^[I]:10);
  Writeln;
  Release(Heap);
  Writeln('Memory after release = ', Memavail)
end.
```

MaxAvail

Syntax

```
function MaxAvail: LongInt:
```

Location

System

Description

MaxAvail returns the maximum undivided amount of memory available on the heap. This is equal to either the total amount of heap space available or the size of the largest disposed dynamic variable, whichever is greater.

If MaxAvail is less than the size of the variable you want to place on the heap, there is little to do but end the program with an out-of-memory error. Turbo Pascal does not have the capability of compacting a fragmented heap.

The example reserves 65,535-byte blocks on the heap although MaxAvail reports at least that much memory available. The program reports the size of the largest available memory space before and after reserving blocks, and after releasing one block by calling FreeMem.

See also

MemAvail

Example

```
program XMaxAvail;
var
  P: Pointer;
begin
  Writeln('Before GetMem, MaxAvail=', MaxAvail);
  while MaxAvail > 65535 do
```

```
      GetMem(P, 65535);
    Writeln('After GetMem,  MaxAvail=', MaxAvail);
    FreeMem(P, 65535);
    Writeln('After FreeMem, MaxAvail=', MaxAvail)
  end.
```

MemAvail

Syntax
```
function MemAvail: LongInt;
```

Location
System

Description
MemAvail returns the number of free bytes available on the heap. Due to fragmented free spaces between objects on the heap, this may be greater than the amount of free space available for individual variables.

See also
MaxAvail

Example
```
program XMemAvail;
begin
  Write('There are ', MemAvail);
  Writeln(' bytes available on the heap');
end.
```

MkDir

Syntax
```
procedure MkDir(Path: <string>);
```

Location
System

Description
MkDir creates a new subdirectory of the name specified by the Path string. This is similar to the DOS MKDIR (MD) command. If Input/Output error checking is off with the {$I–} compiler directive, you can check IoResult after MkDir to determine the success or failure of creating the subdirectory.

See also
ChDir, GetDir, RmDir

Example

```
program XMkDir;
var
  Path: string;
begin
  Write('Create what directory? ');
  Readln(Path);
  if Length(Path) > 0 then
  begin
    {$I-} MkDir(Path); {$I+}
    if IoResult = 0
      then Writeln(Path, ' created')
      else Writeln('Error creating directory')
  end
end.
```

Move

Syntax

```
procedure Move(var Source, Destination: <type>; N: Word);
```

Location

System

Description

Move transfers N bytes of source to destination using fast memory move instructions. The Source and Destination variables may be different or the same types. They also may be the same variable—a large array, for example, in which you want to shift data from one part of the array to another.

Index the source or destination arrays to indicate a starting position. If the source and destination are the same variable, then Move controls the direction of byte transfers to prevent overlapping bytes.

The example fills an array with characters starting with A, displays the array contents, and then moves the first 50 characters to the last 50. This is similar to the way some word processors might move characters during an insertion.

See also

FillChar, SizeOf

Example

```
program XMove;
var
  ChArray: array[1 .. 100] of Char;
```

```
    I: Integer;
begin
  for I := 1 to 100 do
    ChArray[I] := Chr(Ord('@') + I);
  Writeln('Before:');
  for I := 1 to 100 do
    Write(ChArray[I]);
  Writeln;
  Move(ChArray[1], ChArray[50], 50);
  Writeln('After:');
  for I := 1 to 100 do
    Write(ChArray[I]);
  Writeln;
end.
```

MoveRel

Syntax

```
procedure MoveRel(Dx, Dy: Integer);
```

Location
Graph

Description

Calling MoveRel changes the current coordinate by a relative amount equal to
$X + Dx$ and $Y + Dy$. The D in Dx and Dy stands for *delta,* a term that typically
represents a relative change in something.

As the example shows, MoveRel operates invisibly. For an experiment, try
replacing MoveRel with LineRel, which works identically to MoveRel but leaves a trail
behind while moving.

See also
LineRel, LineTo, MoveTo

Example

```
program XMoveRel;
uses Crt, Graph;
var
  I, GraphDriver, GraphMode: Integer;
begin
  GraphDriver := Detect;
  InitGraph(GraphDriver, GraphMode, 'c:\tp\bgi');
  MoveTo(10, GetMaxY div 2);
  for I := 1 to 36 do
```

```
  begin
    SetColor(1 + Random(MaxColors));
    Circle(GetX, GetY, GetX);
    MoveRel(I, 0)
  end;
  repeat until Keypressed;
  CloseGraph
end.
```

MoveTo

Syntax
```
procedure MoveTo(X, Y: Integer);
```

Location
Graph

Description
Use MoveTo to change the current coordinate to a specific display location at (X, Y), without drawing a line or making any other changes to the display.

MoveTo comes in handy for restoring the current coordinate to a previous setting. The example uses this idea in procedure Outline, which draws a white border around the display. By saving the current coordinate in two local variables, Oldx and Oldy, the procedure can restore this coordinate after outlining the screen.

See also
LineTo, MoveRel

Example
```
program XMoveTo;
uses Crt, Graph;
var
  GraphDriver, GraphMode: Integer;
  Y, XMax, YMax: Word;

  procedure Outline;
  var
    Oldx, Oldy: Word;
  begin
    Oldx := GetX;
    Oldy := GetY;
    MoveTo(0, 0);
    LineTo(XMax, 0);
    LineTo(XMax, YMax);
```

```
      LineTo(0, YMax);
      LineTo(0, 0);
      MoveTo(Oldx, Oldy)
    end;

begin
  GraphDriver := Detect;
  InitGraph(GraphDriver, GraphMode, 'c:\tp\bgi');
  XMax := GetMaxX;
  YMax := GetMaxY;
  MoveTo(XMax div 2, YMax div 2);
  Y := YMax div 2;
  Outline;
  while not Keypressed do
  begin
    Delay(50);
    SetColor(1 + Random(MaxColors));
    LineTo(1 + Random(XMax - 2), Y (* 1 + Random(yMax - 2)*) );
    Y := Y + Random(15);
    if Y >= YMax then
    begin
      Y := 1;
      MoveTo(GetX, Y)
    end
  end;
  CloseGraph
end.
```

MsDos

Syntax
```
procedure MsDos(var Regs: Registers);
```

Location
Dos

Description
MsDos calls a standard DOS operating system routine. Variable Regs is a record of type Registers defined in the Dos unit (see Chapter 9).

To call a DOS routine, place the routine's number in Regs.AH, set other fields for this operation, and pass the Regs record to MsDos. When the routine ends, Regs fields will contain any results returned by DOS.

The example shows how to turn on disk-write verification, causing DOS to read and check every disk sector after writing to disk. You might want to use this idea for extra safety in programs that write to disk files. Change AL := 1 to AL:= 0 to turn off verification or use the DOS command, verify OFF.

> **Note:** The Dos unit in Turbo Pascal 5.0 and later versions contains a procedure SetVerify that can turn disk-write verification on and off.

See also
Intr

Example
```
program XMsDos;
uses Dos;
var
  Regs: Registers;
begin
  Writeln('Turn on disk-write verification');
  with Regs do
  begin
    AH := $2E;    { Set Verify Flag }
    AL := 1;      { 1=on, 0=off }
    DL := 0       { Required by DOS 1.0, 2.0 only }
  end;
  MsDos(Regs)     { Call DOS }
end.
```

New

Syntax
```
procedure New(var P: <typed pointer>);
function New(<pointer type> [, C: <constructor>]): Pointer;
```

Location
System

Description
New creates a dynamic variable of P's base type and assigns the address of the first byte in the variable to P. After New(P), the contents of the variable, represented by P^, are uninitialized.

The maximum variable size that each call to New can create is 65,520 bytes, even though the heap might contain much more free space. To create variables larger than this maximum value, call New more than once, and store the resulting pointers in an array or in separate pointer variables.

Unlike some other compilers, Turbo Pascal does not allow allocation of variant record parts by specific tag field values.

Starting with Turbo Pascal 5.5, New is extended in two ways (see the second syntax definition). The first extension, which applies to all uses of New, allows you to write statements such as:

```
p := New(PType);
```

where PType is a pointer type, and P is a pointer variable, usually but not necessarily of type PType. Using New as a function leads to certain dangers. For example, *don't* write expressions such as:

```
if New(PType) then ...
```

That simply throws away heap space by allocating a variable of type PType and then discarding the pointer to that space.

The all-new New also plays a role in object-oriented programming. Objects are often allocated space in heap memory and usually have constructor methods to initialize themselves. Because the constructors must be called for every new instance of the object, New handles both the allocation and initialization steps in one easy motion.

If OPtr is a pointer to an object named OType, which has a constructor named OInit that takes two integer parameters, you can initialize and allocate space for the object with the statement:

```
OPtr := New(OType, OInit(123, 456));
```

See Chapter 15 for more information on object-oriented programming concepts. The example shows the more traditional way to call New.

See also
Dispose, FreeMem, GetMem

Example
```
program XNew;
type
  RealArray = array[1 .. 100] of Real;
var
  P: ^RealArray;
  I: Integer;
begin
  Writeln('Creating array of real numbers on the heap');
  New(P);  { Reserve space for array, assigning its address to P }
  for I := 1 to 100 do     { Assign random values to array }
    P^[I] := Random;
```

```
  for I := 1 to 100 do      { Display values }
    Write(P^[I]:10);
  Writeln
end.
```

NormVideo

Syntax
```
procedure NormVideo;
```

Location
Crt

Description
NormVideo restores text displays to the background and foreground colors originally set when the program started running. Use NormVideo, HighVideo, and LowVideo along with TextColor and TextBackground to display characters in various colors and attributes. Be aware that different monitors and video cards respond differently to the same settings.

      The example displays a table of all possible color combinations, in LowVideo and HighVideo. Notice how NormVideo makes it easy to insert blanks between each combination in the displayed table. You can use the table to select character attributes when designing screens.

See also
HighVideo, LowVideo, TextBackground, TextColor

Example
```
program XNormVideo;
uses Crt;
const
  Blank = ' ';  { Single blank space }
var
  I, BColor, FColor: Integer;
begin
  ClrScr;
  Writeln( 'Text Attributes  Columns=TextColor, Rows=TextBackground');
  Writeln( 'First character=LowVideo, second character=HighVideo');
  Writeln( '------------------------------------------------------------');
  Writeln; Writeln; Write(Blank);
  for I := 0 to 15 do Write(I:4);
  for BColor := 0 to 15 do
  begin
    Writeln;
```

```
        Write(BColor:2);
        for FColor := 0 to 15 do
        begin
          NormVideo;
          Write(Blank);
          TextColor(FColor);
          TextBackground(BColor);
          LowVideo;
          Write(Blank, 'A');
          HighVideo;
          Write('A')
        end;
        NormVideo
      end
  end.
```

NoSound

Syntax
```
procedure NoSound;
```

Location
Crt

Description
NoSound stops the tone started by procedure Sound. Because sound continues after calling Sound, you must call NoSound or the tone will continue—even after the program ends!

The example shows how to design your own bell procedure, which many programmers prefer over using the standard Write(Chr(7)) beep. The delays determine the length and separation of each tone. Try removing NoSound and running the program. Then run the original program to turn off the noise.

See also
Sound

Example
```
program XNoSound;
uses Crt;
var
  I: Integer;
begin
  ClrScr;
  for I := 1 to 10 do
```

```
  begin
    Delay(150);
    Write(#14:4);
    Sound(2000);
    Delay(150);
    NoSound
  end
end.
```

Odd

Syntax

```
function Odd(N: <integer>): Boolean;
```

Location

System

Description

Odd returns true if integer N is an odd number. You also can use Odd to test the least significant bit (lsb) of N in binary. If Odd(N) is true, then lsb = 1, else lsb = 0.

The example shows another way to put this useful function to work. The expression:

```
if Odd(Random(MaxInt))
  then A
  else B;
```

executes A or B about 50% of the time. You might use this idea in a game or a simulation to make 50/50 decisions, as in the example, which flips an imaginary coin, counting the number of heads and tails.

Example

```
program XOdd;
uses Crt;
var
  Done : Boolean; Heads, Tails: LongInt;
begin
  Writeln('Heads I Win, Tails You Lose');
  Writeln;
  Writeln('Flipping a coin.');
  Write(' Press <Enter> to stop...');
  Heads := 0;
  Tails := 0;
  Done := false;
```

```
    repeat
      if Odd(Random(MaxInt))
        then Heads := Heads + 1
        else Tails := Tails + 1;
      if Keypressed then
        Done := (Readkey = Chr(13))
    until Done;
    Writeln;
    Writeln('Heads = ', Heads);
    Writeln('Tails = ', Tails)
  end.
```

Ofs

Syntax
```
function Ofs(V: <ident>): Word;
```

Location
System

Description
Ofs returns the 16-bit offset address where V is located. Usually, V is a variable, but it also can be a procedure or function identifier.

Finding the offset address of pointer variables requires care. Ofs(P) returns the address of the pointer variable itself—in other words, the address where the pointer is stored in memory. Ofs(P^) returns the address of the variable addressed by the pointer. Using the wrong form can produce very hard-to-find bugs.

The example displays the offset address of both a pointer variable (P2) and the number the pointer addresses. The other pointers are not used.

See also
Addr, Seg

Example
```
program XOfs;
var
  P1, P2, P3: ^Real;
begin
  New(P1);
  New(P2);
  New(P3);
  P2^ := Pi;
  Writeln('Offset address of p2  = ', Ofs(P2));
  Writeln('Offset address of p2^ = ', Ofs(P2^))
end.
```

Ord

Syntax
```
function Ord(V: <ordinal>): LongInt;
```

Location
System

Description
Ord returns the ordinal number representing the order of V in a set of scalar values. With an enumerated data type, Ord returns the order of elements as originally declared. If Color = (Red, White, Blue), then Ord(Red) = 0, Ord(White) = 1, and Ord(Blue) = 2.

The ordinal number of a character equals the ASCII value of that character. For example, Ord('A') = 65 and Ord('B') = 66.

The example shows how to use Ord to convert character digits '0' to '9' to equivalent decimal values. Type any character to see the ASCII value. Type a digit key to see the ASCII and decimal values, returned by function ValCh, which uses Ord to convert ASCII digit characters to decimal equivalents. The repeat loop also uses Ord to end when character Ch equals 27, the ASCII value for the Esc key.

See also
Chr

Example
```
program XOrd;
uses Crt;
const
  ASCIIEsc = 27;  { ASCII value for Esc key }
var
  Ch: Char;

  function ValCh(Ch: Char): Byte;
  begin
    ValCh := Ord(Ch) - Ord('0')
  end;

begin
  repeat
    Writeln;
    Write('Type 0..9 or Esc to quit: ');
    Ch := ReadKey;
    Writeln;
    Writeln('The character you typed is : ', Ch);
    Writeln('Its ASCII value is         : ', Ord(Ch));
```

```
      if Ch in ['0'..'9'] then
        Writeln('Its value in decimal is     : ', ValCh(Ch));
    until Ord(Ch) = ASCIIEsc
  end.
```

OutText

Syntax
```
procedure OutText(TextString: string);
```

Location
Graph

Description
Use OutText to display text on graphics displays in the current font, direction, and size set by SetTextStyle and in the justification set by SetTextJustify.

You can pass literal or variable strings to OutText. On-screen, the text appears at the current coordinate, which you can change by calling MoveTo.

See also
OutTextXY, SetTextJustify, SetTextStyle, TextHeight, TextWidth

Example
```
program XOutText;
uses Crt, Graph;
var
  GraphDriver, GraphMode: Integer;
  CharSize, Y: Word;
begin
  GraphDriver := Detect;
  InitGraph(GraphDriver, GraphMode, 'c:\tp\bgi');
  Y := 0;
  Randomize;
  for CharSize := 1 to 8 do
  begin
    SetColor(1 + Random(MaxColors));
    MoveTo(0, Y);
    SetTextStyle(1, 0, CharSize);
    OutText('This is a test. ABCDEFG 1234567890');
    Y := Y + TextHeight('M') + 1
  end;
  repeat until Keypressed;
  CloseGraph
end.
```

OutTextXY

Syntax
```
procedure OutTextXY(X, Y: Integer; TextString: string);
```

Location
Graph

Description
OutTextXY is nearly identical to OutText except for the addition of two parameters, X and Y, representing the coordinate where the first character of string textString appears. The two statements:

```
MoveTo(X, Y);
OutText(S);
```

are equivalent to:

```
OutTextXY(X, Y, S);
```

One difference, however, is that after OutText, CP (current point) changes to the end of the string. After OutTextXY, CP remains unchanged.

See also
OutText

Example
```
program XOutTextXY;
uses Crt, Graph;
var
  GraphDriver, GraphMode: Integer;
  CharSize, Y: Word;
begin
  GraphDriver := Detect;
  InitGraph(GraphDriver, GraphMode, 'c:\tp\bgi');
  Y := 0;
  Randomize;
  for CharSize := 3 to 9 do
  begin
    SetColor(1 + Random(MaxColors));
    SetTextStyle(2, 0, CharSize);
    OutTextXY(0, Y, 'This is a test. ABCDEFG 1234567890');
    Y := Y + TextHeight('M') + 1
  end;
  repeat until Keypressed;
  CloseGraph
end.
```

OvrClearBuf

Syntax
```
procedure OvrClearBuf;
```

Location
Overlay

Description
After calling OvrClearBuf to clear all overlays from the overlay buffer, the next call to a procedure or function in an overlay unit will load the unit from disk or from EMS RAM.

In most programs, there's rarely any good reason to call OvrClearBuf. For debugging custom overlay-loader routines (see OvrReadFunc), you can call OvrClearBuf to force disk reads (or EMS RAM transfers) on the next call to an overlay routine.

If you need extra memory (especially if the overlay buffer is large), you can call OvrClearBuf and then use the buffer memory for other purposes—that is, between calls to routines in overlay units. The overlay buffer is located at OvrHeapOrg:0000 up to but not including the byte at OvrHeapEnd:0000, which is also the base of the heap.

The example configures the Dos unit as an overlay (the only standard Turbo Pascal unit for which this is possible) and then calls two routines in the unit, GetDate before clearing the buffer and DosVersion after. Because this example is so small, you might not see any disk activity.

See also
OvrGetBuf, OvrSetBuf

Example
```pascal
{$O+,F+}    { Use overlays, Generate FAR code }
program XOvrClearBuf;
uses Overlay, Crt, Dos;
{$O Dos}
var
  Version, Year, Month, Day, Weekday: Word;
begin
  OvrInit('XOVRCLEA.OVR');
  if OvrResult <> OvrOk then Halt;
  GetDate(Year, Month, Day, Weekday);
  Writeln('Today''s date is: ', Day, '-', Month, '-', Year);
  Write('Press Enter to load Dos overlay...');
  Readln;
  OvrClearBuf;                    { Empty overlay buffer }
```

```
    Version := DosVersion;     { Reloads Dos unit overlay into buffer }
    Writeln('Dos version is: ', Lo(Version), '.', Hi(Version));
  end.
```

OvrGetBuf

Syntax
```
function OvrGetBuf: LongInt;
```

Location
Overlay

Description
OvrGetBuf returns the size in bytes of the current overlay buffer. Call OvrSetBuf to increase the buffer size. The default buffer size equals the number of bytes in the largest overlay unit.

      The example is in three files: OVERU 1.PAS, OVERU2.PAS, and XOVRGETB.PAS. The first two overlay unit files are used by other overlay examples in this chapter. The third file demonstrates how to call OvrGetBuf to display the overlay buffer size.

> **Note:** You may enter and compile the example programs in Turbo Pascal's IDE, but you must run them from the DOS command line.

See also
OvrSetBuf

Example
```
OVERU1.PAS


{$O+,F+}    { Use overlays, Generate FAR code }
unit OverU1;
interface
procedure WriteHi(N: Word);
implementation
procedure WriteHi(N: Word);
begin
  Write(Hi(N))
end;
end.


OVERU2.PAS
```

```
{$O+,F+}    { Use overlays, Generate FAR code }
unit OverU2;
interface
procedure WriteLo(N: Word);
implementation
procedure WriteLo(N: Word);
begin
  Write(Lo(N))
end;
end.
```

XOVRGETB.PAS

```
{$O+,F+}    { Use overlays, Generate FAR code }
program XOvrGetBuf;
uses Overlay, Dos, OverU1, OverU2;
{$O Dos}
{$O OverU1}
{$O OverU2}
var
  Version: Word;
begin
  OvrInit('XOVRGETB.OVR');
  if OvrResult <> OvrOk then Halt;
   { For test purposes only, the next several statements load
     overlay units (4 times) from disk or from EMS RAM. }
  Write('DOS version = ');
  WriteLo(DosVersion);
  Write('.');
  WriteHi(DosVersion);
  Writeln;
  Writeln('Size of overlay buffer = ', OvrGetBuf, ' bytes');
end.
```

OvrGetRetry

Syntax
```
function OvrGetRetry: LongInt;
```

Location
Overlay

Description

OvrGetRetry returns the size of the probation area, which usually occupies from one-third to half of the total overlay buffer size. Units that fall within this area are placed "on probation," during which time if any statements call procedures and functions in the unit, the unit is given a "reprieve." When buffer space is needed for another overlay, the overlay loader tries to keep reprieved units in memory. This helps to keep frequently used overlays in the buffer for longer times, thus improving program performance by limiting disk reads.

The example displays the size of the probation area before and after calling OvrSetRetry, which changes the probation size. Units OverU1 and OverU2 are from OvrGetBuf's example.

See also

OvrSetRetry

Example

```
{$O+,F+}    { Use overlays, Generate FAR code }
program XOvrGetRetry;
uses Overlay, Dos, OverU1, OverU2;
{$O Dos}
{$O OverU1}
{$O OverU2}
var
  Version: Word;
begin
  OvrInit('XOVRGETR.OVR');
  if OvrResult <> OvrOk then Halt;
{ For test purposes only, the next several statements load
  overlay units (4 times) from disk or from EMS RAM. }
  Writeln('Size of overlay buffer = ', OvrGetBuf, ' bytes');
  Writeln('Size of probation area before = ', OvrGetRetry, ' bytes');
  OvrSetRetry(OvrGetBuf div 3);    { 1/3 total buffer space }
  Write('DOS version = ');
  WriteLo(DosVersion);
  Write('.');
  WriteHi(DosVersion);
  Writeln;
  Writeln('Size of probation area after  = ', OvrGetRetry, ' bytes');
end.
```

OvrInit

Syntax

```
procedure OvrInit(FileName: string);
```

Location
Overlay

Description
All programs that enable overlays must call OvrInit before other statements call procedures and functions in overlay units. The FileName string should be set to the program's .OVR file name. For example, if the main program text is STARS.PAS, Turbo Pascal saves the main code in STARS.EXE and the overlays in STARS.OVR. To initialize overlays for this program, use the statements:

```
OvrInit('STARS.OVR');
if OvrResult <> ovrOk then
begin
  Writeln('Error loading overlays');
  Halt
end;
```

Usually, it is wise to follow OvrInit with a check of the OvrResult variable (typed) constant. If this value does not equal ovrOk, then the overlay file is missing or damaged and the program must not continue.

Turbo Pascal 5.5 and 6.0 allow you to attach an overlay file to the end of the .EXE file. You can then delete the .OVR file. To do this, compile all units and the main program without Turbo Debugger information. Then execute the DOS commands:

```
COPY /B STARS.EXE + STARS.OVR
DEL STARS.OVR
```

Also change the OvrInit parameter to load the .EXE rather than the .OVR file:

```
OvrInit('STARS.EXE');
```

The example demonstrates how to call OvrInit and check for errors. Compile to XOVRINIT.EXE and run. Then delete the XOVRINIT.OVR file and run a second time to see the error message. Units OverU1 and OverU2 are from OvrGetBuf's example.

See also
OvrGetBuf, OvrInitEMS, OvrSetBuf

Example
```
{$O+,F+}    { Use overlays, Generate FAR code }
program XOvrInit;
uses Overlay, Dos, OverU1, OverU2;
{$O Dos}
{$O OverU1}
{$O OverU2}
var
  Version: Word;
```

```
begin
  OvrInit('XOVRINIT.OVR');
  if OvrResult <> OvrOk then
  begin
    Writeln('Overlay error, code ', OvrResult);
    Halt(OvrResult)
  end;{
{ For test purposes only, the next several statements load
  overlay units (4 times) from disk or from EMS RAM. }
  Write('DOS version = ');
  WriteLo(DosVersion);
  Write('.');
  WriteHi(DosVersion);
  Writeln;
end.
```

OvrInitEMS

Syntax
```
procedure OvrInitEMS;
```

Location
Overlay

Description
OvrInitEMS detects whether the system has EMS (Expanded Memory System) RAM. If enough EMS RAM is available, OvrInitEMS loads the program's .OVR overlay file into that memory. Then, rather than reading overlay units from disk, the overlay loader transfers overlays from EMS RAM to the overlay buffer for execution. Because the entire program remains in RAM, performance increases dramatically.

OvrInitEMS does not eliminate the need for a main-memory overlay buffer. But, if EMS RAM is available, you may want to use the smallest buffer possible. There's not much of an advantage to increasing the overlay buffer size with OvrSetBuf if all overlays are stored in EMS RAM. (Transferring overlay units from EMS RAM to the overlay buffer does take some time, so for the best results, you can use both EMS RAM and a large overlay buffer. In most cases, the benefits from such an arrangement are small.)

Checking for errors after calling OvrInitEMS as in the example is optional. If enough EMS RAM is not available to hold overlays, the program uses main memory just as it does if no EMS RAM exists. Units OverU1 and OverU2 are from OvrGetBuf's example.

See also
OvrGetBuf, OvrInit, OvrSetBuf

Example

```
{$O+,F+}    { Use overlays, Generate FAR code }
program XOvrInitEMS;
uses Overlay, Dos, OverU1, OverU2;
{$O Dos}
{$O OverU1}
{$O OverU2}
var
  Version: Word;
begin
  OvrInit('XOVREMS.OVR');
  if OvrResult <> OvrOk then Halt;
  OvrInitEMS;    { Detect and use EMS RAM if available }
  if OvrResult <> OvrOk then
    Writeln('EMS error detected, code ', OvrResult);
{ For test purposes only, the next several statements load
  overlay units (4 times) from disk or from EMS RAM. }
  Write('DOS version = ');
  WriteLo(DosVersion);
  Write('.');
  WriteHi(DosVersion);
  Writeln;
end.
```

OvrReadFunc

Syntax

```
OvrReadFunc = function(OvrSeg: Word): Integer;
```

Location

Overlay

Description

OvrReadFunc is a procedure-type function—in other words, a design for a function that you can write, not a real function in the Overlay unit. Attaching a custom OvrReadFunc function to the Overlay unit traps calls to the overlay loader, letting you add new operations just before overlays are loaded from disk or from EMS RAM. The function must be compiled with the {$F+} far option or by using the **far** keyword in the function declaration.

There are three main reasons for installing an OverReadFunc function:

- To prompt users to insert a disk containing the overlay file.

- To prevent programs from halting due to disk errors while reading overlays.

- To debug overlays by intercepting overlay-loader calls.

To attach a custom overlay-loader function, create a variable of type OvrReadFunc for saving the original overlay-loader address (stockOvrLoader in the example). Then, write a custom function with the same format as OvrReadFunc (see OvrDebugger in the example). Switch on {$F+} or use the **far** keyword to compile this function as a **far** subroutine. The function parameter OvrSeg identifies the overlay to be loaded. Pass this value to the original overlay loader with a statement such as:

```
OvrDebugger := StockOvrLoader(OvrSeg);  { Call overlay loader }
```

This calls the stock overlay loader and returns the result code as OvrDebugger's function value. To check for errors during loading, thus preventing a program from halting if the .OVR file cannot be found, save the stock overlay loader's result code in a temporary variable and loop until the result is zero:

```
repeat
  TempInteger := StockOvrLoader(OvrSeg);
  if TempInteger <> 0 then
    { ... Insert message to check disks, etc. }
until TempInteger = 0;
```

Only if the OvrReadFunc function returns a nonzero value will a runtime error halt the program; therefore, this code prevents accidental interruptions due to overlay problems. (A better example would give people a way to end the program if they cannot correct the overlay problem.)

The example is similar to OvrInit's, but displays several overlay values during each call to the overlay loader. This proves that the overlay loader is intercepting the calls to DosVersion and to WriteLo and WriteHi routines in units OverU1 and OverU2 from OvrGetBuf's example.

See also
OvrInit

Example
```
{$O+,F+}    { Use overlays, Generate FAR code }
program XOvrReadFunc;
uses Overlay, Dos, OverU1, OverU2;
{$O Dos}
{$O OverU1}
{$O OverU2}
var
  Version: Word;
  StockOvrLoader: OvrReadFunc;
```

```
function OvrDebugger(OvrSeg: Word): Integer; far;
begin
  Writeln;
  Writeln(' — — OvrDebugger start');
  Writeln(' OvrTrapCount = ', OvrTrapCount);
  Writeln(' OvrLoadCount = ', OvrLoadCount);
  Writeln(' OvrFileMode  = ', OvrFileMode);
  Writeln(' OvrHeapOrg   = ', OvrHeapOrg, ':0000');
  Writeln(' OvrHeapPtr   = ', OvrHeapPtr, ':0000');
  Writeln(' OvrHeapEnd   = ', OvrHeapEnd, ':0000');
  Writeln(' OvrHeapSize  = ', OvrHeapSize, ' paragraphs');
  Writeln;
  Write('Press Enter to load overlay...');
  Readln;
  OvrDebugger := StockOvrLoader(OvrSeg)    { Call overlay loader }
end;

begin
  OvrInit('XOVRREAD.OVR');
  if OvrResult <> OvrOk then Halt;
  StockOvrLoader := OvrReadBuf;          { Save overlay-loader address }
  OvrReadBuf := OvrDebugger;             { Attach custom function }
{ For test purposes only, the next several statements load
  overlay units (4 times) from disk or from EMS RAM. }
  Write('DOS version = ');
  WriteLo(DosVersion);
  Write('.');
  WriteHi(DosVersion);
  Writeln;
end.
```

OvrSetBuf

Syntax
```
procedure OvrSetBuf(Size: LongInt);
```

Location
Overlay

Description
Call OvrSetBuf to increase the size of the overlay buffer. A larger overlay buffer allows the Overlay unit to store multiple overlays in memory, thus increasing performance by reducing disk reads. Call OverSetBuf as soon as possible after calling OvrInit to

initialize overlays. When also enabling EMS RAM with OvrInitEMS, it is probably not necessary to call OvrSetBuf. If overlays are already in memory, there's little advantage to increasing the overlay buffer size.

OvrSetBuf has no effect in two situations: when the Size value is smaller than the largest overlay unit and after you have executed New to create pointer-addressable variables on the heap, from which the overlay unit takes space for the overlay buffer.

The example doubles the default buffer size by passing to OvrSetBuf a value equal to twice OvrGetBuf, which returns the size of the current buffer. An **if** statement avoids increasing the buffer size if EMS RAM is available. Units OverU1 and OverU2 are from OvrGetBuf's example.

See also
OvrGetBuf, OvrInit, OvrInitEMS

Example

```
{$O+,F+}    { Use overlays, Generate FAR code }
program XOvrSetBuf;
uses Overlay, Dos, OverU1, OverU2;
{$O Dos}
{$O OverU1}
{$O OverU2}
var
  Version: Word;
begin
  OvrInit('XOVRSETB.OVR');
  if OvrResult <> OvrOk then Halt;
  Writeln('Default overlay buffer size = ', OvrGetBuf, ' bytes');
  OvrInitEMS;    { Detect and use EMS RAM if available }
  if OvrResult <> OvrOk then
  begin
    Writeln('EMS RAM not available');
    OvrSetBuf(OvrGetBuf*2);    { Double the buffer size }
    Writeln('Overlay buffer size increased to ', OvrGetBuf, ' bytes')
  end else
    Writeln('Overlays loaded into EMS RAM');
{ For test purposes only, the next several statements load
  overlay units (4 times) from disk or from EMS RAM. }
  Write('DOS version = ');
  WriteLo(DosVersion);
  Write('.');
  WriteHi(DosVersion);
  Writeln;
end.
```

OvrSetRetry

Syntax
```
procedure OvrSetRetry(Size: LongInt);
```

Location
Overlay

Description
Use OvrSetRetry to designate a portion of the overlay buffer as the "probation" area. Normally, the size of this area is zero, making the Overlay unit function as in Turbo Pascal 5.0. Setting the probation area to a positive value enables the "probation-reprieve" overlay memory-management method, first introduced in Turbo Pascal 5.5.

This new buffer-management method helps keep frequently used overlay units in memory for longer periods of time. When a unit's code falls within the designated probation area, any calls to routines in the unit cause the entire unit to be given a reprieve the next time more space is needed for another overlay. (See Chapter 13 for a detailed description of how this method works.)

Borland recommends assigning from one-third to half of the total buffer size to the probation area. For best results, examine the values of OvrTrapCount (the number of intercepted calls to overlays on probation or not in memory) and OvrLoadCount (the number of times overlays are loaded into memory) while experimenting with different probation sizes. Strive for a setting that causes OvrTrapCount to advance more rapidly than OvrLoadCount.

See also
OvrGetRetry

Example
See example for OvrGetRetry.

PackTime

Syntax
```
procedure PackTime(var T: DateTime; var P: LongInt);
```

Location
Dos

Description
Use PackTime to convert date and time values in a DateTime record into a single LongInt value P in the packed format stored with file entries in disk directories. Use UnpackTime to go the other direction, unpacking a LongInt value into a DateTime record.

The example uses PackTime to stuff the current date and time into LongInt variable P, passed to SetFTime to let you update any file to today's date.

See also
GetDate, GetTime, UnpackTime

Example
```
program XPackTime;
uses Dos;
var
  F: file;
  Fname: string;
  Junk: Word;
  TheDate: DateTime;
  P: LongInt;
begin
  Writeln('Change a file''s date and time');
  Write('File name? ');
  Readln(Fname);
  Assign(F, Fname);
  Reset(F);
  with TheDate do
  begin
    GetDate(Year, Month, Day, Junk);
    GetTime(Hour, Min, Sec, Junk)
  end;
  PackTime(TheDate, P);
  SetFTime(F, P);
  Close(F)
end.
```

ParamCount

Syntax
```
function ParamCount: Word;
```

Location
System

Description
ParamCount returns the number of arguments entered after the program name on the DOS command line. Suppose you have the program TEST.EXE on disk. If you run the program from DOS with this command:

```
A>TEST INPUT.TXT OxUTPUT.TXT
```

then ParamCount will equal two. Use the *Run: Parameters* command to perform the equivalent of this command when using Turbo Pascal's integrated compiler. This simulates passing parameters to programs rather than forcing you to return to DOS just to test programs such as these.

One typical use for ParamCount is to know when to display program instructions. If ParamCount is zero and the program requires one or more parameters, then the person who started the program probably needs help. Compile the example to a disk file TEST.EXE and type TEST with and without parameters to see the difference.

See also
EnvCount, EnvStr, GetEnv, ParamStr

Example

```pascal
program XParamCount;
var
  I: Integer;
begin
  if ParamCount = 0 then
  begin { Display instructions }
    Writeln;
    Writeln('Run the program this way:');
    Writeln;
    Writeln('  TEST <p1> <p2> <p3> ... <pn>');
    Writeln;
    Writeln('where <p1>..<pn> are parameters you want');
    Writeln('to pass to TEST.  For example, you could type:');
    Writeln;
    Writeln('  TEST INTEXT.TXT OUTTEXT.TXT')
  end else
  begin { Display parameters }
    Writeln('You typed ', ParamCount, ' parameters:');
    for I := 1 to ParamCount do
      Writeln(I:2, ' : ', ParamStr(I))
  end
end.
```

ParamStr

Syntax
```pascal
function ParamStr(N: Word): string;
```

Location
System

Description

When you are executing a program from DOS, or in memory with optional command-line parameters, ParamStr returns parameter string N, if it exists. Use ParamCount to determine the number of parameters waiting to be read.

The example shows how to use ParamStr to pick up a parameter file name passed to a program from the DOS command line. Compile the program to TEST.EXE and type TEST <filename> to type a text file to the display, similar to the way the DOS TYPE command works. Type TEST alone to see an error message reminding you to type a file name.

Under DOS 3.0 and later versions, ParamStr(0) returns the name of the current program. To assign the program name to a string variable ProgName, write:

```
if Lo(DosVersion) < 3
  then ProgName := ''
  else ProgName := ParamStr(0);
```

See also

EnvCount, EnvStr, GetEnv, ParamCount

Example

```
program XParamStr;
var
  Tf: Text;
  S: string;
begin
  if ParamCount = 0 then
    Writeln('Error: no file name specified')
  else begin
    Assign(Tf, ParamStr(1));
    Reset(Tf);
    while not Eof(Tf) do
    begin
      Readln(Tf, S);
      Writeln(S)
    end;
    Close(Tf)
  end
end.
```

Pi

Syntax

```
function Pi: <real>;
```

Location
System

Description
Pi returns the value of π, previously a constant in earlier Turbo Pascal versions. Because Pi is now a function, its precision changes when you compile a program with the {$N+} directive, enabling math coprocessor data types.

     The example displays the extended value of Pi, enabling a math coprocessor or emulation with the directives {$N+,E+}. Remove the directives and run the example to see Pi's default value. For reference, both values are listed below.

```
Pi = 3.14159265358979E+0000    (Coprocessor or emulation)
Pi = 3.1415926536E+00          (No coprocessor)
```

Example
```
{$N+,E+}    { Enable coprocessor or emulation }
program XPi;
begin
  Writeln('Pi = ', Pi)
end.
```

PieSlice

Syntax
```
procedure PieSlice(X, Y: Integer; StAngle, EndAngle, Radius: Word);
```

Location
Graph

Description
PieSlice draws a filled wedge with the sharp point at coordinate (X,Y). The starting angle (StAngle) and ending angle (EndAngle) represent the width of the wedge, with greater angles running counterclockwise. The Radius changes the wedge length.

     Use SetColor to change the wedge outline. Use SetFillStyle to change the wedge fill color and pattern. The example uses PieSlice to display a chart of the 16 colors available in EGA and VGA displays.

See also
Arc, Circle, Ellipse, GetArcCoords, GetAspectRatio, Sector, SetFillStyle, SetFillPattern

Example
```
program XPieSlice;
uses Crt, Graph;
var
  GraphDriver, GraphMode: Integer;
  Color, StAngle, Radius, XCenter, YCenter: Word;
```

```
begin
  GraphDriver := Detect;
  InitGraph(GraphDriver, GraphMode, 'c:\tp\bgi');
  XCenter := GetMaxX div 2;
  YCenter := GetMaxY div 2;
  Radius := GetMaxX div 4;
  StAngle := 0;
  for Color := 0 to 14 do
  begin
    StAngle := StAngle + 24;
    SetFillStyle(SolidFill, Color);
    PieSlice(XCenter, YCenter, StAngle, StAngle + 24, Radius)
  end;
  repeat until Keypressed;
  CloseGraph
end.
```

Pos

Syntax
```
function Pos(Pattern, Search: <string>): Byte;
```

Location
System

Description
Pos returns the index position where a Pattern exists in the Search string. If Pos does not find Pattern anywhere in Search, the function returns zero.

The example shows a common use for Pos, prompting for file names with a default extension, in this case, .PAS. Run the program and type the name of a Pascal source code file to display. For example, if you type TEST, the program tries to list TEST.PAS. But if you type TEST.TXT, Pos finds the period in the file name and does not add the default extension.

See also
Concat, Copy, Delete, Insert, Length

Example
```
program XPos;
var
  Tf: Text;
  S, Filename: string;
begin
  Write('List what file? [.PAS] ');
```

```
    Readln(FileName);
    if Pos('.', FileName) = 0
      then FileName := FileName + '.PAS';
    Writeln('Listing ', FileName);
    Assign(Tf, FileName);
    Reset(Tf);
    while not Eof(Tf) do
    begin
      Readln(Tf, S);
      Writeln(S)
    end;
    Close(Tf)
  end.
```

Pred

Syntax
```
function Pred(V: <ordinal>): <ordinal>;
```

Location
System

Description
Pred returns the scalar predecessor of V, which can be any ordinal type such as Integer, Char, or an enumerated type of your own making. For example, given the declaration Color = (Red, White, Blue), then Pred(Blue) = White, and Pred(White) = Red. Pred(Red) is undefined. Also, Pred(true) = false, Pred(1) = 0, Pred(2) = 1, and so on.

See also
Succ

Example
```
program XPred;
var
  I: Integer;
begin
  Writeln('Countdown courtesy of Pred(v)');
  Writeln;
  I := 100;
  while I > 0 do
  begin
    Write(I:4);
```

```
      I := Pred(I)
  end
end.
```

Ptr

Syntax
```
function Ptr(Segment, Offset: Word): Pointer;
```

Location
System

Description
Ptr returns a Pointer equal to the 32-bit memory address specified by Segment and Offset. You can assign the function result to any pointer variable.

Use Ptr to create pointers to known locations in memory, as in the example, which points variable LowTime to the low word value of the PC interrupt timer. When you run the program, you see the value at the address in LowTime constantly changing.

See also
Addr, Ofs, Seg

Example
```
program XPtr;
uses Crt;
var
  LowTime: ^Word;
begin
  LowTime := Ptr(0000, $046C);
  while not KeyPressed do
  begin
    GotoXY(1, WhereY);
    Write(LowTime^)
  end
end.
```

PutImage

Syntax
```
procedure PutImage(X, Y: Integer; var BitMap; BitBlt: Word);
```

Location
Graph

Description
PutImage copies a saved graphics image from a variable named BitMap, usually an array of bytes, to the display. The upper-left corner of the image is at coordinate (X,Y). Parameter BitBlt (meaning "bit block transfer" but sometimes called "bit blitter" or "bit blaster") specifies the logical operation used to combine image bits with pixels already on display. Set BitBlt to one of the five constants: NormalPut, XORPut, OrPut, AndPut, NotPut. NormalPut copies the image over anything on display. The other BitBlt values use **xor**, **or**, **and**, or **not** logic to combine bits with display pixels. The image width and height were previously saved by GetImage in BitMap.

Normally, you save images with GetImage and then redisplay them elsewhere with PutImage. The example shows how to use this technique to bounce a red rubber ball around on screen. After drawing the ball, GetImage saves the pixels in a byte array addressed by pointer Image. Then, a **while** loop cycles, displaying the ball with calls to PutImage until you press any key to end the program.

See also
GetImage, ImageSize

Example
```
program XPutImage;
uses Crt, Graph;
const
  Radius = 10;
type
  ByteArray = array[0 .. 0] of Byte;
  ByteArrayPtr = ^ByteArray;
var
  GraphDriver, GraphMode: Integer;
  Xc, Yc, X1, Y1, X2, Y2, XMax, YMax: Integer;
  Diameter, Dx, Dy, X, Y: Integer;
  Image: ByteArrayPtr;
begin
  GraphDriver := Detect;
  InitGraph(GraphDriver, GraphMode, 'c:\tp\bgi');
  XMax := GetMaxX;
  YMax := GetMaxY;
  Xc := XMax div 2;
  Yc := YMax div 2;
  X1 := (Xc - Radius) - 1;
  Y1 := (Yc - Radius) - 4;
  X2 := (Xc + Radius) + 1;
```

```
Y2 := (Yc + Radius) + 4;
Diameter := Radius + Radius;
SetColor(White);                   { Draw red rubber ball }
Circle(Xc, Yc, Radius);
SetFillStyle(SolidFill, Red);
FloodFill(Xc, Yc, White);
GetMem(Image, ImageSize(X1, Y1, X2, Y2));  { Reserve memory }
if Image <> nil then
begin
  GetImage(X1, Y1, X2, Y2, Image^);  { Copy display image }
  ClearViewPort;
  Dx := 1;
  Dy := 1;
  Y := Yc;
  X := Xc;
  while not Keypressed do
  begin
    PutImage(X, Y, Image^, NormalPut);  { Display ball }
    X := X + Dx;
    Y := Y + Dy;
    if (Y >= YMax - Diameter) or(Y <= 0) then Dy := -Dy;
    if (X >= XMax - Diameter) or(X <= 0) then Dx := -Dx
  end
end;
CloseGraph
end.
```

PutPixel

Syntax
```
procedure PutPixel(X, Y: Integer; Pixel: Word);
```

Location
Graph

Description
PutPixel displays a single pixel on the graphics display. The exact format of parameter Pixel depends on the display mode, but you generally can set Pixel to a color constant (0 to 15 for EGA graphics) to display dots of those colors.

The example is similar to the program for Plot. The display fills with a starry-sky pattern, which seems to reach equilibrium after running for a minute or so. The program also gives you a visual way to check Turbo Pascal's random number generator. If the display fills evenly, the generator is probably working.

See also
GetPixel

Example
```
program XPutPixel;
uses Crt, Graph;
var
  GraphDriver, GraphMode: Integer;
  XMax, YMax : Integer; Color: Word;
begin
  GraphDriver := Detect;
  InitGraph(GraphDriver, GraphMode, 'c:\tp\bgi');
  XMax := GetMaxX;
  YMax := GetMaxY;
  while not KeyPressed do
  begin
    if Random(400) > 2
      then Color := 0
      else Color := 1 + Random(MaxColors);
    PutPixel(Random(XMax),     { X }
             Random(YMax),     { Y }
             Color)
  end;
  CloseGraph
end.
```

Random

Syntax
```
function Random: Real;
function Random(Modulus: Word): Word;
```

Location
System

Description
Random returns the next value in a random sequence, optionally seeded (initialized) by Randomize. The first form returns a real number R in the range:

```
0.0 <= R < 1.0
```

The second form returns an integer or word value N in the range:

```
0 <= N < Modulus
```

The Modulus may be any positive whole number from zero to 65,535. You may assign the result to any Byte, ShortInt, Integer, Word, or LongInt variable. Assigning Random(N) to a signed integer variable produces positive values if N is less or equal to MaxInt. If N is greater than MaxInt, both negative and positive integers are produced. This trick does not always have the expected results, though. For example, consider this expression:

```
I := Random(65535);
```

If I is integer, then the expression assigns the equivalent of the range 0 to 65,534. Because the modulus (65,535) is never generated, and because 65,535 in binary equals −1 as a signed integer, this expression skips −1 in the random sequence! To get negative random values correctly, use an expression such as:

```
I := Random(100) - 50;
```

This sets I to a value from −50 to +49, exactly 100 possible values (including −1) evenly distributed over the range.

One common use for Random is to let programs make decisions in simulations. To do this, you might decide that certain operations should occur about 25% of the time, others at 75%, and so on. The example shows how to program such events. It assumes that the expression:

```
if Random(100) < 25
   then DoEvent;
```

will call DoEvent about 25% of the time because Random(100) is about three times more likely to produce values in the range 25 to 99 than it is in the range 0 to 24.

When you run the example, press Enter to see a report of the counts and frequencies of values produced in the range 0 to 24, 0 to 49, 0 to 74, and 0 to 99.

See also
Randomize

Example
```
program XRandom;
uses Crt;
var
  Counts: array[1 .. 4] of LongInt;
  I, N: Integer;
  Ch: Char;
begin
  for I := 1 to 4 do
    Counts[I] := 0;
  Writeln('Counting...');
  while not Keypressed do
  begin
```

```
      N := Random(100);
      if N < 25 then Inc(Counts[1]);
      if N < 50 then Inc(Counts[2]);
      if N < 75 then Inc(Counts[3]);
      Inc(Counts[4])
   end;
   Ch := Readkey;  { throw out keypress }
   for I := 1 to 4 do
     Writeln(I, ' :', Counts[I]:8,
        100.0 * ((1.0 * Counts[I]) / (1.0 * Counts[4])):10:3, ' %')
end.
```

Randomize

Syntax
```
procedure Randomize;
```

Location
System

Description
Call Randomize to seed the random number generator, beginning a new random sequence each time the program runs. If you do not call Randomize, then programs will repeat the same random sequence.

Run the example several times to produce different sets of 10 random numbers. Then, remove Randomize and run the program several more times. Without Randomize, all random number sets are now identical.

See also
Random

Example
```
program XRandomize;
var
  I: Integer;
begin
  Randomize;
  for I := 1 to 10 do
    Write(Random(MaxInt):8);
  Writeln
end.
```

Read

Syntax
```
procedure Read([F: <file>;] V1, V2, ..., Vn);
```

Location
System

Description
Use Read to input one or more variables from a file, which might be a disk file or a device such as a modem or keyboard. If <file> is not specified, Read loads variables from the standard input text file, normally the keyboard.

Read also can read several variables at the same time. The variables do not have to be of the same type. Separate the variable identifiers with commas as in this statement, which reads a character (Ch), an integer (I), and a real number (R):

```
Read(Ch, I, R);
```

When this statement executes, the program pauses for you to type the three items. You can press Enter after typing each item, or you can press Space after the character and integer and press Enter after the real number. The same rule does not hold for string variables, which must be terminated with Enter. For example, the statement:

```
Read(S, I);
```

reads a string (S) and an integer (I). You must press Enter after typing the string (or there must be a carriage return after the string if you are reading from a disk text file). Then you can type, or read from disk, the integer value.

The example shows how to read a text file one character at a time with Read.

See also
ReadKey, Readln, Reset, Write, Writeln

Example
```
program XRead;
var
  Tf: Text;
  Ch: Char;
begin
  Write('Press <Enter> to read file...');
  Read(Ch);
  Assign(Tf, 'XREAD.PAS');
  Reset(Tf);
  while not Eof(Tf) do
```

```
  begin
    Read(Tf, Ch);
    Write(Ch)
  end
end.
```

ReadKey

Syntax
```
function ReadKey: Char;
```

Location

Crt

Description

ReadKey returns one character from the keyboard. The function is particularly convenient for reading control keys, arrow keys, and function keys, when you want complete control over the display. Unlike Read and Readln, ReadKey never displays anything.

To read keyboard commands, you can use ReadKey along with Upcase and Keypressed. If Keypressed is true, then call ReadKey to find out which key was typed. For example, you can write:

```
if Keypressed then
case Upcase(ReadKey) of
  'A' : ChoiceA;
  'B' : ChoiceB;
  'C' : ChoiceC
end;
```

This fragment does not recognize function, arrow, and other special keys, which return two values, a null (ASCII 0) plus a second character representing the key. To do this, first check for a null. Then, use ReadKey a second time to find out which special key was typed. Here the basic steps for reading function and other named keys:

```
if ReadKey = Chr(0) then
  if ReadKey = 'P' then
    DoDownArrow;
```

The statements call DoDownArrow only if you press the down arrow key, which generates the two ASCII characters, null and P. See Table 9.3 for a list of all two-character sequences you can use this way.

The example uses ReadKey in a handy program for checking ASCII values. Use it to discover what characters certain keys produce. Type Esc to quit.

See also
KeyPressed, Read, UpCase

Example

```pascal
program XReadKey;
uses Crt;
var
  Ch: Char;
begin
  Writeln('Display ASCII character values');
  Writeln('Type Esc to quit');
  Writeln;
  repeat
    Write('Char? ');
    Ch := ReadKey;
    Writeln(Ch, ' : ASCII value = ', Ord(Ch));
  until Ch = Chr(27)
end.
```

ReadLn

Syntax

```pascal
procedure Readln([F: Text;] V1, V2, ..., Vn);
```

Location

System

Description

Readln (read line) operates identically to Read, but with one major difference: It can read only from text files. Read can read variables from any kind of file. Readln can read variables only from text files.

Most often you use Readln to read strings when you want someone to type a response to a prompt and press Enter when they are done. For example, this asks you to type a file name:

```pascal
var
  Fname: string;
begin
  Write('File? ');
  Readln(Fname);
  ...
end;
```

Even though Readln reads from text files, you may read variables other than strings. For example, this pauses and waits for you to type a real number:

```
var
  R: Real;
begin
  Write('Value? ');
  Readln(R);
  ...
end;
```

You also can use Readln to read disk text files. Unlike the Read example, though, because Readln reads an entire line at a time into a string variable, no line can exceed the maximum string length of 255 characters.

See also
Read, Reset, Write, Writeln

Example
```
program XReadln;
var
  Tf: Text;
  S: string;
begin
  Write('Press <Enter> to read file...');
  Readln;
  Assign(Tf, 'XREADLN.PAS');
  Reset(Tf);
  while not Eof(Tf) do
  begin
    Readln(Tf, S);
    Writeln(S)
  end
end.
```

Rectangle

Syntax
```
procedure Rectangle(X1, Y1, X2, Y2: Integer);
```

Location
Graph

Description

Rectangle displays a rectangle with its upper-left corner at coordinate (X1,Y1) and its lower coordinate at (X2,Y2). Change the rectangle's color with SetColor.

The example draws randomly colored and sized rectangles until you press any key to stop the program. Lower the Delay value to increase program speed.

See also

Bar, SetColor, SetLineStyle, SetWriteMode

Example

```
program XRectangle;
uses Crt, Graph;
var
  GraphDriver, GraphMode: Integer;
  XMax, YMax: Integer;
begin
  GraphDriver := Detect;
  InitGraph(GraphDriver, GraphMode, 'c:\tp\bgi');
  XMax := GetMaxX;
  YMax := GetMaxY;
  while not Keypressed do
  begin
    Delay(50);
    SetColor(1 + Random(MaxColors));
    Rectangle(Random(XMax), Random(YMax),
              Random(XMax), Random(YMax))
  end;
  repeat until Keypressed;
  CloseGraph
end.
```

RegisterBGIDriver

Syntax

```
function RegisterBGIDriver(Driver: Pointer): Integer;
```

Location

Graph

Description

Call RegisterBGIdriver to register a graphics driver previously loaded into memory. Pass the driver's address in pointer Driver, telling the graphics kernel where to find this driver. If RegisterBGIdriver returns a negative value, then an error occurred and you must not use the loaded driver. Otherwise, when you later initialize the driver with InitGraph, the graphics kernel will use the in-memory copy rather than loading the BGI driver file from disk.

The technique is useful for rapidly switching between two or more graphics drivers and modes. Preloading the drivers onto the heap avoids time-wasting disk reads for every switch.

The example demonstrates how to load two driver files, CGA.BGI and EGAVGA.BGI. Procedure LoadOneDriver reads the file after allocating exactly as much memory as needed to hold the entire file. (The program halts with a runtime error if enough memory is not available.)

The main body of the example calls InitGraph three times, switching between CGA and EGA modes. Press the Space bar to switch. Notice that when you do this, the disk drive light does not come on. To write this same program without preloading and registering the different drivers, you would have to insert CloseGraph commands between the calls to InitGraph.

See also
InitGraph, InstallUserDriver, RegisterBGIFont

Example

```
{ NOTE: This program requires both EGA and CGA video hardware }
program XRegisterBGIdriver;
uses Crt, Graph;
var
  GraphDriver, GraphMode: Integer;

  procedure LoadOneDriver(FileName: string);
  var
    F: file;
    Fp: Pointer;
    Bytes: LongInt;
  begin
    Assign(F, FileName);
    Reset(F, 1);
    Bytes := FileSize(F);
    GetMem(Fp, Bytes);
    BlockRead(F, Fp^, Bytes);
    Close(F);
    if RegisterBGIdriver(Fp) < 0 then
    begin
      Writeln('Error registering ', Filename);
      Writeln('Graphics error : ', GraphErrorMsg(GraphResult));
      Halt
    end
  end;
```

```
procedure DrawLines;
begin
  repeat
    SetColor(1 + Random(GetMaxColor));
    LineTo(Random(GetMaxX), Random(GetMaxY))
  until Keypressed;
  CloseGraph;
  if ReadKey = Chr(27) then Halt
end;

begin
  LoadOneDriver('c:\tp\bgi\cga.bgi');
  LoadOneDriver('c:\tp\bgi\egavga.bgi');
  GraphDriver := CGA; GraphMode := CGAC0;
  InitGraph(GraphDriver, GraphMode, 'c:\tp\bgi');
  DrawLines;
  GraphDriver := EGA; GraphMode := EGAHi;
  InitGraph(GraphDriver, GraphMode, 'c:\tp\bgi');
  DrawLines;
  GraphDriver := CGA; GraphMode := CGAC1;
  InitGraph(GraphDriver, GraphMode, 'c:\tp\bgi');
  DrawLines
end.
```

RegisterBGIFont

Syntax
```
function RegisterBGIFont(Font: Pointer): Integer;
```

Location
Graph

Description
Call RegisterBGIfont to register a graphics font previously loaded into memory. Pass the font's address in pointer Font, telling the graphics kernel where to find this font. If RegisterBGIfont returns a negative value, then an error occurred and you must not use the loaded font. Otherwise, when you later select the font with SetTextStyle, the graphics kernel will use the in-memory copy rather than loading the CHR font file from disk.

The technique is useful when you want to switch between two or more fonts. Preloading the font patterns onto the heap avoids repeated disk reads for every new character style.

The example demonstrates how to load four font files TRIP.CHR, LITT.CHR, SANS.CHR, and GOTH.CHR. Procedure LoadOneFont reads the file after allocating exactly as much memory as needed to hold the entire file. (The program halts with a runtime error if enough memory is not available.)

The main body of the program calls SetTextStyle to switch to a new character style for each string passed to OutText. If the font patterns were not preloaded into memory, each such call would cause the graphics kernel to reload the font file from disk, a time-wasting action the example avoids.

See also
InitGraph, InstallUserFont, RegisterBGIDriver

Example

```pascal
program XRegisterBGIfont;
uses Crt, Graph;
var
  GraphDriver, GraphMode: Integer;

  procedure LoadOneFont(FileName: string);
  var
    F: file;
    Fp: Pointer;
    Bytes: LongInt;
  begin
    Assign(F, FileName);
    Reset(F, 1);
    Bytes := FileSize(F);
    GetMem(Fp, Bytes);
    BlockRead(F, Fp^, Bytes);
    Close(F);
    if RegisterBGIfont(Fp) < 0 then
    begin
      Writeln('Error registering ', Filename);
      Writeln('Graphics error : ', GraphErrorMsg(GraphResult));
      Halt
    end
  end;

begin
  LoadOneFont('c:\tp\bgi\trip.chr');
  LoadOneFont('c:\tp\bgi\litt.chr');
  LoadOneFont('c:\tp\bgi\sans.chr');
```

```
    LoadOneFont('c:\tp\bgi\goth.chr');
    GraphDriver := Detect;
    InitGraph(GraphDriver, GraphMode, 'c:\tp\bgi');
    SetColor(LightBlue);
    MoveTo(10, 50);
    SetBkColor(White);
    OutText('This ');
    SetTextStyle(TriplexFont, HorizDir, 4);
    OutText('program ');
    SetTextStyle(SmallFont, HorizDir, 8);
    OutText('uses ');
    SetTextStyle(SansSerifFont, HorizDir, 3);
    OutText('multiple ');
    SetTextStyle(GothicFont, HorizDir, 5);
    OutText('fonts.');
    repeat until Keypressed;
    CloseGraph
  end.
```

Release

Syntax
```
  procedure Release(var P: Pointer);
```

Location
System

Description
Release resets the heap top to the address of P, previously set by Mark. Any New variables created before Release are invalid. Parameter P may be any pointer type, although it usually is a generic Pointer. Calling Release also erases any disposed areas on the heap, which Turbo Pascal tracks by linking the areas together.

See also
Dispose, FreeMem, GetMem, Mark, New

Example
```
  program XRelease;
  type
    A = array[1 .. 1000] of Real;
    Aptr = ^A;
  var
    Heap: Pointer;
    V: Aptr;
```

```
begin
  Mark(Heap);
  Writeln('Memory before new    =', Memavail:8);
  New(V);
  Writeln('Memory after new     =', Memavail:8);
  Release(Heap);
  Writeln('Memory after release =', Memavail:8)
end.
```

Rename

Syntax
```
procedure Rename(var F: <file>; Filename: <string>);
```

Location
System

Description
Rename changes the directory name of file F to Filename, which may be a literal or variable string. Before renaming, assign the file's current name to file variable F. The file should not be open. Also, to avoid duplicate file names in the same directory, Filename should not already exist. You can check this, as in the example, by resetting the file before renaming. Usually, the file to be renamed is an untyped **file**, but it can be any other file type, too.

See also
Assign, Erase

Example
```
program XRename;
var
  F: file;
  S: string;
begin
  Write('Rename what file? ');
  Readln(S);
  if Length(S) > 0 then
  begin
    Assign(F, S);
    {$I-} Reset(F); {$I+}
    if IoResult <> 0 then
      Writeln('Can''t find ', S)
    else begin
      Write('New name? ');
```

```
      Readln(S);
      if Length(S) > 0
        then Rename(F, S)
    end
  end
end.
```

Reset

Syntax
```
procedure Reset(var F: <file> [; N: Word]);
```

Location
System

Description
Reset opens or resets to the beginning an already open file. Resetting a text file prepares the file for reading only. Resetting other file types prepares for reading and writing. Before resetting, Assign a file path name to F. A null string resets a text file to the standard Input (DOS handle 0).

When F is an untyped **file**, you may use an optional value N to specify the number of bytes that BlockRead and BlockWrite transfer at one time. If you do not specify a value, N defaults to 128. Usually, for best results, set N to 512, the size of one disk sector.

Surround a Reset statement with the compiler directives, {$I–} and {$I+}, turning off automatic Input/Output error detection. Then, check IoResult. If zero, the file is open and ready to use. If not zero, an error occurred and you must not use the file. The example shows how to use this technique to check whether a file exists on disk.

See also
Assign, Close, Rewrite, Truncate

Example
```
program XReset;
var
  F: file;
  FileName: string;
begin
  Write('File? ');
  Readln(FileName);
  if Length(FileName) > 0 then
  begin
```

```
      Assign(F, FileName);
      {$I-} Reset(F); {$I+}
      if Ioresult = 0 then
      begin
        Writeln('File exists!');
        Close(F)
      end else
        Writeln('File does not exist')
    end
  end.
```

RestoreCrtMode

Syntax

```
procedure RestoreCrtMode;
```

Location
Graph

Description
Call RestoreCrtMode to return to the original display screen before calling InitGraph.
After that, call SetGraphMode to go back to the graphics screen.

RestoreCrtMode erases the display and homes the cursor. As the example
shows, you can use this procedure to switch back and forth between graphics and
text screens. Press Enter to switch and Esc to quit. Unfortunately, switching modes
does not preserve any graphics or text previously on display.

See also
CloseGraph, GetGraphMode, SetGraphMode

Example

```
program XRestoreCrtMode;
uses Crt, Graph;
const
  Esc = #27;
var
  GraphDriver, GraphMode: Integer;
  I, XMax, YMax: Word;

  procedure Bubbles;
  var I: Integer;
  begin
    for I := 1 to 100 do
```

```
      begin
        SetColor(Random(1 + GetMaxColor));
        Circle(Random(XMax), Random(YMax), Random(75))
      end
    end;

  begin
    GraphDriver := Detect;
    InitGraph(GraphDriver, GraphMode, 'c:\tp\bgi');
    XMax := GetMaxX;
    YMax := GetMaxY;
    repeat
      SetGraphMode(GraphMode);
      Bubbles;
      if ReadKey <> Esc then
      begin
        RestoreCrtMode;
        Writeln('Press Enter for graphics; Esc to quit...')
      end
    until ReadKey = Esc;
    CloseGraph
  end.
```

Rewrite

Syntax
```
procedure Rewrite(var F: <file> [; N: Word]);
```

Location
System

Description
Rewrite creates a new disk file for output or readies a text device such as a printer or modem. Before rewriting, Assign a file name to file variable F. Rewriting a text file prepares it for writing only. Rewriting other kinds of files prepares for reading and writing.

Rewriting an existing disk file erases the file's contents and creates a new file of the same name, now empty. To prevent accidents, be sure to rewrite existing files only if you want to erase them.

The optional parameter N specifies the number of bytes read by BlockRead or written by BlockWrite when F is an untyped File. If N is not specified, the number defaults to 128. For best results, set N to 512, the size of one disk sector.

Surround a Rewrite statement with the compiler directives, {$I–} and {$I+}, turning off automatic Inout/Output error detection. Then, check IoResult. If zero, then the file is open and ready to use. If not zero, an error occurred, and you must not use the file.

The example shows how to use Rewrite to copy a text file, in this case, creating XREWRITE.BAK from XREWRITE.PAS. Type the program and save as XREWRITE.PAS, then run to create the backup.

See also
Append, Assign, IoResult, Reset, Truncate, Write, Writeln

Example

```
program XRewrite;
var
  InFile, OutFile: Text;
  S: string;
begin
  Writeln('Backing up XREWRITE.PAS...');
  Assign(OutFile, 'XREWRITE.BAK');   { Erase old backup }
  {$I-} Erase(OutFile); {$I+}        { Ignore any error }
  if IoResult <> 0 then
    {do nothing} ;                   { Don't forget the semicolon! }
  Assign(InFile, 'XREWRITE.PAS');    { Open input file  }
  Reset(InFile);
  Rewrite(OutFile);                  { Create output file }
  while not Eof(InFile) do
  begin
    Readln(InFile, S);
    Writeln(OutFile, S);
  end;
  Writeln('done');
  Close(InFile);
  Close(OutFile)
end.
```

RmDir

Syntax
```
procedure RmDir(Path: <string>);
```

Location
System

Description

RmDir removes the subdirectory that Path specifies. If there are any files in the directory, DOS generates an error and does not remove the directory. Use IoResult to detect this error.

RmDir operates identically to the DOS RMDIR and RD commands. The example uses RmDir along with MkDir to create a temporary subdirectory, \TEMP. A program might do this to make certain it has enough space for temporary data files, removing both the files and directory before ending. Before using RmDir, it is important to remove any files in the directory, or you will receive an error.

See also

ChDir, GetDir, MkDir

Example

```
program XRmDir;
var
  Err: Integer;
begin
  Writeln('Creating \TEMP...');
  {$I-} MkDir('\TEMP'); {$I+}
  Err := IoResult;
  if (Err = 0) or (Err = 5 {already exists}) then
  begin
    { Store data in \TEMP subdirectory }
    { Delete files before continuing }
    Writeln('Deleting \TEMP...');
    {$I-} RmDir('\TEMP'); {$I+}
    if IoResult <> 0 then
      Writeln('Error removing \TEMP')
  end
end.
```

Round

Syntax

```
function Round(R : <real>): LongInt;
```

Location

System

Description

Round returns the long integer value of R rounded to the nearest whole number. Round(1.4999) = 1, Round(1.5000) = 2, Round(–1.4999) = –1, Round (–1.5000) = –2, and so on.

You can assign Round's result to any ShortInt, Byte, Integer, or LongInt variable, but you risk receiving a range error for types other than LongInt. The example shows how to avoid this error by checking the real number before rounding. (Although the program checks for negative values, too, the Random statement produces only positive numbers.)

See also
Int, Trunc

Example

```pascal
program XRound;
var
  R: Real;
  I: Integer;
begin
  Randomize;
  R := Random * 50000.0;
  Writeln('R = ', R:0:5);
  if (-32767.0 <= R) and (R <= 32768) then
  begin
    I := Round(R);
    Writeln('I = ', I)
  end else
    Writeln('Result is outside Integer range')
end.
```

RunError

Syntax

```pascal
procedure RunError;
procedure RunError(ErrorCode: Word);
```

Location
System

Description
RunError comes in two flavors: one with no parameters and one with a single Word parameter ErrorCode. Similar to Halt, RunError stops a running program in its tracks. Unlike Halt, RunError simulates a runtime error, just as though the program stopped due to a real critical problem.

Pass the value of any Turbo Pascal runtime error number to RunError to simulate how the program will respond if that error actually occurs. Use the parameterless form of RunError to halt the program with no specific runtime error number. (In that case, a runtime error "0" is reported, even though 0 is not a valid runtime error value.)

One use for RunError is to debug a critical error handler (see Chapter 13, Customizing a Runtime Handler). Executing RunError halts the program and runs the error-handler code.

The example demonstrates another use for RunError—forcing a runtime error to occur after you have replaced Turbo Pascal's normal error-handling logic. Although not shown in the example, you might do this after changing how New and GetMem detect out-of-memory errors (see HeapFunc in this chapter for details). As the example shows, if MaxAvail reports too little memory available, RunError can generate an out-of-memory error (code 1). (Of course, a real program would do this only as a last resort after closing files and performing other duties before shutting down.) To see RunError's result, remove the $ from the top line and insert a $ between { and M in the second.

See also
Exit, Halt

Example
```
{$M 1024, 65535, 65535}    { 64K heap }
{ M 1024,     0,     0}    { Minimum heap }
program XRunError;
const
  Size = 2048;
var
  P: Pointer;
begin
  Writeln('Before: MemAvail=', MemAvail, '  MaxAvail=', MaxAvail);
  if MaxAvail < Size
    then RunError(1)       { Out of memory }
    else GetMem(P, Size); { Allocate heap space }
  Writeln(Size, ' bytes allocated');
  Writeln('After: MemAvail=', MemAvail, '  MaxAvail=', MaxAvail)
end.
```

Sector

Syntax
```
procedure Sector(X, Y: Integer;
  StAngle, EndAngle, XRadius, YRadius: Word);
```

Location
Graph

Description
The strangely named Sector operates like Ellipse, but it fills an ellipse with the current fill pattern and color (see SetFillStyle and SetFillPattern). Use SetColor to

change the ellipse's outline color. The parameters are identical to and have the same effects as the parameters for Ellipse.

The example fills the display with a variety of filled ellipses. Several variables ensure that the program operates correctly with all display types.

See also
Arc, Circle, Ellipse, FillEllipse, GetArcCoords, GetAspectRatio, PieSlice, SetFillStyle, SetFillPattern

Example

```
program XSector;
uses Crt, Graph;
var
  GraphDriver, GraphMode: Integer;
  X, Y, XMax, YMax, XSize, YSize: Integer;
  XSizeD2, YSizeD2, XSizeT2, YSizeT2: Integer;
begin
  Randomize;
  GraphDriver := Detect;
  InitGraph(GraphDriver, GraphMode, 'c:\tp\bgi');
  XMax := GetMaxX;
  YMax := GetMaxY;
  XSize := XMax div 8;
  YSize := YMax div 4;
  XSizeD2 := XSize div 2;
  YSizeD2 := YSize div 2;
  XSizeT2 := XSize * 2;
  YSizeT2 := YSize * 2;
  Y := YSizeD2;
  while Y < (YMax-YSizeD2) do
  begin
    X := XSizeD2;
    while X < (XMax - XSizeD2) do
    begin
      SetColor(1 + Random(MaxColors));
      SetFillStyle(1 + Random(11), 1 + Random(MaxColors));
      Sector(X, Y, Random(360), Random(45),
             XSizeD2 - 6, YSizeD2 - 6);
      X := X + XSize
    end;
    Y := Y + YSize
  end;
  repeat until Keypressed;
  CloseGraph
end.
```

Seek

Syntax
```
procedure Seek(var F: <untyped file>|<typed file>; Rn: LongInt);
```

Location
System

Description
Seek positions the internal file pointer to record Rn in file F so that the next read or write to the file occurs at position Rn. The file must be open before seeking. You can use any file type except Text. To Seek in text files, declare the file variable as a **file of** Char.

The first record in all files is numbered 0; therefore, seeking to record 0 is similar to resetting the file to its beginning. Seeking to one record beyond the last record in a file prepares for expanding existing files. Use this method when you want to append nontext files.

The example shows how to seek characters in a text file, reading the program's own text (XSEEK.PAS) and displaying the thirteenth character, k. Because the first record—or character in this case—is number 0, seeking to 12 locates the thirteenth, not the twelfth, record.

See also
FilePos, SeekEof, SeekEoln

Example
```
program XSeek;
var
  Tf: file of Char;
  Ch: Char;
begin
  Assign(Tf, 'XSEEK.PAS');
  Reset(Tf);
  Seek(Tf, 12);
  Read(Tf, Ch);
  Writeln('Ch=', Ch);
  Close(Tf)
end.
```

SeekEof

Syntax
```
function SeekEof(var F: Text): Boolean;
```

Location
System

Description
This function is similar to Eof except that SeekEof looks ahead for the end of file marker ^Z (ASCII 26), skipping tabs, blanks, and end-of-line carriage return and line-feed characters. File F must be Text. It cannot be **file of** Char.

The function is true when it finds a ^Z (ASCII 26) ahead of the current character or at the physical end of the file, whichever comes first.

When reading text files, SeekEof helps you to avoid reading extra blank lines after the last line of text. The example shows how to do this. Run the program and then type the name of any text file for a report on the total number of lines plus the total number of nonblank lines.

See also
Eof, SeekEoln

Example
```pascal
program XSeekEof;
var
  Tf: Text;
  C1, C2: LongInt;
  S: string;
begin
  Write('File name? ');
  Readln(S);
  Assign(Tf, S);
  Reset(Tf);
  C1 := 0;
  C2 := 0;
  while not Eof(Tf) do        { Read all lines }
  begin
    Readln(Tf, S);
    Inc(C1)
  end;
  Reset(Tf);
  while not SeekEof(Tf) do    { Read only non-blank lines }
  begin
    Readln(Tf, S);
    Inc(C2)
  end;
  Writeln;
  Writeln;
  Writeln('Total number of lines     = ', C1);
  Writeln('Number of non-blank lines = ', C2)
end.
```

SeekEoln

Syntax
```
function SeekEoln(var F: Text): Boolean;
```

Location
System

Description
This function is similar to Eoln except that SeekEoln looks ahead for the end-of-line carriage return and line feed markers, skipping tabs and blanks. When reading text files, SeekEoln avoids reading extra blank characters after the last significant character on each line. File F must be type Text. It cannot be **file of** Char.

The function is true when it finds a carriage return (ASCII 13) and line feed (ASCII 10) ahead of the current character. It also is true at the physical end of the file.

The example reads any text file, ignoring blanks and control characters. Change SeekEoln to Eoln to see the differences between these similar functions.

See also
Eoln, SeekEof

Example
```
program XSeekEoln;
var
  Tf: Text;
  Ch: Char;
  Filename: string;
begin
  Write('File name? ');
  Readln(Filename);
  Assign(Tf, Filename);
  Reset(Tf);
  while not Eof(Tf) do
  begin
    while not SeekEoln(Tf) do
    begin
      Read(Tf, Ch);
      Write(Ch)
    end;
    Readln(Tf);
    Writeln
  end;
  Close(Tf)
end.
```

Seg

Syntax
```
function Seg(V: <ident>): Word;
```

Location
System

Description
Seg returns the segment address of a variable, procedure, or function, V. Finding the address of pointer variables requires care. Seg(P) returns the segment of the pointer variable itself. Seg(P^) returns the segment address of the variable addressed by the pointer.

The example displays the segment address of a variable and a procedure. When you run the program, you see these values are different, proving that Turbo Pascal stores its global variables and procedure code in different memory segments.

See also
Addr, CSeg, DSeg, Ofs, SSeg

Example
```pascal
program XSeg;
var
  I: Integer;

  procedure X;
  begin
    Writeln('x')
  end;

begin
  Writeln('Seg(I)    = ', Seg(I));
  Writeln('Seg(X)    = ', Seg(X))
end.
```

SetActivePage

Syntax
```
procedure SetActivePage(Page: Word);
```

Location
Graph

Description

SetActivePage tells the Turbo Pascal graphics kernel on which memory page to draw. The procedure works only on systems with multiple graphics pages, such as EGA, VGA, and Hercules. It does not work with CGA graphics.

Together, SetActivePage and SetVisualPage make it easy to design smooth animation sequences with a technique known as page swapping or ping-ponging. The idea is to draw new graphics on an invisible page while viewing the most recent frame. Then, switch frames bringing the new graphics into view and preparing to draw on the other page.

The example demonstrates the difference page swapping makes, expanding a circle, with each new outline a different frame in the animation. To see how page swapping smooths the action, initialize variable visual to 0, drawing and displaying on the same graphics page. Without page swapping, you can see each circle being formed. With page swapping, all drawing occurs backstage—you see only the results.

See also

SetVisualPage

Example

```pascal
program XSetActivePage;
uses Crt, Graph;
var
  GraphDriver, GraphMode: Integer;
  Radius, Xc, Yc: Word;
  Active, Visual, Temp: Word;
begin
{ Note: Requires multipage EGA or VGA display }
  GraphDriver := EGA;   { or VGA }
  GraphMode := EGAHi;   { and VGAMed }
  InitGraph(GraphDriver, GraphMode, 'c:\tp\bgi');
  Xc := GetMaxX div 2;
  Yc := GetMaxY div 2;
  Radius := 10;
  Active := 0;
  Visual := 1;
  while not Keypressed do
  begin
    SetActivePage(Active);
    SetVisualPage(Visual);
    ClearViewPort;
    SetColor(1 + Random(GetMaxColor));
    Circle(Xc, Yc, Radius);
    SetVisualPage(Active);
    Temp := Active;
```

```
      Active := Visual;
      Visual := Temp;
      Radius := Radius + 10;
      if Radius > Yc then
         Radius := 10
   end;
   CloseGraph
end.
```

SetAllPalette

Syntax
```
procedure SetAllPalette(var Palette);
```

Location
Graph

Description
Use SetAllPalette to change the actual colors you see for the color values you pass to SetColor. A palette is merely a translation between these color values and the values passed to the graphics hardware.

The palette parameter is untyped to allow it to grow or shrink to the exact size you need for different video graphics modes. Usually, though, palette is of type PaletteType, defined in the Graph unit as:

```
PaletteType = record
   Size: Byte;
   Colors: array[ 0 .. maxColors] of ShortInt
end;
```

The size byte tells how many values follow in the Colors array. Each array index is a different color, from zero to maxColors, a constant also defined in Graph. (Use GetMaxColor to discover the maximum color value for different modes.) By inserting a new color value into the colors array, you tell Turbo Pascal to convert one color to another. Passing the whole record to SetAllPalette instantly changes any graphics now on display to the new colors.

The example shows how to use SetAllPalette to achieve an animation effect simply by scrambling palette colors until you press a key to stop the program.

Setting any palette color to –1 tells Turbo Pascal not to change that setting. The example uses this technique to preserve the background color (Colors[0]) without having to know what that color value is.

See also
GetPalette, SetPalette, SetRGBPalette

Example

```
program XSetAllPalette;
uses Crt, Graph;
var
  GraphDriver, GraphMode: Integer;
  I, CMax, XMax, YMax: Integer;
  Palette: PaletteType;
begin
  GraphDriver := Detect;
  InitGraph(GraphDriver, GraphMode, 'c:\tp\bgi');
  XMax := GetMaxX;
  YMax := GetMaxY;
  CMax := GetMaxColor;
  Randomize;
  for I := 1 to 75 do
  begin
    SetColor(1 + Random(CMax));
    Circle(Random(XMax), Random(YMax), Random(100))
  end;
  Palette.Size := CMax + 1;  { Number of colors in palette }
  Palette.Colors[0] := -1;   { No change to background color }
  while not KeyPressed do
  begin
    Delay(150);
    for I := 1 to CMax do
      Palette.Colors[I] := Random(CMax + 1);
    SetAllPalette(Palette)
  end;
  CloseGraph
end.
```

SetAspectRatio

Syntax

```
procedure SetAspectRatio(XAsp, YAsp: Word);
```

Location

Graph

Description

The Graph unit keeps an internal value called the *aspect ratio,* which compensates for the fact that pixels on most PC graphics displays are not perfectly square. If a display's aspect ratio were not taken into account, circles would not be round because horizontal and vertical radii of the same numbers of pixels would have different visible lengths.

In some custom and VGA display modes, pixels are square (a ratio of 1/1). No compensation is required on such displays to draw round circles. On other displays, the ratio is anything but square. Among other default ratios, Graph unit uses 4167/10,000 for CGA and 7750/10,000 for EGA displays.

Most the time, these defaults work well. But monitors are often misaligned, and in such cases, SetAspectRatio can make helpful adjustments. A graphics program might provide aspect-ratio variables as an optional service to let users fine-tune their displays.

The example program draws circles with several different aspect ratios in effect. See Chapter 11 for more information about this subject.

See also
GetAspectRatio

Example

```pascal
program XSetAspectRatio;
uses Graph;
var
  GraphDriver, GraphMode: Integer;

  procedure RoundAbout;
  var
    Ch: Char;  { Throw-away character }
    XAsp, YAsp: Word;
  begin
    GetAspectRatio(XAsp, YAsp);
    Writeln('X=', XAsp, ' Y=', YAsp,
      ' Ratio=', (1.0 * XAsp) / YAsp);
    Circle(GetMaxX - (GetMaxX div 3),
      GetMaxY div 2, GetMaxY div 4);
    Readln
  end;

begin
  GraphDriver := Detect;
  InitGraph(GraphDriver, GraphMode, 'c:\tp\bgi');
  RoundAbout;
  SetAspectRatio(1, 1);
  RoundAbout;
  SetAspectRatio(1, 2);
  RoundAbout;
  SetAspectRatio(2, 1);
```

```
    RoundAbout;
    SetAspectRatio(3, 2);
    RoundAbout;
    CloseGraph
end.
```

SetBkCol

Syntax
```
procedure SetBkColor(Color: Word);
```

Location
Graph

Description
Call SetBkColor to change the background color. Parameter Color selects a color value from the current palette (see SetAllPalette). Set Color to zero to change the background to black, the default color for all graphics modes.

The example cycles the graphics display through all possible background colors for the default palette. Press any key to end the program.

See also
GetBkColor, GetColor, SetColor

Example
```
program XSetBkColor;
uses Crt, Graph;
var
  GraphDriver, GraphMode: Integer;
  Color: Word;
begin
  GraphDriver := Detect;
  InitGraph(GraphDriver, GraphMode, 'c:\tp\bgi');
  while not Keypressed do
  begin
    Color := 0;
    while Color <= GetMaxColor do
    begin
      SetBkColor(Color);
      Delay(500);
      if Keypressed
        then Color := GetMaxColor;
      Inc(Color)
```

```
        end
      end;
    CloseGraph
  end.
```

SetCBreak

Syntax
```
procedure SetCBreak(Break: Boolean);
```

Location
Dos

Description
Call SetCBreak to turn on DOS's Ctrl-Break switch (break = true) or to turn it off (break = false). Normally, you should leave the switch off. But, if you want to be able to interrupt programs at any time a DOS function is called—useful during debugging, especially in programs that tend to get "locked up"—turn on Ctrl-Break by passing true to SetCBreak. With Ctrl-Break off, pressing Ctrl-C or Ctrl-Break keys interrupts a program only during console Input/Output, printing, or communications. (Most communications programs do not call DOS for serial Input/Output, thus bypassing the Ctrl-Break switch.)

The example demonstrates how to use SetCBreak along with its sister procedure GetCBreak, which returns the current Ctrl-Break switch setting.

See also
GetCBreak

Example
```
program XSetCBreak;
uses Crt, Dos;
var
  Break: Boolean;
begin
  GetCBreak(Break);
  Writeln('Control-Break checking is: ', Break);
  SetCBreak(not Break);
  GetCBreak(Break);
  Writeln('Control-Break checking is: ', Break);
  SetCBreak(False);
  GetCBreak(Break);
  Writeln('Control-Break checking is: ', Break);
end.
```

SetColor

Syntax
```
procedure SetColor(Color: Word);
```

Location
Graph

Description
Pass a color number to SetColor to change the color used by LineTo, LineRel, Line, Rectangle, DrawPoly, Arc, Circle, Ellipse, PieSlice (outline only), OutText, and OutTextXY.

Parameter Color is an index into the current color palette, not a color value as stored in video display memory. Due to this, the actual color you see might not match one of the color constants listed in the Graph unit. For example, if you write SetColor(Red), you could see a different color if you had previously changed the palette or if the hardware does not display red for this color number.

The example displays a series of bars in all possible colors for the graphics mode on your computer. The first bar is the same as the background and is, therefore, invisible.

See also
GetBkColor, GetColor, GetMaxColor, SetBKColor

Example
```
program XSetColor;
uses Crt, Graph;
var
  GraphDriver, GraphMode: Integer;
  X, XMax, YMax, Color, Width, Height: Word;
begin
  GraphDriver := Detect;
  InitGraph(GraphDriver, GraphMode, 'c:\tp\bgi');
  XMax := GetMaxX;
  YMax := GetMaxY;
  Width := (Succ(XMax) div Succ(GetMaxColor)) div 2;
  Height := (Succ(YMax) div 4);
  X := 0;
  for Color := 0 to GetMaxColor do
  begin
    SetColor(Color);
    Rectangle(X, YMax, X+Width, Height);
    SetFillStyle(LtSlashFill, Color);
    FloodFill(X + 1, YMax - 1, Color);
```

```
      X := X + Width + Width
   end;
   repeat until KeyPressed;
   CloseGraph
end.
```

SetDate

Syntax

```
procedure SetDate(Year, Month, Day: Word);
```

Location

Dos

Description

Call SetDate to change the computer's system date. Parameter Year must be the full year—1987 or 1999, for example. Parameter Month should be in the range 1 to 12, and Day should be the month's day number.

    The example finds the day of the week for any date by setting the system date and then calling the Dos unit routine GetDate. Before the program ends, it calls SetDate a second time to reset today's date. (Do not trust the results of this example too much. The program's accuracy is only as good as DOS's date routines, which may have bugs on some early systems and which may not be able to handle dates before January 1, 1980.)

See also

GetDate, GetTime, SetTime

Example

```
program XSetDate;
uses Dos;
const
  DayNames: array[0 .. 6] of string[3] =
    ('Sun', 'Mon', 'Tue', 'Wed', 'Thu', 'Fri', 'Sat');
var
  Oldyear, Oldmonth, Oldday, Olddayofweek: Word;
  Newyear, Newmonth, Newday, Newdayofweek: Word;
  Year, Month, Day: Word;
begin
  GetDate(Oldyear, Oldmonth, Oldday, Olddayofweek);
  Write('Year? (ex. 1987) : '); Readln(Year);
  Write('Month? (ex. 11)  : '); Readln(Month);
  Write('Day? (ex. 25)    : '); Readln(Day);
```

```
    SetDate(Year, Month, Day);
    GetDate(Newyear, Newmonth, Newday, Newdayofweek);
    Writeln('Day of week : ', DayNames[Newdayofweek]);
    SetDate(Oldyear, Oldmonth, Oldday)
end.
```

SetFAttr

Syntax
```
procedure SetFAttr(var F; Attr: Word);
```

Location
Dos

Description
SetFAttr stores the attribute value Attr along with a file name in a disk directory. It changes nothing in the file itself; only the file's directory entry. By changing the attribute, you can hide files, modify the archive bit—which tells if the file was recently backed up—or mark the file read-only, preventing it from being deleted or changed.

Before using SetFAttr, assign a file name to any file variable. Then pass the file variable (F) and a Word variable (Attr) to GetFAttr. The file must not be open.

To preserve other attribute settings, use GetFAttr before calling SetFAttr. Add or subtract combinations of the constant values:

```
ReadOnly  = $01    Hidden   = $02
SysFile   = $04    VolumeID = $08
Directory = $10    Archive  = $20
```

To test whether a file has a certain attribute combination, **and** the attribute with the sum of one or more constants. If the result is zero, then the file does not have the attributes. If not zero, then the file has at least one of the settings.

To change an attribute, **or** the sum of one or more constant values to turn on attributes, or **not-and** the sum to turn off attributes.

The example shows how to use these techniques to first check whether a file TEST.TXT has ReadOnly or Hidden attributes. If not, the program turns on these settings by **or**ing them into the file's current attribute bits; otherwise, it turns the settings off by **not-and**ing the settings. Run the program once to hide TEST.TXT in the directory and to mark it read-only, preventing you from deleting it. Run the program again to reset the file's attributes to normal. You need a test file named TEST.TXT for the example to work.

See also
GetFAttr, GetFTime, SetFTime

Example

```
program XSetFAttr;
uses DOS;
var
  F: file;
  Attr, Settings: Word;
begin
  Assign(F, 'TEST.TXT');
  GetFAttr(F, Attr);
  Settings := ReadOnly+Hidden;
  if (Attr and Settings) = 0
    then SetFAttr(F, (Attr or Settings))      { Turn on }
    else SetFAttr(F, (Attr and not Settings)) { Turn off }
end.
```

SetFillPattern

Syntax

```
procedure SetFillPattern(Pattern: FillPatternType; Color: Word);
```

Location

Graph

Description

SetFillPattern changes the bit pattern and color used by Bar, Bar3D, FillEllipse, FillPoly. FloodFill, PieSlice, and Sector. The pattern is a variable of this type:

```
FillPatternType = array[1 .. 8] of Byte;
```

Insert bit pattern bytes into the pattern array and call SetFillPattern with a color value. In the example, a **repeat** loop cycles until you press any key to quit. Each time through the loop, an inner **for** loop rotates to the left the bits in the pattern array. Filling a bar with this pattern causes an undulating animation that would be difficult to achieve with other methods.

See also

GetFillPattern, GetFillSettings

Example

```
program XSetFillPattern;
uses Crt, Graph;
var
  GraphDriver, GraphMode: Integer;
  Xc, Yc, X1, Y1, X2, Y2: Integer;
  Pattern: FillPatternType;
  I: Byte;
```

```
begin
  GraphDriver := Detect;
  InitGraph(GraphDriver, GraphMode, 'c:\tp\bgi');
  Xc := GetMaxX div 2;
  Yc := GetMaxY div 2;
  for I := 1 to 8 do
    Pattern[I] := I;
  X1 := Xc - 50; Y1 := Yc - 50;
  X2 := Xc + 50; Y2 := Yc + 50;
  repeat
    SetFillPattern(Pattern, Red);
    Bar(X1, Y1, X2, Y2);
    for I := 1 to 8 do
      Pattern[I] := (Pattern[I] shl 1) or Pattern[I] shr 7
  until Keypressed;
  CloseGraph
end.
```

SetFillStyle

Syntax
```
procedure SetFillStyle(Pattern: Word; Color: Word);
```

Location
Graph

Description
Call SetFillStyle to select one of several predefined fill patterns for Bar, Bar3D, FillEllipse, FillPoly, FloodFill, PieSlice, and Sector. Pass a Color number plus one of these Pattern constants, as defined in the Graph unit's interface:

```
EmptyFill       = 0;    { fills area in background color }
SolidFill       = 1;    { fills area in solid fill color }
LineFill        = 2;    { --- fill }
LtSlashFill     = 3;    { /// fill }
SlashFill       = 4;    { /// fill with thick lines }
BkSlashFill     = 5;    { \\\ fill with thick lines }
LtBkSlashFill   = 6;    { \\\ fill }
HatchFill       = 7;    { light hatch fill }
XHatchFill      = 8;    { heavy cross hatch fill }
InterleaveFill  = 9;    { interleaving line fill }
WideDotFill     = 10;   { widely spaced dot fill }
CloseDotFill    = 11;   { closely spaced dot fill }
Userfill        = 12;   { user defined fill }
```

The example displays randomly colored and sized bars using all possible fill patterns except zero, which fills in the background color. Press any key to end the demonstration.

See also
GetFillSettings, SetFillPattern

Example

```pascal
program XSetFillStyle;
uses Crt, Graph;
var
  GraphDriver, GraphMode: Integer;
  XMax, YMax: Integer;
begin
  GraphDriver := Detect;
  InitGraph(GraphDriver, GraphMode, 'c:\tp\bgi');
  XMax := GetMaxX;
  YMax := GetMaxY;
  while not Keypressed do
  begin
    SetFillStyle(1 + Random(11), 1 + Random(GetMaxColor));
    Bar(Random(XMax), Random(YMax),
      Random(XMax), Random(YMax))
  end;
  CloseGraph
end.
```

SetFTime

Syntax

```pascal
procedure SetFTime(var F; Time: LongInt);
```

Location
Dos

Description
Call SetFTime to change the date and time for a file's directory entry. The procedure never changes the file itself, only the date and time you see when listing the file name with the DOS DIR command.

File F must be open. Parameter Time must be in the packed format required by DOS. To set a specific time, assign fields in a DateTime record and call PackTime to convert the record to the packed long integer value. Then call SetFTime to change the file date and time.

If you write to a file and then call SetFTime, when you close the file, DOS will update the date and time, erasing your change. To avoid this problem, Reset the file you want to change. As long as you do not write to the file, Close will not update the date and time.

The example changes TEST.TXT's date to last year by reading the file's date and time with GetFTime, unpacking the long integer value into a DateTime record, subtracting one from the year field, repacking, and then calling SetFTime.

See also
GetFTime, PackTime, SetFAttr

Example

```
program XSetFTime;
uses Dos;
var
  F: file;
  Time: LongInt;
  Daterec: DateTime;
begin
  Assign(F, 'TEST.TXT');
  Reset(F);
  GetFTime(F, Time);
  UnPackTime(Time, Daterec);
  with Daterec do
    Year := Year - 1;
  PackTime(Daterec, Time);
  SetFTime(F, Time);
  Close(F)
end.
```

SetGraphBufSize

Syntax
```
procedure SetGraphBufSize(BufSize: Word);
```

Location
Graph

Description
Before calling InitGraph, if you plan to fill complex polygons or other shapes with patterns, you might have to expand a special memory buffer set aside by the graphics kernel. Pass to SetGraphBufSize the number of bytes in BufSize that you want to reserve for the kernel's fill work space.

Normally, you rarely need to increase the default setting of 4K, large enough to fill polygons with over 600 points. You might call SetGraphBufSize as in the example, though, to reduce the buffer size and gain a little extra memory for other purposes when filling relatively uncomplicated shapes.

See also
FloodFill, FillPoly

Example

```pascal
program XSetGraphBufSize;
uses Crt, Graph;
const
  NumPoints = 75;
var
  GraphDriver, GraphMode: Integer;
  I, XMax, YMax: Integer;
  PolyPoints: array[1 .. NumPoints] of PointType;
begin
  Randomize;
  SetGraphBufSize(1024);   { 1/4 the normal 4K allotment }
  GraphDriver := Detect;
  InitGraph(GraphDriver, GraphMode, 'c:\tp\bgi');
  XMax := GetMaxX;
  YMax := GetMaxY;
  for I := 1 to NumPoints do
  begin
    PolyPoints[I].X := Random(XMax);
    PolyPoints[I].Y := Random(YMax)
  end;
  SetFillStyle(XHatchFill, LightMagenta);
  FillPoly(NumPoints, PolyPoints);
  repeat until Keypressed;
  CloseGraph
end.
```

SetGraphMode

Syntax
```pascal
procedure SetGraphMode(Mode: Integer);
```

Location
Graph

Description

Call SetGraphMode to restore a previous graphics mode after switching to a text screen. Parameter Mode should be the value returned by GetGraphMode, although it also can be a different value if you want to switch between various graphics modes in the same program.

The example shows one way to use SetGraphMode. The program begins normally, automatically detecting and initializing a graphics display. It then saves the current graphics mode in Oldmode and calls RestoreCrtMode to return to the text screen. After displaying a message, SetGraphMode returns to the graphics display until you press a key to end the example.

See also

GetGraphMode, GetModeRange, GraphResult, InitGraph, RestoreCRTMode

Example

```pascal
program XSetGraphMode;
uses Crt, Graph;
var
  GraphDriver, GraphMode: Integer;
  I, Oldmode, XMax, YMax: Integer;
begin
  GraphDriver := Detect;
  InitGraph(GraphDriver, GraphMode, 'c:\tp\bgi');
  if GraphResult = GrOk then
  begin
    XMax := GetMaxX;
    YMax := GetMaxY;
    Oldmode := GetGraphMode;
    RestoreCrtMode;
    Writeln('Ready for graphics!');
    Writeln;
    Write('Press <Enter> to continue...');
    Readln;
    SetGraphMode(Oldmode);
    repeat
      SetColor(Random(1+GetMaxColor));
      Rectangle(Random(XMax), Random(YMax),
        Random(XMax), Random(YMax));
    until Keypressed;
    CloseGraph
  end
end.
```

SetIntVec

Syntax

```
procedure SetIntVec(IntNo: Byte; Vector: Pointer);
```

Location
Dos

Description
Interrupt vectors are the addresses of routines you want to run when a specific interrupt occurs. The interrupt itself is identified by a number ranging from zero to hex $FF. Programs can interrupt themselves through software interrupts—a call to a DOS function, for example. Or, programs can be interrupted by hardware-generated interrupts—perhaps from a keypress or an incoming character from a modem.

Call SetIntVec to change the vector address of any PC interrupt. Because many computer operations depend on the correct vectors, changing vectors indiscriminately can cause serious problems. For instance, if you fiddle with the absolute disk read and write vectors, hex $25 and $26, you could temporarily lose the ability to use your disk drives.

The example shows how to set a pointer variable, Address, to a specific location. In your own programs, replace the first 0000 with the segment and the second 0000 with the offset addresses of your interrupt routine. Then pass the interrupt number (here $60) plus the address to SetIntVec. After that, when this interrupt occurs, your interrupt routine will begin running.

See also
GetIntVec, Intr, MsDos

Example

```
program XSetIntVec;
uses Dos;
var
  Address: Pointer;
begin
  Address := Ptr(0000, 0000);
  SetIntVec($60, Address)
end.
```

SetLineStyle

Syntax

```
procedure SetLineStyle(LineStyle: Word; Pattern: Word; Thickness: Word);
```

Location
Graph

Description
Call SetLineStyle to change the thickness and bit pattern used by LineTo, LineRel, Line, Rectangle, and DrawPoly. Arc, Circle, Ellipse, and PieSlice outlines are always solid—you cannot change their line styles with SetLineStyle.

Parameter LineStyle may be one of the following constant values:

```
SolidLn    = 0;
DottedLn   = 1;
CenterLn   = 2;
DashedLn   = 3;
UserBitLn  = 4;
```

Parameter Thickness may be normWidth (1) or thickWidth (3). As the example proves, a thickness of two does not draw a double-width line as you might expect. Only thicknesses of 1 and 3 have any effect.

If you set parameter LineStyle to the constant UserBitLn, lines are drawn with the bits in parameter pattern. SetLineStyle ignores pattern for any other lineStyle value. For example, to draw a finely dotted horizontal line with the repeating binary pattern 01010101 . . . , you could write:

```
pattern := $5555;
SetLineStyle(UserBitLn, Pattern, NormWidth);
SetColor(Red);
Line(0, 10, GetMaxX, 10);
```

The example displays test lines in all possible standard settings. Notice that line thicknesses of 1 and 2 draw identical lines.

See also
GetLineSettings, Line, LineRel, LineTo, SetWriteMode

Example
```
program XSetLineStyle;
uses Crt, Graph;
var
  GraphDriver, GraphMode: Integer;
  Y, XMax, YMax: Word;
  LineStyle, Pattern, Thickness: Word;
  LsStr, PStr, TStr: string[8];
begin
  GraphDriver := Detect;
  InitGraph(GraphDriver, GraphMode, 'c:\tp\bgi');
  XMax := GetMaxX;
  YMax := GetMaxY;
```

```
Y := 4;
Pattern := 0;  { Ignored unless lineStyle = UserBitLn }
for Thickness := 1 to 3 do
  for LineStyle := 0 to 3 do
  begin
    SetColor(Red);
    SetLineStyle(LineStyle, Pattern, Thickness);
    Line(0, Y, XMax, Y);
    Str(LineStyle, LsStr);
    Str(Pattern, PStr);
    Str(Thickness, TStr);
    SetColor(White);
    OutTextXY(0, Y + 8,
      'Style='+LsStr+'  Pattern='+PStr+'  Thickness='+TStr);
    Y := Y + 28
  end;
repeat until Keypressed;
CloseGraph
end.
```

SetPalette

Syntax
```
procedure SetPalette(ColorNum: Word; Color: ShortInt);
```

Location
Graph

Description
As described in the description to SetAllPalette, color numbers are translated to the actual color values stored in the video display memory to produce certain hues on-screen. The translations between color numbers and the hues they produce are stored in a palette. Use SetPalette to change one palette entry, affecting the color you see (Color) for a specified color number (ColorNum).

The example demonstrates how to use this procedure to produce an interesting illusion. By rotating all but palette entry zero (representing the background color), lines take on the colors of their neighbors. Because changing palette entries has an immediate visual effect, the lines seem to move.

See also
GetPalette, SetAllPalette, SetColor, SetRGBPalette

Example

```pascal
program XSetPalette;
uses Crt, Graph;
var
  GraphDriver, GraphMode: Integer;
  Maxcolor, Temp, C, Y, XMax, YMax: Word;
  Colors: array[0 .. 15] of Word;
begin
  GraphDriver := Detect;
  InitGraph(GraphDriver, GraphMode, 'c:\tp\bgi');
  XMax := GetMaxX;
  YMax := GetMaxY;
  Y := 0;
  MaxColor := GetMaxColor;
  SetLineStyle(SolidLn, 0, ThickWidth);
  for C := 0 to MaxColor do
  begin
    Colors[C] := C;                { Save colors in array }
    SetColor(C);
    Y := Y + 20;
    Line(0, Y, XMax, Y)          { Fill screen with lines }
  end;
  while not Keypressed do         { "Rotate" colors }
  begin
    Delay(300);                    { Adjust to change speed }
    Temp := Colors[1];
    for C := 1 to MaxColor do
    begin
      if C = MaxColor
        then Colors[C] := Temp
        else Colors[C] := Colors[C+1];
      SetPalette(C, Colors[C])
    end
  end;
  CloseGraph
end.
```

SetRGBPalette

Syntax

```pascal
procedure SetRGBPalette(ColorNum, RedValue, GreenValue,
  BlueValue: Integer);
```

Location
Graph

Description
Use this special Graph procedure to set the red, green, and blue (RGB) color values for IBM-8514 256-color displays. Set colorNum to the palette index value you want to change, in the range 0 to 255. For compatibility with other display formats, the first 16 (index values 0 to 15) IBM-8514 palette entries match EGA and VGA display colors. Use SetRGBPalette to modify these colors.

Only the least-significant 6 bits of the low bytes in each of the three Integer parameters, redValue, greenValue, and blueValue, are used, limiting color values to the range 0 to 64.

It is possible to use SetRGBPalette to modify some VGA display colors, but in this case, Borland specifies that colorNum should be limited to the values 0 to 15, even for 256-color displays. At this time, better control of 256-color VGA displays is available only with a special version of the BGI Graph unit, which Borland distributes free of charge on bulletin boards and time-share services such as Compuserve.

The example examines the automatically selected graphics driver (GraphDriver) and calls either SetRGBPalette or SetPalette to modify the displayed colors of vertical lines drawn in all available colors. Because palette entries control the colors of pixels already on display, the effects of modifying the palette values are instantaneous.

See also
GetPalette, SetAllPalette, SetPalette

Example
```
program XSetRGBPalette;
uses Crt, Graph;
var
  GraphDriver, GraphMode: Integer;
  X, XMax, YMax, Color, Width, Height: Word;
begin
  GraphDriver := Detect;
  InitGraph(GraphDriver, GraphMode, 'c:\tp\bgi');
  XMax := GetMaxX;
  YMax := GetMaxY;
  Width := (Succ(XMax) div Succ(GetMaxColor)) div 2;
  Height := (Succ(YMax) div 4);
  X := 0;
  for Color := 0 to GetMaxColor do
  begin
    SetColor(Color);
    Line(X, YMax, X, Height);
    Line(X + 1, YMax, X + 1, Height);
    X := X + (Width * 2)
  end;
```

```
    while not Keypressed do
      for Color := 1 to GetMaxColor do
        if GraphDriver = IBM8514
          then SetRGBPalette(Color, Random(65), Random(65), Random(65))
          else SetPalette(Color, Random(GetMaxColor + 1));
    CloseGraph
  end.
```

SetTextBuf

Syntax
```
procedure SetTextBuf(var F: Text; var Buf[; Size: Word]);
```

Location
System

Description
When reading and writing large text files, you might be able to improve Input/Output speed by increasing the size of the buffer Turbo Pascal fills with characters on their way to and from disk.

Normally, text files have a 128-byte buffer, large enough for most purposes. To increase buffer size, declare a variable, usually an array of Byte or Char, and pass the variable along with the file to SetTextBuf. Do this either before or immediately after resetting or rewriting the file. Changing the text buffer after reading or writing text might accidentally discard information stored in the default buffer.

Unless you add a size parameter, Turbo Pascal uses the entire buffer. In other words, the default condition is:

```
SetTextBuf(F, Buffer, SizeOf(Buffer));
```

Usually, this is best. To use only part of a buffer, pass the number of bytes as the third parameter. For example, to use 512 bytes of a buffer, you could write:

```
SetTextBuf(F, Buffer, 512);
```

Use the example to experiment reading large text files. Change the buffer size (or remove the SetTextBuf statement) and notice how long it takes to read through a file. Also, watch your disk drive light. With larger buffer sizes, you should see less disk activity, which usually means better program speed.

See also
Assign, Close, Reset

Example
```
program XSetTextBuf;
var
```

```
  Tf: Text;
  Buf: array[0 .. 1023] of Char;
  FileName, S: string;
begin
  Write('Display what text file? ');
  Readln(FileName);
  Assign(Tf, FileName);
  SetTextBuf(Tf, Buf);    { Use entire buffer }
  Reset(Tf);
  while not Eof(Tf) do
  begin
    Readln(Tf, S);
    Writeln(S)
  end;
  Close(Tf)
end.
```

SetTextJustify

Syntax
```
procedure SetTextJustify(Horiz, Vert: Word);
```

Location
Graph

Description
Call SetTextJustify to change where OutText displays text in relation to the current point (CP) or to the coordinate passed to OutTextXY. For the Horiz parameter, use one of these constants:

```
LeftText    = 0;
CenterText  = 1;
RightText   = 2;
```

For the Vert parameter, use one of these constants:

```
BottomText  = 0;
CenterText  = 1;
TopText     = 2;
```

The example helps explain how SetTextJustify affects the appearance of text on-screen. Run the program and press Enter several times to display a message. A white dot shows the current point in relation to where text appears for various justification settings.

See also

GetTextSettings, OutText, OutTextXY, SetUserCharSize, TextHeight, TextWidth

Example

```pascal
program XSetTextJustify;
uses Crt, Graph;
var
  GraphDriver, GraphMode: Integer;
  XCenter, YCenter: Word;
  Horiz, Vert: Integer;
begin
  GraphDriver := Detect;
  InitGraph(GraphDriver, GraphMode, 'c:\tp\bgi');
  XCenter := GetMaxX div 2;
  YCenter := GetMaxY div 2;
  for Vert := 0 to 2 do
    for Horiz := 0 to 2 do
    begin
      SetTextJustify(Horiz, Vert);
      ClearViewPort;
      SetColor(Magenta);
      OutTextXY(XCenter, YCenter, 'Happy New Year!');
      SetColor(White);
      Rectangle(XCenter, YCenter, XCenter + 1, YCenter + 1);
      if ReadKey = CHR(27) then
      begin
        CloseGraph;
        Halt
      end
    end;
  CloseGraph
end.
```

SetTextStyle

Syntax

```pascal
procedure SetTextStyle(Font, Direction: Word; Size: Word);
```

Location

Graph

Description

SetTextStyle changes three text characteristics: the font, the direction, and the size.

To select a different font, use one of these constants:

```
DefaultFont    = 0;
TriplexFont    = 1;
SmallFont      = 2;
SansSerifFont  = 3;
GothicFont     = 4;
```

The default font is an 8 x 8 bit-mapped image. The other fonts are stroked (vectored). If the font is not in memory, SetTextStyle attempts to load the associated CHR file from disk, in the path specified for InitGraph. If the font file is not on disk, SetTextStyle returns an error through GraphResult.

The Direction and Size parameters let you display text horizontally or vertically and scale characters to different sizes. Set Direction to either of the constants HorizDir or VertDir. Set Size to any positive value greater than zero. The actual size you see on-screen has no relation to the point sizes (typically in 1/72 inch increments) used in typesetting. Using the same Size values for different fonts does not draw characters in the same relative sizes on-screen.

The example displays two messages in vertical and horizontal directions. Notice how TextWidth and TextHeight position the text.

See also
GetTextSettings, OutText, OutTextXY, SetTextJustify, SetUserCharSize, TextHeight, TextWidth

Example
```
program XSetTextStyle;
uses Crt, Graph;
const
  Size = 4;
var
  GraphDriver, GraphMode: Integer;
  X, Y: Word;
begin
  GraphDriver := Detect;
  InitGraph(GraphDriver, GraphMode, 'c:\tp\bgi');
  X := TextWidth('M') * 4;
  Y := TextHeight('M') * 2;
  SetTextStyle(SansSerifFont, VertDir, Size);
  OutTextXY(X, Y, 'Going up');
  SetTextStyle(SansSerifFont, HorizDir, Size);
  OutTextXY(X, Y, '   Stepping out');
  repeat until Keypressed;
  CloseGraph
end.
```

SetTime

Syntax

```
procedure SetTime(Hour, Minute, Second, Sec100: Word);
```

Location
Dos

Description
Call SetTime to change the computer's system time to the Hour, Minute, Second, and Sec100 (hundredths of seconds) specified by these parameters.

As the example demonstrates, programs can set the time to zero, perform an operation to be timed (a nested **for** loop here), and then call GetTime to read the result. The program displays how long it takes to cycle one million times—an important benchmark of the computer processor's speed and Turbo Pascal's **for** loop overhead. After running this program, you might want to reset your computer's clock to the current time. To do this, either reboot or use the DOS TIME command.

See also
GetDate, GetTime, PackTime, SetDate

Example

```
program XSetTime;
uses DOS;
var
  I, J: Integer;
  Hour, Minute, Sec, Sec100: Word;
begin
  SetTime(0, 0, 0, 0);
  for I := 1 to 100 do
    for J := 1 to 10000 do { nothing } ;
  GetTime(Hour, Minute, Sec, Sec100);
  Writeln('Hours     = ', Hour);
  Writeln('Minutes   = ', Minute);
  Writeln('Seconds   = ', Sec);
  Writeln('Hundredths = ', Sec100)
end.
```

SetUserCharSize

Syntax

```
procedure SetUserCharsize(MultX, DivX, MultY, DivY: Word);
```

Location
Graph

Description
Most the time, you can select character font sizes by passing a size number to SetTextStyle. For better control, use SetUserCharSize, which lets you adjust the horizontal and vertical ratio used to draw characters.

Parameters MultX and DivX control the horizontal size. Parameters MultY and DivY control the vertical. Use a ratio less than one to shrink characters to less than their usual dimensions. For example, if MultX/DivX equals 0.25, then characters will be displayed one fourth their normal width. Likewise, if MultY/DivY equals 3.5, then characters display about $3\frac{1}{2}$ times their normal height.

After calling SetUserCharSize, you must call SetTextStyle to select a character font and direction. Pass the constant UserCharSize as the third SetTextStyle parameter, telling the graphics kernel to use your ratio rather than the default. Because SetTextStyle loads a font CHR file from disk, you might want to preload and register the font ahead of time (see RegisterBGIfont), especially if you switch ratios frequently.

The example displays two messages, the first 3.5 times as tall as usual (7/2), and the second about 2.7 (8/3) times as wide on EGA or better systems and about 1.4 (4/3) times as wide on CGA displays. Try experimenting with different ratios in the three calls to SetUserCharSize.

See also
SetTextStyle, OutText, OutTextXY, TextHeight, TextWidth

Example
```
program XSetUserCharSize;
uses Crt, Graph;
var
  GraphDriver, GraphMode: Integer;
begin
  GraphDriver := Detect;
  InitGraph(GraphDriver, GraphMode, 'c:\tp\bgi');
  SetUserCharSize(1, 1, 7, 2);
  SetTextStyle(SansSerifFont, HorizDir, UserCharSize);
  OutTextXY(0, 50, 'Tall in the saddle');
  if GraphDriver = CGA
    then SetUserCharSize(4, 3, 1, 1)
    else SetUserCharSize(8, 3, 1, 1);
  SetTextStyle(SansSerifFont, HorizDir, UserCharSize);
  OutTextXY(0, 150, 'Wide in the ride');
  repeat until Keypressed;
  CloseGraph
end.
```

SetVerify

Syntax
```
procedure SetVerify(Verify: Boolean);
```

Location
Dos

Description
When the DOS *verify* switch is true, disk writes are followed by automatic disk reads to verify that data written to disk probably was stored correctly. When the verify switch is false, disk writes are not followed by disk reads. Because write-verification slows disk Input/Output considerably, most people leave this switch off.

Call function SetVerify to change the switch setting (similar to the way the DOS VERIFY command works). Call the related GetVerify procedure to inspect the state of the DOS verify switch. The example toggles the switch on and off.

See also
GetVerify

Example
```
program XSetVerify;
uses Dos;
var
  Verify: Boolean;
begin
  GetVerify(Verify);
  Verify := not Verify;
  SetVerify(Verify);
  Writeln('Verify switch is: ', Verify)
end.
```

SetViewPort

Syntax
```
procedure SetViewPort(X1, Y1, X2, Y2: Integer; Clip: Boolean);
```

Location
Graph

Description
Changing the graphics viewport with SetViewPort defines the boundaries of the visible portion of the display. Coordinate (X1,Y1) represents the top-left corner of the new display window and (X2,Y2) represents the bottom-right corner. If Clip is

true, then lines drawn outside of the new boundaries are invisible. If it is false, then lines are not restricted to the window boundaries. In place of true and false, you can use the Graph constants, clipOn and clipOff.

After calling SetViewPort, the top-left corner of the new window has the coordinate (0,0), not (X1,Y1). You can use this fact to shift the origin—the anchor point or home position of the logical coordinate grid. Negative coordinate values lie to the left and above the origin. Positive coordinate values lie to the right and below. Shifting the viewport to center (0,0) sometimes makes graphics programs easier to write. To do this, execute the instructions:

```
xCenter := GetMaxX div 2;
yCenter := GetMaxY div 2;
SetViewPort(XCenter, YCenter, GetMaxX, GetMaxY, clipOff);
```

See also
ClearViewPort, GetViewSettings

Example
```
program XSetViewPort;
uses Crt, Graph;
var
  GraphDriver, GraphMode: Integer;
  XCenter, YCenter, Xcd2, Ycd2: Integer;
begin
  GraphDriver := Detect;
  InitGraph(GraphDriver, GraphMode, 'c:\tp\bgi');
  XCenter := GetMaxX div 2;
  YCenter := GetMaxY div 2;
  Xcd2 := XCenter div 2;
  Ycd2 := YCenter div 2;
  Randomize;
  SetViewPort(XCenter - Xcd2, YCenter - Ycd2,
    XCenter + Xcd2, YCenter + Ycd2, ClipOn);
  while not Keypressed do
  begin
    SetColor(1 + Random(GetMaxColor));
    LineTo(Random(GetMaxX) - Xcd2, Random(GetMaxY) - Ycd2)
  end;
  CloseGraph
end.
```

SetVisualPage

Syntax
```
procedure SetVisualPage(Page: Word);
```

Location
Graph

Description
In graphics modes that support multiple pages, SetVisualPage brings the display numbered Page into view. When combined with SetActivePage, this procedure lets you view one graphics display while drawing on another. Rapidly flopping the two pages—viewing the previously hidden page and drawing on the one now invisible—can produce smooth animations, similar to the effect of flipping the pages in an animated cartoon book.

See also
SetActivePage

Example
See example for SetActivePage.

SetWriteMode

Syntax
```
procedure SetWriteMode(WriteMode: Integer);
```

Location
Graph

Description
To change the logic by which Graph combines pixels in lines and other shapes with existing pixels, pass one of the following values to SetWriteMode:

```
CopyPut  = 0;
XORPut   = 1;
ORPut    = 2;
ANDPut   = 3;
NOTPut   = 4;
```

The Graph unit defines these constants to add readability to programs. For example, to change the write mode to ANDPut, execute the statement:

```
SetWriteMode(ANDPut);
```

Each write-mode method has a different effect. The default value CopyPut causes new pixels to overwrite existing shapes. The other values combine new pixels according to the rules of Boolean logic operators **xor**, **or**, **and**, and **not** (see Chapter 2).

One of the more useful of these values is XORPut, which has the property of being able to toggle bits on and off without prior knowledge of the original bit value. When applied to graphics, this property lets programs draw shapes on top of other shapes and then remove the topmost shape simply by redrawing that shape. As if by magic, the shape below remains untouched by the operation.

The example demonstrates the effect of drawing lines with the write mode set to XORPut. First, the program fills the screen with a complex background pattern, drawn by the Bar procedure. Then, an array of color and coordinate values is filled with random values. A **for** loop uses these values to draw ten lines over the complex background. Another **for** loop then redraws the same lines in reverse. Press Enter repeatedly to see how XORPut allows these lines to remove themselves from the display, completely restoring other lines and the background pattern below.

See also
SetLineStyle

Example

```
program XSetWriteMode;
uses Crt, Graph;

type
  Rec = record
    Color: Word;
    X1, Y1, X2, Y2: Integer
  end;

var
  GraphDriver, GraphMode: Integer;
  I: Integer;
  V: array[1 .. 10] of Rec;

  procedure SetValues(I, C: Word; X, Y, Xx, Yy: Integer);
  begin
    with V[I] do
    begin
      Color := C;
      X1 := X;
      Y1 := Y;
      X2 := Xx;
```

```
      Y2 := Yy
    end
  end;

begin
  GraphDriver := Detect;
  InitGraph(GraphDriver, GraphMode, 'c:\tp\bgi');
  SetFillStyle(XHatchFill, Red);
  Bar(0, 0, GetMaxX, GetMaxY);
  for I := 1 to 10 do
    SetValues(I, 1 + Random(GetMaxColor),
      Random(GetMaxX), Random(GetMaxY),
      Random(GetMaxX), Random(GetMaxY));
  SetWriteMode(XORPut);
  SetLineStyle(SolidLn, 0, ThickWidth);
  for I := 1 to 10 do with V[I] do
  begin
    SetColor(Color);
    Line(X1, Y1, X2, Y2)
  end;
  for I := 10 downto 1 do with V[I] do
  begin
    Readln;
    SetColor(Color);
    Line(X1, Y1, X2, Y2)
  end;
  repeat until Keypressed;
  CloseGraph
end.
```

Sin

Syntax
```
function Sin(R: <real>): <real>;
```

Location
System

Description
Sin returns the sine of R, which must be expressed in radians. The example requires a graphics display.

See also
ArcTan, Cos

Example
```pascal
program XSin;
uses Crt, Graph;
var
  GraphDriver, GraphMode: Integer;
  X, Y, Yc: Integer;

  function Radians(Angle: Integer): Real;
  begin
    Radians := Abs(Angle mod 360) * Pi / 180.0
  end;

begin
  GraphDriver := Detect;
  InitGraph(GraphDriver, GraphMode, 'c:\tp\bgi');
  Yc := GetMaxY div 2;
  for X := 0 to GetMaxX do
    PutPixel(X, Yc + Round(Yc * Sin(Radians(X))), Green);
  repeat until Keypressed;
  CloseGraph
end.
```

SizeOf

Syntax
```pascal
function SizeOf(V: <type>¦<file>): Word;
```

Location
System

Description
SizeOf returns the size in bytes of a variable or data type V. Use this function with Move and FillChar to prevent accidentally overwriting memory beyond addresses occupied by variables.

The example displays a chart of Turbo Pascal's common data types along with the number of bytes variables of those types occupy in memory.

See also
FillChar, GetMem, Move

Example

```
program XSizeOf;
begin
  Writeln('Types           Bytes');
  Writeln('==================');
  Writeln('Byte ........ ', Sizeof(Byte));
  Writeln('ShortInt .... ', Sizeof(ShortInt));
  Writeln('Integer ..... ', Sizeof(Integer));
  Writeln('Word ........ ', Sizeof(Word));
  Writeln('LongInt ..... ', Sizeof(LongInt));
  Writeln('Real ........ ', Sizeof(Real));
  Writeln('Char ........ ', Sizeof(Char));
  Writeln('Boolean ..... ', Sizeof(Boolean))
end.
```

Sound

Syntax

```
procedure Sound(Hz: Word);
```

Location

Crt

Description

Sound turns on tone with a frequency of approximately Hz (hertz) cycles per second. The tone stays on while other statements execute until you call NoSound.

See also

NoSound

Example

```
program XSound;
uses Crt;
var
  Frequency: Integer;
begin
  while not Keypressed do
  begin
    Write('Whoop...');
    for Frequency := 500 to 900 do
    begin
      Delay(1);
      Sound(Frequency)
    end;
```

```
      NoSound;
      Delay(75)
   end
end.
```

SPtr

Syntax
```
function SPtr: Word;
```

Location
System

Description
SPtr returns the 16-bit value of the processor stack pointer, which decreases toward zero as the program uses stack space for local variables and also for procedure and function calls. You might examine the stack pointer in a program that turns off stack checking with the compiler directive {$S–} to see if your memory fuel tank is getting low.

The example calls a recursive bean counter, counting up to 10 and displaying the stack pointer at each level in the recursion. Function SSeg returns the stack segment value, which never changes. When you run the program, you see a display similar to this:

```
Beans  =  0  SPtr  = 5643  :3FBA
Beans  =  1  SPtr  = 5643  :3FC0
Beans  =  2  SPtr  = 5643  :3FC6
Beans  =  3  SPtr  = 5643  :3FCC
Beans  =  5  SPtr  = 5643  :3FD8
Beans  =  7  SPtr  = 5643  :3FE4
Beans  =  9  SPtr  = 5643  :3FF0
Beans  = 10  SPtr  = 5643  :3FF6
```

See also
SSeg

Example
```
program XSPtr;

   function WHex(V: Word) : Char;
   const
      Digits: array[0 .. 15] of Char = '0123456789ABCDEF';
   begin
```

```
      Write(Digits[Hi(V) div 16],
            Digits[Hi(V) mod 16],
            Digits[Lo(V) div 16],
            Digits[Lo(V) mod 16]);
    WHex := Chr(0) { Null, so WHex can go in Write statements }
  end;


  procedure BeanCounter(Beans: Integer);
  begin
    if Beans > 0
      then BeanCounter(Beans - 1);
    Writeln('Beans =', Beans:3,
      '  SPtr = ', WHex(SSeg), ':', WHex(SPtr))
    end;


begin
  BeanCounter(10)
end.
```

Sqr

Syntax

```
function Sqr(N: <number>): <number>;
```

Location

System

Description

Sqr returns the square of an integer or real number. The result, which is of the same type as its parameter, is equivalent to N * N.

The square of even small integers may produce unexpected results. For example, Sqr(250) is –3036, not 62,500, which is greater than the largest possible positive Integer value. Because any value squared is a positive number, you can usually avoid this problem by assigning Sqr to a Word or LongInt variable rather than to an Integer or ShortInt.

See also

Sqrt

Example

```
program XSqr;
const Number = 212;
var
```

```
    Int: Integer;
    Long: LongInt;
  begin
    Int := Number;
    Int := Sqr(Int);
    Long := Sqr(Number);
    Writeln('Sqr(number):');
    Writeln('----------------------');
    Writeln('Integer result = ', Int);
    Writeln('LongInt result = ', Long)
  end.
```

Sqrt

Syntax

```
function Sqrt(R: <real>): <real>;
```

Location

System

Description

Sqrt returns the square root of a real number R. Unlike some functions that return the type of their arguments, Sqrt always returns a real-number result.

See also

Sqr

Example

```
program XSqrt;
var
  R: Real;
begin
  Write('Square root of ? ');
  Readln(R);
  Writeln('  _____');        { 2 blanks + 8 underlines }
  Writeln('\/', R:0:3, '=':8, Sqrt(R):10:3)
end.
```

SSeg

Syntax

```
function SSeg: Word;
```

Location

System

Description

SSeg returns the value of the stack segment register, SS. This equals the base address where local variables (those declared inside procedures and functions) are stored along with return addresses.

See also

CSeg, DSeg, SPtr

Example

See example for SPtr.

Str

Syntax

```
procedure Str(I[:N]: <integer>; var S: <string var>);
procedure Str(R[:N[:D]]: <real>; var S: <string var>);
```

Location

System

Description

Str converts real number values R or integer values I to string variables S. Optional formatting expressions right justify values in N columns and D decimal places within the string.

You can specify the maximum number of decimals only for real numbers. For example, Str(R:8:2, S) converts real number R to string S in eight columns with two decimal places. This is identical to the numeric formatting rules for numbers in Write and Writeln statements.

The example displays several numbers as strings, using a variety of formatting options. The first two Writeln statements display a column reference line.

See also

Val, Write, Writeln

Example

```
program XStr;
var
  S: string;
begin
  Writeln('0         1         2         3');
  Writeln('0123456789012345678901234567890123456789');
  Str(Pi, S); Writeln(S);
  Str(Pi:8:2, S); Writeln(S);
```

```
    Str(Maxint, S); Writeln(S);
    Str(255:6, S); Writeln(S);
end.
```

Succ

Syntax
```
function Succ(V: <ordinal>): <ordinal>;
```

Location
System

Description
Succ returns the scalar successor of V. For example, if you type Color = (Red, White, Blue), then Succ(White) = Blue, and Succ(Red) = White. Succ(Blue) is undefined. Also, Succ(false) = true, and Succ(0) = 1, Succ(1) = 2, and so on.

See also
Pred

Example
```
program XSucc;
var
  I: Integer;
begin
  Writeln('Counting via Succ()');
  Writeln;
  I := 0;
  while I < 100 do
  begin
    I := Succ(I);
    Write(I:8)
  end;
  Writeln
end.
```

Swap

Syntax
```
function Swap(I: <integer>): <integer>;
```

Location
System

Description

Swap exchanges the high (most significant) and low (least significant) bytes of a 16-bit Integer or Word variable. You also can swap other integer types such as ShortInt and Byte, but the results are not particularly useful for these single-byte quantities.

See also

Hi, Lo

Example

```
program XSwap;
uses Crt;
var
  S: Shortint;
  I: Integer;
  L: Longint;
  B: Byte;
  W: Word;
begin
  S := 15; S := Swap(S); Writeln('S=', S);
  B := 255; B := Swap(B); Writeln('B=', B);
  I := 240; I := Swap(I); Writeln('I=', I);
  W := 240; W := Swap(W); Writeln('W=', W);
  L := 900000; L := Swap(L); Writeln('L=', L)
end.
```

SwapVectors

Syntax

```
procedure SwapVectors;
```

Location

Dos

Description

When a program begins, Turbo Pascal's System unit copies a series of low-memory interrupt vectors, which address critical ROM and DOS routines such as the keyboard interrupt handlers. Some of these vectors are then replaced with the addresses of Turbo Pascal's own critical code. Later, just before the program hands control back to DOS, the System unit restores the original vectors. If you need to do this at other times, call SwapVectors.

The example uses SwapVectors to restore interrupt vectors before calling Exec to execute a DOS command. This lets DOS use its own critical routines. A second call to SwapVectors restores the Turbo Pascal vectors before the program continues.

See also
Exec

Example
```
{$M 1024, 0, 0}
program XSwapVectors;
uses Dos;
begin
  Writeln('Press Enter for wide directory...');
  Readln;
  SwapVectors;
  Exec(GetEnv('COMSPEC'), '/C DIR *.* /W');
  SwapVectors;
  Writeln;
  Writeln('Press Enter to continue...');
  Readln;
    { ... continue program }
end.
```

TextBackground

Syntax
```
procedure TextBackground(Color: Byte);
```

Location
Crt

Description
TextBackground selects the background color of the entire text display, regardless of the current window boundaries. After TextBackground, ClrScr clears the screen to the new Color. Characters with the same TextColor as the background are invisible.

See also
HighVideo, LowVideo, NormVideo, TextColor

Example
```
program XTextBackground;
uses Crt;
var
  Ch: Char;
  Color: Byte;
```

```
begin
  ClrScr;
  for Color := 0 to 15 do
  begin
    TextBackGround(Color);
    Writeln;
    if Color < 8
      then LowVideo
      else HighVideo;
    for Ch := 'A' to 'Z' do
      Write(Ch:2)
  end;
  Writeln
end.
```

TextColor

Syntax
```
procedure TextColor(Color: Byte);
```

Location
Crt

Description
TextColor selects the foreground Color for displaying characters. Characters with the same color as the background are invisible.

See also
HighVideo, LowVideo, NormVideo, TextBackground

Example
```
program XTextColor;
uses Crt;
var
  Ch: Char;
  Color: Byte;
begin
  ClrScr;
  for Color := 0 to 15 do
  begin
    TextBackground(Color);
    Writeln;
    for Ch := 'A' to 'Z' do
    begin
```

```
        TextColor(Ord(Ch) mod 16);
        Write(Ch:2)
      end
    end;
    Writeln
  end.
```

TextHeight

Syntax
```
function TextHeight(TextString: <string>): Word;
```

Location
Graph

Description
TextHeight returns the height in pixels of a literal or variable string. Use this value
to space text vertically, or, as in the example, to draw boxes around text in different
fonts and sizes.

See also
OutText, OutTextXY, SetTextStyle, SetUserCharSize, TextWidth

Example
```
program XTextHeight;
uses Crt, Graph;
const
  Message = 'Happy Holidays';
var
  GraphDriver, GraphMode: Integer;
  XCenter, YCenter, X1, X2, Y1, Y2, H, W: Integer;
begin
  GraphDriver := Detect;
  InitGraph(GraphDriver, GraphMode, 'c:\tp\bgi');
  XCenter := GetMaxX div 2;
  YCenter := GetMaxY div 2;
  SetTextJustify(CenterText, CenterText);
  SetTextStyle(TriplexFont, HorizDir, 4);
  H := TextHeight(Message) + 4;
  W := TextWidth(Message) + 4;
  X1 := XCenter - (W div 2);
  X2 := XCenter + (W div 2);
  Y1 := YCenter - (H div 2);
  Y2 := YCenter + (H div 2);
```

```
    SetColor(Red);
    Rectangle(X1, Y1, X2, Y2);
    SetColor(Green);
    OutTextXY(XCenter, YCenter, Message);
    repeat until Keypressed;
    CloseGraph
  end.
```

TextMode

Syntax
```
procedure TextMode(Mode: Word);
```

Location
Crt

Description
TextMode selects a text display mode. Pass one of the following constants to TextMode's Mode parameter:

```
BW40     --    40  columns, monochrome
CO40     --    40  columns, color
BW80     --    80  columns, monochrome
CO80     --    80  columns, color
Mono     --    MDA or Hercules only
Font8x8  --    EGA 43-line or VGA 50-line modes
```

You also can use C40 in place of CO40 and C80 in place of CO80, provided for compatibility with Turbo Pascal version 3.0 programs.

When programs begin and every time you call TextMode, the display mode is stored in the Crt Word variable, LastMode. Passing LastMode to TextMode, then, does not return to the previous text display as you might expect.

As the example demonstrates, add the special constant Font8x8 to CO80 to turn on 43-line EGA or 50-line VGA displays. Do not run this program unless you have EGA or VGA video. Then, to return to the previous display, use the statement:

```
TextMode(Lo(LastMode));
```

See also
Lo, RestoreCrtMode

Example
```
{ Note: Requires EGA or VGA video card }

program XTextMode;
uses Crt;
```

```
var
  Color: Integer;
begin
  TextMode(CO80 + Font8x8);  { EGA=43 lines, VGA=50 lines }
  ClrScr;
  Writeln('   Tiny Text Color Demonstration');
  Writeln('-------------------------------------');
 for Color := 0 to 15 do
  begin
    NormVideo;
    Write('Color=', Color:2);
    TextColor(Color);
    Write('   Normal video   ');
    HighVideo;
    Writeln('High video')
  end;
  repeat until Keypressed;
  TextMode(Lo(LastMode))  { Restore original display }
end.
```

TextWidth

Syntax
```
function TextWidth(TextString: <string>): Word;
```

Location
Graph

Description
TextWidth returns the width of TextString in pixels. Use this function along with TextHeight to design graphics text displays in different fonts and sizes. The example is a primitive text editor—actually just a typing demonstration—that shows one way to simulate carriage returns and line feeds on graphics displays.

See also
OutText, OutTextXY, SetTextStyle, TextHeight

Example
```
program XTextWidth;
uses Crt, Graph;
var
  GraphDriver, GraphMode: Integer;
  XMax, YMax: Integer;
  Ch: Char;
```

```
begin
  GraphDriver := Detect;
  InitGraph(GraphDriver, GraphMode, 'c:\tp\bgi');
  XMax := GetMaxX;
  YMax := GetMaxY;
  SetTextStyle(SansSerifFont, HorizDir, 4);
  OutTextXY(0, 0, 'Type Esc to quit...');
  MoveTo(0, TextHeight('M') + 6);
  repeat
    Ch := ReadKey;
    OutText(Ch);
    if (Ch = Chr(13)) or(GetX + TextWidth('M') > XMax) then
    begin { carriage return, line feed }
      MoveTo(0, GetY + TextHeight('M') + 6);
      if GetY + TextHeight('M') >= YMax
        then ClearViewPort { new page }
    end
  until Ch = Chr(27);
  CloseGraph
end.
```

Trunc

Syntax
```
function Trunc(R: <real>): LongInt;
```

Location
System

Description
Trunc returns the LongInt equivalent value of a real number R minus R's fractional part. The function operates similarly to Int, but returns a LongInt rather than a real-number result.

If you attempt to assign Trunc to an Integer variable, and if range checking is turned on with the compiler directive {$R+}, a runtime error 201 halts the program. With range checking off ({$R−}), this error is not detected and the program does not halt, although the assigned value is meaningless. To avoid this problem, test R before passing to Trunc. For example:

```
if (-32768.0 <= R) and (R <= 32767.0)
  then N := Trunc(R)
  else Writeln('Real number out of range')
```

See also
Frac, Int, Round

Example

```pascal
program XTrunc;
var
  I: Integer;
  R: Real;
begin
  Randomize;
  for I := 1 to 20 do
  begin
    R := Random * 20000;
    Writeln('R=', R:11:4, '  Trunc(R)=', Trunc(R):6)
  end
end.
```

Truncate

Syntax

```pascal
procedure Truncate(var F: <file>);
```

Location
System

Description
Use Truncate to delete from the current file marker to the end of the file. The present file marker then becomes the new end of file, and all information beyond that point is permanently lost. File F may be any type except Text. To truncate text files, use **file of** Char.

The example creates a file of 100 numbers and then truncates from record number 50 to the end of the file. Remember that the first record is number 0. Seeking to record 50, then, locates the fifty-first record—the first to be truncated in this test.

See also
Close, Reset, Rewrite, Seek

Example

```pascal
program XTruncate;
var
  F: file of Integer;
  I: Integer;

  procedure DisplayFile;
```

```
    var
      N: Integer;
    begin
      Reset(F);
      while not EOF(F) do
      begin
        Read(F, N);
        Write(N:8)
      end;
      Writeln;
      Writeln
    end;

begin
  Assign(F, 'TEST.DAT');    { Create file of 100 numbers }
  Rewrite(F);
  for I := 1 to 100 do
    Write(F, I);
  Writeln('Before truncating:');
  DisplayFile;
  Seek(F, 50);      { Delete all records from #50 to end of file }
  Truncate(F);
  Writeln('After truncating:');
  DisplayFile;
  Close(F)
end.
```

TypeOf

Syntax
```
function TypeOf(<type identifier>): Pointer;
```

Location
System

Description
TypeOf returns the address of an object type's VMT (Virtual Method Table). Be sure
to set type identifer to the name of an object type—not to the name of a variable
(instance) of that type.

The VMT stores the addresses of virtual methods defined in the object. It also
stores the size of an instance of this object type. Only objects with one or more virtual
methods or a constructor have VMTs.

TypeOf is required by streams—a way to read and write other objects in disk files (see Chapter 17).

Example

See ADDRU.PAS.PAS (Program 17-9) and PERSONU.PAS (Program 17-10) in Chapter 17.

UnpackTime

Syntax
```
procedure UnpackTime(P: LongInt; var T: DateTime);
```

Location
Dos

Description
Call UnpackTime with a long integer P equal to the packed date and time format, as returned by GetFTime. Also pass a DateTime record R. The procedure unpacks the encoded date and time into the record fields, Year, Month, Day, Hour, Min, and Sec.

See also
GetFTime, GetTime, PackTime, SetFTime, SetTime

Example
See example for GetFTime.

UpCase

Syntax
```
function UpCase(Ch: Char): Char;
```

Location
System

Description
UpCase converts character Ch from lower- to uppercase. The function affects only characters in the range a to z. Punctuation, digits, and uppercase characters return unchanged.

The equivalent DnCase (upper- to lowercase) function, not in Turbo Pascal, is shown in the example.

See also
Chr, Ord

Example

```
program XUpCase;
const
  Blank = ' ';
var
  Ch: Char;

  function DnCase(Ch: Char): Char;
  begin
    if ('A' <= Ch) and(Ch <= 'Z')
      then DnCase := Chr(Ord(Ch) + 32)
  end;

begin
  Writeln('Ch:UpCase');
  for Ch := 'a' to 'z' do
    Write(Ch, UpCase(Ch), Blank);
  Writeln;
  Writeln;
  Writeln('Ch:DnCase');
  for Ch := 'A' to 'Z' do
    Write(Ch, DnCase(Ch), Blank);
  Writeln
end.
```

Val

Syntax

```
procedure Val(S: <string>; var N: <number>; var E: Integer);
```

Location

System

Description

Val converts string S to a real or integer number N. If N is a real number, then the string may be in scientific notation and may or may not have a decimal part. If N is an integer, the string must be a whole number. Val returns an error code in integer variable E equal to the index position in string S where Val finds a bad character. If E is zero, then the conversion was successful.

When you run the example, type a number like 3.14159 to convert from a string to a Real variable. Type errors like 3.14QB6 to see how the **else** clause handles bad characters.

See also

Str

Example

```
program XVal;
var
  R: Real;
  S: string;
  E: Integer;
begin
  Write('Enter a number: ');
  Readln(S);
  Val(S, R, E);
  if E = 0
    then Writeln('No errors.  Value = ', R)
    else Writeln('^':16 + E, '--- Error!')
end.
```

WhereX

Syntax

```
function WhereX: Byte;
```

Location

Crt

Description

WhereX returns the horizontal cursor coordinate. As the example shows, this function and its brother WhereY are useful for writing procedures to move the cursor around the screen or in a text window.

Another use for WhereX is to move the cursor up or down a few lines without changing its column position. For example, this statement moves the cursor up four lines:

```
GotoXY(WhereX, WhereY - 4);
```

See also

GotoXY, WhereY, Window

Example

```
program XWhereXY;
uses Crt;
var
```

```
    X, I: Integer;

    procedure GoUp;
    begin
      Gotoxy(WhereX, WhereY - 1);
    end;

    procedure GoLeft;
    begin
      Gotoxy(WhereX - 1, WhereY)
    end;

begin
  ClrScr;
  GotoXY(40, 12);
  Write(' <-- Center of screen');
  GotoXY(40, 12);
  for I := 1 to 4 do GoUp;
  for I := 1 to 15 do GoLeft;
  X := WhereX;
  Write(' <-- Up 4, left 15');
  GotoXY(X, WhereY);
  repeat until Keypressed
end.
```

WhereY

Syntax
```
function WhereY: Byte;
```

Location
Crt

Description
WhereY returns the vertical cursor coordinate. Along with WhereX, this function is useful for writing procedures to move the cursor around the screen.

See also
GotoXY, WhereX, Window

Example
See example for WhereX.

Window

Syntax

```
procedure Window(X1, Y1, X2, Y2: Byte);
```

Location

Crt

Description

Window sets the text display window to the upper-left corner (X1, Y1) and lower-right corner (X2, Y2). Window(1, 1, 80, 25) resets the display to its maximum opening.

After changing the window, output to the display is restricted to the new borders. Scrolling occurs inside the window and does not disturb text elsewhere on the screen. Screen operations like ClrScr, ClrEol, and GotoXY operate in the current window. In other words, GotoXY(1, 1) locates the upper-left corner of the new window, not necessarily the upper-left corner of the display.

Window does not save text *behind* the window. After you write to a new window, anything on the screen at the same position is lost.

The example displays randomly selected and colored text in three windows that scroll separately. Notice that the program must keep track of the cursor location in each window and that it must execute GotoXY after Window to place the cursor inside the window before displaying text there.

See also

ClrEol, ClrScr, DelLine, InsLine, GotoXY, WhereX, WhereY

Example

```
program XWindow;
uses Crt;
var
  Y1, Y2, Y3: Integer;

  procedure RandText;
  var
    I: Integer;
  begin
    Delay(75);
    for I := 1 to 25 do
    begin
      TextColor(1 + Random(15));
      Write(Chr(32 + Random(144)))
    end;
```

```
      Writeln
    end;

  begin
    ClrScr;
    Y1 := 11;
    Y2 := 11;
    Y3 := 13;
    while not Keypressed do
    begin
      Window(1, 1, 26, 11);
      GotoXY(1, Y1);
      RandText;
      Y1 := WhereY;
      Window(20, 13, 45, 23);
      GotoXY(1, Y2);
      RandText;
      Y2 := WhereY;
      Window(50, 5, 75, 17);
      GotoXY(1, Y3);
      RandText;
      Y3 := WhereY
    end
  end.
```

Write

Syntax
```
procedure Write([F: <file>;] V1, V2, ..., Vn);
```

Location
System

Description
Use Write to send values to an output file, which might be the display, the printer, a modem, or a disk file. If <file> is not specified, Write and Writeln default to the standard Output, normally the console. For text, the output file may be redirected from the DOS command line if you do not use the Crt unit. In programs that use Crt, Write (and Writeln) display text much faster but cannot be redirected.

Separate multiple items with commas inside Write's parentheses. The items may be of different types. When writing to text files, the items may be literal constants or variables. When writing to data files, items must be variables.

When writing to text files or to the default Output, Boolean variables automatically convert to the strings 'TRUE' and 'FALSE'.

Optional formatting commands write integer, real, and string variables in fixed column widths. The command I:N right justifies integer I or string S in N columns, while R:N:D right justifies real number R with D decimal places in N columns.

When writing data files, Write transfers one or more records to the current file position.

See also
Assign, Read, Readln, Rewrite, Writeln

Example
```
program XWrite;
const
  N = 1234;
  S = 'The Write Stuff';
begin
  Write('Pi=', Pi:1:8, ' N=', N, ' S=', S)
end.
```

Writeln

Syntax
```
procedure Writeln([F: <file>;] V1, V2, ..., Vn);
```

Location
System

Description
Writeln operates identically to Write except for two differences: You can use this procedure only with text files (including text devices like the display console and a printer), and after the last item written, Writeln appends carriage return and line feed control characters.

Normally, use Writeln when you want to display text and send the cursor to the start of a new line. Use Write when you want to display text and leave the cursor positioned after the last character written. Use Writeln with no parameters to start a new line without displaying any text.

Like Write, Writeln can handle any number of parameters, which can be strings, characters, or simple types that Turbo Pascal can convert to text. When writing items such as real numbers or integers, remember that these are converted to a character format.

In programs that do not use the Crt unit, Writeln's output can be redirected from the DOS command line. To test this, compile the example to a disk file,

XWRITELN.EXE. Typing XWRITELN alone sends text to the default output, the display. Typing XWRITELN > PRN sends the output to the printer. Typing XWRITELN > TEST.TXT sends the output to a disk text file, TEST.TXT.

See also
Append, Assign, Read, Readln, Rewrite, Write

Example
```
program XWriteln;
begin
  Writeln('You can redirect this text to a file.');
  Writeln('Follow the instructions in the description.');
  Writeln('That''s all folks!')
end.
```

Appendixes

A   Turbo Pascal Railroad Diagrams

B   Memory Map

C   Options and Directives

D   ASCII Character Codes

E   Operator Precedence

A

Turbo Pascal Railroad Diagrams

A

Turbo Pascal Railroad Diagrams

The following railroad diagrams describe the syntax of Turbo Pascal. Portions of the same diagrams appear throughout the book, sometimes in slightly altered form. See Chapter 1 for a description on how to read and use railroad diagrams.

letter

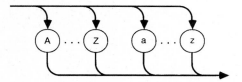

digit

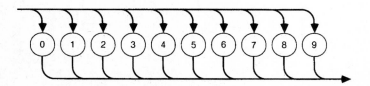

hex digit

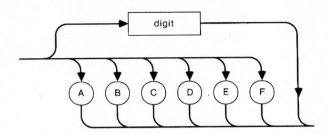

identifier

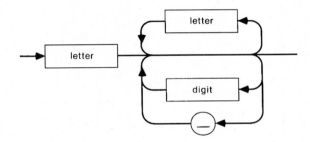

unsigned integer

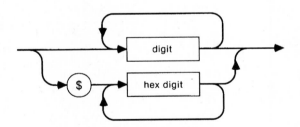

Appendix A

unsigned number

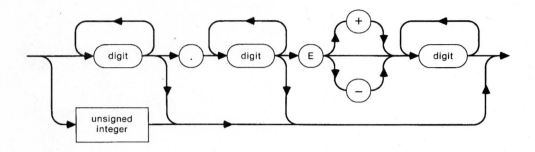

string constant

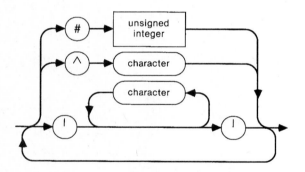

unsigned constant

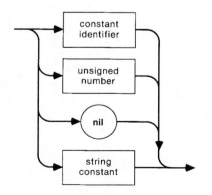

constant

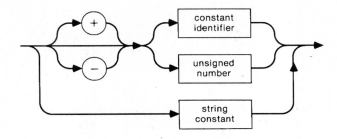

simple type

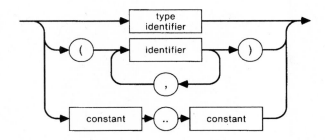

field list

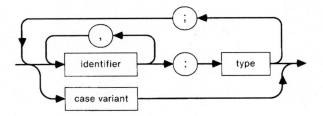

case variant

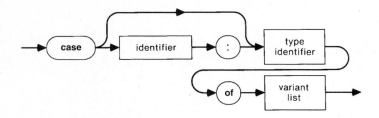

variant list

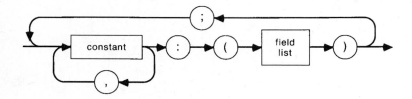

data type

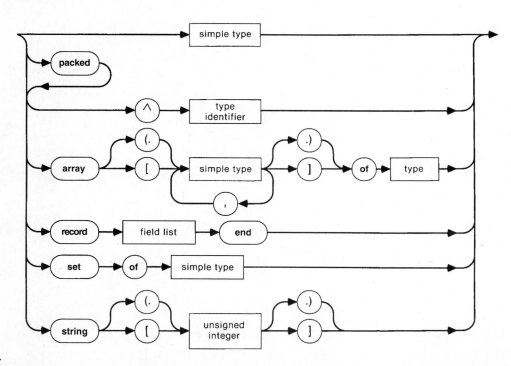

file type

type

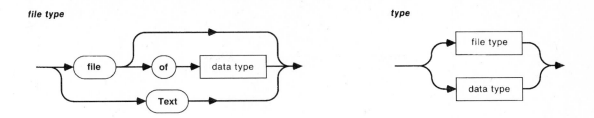

factor

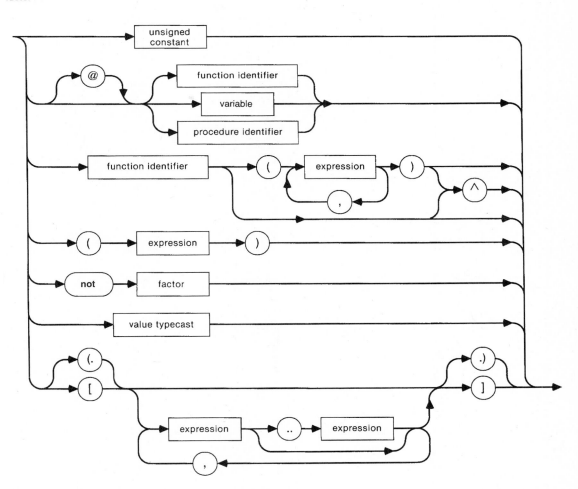

value typecast

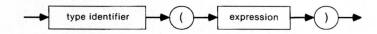

variable typecast

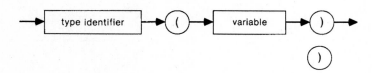

term

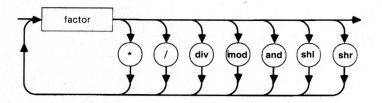

simple expression

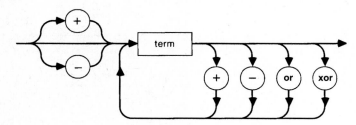

expression

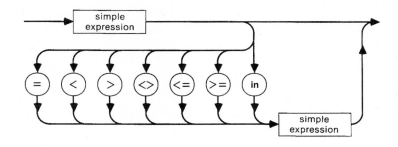

variable

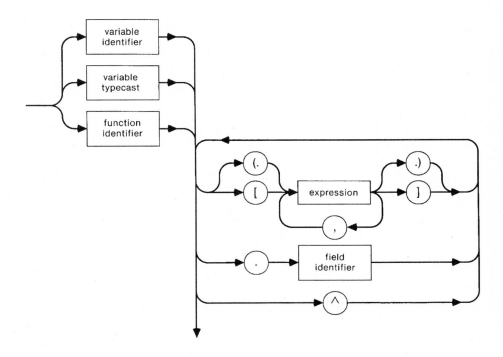

inline element

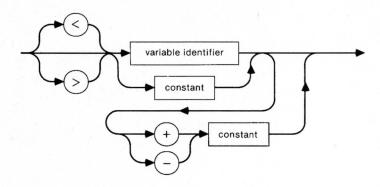

inline directive

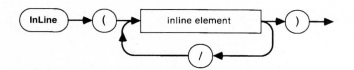

procedure body

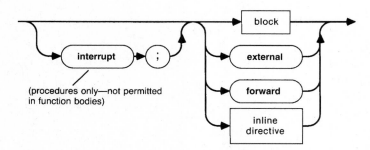

(procedures only—not permitted
in function bodies)

parameter list

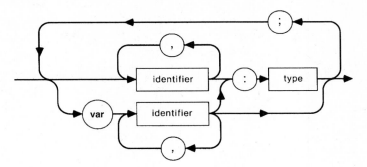

parameters

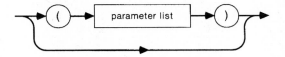

function declaration

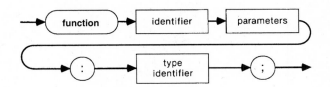

procedure declaration

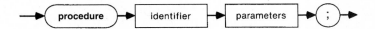

absolute address

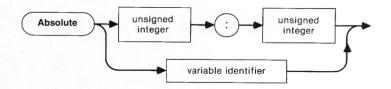

variable declaration

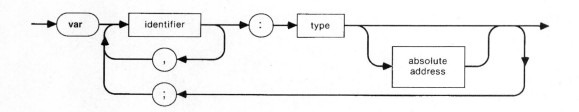

type declaration

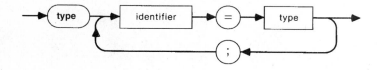

set constant

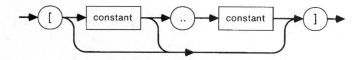

record constant

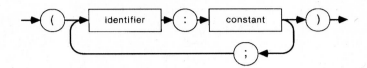

array constant

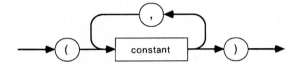

variable (typed) constant

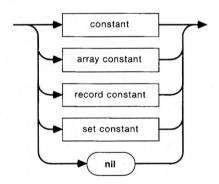

constant declaration

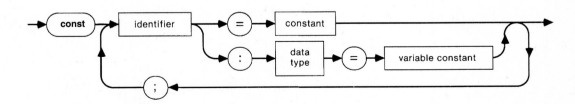

label declaration

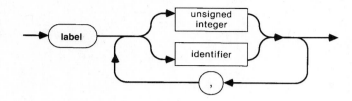

for statement

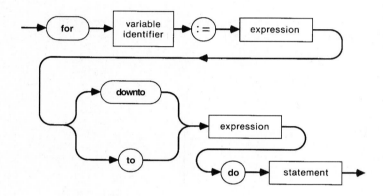

repeat statement

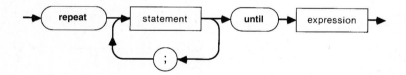

while statement

case statement

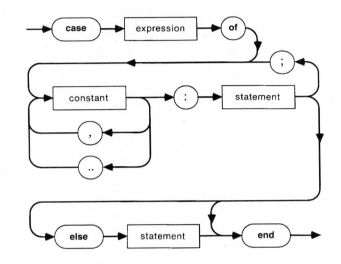

if statement

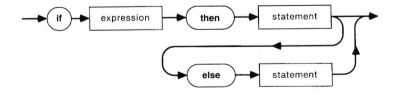

statement

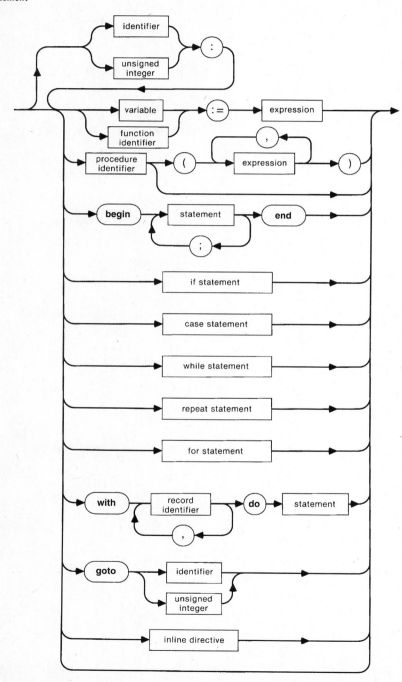

block

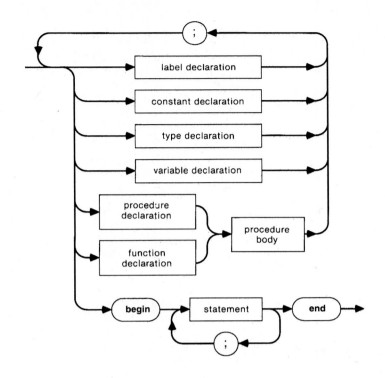

interface part

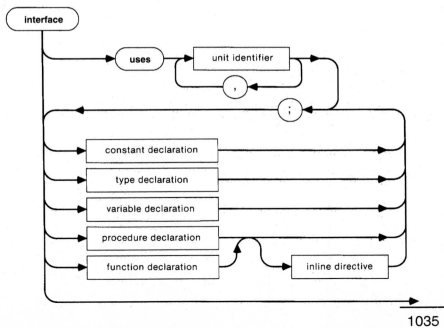

unit

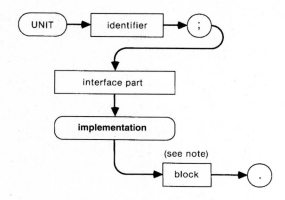

Note: BEGIN Statement; ...; Statement optional

program

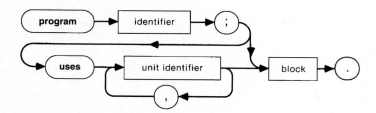

Object-Oriented Diagrams

procedure method

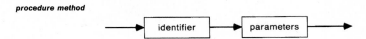

function method

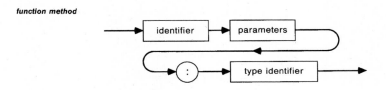

method heading

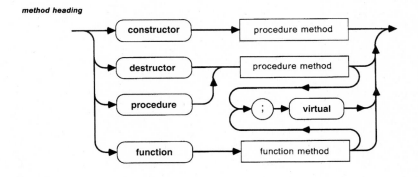

method

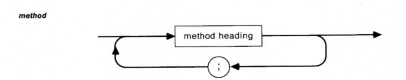

instance variables

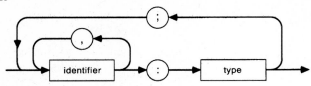

object type

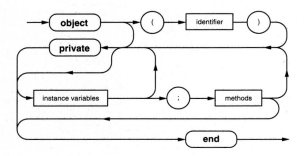

B

Memory Map

B

Memory Map

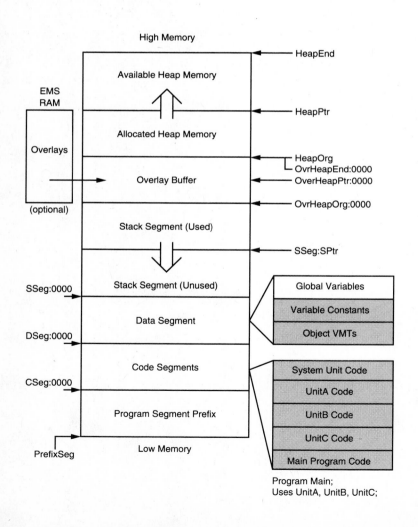

Shaded areas represent the compiled .EXE file image as stored on disk. (Overlay units may be attached to this image.) Other areas are allocated at runtime. The main program and each unit occupy distinct code segments up to 64K; therefore, the value of CSeg (register CS) changes depending on which module's code is executing. DSeg (register DS) and SSeg (register SS) do not change during normal program runs. The top of the stack is located at SSeg:SPtr. The data segment contains global variables, which are allocated at runtime. It also contains variable (typed) constants and Virtual Method Tables (VMTs), both of which are stored in the .EXE file. DOS creates the 256-byte Program Segment Prefix when it loads the program into RAM. PrefixSeg addresses this memory.

The occupied heap of dynamic variables created by New and GetMem grows up from the start of the heap (HeapOrg). Space between HeapPtr and HeapEnd has never been used.

The overlay buffer begins at OvrHeapOrg and extends to the start of the heap. OvrHeapEnd marks the top of the overlay buffer. OverHeapPtr floats between these areas as new overlays are loaded into the buffer. These three Word values address paragraph boundaries at offset addresses of 0000. See Chapter 10 for more information on the layout of the overlay buffer.

C

Options and Directives

C

The following tables, C-1 through C-4, list Turbo Pascal's options and directives: switched, command-line, and parameter.

Switched Options

Switched options consist of a dollar sign, a letter (which may be in upper- or lowercase), and either a plus sign (to enable a setting) or a minus sign (to turn a setting off). There are three ways to use a switched option:

- In the program's text, surround an option with braces or the alternate double-character symbols (* and *). For example, to turn off word align-ment, you can insert the option {$A–}, or you can write (*$A–*), which means the same. You can also specify multiple options separated with commas like this: {$F+,I–,N+}.

- When compiling programs with the IDE, you may use the *Options:Compiler* command to select an equivalent setting as listed in the table's second column. Any directives embedded in the program's text take precedence over options selected in the IDE.

- When using the command-line compiler, specify options as /$X+ or /$X–, where X is an option letter. For example, from a DOS prompt, you can enter the command **tpc /$B+ name** to compile the program file NAME.PAS and select full Boolean expression evaluation. You may use the identical options with the protected-mode command-line compiler TPCX.EXE and the nonprotected-mode TPC.EXE.

To the right of the Default column, Table C-1 shows whether an option is global or local. Global options apply to an entire module and should be entered once near

1044

the top of the file, preferably above a **program** or **unit** declaration. Local options may be entered one or more times between any statement or outside of any code-generating block.

Table C-1 Switched options

Options	Options:Compiler Dialog Setting	Default	Use	Comments
$A +/−	Word align data: Word (+) or Byte (−)	+	Global	No effect on 8088-based systems. Use $A+ to align data at even addresses for fast access on 80x86-based PCs.
$B +/−	Complete Boolean eval: Short Circuit (−) or Complete (+)	−	Local	Default setting short-circuits Boolean expression (**and** and **or**) evaluation when result is known. Use $B+ to evaluate all parts of Boolean expressions (not recommended in most cases).
$D +/−	Debug information	+	Global	Adds debugging information (symbols and line numbers) to compiled code so the debugger can single-step statements, display variables, and so on. Turn off to reduce code-file size.
$E +/−	Emulation	+	Global	Default setting links code to a software math-coprocessor emulator for systems lacking a hardware coprocessor.

continued

Table C-1 continued

Options	Options:Compiler Dialog Setting	Default	Use	Comments
$F +/–	Force far calls	–	Local	Switch to $F+ to force far calls to subroutines, and to insert a **far** assembly language instruction at the ends of those routines.
$G +/–	286 instructions	–	Local	Use $G+ only for code to be executed on 80286 or a compatible system (for example, an 80386- or 80486-based PC).
$I +/–	I/O checking	+	Local	Insert {$I–} and {$I+} directives around I/O statements, then use IOResult function to test for an error.
$L +/–	Local symbols	+	Global	Default setting includes all local symbols in compiled output for use in the debugger. Switch off to conserve memory (at the expense of not being able to view local symbols).
$N +/–	8087/80287	–	Global	Use $N+ only if an 80x87 math coprocessor will be present when the program runs and if your code uses floating point expressions. Despite the option's name, it works with all versions of math coprocessors, not only 8087s and 80287s.

Options	Options:Compiler Dialog Setting	Default	Use	Comments
$O +/–	Overlays allowed	–	Global	Change to $O+ to permit a unit to be used as an overlay module.
$R +/–	Range checking	–	Local	Use $R+ to enable range checking for array indexes and subrange values. This option also inserts checks into the code to determine whether an object's constructor has been called before any statement that calls a virtual method in that object. These checks take time, so use $R– for better code performance.
$S +/–	Stack checking	+	Local	Normally leave on to help prevent crashes due to lack of stack space, but turn off with $S– for critical subroutines that must run as fast as possible.
$V +/–	Strict var-strings: Strict (+) or Relaxed (–)	+	Local	In default state, string arguments must match the lengths of declared string parameters. Use $V– to defeat string-length checks, but in that case, risk overwriting ends of strings.

continued

Table C-1 continued

Options	Options:Compiler Dialog Setting	Default	Use	Comments
$X +/−	Extended syntax	+	Global	Enables non-system functions to be called as though they were procedures (ignore the function result).

Command-Line Options

Command-line options select additional compiler features. Like switches, most command-line options have equivalent settings that you can select with an appropriate menu command as listed in the table. Unlike switches, the command-line options have no equivalent text forms that you can insert into a program listing.

When using either the TPC or TPCX command-line compilers, precede options with a slash character. Separate multiple options with blanks. For example, the command **tpc /B /L name** compiles NAME.PAS with the /B and /L options. (You may also list options following the file name.)

Some options stand alone—for example, /B and /L. Others require one or more arguments. There may not be any spaces between such option letters and their arguments. For example, the command **tpc /Ec:\bin name** tells the compiler to compile NAME.PAS and write its .EXE code file to the directory C:\BIN. (For clarity, it helps to write the option in uppercase and its argument in lowercase as shown here, although you may type options and arguments in upper- or lowercase as you wish.)

Arguments listed in Table C-2 are:

- **adr:** An address in the form SEG:OFS, where SEG is a segment address and OFS is an offset from that segment's base. The only option that uses an address argument is /F, which recompiles a module to locate the source of a runtime error. If you receive a runtime error, note the reported address and enter a command such as **tpc /F079E:67AF name** to search for an error at address 079E:67AF in NAME.PAS.

- **dir:** A directory path name, which may include a drive letter and colon. Separate multiple directory paths with semicolons and no spaces. For example, to specify the two directories C:\LIB and C:\PROJ\LIB as locations where the compiler can find compiled .TPU files, you can enter a command such as **tpc /Uc:\lib;c:\proj\lib name**.

- **sym:** Any symbol that begins with a letter and includes letters, digits, or underlines. A symbol is typically used in a conditional directive such as {$IFDEF sym}. To define a symbol named *debugging,* perhaps to enable special debugging sections in a program, you can type a command such as **tpc /Ddebugging name**.

Table C-2 Command-line options

Option	Menu Command	Comments
/B	Compile:Build	Unconditionally compiles or recompiles a program or unit and all subunits if any. Using this option may increase the length of time it takes to compile a module, but ensures that every submodule belonging to a program or unit will be compiled.
/D sym	Options:Compiler, Conditional defines	Defines a conditional symbol. Equivalent to a $D symbol conditional option.
/E dir	Options:Directories, EXE and TPU Directory	Specifies directory path where the compiler should write .EXE and .TPU code files.
/F adr	Search:Find error	Replace adr with the address of a runtime error to locate the statement where the error occurred. Recompiles program, then reports the error's location.
/GS	Options:Linker, Map file: Segments	Generates a limited map file of segment address information.
/GP	Options:Linker, Map file: Publics	Generates a limited map file of public symbols.
/GD	Options:Linker, Map file: Detailed	Generates a detailed map file with line number information.

continued

Table C-2 continued

Option	Menu Command	Comments
/I dir	Options:Directories, Include directories	Specifies directory path where include files (.INC) are stored.
/L	Options:Linker, Link buffer: Memory (default) or Disk (equivalent to /L)	Tells the compiler to use a disk buffer for storing linker information, thus conserving memory and allowing larger programs to be linked, but at a slower speed. Takes effect only when linking compiled units to a program module.
/M	Compile:Make	Conditionally compiles or recompiles a program or unit along with any other units that have been modified since the most recent compilation. Using this option helps to prevent recompiling modules that have not been changed, and thus can speed compilation for a multimodule program.
/O dir	Options:Directories, Object directories	Specifies directory path where object-code files (.OBJ) are stored.
/Q	n/a	Tells compiler to "be quiet," that is, not to display as much information as it normally does while compiling. Reduces screen clutter when executing the compiler from a batch or "make" file.
/T dir	n/a	Specifies "Turbo" directory path where configuration files (TPC.CFG) and the library file (TURBO.TPL) are stored. The compiler always searches the current directory and the one containing the compiler's .EXE file for these files. You need to use this option only if you store configuration and library files in a different location.

Option	Menu Command	Comments
/U dir	Options:Directories, Unit directories	Specifies directory path where compiled unit files (.TPU) are stored.
/V	Options:Debugger, Debugging, Standalone	Adds debugging information to compiled module. Use this option to prepare for debugging a program with the stand-alone Turbo Debugger. This option is not required for debugging with the IDE's built-in debugger.

Parameter Options

Turbo Pascal's parameter options are similar to its switches, but instead of plus or minus, are followed by a space and one or more arguments. Except for the $M memory option, you may use these options only in the program text—the other options have no equivalent menu commands or command-line forms. For example, if you enter this directive into a program

```
{$I commons.inc}
```

the compiler (either the integrated or command-line version) will include the contents of COMMONS.INC. at the option's location.

You may surround parameter options with braces or with the alternate comment brackets (* and *). The directive {$L filename} has the identical effect as (*$L filename*).

Table C-3 Parameter options

Option	Comments
$I filename	Include the contents from the file named *filename* at the location where the directive appears. The effect is identical to what would happen if that file's contents existed at this location.

continued

Table C-3 continued

Option	Comments
$L filename	Link the code file named *filename* into the compiled module. Normally used to load an object-code file (with the extension .OBJ) created by an assembler and containing external procedures and functions written in assembly language.
$M stacksize,heapmin, heapmax	Set stacksize to a value from 1024 to 65536, specifying the number of bytes of stack space to reserve for the program. Set heapmin and heapmax to values from 0 to 655360, specifying the minimum and maximum number of bytes of heap space to reserve for the program. The amount of heap space actually available at runtime depends on the amount of memory available, but will be no less than heapmin and no more than heapmax. $M does nothing in a unit.
$O unitname	Use only in a program—has no effect in a unit. Specifies unitname to be an overlay module. For this directive to work, the specified unit (or units) must have been compiled with the $O+ switched option and the Overlay unit must be specified in the program's **uses** declaration.

Conditional Compilation Directives

Use conditional compilation directives to select portions of a program to compile based on certain conditions. For example, if a program includes the directive

```
{$DEFINE debugging}
```

then, later in the code, you can select between two sections by using the IFDEF directive like this:

```
{$IFDEF debugging}
  Writeln('Debugging is in effect!');
{$ENDIF}
```

Only if the debugging symbol is defined by a DEFINE directive or a command-line /D option will the Writeln statement be compiled. If debugging is not defined, the compiler skips over the statement as though it wasn't there.

It's important to realize that a symbol is "defined" if that symbol exists. Such symbols are not variables, and they have no values. The expression

```
{$IFDEF debugging}
```

does *not* examine debugging's value (since it has no value). It merely tests whether a preceding DEFINE directive or /D command-line option has defined debugging.

Table C-4 Conditional compilation directives

Directive	Comments
DEFINE symbol	Defines *symbol*, which may be any legal identifier, for use in another conditional compilation directive. After the directive {$DEFINE symbol}, the expression {$IFDEF symbol} will be true.
UNDEF symbol	Undefines *symbol*. After the directive {$UNDEF symbol}, the expression {$IFDEF symbol} will be false.
IFDEF symbol	Evaluates to true if *symbol* was previously defined. If this directive evaluates to true, the compiler will begin compiling the lines that follow. If the directive evaluates to false, the compiler will skip subsequent lines until another directive ends or changes the condition.
IFNDEF symbol	Similar to IFDEF, but negates the result. If a symbol is defined with the directive {$DEFINE symbol}, the directive {$IFNDEF symbol} will be false. If a symbol has never been defined, or has been undefined with UNDEF, then {$IFNDEF symbol} will be true.
IFOPT option	If the listed switched option is in effect, IFOPT evaluates to true, causing the compiler to compile subsequent lines. For example, the directive {$IFOPT X+} is true if the $X+ switched option is currently active.

continued

Table C-4 continued

Directive	Comments
ELSE	Use along with IFDEF, IFNDEF, and IFOPT to compile or not compile an alternate section of a program.
ENDIF	Ends an IFDEF, IFNDEF, IFOPT, or ELSE directive.

D

ASCII Character Codes

D

ASCII Character Codes

ASCII Dec	Value Hex	ASCII Character	ASCII Dec	Value Hex	ASCII Character
000	00	null	021	15	§
001	01	☺	022	16	–
002	02	☻	023	17	↨
003	03	♥	024	18	↑
004	04	♦	025	19	↓
005	05	♣	026	1A	→
006	06	♠	027	1B	←
007	07	•	028	1C	∟
008	08	◘	029	1D	↔
009	09	○	030	1E	▲
010	0A	◙	031	1F	▼
011	0B	♂	032	20	SP
012	0C	♀	033	21	!
013	0D	♪	034	22	"
014	0E	♫	035	23	#
015	0F	¤	036	24	$
016	10	►	037	25	%
017	11	◄	038	26	&
018	12	↕	039	27	'
019	13	‼	040	28	(
020	14	¶	041	29	)

ASCII Dec	Value Hex	ASCII Character	ASCII Dec	Value Hex	ASCII Character
042	2A	*	083	53	S
043	2B	+	084	54	T
044	2C	,	085	55	U
045	2D	–	086	56	V
046	2E	.	087	57	W
047	2F	/	088	58	X
048	30	0	089	59	Y
049	31	1	090	5A	Z
050	32	2	091	5B	[
051	33	3	092	5C	\
052	34	4	093	5D	]
053	35	5	094	5E	^
054	36	6	095	5F	–
055	37	7	096	60	`
056	38	8	097	61	a
057	39	9	098	62	b
058	3A	:	099	63	c
059	3B	;	100	64	d
060	3C	<	101	65	e
061	3D	=	102	66	f
062	3E	>	103	67	g
063	3F	?	104	68	h
064	40	@	105	69	i
065	41	A	106	6A	j
066	42	B	107	6B	k
067	43	C	108	6C	l
068	44	D	109	6D	m
069	45	E	110	6E	n
070	46	F	111	6F	o
071	47	G	112	70	p
072	48	H	113	71	q
073	49	I	114	72	r
074	4A	J	115	73	s
075	4B	K	116	74	t
076	4C	L	117	75	u
077	4D	M	118	76	v
078	4E	N	119	77	w
079	4F	O	120	78	x
080	50	P	121	79	y
081	51	Q			
082	52	R			

ASCII Dec	Value Hex	ASCII Character	ASCII Dec	Value Hex	ASCII Character
122	7A	z	157	9D	¥
123	7B	{	158	9E	Pt
124	7C	¦	159	9F	ƒ
125	7D	}	160	A0	á
126	7E	~	161	A1	í
127	7F	Δ	162	A2	ó
128	80	Ç	163	A3	ú
129	81	ü	164	A4	ñ
130	82	é	165	A5	Ñ
131	83	â	166	A6	ª
132	84	ä	167	A7	º
133	85	à	168	A8	¿
134	86	å	169	A9	⌐
135	87	ç	170	AA	¬
136	88	ê	171	AB	½
137	89	ë	172	AC	¼
138	8A	è	173	AD	¡
139	8B	ï	174	AE	«
140	8C	î	175	AF	»
141	8D	ì	176	B0	░
142	8E	Ä	177	B1	▒
143	8F	Å	178	B2	▓
144	90	É	179	B3	│
145	91	æ	180	B4	┤
146	92	Æ	181	B5	╡
147	93	ô	182	B6	╢
148	94	ö	183	B7	╖
149	95	ò	184	B8	╕
150	96	û	185	B9	╣
151	97	ù	186	BA	║
152	98	ÿ	187	BB	╗
153	99	Ö	188	BC	╝
154	9A	Ü	189	BD	╜
155	9B	¢	190	BE	╛
156	9C	£	191	BF	┐

ASCII Dec	Value Hex	ASCII Character	ASCII Dec	Value Hex	ASCII Character
192	C0	∟	224	E0	α
193	C1	⊥	225	E1	β
194	C2	⊤	226	E2	Γ
195	C3	├	227	E3	π
196	C4	─	228	E4	Σ
197	C5	+	229	E5	σ
198	C6	╞	230	E6	μ
199	C7	╟	231	E7	τ
200	C8	╚	232	E8	Φ
201	C9	╔	233	E9	θ
202	CA	╩	234	EA	Ω
203	CB	╦	235	EB	δ
204	CC	╠	236	EC	∞
205	CD	=	237	ED	ø
206	CE	╬	238	EE	∈
207	CF	╧	239	EF	∩
208	D0	╨	240	F0	≡
209	D1	╤	241	F1	±
210	D2	╥	242	F2	≥
211	D3	╙	243	F3	≤
212	D4	╘	244	F4	⌠
213	D5	╒	245	F5	⌡
214	D6	╓	246	F6	÷
215	D7	╫	247	F7	≈
216	D8	╪	248	F8	°
217	D9	┘	249	F9	•
218	DA	┌	250	FA	·
219	DB	█	251	FB	√
220	DC	▄	252	FC	η
221	DD	▌	253	FD	²
222	DE	▐	254	FE	■
223	DF	▀	255	FF	

E

Operator Precedence

E

Table E-1 Operator Precedence

Level	Operator	Description	Allowed operand types
1:	@	Address of	Procedure, Function, Variable
	–	Unary minus	Integer Real
	not	Negate	Boolean, Integer
2:	*	Times	Integer Real, Set
	/	Divide	Real, Set
	div	Integer divide	Integer
	mod	Modulus	Integer
	and	Logical **and**	Boolean, Integer
	shl	Shift left	Integer
	shr	Shift right	Integer
3:	+	Plus	Integer, Real, String, Set
	–	Minus	Integer, Real, Set
	or	Logical **or**	Boolean, Integer
	xor	Exclusive **or**	Boolean, Integer
4:	=	Equal	All
	< >	Not equal	All
	<	Less than	All
	>	Greater than	All
	< =	Less or equal	All
	> =	Greater or equal	All
	in	Set membership	**set**

Notes: Operators at level 1 have higher precedences than operators at level 2, operators at level 2 have higher precedences than operators at level 3, and so on. Integer types include Byte, ShortInt, Word, Integer, and LongInt. Real types include Single, Double, Extended, and Comp—which require a math coprocessor—and Real which is always available.

Bibliography

Brooks, Frederick P. *The Mythical Man-Month*. Addison-Wesley, 1975. Amusing collection of essays on managing large software projects.

Duncan, Ray. *Advanced MS-DOS*. Microsoft Press, 1986. You won't find a better DOS reference. Also discusses routines in the PC ROM BIOS. Requires knowledge of assembly language and some C.

Grogono, Peter. *Programming in Pascal*. Rev ed. Addison-Wesley, 1980. Introduction to programming in standard Pascal. Many good examples.

Jensen, Kathleen, and Wirth, Niklaus. *Pascal User Manual and Report,* 2nd ed. Springer-Verlag, 1974. The classic Pascal reference. Part one, The User Manual, written by Jensen, is a concentrated overview of programming in Pascal and contains many short examples. The Report, written by Pascal inventor, Niklaus Wirth, describes the syntax of standard Pascal. Pretty much out-of-date by now, but worth a look.

Kernighan, Brian W., and Plauger, P.J. *Software Tools in Pascal*. Addison-Wesley, 1981. Practical guide to software development with emphasis on writing useful programs in Pascal.

Knuth, Donald E. *The Art of Computer Programming, Vols. 1, 2, 3,* 2nd ed. Addison-Wesley, 1973. Penultimate reference for professional programmers and students working in any computer language.

Ledgard, Henry F., et al. *Pascal With Style; Programming Proverbs*. Hayden Book Company, 1979. Thoughtful hints and suggestions for developing a good programming style.

Liffick, W. Blaise. *The BYTE Book of Pascal.* BYTE Publications, 1979. Looks at Pascal compiler design. Contains many programs, from text formatters to chess, written for a variety of Pascal compilers.

Schmucker, Kurt J. *Object-Oriented Programming for the Macintosh.* Object Pascal for the Mac and Turbo Pascal OOP extensions share some of the same concepts and forms, although the two languages are not source-code compatible. Still, this is a good book if you want to learn more about OOP.

Swan, Tom. *Mastering Turbo Assembler.* SAMS, 1990. The author's book on Borland's Turbo Assembler.

Swan, Tom. *Mastering Turbo Debugger.* Hayden Books, 1990. The author's book on Borland's Turbo Debugger.

Swan, Tom. *Learning C++.* SAMS, 1991. The author's book on C++. Includes a version of Zortech C++ on disk.

Swan, Tom. *Turbo Pascal for Windows 3.0 Programming.* Bantam Books, 1991. The author's book on Borland's Turbo Pascal for Windows.

Wiener, Richard S., and Pinson, Lewis J. *An Introduction to Object-Oriented Programming and C++.* Addison-Wesley, 1988. Although this book contains no Pascal programs, it describes OOP concepts in C++, upon which Turbo Pascal's OOP extensions are based. Requires a strong knowledge of C.

Wirth, Niklaus. *Algorithms + Data Structures = Programs.* Prentice-Hall, 1976. Still one of the best books on advanced Pascal programming.

Answers to
Selected Exercises

The exercises at the ends of chapters were chosen to illustrate various Pascal features discussed in the chapters. The answers in this section will help you to fine-tune your understanding of details that may give you trouble on a first reading. Of course, no book has all the answers and this book is no exception. You will, therefore, find a few missing numbers and several missing chapters in the material that follows.

Chapter 1

1-1.

```pascal
program Alphabet;
begin
  Writeln('Pack my box with five dozen liquor jugs.')
end.
```

1-2.

```pascal
program Announcement;
begin
  Writeln('"It''s eleven o''clock," she said,');
  Writeln('"Why aren''t you in bed?"')
end.
```

1-5.

```pascal
program Triplicate;
var
  S: string[20];
begin
  Write('Enter any string: ');
  Readln(S);
  Writeln(S, S, S)
end.
```

Chapter 2

2-1.

```
program WaterWeight;
const
  LbsPerGallon = 8.33;
var
  Gallons: Real;
begin
  Writeln('Weight of water');
  Writeln;
  Write('Number of gallons? ');
  Readln(Gallons);
  Writeln('Weight = ', Gallons * LbsPerGallon:8:2, ' pounds.')
end.
```

2-2.

```
program Fahrenheit;
var
  Fdegrees, Cdegrees: Real;
begin
  Writeln('Celsius to Fahrenheit conversion');
  Writeln;
  Write('Degrees Celsius? ');
  Readln(Cdegrees);
  Fdegrees := ((Cdegrees * 9.0) / 5.0) + 32.0;
  Writeln('Degrees Fahrenheit = ', Fdegrees:8:2)
end.
```

2-3.

```
{ Boiling point of water at various altitudes }
{ Author: Tom Swan }
program Water;
const
  Factor = 550;        { One degree less per Factor feet }
  BoilingPoint = 212; { Degrees Fahrenheit }
var
  Altitude, Temperature: Real;
begin
  Writeln('Boiling point of water');
  Writeln;
```

```
    Write('Altitude? ');
    Readln(Altitude);
    Temperature := BoilingPoint - (Altitude / Factor);
    Writeln('Temperature = ', Temperature:8:2, ' degrees Fahrenheit')
  end.
```

2-4.

The number of decimal places is declared as a variable constant. This makes it easy to specify a default value of two. Another possibility would be to declare Decimals as an Integer variable, initializing with the assignment statement Decimals := 2.

```
{ Modified for variable number of decimal places }
program WaterWeight;
const
  LbsPerGallon = 8.33;
  Places = 8;                 { Fixed number columns }
  Decimals: Integer = 2;   { Variable decimal places }
var
  Gallons: Real;
begin
  Writeln('Weight of water');
  Writeln;
  Write('Number of gallons? ');
  Readln(Gallons);
  Write('Number of decimal places? ');
  Readln(Decimals);
  Writeln('Weight = ',
    Gallons * LbsPerGallon:Places:Decimals, ' pounds.')
end.
```

Chapter 3

3-1.

```
program WhileCountDown;
var
  I: Integer;
begin
  Writeln('While countdown');
  I := 10;
  while I > 0 do
```

```
    begin
      Writeln(I);
      I := I - 1
    end
  end.
```

3-2.

```
  program Celsius2;
  var
    Fdegrees, Cdegrees: Real;
    Answer: Char;
  begin
    Writeln('Fahrenheit to Celsius conversion');
    Writeln;
    repeat
      Write('Degrees Fahrenheit ? ');
      Readln(Fdegrees);
      Cdegrees := ((Fdegrees - 32.0) * 5.0) / 9.0;
      Writeln('Degrees Celsius = ', Cdegrees:8:2);
      Writeln;
      Write('Another (Y/N)? ');
      Readln(Answer)
    until (Answer <> 'Y') and (Answer  <> 'y')
  end.
```

3-3.

```
program Color3;
var
  Choice: Integer;
  UserQuits: Boolean;
begin
  Writeln('Complementary Colors #3');
  UserQuits := false;
  repeat
    Writeln;
    Writeln(' 1=Blue         2=Green       3=Orange       4=Purple');
    Writeln(' 5=Red          6=Yellow      7=Yellow-green 8=Red-purple');
    Writeln(' 9=Blue-green 10=Red-orange 11=Blue-purple  12=Yellow-orange');
    Writeln;
    Write('Color? (0 to quit) ');
    Readln(Choice);
    Write('Complement is: ');
    case Choice of
```

```
 0: UserQuits := true;
 1: Writeln('Orange');
 2: Writeln('Red');
 3: Writeln('Blue');
 4: Writeln('Yellow');
 5: Writeln('Green');
 6: Writeln('Purple');
 7: Writeln('Red-purple');
 8: Writeln('Yellow-green');
 9: Writeln('Red-orange');
10: Writeln('Blue-green');
11: Writeln('Yellow-orange');
12: Writeln('Blue-purple')
      else Writeln('Error: try again.')
    end
  until UserQuits
end.
```

3.4.

There are many correct answers to writing a factorial program. The answer below is easy to understand, but it may not be the most efficient solution.

```
program Fact;
var
  Value: Integer;
  Result: Real;
begin
  repeat
    Write('Value? (-1 to end) ');
    Readln(Value);
    if Value >= 0 then
    begin
      Result := 1;
      while Value > 0 do
      begin
        Result := Result * Value;
        Value := Value - 1
      end;
      Writeln('Factorial = ', Result:1:0)
    end
  until Value = -1
end.
```

3-5.

If you had trouble with this one, enter and run the answer here, then "play computer," writing down the variables on paper while executing the program statements by hand. This should help explain how the program works. The method is called a "binary search" because of the way the high and low guesses are divided by two in line 10 to form new guesses. This narrowing down of possibilities is guaranteed to compute the correct result in seven attempts or less. Any more than that and the program knows you're cheating.

```
program NumberGame;
var
   Answer, High, Low, Guess: Integer;
begin
  Writeln('Think of a number from 1 to 100');
  Write('then press return...');
  Readln;
  High := 100;
  Low := 1;
  repeat
    Guess := (Low + High) div 2;
    Write('I guess ', Guess, '. 1=Correct, 2=Low, 3=High ? ');
    Readln(Answer);
    if Answer = 2 then
      Low := Guess + 1
    else if Answer = 3 then
      High := Guess - 1
  until (High < Low) or (Answer = 1);
  if Answer = 1 then
    Writeln('I win!')
  else Writeln('You cheated!!!')
end.
```

Chapter 4

4-1.

```
program Area;
var
   Selection: Integer;

procedure Square;
```

```
      var
        A, B: Real;
      begin
        Writeln('Square');
        Write('Length side A? ');
        Readln(A);
        Write('Length side B? ');
        Readln(B);
        Writeln('Area=', A * B:1:2)
      end;

      procedure Pyramid;
      var
        N, B, H: Real;
      begin
        Writeln('Pyramid');
        Write('Number of faces? ');
        Readln(N);
        Write('Length of base? ');
        Readln(B);
        Write('Height? ');
        Readln(H);
        Writeln('Area=', ((N * B * H) / 2):1:2)
      end;

      procedure Cube;
      var
        A: Real;
      begin
        Writeln('Cube');
        Write('Length of one side? ');
        Readln(A);
        Writeln('Area=', 6 * Sqr(A):1:2)
      { Note: Sqr(N) is a predeclared function. }
      end;

      procedure Cylinder;
      var
        R, H: Real;
      begin
        Writeln('Cylinder');
        Write('Radius? ');
        Readln(R);
        Write('Height? ');
```

```pascal
    Readln(H);
    Writeln('Area=', ((2 * Pi * R) * H):1:2)
  end;

begin
  Writeln('Compute the area');
  Writeln;
  Write('1=square, 2=pyramid, 3=cube, 4=cylinder? ');
  Selection := 0; { End on pressing Enter }
  Readln(Selection);
  case Selection of
    1: Square;
    2: Pyramid;
    3: Cube;
    4: Cylinder
  end
end.
```

4-2.

```pascal
program Current;
var
  Voltage, Resistance: Real;

function Amperes: Real;
begin
  Amperes := Voltage / Resistance
end;

begin
  Writeln('Calculate current in Amperes');
  Write('Voltage? ');
  Readln(Voltage);
  Write('Resistance (ohms)? ');
  Readln(Resistance);
  Writeln('Current = ', Amperes:1:2, ' amperes')
end.
```

4-3.

Six functions are used in this version of the program. The first three functions calculate E, I, and R. The next three prompt for volts, amperes, and ohms.

```pascal
program OhmsLaw;
var
  Choice: Char;
```

```
{ Solve for E = voltage }
function E(Amps, Ohms: Real): Real;
begin
  E := Amps * Ohms
end;

{ Solve for I = current }
function I(Volts, Ohms: Real): Real;
begin
  I := Volts / Ohms
end;

{ Solve for R = resistance }
function R(Volts, Amps: Real): Real;
begin
  R := Volts / Amps
end;

{ Prompt for voltage }
function Voltage: Real;
var
  N: Real;
begin
  Write('Volts? ');
  Readln(N);
  Voltage := N
end;

{ Prompt for current }
function Current: Real;
var
  N: Real;
begin
  Write('Current (amps)? ');
  Readln(N);
  Current := N
end;

{ Prompt for resistance }
function Resistance: Real;
var
  N: Real;
```

```
begin
  Write('Resistance (ohms)? ');
  Readln(N);
  Resistance := N
end;

begin
  Writeln('Welcome to Ohm''s Law');
  repeat
    Writeln;
    Write('E=voltage, I=current, R=resistance or Q=quit? ');
    Readln(Choice);
    case Upcase(Choice) of
      'E': Writeln(E(Current, Resistance):1:2, ' volts');
      'I': Writeln(I(Voltage, Resistance):1:2, ' amperes');
      'R': Writeln(R(Voltage, Current   ):1:2, ' ohms')
    end
  until Upcase(Choice) = 'Q'
end.
```

4-6.

Make the following changes to Program 4-7 to print the alphabet in normal order.

```
 7:  if Ch > 'A' then B(Ch);
13:  A(Pred(Ch))
17:  A('Z')
```

4-7.

```
program TestPETC;

{ Press Enter To Continue }
procedure PETC;
var
  Ch: Char;
begin
  Writeln;
  Write('Press Enter to continue...');
  Readln
end;

begin
  Writeln('Test PETC procedure');
  PETC;
  Writeln('Program continues')
end.
```

Chapter 5

5-1.

```
program DateCheck;
type
  DateRec =
    record
      Year: Integer;
      Month: 1 .. 12;
      Day: 0 .. 31
    end;
var
  TestDate: DateRec;

{ True if date is a leap year. From Program 3-12. }
function LeapYear(var Date: DateRec): Boolean;
begin
  with Date do
    if Year mod 100 = 0
      then LeapYear := (Year mod 400) = 0
      else LeapYear := (Year mod   4) = 0
end;

{ True if Date is legal }
function GoodDate(var Date: DateRec): Boolean;
const
  Days: array[1 .. 12] of Byte =
    (31, 28, 31, 30, 31, 30, 31, 31, 31, 31, 30, 31);
var
  LastDay: Integer;
begin
  with Date do
  begin
    if LeapYear(Date)
      then Days[2] := 29
      else Days[2] := 28;
    GoodDate :=
      (Year  >=  0) and
      (Month >=  1) and
      (Month <= 12) and
      (Day   >=  1) and
      (Day   <= Days[Month])
```

```
      end
    end;

    begin
      with TestDate DO
      begin
        Write('Year? ');
        Readln(Year);
        Write('Month? ');
        Readln(Month);
        Write('Day? ');
        Readln(Day)
      end;
      if GoodDate(TestDate)
        then Writeln('Date may be okay')
        else Writeln('Date is not okay')
    end.
```

5-2.

```
    program TFOrdinals;

    procedure BooleanOrd(B: Boolean);
    begin
      Writeln('Ordinal value of ', B, ' = ', Ord(B))
    end;

    begin
      BooleanOrd(true);
      BooleanOrd(false);
      BooleanOrd(not true);
      BooleanOrd(not(not true and not false))
    end.
```

5-3.

```
    program VertAndDiag;
    var
      I: Integer;
      S: string[80];
    begin
      Write('String? ');
      Readln(S);
      Writeln;
      Writeln('Vertical:');
```

```
      for I := 1 to Length(S) do
        Writeln(S[I]);
      Writeln;
      Writeln('Press Enter...');
      Readln;
      Writeln('Diagonal');
      for I := 1 to Length(S) do
        Writeln(S[I]:I)
    end.
```

5-5.

To solve this problem, you first need to decide on the kind of index to use. You might start with an enumerated data type:

```
type
  City = (Atlanta, Baltimore, Boston, Chicago,
    Dallas, LosAngeles, NewYork);
```

Next, declare the mileage array indexed by the new type.

```
var
  Miles: array[City, City] of Real;
```

Defining the data structures often simplifies writing the program. To assign mileages, you could use assignments like these:

```
Miles[Atlanta, Dallas] := 822;
Miles[Chicago, Boston] := 1004;
```

With these suggestions as starting points, you should be able to finish the program.

5-8.

Depending on how you enter names, sorting by last name can be tricky. Everything proceeds smoothly as long as all entries are in last-name-first order. Because assumptions such as these are prime sources of program bugs, a better solution is to use separate fields in the Member record for last names, first names, and middle initials. Because you can then directly compare two last names, this makes sorting easier. Another problem arises if names are in upper- and lowercase. To deal with this problem, you may have to convert to all uppercase before sorting. (Converting fields to uppercase before comparing in the sort procedure causes operating times to suffer. Why?)

5-10.

This is easily done with a **set of** DaysOfWeek.

```
type
  DaySet = set of DaysOfWeek;
```

```
  Employee =
  record
    Name: string[40];
    Days: DaySet
  end;
```

Then, to record the days an employee works is a simple assignment. Assume A is an array of Employee records indexed by Number.

```
A[Number].Days := [Mon .. Wed, Fri, Sat];
```

It's now easy to print the chart. A nested **for** loop seems best.

```
Writeln('  #  Sun  Mon  Tue  Wed  Thu  Fri  Sat');
for Number := 1 to LastEmployee do
begin
  Writeln;
  Write(Number:3);
  for Day := Sun to Sat do
    if Day in A[Number].Days
      then Write('*':5)
      else Write(' ':5)
end;
```

Chapter 6

6-1.

```
program SdrawKcab;
var
  InFile: Text;
  FileName: string[64];
  OneLine: string[132];
  I: Integer;
begin
  Write('File name? ');
  Readln(FileName);
  Assign(InFile, FileName);
  Reset(InFile);
  while not eof(InFile) do
  begin
    Readln(InFile, OneLine);
    for I := Length(OneLine) downto 1 do
      Write(OneLine[I]);
```

```
      Writeln
    end
  end.
```

6-3.

The simplest approach is to use a constant maximum number of lines for each new output file. For example:

```
while not Eof(InFile) do
begin
  StartOutput;
  for I := 1 to MaxLines do
    if not Eof(InFile) then
    begin
      Readln(InFile, OneLine);
      Writeln(OutFile, OneLlne)
    end;
  Close(OutFile)
end;
```

The procedure StartOutput has to create the new output file. Most important is to give each file a new name. FileNumber is a global integer variable.

```
procedure StartOutput;
begin
  FileNumber := FileNumber + 1;
  Str(FileNumber, S);
  Assign(OutFile, FileName + '.' + S);
  Rewrite(OutFile)
end;
```

6-4.

You can improve program speed by not resetting the input file if line numbers are greater than the last line read. This is a trick employed by word-processing programs. When you advance, say, from page 10 to page 11, there is no reason to reread the previous pages again. For clarity, the changes to Program 6-10 are in uppercase.

```
program SeekStrings;
var
  TextFile: Text;
  FileName: string[14];
  LineNumber, I: Integer;
```

```
    OneLine: string[80];
    OLDLINE: Integer;
begin
  Writeln;
  Write('Seek strings in what file? ');
  Readln(FileName);
  Assign(TextFile, FileName);
  Reset(TextFile);
  OLDLINE := 0;
  repeat
    Writeln;
    Write('Line number? (0 to quit) ');
    Readln(LineNumber);
    if LineNumber > 0 then
    begin
      if OLDLINE > LINENUMBER then
      begin
        Reset(TextFile);
        OLDLINE := 0
      end;
      for I := OLDLINE + 1 to LineNumber do
        Readln(TextFile, OneLine);
      Writeln(LineNumber, ': ', OneLine);
      OLDLINE := LINENUMBER
    end
  until LineNumber = 0;
  Close(TextFile)
end.
```

6-5.

There is no single correct answer here, although some encryption methods are better than others. Basically, you need to read blocks of data, change each byte according to a formula, and write the blocks back to disk. After reading a block, a simple **for** loop converts the bytes.

```
for I := 0 to 511 do
  Encrypt(Block[I]);
```

Of course, that doesn't say anything about the encryption method. You could add a constant value to each byte; use a translation table that says A is T, B is C, C is Q, and so on; or mathematically change each byte some other way. Chapter 12, for example, discusses logical operations on integers. One of those operations is called the *exclusive or*, written **xor**. You could use **xor** to write the simple encryption loop like this:

```
for I := 0 to 511 DO
  Block[I] := Block[I] xor Key[1 + I mod Length(Key)];
```

Chapter 7

7-1.

You can store any kind of data in a linked list. The link fields are the same; just change the other fields in the record. This declaration links 80-character strings.

```
ItemPointer = ^Item;
Item = record
  NextItem: ItemPointer;
  OneString: string[80]
end;
```

You can then treat OneString fields as you do any other string variables. ItemRec is a variable of type Item.

```
New(ItemRec);
Readln(InFile, ItemRec^.OneString);
```

Notice how the caret tells Pascal you want to access the data stored at the address of ItemRec. That data is a record; therefore, you can use a period as shown to access individual fields.

7-3.

There are two ways to exchange data in a circular list. Assuming each item of the list stores its data directly, you can shuffle the two items' pointers, thus exchanging their positions. Or, if the data is addressed by another pointer, you can swap the two data pointers in the items—a simpler and faster approach.

The following fragments implement the first and more difficult solution. For storing items on the list, the program uses these declarations:

```
type
  ItemPointer = ^Item;
  Item = record
    Data: string[20];  { Or any other data to be stored in the list }
    Left, Right: ItemPointer
  end;
```

Two support procedures, InsertItem and UnlinkItem, add new items to a list and remove old items. InsertItem attaches a new item (addressed by the NewItem pointer) onto the list addressed by P. UnlinkItem detaches an item addressed by P from its list, but does not dispose of that item. Here are the two procedures:

```
procedure InsertItem(var P: ItemPointer; NewItem: ItemPointer);
begin
  Newitem^.Left := P;
  NewItem^.Right := P^.Right;
  P^.Right^.Left := NewItem;
  P^.Right := NewItem
end;

procedure UnlinkItem(P: ItemPointer);
begin
  P^.Left^.Right := P^.Right;
  P^.Right^.Left := P^.Left
end;
```

Next comes the Swap procedure, which takes two parameters, A and B, addressing the two items to be swapped. The first two **if** statements handle the special conditions where A and B are adjacent in the list.

The main algorithm works by unlinking item B, linking it to the right of item A, then unlinking A and relinking A to the right of B's former position. Performing those actions on adjacent items would in some cases leave the items in their original positions, thus adjacent items must be treated specially. (The procedure assumes that the list has at least two items and that A and B address different items in the list.)

```
procedure Swap(A, B: ItemPointer);
var
  C: ItemPointer;
begin
  if A^.Left = B then
  begin                     { Adjacent items, B to left of A }
    UnlinkItem(B);
    InsertItem(A, B)
  end else
  if A^.Right = B then
  begin                     { Adjacent items, B to right of A }
    UnlinkItem(A);
    InsertItem(B, A)
  end else
  begin                     { Nonadjacent items }
    C := B^.Left;
    UnlinkItem(B);
    InsertItem(A, B);
    if A <> C then
    begin
      UnlinkItem(A);
```

```
        InsertItem(C, A)
      end
    end
  end;
```

Chapter 12

12-1.

```
program Hypotenuse;
var
  A, B: Real;

procedure GetNum(var R: Real);
var
  S: string[20];
  E: Integer;
begin
  repeat
    Readln(S);
    Val(S, R, E);
    if E <> 0 then
      Writeln('Error in number, try again. . .')
  until E = 0
end;

begin
  Writeln('Find the Hypotenuse of a right triangle');
  Writeln;
  Writeln('Enter length of side A');
  GetNum(A);
  Writeln('Enter length of side B');
  GetNum(B);
  Writeln('Hypotenuse = ', Sqrt(A * A + B * B):8:2)
end.
```

12-5.

Octal (base 8) digits range from 0 to 7. Because this takes three bits (in binary 000 to 111), you must imagine an eight-bit byte to have a zero bit to its left, making a total of nine bits. The value 255 decimal ($FF hexadecimal or 1111 1111 in binary) is, therefore, 377 in octal or, with its imaginary bit, 011 111 111 in binary. The answer uses divisions to isolate groups of three bits in bytes. This works because divisors that are powers of two (64 and 8 in the answer) have the effect of shifting left all the bits in a byte. Thus, 64 or 2^6 shifts bits six places left; 8 or 2^3 shifts three places, and so on.

```pascal
program OctalTest;
var
  Value: Integer;

function OctalDigit(N: Byte): Byte;
begin
  OctalDigit := N mod 8
end;

procedure OctalByte(N: Byte);
begin
  Write(' ',  OctalDigit(N div 64),
    OctalDigit(N div 8 ),
    OctalDigit(N))
end;

begin
  Writeln('Octal notation');
  Writeln;
  Write('Value? ');
  Readln(Value);
  OctalByte(Hi(Value));
  OctalByte(Lo(Value))
end.
```

Chapter 15

15.1

```pascal
DiskDrive = object
    Speed: Integer;
    Open: Boolean;
    DiskInserted: Boolean;
    constructor Init;
    destructor Done;
    procedure InsertDisk;
    procedure EjectDisk;
    function IsOpen: Boolean;
    procedure SetSpeed(S: Integer)
  end;
```

There are other possibilities. This exercise is designed to have you think about the properties of a diskette drive and how to represent those properties with an OOP object. Simulating real-world objects like disk drives and motors is one of OOP's primary uses.

15-2.

A constructor initializes a link between an object and its VMT in objects that define one or more virtual methods. Constructors also allocate space via New for dynamic objects in heap memory. In addition to these standard effects, constructors may also perform other object initializations.

15-3.

When called via Dispose, a destructor disposes the memory occupied by a dynamic object instance on the heap. In addition, destructors may perform other cleanup chores.

15-4.

Object types may define an unlimited number of constructors and destructors.

15-5.

A static method's address is known at compile time. A virtual method's address must be looked up at runtime from the object's VMT. Replaced static methods in descendant objects can't be called by method implementations in the object's ancestors. Replaced virtual methods can be called by an ancestor's precompiled code.

Program Index

Index

A

B

C

E

G

J

JMP machine language instruction, 553, 561
JNE machine language instruction, 561
Jumps in BASM, 560-561
Justifying text displays, 370-372, 914, 982-983

K

Keep procedure, 891-892
Kernels, 318
Key words, 3, 7
Keyboard
  buffer for, 892
  character input with, 940-941
  and Crt unit, 251-254
  device file name for, 147
  flag byte for, 404-406
  and ReadKey, 940
  as typewriter, 153
  See also Read procedure; Readln procedure
Keypressed function, 251, 892-893, 940
Keypresses, ExecView for, 697
Keys for objects, 736-739
Kilometers, converting, from miles, 30

L

/L command-line option, 1046
$L compiler directive, 570, 1052

Labels and **label** declarations
  in BASM, 560-561
  in dialog boxes, 701
  with **goto**, 60-61
  railroad diagram for, 1031
Large-program development, 439-447
  and Exec, 817
  and units, 303-306
LastMode variable, 243, 245-246
Late binding of objects, 599, 631-632
LDS machine language instruction, 555
Leading zeros
  for hexadecimal values, 553
  for real numbers, 16-17
Leap year, program to determine, 51-52
Leave machine language instruction, 515
Leaves with trees, 202-203
Left arrow key, 11, 253
LeftText constant, 370, 982
Length of strings, 19
  in collections, 731
  Length function for, 109-110, 219-223, 893
  maximum, 5
  setting, 222-223
  and $V compiler directive, 228, 1047
LES machine language instruction, 539
Less than signs (<)
  as comparison operator, 22
  with inline statements, 544
  for least significant byte, 881
  with not equal operator, 22, 28
  precedence of, 1062
  with sets, 134
Letters, railroad diagram for, 1020
Library files and units, 238, 284, 302-303

Q

R

T

U

V

W

X

$X compiler directive, 516-517, 642-643, 1048
XMS memory manager, 514
XON-XOFF protocol, 570-573
xor logical operator, 20-21, 403-404, 1062
XORPut constant, 345-346, 364, 934

Y

Year and system date, 263-264
  and file date, 267
  with GetDate, 840-841
  setting, 968
  unpacking, 1008
Yellow constant, 254

Z

Zeros
  for hexadecimal values, 553
  for real numbers, 16-17
Zoom buttons for windows, 688